CLYMER®

HONDA

VT750 SHADOW CHAIN DRIVE • 1998-2006

D1560443

CLYMER®

P.O. Box 12901, Overland Park, Kansas 66282-2901

Copyright ©2006 Prism Business Media Inc.

FIRST EDITION
First Printing August, 2004

SECOND EDITION
First Printing June, 2005

THIRD EDITION
First Printing October, 2006

Printed in U.S.A.

CLYMER and colophon are registered trademarks of Prism Business Media Inc.

ISBN-10: 1-59969-083-7

ISBN-13: 978-1-59969-083-4

Library of Congress: 2006934606

AUTHOR: Ron Wright.

TECHNICAL PHOTOGRAPHY: Ron Wright. Special thanks to Clawson Motorsports in Fresno, California for their assistance.

TECHNICAL ILLUSTRATION: Steve Amos.

WIRING DIAGRAMS: Bob Meyer and Lee Buell.

EDITOR: James Grooms.

PRODUCTION: Julie Jantzer-Ward.

TOOLS AND EQUIPMENT: K&L Supply Co. at www.klsupply.com.

COVER: Mark Clifford Photography at www.markclifford.com.

Chapter One
General Information

1

Chapter Two
Troubleshooting

2

Chapter Three
Periodic Lubrication, Maintenance and Tune-up

3

Chapter Four
Engine Top End

4

Chapter Five
Engine Lower End

5

Chapter Six
Clutch and External Shift Mechanism

6

Chapter Seven
Transmission and Internal Shift Mechanism

7

Chapter Eight
Fuel and Emission Control Systems

8

Chapter Nine
Electrical System

9

Chapter Ten
Cooling System

10

Chapter Eleven
Wheels, Tires and Drive Chain

11

Chapter Twelve
Front Suspension and Steering

12

Chapter Thirteen
Rear Suspension

13

Chapter Fourteen
Brakes

14

Chapter Fifteen
Body and Exhaust System

15

Index

16

Wiring Diagrams

17

CLYMER®

Publisher Shawn Etheridge

EDITORIAL

Managing Editor
James Grooms

Associate Editors
Richard Arens
Steven Thomas

Authors
Jay Bogart
Jon Engleman
Michael Morlan
George Parise
Mark Rolling
Ed Scott
Ron Wright

Illustrators
Steve Amos
Errol McCarthy
Mitzi McCarthy

Group Production Manager
Dylan Goodwin

Senior Production Editors
Greg Araujo
Darin Watson

Production Editors
Julie Jantzer-Ward
Justin Marciniak
Holly Messinger

Associate Production Editor
Susan Hartington

Technical Illustrator
Bob Meyer

MARKETING/SALES AND ADMINISTRATION

Sales Channel & Brand Marketing Coordinator
Melissa Abbott Mudd

Art Director
Chris Paxton

Sales Managers
Justin Henton
Dutch Sadler
Matt Tusken

Business Manager
Ron Rogers

Customer Service Manager
Terri Cannon

Customer Service Representatives
Felicia Dickerson
Courtney Hollars
April LeBlond

Warehouse & Inventory Manager
Leah Hicks

PRiSM
BUSINESS MEDIA™
P.O. Box 12901, Overland Park, KS 66282-2901 • 800-262-1954 • 913-967-1719

The following books and guides are published by Prism Business Media

More information available at *clymer.com*

CONTENTS

QUICK REFERENCE DATA . . . . **IX**

CHAPTER ONE
GENERAL INFORMATION **1**

Manual organization
Warnings, cautions and notes
Safety
Serial numbers
Fasteners
Shop supplies

Basic tools
Precision measuring tools
Electrical system fundamentals
Special tools
Basic service methods
Storage

CHAPTER TWO
TROUBLESHOOTING **34**

Engine operating requirements
Starting the engine
Engine will not start
Poor engine performance
Fuel system
Engine
Engine lubrication

Cylinder leakdown test
Clutch
Gearshift linkage
Transmission
Electrical testing
Front suspension and steering
Brake system

CHAPTER THREE
PERIODIC LUBRICATION, MAINTENANCE AND TUNE-UP **58**

Fuel type
Tune-Up
Cylinder identification and firing order
Air filter
Crankcase breather inspection
Engine compression test
Spark plugs
Ignition timing inspection
Valve clearance
Carburetor
Fuel hose inspection
Throttle cable
Clutch cable adjustment
Speedometer cable lubrication

Engine oil and filter
Cooling system
Emission control systems inspection
Battery
Tires and wheels
Steering bearing inspection
Front suspension inspection
Rear suspension inspection
Brakes
Drive chain
Lights and horn
Sidestand and ignition cut-off
 switch inspection
Fastener inspection

CHAPTER FOUR
ENGINE TOP END **98**

Servicing the engine in the frame
Cylinder head covers
Camshafts
Cam chain tensioner and cam chain
Cylinder head

Valves and valve components
Cylinder
Piston and piston rings
Cylinder stud replacement

CHAPTER FIVE
ENGINE LOWER END **145**

Shop cleanliness
Servicing engine in frame
Engine
Crankcase

Crankcase seal and bearing replacement
Crankshaft
Connecting rods
Oil pump

CHAPTER SIX
CLUTCH AND EXTERNAL SHIFT MECHANISM **172**

Clutch cable replacement
Right crankcase cover
Clutch release lever

Clutch
Primary drive gear
External shift mechanism

CHAPTER SEVEN
TRANSMISSION AND INTERNAL SHIFT MECHANISM **193**

Transmission operation
Transmission

Internal shift mechanism

CHAPTER EIGHT
FUEL AND EMISSION CONTROL SYSTEMS 207

Fuel system precautions
Fuel hose identification
Air filter housing
Air filter chamber
Sub-air filter element
Carburetor operation
Carburetor service
Carburetor adjustment
Carburetor heater
  and air temperature switch

Throttle cable replacement
Choke cable replacement
Fuel filter
Fuel pump
Fuel tank
Crankcase breather system
Evaporative emission control system
  (California models)

CHAPTER NINE
ELECTRICAL SYSTEM 244

Electrical component replacement
Electrical connectors
Electrical component location
Battery
Charging system
Stator coil and left crankcase cover
Flywheel, starter clutch and
  starter reduction gears
Ignition system troubleshooting
Ignition coils
Ignition pulse generator
Ignition pulse generator rotor
Ignition control module (ICM)
Starting system troubleshooting
Starter
Starter relay switch
Clutch diode
Lighting system
Headlight housing
Speedometer assembly

Speedometer/speed sensor
Coolant temperature circuit troubleshooting
Coolant temperature switch testing
  and replacement
Fan motor switch
Oil pressure indicator
  and oil pressure switch
Neutral indicator and neutral switch
Sidestand switch
Clutch switch
Front brake light switch
Rear brake light switch
Ignition switch
Handlebar switch
Switch continuity test
Turn signal relay
Horn
Fuses
Wiring diagrams

CHAPTER TEN
COOLING SYSTEM 312

Temperature warning system
Cooling system inspection
Radiator
Cooling fan

Coolant reserve tank
Thermostat
Thermostat housing
Water pump

CHAPTER ELEVEN
WHEELS, TIRES AND DRIVE CHAIN **325**

Motorcycle lift
Front wheel
Speedometer gear and cable
Rear wheel
Driven flange
Front and rear hubs

Wheel service
Tire safety
Tire changing
Wheel balance
Drive and driven sprockets
Drive chain

CHAPTER TWELVE
FRONT SUSPENSION AND STEERING **356**

Handlebar
Handlebar grips and weights
Front fork
Steering head and stem

Steering bearing preload check
Steering head bearing race replacement
Steering stem bearing race replacement

CHAPTER THIRTEEN
REAR SUSPENSION **385**

Shock absorber

Rear swing arm

CHAPTER FOURTEEN
BRAKES **396**

Brake fluid selection
Preventing brake fluid damage
Brake service
Front brake pads
Front caliper
Front master cylinder

Front brake hose replacement
Front brake disc
Brake bleeding
Brake fluid draining
Rear drum brake
Rear brake pedal

CHAPTER FIFTEEN
BODY AND EXHAUST SYSTEM **423**

Seat
Side covers
Steering covers (VT750C)
Front fender

Rear fender
Grab rail
Exhaust system

INDEX **430**

WIRING DIAGRAMS **437**

QUICK REFERENCE DATA

MOTORCYCLE INFORMATION

MODEL:_____ YEAR:_____

VIN NUMBER:_____

ENGINE SERIAL NUMBER:_____

CARBURETOR SERIAL NUMBER OR I.D. MARK:_____

COLOR CODE:_____

TIRE INFLATION PRESSURE*

	Front psi (kPa)	Rear psi (kPa)
Rider	29 (200)	29 (200)
Maximum weight capacity	29 (200)	36 (250)

* The tire inflation pressures listed here are for original equipment tires. Aftermarket tires may require different inflation pressure. Refer to tire manufacturer's specifications.

RECOMMENDED LUBRICANTS AND FUEL

Brake fluid	DOT 4
Control cables	Cable lubricant
Cooling system	Honda HP Coolant or equivalent[1]
Drive chain	Drive chain lubricant specified for O-ring use or No. 80-90 gear oil.
Engine oil	
Classification	
JASO T 903 standard classification	MA
API classification	SG or higher[2]
Viscosity classification	SAE 10W-40
Fork oil	Pro Honda Suspension Fluid SS-8 or equivalent 10 wt fork oil
Fuel	Unleaded gasoline with a pump octane number of 86 or higher[3]

1. Coolant must not contain silicate inhibitors as they can cause premature wear to the water pump seals. See text for further information.
2. API SG or higher classified oils not specified as ENERGY CONSERVING can be used. See text for additional information.

ENGINE OIL CAPACITY

	Liters	U.S. qt.
Change engine oil only	2.2	2.32
Engine oil and filter change	2.4	2.54
Engine disassembly	2.9	3.06

COOLANT CAPACITY

	Liters	U.S. qt.
Radiator and engine	1.75	1.85
Reserve tank	0.4	0.42

MAINTENANCE SPECIFICATIONS

Brake pedal free play	20-30 mm (3/4-1 1/4 in.)
Brake pedal height	
VT750C	50 mm (2.0 in.) above top of footpeg
VT750DC	–
Carburetor synchronization	
Base carburetor	No. 1
Maximum vacuum difference	27 kPa (200 mm Hg 0.7 in. Hg)
Clutch lever free play	10-20 mm (3/8-3/4 in.)
Cylinder number	No. 1 (rear)
	No. 2 (front)
Drive chain free play	15-35 mm (19/32-1 3/8 in.)
Engine compression	1275 ± 98 kPa (185 ± 14 psi) @ 400 rpm
Engine idle speed	
2001-2003	1000 ± 100 rpm
2004-2005	
49-state/Canada	1000 ± 100 rpm
California	1200 ± 100 rpm
2006-on	1200 ± 100 rpm
Engine oil pressure	530 kPa (77 psi) @ 5500 rpm/80° C (176° F)
Firing order	Front (308°), rear (412°)
Ignition timing	
F mark	
VT750C	8° BTDC @ 1000 rpm
VT750DC	6° BTDC @ 1000 rpm
Spark plug gap	0.8-0.9 mm (0.031-0.035 in.)
Spark plug type	
NGK	
Standard	DPR8EA-9
Cold climate*	DPR7EA-9
Extended high speed riding	DPR9EA-9
Denso	
Standard	X24EPR-U9
Cold climate*	X22EPR-U9
Extended high speed riding	X2 EPR-U9
Valve clearance	
Intake	0.13-0.17 mm (0.005-0.007 in.)
Exhaust	0.18-0.22 mm (0.007-0.009 in.)
Throttle grip free play	2-6 mm (5/64-1/4 in.)

* Ambient temperature below 5° C (41° F).

CHAPTER ONE

GENERAL INFORMATION

This detailed and comprehensive manual covers the Honda VT750 series from 1998-2006.

The text provides complete information on maintenance, tune-up, repair and overhaul. Hundreds of original photographs and illustrations created during the complete disassembly of the motorcycle guide the reader through every job. All procedures are in step-by-step form and designed for the reader who may be working on the motorcycle for the first time.

MANUAL ORGANIZATION

A shop manual is a tool and as in all Clymer manuals, the chapters are thumb tabbed for easy reference. Main headings are listed in the table of contents and the index. Frequently used specifications and capacities from the tables at the end of each individual chapter are listed in the *Quick Reference Data* section at the front of the manual. Specifications and capacities are provided in U.S. Standard and metric units of measure.

Some procedures have references to headings in other chapters or sections of the manual. When a specific heading is called out it in a step it will be *italicized* as it appears in the manual. If a sub-heading is indicated as being "in this section" it is located within the same main heading. For example, the sub-heading *Handling Gasoline Safely* is located within the main heading *SAFETY.*

This chapter provides general information on shop safety, tools and their usage, service funda-

mentals and shop supplies. **Tables 1-9**, at the end of the chapter, list the following:

Table 1 lists engine and frame serial numbers.
Table 2 lists motorcycle dimensions.
Table 3 lists motorcycle weight.
Table 4 lists fuel tank capacity.
Table 5 lists metric, inch and fractional equivalents.
Table 6 lists conversion formulas.
Table 7 lists general torque specifications.
Table 8 lists technical abbreviations.
Table 8 lists metric tap and drill sizes.

Chapter Two provides methods for quick and accurate diagnosis of problems. Troubleshooting procedures present typical symptoms and logical methods to pinpoint and repair the problem.

Chapter Three explains all routine maintenance necessary to keep the motorcycle running well. Chapter Three also includes recommended tune-up procedures, eliminating the need to constantly consult the chapters on the various assemblies.

Subsequent chapters describe specific systems such as engine, transmission, clutch, drive system, fuel system, suspension, brakes, body components and exhaust system.

WARNINGS, CAUTIONS AND NOTES

The terms WARNING, CAUTION and NOTE have specific meanings in this manual.

A WARNING emphasizes areas where injury or even death could result from negligence. Mechanical damage may also occur. WARNINGS *are to be taken seriously.*

A CAUTION emphasizes areas where equipment damage could result. Disregarding a CAUTION could cause permanent mechanical damage, though injury is unlikely.

A NOTE provides additional information to make a step or procedure easier or clearer. Disregarding a NOTE could cause inconvenience, but would not cause equipment damage or injury.

SAFETY

Professional mechanics can work for years and never sustain a serious injury or mishap. Follow these guidelines and practice common sense to safely service the motorcycle.

1. Do not operate the motorcycle in an enclosed area. The exhaust gasses contain carbon monoxide, an odorless, colorless, and tasteless poisonous gas. Carbon monoxide levels build quickly in small enclosed areas and can cause unconsciousness and death in a short time. Make sure the work area is properly ventilated or operate the motorcycle outside.

2. *Never* use gasoline or any extremely flammable liquid to clean parts. Refer to *Cleaning Parts* and *Handling Gasoline Safely* in this section.

3. *Never* smoke or use a torch in the vicinity of flammable liquids, such as gasoline or cleaning solvent.

4. If welding or brazing on the motorcycle, remove the fuel tank, fuel body and shocks to at least 50 ft. (15 m) away.

5. Use the correct type and size of tools to avoid damaging fasteners.

6. Keep tools clean and in good condition. Replace or repair worn or damaged equipment.

7. When loosening a tight fastener, be guided by what would happen if the tool slipped.

8. When replacing fasteners, make sure the new fasteners are the same size and strength as the original ones.

9. Keep the work area clean and organized.

10. Wear eye protection *any time* the safety of the eyes is in question. This includes procedures that involve drilling, grinding, hammering, compressed air and chemicals.

11. Wear the correct clothing for the job. Tie up or cover long hair so it cannot catch in moving equipment.

12. Do not carry sharp tools in clothing pockets.

13. Always have an approved fire extinguisher available. Make sure it is rated for gasoline (Class B) and electrical (Class C) fires.

14. Do not use compressed air to clean clothes, the motorcycle or the work area. Debris may be blown into the eyes or skin. *Never* direct compressed air at anyone. Do not allow children to use or play with any compressed air equipment.

15. When using compressed air to dry rotating parts, hold the part so it cannot rotate. Do not allow the force of the air to spin the part. The air jet is capable of rotating parts at an extreme speed. The part may become damaged or disintegrate, causing serious injury.

16. Do not inhale the dust created by brake pad and clutch wear. These particles may contain asbestos. In addition, some types of insulating materials and gaskets may contain asbestos. Inhaling asbestos particles is hazardous to health.

17. Never work on the motorcycle while someone is working under it.

18. When placing the motorcycle on a stand, make sure it is secure before walking away.

Handling Gasoline Safely

Gasoline is a volatile flammable liquid and is one of the most dangerous items in the shop. Because gasoline is used so often, many people forget it is hazardous. Only use gasoline as fuel for gasoline internal combustion engines. Keep in mind when working on a motorcycle that gasoline is always present in the fuel tank, fuel line and fuel body. To avoid a disastrous accident when working around the fuel system, carefully observe the following precautions:

1. *Never* use gasoline to clean parts. Refer to *Cleaning Parts* in this section.

2. When working on the fuel system, work outside or in a well-ventilated area.

3. Do not add fuel to the fuel tank or service the fuel system while the motorcycle is near open flames, sparks or where someone is smoking. Gasoline vapor is heavier than air, it collects in low areas and is more easily ignited than liquid gasoline.

4. Allow the engine to cool completely before working on any fuel system component.

5. Do not store gasoline in glass containers. If the glass breaks, a serious explosion or fire may occur.

6. Immediately wipe up spilled gasoline with rags. Store the rags in a metal container with a lid until they can be properly disposed of, or place them outside in a safe place for the fuel to evaporate.

7. Do not pour water onto a gasoline fire. Water spreads the fire and makes it more difficult to put out. Use a class B, BC or ABC fire extinguisher to extinguish the fire.

8. Always turn off the engine before refueling. Do not spill fuel onto the engine or exhaust system. Do not overfill the fuel tank. Leave an air space at the top of the tank to allow room for the fuel to expand due to temperature fluctuations.

Cleaning Parts

Cleaning parts is one of the more tedious and difficult service jobs performed in the home garage. Many types of chemical cleaners and solvents are available for shop use. Most are poisonous and extremely flammable. To prevent chemical exposure, vapor buildup, fire and serious injury, observe each product warning label and note the following:

1. Read and observe the entire product label before using any chemical. Always know what type of chemical is being used and whether it is poisonous and/or flammable.

2. Do not use more than one type of cleaning solvent at a time. If mixing chemicals is required, measure the proper amounts according to the manufacturer.

3. Work in a well-ventilated area.

4. Wear chemical-resistant gloves.

5. Wear safety glasses.

6. Wear a vapor respirator if the instructions call for it.

7. Wash hands and arms thoroughly after cleaning parts.

8. Keep chemical products away from children and pets.

9. Thoroughly clean all oil, grease and cleaner residue from any part that must be heated.

10. Use a nylon brush when cleaning parts. Metal brushes may cause a spark.

11. When using a parts washer, only use the solvent recommended by the manufacturer. Make sure the parts washer is equipped with a metal lid that lowers in case of fire.

Warning Labels

Most manufacturers attach information and warning labels to the motorcycle. These labels contain instructions that are important to safety when operating, servicing, transporting and storing the motorcycle. Refer to the owner's manual for the description and location of labels. Order replacement labels from the manufacturer if they are missing or damaged.

SERIAL NUMBERS

Serial numbers are stamped on various locations on the frame, engine, transmission and fuel body. Record these numbers in the *Quick Reference Data* section in the front of the manual. Have these numbers available when ordering parts.

The VIN number label (**Figure 1**) is located on the left side of the steering head.

The frame serial number (**Figure 2**) is stamped on the right side of the steering head.

The engine serial number (**Figure 3**) is stamped on a raised pad on the right crankcase.

The carburetor identification number (**Figure 4**) is located on the intake side of the carburetor body.

The color label code (**Figure 5**, typical) is located on the frame behind the left side cover.

FASTENERS

Proper fastener selection and installation is important to ensure the motorcycle operates as designed and can be serviced efficiently. The choice of original equipment fasteners is not arrived at by chance. Make sure replacement fasteners meet all the same requirements as the originals.

Threaded Fasteners

Threaded fasteners secure most of the components on the motorcycle. Most are tightened by turning them clockwise (right-hand threads). If the normal rotation of the component being tightened would loosen the fastener, it may have left-hand threads. If a left-hand threaded fastener is used, it is noted in the text.

Two dimensions are required to match the thread size of the fastener: the number of threads in a given distance and the outside diameter of the threads.

The two systems currently used to specify threaded fastener dimensions are the U.S. Standard system and the metric system (**Figure 6**). Pay particular attention when working with unidentified fasteners; mismatching thread types can damage threads.

> *NOTE*
> *To ensure that the fastener threads are not mismatched or cross-threaded, start all fasteners by hand. If a fastener is hard to start or turn, determine the cause before tightening with a wrench.*

The length (L, **Figure 7**), diameter (D) and distance between thread crests (pitch) (T) classify metric screws and bolts. A typical bolt may be identified by the numbers, 8—1.25 × 130. This indicates the bolt has a diameter of 8 mm, the distance between thread crests is 1.25 mm and the length is 130 mm. Always measure bolt length as shown in L, **Figure 7** to avoid purchasing replacements of the wrong length.

The numbers located on the top of the fastener (**Figure 7**) indicate the strength of metric screws and bolts. The higher the number, the stronger the fastener is. Unnumbered fasteners are the weakest.

Many screws, bolts and studs are combined with nuts to secure particular components. To indicate the size of a nut, manufacturers specify the internal diameter and the thread pitch.

The measurement across two flats on a nut or bolt indicates the wrench size.

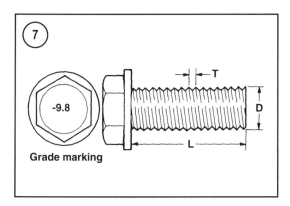

U.S. Standard   Metric

60°   60°

(7)

-9.8

Grade marking

WARNING
Do not install fasteners with a
strength classification lower than
what was originally installed by the
manufacturer. Doing so may cause
equipment failure and/or damage.

Torque Specifications

The materials used in the manufacturing of the motorcycle may be subjected to uneven stresses if the fasteners of the various subassemblies are not installed and tightened correctly. Fasteners that are improperly installed or work loose can cause extensive damage. It is essential to use an accurate torque wrench as described in this chapter and with the torque specifications in this manual.

Specifications for torque are provided in Newton-meters (N•m), foot-pounds (ft.-lb.) and inch-pounds (in.-lb.). Refer to **Table 7** for general torque specifications. To use **Table 7**, first determine the size of the fastener as described in *Threaded Fasteners* in this section. Torque specifications for specific components are at the end of the appropriate chapters. Torque wrenches are covered in the *Basic Tools* section.

Self-Locking Fasteners

Several types of bolts, screws and nuts incorporate a system that creates interference between the two fasteners. Interference is achieved in various ways. The most common type is the nylon insert nut and a dry adhesive coating on the threads of a bolt.

Self-locking fasteners offer greater holding strength than standard fasteners, which improves their resistance to vibration. All self-locking fasteners cannot be reused. The materials used to form the lock become distorted after the initial installation and removal. Discard and replace self-locking fasteners after their removal. Do not replace self-locking fasteners with standard fasteners.

Washers

The two basic types of washers are flat washers and lockwashers. Flat washers are simple discs with a hole to fit a screw or bolt. Lockwashers are used to prevent a fastener from working loose. Washers can be used as spacers and seals or can help distribute fastener load and prevent the fastener from damaging the component.

As with fasteners, when replacing washers make sure the replacement washers are of the same design and quality.

Cotter Pins

A cotter pin is a split metal pin inserted into a hole or slot to prevent a fastener from loosening. In certain applications, such as the rear axle on an ATV or motorcycle, the fastener must be secured in this way. For these applications, a cotter pin and castellated (slotted) nut is used.

To use a cotter pin, first make sure the diameter is correct for the hole in the fastener. After correctly tightening the fastener and aligning the holes, insert the cotter pin through the hole and bend the ends over the fastener (**Figure 8**). Unless instructed to do so, never loosen a tightened fastener to align the holes. If the holes do not align, tighten the fastener enough to achieve alignment.

Cotter pins are available in various diameters and lengths. Measure the length from the bottom of the head to the tip of the shortest pin.

Snap Rings and E-clips

Snap rings (**Figure 9**) are circular-shaped metal retaining clips. They are required to secure parts and gears in place on parts such as shafts, pins or rods. External type snap rings are used to retain items on shafts. Internal type snap rings secure parts within housing bores. In some applications, in addition to securing the component(s), snap rings of varying thicknesses also determine endplay. These are usually called selective snap rings.

The two basic types of snap rings used are machined and stamped snap rings. Machined snap rings (**Figure 10**) can be installed in either direction because both faces have sharp edges. Stamped snap rings (**Figure 11**) are manufactured with a sharp and round edge. When installing a stamped snap ring in a thrust application, install the sharp edge facing away from the part producing the thrust.

E-clips are used when it is not practical to use a snap ring. Remove E-clips with a flat blade screwdriver by prying between the shaft and E-clip. To install an E-clip, center it over the shaft groove and push or tap it into place.

Observe the following when installing snap rings:

1. Remove and install snap rings with snap ring pliers. Refer to *Snap Ring Pliers* in this chapter.
2. In some applications it may be necessary to replace snap rings after removing them.
3. Compress or expand snap rings only enough to install them. If overly expanded, they lose their retaining ability.
4. After installing a snap ring, make sure it seats completely.
5. Wear eye protection when removing and installing snap rings.

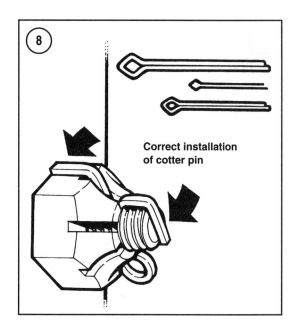

Correct installation of cotter pin

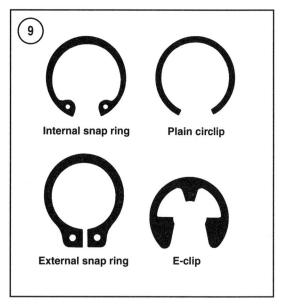

Internal snap ring　　Plain circlip

External snap ring　　E-clip

SHOP SUPPLIES

Lubricants and Fluids

Periodic lubrication helps ensure a long service life for any type of equipment. Using the correct type of lubricant is as important as performing the lubrication service, although in an emergency the wrong type is better than not using one. The following section describes the types of lubricants most often required. Make sure to follow the manufacturer's recommendations for lubricant types.

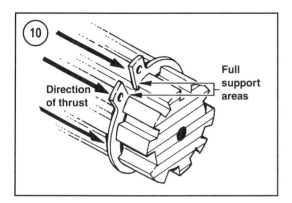

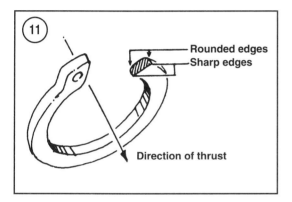

Engine oils

Engine oil for four-stroke motorcycle engine use is classified by three standards: the American Petroleum Institute (API) service classification, the Society of Automotive Engineers (SAE) viscosity rating and the Japanese Automobile Standards Organization (JASO) T 903 Standard rating.

The API and SAE information is on all oil container labels. The JASO information is found on oil containers sold by the oil manufacturer specifically for motorcycle use. Two letters indicate the API service classification. The number or sequence of numbers and letter (10W-40 for example) is the oil's viscosity rating. The API service classification and the SAE viscosity index are not indications of oil quality.

The API service classification indicates that the oil meets specific lubrication standards. The first letter in the classification S indicates that the oil is for gasoline engines. The second letter indicates the standard the oil satisfies.

The JASO certification label identifies two separate oil classifications and a registration number to ensure the oil has passed all JASO certification standards for use in four-stroke motorcycle engines. The classifications are: MA (high friction applications) and MB (low friction applications). Only oil that has passed JASO standards can carry the JASO certification label.

NOTE
*Refer to **Engine Oil and Filter** in Chapter Three for further information on API, SAE and JASO ratings.*

Always use an oil with a classification recommended by the manufacturer. Using an oil with a different classification can cause engine damage.

Viscosity is an indication of the oil's thickness. Thin oils have a lower number while thick oils have a higher number. Engine oils fall into the 5- to 50-weight range for single-grade oils.

Most manufacturers recommend multi-grade oil. These oils perform efficiently across a wide range of operating conditions. Multi-grade oils are identified by a *W* after the first number, which indicates the low-temperature viscosity.

Engine oils are most commonly mineral (petroleum) based, but synthetic and semi-synthetic types are used more frequently. When selecting engine oil, follow the manufacturer's recommendation for type, classification and viscosity when selecting engine oil.

Greases

Grease is lubricating oil with thickening agents added to it. The National Lubricating Grease Institute (NLGI) grades grease. Grades range from No. 000 to No. 6, with No. 6 being the thickest. Typical multipurpose grease is NLGI No. 2. For specific applications, manufacturers may recommend water-resistant type grease or one with an additive such as molybdenum disulfide (MoS_2).

Brake fluid

Brake fluid is the hydraulic fluid used to transmit hydraulic pressure (force) to the wheel brakes. Brake fluid is classified by the Department of Transportation (DOT). Current designations for brake fluid are DOT 3, DOT 4 and DOT 5. This classification appears on the fluid container.

Each type of brake fluid has its own definite characteristics. Do not intermix different types of brake fluid as this may cause brake system failure. DOT 5 brake fluid is silicone based. DOT 5 is not compatible with other brake fluids or in systems for which it was not designed. Mixing DOT 5 fluid with other fluids may cause brake system failure. When adding brake fluid, *only* use the fluid recommended by the manufacturer.

Brake fluid damages any plastic, painted or plated surface it contacts. Use extreme care when working with brake fluid, and remove any spills immediately with soap and water.

Hydraulic brake systems require clean and moisture-free brake fluid. Never reuse brake fluid. Keep containers and reservoirs properly sealed.

> *WARNING*
> *Never put a mineral-based (petroleum) oil into the brake system. Mineral oil causes rubber parts in the system to swell and break apart, causing complete brake failure.*

Coolant

Coolant is a mixture of water and antifreeze used to dissipate engine heat. Ethylene glycol is the most common form of antifreeze. Check the motorcycle manufacturer's recommendations (Chapter Three) when selecting antifreeze. Most require one that is specifically designed for use in aluminum engines. These types of antifreeze have additives that inhibit corrosion.

Only mix distilled water with antifreeze. Impurities in tap water may damage internal cooling system passages.

Chain lubricant

Many types of chain lubricants are available. Which type to use depends on the type of chain.

On O-ring (sealed) chains, the lubricant keeps the O-rings pliable and prevents corrosion. The actual chain lubricant is enclosed in the chain by the O-rings. Recommended types include aerosol sprays specifically designed for O-ring chains and conventional engine and gear oils. When using a spray lubricant, check that it is suitable for O-ring chains.

Do not use high-pressure washers, solvents or gasoline to clean an O-ring chain. Only clean with kerosene.

Cleaners, Degreasers and Solvents

Many chemicals are available to remove oil, grease and other residue from the motorcycle. Before using cleaning solvents, consider how they will be used and disposed of, particularly if they are not water-soluble. Local ordinances may require special procedures for the disposal of many types of cleaning chemicals. Refer to *Cleaning Parts* in this chapter for more information.

Use brake parts cleaner to clean brake system components. Brake parts cleaner leaves no residue. Use electrical contact cleaner to clean electrical connections and components without leaving any residue. Carburetor cleaner is a powerful solvent used to remove fuel deposits and varnish from fuel system components. Use this cleaner carefully, as it may damage finishes.

Generally, degreasers are strong cleaners used to remove heavy accumulations of grease from engine and frame components.

Most solvents are designed to be used with a parts washing cabinet for individual component cleaning. For safety, use only nonflammable or high flash point solvents.

Gasket Sealant

Sealant is used in combination with a gasket or seal and occasionally alone. Follow the manufacturer's recommendation when using a sealant. Use extreme care when choosing a sealant different from the type originally recommended. Choose a sealant based on its resistance to heat and various fluids, and the sealing capability.

Common sealant is RTV, or room temperature vulcanizing sealant. This sealant cures at room temperature over a specific time period. This allows the repositioning of components without damaging gaskets.

Moisture in the air causes the RTV sealant to cure. Always install the tube cap as soon as possible after applying RTV sealant. RTV sealant has a limited shelf life and will not cure properly if the shelf life has expired. Keep partial tubes sealed and discard them if they have surpassed the expiration date.

Applying RTV sealant

Clean all old gasket residue from the mating surfaces. Remove all gasket material from blind threaded holes to avoid inaccurate bolt torque. Spray the mating surfaces with aerosol parts cleaner and wipe with a lint-free cloth. The area must be clean for the sealant to adhere.

Apply RTV sealant in a continuous bead 2-3 mm (0.08-0.12 in.) thick. Circle all the fastener holes unless otherwise specified. Do not allow any sealant to enter these holes. Assemble and tighten the fasteners to the specified torque within the time frame recommended by the RTV sealant manufacturer.

Gasket Remover

Aerosol gasket remover can help remove stubborn gaskets. This product can speed up the removal process and prevent damage to the mating surface that may be caused by using a scraping tool. Most of these types of products are very caustic. Follow the gasket remover manufacturer's instructions for use.

Threadlocking Compound

A threadlocking compound is a fluid applied to the threads of fasteners. After tightening the fastener, the fluid dries and becomes a solid filler between the threads. This makes it difficult for the fastener to work loose from vibration or heat expansion and contraction. Some threadlocking compounds also provide a seal against fluid leakage.

Before applying a threadlocking compound, remove any old compound from both thread areas and clean them with aerosol parts cleaner. Use the compound sparingly. Excess fluid can run into adjoining parts.

> *CAUTION*
> *Threadlocking compounds are anaerobic and stress, crack and attack most plastic parts and surfaces. Use caution when using these products in areas where plastic components are located.*

Threadlocking compounds are available in different strength, temperature and repair applications.

Follow the manufacturer's recommendations regarding compound selection.

BASIC TOOLS

Most of the procedures in this manual can be carried out with simple hand tools and test equipment familiar to the home mechanic. Always use the correct tools for the job at hand. Keep tools organized and clean. Store them in a tool chest with related tools organized together.

Some of the procedures in this manual specify special tools. In many cases the tool is illustrated in use. Those with a large tool kit may be able to use a suitable substitute or fabricated replacement. However, in some cases, the specialized equipment or expertise may make it impractical for the home mechanic to attempt the procedure. When necessary, such operations come with the recommendation to have a dealership or specialist perform the task. It may be less expensive to have a professional perform these jobs, especially when considering the cost of equipment.

Quality tools are essential. The best are constructed of high-strength alloy steel. These tools are light, easy to use and resistant to wear. Their working surface is devoid of sharp edges and the tool is carefully polished. They have an easy-to-clean finish and are comfortable to use. Quality tools are a good investment.

When purchasing tools to perform the procedures covered in this manual, consider the tool's potential frequency of use. If a tool kit is just now being started, consider purchasing a basic tool set from a quality tool supplier. These sets are available in many tool combinations and offer substantial savings when compared to individually purchased tools. As work experience grows and tasks become more complicated, specialized tools can be added.

Screwdrivers

Screwdrivers of various lengths and types are mandatory for the simplest tool kit. The two basic types are the slotted tip (flat blade) and the Phillips tip. These are available in sets that often include an assortment of tip sizes and shaft lengths.

As with all tools, use a screwdriver designed for the job. Make sure the size of the tip conforms to the size and shape of the fastener. Use them only for driving screws. Never use a screwdriver for prying or chiseling metal. Repair or replace worn or damaged screwdrivers. A worn tip may damage the fastener, making it difficult to remove.

Phillips-head screws are often damaged by incorrectly fitting screwdrivers. Quality Phillips screwdrivers are manufactured with their crosshead tip machined to Phillips Screw Company specifications. Poor quality or damaged Phillips screwdrivers can back out (camout) and round over the screw head. In addition, weak or soft material screws can make removal difficult.

The best type of screwdriver to use on Phillips screws is the ACR Phillips II screwdriver, patented by the Phillips Screw Company. ACR stands for the horizontal anti-camout ribs found on the driving faces or flutes of the screwdrivers tip (**Figure 12**). ACR Phillips II screwdrivers were designed as part of a manufacturing drive system to be used with ACR Phillips II screws, but they work well on all common Phillips screws. A number of tool companies offer ACR Phillips II screwdrivers in different tip sizes and interchangeable bits to fit screwdriver bit holders.

> *NOTE*
> *Another way to prevent camout and to increase the grip of a Phillips screwdriver is to apply valve grinding compound or Permatex Screw & Socket Gripper onto the screwdriver tip. After loosening/tightening the screw, clean the screw recess to prevent engine oil contamination.*

Wrenches

Open-end, box-end and combination wrenches (**Figure 13**) are available in a variety of types and sizes.

The number stamped on the wrench refers to the distance between the work areas. This size must match the size of the fastener head.

The box-end wrench is an excellent tool because it grips the fastener on all sides. This reduces the chance of the tool slipping. The box-end wrench is designed with either a 6- or 12-point opening. For stubborn or damaged fasteners, the 6-point provides superior holding ability because it contacts the fastener across a wider area at all six edges. For general use, the 12-point works well. It allows the wrench to be removed and reinstalled without moving the handle over such a wide arc.

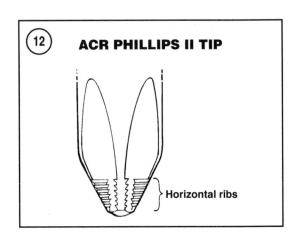

ACR PHILLIPS II TIP

Horizontal ribs

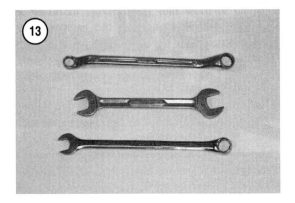

An open-end wrench is fast and works best in areas with limited overhead access. It contacts the fastener at only two points and is subject to slipping if under heavy force or if the tool or fastener is worn. A box-end wrench is preferred in most instances, especially when breaking loose and applying the final tightness to a fastener.

The combination wrench has a box-end on one end and an open-end on the other. This combination makes it a convenient tool.

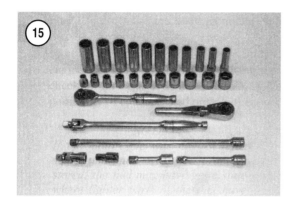

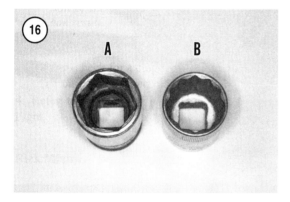

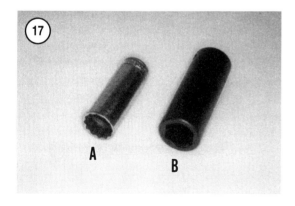

Adjustable Wrenches

An adjustable wrench or Crescent wrench (**Figure 14**) can fit nearly any nut or bolt head that has clear access around its entire perimeter. An adjustable wrench is best used as a backup wrench to keep a large nut or bolt from turning while the other end is being loosened or tightened with a box-end or socket wrench.

Adjustable wrenches contact the fastener at only two points, which makes them more subject to slipping off the fastener. Because one jaw is adjustable

and may become loose only aggravates this shortcoming. Make certain the solid jaw is the one transmitting the force.

Socket Wrenches, Ratchets and Handles

Sockets that attach to a ratchet handle (**Figure 15**) are available with 6-point (A, **Figure 16**) or 12-point (B) openings and different drive sizes. The drive size indicates the size of the square hole that accepts the ratchet handle. The number stamped on the socket is the size of the work area and must match the fastener head.

As with wrenches, a 6-point socket provides superior-holding ability, while a 12-point socket needs to be moved only half as far to reposition it on the fastener.

Sockets are designated for either hand or impact use. Impact sockets are made of thicker material for more durability. Compare the size and wall thickness of a 19-mm hand socket (A, **Figure 17**) and the 19-mm impact socket (B). Use impact sockets when using an impact driver or air tools. Use hand sockets with hand-driven attachments.

> *WARNING*
> *Do not use hand sockets with air or impact tools because they may shatter and cause injury. Always wear eye protection when using impact or air tools.*

Various handles are available for sockets. Use the speed handle for fast operation. Flexible ratchet heads in varying lengths allow the socket to be turned with varying force, and at odd angles. Extension bars allow the socket setup to reach difficult areas. The ratchet is the most versatile. It allows the user to install or remove the nut without removing the socket.

Sockets combined with any number of drivers make them undoubtedly the fastest, safest and most convenient tool for fastener removal and installation.

Impact Driver

An impact driver provides extra force for removing fasteners by converting the impact of a hammer into a turning motion. This makes it possible to remove stubborn fasteners without damaging them.

Impact drivers and interchangeable bits (**Figure 18**) are available from most tool suppliers. When using a socket with an impact driver, make sure the socket is designed for impact use. Refer to *Socket Wrenches, Ratchets and Handles* in this section.

> *WARNING*
> *Do not use hand sockets with air or impact tools because they may shatter and cause injury. Always wear eye protection when using impact or air tools.*

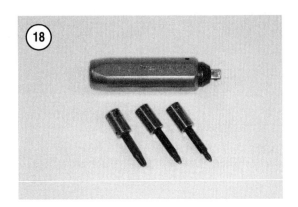

Allen Wrenches

Use Allen or setscrew wrenches (**Figure 19**) on fasteners with hexagonal recesses in the fastener head. These wrenches are available in L-shaped bar, socket and T-handle types. A metric set is required when working on most motorcycles. Allen bolts are sometimes called socket bolts.

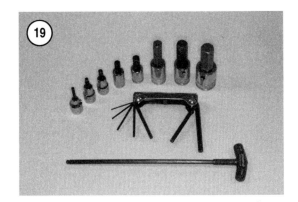

Torque Wrenches

Use a torque wrench with a socket, torque adapter or similar extension to tighten the fastener to a measured torque. Torque wrenches come in several drive sizes (1/4, 3/8, 1/2 and 3/4) and have various methods of reading the torque value. The drive size indicates the size of the square drive that accepts the socket, adapter or extension. Common methods of reading the torque value are the deflecting beam, the dial indicator and the audible click (**Figure 20**). When choosing a torque wench, consider the torque range, drive size and accuracy. The torque specifications in this manual provide an indication of the range required. A torque wrench must be properly cared for to remain accurate. Store torque wrenches in cases or separate padded drawers within a toolbox. Follow the manufacturer's instructions for their care and calibration.

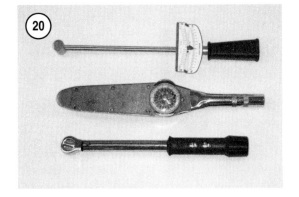

Torque Adapters

Torque adapters or extensions extend or reduce the reach of a torque wrench. The torque adapter shown in **Figure 21** is used to tighten a fastener that cannot be reached because of the size of the torque wrench head, drive and socket. If a torque adapter changes the effective lever length (**Figure 22**), the

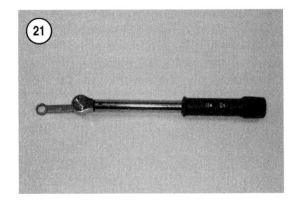

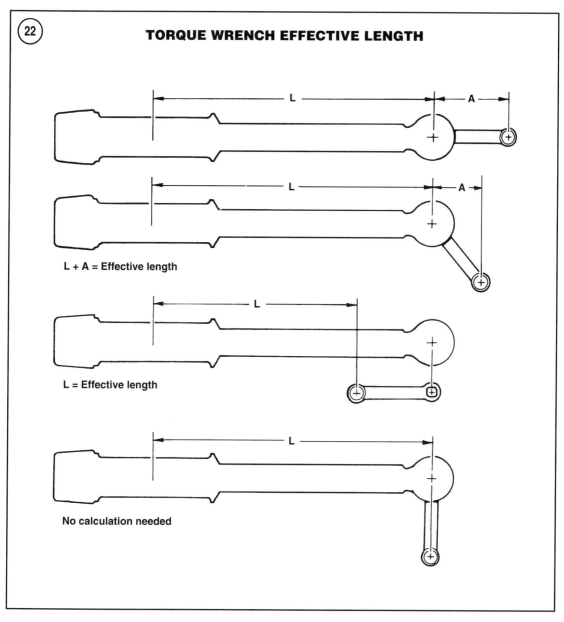

TORQUE WRENCH EFFECTIVE LENGTH

L + A = Effective length

L = Effective length

No calculation needed

torque reading on the wrench will not equal the actual torque applied to the fastener. It is necessary to recalibrate the torque setting on the wrench to compensate for the change of lever length. When using a torque adapter at a right angle to the drive head, calibration is not required because the effective length has not changed.

To recalculate a torque reading when using a torque adapter, use the following formula and refer to **Figure 22**.

$$TW = \frac{TA \times L}{L + A}$$

TW is the torque setting or dial reading on the wrench.

TA is the torque specification and the actual amount of torque that is applied to the fastener.

A is the amount the adapter increases (or in some cases reduces) the effective lever length as measured along the centerline of the torque wrench.

L is the lever length of the wrench as measured from the center of the drive to the center of the grip.

The effective length is the sum of L and A.

Example:

TA = 20 ft.-lb.

A = 3 in.

L = 14 in.

TW = $\frac{20 \times 14}{14 + 3} = \frac{280}{17}$ = 16.5 ft.-lb.

In this example, the torque wrench would be set to the recalculated torque value (TW = 16.5 ft.-lb.). When using a beam-type wrench, tighten the fastener until the pointer aligns with 16.5 ft.-lb. In this example, although the torque wrench is set to 16.5 ft.-lb., the actual torque is 20 ft.-lb.

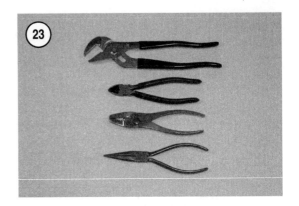

Pliers

Pliers come in a wide range of types and sizes. Pliers are useful for holding, cutting, bending, and crimping. Do not use them to turn fasteners. **Figures 23** and **Figure 24** show several types of useful pliers. Each design has a specialized function. Slip-joint pliers are general-purpose pliers used for gripping and bending. Diagonal cutting pliers are needed to cut wire and can be used to remove cotter pins. Use needlenose pliers to hold or bend small objects. Locking pliers (**Figure 24**) hold objects very tightly. They have many uses ranging from holding two parts together to gripping the end of a broken stud. Use caution when using locking pliers, as the sharp jaws will damage the objects they hold.

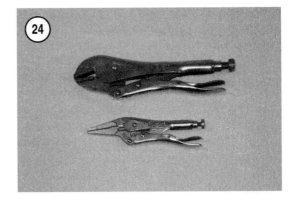

Snap Ring Pliers

Snap ring pliers are specialized pliers with tips that fit into the ends of snap rings to remove and install them.

Snap ring pliers (**Figure 25**) are available with a fixed action (either internal or external) or convertible (one tool works on both internal and external snap rings). They may have fixed tips or interchangeable ones of various sizes and angles. For general use, select a convertible type pliers with interchangeable tips (**Figure 25**).

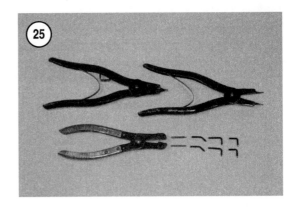

> *WARNING*
> *Snap rings can slip and fly off when removing and installing them. In addition, the snap ring pliers' tips may break. Always wear eye protection when using snap ring pliers.*

Hammers

Various types of hammers are available to fit a number of applications. Use a ball-peen hammer to strike another tool, such as a punch or chisel. Use soft-faced hammers when a metal object must be struck without damaging it. *Never* use a metal-faced hammer on engine and suspension components because damage occurs in most cases.

Always wear eye protection when using hammers. Make sure the hammer face is in good condition and the handle is not cracked. Select the correct

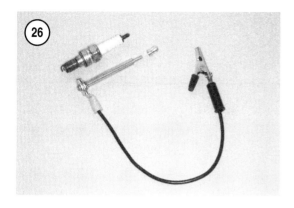

hammer for the job and make sure to strike the object squarely. Do not use the handle or the side of the hammer to strike an object.

Ignition Grounding Tool

Some test procedures require turning the engine over without starting it. To prevent damage to the ignition system from excessive resistance or the possibility of fuel vapor being ignited by an open spark, remove the spark plug caps and ground them directly to a good engine ground with the tool shown in **Figure 26**.

Make the tool shown from a No. 6 screw and nut, two washers, length of tubing, alligator clip, electrical eyelet and a length of wire. Two tools are required to ground both plug caps for each cylinder.

PRECISION MEASURING TOOLS

The ability to accurately measure components is essential to successfully rebuild an engine. Equipment is manufactured to close tolerances, and obtaining consistently accurate measurements is essential to determining which components require replacement or further service.

Each type of measuring instrument is designed to measure a dimension with a certain degree of accuracy and within a certain range. When selecting the measuring tool, make sure it is applicable to the task.

As with all tools, measuring tools provide the best results if cared for properly. Improper use can damage the tool and cause inaccurate results. If any measurement is questionable, verify the measurement using another tool. A standard gauge is usually provided with measuring tools to check accuracy and calibrate the tool if necessary.

Precision measurements can vary according to the experience of the person performing the procedure. Accurate results are only possible if the mechanic possesses a feel for using the tool. Heavy-handed use of measuring tools produces less accurate results. Hold the tool gently by the fingertips to easily feel the point at which the tool contacts the object. This feel for the equipment produces more accurate measurements and reduces the risk of damaging the tool or component. Refer to the following sections for specific measuring tools.

Feeler Gauge

Use the feeler or thickness gauge (**Figure 27**) to measure the distance between two surfaces.

A feeler gauge set consists of an assortment of steel strips of graduated thickness. Each blade is marked with its thickness. Blades can be of various lengths and angles for different procedures.

A common use for a feeler gauge is to measure valve clearance. Use wire (round) type gauges to measure spark plug gap.

Calipers

Calipers (**Figure 28**) are excellent tools for obtaining inside, outside and depth measurements. Although not as precise as a micrometer, they allow reasonable precision, typically to within 0.05 mm (0.001 in.). Most calipers have a range up to 150 mm (6 in.).

Calipers are available in dial, vernier or digital versions. Dial calipers have a dial readout that provides convenient reading. Vernier calipers have marked scales that must be compared to determine the measurement. The digital caliper uses a LCD to show the measurement.

Properly maintain the measuring surfaces of the caliper. There must not be any dirt or burrs between the tool and the object being measured. Never force the caliper closed around an object. Close the caliper around the highest point to remove it with a slight drag. Some calipers require calibration. Always refer to the manufacturer's instructions when using a new or unfamiliar caliper.

To read a vernier caliper refer to **Figure 29**. The fixed scale is marked in 1-mm increments. Ten individual lines on the fixed scale equal 1 cm. The moveable scale is marked in 0.05 mm (hundredth) increments. To obtain a reading, establish the first number by the location of the 0 line on the movable scale in relation to the first line to the left on the fixed scale. In this example, the number is 10 mm. To determine the next number, note which of the lines on the movable scale align with a mark on the fixed scale. A number of lines will seem close, but only one will align exactly. In this case, 0.50 mm is the reading to add to the first number. The result of adding 10 mm and 0.50 mm is a measurement of 10.50 mm.

Micrometers

A micrometer is an instrument designed for linear measurement using the decimal divisions of the inch or meter (**Figure 30**). While there are many types and styles of micrometers, most of the procedures in this manual call for an outside micrometer. Use the outside micrometer to measure the outside diameter of cylindrical forms and the thickness of materials.

A micrometer's size indicates the minimum and maximum size of a part it can measure. The usual sizes (**Figure 31**) are 0-25 mm (0-1 in.), 25-50 mm (1-2 in.), 50-75 mm (2-3 in.) and 75-100 mm (3-4 in.).

Micrometers that cover a wider range of measurements are available. These use a large frame with interchangeable anvils of various lengths. This type of micrometer offers a cost savings, but its overall size may make it less convenient.

Reading

When reading a micrometer, numbers are taken from different scales and added together. The fol-

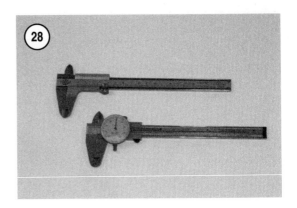

lowing sections describe how to read the measurements of various types of outside micrometers.

For accurate results, properly maintain the measuring surfaces of the micrometer. There cannot be any dirt or burrs between the tool and the measured object. Never force the micrometer closed around an object. Close the micrometer around the highest point to remove with a slight drag. **Figure 32** shows the markings and parts of a standard metric micrometer.

Metric micrometer

The standard metric micrometer is accurate to one one-hundredth of a millimeter (0.01-mm). The sleeve line is graduated in millimeter and half millimeter increments. The marks on the upper half of the sleeve line equal 1.00 mm. Each fifth mark above the sleeve line is identified with a number. The number sequence depends on the size of the micrometer. A 0-25 mm micrometer, for example, has sleeve marks numbered 0 through 25 in 5-mm increments. This numbering sequence continues with larger micrometers. On all metric micrometers, each mark on the lower half of the sleeve equals 0.50 mm.

The tapered end of the thimble has 50 lines marked around it. Each mark equals 0.01 mm. One complete turn of the thimble aligns its 0 mark with the first line on the lower half of the sleeve line or 0.50 mm.

When reading a metric micrometer, add the number of millimeters and half-millimeters on the sleeve line to the number of one one-hundredth millimeters on the thimble. Perform the following steps while referring to **Figure 33**.

1. Read the upper half of the sleeve line and count the number of lines visible. Each upper line equals 1 mm.

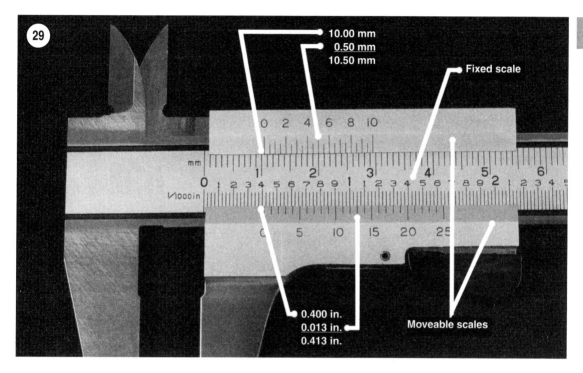

10.00 mm
0.50 mm
10.50 mm

Fixed scale

Moveable scales

0.400 in.
0.013 in.
0.413 in.

DECIMAL PLACE VALUES*

0.1	Indicates 1/10 (one tenth of an inch or millimeter)
0.010	Indicates 1/100 (one one-hundreth of an inch or millimeter)
0.001	Indicates 1/1,000 (one one-thousandth of an inch or millimeter)

*This chart represents the values of figures placed to the right of the decimal point. Use it when reading decimals from one-tenth to one one-thousandth of an inch or millimeter. It is not a conversion chart (for example: 0.001 in. is not equal to 0.001 mm).

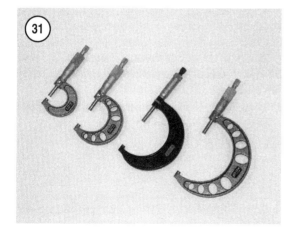

2. See if the half-millimeter line is visible on the lower sleeve line. If so, add 0.50 mm to the reading in Step 1.

3. Read the thimble mark that aligns with the sleeve line. Each thimble mark equals 0.01 mm.

NOTE
If a thimble mark does not align exactly with the sleeve line, estimate the amount between the lines. For accurate readings in two-thousandths of a millimeter (0.002 mm), use a metric vernier micrometer.

4. Add the readings from Steps 1-3.

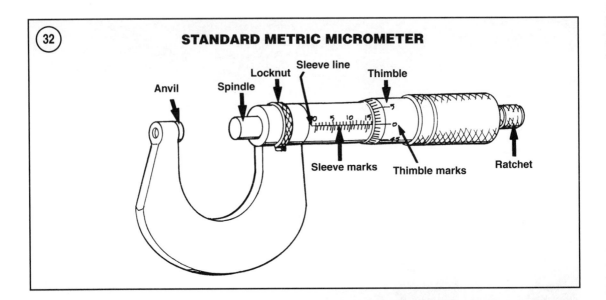

STANDARD METRIC MICROMETER

Anvil · Spindle · Locknut · Sleeve line · Thimble · Sleeve marks · Thimble marks · Ratchet

Adjustment

Before using a micrometer, check its adjustment as follows:

1. Clean the anvil and spindle faces.

2A. To check a 0-1 in. or 0-25 mm micrometer:

   a. Turn the thimble until the spindle contacts the anvil. If the micrometer has a ratchet stop, use it to ensure that the proper amount of pressure is applied.

   b. If the adjustment is correct, the 0 mark on the thimble will align exactly with the 0 mark on the sleeve line. If the marks do not align, the micrometer is out of adjustment.

   c. Follow the manufacturer's instructions to adjust the micrometer.

2B. To check a micrometer larger than 1 in. or 25 mm use the standard gauge supplied by the manufacturer. A standard gauge is a steel block, disc or rod that is machined to an exact size.

   a. Place the standard gauge between the spindle and anvil, and measure its outside diameter or length. If the micrometer has a ratchet stop, use it to ensure that the proper amount of pressure is applied.

   b. If the adjustment is correct, the 0 mark on the thimble will align exactly with the 0 mark on the sleeve line. If the marks do not align, the micrometer is out of adjustment.

   c. Follow the manufacturer's instructions to adjust the micrometer.

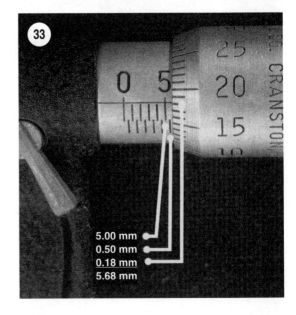

5.00 mm
0.50 mm
0.18 mm
5.68 mm

Care

Micrometers are precision instruments. They must be used and maintained with great care. Note the following:

1. Store micrometers in protective cases or separate padded drawers in a toolbox.

2. When in storage, make sure the spindle and anvil faces do not contact each other or an other object. If they do, temperature changes and corrosion may damage the contact faces.

3. Do not clean a micrometer with compressed air. Dirt forced into the tool causes wear.

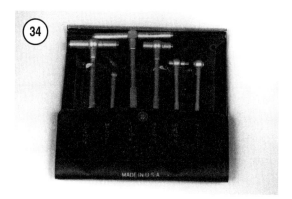

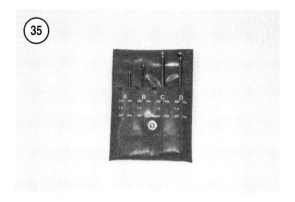

carefully insert the gauge into the bore. Carefully move the gauge in the bore to make sure it is centered. Tighten the knurled end of the gauge to hold the movable post in position. Remove the gauge and measure the length of the posts. Telescoping gauges are typically used to measure cylinder bores.

To use a small-bore gauge, select the correct size gauge for the bore. Carefully insert the gauge into the bore. Tighten the knurled end of the gauge to carefully expand the gauge fingers to the limit within the bore. Do not overtighten the gauge because there is no built in release. Excessive tightening can damage the bore surface and the tool. Remove the gauge and measure the outside dimension (**Figure 36**). Small bore gauges are typically used to measure valve guides.

Dial Indicator

A dial indicator (**Figure 37**) is a gauge with a dial face and needle used to measure variations in dimensions and movements. Measuring brake rotor runout is a typical use for a dial indicator.

Dial indicators are available in various ranges and graduations and with three basic types of mounting bases: magnetic, clamp, or screw-in stud. When purchasing a dial indicator, select the magnetic stand (**Figure 37**) type with a continuous dial.

4. Lubricate micrometers with WD-40 to prevent corrosion.

Telescoping and Small Bore Gauges

Use telescoping gauges (**Figure 34**) and small bore gauges (**Figure 35**) to measure bores. Neither gauge has a scale for direct readings. Use an outside micrometer to determine the reading.

To use a telescoping gauge, select the correct size gauge for the bore. Compress the movable post and

Cylinder Bore Gauge

A cylinder bore gauge is similar to a dial indicator. The gauge set shown in **Figure 38** consists of a dial indicator, handle and different length adapters (anvils) to fit the gauge to various bore sizes. Use the bore gauge to measure bore size, taper and out-of-round. When using a bore gauge, follow the manufacturer's instructions.

Compression Gauge

A compression gauge (**Figure 39**) measures combustion chamber (cylinder) pressure, usually in psi or kg/cm^2. Insert or screw the gauge adapter into the spark plug hole to obtain the reading. Disable the engine so it does not start, and hold the throttle in the wide-open position when performing a compression test. An engine that does not have adequate compression cannot be properly tuned. Refer to Chapter Three.

Multimeter

A multimeter (**Figure 40**) is an essential tool for electrical system diagnosis. The voltage function indicates the voltage applied or available to various electrical components. The ohmmeter function tests circuits for continuity, or lack of continuity, and measures the resistance of a circuit.

Some manufacturers' specifications for electrical components are based on results using a specific test meter. Results may vary if using a meter not recommend by the manufacturer is used. Such requirements are noted when applicable.

Ohmmeter (analog) calibration

Each time an analog ohmmeter is used or if the scale is changed, the ohmmeter must be calibrated.

Digital ohmmeters do not require calibration.
1. Make sure the meter battery is in good condition.
2. Make sure the meter probes are in good condition.
3. Touch the two probes together and observe the needle location on the ohms scale.
4. The needle must align with the 0 mark to obtain accurate measurements.
5. If necessary, rotate the meter ohms adjust knob until the needle and 0 mark align.

ELECTRICAL SYSTEM FUNDAMENTALS

A thorough study of the many types of electrical systems used in today's motorcycles is beyond the scope of this manual. However, a basic understanding of electrical basics is necessary to perform sim-

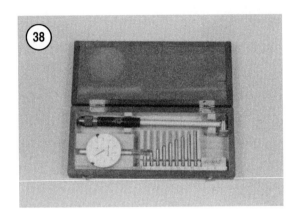

ple diagnostic tests. Refer to *Electric Testing* in Chapter Two for specific procedures.

Voltage

Voltage is the electrical potential or pressure in an electrical circuit and is expressed in volts. The more pressure (voltage) in a circuit, the more work can be performed.

Direct current (DC) voltage means the electricity flows in one direction. All circuits powered by a battery are DC circuits.

Alternating current (AC) means the electricity flows in one direction momentarily and then switches to the opposite direction. Alternator output is an example of AC voltage. This voltage must be changed or rectified to direct current to operate in a battery powered system.

Resistance

Resistance is the opposition to the flow of electricity within a circuit or component and is measured in ohms. Resistance causes a reduction in available current and voltage.

Resistance is measured in an inactive circuit with an ohmmeter. The ohmmeter sends a small amount of current into the circuit and measures how difficult it is to push the current through the circuit.

An ohmmeter, although useful, is not always a good indicator of a circuit's actual ability under operating conditions. This is because of the low voltage (6-9 volts) the meter uses to test the circuit. The voltage in an ignition coil secondary winding can be several thousand volts. Such high voltage can cause

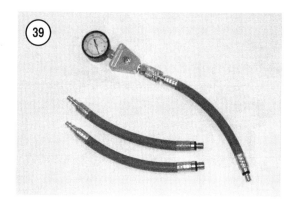

the coil to malfunction, even though it tests acceptable during a resistance test.

Resistance generally increases with temperature. Perform all testing with the component or circuit at room temperature. Resistance tests performed at high temperatures may indicate high-resistance readings and cause the unnecessary replacement of a component.

Amperage

Amperage is the unit of measurement for the amount of current within a circuit. Current is the actual flow of electricity. The higher the current, the more work can be performed up to a given point. If the current flow exceeds the circuit or component capacity, it damages the system.

SPECIAL TOOLS

Some of the procedures in this manual require special tools. These are described in the appropriate chapter and are available from either the manufacturer or a tool supplier.

In many cases, an acceptable substitute may be found in an existing tool kit. Another alternative is to make the tool. Many schools with a machine shop curriculum welcome outside work that can be used as practical shop applications for students.

BASIC SERVICE METHODS

Most of the procedures in this manual are straightforward and can be performed by anyone reasonably competent with tools. However, consider personal capabilities carefully before attempting any operation involving major disassembly of the engine.

1. Front, in this manual, refers to the front of the motorcycle. The front of any component is the end closest to the front of the motorcycle. The left and right sides refer to the position of the parts as viewed by the rider sitting on the seat facing forward.

2. Whenever servicing an engine or suspension component, secure the motorcycle in a safe manner.

3. Tag all similar parts for location and mark all mating parts for position. Record the number and thickness of any shims as they are removed. Identify parts by placing them in sealed and labeled plastic sandwich bags.

4. Tag disconnected wires and connectors with masking tape and a marking pen. Do not rely on memory alone.

5. Protect finished surfaces from physical damage or corrosion. Keep gasoline and other chemicals off painted surfaces.

6. Use penetrating oil on frozen or tight bolts. Avoid using heat where possible. Heat can warp, melt or affect the temper of parts. Heat also damages the finish of paint and plastics.

7. When a part is a press fit or requires a special tool for removal, the information or type of tool is identified in the text. Otherwise, if a part is difficult to remove or install, determine the cause before proceeding.

8. To prevent objects or debris from falling into the engine, cover all openings.

9. Read each procedure thoroughly and compare the illustrations to the actual components before starting the procedure. Perform the procedure in sequence.

10. Recommendations are occasionally made to refer service to a dealership or specialist. In these

cases, the work can be performed more economically by the specialist than by the home mechanic.

11. The term *replace* means to discard a defective part and replace it with a new part. *Overhaul* means to remove, disassemble, inspect, measure, repair and/or replace parts as required to recondition an assembly.

12. Some operations require the use of a hydraulic press. If a press is not available, have these operations performed by a shop equipped with the necessary equipment. Do not use makeshift equipment that may damage the motorcycle.

13. Repairs are much faster and easier if the motorcycle is clean before starting work. Degrease the motorcycle with a commercial degreaser; follow the directions on the container for the best results. Clean all parts with cleaning solvent as they are removed.

> *CAUTION*
> *Do not direct high-pressure water at steering bearings, fuel hoses, wheel bearings, suspension and electrical components. The water forces the grease out of the bearings and possibly damages the seals.*

14. If special tools are required, have them available before starting the procedure. When special tools are required, they are described at the beginning of the procedure.

15. Make diagrams of similar-appearing parts. For instance, crankcase bolts are often not the same lengths. Do not rely on memory alone. Carefully laid out parts can become disturbed, making it difficult to reassemble the components correctly without a diagram.

16. Make sure all shims and washers are reinstalled in the same location and position.

17. Whenever rotating parts contact a stationary part, look for a shim or washer.

18. Use new gaskets if there is any doubt about the condition of old ones.

19. If using self-locking fasteners, replace them with new ones. Do not install standard fasteners in place of self-locking ones.

20. Use grease to hold small parts in place if they tend to fall out during assembly. Do not apply grease to electrical or brake components.

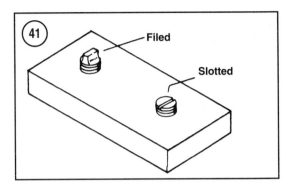

Filed

Slotted

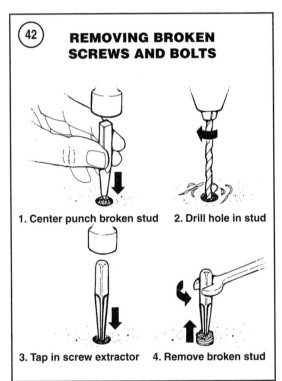

REMOVING BROKEN SCREWS AND BOLTS

1. Center punch broken stud

2. Drill hole in stud

3. Tap in screw extractor

4. Remove broken stud

Removing Frozen Fasteners

If a fastener cannot be removed, several methods may be used to loosen it. First, apply penetrating oil such as Liquid Wrench or WD-40. Apply it liberally and let it penetrate for 10-15 minutes. Rap the fastener several times with a small hammer. Do not hit it hard enough to cause damage. Reapply the penetrating oil if necessary.

For frozen screws, apply penetrating oil as described, then insert a screwdriver in the slot and rap the top of the screwdriver with a hammer. This loosens the rust so the screw can be removed in the normal way. If the screw head is too damaged to use

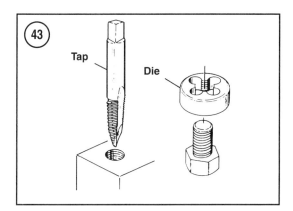

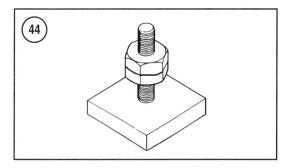

this method, grip the head with locking pliers and twist the screw out.

Avoid applying heat unless specifically instructed because it may melt, warp or remove the temper from parts.

Removing Broken Fasteners

If the head breaks off a screw or bolt, several methods are available for removing the remaining portion. If a large portion of the remainder projects out, try gripping it with locking pliers. If the projecting portion is too small, file it to fit a wrench or cut a slot (**Figure 41**) in it to fit a screwdriver.

If the head breaks off flush, use a screw extractor. To do this, centerpunch the exact center of the remaining portion of the screw or bolt. Drill a small hole in the screw and tap the extractor into the hole. Back the screw out with a wrench on the extractor (**Figure 42**).

Repairing Damaged Threads

Occasionally threads are stripped through carelessness or impact damage. Often the threads can be repaired by running a tap (for internal threads on

nuts) or die (for external threads on bolts) through the threads (**Figure 43**). To clean or repair spark plug threads, use a spark plug tap.

If an internal thread is damaged, it may be necessary to install a Helicoil or some other type of thread insert. Follow the manufacturer's instructions when installing the insert.

If it is necessary to drill and tap a hole, refer to **Table 9** for metric tap and drill sizes.

Stud Removal/Installation

A stud removal tool is available from most tool suppliers. This tool makes the removal and installation of studs easier. If one is not available and the threads on the stud are not damaged, thread two nuts onto the stud and tighten them against each other (**Figure 44**). Remove the stud by turning the lower nut.

1. Measure the height of the stud above the surface.
2. Thread the stud removal tool onto the stud and tighten it or thread two nuts onto the stud.
3. Remove the stud by turning the stud remover or the lower nut.
4. Remove any threadlocking compound from the threaded hole. Clean the threads with an aerosol parts cleaner.
5. Install the stud removal tool onto the new stud or thread two nuts onto the stud.
6. Apply threadlocking compound to the threads of the stud.
7. Install the stud and tighten with the stud removal tool or the top nut.
8. Install the stud to the height noted in Step 1 or its torque specification.
9. Remove the stud removal tool or the two nuts.

Removing Hoses

When removing stubborn hoses, do not exert excessive force on the hose or fitting. Remove the hose clamp and carefully insert a small screwdriver or pick tool between the fitting and hose. Apply a spray lubricant under the hose and carefully twist the hose off the fitting. Clean the fitting of any corrosion or rubber hose material with a wire brush. Clean the inside of the hose thoroughly. Do not use any lubricant when installing the hose (new or old). The lubricant may allow the hose to come off the fitting, even with the clamp secure.

Bearings

Bearings are used in the engine and transmission assembly to reduce power loss, heat and noise resulting from friction. Because bearings are precision parts, they must be maintained with proper lubrication and maintenance. If a bearing is damaged, replace it immediately. When installing a new bearing, take care to prevent damaging it. Bearing replacement procedures are included in the individual chapters where applicable; however, use the following sections as a guideline.

NOTE
Unless otherwise specified, install bearings with the manufacturer's mark or number facing outward.

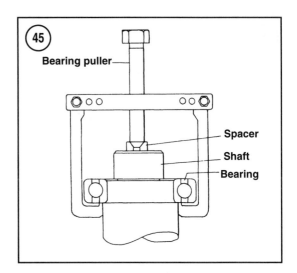

Removal

While bearings are normally removed only when damaged, there may be times when it is necssary to remove a bearing that is in good condition. However, improper bearing removal damages the bearing and possibly the shaft or case half.

1. Before removing the bearings, note the following:
   a. Refer to the bearing replacement procedure in the appropriate chapter for any special instructions.
   b. Remove any seals that interfere with bearing removal. Refer to *Seals* in this chapter.
   c. When removing more than one bearing, identify the bearings before removing them. Refer to the bearing manufacturer's numbers on the bearing.
   d. Note and record the direction in which the bearing numbers face for proper installation.
   e. Remove any set plates or bearing retainers before removing the bearings.

2. When using a puller to remove a bearing from a shaft, take care that the shaft is not damaged. Always place a piece of metal between the end of the shaft and the puller screw. In addition, place the puller arms next to the inner bearing race. See **Figure 45**.

3. When using a hammer to remove a bearing from a shaft, do not strike the hammer directly against the shaft. Instead, use a brass or aluminum rod between the hammer and shaft (**Figure 46**) and make sure to support both bearing races with wooden blocks as shown.

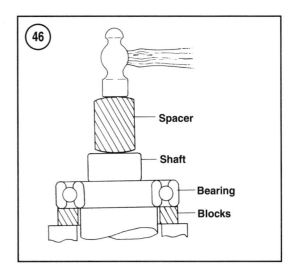

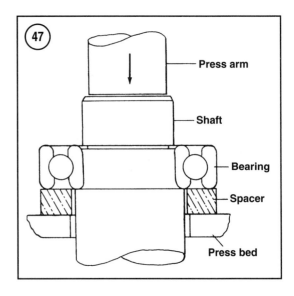

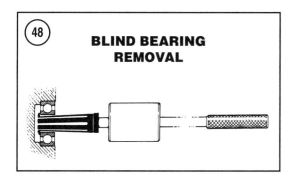

BLIND BEARING REMOVAL

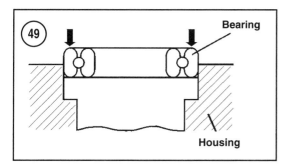

Bearing

Housing

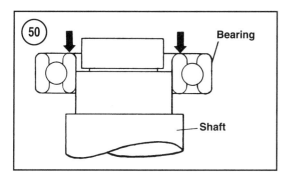

Bearing

Shaft

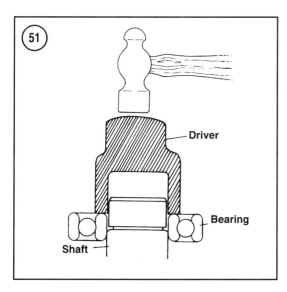

Driver

Bearing

Shaft

4. The ideal method of bearing removal is with a hydraulic press. Note the following when using a press:

a. Always support the inner and outer bearing races with a suitable size wooden or aluminum ring (**Figure 47**). If only the outer race is supported, pressure applied against the balls and/or the inner race damages them.

b. Always make sure the press arm (**Figure 47**) aligns with the center of the shaft. If the arm is not centered, it may damage the bearing and/or shaft.

c. The moment the shaft is free of the bearing, it drops to the floor. Secure or hold the shaft to prevent it from falling.

d. When removing bearings from a housing, support the housing with 4 × 4 in. wooden blocks to prevent damage to gasket surfaces.

5. Use a blind bearing puller to remove bearings installed in blind holes (**Figure 48**).

Installation

1. When installing a bearing in a housing, apply pressure to the *outer* bearing race (**Figure 49**). When installing a bearing on a shaft, apply pressure to the *inner* bearing race (**Figure 50**).

2. When installing a bearing as described in Step 1, some type of driver is required. Never strike the bearing directly with a hammer or the bearing becomes damaged. When installing a bearing, use a piece of pipe or a driver with a diameter that matches the bearing inner race. **Figure 51** shows the correct way to use a driver and hammer to install a bearing.

3. Step 1 describes how to install a bearing in a case half or over a shaft. However, when installing a bearing over a shaft and into the housing at the same time, a tight fit is required for both outer and inner bearing races. In this situation, install a spacer underneath the driver tool so pressure is applied evenly across both races. Refer to **Figure 52**. If the outer race is not supported as shown, the balls push against the outer bearing race and damage it.

Interference fit

1. Follow this procedure when installing a bearing over a shaft. When a tight fit is required, the bearing inside diameter is smaller than the shaft. In this case, driving the bearing on the shaft using normal

methods may cause bearing damage. Instead, heat the bearing before installation. Note the following:

   a. Secure the shaft so it is ready for bearing installation.

   b. Clean all residues from the bearing surface of the shaft. Remove burrs with a file.

   c. Fill a suitable pot or beaker with clean mineral oil. Place a thermometer rated above 120° C (248° F) in the oil. Support the thermometer so it does not rest on the bottom or side of the pot.

   d. Remove the bearing from its wrapper and secure it with a piece of heavy wire bent to hold it in the pot. Hang the bearing in the pot so it does not touch the bottom or sides of the pot.

   e. Turn the heat on and monitor the thermometer. When the oil temperature rises to approximately 120° C (248° F), remove the bearing from the pot and quickly install it. If necessary, place a socket on the inner bearing race and tap the bearing into place. As the bearing chills, it will tighten on the shaft, so installation must be done quickly. Make sure the bearing is installed completely.

2. Follow this step when installing a bearing in a housing. Bearings are generally installed in a housing with a slight interference fit. Driving the bearing into the housing using normal methods may damage the housing or cause bearing damage. Instead, heat the housing before the bearing is installed. Note the following:

CAUTION
Before heating the housing in this procedure, wash the housing thoroughly with detergent and water. Rinse and rewash the cases as required to remove all traces of oil and other chemical deposits.

   a. Heat the housing to approximately 100° C (212° F) in an oven or on a hot plate. To check it is the proper temperature, place tiny drops of water on the housing; if they sizzle and evaporate immediately, the temperature is correct. Heat only one housing at a time.

CAUTION
Do not heat the housing with a propane or acetylene torch. Never bring a flame into contact with the bearing or housing. The direct heat destroys

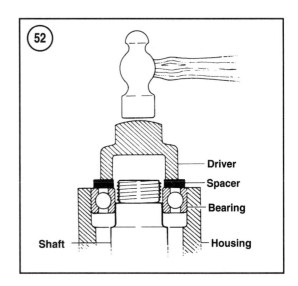

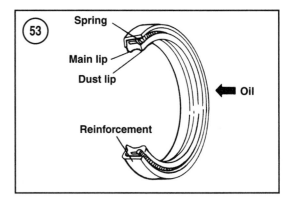

the case hardening of the bearing and likely warps the housing.

   b. Remove the housing from the oven or hot plate, and hold onto the housing with a kitchen potholder, heavy gloves or heavy shop cloth.

NOTE
Remove and install the bearings with a suitable size socket and extension.

   c. Hold the housing with the bearing side down and tap the bearing out. Repeat for all bearings in the housing.

   d. Before heating the bearing housing, place the new bearing in a freezer if possible. Chilling a bearing slightly reduces its outside diameter while the heated bearing housing assembly is slightly larger due to heat expansion. This makes bearing installation easier.

NOTE
Always install bearings with the manufacturer's mark or number facing outward.

e. While the housing is still hot, install the new bearing(s) into the housing. Install the bearings by hand, if possible. If necessary, lightly tap the bearing(s) into the housing with a socket placed on the outer bearing race (**Figure 49**). Do not install new bearings by driving on the inner-bearing race. Install the bearing(s) until it seats completely.

Seal Replacement

Seals (**Figure 53**) contain oil, water, grease or combustion gasses in a housing or shaft. Improper removal of a seal can damage the housing or shaft. Improper installation of the seal can damage the seal. Note the following:
1. Prying is generally the easiest and most effective method of removing a seal from the housing. However, always place a rag underneath the pry tool (**Figure 54**) to prevent damage to the housing.
2. Pack waterproof grease in the seal lips before the seal is installed.

3. In most cases, install seals with the manufacturer's numbers or marks face out.
4. Install seals either by hand or with tools. Center the seal in its bore and install it by hand. If not, install the seal with a socket or bearing driver placed on the outside of the seal as shown in **Figure 55**. Drive the seal squarely into the housing until it is flush with its mounting bore. Never install a seal by hitting against the top of the seal with a hammer.

STORAGE

Several months of non-use can cause a general deterioration of the motorcycle. This is especially true in areas of extreme temperature variations. This deterioration can be minimized with careful preparation for storage. A properly stored motorcycle is much easier to return to service.

Storage Area Selection

When selecting a storage area, consider the following:
1. The storage area must be dry. A heated area is best, but not necessary. It should be insulated to minimize extreme temperature variations.
2. If the building has large window areas, mask them to keep sunlight off the motorcycle.
3. Avoid storage areas close to saltwater.
4. Consider the area's risk of fire, theft or vandalism. Check with an insurer regarding motorcycle coverage while in storage.

Preparing the Motorcycle for Storage

The amount of preparation a motorcycle should undergo before storage depends on the expected length of non-use, storage area conditions and personal preference. Consider the following as the minimum requirement:
1. Wash the motorcycle thoroughly. Remove all dirt, mud and road debris.
2. Start the engine and allow it to reach operating temperature. Drain the engine oil regardless of the riding time since the last service. Fill the engine with the recommended type and quantity of oil.
3. Fill the fuel tank completely.
4. Remove one spark plug from each cylinder head. Ground the spark plug caps to the engine. Refer to *Ignition Ground Tool* in this chapter. Pour a teaspoon

(15-20 ml) of engine oil into the cylinders. Place a rag over the openings and slowly turn the engine over to distribute the oil. Reinstall the spark plugs.

5. Remove the battery. Store the battery in a cool and dry location. Charge the battery once a month. Refer to *Battery* in Chapter Nine for information on battery charging and service.

6. Cover the exhaust and intake openings.

7. Apply a protective substance to the plastic and rubber components, including the tires. Follow the manufacturer's instructions for each type of product being used.

8. Place the motorcycle on a stand. Rotate the front tire periodically to prevent a flat spot from developing and damaging the tire.

9. Cover the motorcycle with old bed sheets or something similar. Do not cover it with any plastic material that traps moisture.

Returning the Motorcycle to Service

The amount of service required when returning a motorcycle to service after storage depends on the length of non-use and storage conditions. In addition to performing the reverse of the above procedure, make sure the brakes, clutch, throttle and engine stop switch work properly before operating the motorcycle. Refer to Chapter Three and evaluate the service intervals to determine which areas require service.

Table 1 ENGINE AND FRAME SERIAL NUMBERS

Model	Starting engine serial number	Starting frame serial number
1998 VT750C		
49-state	RC44E-2000001-on	RC440-WM000001-on
California	RC44E-2000001-on	RC441-WM000001-on
1998 VT750CD		
49-state	RC44E-2000001-on	RC443-WM000001-on
California	RC44E-2000001-on	RC444-WM000001-on
1998 VT750CD2		
49-state	RC44E-2000001-on	RC446-WM000001-on
California	RC44E-2000001-on	RC447-WM000001-on
1999 VT750C		
49-state	RC44E-2200001-on	RC440-XM100001-on
California	RC44E-2200001-on	RC441-XM100001-on
1999 VT750CD		
49-state	RC44E-2200001-on	RC443-XM100001-on
California	RC44E-2200001-on	RC444-XM100001-on
1999 VT750CD2		
49-state	RC44E-2200001-on	RC446-XM1000001-on
California	RC44E-2200001-on	RC447-XM1000001-on
2000 VT750C		
49-state	RC44E-4000001-on	JH2RC440-YM200001-on
49-state	RC44E-4100001-on	JH2RC440-YK300001-on
California	RC44E-4000001-on	JH2RC441-YM200001-on
California	RC44E-4100001-on	JH2RC441-YK300001-on
2000 VT750CD		
49-state	RC44E-4100001-on	JH2RC443-YK300001-on
49-state	RC44E-4000001-on	JH2RC443-YM200001-on
California	RC44E-4100001-on	JH2RC444-YK300001-on
California	RC44E-4000001-on	JH2RC444-YM200001-on
(continued)		

Table 1 ENGINE AND FRAME SERIAL NUMBERS (continued)

Model	Starting engine serial number	Starting frame serial number
2000 VT750CD2		
49-state	RC44E-4000001-on	JH2RC446-YM200001-on
49-state	RC44E-4100001-on	JH2RC446-YK300001-on
California	RC44E-4100001-on	JH2RC447-YK300001-on
California	RC44E-4000001-on	JH2RC447-YM200001-on
2001 VT750CD		
49-state	RC44E-4200001-on	JH2RC443-1K400001-on
California	RC44E-4200001-on	JH2RC444-1K400001-on
2001 VT750CD2		
49-state	RC44E-4200001-on	JH2RC446-1K400001-on
California	RC44E-4200001-on	JH2RC447-1K400001-on
2002 VT750CDA		
49-state	RC44E-4360001-on	JH2RC443-2M610001-on
49-state	RC44E-4300001-on	JH2RC443-2K600001-on
California	RC44E-4360001-on	JH2RC444-2M610001-on
California	RC44E-4300001-on	JH2RC444-2K600001-on
2002 VT750CDB		
49-state	RC44E-4360001-on	JH2RC44J-2M010001-on
49-state	RC44E-4300001-on	JH2RC44J-2K000001-on
California	RC44E-4360001-on	JH2RC44K-2M010001-on
California	RC44E-4300001-on	JH2RC44K-2K000001-on
2002 VT750CDC		
49-state	RC44E-4300001-on	JH2RC446-2K600001-on
49-state	RC44E-4360001-on	JH2RC446-2M610001-on
California	RC44E-4300001-on	JH2RC447-2K600001-on
California	RC44E-4360001-on	JH2RC447-2M610001-on
2002 VT750CDD		
49-state	RC44E-4360001-on	JH2RC44F-2M010001-on
49-state	RC44E-4300001-on	JH2RC44F-2K000001-on
California	RC44E-4360001-on	JH2RC44H-2M010001-on
California	RC44E-4300001-on	JH2RC44H-2K000001-on
2003 VT750CDA		
49-state	RC44E-4460001-on	JH2RC443-3M700001-on
California	RC44E-4460001-on	JH2RC444-3M700001-on
2003 VT750CDB		
49-state	RC44E-4460001-on	JH2RC44J-3M100001-on
California	RC44E-4460001-on	JH2RC44K-3M100001-on
2003 VT750CDC		
49-state	RC44E-4460001-on	JH2RC446-3M700001-on
California	RC44E-4460001-on	JH2RC447-3M700001-on
2003 VT750CDD		
49-state	RC44E-4460001-on	JH2RC44F-3M100001-on
California	RC44E-4460001-on	JH2RC44H-3M100001-on
2001 VT750DC		
49-state	RC44E-6150001-on	JH2RC440-1K500001-on
California	RC44E-6150001-on	JH2RC441-1K500001-on
2002 VT750DC		
49-state	RC44E-6180001-on	JH2RC440-2M610001-on
California	RC44E-6180001-on	JH2RC441-2M600001-on
2003 VT750DCA		
49-state	RC44E-6370001-on	JH2RC440-3M700001-on
California	RC44E-6370001-on	JH2RC441-3M700001-on
2004-2006	NA	

Table 2 MOTORCYCLE DIMENSIONS

	mm	in.
Footpeg height		
VT750C models	302	11.9
VT750DC	Not specified	
Ground clearance		
VT750C	145	5.7
VT750DC	140	5.5
Overall height		
VT750C	1135	44.7
VT750CD/CD2		
1998-2000	1135	44.7
2001-on	1110	43.7
VT750C3/CD3	1110	43.7
VT750DC	1070	42.1
Overall length		
VT750C	2450	96.5
VT750DC	2335	91.9
Overall width		
VT750C	980	38.6
VT750DC	800	31.5
Seat height		
VT750C	700	27.6
VT750DC	675	26.6
Wheelbase		
VT750C	1615	63.6
VT750DC	1645	64.8

Table 3 MOTORCYCLE WEIGHT SPECIFICATIONS

	kg	lb.
Curb weight		
VT750C	246	542.0
VT750DC		
49 state	235.4	519.0
California	236.3	520.0
Dry weight		
VT750C	229	505.0
VT750DC		
49 state	224.5	494.5
California	225.7	497.6
Maximum weight capacity		
VT750C	170	375.0
VT750DC	166	366.0

Table 4 FUEL TANK CAPACITY

Fuel tank	
VT750C	14.0 L (3.7 U.S. gal.)
VT750DC	13.0 L (3.42 U.S. gal.)
Reserve	
VT750C	3.6 L (0.95 U.S. gal.)
VT750DC	4.0 L (1.06 U.S. gal.)

Table 5 METRIC, INCH AND FRACTIONAL

mm	in.	Nearest fraction	mm	in.	Nearest fraction
1	0.0394	1/32	26	1.0236	1 1/32
2	0.0787	3/32	27	1.0630	1 1/16
3	0.1181	1/8	28	1.1024	1 3/32
4	0.1575	5/32	29	1.1417	1 5/32
5	0.1969	3/16	30	1.1811	1 3/16
6	0.2362	1/4	31	1.2205	1 7/32
7	0.2756	9/32	32	1.2598	1 1/4
8	0.3150	5/16	33	1.2992	1 5/16
9	0.3543	11/32	34	1.3386	1 11/32
10	0.3937	13/32	35	1.3780	1 3/8
11	0.4331	7/16	36	1.4173	1 13/32
12	0.4724	15/32	37	1.4567	1 15/32
13	0.5118	1/2	38	1.4961	1 1/2
14	0.5512	9/16	39	1.5354	1 17/32
15	0.5906	19/32	40	1.5748	1 9/16
16	0.6299	5/8	41	1.6142	1 5/8
17	0.6693	21/32	42	1.6535	1 21/32
18	0.7087	23/32	43	1.6929	1 11/16
19	0.7480	3/4	44	1.7323	1 23/32
20	0.7874	25/32	45	1.7717	1 25/32
21	0.8268	13/16	46	1.8110	1 13/16
22	0.8661	7/8	47	1.8504	1 27/32
23	0.9055	29/32	48	1.8898	1 7/8
24	0.9449	15/16	49	1.9291	1 15/16
25	0.9843	31/32	50	1.9685	1 31/32

Table 6 CONVERSION FORMULAS

Multiply:	By:	To get the equivalent of:
Length		
Inches	25.4	Millimeter
Inches	2.54	Centimeter
Miles	1.609	Kilometer
Feet	0.3048	Meter
Millimeter	0.03937	Inches
Centimeter	0.3937	Inches
Kilometer	0.6214	Mile
Meter	3.281	Feet
Fluid volume		
U.S. quarts	0.9463	Liters
U.S. gallons	3.785	Liters
U.S. ounces	29.573529	Milliliters
Imperial gallons	4.54609	Liters
Imperial quarts	1.1365	Liters
Liters	0.2641721	U.S. gallons
Liters	1.0566882	U.S. quarts
Liters	33.814023	U.S. ounces
Liters	0.22	Imperial gallons
Liters	0.8799	Imperial quarts
Milliliters	0.033814	U.S. ounces
Milliliters	1.0	Cubic centimeters
Milliliters	0.001	Liters

(continued)

Table 6 CONVERSION FORMULAS (continued)

Multiply:	By:	To get the equivalent of:
Torque		
Foot-pounds	1.3558	Newton-meters
Torque		
Foot-pounds	0.138255	Meters-kilograms
Inch-pounds	0.11299	Newton-meters
Newton-meters	0.7375622	Foot-pounds
Newton-meters	8.8507	Inch-pounds
Meters-kilograms	7.2330139	Foot-pounds
Volume		
Cubic inches	16.387064	Cubic centimeters
Cubic centimeters	0.0610237	Cubic inches
Temperature		
Fahrenheit	$(°F - 32) \times 0.556$	Centigrade
Centigrade	$(°C \times 1.8) + 32$	Fahrenheit
Weight		
Ounces	28.3495	Grams
Pounds	0.4535924	Kilograms
Grams	0.035274	Ounces
Kilograms	2.2046224	Pounds
Pressure		
Pounds per square inch	0.070307	Kilograms per square centimeter
Kilograms per square centimeter	14.223343	Pounds per square inch
Kilopascals	0.1450	Pounds per square inch
Pounds per square inch	6.895	Kilopascals
Speed		
Miles per hour	1.609344	Kilometers per hour
Kilometers per hour	0.6213712	Miles per hour

Table 7 GENERAL TORQUE SPECIFICATIONS

Fastener size or type	N•m	ft.-lb.	in.-lb.
5 mm screw	4	–	35
5 mm bolt and nut	5	–	44
6 mm screw	9	–	80
6 mm bolt and nut	10	–	88
6 mm flange bolt (8 mm head, small flange)	9	–	80
6 mm flange bolt (10 mm head) and nut	12	–	106
8 mm bolt and nut	22	16	–
8 mm flange bolt and nut	27	20	–
10 mm bolt and nut	35	26	–
10 mm flange bolt and nut	40	29	–
12 mm bolt and nut	55	40	–

Table 8 TECHNICAL ABBREVIATIONS AND ACRONYMS

ABDC	After bottom dead center
API	American Petroleum Institute
ATDC	After top dead center
BBDC	Before bottom dead center
BDC	Bottom dead center
BTDC	Before top dead center

(continued)

Table 8 TECHNICAL ABBREVIATIONS AND ACRONYMS (continued)

C	Celsius (centigrade)
cc	Cubic centimeters
cid	Cubic inch displacement
CDI	Capacitor discharge ignition
cu. in.	Cubic inches
F	Fahrenheit
ft.	Feet
ft.-lb.	Foot-pounds
gal.	Gallons
H/A	High altitude
hp	Horsepower
ICM	Ignition control module
in.	Inches
in.-lb.	Inch-pounds
JASO	Japanese Automobile Standard Organization
kg	Kilograms
kgm	Kilogram meters
km	Kilometer
kPa	Kilopascals
L	Liter
LED	Light emitting diode
m	Meter
ml	Milliliter
mm	Millimeter
MTBE	Methyl Tertiary Butyl Ether
N/A	Not available
N•m	Newton-meters
OE	Original equipment
oz.	Ounces
psi	Pounds per square inch
pt.	Pint
qt.	Quart
rpm	Revolutions per minute
SAE	Society of Automotive Engineers
SE	Starting enrichment

Table 9 METRIC TAP AND DRILL SIZES

Metric size	Drill equivalent	Decimal fraction	Nearest fraction
3 × 0.50	No. 39	0.0995	3/32
3 × 0.60	3/32	0.0937	3/32
4 × 0.70	No. 30	0.1285	1/8
4 × 0.75	1/8	0.125	1/8
5 × 0.80	No. 19	0.166	11/64
5 × 0.90	No. 20	0.161	5/32
6 × 1.00	No. 9	0.196	13/64
7 × 1.00	16/64	0.234	15/64
8 × 1.00	J	0.277	9/32
8 × 1.25	17/64	0.265	17/64
9 × 1.00	5/16	0.3125	5/16
9 × 1.25	5/16	0.3125	5/16
10 × 1.25	11/32	0.3437	11/32
10 × 1.50	R	0.339	11/32
11 × 1.50	3/8	0.375	3/8
12 × 1.50	13/32	0.406	13/32
12 × 1.75	13/32	0.406	13/32

CHAPTER TWO

TROUBLESHOOTING

The troubleshooting procedures described in this chapter provide typical symptoms and logical methods for isolating the cause(s). There may be several ways to solve a problem, but only a systematic approach is successful to avoid wasted time and possibly unnecessary parts replacement.

Gather as much information as possible to aid in diagnosis. Never assume anything and do not overlook the obvious. Make sure the engine start switch is in RUN and there is fuel in the tank. Learning to recognize symptoms makes troubleshooting easier. In most cases, expensive and complicated test equipment is not needed to determine whether repairs can be performed at home. On the other hand, be realistic and do not start procedures that are beyond the experience and equipment available. If the motorcycle does require the attention of a professional, describe symptoms and conditions accurately and fully. The more information a technician has available, the easier it is to diagnose the problem.

Proper lubrication, maintenance and periodic tune-ups reduce the chance of problems occurring. However, even with the best of care the motorcycle may require troubleshooting.

ENGINE OPERATING REQUIREMENTS

An engine needs the correct air/fuel mixture, compression and a spark at the right time to run properly. If one of these is missing, the engine will not run. **Figure 1** explains basic four-stroke engine operation. This is helpful when troubleshooting the engine.

STARTING THE ENGINE

When experiencing engine-starting troubles, it is easy to work out of sequence and forget basic starting procedures. The following sections describe the recommended starting procedures.

Starting Notes

1. A sidestand ignition cut-off system is used on all models. The position of the sidestand can affect engine starting. Note the following:
   a. The engine cannot turn over when the sidestand is down and the transmission is in gear.
   b. The engine can turn over when the sidestand is down and the transmission is in neutral.

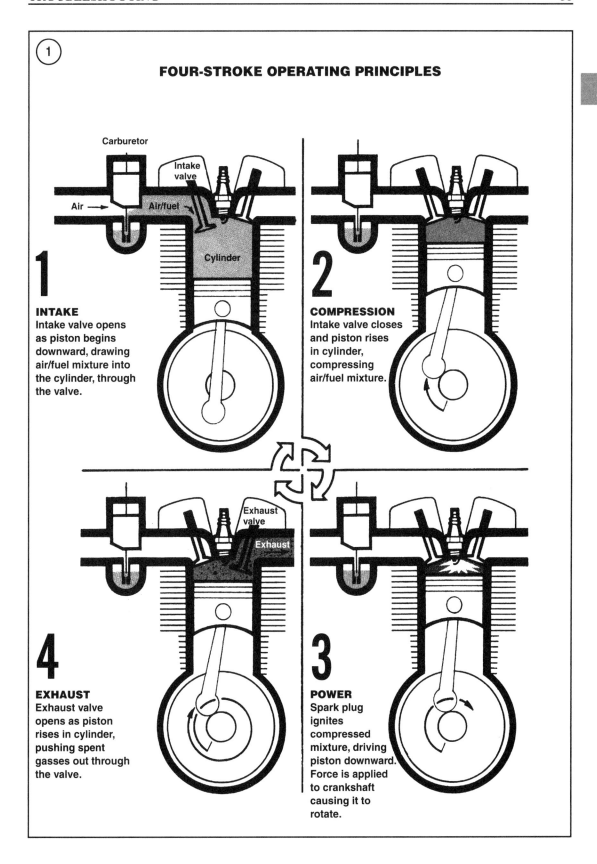

(1)

FOUR-STROKE OPERATING PRINCIPLES

2

Carburetor

Intake valve

Air →

Air/fuel

Cylinder

1

INTAKE
Intake valve opens
as piston begins
downward, drawing
air/fuel mixture into
the cylinder, through
the valve.

2

COMPRESSION
Intake valve closes
and piston rises
in cylinder,
compressing
air/fuel mixture.

Exhaust valve

Exhaust

4

EXHAUST
Exhaust valve
opens as piston
rises in cylinder,
pushing spent
gasses out through
the valve.

3

POWER
Spark plug
ignites
compressed
mixture, driving
piston downward.
Force is applied
to crankshaft
causing it to
rotate.

The engine stops when the transmission is shifted into gear with the sidestand down.

c. The engine can turn over when the sidestand is up and the transmission is in neutral or in gear with the clutch lever pulled in.

2. Before starting the engine, shift the transmission into neutral and confirm the engine stop switch is in the RUN position (A, **Figure 2**).

3. Turn the ignition switch on and confirm the following:

a. The neutral indicator light is on (when transmission is in neutral).

b. The low oil pressure indicator is on. The indicator should go off a few seconds after the engine starts. If the light stays on, turn the engine off and check the oil level (Chapter Three).

NOTE
The low oil pressure indicator comes on when the ignition switch is turned on to show the indicator is working correctly. If the indicator did not come on after turning on the ignition switch, refer to **Oil Pressure Indicator and Oil Pressure Switch** *in Chapter Nine.*

4. Turn the fuel valve on (**Figure 3**, typical).

5. While not part of the starting procedure, the following information is useful in preventing component damage:

a. Running the engine at a fast idle speed for more than 5 minutes and/or repeatedly snapping the throttle on and off at normal air temperature may cause the exhaust pipes to discolor.

b. Excessive choke use can cause an excessively rich fuel mixture. This condition can wash oil off the piston and cylinder surfaces and cause piston and cylinder scuffing.

6. The engine is now ready to start. Refer to *Starting Procedure* in this section.

Starting Procedure

NOTE
Do not operate the starter for more than 5 seconds at a time. Wait approximately 10 seconds between starting attempts.

Engine cold with air temperature between 10-25° C (50-95° F)

1. Review *Starting Notes* in this section.

2. Place the engine stop switch (A, **Figure 2**) in the RUN position.

3. Turn the fuel valve on (**Figure 3**, typical).

4. Turn the ignition switch on.

5. Pull the choke lever (**Figure 4**) to the fully on position.

6. Operate the starter button (B, **Figure 2**) and start the engine. Do not open the throttle when pressing the starter button.

NOTE
When the engine is started with the throttle open and the choke on, a lean mixture results and causes hard starting.

7. With the engine running, operate the choke lever as required to keep the engine idling.

8. After approximately 30 seconds, push the choke lever to the fully off position (**Figure 4**). If the idle is rough, open the throttle lightly until the engine warms up.

Cold engine with air temperature of
10° C (50° F) or lower

1. Review *Starting Notes* in this section.
2. Place the engine stop switch (A, **Figure 2**) in the RUN position.
3. Turn the fuel valve on (**Figure 3**).
4. Turn the ignition switch on.
5. Pull the choke lever (**Figure 4**) to the fully on position.
6. Operate the starter button (B, **Figure 2**) and start the engine. Do not open the throttle when pressing the starter button.
7. Once the engine is running, open the throttle slightly to help warm the engine. Continue warming the engine until the choke can be turned off and the engine responds to the throttle cleanly.

Warm engine and/or high air temperature
35° C (95° F) or higher

1. Review *Starting Notes* in this section.
2. Place the engine stop switch (A, **Figure 2**) in the RUN position.
3. Turn the fuel valve on (**Figure 3**).
4. Turn the ignition switch on.
5. Open the throttle slightly and depress the starter button (B, **Figure 2**). Do not use the choke.

Engine flooded

If the engine does not start after a few attempts, it may be flooded. If a gasoline smell is present after attempting to start the engine, and the engine did not start, the engine is probably flooded. To start a flooded engine, perform the following:
1. Review *Starting Notes* in this section.

2. Place the engine stop switch (A, **Figure 2**) in the RUN position.
3. Turn the fuel valve on (**Figure 3**).
4. Turn the ignition switch on.
5. Turn the choke (**Figure 4**) off.
6. Open the throttle completely and depress the starter button (B, **Figure 2**) for 5 seconds. Note the following:
    a. If the engine starts but idles roughly, vary the throttle position slightly until the engine idles and responds smoothly.
    b. If the engine does not start, turn the ignition switch off and wait approximately 10 seconds. Then repeat the steps under the warm engine starting procedure in this section. If the engine still does not start, refer to *Engine Will Not Start* in this chapter.

ENGINE WILL NOT START

Identifying the Problem

If the engine does not start, perform the following steps in order while remembering the *Engine Operating Requirements* described in this chapter. If the engine fails to start after performing these checks, refer to the troubleshooting procedures indicated in the steps. If the engine starts, but idles or runs roughly, refer to *Poor Engine Performance* in this chapter.

NOTE
An accidentally triggered anti-theft device can cut-off power to the ignition system or starter, depending on how it is wired. If such a device is installed, check its operation for a short circuit.

1. Refer to *Starting the Engine* in this chapter to make sure all switch positions and starting procedures are correct.
2. If the starter does not turn over, perform these quick tests to isolate the starter problem:
    a. Turn the ignition switch on and shift the transmission into neutral. The headlight should come on. If not, check the main fuse and appropriate subfuse (Chapter Nine). If the fuses are good, check the battery cables for a loose or contaminated connection. If good, check the battery (Chapter Nine).

b. If the headlight came on, push the starter button to start the engine. The solenoid should click. If not, the problem is in the wiring to the solenoid, ignition switch, or the solenoid is faulty.

c. If the solenoid did click but the starter did not turn the engine over, the problem may be due to excessive voltage drop in the starter circuit, or the starter is damaged. This could be due to worn brushes or a shorted commutator. The problem can also be in the starter drive system or engine. Refer to *Starting System Troubleshooting* in Chapter Nine.

d. If the problem still exists, refer to the appropriate starter procedure in this section.

3. If the starter turns over, and the engine seems flooded, refer to *Engine Flooded* under *Starting The Engine* in this chapter. If the engine is not flooded, continue with Step 4.

4. Remove the cap from the fuel tank and make sure the fuel tank has a sufficient amount of fuel to start the engine.

5. If there is sufficient fuel in the fuel tank, remove one of the spark plugs immediately after attempting to start the engine. The plug's insulator should be wet, indicating that fuel is reaching the engine. If the plug tip is dry, fuel is not reaching the engine. Confirm this condition by checking a spark plug from the other cylinder. A faulty fuel flow problem causes this condition. Refer to *Fuel System* in this chapter. If there is fuel on each spark plug and the engine does not start, the engine may not have adequate spark. Continue with Step 6.

NOTE
When examining the spark plug caps in the following steps, check for the presence of water in the plug caps.

6. Make sure each spark plug wire is secure. Push the spark plug caps and slightly rotate them to clean the electrical connection between the plug and the connector. If the engine does not start, continue with Step 7.

NOTE
Cracked or damaged spark plug caps and cables can cause intermittent problems that are difficult to diagnose. If the engine occasionally misfires or cuts out, use a spray bottle to wet the spark plug cables and caps

while the engine is running. Water that enters a damaged cap or cable causes an arc through the insulating material, causing an engine misfire.

7. Perform the *Spark Test* in this section. If there is a strong spark at each plug, perform Step 8. If there is no spark or if the spark is very weak, refer to *Ignition System Troubleshooting* in Chapter Nine.

NOTE
Performing a spark test is the quickest way to isolate an ignition or fuel system problem. If a spark is recorded at each plug wire, there is sufficient voltage at each plug and the ignition system is working correctly. Refer to **Fuel System** *in this chapter.*

8. If the fuel and ignition systems are working correctly, perform a leakdown test (this chapter) and cylinder compression test (Chapter Three). If the leakdown test indicates a problem with a cylinder(s), or the compression is low, refer to *Low Engine Compression* under *Engine* in this chapter.

Spark Test

Perform a spark test to determine if the ignition system is producing adequate spark. This test should be performed with a spark tester. A spark tester looks like a spark plug with an adjustable gap between the center electrode and grounded base. Because the voltage required to jump the spark tester gap is sufficiently larger than that of a normally gapped spark plug, the test results are more accurate than with a spark plug. Do not assume that because a spark jumped across a spark plug gap, the ignition system is working correctly.

This test should be performed on a cold and hot engine, if possible. If the test results are positive for each test, the ignition system is working correctly.

NOTE
The spark tester used in this procedure is available from Motion Pro (part No. 08-0122) and can be purchased through motorcycle dealerships.

CAUTION
After removing the spark plug caps and before removing the spark plugs

in Step 1, clean the area around each spark plug with compressed air. Dirt that falls into the cylinder causes rapid engine wear.

NOTE
When disconnecting the spark plug caps in Step 1, check for the presence of water in the plug caps.

1. Disconnect the spark plug caps.
2. Inspect each spark plug for damage.
3. Connect a spark tester to one of the spark plug caps. Ground the spark tester base (or spark plug) to the cylinder head (**Figure 5**). Position the spark tester or spark plug firing tip away from the open spark plug holes. Position the spark tester so the electrodes are visible.

WARNING
Mount the spark tester and spark plugs away from the spark plug holes in the cylinder head so the spark plugs or tester cannot ignite the gasoline vapors in the cylinder. If the engine is flooded, do not perform this test. The firing of the spark plugs or spark tester can ignite fuel ejected through the spark plug holes.

4. Connect a separate spark plug or a grounding tool to each remaining spark plug cap to ground the ignition system.

NOTE
*Refer to **Ignition Grounding Tool** in Chapter One.*

5. With the transmission in neutral, turn the ignition system to on and the engine stop switch (A, **Figure 2**) to the RUN position.

WARNING
Do not hold the spark tester, spark plug or connector or a serious electrical shock may result.

6. Push the starter button to turn the engine over. A fat blue spark must be evident between the spark tester terminals. Repeat for the other cylinder.
7. If there is a spark at each plug wire, the ignition system is functioning properly. Check for one or more of the following possible malfunctions:
   a. Faulty fuel system component.
   b. Flooded engine.
   c. Engine damage (low compression).
8. If the spark was weak or if there was no spark at one or more plugs, note the following:
   a. If there is no spark at all the plugs, perform the peak voltage checks described under *Ignition System Troubleshooting* in Chapter Nine.
   b. If there is no spark at one spark plug only, and the plug is good, there is a problem with the spark plug wire or plug cap. Tighten the spark plug cap and repeat the test.
   c. If there is no spark with one ignition group (two spark plugs, same ignition coil), switch the ignition coils and retest. If there is now spark (both spark plugs), the ignition coil is faulty.

Starter Does Not Turn Over

If the engine does not turn over, the battery or starting system is usually at fault. Check the following steps in order:
1. Refer to *Starting the Engine* in this chapter for proper switch and sidestand operation.
2. Check the condition of the main fuse and the ignition/starter subfuse (Chapter Nine).
3. Check for loose, contaminated or damaged battery cables. Check for damaged battery posts.
4. Discharged or damaged battery. Check the battery and battery cables as described in Chapter Nine.
5. Damaged sidestand switch (Chapter Nine).
6. Damaged starter, starter solenoid or starter switch. Test the starting circuit as described in Chapter Nine to isolate the problem.
7. Ignition system failure. Perform the peak voltage tests in Chapter Nine.
8. Engine damage.

Starter Turns Over Slowly

For the starter to work correctly, the battery must be 75 percent charged and the battery cables cleaned and in good condition. Inspect and test the battery as described in Chapter Nine.

Starter Turns Over Correctly,
but Engine Does Not Start

If the starter turns over correctly, the battery and starting circuit are working correctly. Perform the *Spark Test* in this chapter to isolate the problem to the fuel or ignition system. If the ignition and fuel systems are working correctly, the engine may not have enough compression to start. Refer to *Low Engine Compression* under *Engine* in this chapter.

POOR ENGINE PERFORMANCE

If the engine runs, but performance or drivability is unsatisfactory, refer to the following section that best describes the symptoms.

Engine Starts but Stalls
and is Difficult to Restart

Check for the following:
1. Incorrect choke operation. This can be due to improper use or because the choke valve is stuck in the carburetor.
2. Open the fuel fill cap. If air is sucked into the tank, the fuel tank breather system is plugged. Note the following:
    a. On 49 State and Canada models, the fuel tank breather hose is connected onto the bottom of the fuel tank. Disconnect and clean the hose and the fitting on the fuel tank.
    b. On California models, check the Evaporative emission (EVAP) No. 1 hose. This hose is connected between the fuel tank and the charcoal canister. Disconnect and clean both hose ends and hose fittings. Check the charcoal canister for gasoline.
3. When the ignition switch is first turned on, the fuel pump should run for approximately 2 seconds. Check for a faulty fuel pump or fuel pump system if the pump does not run when the ignition switch is turned on.
4. Plugged fuel feed hose or fuel filter.

5. Incorrect carburetor adjustment.
6. Incorrect float level adjustment.
7. Plugged carburetor jets.

NOTE
If a warm or hot engine starts with the choke on, or if a cold engine starts and runs until the choke is off, the pilot jets are probably plugged.

8. Contaminated or stale fuel.
9. Clogged air filter.
10. Intake air leak.
11. Plugged exhaust system. Check both mufflers, especially if the motorcycle was just returned from storage.
12. Emission control system (California models):
    a. Damaged EVAP CAV control valve.
    b. Damaged EVAP purge control valve.
    c. Plugged or disconnected emission control hose.
13. Faulty ignition system component.

Engine Backfires, Cuts Out
or Misfires During Acceleration

A backfire occurs when fuel is burned or ignited in the exhaust system. A lean air/fuel mixture can cause these engine performance problems.
1. Check for the following conditions:
    a. Incorrect float level adjustment.
    b. Plugged pilot jets or pilot system.
    c. Vacuum leak.
2. Damaged air cut-off valve (installed in each carburetor).
3. Loose exhaust pipe-to-cylinder head connection.
4. Intake air leak.
5. Incorrect ignition timing or a damaged ignition system can cause these conditions. Perform the peak voltage tests in Chapter Nine to isolate the damaged ignition system component. Check the ignition timing as described in Chapter Three.

NOTE
The ignition timing is controlled by the ICM and cannot be adjusted. Checking the ignition timing is used as an aid to diagnose engine and drivability problems.

6. Check the following engine components:

a. Broken valve springs.

b. Stuck or leaking valves.

c. Worn or damaged camshaft lobes.

d. Incorrect valve timing due to incorrect camshaft installation or a mechanical failure.

Engine Backfires on Deceleration

If the engine backfires when the throttle is released, check the following:

1. Damaged air cut-off valve (installed in each carburetor).

2. Lean carburetor pilot system.

3. Loose exhaust pipe-to-cylinder head connection.

4. Damaged EVAP CAV control valve on California models.

5. Faulty ignition system component.

6. Check the following engine components:

a. Broke valve springs.

b. Stuck or leaking valves.

c. Worn or damaged camshaft lobes.

d. Incorrect valve timing due to incorrect camshaft installation or a mechanical failure.

Poor Fuel Mileage

1. Clogged fuel system.

2. Faulty thermostat.

3. Dirty or clogged air filter.

4. Incorrect ignition timing.

5. Vacuum leak.

6. Damaged EVAP CAV control valve on California models.

Engine Does Not Idle or Idles Roughly

1. Clogged air filter element.

2. Poor fuel flow resulting from a partially clogged fuel valve, fuel filter or fuel hose.

3. Contaminated or stale fuel.

4. Incorrect carburetor adjustment.

5. Leaking head gasket(s) or vacuum leak.

6. Intake air leak.

7. Incorrect ignition timing (defective ICM or ignition pulse generator).

8. Low engine compression.

Low Engine Power

1. Support the motorcycle on a stand with the rear wheel off the ground, and then spin the rear wheel by hand. If the wheel spins freely, perform Step 2. If the wheel does not spin freely, check for the following conditions:

a. Dragging brakes.

NOTE
After riding the motorcycle, come to a stop on a level surface in a safe area away from all traffic. Turn the engine off and shift the transmission into neutral. Walk or push the motorcycle forward. If the motorcycle is harder to push than normal, check for dragging brakes.

b. Damaged or binding drive chain.

c. Damaged wheel bearings.

2. Test ride the motorcycle and accelerate quickly from first to second gear. If the engine speed increased according to throttle position, perform Step 3. If the engine speed did not increase, check for one or more of the following problems:

a. Slipping clutch.

b. Warped clutch plates/discs.

c. Worn clutch plates/discs.

d. Weak or damaged clutch springs.

3. Test ride the motorcycle and accelerate lightly. If the engine speed increased according to throttle position, perform Step 4. If the engine speed did not increase, check for one or more of the following problems:

a. Clogged air filter.

b. Restricted fuel flow.

c. Pinched fuel tank breather hose.

d. Clogged or damaged muffler. Tap the mufflers with a rubber mallet to check for loose or broken baffles.

NOTE
A clogged muffler or exhaust system prevents some of the burned exhaust gasses from exiting the exhaust port at the end of the exhaust stroke. This condition affects the incoming air/fuel mixture on the intake stroke and reduces engine power.

4. Check for retarded ignition timing as described in Chapter Three. A decrease in power results when the plugs fire later than normal.

5. Check for one or more of the following problems:

    a. Low engine compression.

    b. Worn spark plugs.

    c. Fouled spark plug(s).

    d. Incorrect spark plug heat range.

    e. Weak ignition coil(s).

    f. Incorrect ignition timing (defective ICM or ignition pulse generator).

    g. Plugged carburetor passages.

    h. Incorrect oil level (too high or too low).

    i. Contaminated oil.

    j. Worn or damaged valve train assembly.

    k. Engine overheating. Refer to *Engine Overheating* in this chapter.

6. If the engine knocks when it is accelerated or when running at high speed, check for one or more of the following:

    a. Incorrect type of fuel.

    b. Lean fuel mixture.

    c. Advanced ignition timing (defective ICM).

NOTE
Other signs of advanced ignition timing are engine overheating and hard or uneven engine starting.

    d. Excessive carbon buildup in combustion chamber.

    e. Worn pistons and/or cylinder bores.

Poor Idle or Low Speed Performance

1. Check for an incorrect pilot screw adjustment.

2. Check for damaged or loose intake manifold and air filter housing hose clamps. These conditions cause an air leak.

3. Perform the spark test in this chapter. Note the following:

    a. If the spark is good, go to Step 4.

    b. If the spark is weak, refer to *Ignition System Troubleshooting* in Chapter Nine.

4. Check the ignition timing as described in Chapter Three. If ignition timing is correct, perform Step 5. If the timing is incorrect, refer to *Ignition System Troubleshooting* in Chapter Nine.

5. Check the fuel system as described under *Fuel System* in this chapter.

Poor High Speed Performance

1. Check ignition timing as described in Chapter Three. If ignition timing is correct, perform Step 2. If the timing is incorrect, refer to *Ignition System Troubleshooting* in Chapter Nine.

2. Check the fuel system as described under *Fuel System* in this chapter.

3. Check the valve clearance as described in Chapter Three. Note the following:

    a. If the valve clearance is correct, perform Step 4.

    b. If the clearance is incorrect, readjust the valves.

4. Incorrect valve timing and worn or damaged valve springs can cause poor high-speed performance. If the camshafts were timed just before the motorcycle experienced this type of problem, the cam timing may be incorrect. If the cam timing was not set or changed, and all of the other inspection procedures in this section failed to locate the problem, inspect the camshafts and valve assembly.

FUEL SYSTEM

The following section isolates common fuel system problems under specific complaints. If the starter turns over and there is spark at each spark plug, poor fuel flow may be preventing the correct amount of fuel from being supplied to the spark plugs. Troubleshoot the fuel system as follows:

1. Open the fuel fill cap. If air is sucked into the tank, the fuel tank breather system is plugged. Note the following:

    a. On 49 State and Canada models, the fuel tank breather hose is connected onto the bottom of the fuel tank.

    b. On California models, check the Evaporative emission (EVAP) No. 1 hose. This hose is connected between the fuel tank and the charcoal canister.

2. Make sure there is a sufficient amount of fuel in the tank.

3. After attempting to start the engine, remove one of the spark plugs (Chapter Three) and check for the presence of fuel on the plug tip. Note the following:

    a. If there is no fuel visible on the plug, remove another spark plug. If there is no fuel on this plug, check for a clogged fuel filter or fuel line. If all of these are good, continue with Step 4.

b. If there is fuel present on the plug tip, and the engine has spark at all of the spark plugs, check for an excessive intake air leak or the possibility of contaminated or stale fuel.

NOTE
If the motorcycle was not used for some time and was not properly stored, the fuel may have gone stale where lighter parts of the fuel have evaporated. Depending on the condition of the fuel, a no-start condition can result.

c. If there is an excessive amount of fuel on the plug, check for a clogged air filter or flooded carburetor (incorrect float level).

4. Refer to *Fuel Pump System Test* in Chapter Eight.

Rich Mixture

The following conditions can cause a rich air/fuel mixture:
1. Clogged air filter.
2. Choke valve stuck open.
3. Float level too high.
4. Contaminated float valve seat.
5. Worn or damaged float valve and seat.
6. Leaking or damaged float.
7. Clogged carburetor jets.
8. Damaged vacuum piston/diagram.
9. Faulty EVAP purge control valve (California models).

Lean Mixture

The following conditions can cause a lean air/fuel mixture:
1. Intake air leak.
2. Float level too low.
3. Clogged fuel line.
4. Partially restricted fuel tank breather hose.
5. Damaged vacuum piston/diaphragm.
6. Plugged carburetor air vent hose.
7. Damaged float.
8. Damaged float valve.

ENGINE

Engine Smoke

The color of engine smoke can help diagnosis engine problems or operating conditions.

Black smoke

Black smoke is an indication of a rich air/fuel mixture where an excessive amount of fuel is being burned in the combustion chamber.

Blue smoke

Blue smoke indicates the engine is burning oil in the combustion chamber as it leaks past worn valve stem seals and piston rings. Excessive oil consumption is another indicator of an engine that is burning oil. Perform a compression test (Chapter Three) to isolate the problem.

White smoke or steam

It is normal to see white smoke or steam from the exhaust after first starting the engine in cold weather. This is condensed steam formed by the engine during combustion. If the motorcycle is ridden far enough, the water cannot collect in the crankcase and is not a problem. Once the engine heats up to normal operating temperature, the water evaporates and exits the engine through the crankcase vent system. However, if the motorcycle is ridden for short trips or repeatedly started and stopped and allowed to cool off without the engine getting warm enough, water starts to collect in the crankcase. With each short run of the engine, more water collects. As this water mixes with the oil in the crankcase, sludge is produced. Water sludge can eventually cause engine damage as it circulates through the lubrication system and blocks off oil passages. Water draining from drain holes in exhaust pipes indicates water buildup.

Large amounts of steam can also be caused by a cracked cylinder head or cylinder block surface that allows antifreeze to leak into the combustion chamber. Perform a coolant pressure test as described in Chapter Ten.

Low Engine Compression

Problems with the engine top end affect engine performance and drivability. When the engine is suspect, perform the leakdown procedure in this chapter and make a compression test as described in Chapter Three. Interpret the results as described in each procedure to troubleshoot the suspect area. An engine can lose compression through the following areas:

1. Valves:
   a. Incorrect valve adjustment.
   b. Incorrect valve timing.
   c. Worn or damaged valve seats (valve and/or cylinder head).
   d. Bent valves.
   e. Weak or broken valve springs.
2. Cylinder head:
   a. Loose spark plug or damaged spark plug hole.
   b. Damaged cylinder head gasket.
   c. Warped or cracked cylinder head.

Engine Overheating (Cooling System)

> *WARNING*
> *Do not remove the radiator cap or coolant drain plug, or do not disconnect any coolant hose immediately after or during engine operation. Scalding fluid and steam may be blown out under pressure and cause serious injury. When the engine has been operated, the coolant is very hot and under pressure. Attempting to remove the items when the engine is hot can cause the coolant to spray violently from the radiator, water pump or hose, causing burns and injury on contact.*

1. Low coolant level.
2. Air in cooling system.
3. Clogged radiator, hose or engine coolant passages.
4. Thermostat stuck closed.
5. Worn or damaged radiator cap.
6. Open or short circuit in the cooling system wiring harness. Test the cooling system electrical system as described in Chapter Nine.
7. Damaged water pump.
8. Damaged coolant temperature indicator.
9. Radiator fan inoperative.
10. Damaged water pump.

Engine Overheating (Engine)

1. Improper spark plug heat range.
2. Low oil level.
3. Oil not circulating properly.
4. Valves leaking.
5. Heavy engine carbon deposits in combustion chamber.
6. Dragging brake(s).
7. Clutch slipping.

Engine Temperature Too Low

Thermostat stuck open.

Preignition

Preignition is the premature burning of fuel and is caused by hot spots in the combustion chambers. Glowing deposits in the combustion chambers, inadequate cooling or an overheated spark plug(s) can all cause preignition. This is first noticed as a power loss but eventually causes damage to the internal parts of the engine because of higher combustion chamber temperatures.

Detonation

Commonly called spark knock or fuel knock, detonation is the violent explosion of fuel in the combustion chamber before the proper time of ignition. Engine damage can result. Use of low octane gasoline is a common cause of detonation.

Even when using a high octane gasoline, detonation can occur. Other causes are over-advanced ignition timing, lean air/fuel mixture at or near full throttle, inadequate engine cooling or the excessive accumulation of carbon deposits in the combustion chamber (cylinder head and piston crowns).

Power Loss

Refer to *Poor Engine Performance* in this chapter.

Engine Noises

Unusual noises are often the first indication of a developing problem. Investigate any new noises as soon as possible. Something that may be a minor problem, if corrected, could prevent the possibility of more extensive damage.

Use a mechanic's stethoscope or a small section of hose held near your ear (not directly on your ear) with the other end close to the source of the noise to isolate the location. Determining the exact cause of a noise can be difficult. If this is the case, consult a professional mechanic to determine the cause. Do not disassemble major components until all other possibilities have been eliminated.

Consider the following when troubleshooting engine noises:
1. A knocking or pinging during acceleration is caused by using a lower octane fuel than recommended. It may also be caused by poor fuel. Pinging can also be caused by an incorrect spark plug heat range or carbon buildup in the combustion chamber.
2. A slapping or rattling noises at low speed or during acceleration may be caused by excessive piston-to-cylinder wall clearance (piston slap).

NOTE
Piston slap is easier to detect when the engine is cold and before the pistons have expanded. Once the engine has warmed up, piston expansion reduces piston-to-cylinder clearance.

3. A knocking or rapping while decelerating is usually caused by excessive rod bearing clearance.
4. Persistent knocking and vibration occurring every crankshaft rotation is usually caused by worn rod or main bearing(s). It can also be caused by broken piston rings or damaged piston pins.
5. A rapid on-off squeal may be a compression leak around the cylinder head gasket or spark plug(s).
6. If the valve train is noisy, check for the following:
   a. Excessive valve clearance.
   b. Worn or damaged camshaft.
   c. Damaged camshaft.
   d. Worn or damaged valve train components.
   e. Valve sticking in guide.
   f. Broken valve spring.
   g. Low oil pressure.
   h. Clogged cylinder oil hole or oil passage.

ENGINE LUBRICATION

An improperly operating engine lubrication system quickly leads to engine seizure. Check the engine oil level and oil pressure as described in Chapter Three. Oil pump service is described in Chapter Five.

High Oil Consumption or Excessive Exhaust Smoke

1. Worn valve guides/seals.
2. Worn or damaged piston rings.

Low Oil Pressure

1. Low oil level.
2. Worn or damaged oil pump.
3. Clogged oil strainer screen.
4. Clogged oil filter.
5. Internal oil leakage.
6. Oil pressure relief valve stuck open.
7. Incorrect type of engine oil.

High Oil Pressure

1. Oil pressure relief valve stuck closed.
2. Clogged oil filter.
3. Clogged oil gallery or metering orifices.

No Oil Pressure

1. Low oil level.
2. Oil pressure relief valve stuck closed.
3. Damaged oil pump.
4. Damaged oil pump sprocket(s) or chain.
5. Incorrect oil pump installation.
6. Internal oil leak.

Oil Pressure Indicator Stays On

1. Low oil pressure.
2. No oil pressure.
3. Damaged oil pressure switch.
4. Short circuit in warning lamp circuit.

Oil Level Too Low

1. Oil level not maintained at correct level.

2. Worn piston rings.

3. Worn cylinder.

4. Worn valve guides.

5. Worn valve stem seals.

6. Piston rings incorrectly installed during engine overhaul.

7. External oil leakage.

8. Oil leaking into the cooling system.

Oil Contamination

1. Blown head gasket, which allows coolant to leak into the engine.

2. Coolant leak.

3. Oil and filter not changed at specified intervals or when operating conditions demand more frequent changes.

CYLINDER LEAKDOWN TEST

A cylinder leakdown test can locate engine problems from leaking valves, blown head gaskets or broken, worn or stuck piston rings. This test is performed by applying compressed air to the cylinder and then measuring the percent of leakage. A cylinder leakdown tester (**Figure 6**) and air compressor is required to perform this test.

Follow the manufacturer's directions along with the following information when performing a cylinder leak down test:

1. Start and run the engine until it is warm. Turn the engine off.

2. Remove one of the front cylinder spark plugs. Refer to *Spark Plugs* in Chapter Three.

3. Set the front cylinder piston to TDC on its compression stroke. Refer to *Valve Clearance* in Chapter Three.

> *WARNING*
> *Make sure the piston is exactly at TDC on its compression stroke. The crankshaft may rotate when compressed air is applied to the cylinder. Remove any tools attached to the end of the crankshaft. To prevent the engine from turning over as compressed air is applied to the cylinder, shift the transmission into fifth gear and have an assistant apply the rear brake.*

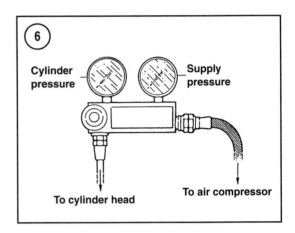

4. Thread the test adapter into the front cylinder spark plug hole. Connect the air compressor hose to the tester (**Figure 7**) following the manufacturer's instructions.

5. Apply compressed air to the leakdown tester and make a cylinder leakage test following the manufacturer's instructions. Read the percent of leakage on the gauge, following the manufacturer's instructions. Record the reading and note the following:

> *NOTE*
> *If there is an immediate high loss of air through the valves, either the engine is not at TDC on its compression stroke or there is major engine damage. Rotate the crankshaft counterclockwise one full turn and realign the **FT** mark on the flywheel with the index mark on the left crankcase cover.*

a. For a new or rebuilt engine, a leakage rate of 0- to- 5 percent per cylinder is desired. A leakage rate of 6- to- 14 percent is acceptable and means the engine is in good condition.

b. If testing a used engine, the critical rate is not the percent of leakage for each cylinder, but instead the difference between the cylinders. On a used engine, a leakage rate of 10 percent or less between cylinders is satisfactory.

c. A leakage rate exceeding 10 percent between cylinders points to an engine that is in poor condition and requires further inspection and possible repair.

6. After checking the percent of leakage and with air pressure still applied to the combustion chamber, listen for air escaping from the following areas. If

necessary, use a mechanic's stethoscope to pinpoint the source.

    a. Air leaking through the exhaust pipe indicates a leaking exhaust valve.

    b. Air leaking through the carburetor or air filter indicates a leaking intake valve.

    c. Air leaking through the crankcase breather tube suggests worn piston rings or a worn cylinder bore.

    d. Air leaking into the cooling system causes the coolant to bubble in the radiator. When this condition is indicated, check for damaged cylinder head gaskets and warped cylinder head or cylinder block surfaces.

7. Remove the leakdown tester and repeat these steps for the rear cylinder. Set the rear cylinder at TDC on its compression stroke.

8. After testing each cylinder, reinstall the spark plug and reconnect the spark plug cap.

CLUTCH

Clutch troubleshooting is listed in this section. Clutch service is covered in Chapter Six.

No Pressure at Clutch Lever

1. Incorrect clutch adjustment.
2. Broken clutch cable.
3. Damaged clutch release mechanism.

Clutch Lever Difficult to Pull In

1. Dry or damaged clutch cable.
2. Kinked or stuck clutch cable.
3. Incorrect clutch cable routing.

4. Damaged clutch release mechanism.
5. Damaged right crankcase cover.
6. Damaged clutch release plate bearing.

Rough Clutch Operation

Worn, grooved or damaged clutch hub and clutch housing slots.

Clutch Slip

If the engine speed increases without an increase in motorcycle speed, the clutch is probably slipping. The main causes of clutch slippage are:
1. No clutch lever free play.
2. Worn clutch plates.
3. Weak clutch springs.
4. Sticking or damaged clutch release mechanism.
5. Clutch plates contaminated by engine oil additive.

Clutch Drag

If the clutch does not disengage or if the motorcycle creeps with the transmission in gear and the clutch disengaged, the clutch is dragging. Some main causes of clutch drag are:
1. Excessive clutch lever free play.
2. Warped clutch plates.
3. Damaged clutch release mechanism
4. Loose clutch housing nut.
5. High oil level.
6. Incorrect oil viscosity.
7. Engine oil additive being used.
8. Damaged clutch hub and clutch housing splines.

GEARSHIFT LINKAGE

The gearshift linkage assembly connects the shift pedal (external shift mechanism) to the shift drum (internal shift mechanism). Refer to Chapter Seven to identify the components called out in this section.

Transmission Jumps Out of Gear

1. Damaged stopper arm.
2. Damaged stopper arm spring.
3. Worn or damaged shift drum cam.
4. Damaged gearshift arm spring.

5. Loose or damaged shift drum.
6. Bent shift fork shaft(s).
7. Bent or damaged shift fork(s).
8. Worn gear dogs or slots.

Difficult Shifting

1. Incorrect clutch operation.
2. Incorrect oil viscosity.
3. Loose or damaged stopper arm assembly.
4. Bent shift fork shaft(s).
5. Bent or damaged shift fork(s).
6. Worn gear dogs or slots.
7. Damaged shift drum grooves.
8. Damaged gearshift spindle.
9. Incorrect gearshift linkage installation.

Shift Pedal Does Not Return

1. Bent gearshift spindle.
2. Bent gearshift arm.
3. Weak or damaged gearshift arm return spring.
4. Shift shaft incorrectly installed (return spring incorrectly indexed around pin).

Excessive Engine/Transmission Noise

1. Damaged primary drive and driven gears or bearing.
2. Damaged transmission bearings or gears.

TRANSMISSION

Transmission symptoms are sometimes difficult to distinguish from clutch symptoms. Basic transmission troubleshooting is listed below. Refer to Chapter Seven for transmission service procedures. Before working on the transmission, make sure the clutch and gearshift linkage assembly are not causing the problem.

Difficult Shifting

1. Incorrect clutch operation.
2. Bent shift fork(s).
3. Damaged shift fork guide pin(s).
4. Bent shift fork shaft(s).
5. Bent gearshift spindle.
6. Damaged shift drum grooves.

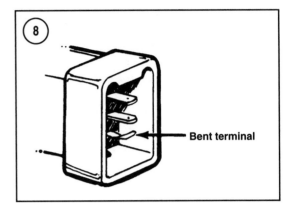

Jumps Out of Gear

1. Loose or damaged shift drum stopper arm.
2. Bent or damaged shift fork(s).
3. Bent shift fork shaft(s).
4. Damaged shift drum grooves.
5. Worn gear dogs or slots.
6. Weak or damaged gearshift arm return spring.

Incorrect Shift Lever Operation

1. Bent shift pedal or linkage.
2. Stripped shift pedal splines.
3. Damaged shift linkage.
4. Damaged gearshift spindle.

Excessive Gear Noise

1. Worn or damaged transmission bearings.
2. Worn or damaged gears.
3. Excessive gear backlash.

ELECTRICAL TESTING

This section describes basic electrical testing and the use of test equipment.

Electrical testing can be time-consuming and frustrating without proper knowledge and a suitable plan. Refer to the color wiring diagrams at the end of the manual for component and connector identification. Use the wiring diagrams to determine how the circuit should work by tracing the current paths from the power source through the circuit components to ground. Also check any circuits that share the same fuse, ground or switch. If the other circuits work properly and the shared wiring is good, the cause must be in the wiring used only by the suspect

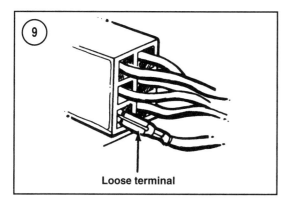

Loose terminal

circuit. If all related circuits are faulty at the same time, the probable cause is a poor ground connection or blown fuse(s).

As with all troubleshooting procedures, analyze typical symptoms in a systematic manner. Never assume anything and do not overlook the obvious, such as a blown fuse or an electrical connector that has separated. Test the simplest and most obvious items first and try to make tests at easily accessible points on the motorcycle.

Electrical Component Replacement

Most motorcycle dealerships and parts suppliers do not accept the return of any electrical part. If you cannot determine the *exact* cause of any electrical system malfunction, have a Honda dealership retest that specific system to verify your test results. If you purchase a new electrical component(s), install it, and find the system still does not work properly, you probably cannot return the unit for a refund.

Consider any test results carefully before replacing a component that tests only *slightly* out of specification, especially resistance. A number of variables can affect test results dramatically. These include the testing meter's internal circuitry, ambient temperature and conditions under which the machine has been operated. All instructions and specifications have been checked for accuracy, but successful test results depend a great degree on individual accuracy.

Preliminary Checks and Precautions

Before starting any electrical troubleshooting, perform the following:

1. Check the main fuse (Chapter Nine). If the fuse is blown, replace it.

2. Check the subfuses mounted in the fuse box (Chapter Nine). Inspect the suspected fuse, and replace it if blown.

3. Inspect the battery. Make sure it is fully charged, and that the battery leads are clean and securely attached to the battery terminals. Refer to *Battery* in Chapter Nine.

4. Disconnect each electrical connector in the suspect circuit and make sure there are no bent terminals in the electrical connector (**Figure 8**). A bent terminal does not connect to the mating terminal, causing an open circuit.

5. Make sure the terminals on the end of each wire are pushed all the way into the plastic housing (**Figure 9**). If not, carefully push them in with a narrow blade screwdriver.

6. Check all electrical wires where they enter the individual metal terminals in both the male and female plastic housings.

7. Make sure all terminals within the housing are clean and free of corrosion. Clean them, if necessary, and pack the connectors with dielectric grease.

8. Push the connector halves together. Make sure the connectors are fully engaged and locked together.

9. Never pull the electrical wires when disconnecting an electrical connector. Pull only on the connector plastic housing.

> *NOTE*
> *Always consider electrical connectors the weak link in the electrical system. Dirty, loose-fitting and corroded connectors cause numerous electrical related problems, especially on high-mileage motorcycles. When troubleshooting an electrical problem, carefully inspect the connectors and wiring harness.*

10. Never use a self-powered test light on circuits that contain solid-state devices. The solid-state devices may be damaged.

Intermittent Problems

Intermittent problems are problems that do not occur all the time and can be difficult to locate. For example, when a problem only occurs when the motorcycle is ridden over rough roads (vibration) or in wet conditions (water penetration), it is intermittent. To locate and repair intermittent problems, you need to simulate the condition when testing the components. Note the following:

1. Vibration—This is a common problem with loose or damaged electrical connectors.

   a. Perform a continuity test as described in the appropriate service procedure or refer to *Continuity Testing* in this chapter.

   b. Lightly pull or wiggle the connectors while repeating the test. Do the same when checking the wiring harness and individual components, especially where the wires enter a housing or connector.

   c. A change in meter readings indicates a poor connection. Find and repair the problem or replace the part. Check for wires with cracked or broken insulation.

NOTE
An analog ohmmeter is useful when making this type of test. Slight needle movements are apparent to indicate a loose connection.

2. Heat—This is another common problem with connectors or plugs that have loose or poor connections. As these connections heat up, the connection or joint expands and separates, causing an open circuit. Other heat related problems occur when a component creates its own heat as it starts to fail or go bad.

   a. Troubleshoot the problem to help isolate the problem or area.

   b. To check a connector, perform a continuity test as described in the appropriate service procedure or refer to *Continuity Testing* in this chapter. Repeat the test while heating the connector with a heat gun or hair dryer. If the meter reading was normal (continuity) when the connector was cold, then fluctuated or read infinity when heat was applied, the connection is bad.

   c. To check a component, allow the engine to cool, then start and run the engine. Note operational differences when the engine is cold and hot.

   d. If the engine does not start, isolate and remove the component; first test it at room temperature and then after heating it with a hair

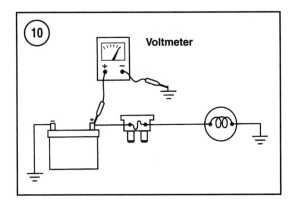

dryer. A change in meter readings indicates a temperature problem.

CAUTION
A heat gun or hair dryer quickly raises the heat of the component being tested. Do not apply heat directly to the ICM or use heat in excess of 60° C (140° F) on any electrical component. If available, monitor heat with an infrared thermometer.

3. Water—When the problem occurs when riding in wet conditions or in areas with high humidity, start and run the engine in a dry area. Then, with the engine running, spray water onto the suspected component. Often times, water related problems repair themselves after the component becomes hot enough to dry itself, adding to the frustration.

Test Light or Voltmeter

A test light can be constructed from a 12-volt light bulb with a pair of test leads carefully soldered to the bulb. To check for battery voltage in a circuit, attach one lead to ground and the other lead to various points along the circuit. The bulb lights when battery voltage is present.

A voltmeter is used in the same manner as the test light to find out if battery voltage is present in any given circuit. The voltmeter, unlike the test light, also indicates how much voltage is present at each test point. When using a voltmeter, attach the positive lead to the component or wire to be checked and the negative lead to a good ground (**Figure 10**). When purchasing a digital voltmeter, select one with a minimum impedance of 10M ohms/DCV.

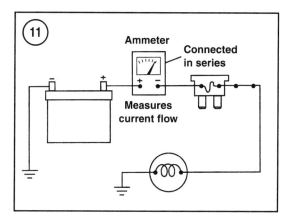

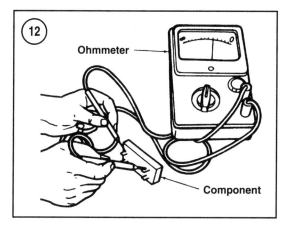

CAUTION
Do not use a self-powered test light with an incandescent bulb to test electronic equipment or circuits with solid-state devices. Because this type of test light uses a battery and applies voltage to the circuit during the test, the current draw can damage the component. Instead, use an LED test light or a digital multimeter with a minimum impedance of 10M ohms/DCV.

1. Touch the test leads together to make sure the light bulb goes on. If not, correct the problem before using it in a test procedure.
2. Disconnect the motorcycle's battery or remove the fuse(s) that protects the circuit to be tested.
3. Select two points within the circuit where there should be continuity.
4. Attach one lead of the self-powered test light to each point.
5. If there is continuity, the self-powered test light bulb comes on.
6. If there is no continuity, the self-powered test light bulb does not come on, indicating an open circuit.

Ohmmeter

An ohmmeter measures the resistance (in ohms) to current flow in a circuit or component. Like the self-powered test light, an ohmmeter contains its own power source and should not be connected to a live circuit.

Ohmmeters may be analog type (needle scale) or digital type (LCD or LED readout). Both types of ohmmeters have a switch that allows the user to select different ranges of resistance for accurate readings. The analog ohmmeter also has a set-adjust control, which is used to zero or calibrate the meter (digital ohmmeters do not require calibration).

An ohmmeter is used by connecting its test leads to the terminals or leads of the circuit or component to be tested (**Figure 12**). If using an analog meter, calibrate it by touching the test leads together and turning the set-adjust knob until the meter needle reads zero. When the leads are uncrossed, the needle should move to the other end of the scale indicating infinite resistance.

During a continuity test, a reading of infinity indicates there is an open in the circuit or component.

Ammeter

An ammeter measures the flow of current (amps) in a circuit (**Figure 11**). When connected in series in a circuit, the ammeter determines if current is flowing through the circuit and if that current flow is excessive because of a short in the circuit. Current flow is often referred to as current draw. Comparing actual current draw in the circuit or component to the manufacturer's specified current draw provides useful diagnostic information.

Self-powered Test Light (Continuity Tester)

A self-powered test light can be constructed from a 12-volt light bulb, a pair of test leads and a 12-volt battery. When the test leads are touched together the light bulb should go on.

Use a self-powered test light as follows:

A reading of zero indicates continuity, which means no measurable resistance is in the circuit or component being tested. If the meter needle falls between these two ends of the scale, this indicates the actual resistance to current flow that is present. To determine the resistance, multiply the meter reading by the ohmmeter scale. For example, a meter reading of 5 multiplied by the R × 1000 scale is 5000 ohms of resistance.

CAUTION
Never connect an ohmmeter to a circuit that has power applied to it. Always disconnect the battery negative lead before using an ohmmeter.

Jumper Wire

A jumper wire is a simple way to bypass a potential problem and isolate it to a particular point in a circuit. If a faulty circuit works properly with a jumper wire installed, an open circuit exists between the two jumper points.

To troubleshoot with a jumper wire, first use the wire to determine if the problem is on the ground side or the load side of a device. Test the ground by connecting a jumper between the lamp and a good ground. If the lamp comes on, the problem is the connection between the lamp and ground. If the lamp does not come on with the jumper installed, the lamp's connection to ground is good and the problem is between the lamp and the power source.

To isolate the problem, connect the jumper between the battery and the lamp. If it comes on, the problem is between these two points. Next connect the jumper between the battery and the fuse side of the switch. If the lamp comes on, the switch is good. By successively moving the jumper from one point to another, the problem can be isolated to a particular place in the circuit.

Pay attention to the following when using a jumper wire:
1. Make sure the jumper wire gauge (thickness) is the same as that used in the circuit being tested. A smaller gauge wire could rapidly overheat and melt.
2. Install insulated boots over alligator clips. This prevents accidental grounding, sparks or possible shock when working in cramped quarters.
3. Jumper wires are temporary test measures only. Do not leave a jumper wire installed as a permanent

solution. This creates a severe fire hazard that could easily lead to complete loss of the motorcycle.
4. When using a jumper wire always install an inline fuse/fuse holder (available at most auto supply stores or electronic supply stores) to the jumper wire. Never use a jumper wire across any load (a component that is connected and turned on). This would result in a direct short and blows the fuse(s).

Voltage Testing

Unless otherwise specified, make all voltage tests with the electrical connectors still connected. Insert the test leads into the backside of the connector and make sure the test lead touches the electrical wire or metal terminal within the connector housing. If the test lead only touches the wire insulation, you get a false reading.

Always check both sides of the connector because one side may be loose or corroded, thus preventing electrical flow through the connector. This type of test can be performed with a test light or a voltmeter. A voltmeter gives the best results.

NOTE
If using a test light, it does not make any difference which test lead is attached to ground.

1. Attach the voltmeter negative test lead to a good ground (bare metal). Make sure the part used for ground is not insulated with a rubber gasket or rubber grommet.
2. Attach the voltmeter positive test lead to the point (electrical connector, etc.) to be tested (**Figure 10**).
3. Turn the ignition switch on. If using a test light, the test light will come on if voltage is present. If using a voltmeter, note the voltage reading. The reading should be within 1 volt of battery voltage. If the voltage is less there is a problem in the circuit.

Voltage Drop Testing

The wires, cables, connectors and switches in an electrical circuit are designed to carry current with low resistance. This ensures that current can flow through the circuit with a minimum loss of voltage. Voltage drop indicates where there is resistance in a circuit. A higher-than-normal amount of resistance in a circuit decreases the flow of current and causes

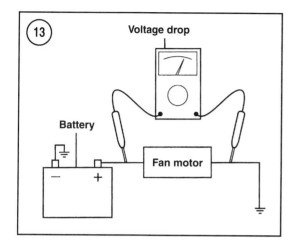

the voltage to drop between the source and destination in the circuit.

Because resistance causes voltage to drop, use a voltmeter to measure voltage drop when current is running through the circuit. If the circuit has no resistance, there is no voltage drop so the voltmeter indicates 0 volts. The greater the resistance in a circuit, the greater the voltage drop reading.

To perform a voltage drop:

NOTE
When checking the voltage drop in the starter circuit, refer to **Starting System Troubleshooting** *in Chapter Nine.*

1. Connect the positive meter test lead to the electrical source (where electricity is coming from).
2. Connect the voltmeter negative test lead to the electrical load (where the electricity is going). See **Figure 13**.
3. If necessary, activate the component(s) in the circuit. For example, if checking the voltage in the starter circuit, it is necessary to push the starter button. If checking the voltage drop in the front brake light switch circuit, apply the front brake lever.
4. Read the voltage drop (difference in voltage between the source and destination) on the voltmeter. Note the following:

   a. The voltmeter should indicate 0 volts. If there is a drop of 0.5 volts or more, there is a problem within the circuit. A voltage drop reading of 12 volts indicates an open circuit.

   b. A voltage drop of 1 or more volts indicates that a circuit has excessive resistance.

   c. For example, consider a starting problem where the battery is fully charged but the starter turns over slowly. Voltage drop would be the difference in the voltage at the battery (source) and the voltage at the starter (destination) as the engine is being started (current is flowing through the battery cables). A corroded battery cable would cause a high voltage drop (high resistance) and slow engine cranking.

   d. Common sources of voltage drop are loose or contaminated connectors and poor ground connections.

Peak Voltage Testing

Peak voltage tests check the voltage output of the ignition coil and ignition pulse generator at normal cranking speed. These tests make it possible to identify ignition system problems quickly and accurately.

Peak voltage tests require a peak voltage adapter or tester. Refer to *Ignition System Troubleshooting* in Chapter Nine.

Continuity Testing

Use a continuity test to determine the integrity of a circuit, wire or component. A circuit has continuity if it forms a complete circuit; that is if there are no opens in either the electrical wires or components within the circuit. An open circuit, on the other hand, has no continuity.

This type of test can be performed with a self-powered test light or an ohmmeter. An ohmmeter gives the best results. If using an analog ohmmeter, calibrate the meter by touching the leads together and turning the calibration knob until the meter reads zero.

1. Disconnect the negative battery cable.
2. Attach one test lead (test light or ohmmeter) to one end of the part of the circuit to be tested.
3. Attach the other test lead to the other end of the part or the circuit to be tested.
4. The self-powered test light comes on if there is continuity. An ohmmeter reads 0 or very low resistance if there is continuity. A reading of infinite resistance indicates no continuity or the circuit is open.

Testing for a Short with a Self-powered Test Light or Ohmmeter

1. Disconnect the negative battery cable.
2. Remove the blown fuse from the fuse panel.
3. Connect one test lead of the test light or ohmmeter to the load side (battery side) of the fuse terminal in the fuse panel.
4. Connect the other test lead to a good ground (bare metal). Make sure the part used for a ground is not insulated with a rubber gasket or rubber grommet.
5. With the self-powered test light or ohmmeter attached to the fuse terminal and ground, wiggle the wiring harness relating to the suspect circuit at 6 in. (15.2 cm) intervals. Start next to the fuse panel and work your way away from the fuse panel. Watch the self-powered test light or ohmmeter as you progress along the harness.
6. If the test light blinks or the needle on the ohmmeter moves, there is a short-to-ground at that point in the harness.

Testing For a Short with a Test Light or Voltmeter

1. Remove the blown fuse from the fuse panel.
2. Connect the test light or voltmeter across the fuse terminals in the fuse panel. Turn the ignition switch on and check for battery voltage.
3. With the test light or voltmeter attached to the fuse terminals, wiggle the wiring harness relating to the suspect circuit at 6 in. (15.2 cm) intervals. Start next to the fuse panel and work systematically away from the panel. Watch the test light or voltmeter as you progress along the harness.
4. If the test light blinks or if the needle on the voltmeter moves, there is a short-to-ground at that point in the harness.

FRONT SUSPENSION AND STEERING

Steering is Sluggish

1. Incorrect steering stem adjustment (too tight).
2. Damaged steering head bearings.
3. Tire pressure too low.
4. Damaged tire.

Motorcycle Steers to One Side

1. Bent axle.
2. Bent frame.
3. Worn or damaged wheel bearings.
4. Worn or damaged swing arm pivot bearings.
5. Damaged steering head bearings.
6. Bent swing arm.
7. Incorrectly installed wheels.
8. Front and rear wheels are not aligned.
9. Front fork legs positioned unevenly in steering stem.
10. Damaged tire.

Front Suspension Noise

1. Loose mounting fasteners.
2. Damaged fork(s).
3. Low fork oil capacity.

Front Wheel Wobble/Vibration

1. Loose front wheel axle.
2. Loose or damaged wheel bearing(s).
3. Damaged wheel rim(s).
4. Damaged tire(s).
5. Flat spot on tire.

NOTE
If the motorcycle is put in storage for a considerable amount of time, the weight placed on the front tire can cause the tire to flatten on the spot resting against the floor.

6. Unbalanced tire and wheel assembly.
7. Loose or damaged spokes.

Hard Suspension (Front Fork)

1. Excessive tire pressure.
2. Damaged steering head bearings.
3. Incorrect steering head bearing adjustment.
4. Bent fork tubes.
5. Binding slider.

NOTE
If a fork brace was installed onto the fork tubes, make sure it was installed correctly.

6. Incorrect weight fork oil.
7. Fork oil level too high.
8. Plugged fork oil passage.

Hard Suspension
(Rear Shock Absorber)

1. Excessive rear tire pressure.
2. Bent damper rod.
3. Incorrect shock adjustment.
4. Damaged shock absorber bushing(s).
5. Damaged swing arm pivot bearings.

Soft Suspension
(Front Fork)

1. Insufficient tire pressure.
2. Insufficient fork oil level or fluid capacity.
3. Incorrect oil viscosity.
4. Weak or damaged fork springs.

Soft Suspension
(Rear Shock Absorber)

1. Insufficient rear tire pressure.
2. Weak or damaged shock absorber spring.
3. Damaged shock absorber.
4. Incorrect shock absorber adjustment.
5. Leaking damper unit.

BRAKE SYSTEM

The front and rear brake units are critical to riding performance and safety. Inspect the front and rear brakes frequently and repair any problem immediately. When replacing or refilling the front disc brake fluid, use only DOT 4 brake fluid from a closed container. Refer to Chapter Three for additional information on brake fluid selection and routine brake inspection and service.

Always check the brake operation before riding the motorcycle.

Front Disc Brake

Soft or spongy brake lever

Operate the front brake lever or rear brake pedal and check to see if the lever travel distance in-creases. If the lever travel does increase while being operated or feels soft or spongy, there may be air in the brake line. In this condition, the brake system is not capable of producing sufficient brake force. When an increase in lever travel is noticed or when the brake feels soft or spongy, check the following possible causes:

1. Air in system.

NOTE
If the brake level in the reservoir drops too low, air can enter the hydraulic system through the master cylinder. Air can also enter the system from loose or damaged hose fittings. Air in the hydraulic system causes a soft or spongy brake lever action. This condition is noticeable and reduces brake performance. When it is suspected that air has entered the hydraulic system, flush the brake system and bleed the brakes as described in Chapter Fourteen.

NOTE
If different handlebars were installed, an extreme bar angle may affect the brake fluid level in the reservoir. Check the fluid level with the handlebar in both left and right lock positions.

2. Low brake fluid level.

NOTE
As the brake pads wear, the brake fluid level in the master cylinder reservoir drops. Whenever adding brake fluid to the reservoir, visually check the brake pads for wear. If it does not appear that there is an increase in pad wear, check the brake hoses, lines and banjo bolts for leaks.

3. Leak in the brake system.
4. Contaminated brake fluid.
5. Plugged brake fluid passages.
6. Damaged brake lever assembly.
7. Worn or damaged brake pads.
8. Worn or damaged brake disc.
9. Warped brake disc.
10. Contaminated brake pads and disc.

NOTE
A leaking fork seal can allow oil to contaminate the brake pads and disc.

11. Worn or damaged master cylinder cups and/or cylinder bore.
12. Worn or damaged brake caliper piston seals.
13. Contaminated master cylinder assembly.
14. Contaminated brake caliper assembly.
15. Brake caliper not sliding correctly on slide pins.
16. Sticking master cylinder piston assembly.
17. Sticking brake caliper pistons.

Brake drag

When the brakes drag, the brake pads are not capable of moving away from the brake disc when the brake lever is released. Any of the following causes, if they occur, would prevent correct brake pad movement and cause brake drag.
1. Warped or damaged brake disc.
2. Brake caliper not sliding correctly on slide pins.
3. Sticking or damaged brake caliper pistons.
4. Contaminated brake pads and disc.
5. Plugged master cylinder port.
6. Contaminated brake fluid and hydraulic passages.
7. Restricted brake hose joint.
8. Loose brake disc mounting bolts.
9. Damaged or misaligned wheel.
10. Incorrect wheel alignment.
11. Incorrectly installed brake caliper.
12. Damaged front wheel.

Hard brake lever operation

When the brakes are applied and there is sufficient brake performance but the operation of brake lever feels excessively hard, check for the following possible causes:
1. Clogged brake hydraulic system.
2. Sticking caliper piston.
3. Sticking master cylinder piston.
4. Glazed or worn brake pads.
5. Mismatched brake pads.
6. Damaged front brake lever.
7. Brake caliper not sliding correctly on slide pins.
8. Worn or damaged brake caliper seals.

Front brake grabs

1. Damaged brake pad pin bolt. Look for steps or cracks along the pad pin bolt surface.
2. Contaminated brake pads and disc.
3. Incorrect wheel alignment.
4. Warped brake disc.
5. Loose brake disc mounting bolts.
6. Brake caliper not sliding correctly on slide pins.
7. Mismatched brake pads.
8. Damaged wheel bearings.

Brake squeal or chatter

1. Contaminated brake pads and disc.
2. Incorrectly installed brake caliper.
3. Warped brake disc.
4. Incorrect wheel alignment.
5. Mismatched brake pads.
6. Incorrectly installed brake pads.

Leaking brake caliper

1. Damaged dust and piston seals.
2. Damaged cylinder bore.
3. Loose caliper body bolts.
4. Loose banjo bolt.
5. Damaged banjo bolt washers.
6. Damaged banjo bolt threads in caliper body.

Leaking master cylinder

1. Damaged piston secondary seal.
2. Damaged piston snap ring and/or snap ring groove.
3. Worn or damaged master cylinder bore.
4. Loose banjo bolt.
5. Damaged banjo bolt washers.
6. Damaged banjo bolt threads in master cylinder body.
7. Loose or damaged reservoir cap.

Rear Drum Brake

Poor brake performance

1. Incorrect brake adjustment.
2. Worn brake shoe linings or brake drum.
3. Contaminated brake drum and brake shoe linings.
4. Worn brake cam.

5. Brake panel cracked at brake cam operating area.

6. Brake arm and brake cam splines stripped or improperly indexed.

7. Bent or damaged brake rod.

8. Loose or missing parts at brake rod and brake pedal assembly.

Brake drag

1. Incorrect brake adjustment.

2. Contaminated brake drum and brake shoe linings.

3. Weak or damaged brake return springs.

4. Weak or damaged brake rod return spring.

5. Damaged brake shoes.

6. Warped brake drum.

7. Incorrect brake cam and brake arm alignment.

Brake grabs

1. Contaminated brake drum.

2. Contaminated brake shoe linings.

3. Weak or damaged brake return springs.

4. Warped brake drum.

5. Incorrect brake cam and brake arm alignment.

Brake squeals or chatters

1. Contaminated brake drum.

2. Contaminated brake linings.

3. Warped brake drum.

4. Damaged brake shoes.

NOTE
If the brake rod chatters when the motorcycle is rolled backward while the rear brake is applied, check the brake stopper arm where it is bolted onto the brake panel. If the stopper arm mounting bolt and nut are tight, check for excessive clearance between the stopper arm mounting bolt and its mounting bore in the brake panel.

Hard rear brake pedal operation or slow brake pedal return

1. Weak or damaged brake shoe return springs.

2. Contaminated brake drum.

3. Contaminated brake linings.

4. Incorrect brake adjustment.

5. Incorrect brake assembly.

6. Damaged brake cam or backing plate.

7. Damaged rear brake pedal assembly.

8. Damaged brake rod.

CHAPTER THREE

PERIODIC LUBRICATION, MAINTENANCE AND TUNE-UP

This chapter describes lubrication, maintenance and tune-up procedures.

To maximize the service life of the motorcycle and gain the utmost in safety and performance, it is necessary to perform periodic inspections and maintenance. Minor problems found during routine service can be corrected before they develop into major ones. A neglected motorcycle is unreliable and may be dangerous to ride.

Table 1 lists the recommended lubrication, maintenance and tune-up intervals. When operating the motorcycle in extreme conditions, it may be appropriate to reduce the time interval between some maintenance items.

For convenience, most of the services listed in **Table 1** are described in this chapter. Procedures that require more than minor disassembly or adjustment are covered in the appropriate chapter.

Before servicing the motorcycle, make sure the procedures and the required skills are thoroughly understood. If your experience and equipment are limited, start by performing basic procedures. Perform more involved tasks as you gain further experience and acquire the necessary tools.

FUEL TYPE

The VT750 engine requires gasoline with a pump octane number of 86 or higher. Using a gasoline with a lower octane number can cause pinging or spark knock and lead to engine damage.

When choosing gasoline and filling the fuel tank, note the following:

1. When filling the tank, do not overfill it. No fuel should be in the filler neck (tube located between the fuel cap and tank).

2. In some areas of the United States and Canada, oxygenated fuels are used to reduce exhaust emissions. If using oxygenated fuel, make sure it meets the minimum octane requirements. Oxygenated fuels can damage plastic and paint. Do not spill fuel onto the fuel tank during filling. Wipe up spills with a soft cloth.

3. An ethanol (ethyl or grain alcohol) gasoline that contains more than 10 percent ethanol by volume may cause engine starting and performance related problems. Gasoline containing ethanol may be sold under the name Gasohol.

4. A methanol (methyl or wood alcohol) gasoline that contains more than 5 percent methanol by volume may cause engine starting and performance related problems. Gasoline that contains methanol must have corrosion inhibitors to protect the metal, plastic and rubber parts in the fuel system from damage.

5. Gasoline that contains more than 15 percent Methyl Tertiary Butyl Ether (MTBE) should not be used.

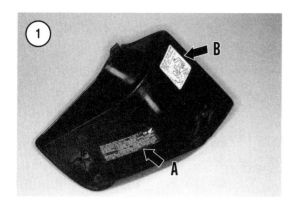

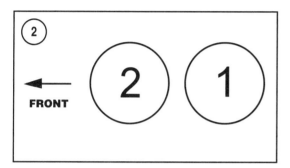

TUNE-UP

Perform the following tune-up procedures at the intervals specified in **Table 1**. More frequent tune-ups may be required if the motorcycle is operated primarily in stop-and-go traffic or in areas were there is a large amount of blowing dirt and dust.

The Motorcycle Emission Control Information label attached to the inside of the left cover (A, **Figure 1**) lists tune-up information. Refer to **Table 6** for tune-up specifications. On California models, the vacuum hose routing diagram (B, **Figure 1**) is useful when identifying hoses used in the emission control system.

NOTE
If the specifications on the Motorcycle Emission Control Information label differ from those in Table 6, use those on the label.

To perform a tune-up, service the following items as described in this chapter:
1. Air filter.
2. Spark plugs.
3. Engine compression.
4. Ignition timing.
5. Valve clearance.
6. Engine oil and filter.
7. Cooling system.
8. Wheels and tires.
9. Suspension components.
10. Brake system.
11. Drive chain.
12. Fasteners.

**CYLINDER IDENTIFICATION
AND FIRING ORDER**

Figure 2 identifies the cylinder numbers. The cylinder firing order is 2 (front), 1 (rear).

AIR FILTER

The air filter removes dust and abrasive particles from the air before the air enters the engine. A clogged air filter decreases the efficiency and life of the engine. With a damaged air filter, very fine particles could enter the engine and cause rapid wear of the piston rings, cylinder and bearings. Never run the motorcycle without the air filter element installed.

Replace the air filter element at the service interval specified in **Table 1**.

NOTE
The service intervals specified in Table 1 should be followed with general use. However, replace the air filter more often if dusty areas are frequently encountered.

Replacement

1. Remove the bolts and the air filter cover (**Figure 3**).

2. Remove the air filter (**Figure 4**).

> *NOTE*
> *The air filter element contains a dust adhesive. Do not clean the filter element (**Figure 5**) with air or any type of chemical cleaner or water.*

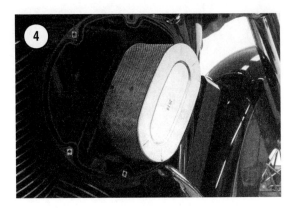

3. Inspect the air filter element (A, **Figure 5**) for an excessive amount of dirt and possible damage. Check for holes or shredded filter seams. Check the foam seal on the bottom of the filter (B, **Figure 5**) for cuts, crushed or contaminated areas that would prevent the foam seal from sealing tightly. Do not run the motorcycle with a damaged air filter element or one that has been cleaned. Both conditions may allow dirt to enter the engine. If the element is good, use it until the indicated time for replacement listed in **Table 1**.

4. Inspect the air box for dirt and debris that may have passed through the element. Wipe the inside of the air box and the air filter cover with a clean cloth.

5. Check that the rubber seal seats fully in the air box cover groove. Replace the seal if deteriorated or damaged.

6. Install the air filter element (**Figure 4**) and secure with the air filter cover and mounting screws.

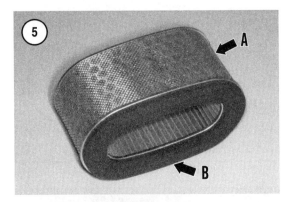

CRANKCASE BREATHER INSPECTION

The engine is equipped with a closed crankcase breather system to prevent fumes and gasses from being vented into the atmosphere. However, under various operating conditions, contaminants (water and blow-by gas) that are not burned in the combustion chamber collect in the air box. To remove these contaminants, the air box is equipped with a transparent drain tube (**Figure 6**). At the interval specified in **Table 1**, inspect the drain tube for fluid, and if necessary, disconnect the drain tube and drain the contaminants into a container. Reinstall the drain tube securely onto the air box. Check the drain tube more frequently after riding the motorcycle in rain, after riding long distances under full-throttle, if the motorcycle is washed frequently or after the motorcycle is dropped on its side.

ENGINE COMPRESSION TEST

A cranking compression test is one of the quickest ways to check the internal condition of the engine (piston rings, pistons, head gasket, valves and cylinders). Check compression at each tune-up, record it in the maintenance log at the end of the manual, and compare it with the reading obtained at the next tune-up.

Use the spark plug tool included in the motorcycle's tool kit and a screw-in type compression gauge with a flexible adapter (**Figure 7**). Before using the gauge, check that the rubber gasket on the end of the adapter is not cracked or damaged; this gasket seals the cylinder to ensure accurate compression readings.

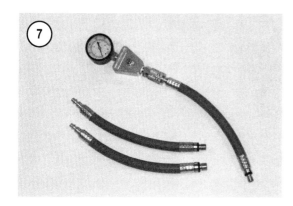

1. Make sure the battery is fully charged to ensure proper engine cranking speed (400 rpm).

2. Run the engine until it reaches normal operating temperature, and then turn it off.

3. Disconnect both spark plug caps from each cylinder.

4. Remove one spark plug from the front cylinder.

5. Lubricate the threads of the compression gauge adapter with a *small* amount of antiseize compound and carefully thread the gauge into one of the spark plug hole (**Figure 8**). Tighten the hose by hand to form a good seal.

CAUTION
*When the spark plug leads are disconnected, the electronic ignition produces the highest voltage possible. This can damage the ICM or other ignition component. To protect the ignition system, install a grounding tool in each spark plug cap. Refer to **Ignition Grounding Tool** in Chapter One. Do not crank the engine more than necessary.*

6. Move the engine stop switch to RUN, and turn the ignition switch on. Open the throttle completely and using the starter, crank the engine over while reading the compression gauge until there is no further rise in pressure. The compression reading should increase on each stroke. Maximum pressure is usually reached within 4-7 seconds of engine cranking. Record the reading.

NOTE
If a cylinder requires a longer cranking time to reach its maximum compression reading, there is a problem with that cylinder.

7. Install the spark plug.

8. Repeat for the rear cylinder.

9. When interpreting the results, also note the difference between the readings. **Table 6** lists the standard compression pressure reading. Low compression indicates worn or broken rings, leaking or sticky valves, blown head gasket or a combination of all three. Readings that are lower than normal, but are relatively even among both cylinders indicates piston, ring and cylinder wear. Note the following:

   a. If the compression readings do not differ between cylinders by more than 10 percent, the rings and valves are in good condition.

   b. If a low reading (10 percent or more) is obtained on one of the cylinders, it indicates valve or ring trouble. To determine which, perform a wet compression test. Pour about a teaspoon of engine oil into the spark plug hole. Repeat the compression test and record the reading. If the compression increases significantly, the valves are good but the rings are defective on that cylinder. If compression does not increase, the valves require servicing.

NOTE
An engine with low compression cannot be tuned to maximum performance.

10. Reverse Steps 1-5 to complete installation. Reinstall the spark plugs and caps as described under *Spark Plugs* in this chapter.

SPARK PLUGS

Inspect and replace the spark plugs at the service intervals specified in **Table 1**.

Removal

Careful removal of the spark plug is important in preventing grit from entering the combustion chamber. It is also important to know how to remove a plug that is seized or is resistant to removal. Forcing a seized plug can destroy the threads in the cylinder head.

During removal, label each spark plug with its cylinder number (**Figure 2**) and position in the cylinder head.

1. On VT750DC models, remove the front cylinder left side overhead cover and the rear cylinder right side overhead cover.

2. Blow away any dirt that has accumulated around the spark plug hole.

> *CAUTION*
> *Dirt that falls through the spark plug hole causes engine wear and damage.*

3. Grasp the spark plug cap boot (**Figure 9**) and twist it slightly to break it loose, then pull it from the spark plug.

4. Fit a spark plug wrench onto the spark plug and remove it by turning the wrench counterclockwise. If the plug is seized or drags excessively during removal, stop and perform the following:

    a. Apply penetrating lubricant, such as Liquid Wrench or WD-40 and allow it to stand for about 15 minutes.

    b. If the plug is completely seized, apply moderate pressure in both directions with the wrench. Only attempt to break the seal so the lubricant can penetrate under the spark plug and into the threads. If this does not work and the engine still starts, install the spark plug cap and start the engine. Allow it to completely warm up. The heat of the engine may be enough to expand the parts and allow the plug to be removed.

    c. When a spark plug is loose but drags excessively during removal, apply penetrating lubricant around the spark plug threads. Turn the plug in (clockwise) to help distribute the lubricant onto the threads. Slowly remove the plug, working it in and out of the cylinder head while continuing to add lubricant. Do not reuse the spark plug.

    d. Inspect the threads in the cylinder head for damage. Clean and true the threads with a

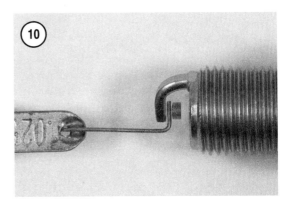

spark plug thread-chaser. Apply a thick grease onto the thread-chaser threads before using it. The grease helps trap some of the debris cut from the threads to prevent it from falling into the engine.

> *NOTE*
> *Damaged spark plug threads require removal of the cylinder head (Chapter Four) and repair.*

5. Inspect the plug carefully. Look for a damaged porcelain cover, excessively eroded electrodes, and excessive carbon or oil fouling. Refer to *Reading/Inspection* in this section.

> *CAUTION*
> *The porcelain cover found on the top of the spark plug, actually extends into the plug shell to prevent the spark from grounding through the plug shell and threads. The porcelain cover can be easily damaged from mishandling. Make sure the spark plug socket fits the plug fully before turning the plug.*

6. Repeat for each spark plug.

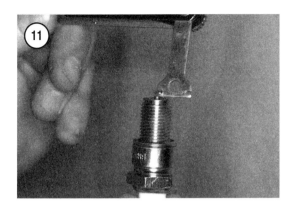

Gap and Installation

Gap used and new spark plugs to ensure a reliable, consistent spark. Use a spark plug gapping tool and a wire feeler gauge as described in this procedure.

1. Remove the new spark plug from the box. Remove the terminal adapter installed onto the end of the plug.

2. Refer to the spark plug gap listed in **Table 6**. Insert a wire feeler gauge between the center and side electrode (**Figure 10**, typical). If there is a slight drag, the setting is correct. If the gap is too large or small, adjust the gap by bending the ground electrode with a gapping tool (**Figure 11**) to achieve the required gap.

> *NOTE*
> *Do not use a blade type feeler gauge to check the spark plug gap on a used spark plug or too large of a gap results.*

3. Wipe a *small* amount of antiseize compound onto the plug threads before installing the spark plug. Do not get the compound on the electrodes.

4. Screw the spark plug in by hand until it seats. Little effort should be required. If force is necessary, the plug may be cross-threaded. Unscrew it and try again.

5. Tighten the spark plug to 14 N•m (124 in.-lb.) or use a spark plug wrench and tighten the plug an additional 1/4-1/2 turn after the gasket makes contact with the cylinder head. If installing an old, re-gapped spark plug and gasket, only tighten the plug an additional 1/8-1/4 turn.

> *NOTE*
> *Do not overtighten the spark plug. This may crush the gasket and cause a compression leak.*

6. Align and press the cap (**Figure 9**) onto the spark plug.

> *CAUTION*
> *Position the spark plug wires so they do not contact the exhaust pipe.*

7. On VT750DC models, install the overhead covers.

Selection

The proper spark plug is important to obtain maximum performance and reliability. The condition of a used spark plug can reveal a lot about engine condition and carburetion. **Table 6** lists the recommended spark plug.

Spark plugs are available in several heat ranges to accommodate the load and performance demands placed on the engine. The standard spark plug recommended by the manufacturer is usually a medium heat-range plug that operates well over a wide range of engine speeds.

> *NOTE*
> *A hotter or colder spark plug does not make a hotter or colder spark. Heat range numbers describe how effectively plugs resist the transfer of heat into cylinder heads.*

Heat range is determined by the length, shape, thickness and chemical composition of a spark plug's lower insulator.

If the engine is run in hot climates, at high speed or under heavy loads for prolonged periods, a spark plug with a colder heat range may be required. A colder plug quickly transfers heat away from its firing tip and to the cylinder head. This is accomplished by a short path up the ceramic insulator and into the body of the spark plug (**Figure 12**). By transferring heat quickly, the plug remains cool enough to avoid overheating and preignition problems. If the engine is run slowly for prolonged periods, this type of plug may foul and cause poor performance. A colder plug does not cool down a hot engine.

If the engine is run in cold climates or at a slow speed for prolonged periods, a spark plug with a hotter heat range may be required. A hotter plug slowly transfers heat away from its firing tip and to the cylinder head. This is accomplished by a long path up the ceramic insulator and into the body of the plug (**Figure 12**). By transferring heat slowly, the plug remains hot enough to avoid fouling and buildup. If the engine is run in hot climates for fast or prolonged periods, this type of plug may overheat, cause preignition problems and possibly melt the electrode. Damage to the piston and cylinder assembly is possible.

If the engine is unmodified, changing to a different heat range plug is normally not required. However, if the engine's performance characteristics have been changed, a different heat range play may be necessary.

When installing a different heat range plug, go *one step* hotter or colder from the recommended plug. Do not try to correct poor carburetor or ignition problems by using different spark plugs. This only compounds the existing problem(s) and possibly leads to engine damage.

The reach (length) of a plug is also important (**Figure 13**). A shorter-than-normal plug causes difficult starting, carbon buildup on the exposed cylinder head threads, and reduces engine performance. These same conditions can occur if the correct length plug is used without a gasket. Trying to thread a spark plug into threads with carbon buildup may damage the threads in the cylinder head.

Reading/Inspection

The spark plug is an excellent indicator of how the engine is operating. By correctly evaluating the condition of the plug, engine problems can be diagnosed. After removing the spark plug, compare the firing tip with the ones shown in **Figure 14**, typical. The following section provide a description, as well as common causes, for each of the conditions.

> *CAUTION*
> *In all cases, when a spark plug is abnormal, find the cause of the problem before continuing engine operation. Engine damage is possible when abnormal plug readings are ignored.*

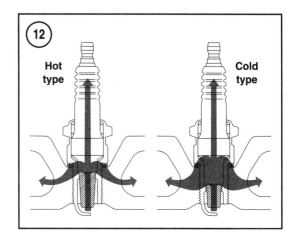

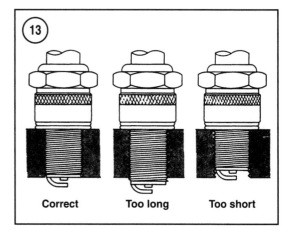

Normal condition

The plug has a light tan or gray deposits on the tip. No erosion of the electrodes or abnormal gap is evident. This indicates an engine that has properly adjusted carburetion, ignition timing and proper fuel mixture. This heat range of plug is appropriate for the conditions in which the engine has been operated. The plug can be reused.

Oil fouled

The plug is wet with black, oily deposits on the electrodes and insulator. The electrodes do not show wear.

1. Incorrect carburetor jetting.
2. Float level set too high.
3. Clogged air filter.
4. Faulty ignition component.
5. Spark plug heat range too cold.

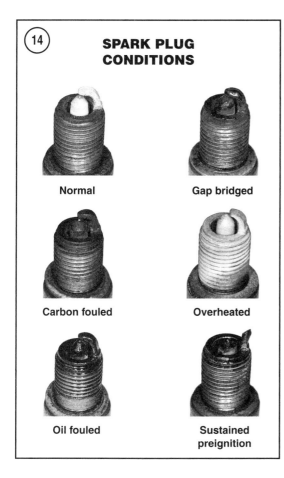

SPARK PLUG CONDITIONS

Normal

Gap bridged

Carbon fouled

Overheated

Oil fouled

Sustained preignition

6. Low engine compression (worn piston rings or valve guides).

7. Engine not properly broken in.

Carbon fouled

The plug is black with a dry, sooty deposit on the entire plug surface. This dry sooty deposit is conductive and can create electrical paths that bypass the electrode gap. This often causes misfiring of the plug.

1. Rich fuel mixture.

2. Spark plug heat range too cold.

3. Clogged air filter.

4. Faulty ignition component.

5. Low engine compression.

6. Prolonged idling.

Overheating

The plug is dry and the insulator has a white or light gray cast. The insulator may also appear blistered. The electrodes may have a burnt appearance.
1. Lean fuel mixture.
2. Spark plug heat range too hot.
3. Faulty ignition component.
4. Air leak.
5. Overtightened spark plug.
6. No crush washer on spark plug.
7. Engine lubrication system malfunction.

Gap bridging

The plug is clogged with deposits between the electrodes. The engine can run with a bridged spark plug, but it misfires.
1. Incorrect oil type.
2. Incorrect fuel or fuel contamination.
3. Excessive carbon deposits in combustion chamber.

Preignition

The plug electrodes are excessively eroded or melted. This condition can lead to engine damage.
1. Faulty ignition system component.
2. Spark plug heat range too hot.
3. Air leak.
4. Excessive carbon deposits in combustion chamber.

Worn out

The plug electrodes are rounded from normal combustion. There is no indication of abnormal combustion or engine conditions. Replace the plug.

IGNITION TIMING INSPECTION

The engine is equipped with a fully transistorized ignition system. Periodically check the timing to make sure all ignition components are operating correctly. Because of the solid state design, problems with the ignition system are rare and adjusting the ignition timing is neither necessary nor possible. If there seems to be an ignition-related problem, check the ignition timing to confirm the condition of the ignition system or a related problem.

Incorrect ignition timing can cause a drastic loss of engine performance. It may also cause overheating.

> **WARNING**
> *Do not start and run the motorcycle in an enclosed area. The exhaust gasses contain carbon monoxide, a colorless, odorless, poisonous gas. The carbon monoxide levels build quickly in an enclosed area and can cause unconsciousness and death in a short time.*

1. Start the engine and let it reach normal operating temperature. Shut the engine off.

2. Remove the timing hole cap (A, **Figure 15**) and its O-ring to access the flywheel timing marks.

3. Connect a timing light to one of the rear cylinder's spark plug wires following the manufacturer's instructions.

4. Start the engine and set the idle speed as described in this chapter.

5. Check the ignition timing as follows:

   a. Aim the timing light at the timing hole and pull the trigger. The ignition timing is correct if the *F* mark on the flywheel aligns with the index mark on the left crankcase cover (**Figure 16**).

   b. Increase the engine speed and check the ignition timing again. The ignition timing is correct if the advance marks on the flywheel align with the index mark on the left crankcase cover (**Figure 17**).

   c. Turn the engine off.

6. Connect a timing light to one of the front cylinder's spark plug wires following the manufacturer's instructions. Repeat Step 5.

7. Turn the engine off and disconnect the timing light.

8. If the timing is incorrect, there is a problem with one or more ignition system components. Refer to *Ignition System Troubleshooting* in Chapter Nine. There is no method of adjusting ignition timing.

9. Lubricate the timing hole cap threads (A, **Figure 15**) and O-ring with grease and tighten to the following:

   a. On VT750C models, 10 N•m (88 in.-lb.).

   b. On VT750DC models, 15 N•m (133 in.-lb.).

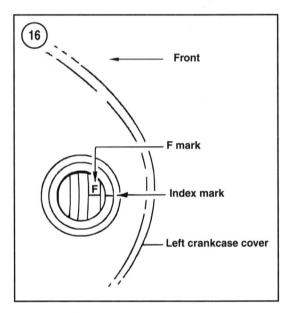

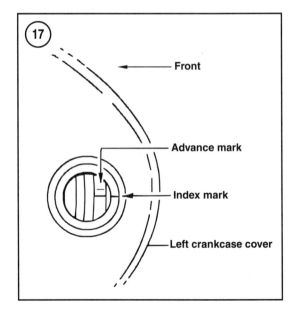

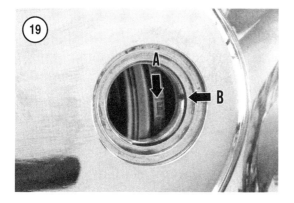

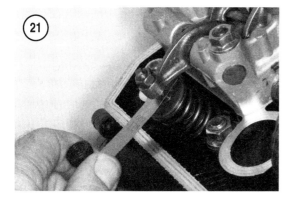

VALVE CLEARANCE

Inspection

The valve clearance for all models is listed in **Table 6**. Check and adjust the front cylinder valves first and then the rear cylinder valves. Refer to **Figure 2** for cylinder numbers.

> *NOTE*
> *Check and adjust the valve clearance with the engine cold (below 35° C [95° F]).*

1. Support the motorcycle on a stand so the seat is level. This makes it easier to view the flywheel timing marks.
2. Remove the front and rear cylinder head covers. Refer to Chapter Four.
3. Remove the timing (A, **Figure 15**) and crankshaft (B) hole caps from the left crankcase cover. The left crankcase cover must be installed on the engine to view the flywheel timing marks.
4. Remove the spark plugs as described in this chapter. This makes it easier to turn the engine by hand. Cover the spark plug openings to prevent small items from falling into the engine.
5. Set the front cylinder piston at TDC on its compression stroke as follows:
   a. Turn the crankshaft (**Figure 18**) counterclockwise and align the *FT* mark (A, **Figure 19**) on the flywheel with the index mark on the left crankcase cover (B).
   b. Try to move each front cylinder head rocker arm (**Figure 20**) by hand. The exhaust rocker arm and both intake rocker arms should have some free play. If all three rocker arms are tight (no free play), rotate the engine 360° (1 full turn) and realign the *FT* mark.
6. Measure the clearance of the exhaust valve and both intake valves as follows:
   a. Refer to **Table 6** to select the correct feeler gauges for the valve to be checked.
   b. Insert the feeler gauge between the adjusting screw and the end of the valve stem (**Figure 21**). When the clearance is correct, there is a slight drag on the feeler gauge when it is inserted and withdrawn.
   c. If there is too much or too little drag, adjust the valve clearance as described in this section.

d. When the front cylinder head valve clearances are correct, continue with Step 7 to check the rear cylinder head valve clearances.

7. Turn the crankshaft counterclockwise 308° and align the *RT* mark (A, **Figure 22**) on the flywheel with the index mark on the right crankcase cover (B). Check that the rear cylinder head piston is at TDC on its compression stroke as described in Step 5. If all three rocker arms are tight (no free play), rotate the engine 360° (1 turn) and realign the *RT* mark. Check the valve clearances as described in Step 6.

8. When the clearance of each valve is within specification, reverse Steps 1-4. Note the following:
   a. Reinstall the spark plugs as described in this chapter.
   b. Install the cylinder head covers as described in Chapter Four.
   c. Lubricate the timing and crankshaft hole cap threads and O-ring with grease and tighten as specified in **Table 7**.
   d. Check carburetor synchronization as described in this chapter.

Adjustment

1. Set the cylinder to TDC on its compression stroke as described above.
2. Loosen the locknut (A, **Figure 23**) on the valve adjusting screw.
3. Turn the adjusting screw (B, **Figure 23**) until the valve clearance (drag on feeler gauge) is correct.
4. Lubricate the adjusting screw and nut with engine oil.
5. Hold the adjusting screw to prevent it from turning and tighten the locknut to 23 N•m (17 ft.-lb.).
6. Recheck the valve clearance. If the clearance changed when the locknut was tightened, loosen the locknut and repeat the adjusting procedure.

CARBURETOR

Starting Enrichment Valve (Choke) Cable Inspection and Adjustment

Each carburetor is equipped with a manually operated starting enrichment (SE) valve assembly to richen the air/fuel mixture when starting a cold engine. The system consists of an SE valve installed inside each carburetor, cables and a hand-operated

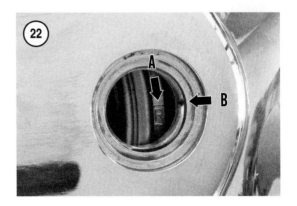

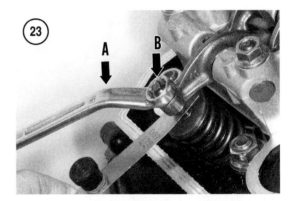

SE knob (**Figure 24**). With the SE knob pushed in, the SE valves should be closed. With the SE knob pulled out, the SE valves should be open.

SE valves that fail to open or close correctly can cause engine starting and drivability problems.

1. If there is a problem and an SE valve is suspected, note the following:
   a. If the engine is difficult to start when cold, but starts easily once it has warmed up, check for an SE valve that is not fully opening when the SE knob is pulled out. Pull the knob out and

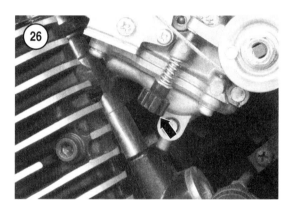

3

check for any creeping. Check the cables for damage.

b. If the engine starts but idles or runs roughly, check for an SE valve that is not completely closing when the SE knob is pushed in.

NOTE
Refer to Chapter Eight to check the SE valve and cable assembly.

2. At the interval specified in **Table 1**, check the SE valve operation as follows:

a. Operate the SE knob (**Figure 24**) by hand. The SE knob should move the SE valve between its fully closed and fully open positions without binding. The SE knob should also stay in its fully closed or fully open position without creeping. If the SE knob does not stay in position, adjust tension on the cable by turning the plastic nut behind the knob as described in substep b and substep c.

b. Pull the SE knob out, then pull the rubber cover (A, **Figure 25**) located behind the knob away from the plastic nut.

c. Turn the plastic nut (B, **Figure 25**) as required to tension the cable. Adjust the nut un-

til the SE knob remains stationary when it is pulled all the way out. The knob must move without any roughness or binding.

NOTE
Although the SE cable operates under tension, the cable can be lubricated with oil after removing it from the carburetors. Refer to Chapter Eight.

Idle Mixture Adjustment

The idle mixture (pilot screw) is preset and should not be reset during a tune-up. Do not adjust the pilot screws unless the carburetors have been overhauled. Refer to *Pilot Screw Adjustment* in Chapter Eight.

Idle Speed Adjustment

The engine idle speed is adjusted by turning the throttle stop screw (**Figure 26**) on the left side of the engine.

1. Start the engine and let it warm up approximately 2-3 minutes.

2. Support the motorcycle on its sidestand. Turn the engine off.

3. Connect a portable tachometer following the manufacturer's instructions.

4. Make sure the SE knob (**Figure 24**) is pushed all the way in before adjusting the idle speed.

5. Restart the engine and set the idle speed (**Table 6**) by turning the throttle stop screw (**Figure 26**).

6. Open and close the throttle a couple times. Check for variation in idle speed and readjust if necessary.

WARNING
With the engine idling, move the handlebar from side to side. If idle speed increases during this movement, the throttle cable needs adjusting or may be incorrectly routed through the frame. Correct this problem immediately. Do not ride the motorcycle in this unsafe condition.

NOTE
If the engine runs roughly at idle, first check for a dirty or contaminated air filter element. Then check for an SE valve (choke) that is not fully closing

7. Turn the engine off and disconnect the portable tachometer.

Synchronization

Synchronizing the carburetors adjusts the throttle plates so they open at the same time. This ensures that both carburetors deliver the same air/fuel mixture to both cylinders. A linkage assembly connects the throttle plates to each other. When this linkage goes out of adjustment, the throttle plates open at different intervals, causing poor engine idle, lack of throttle response (hesitation, stumble) and other drivability problems.

When the carburetors are properly synchronized, the engine warms up faster and there is an improvement in idle speed performance, throttle response and mileage.

A carburetor tuner, like the Motion Pro Deluxe Carb tuner shown in **Figure 27** (part No. 08-0009), is required to check carburetor synchronization.

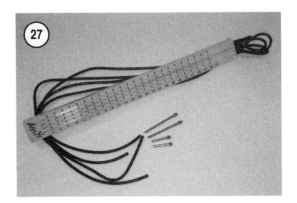

NOTE
*For a description of the Motion Pro Deluxe Carb Turner and other tools, refer to **www.motionpro.com**.*

1. Start the engine and let it warm up to normal operating temperature. Turn the engine off.
2. Support the motorcycle on its sidestand.
3. Remove the fuel tank (Chapter Eight).
4. Remove the air filter housing (Chapter Eight).
5. Connect a remote fuel tank to the carburetor. Open the fuel valve to fill the fuel line. Repair any fuel leaks before starting the engine.
6. Remove the rear cylinder head left side fin (**Figure 28**). Reconnect the spark plug cap.
7. Remove the screw and washer from each cylinder head intake port. Refer to **Figure 29** (front) and **Figure 30** (rear).
8. Install the vacuum gauge adapters into the intake ports (**Figure 31**, typical).

WARNING
Mercury is poisonous. When using a mercury carburetor tuner, follow the manufacturer's handling instructions.

9. Connect the carburetor tuner to the vacuum gauge adapters.

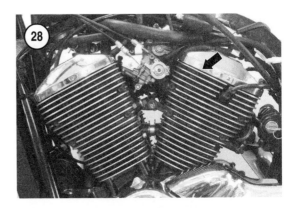

3

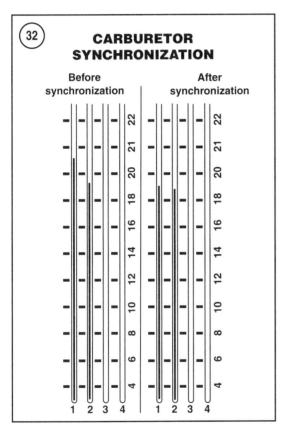

CARBURETOR SYNCHRONIZATION

Before synchronization	After synchronization

NOTE
When using a mercury carburetor tuner, do not increase the idle speed above 3500 rpm and/or drop the idle speed suddenly. The abrupt change in vacuum pressure may draw mercury into the engine. Refer to the manufacturer's instructions.

10. Start the engine and set the idle speed (**Table 6**) with the throttle stop screw (**Figure 26**).

NOTE
With the fuel tank removed and the engine running at idle speed, listen for any hissing or other sounds indicating a disconnected or damaged vacuum hose. Reconnect or repair any damaged hoses before continuing.

11. With the engine running at idle speed, check the gauge readings (**Figure 32**). If the difference in gauge readings is 27 mm Hg (0.7 in. Hg) or less between the two cylinders, the carburetors are considered synchronized. Note the following:

    a. If the carburetors are not synchronized, continue with Step 12.

    b. If the carburetors are synchronized, go to Step 13.

NOTE
Figure 33 shows the carburetor synchronization adjusting screw with the carburetor removed for clarity. The base carburetor is the No. 1 (rear) carburetor.

12. Using a screwdriver through the frame hole (**Figure 34**), turn the synchronization adjusting screw (**Figure 33**) to adjust the carburetors so the

gauge readings are as close to each other as possible (**Figure 32**, typical). Snap the throttle a few times to move the throttle linkage, and make sure the adjustment does not change.

NOTE
If the synchronizing screw is hard to turn or is non-responsive, check the linkage assembly for an excessive amount of dirt or other residue buildup. Spray the screw with a carburetor cleaner. If this does not help, check for damaged linkage components (springs, rods, clevis pins).

13. Slowly increase the engine speed to 3000 rpm. Both cylinder gauge readings should change but both should still register nearly the same reading. If both cylinder gauge readings are close or nearly identical at idle speed, but change unevenly when the engine speed is increased, a problem exists that is causing a change in the readings. Consider the following possible problems:
   a. Intake manifold air leak.
   b. Worn carburetor throttle valves or carburetor bores.
   c. Restricted exhaust system.
   d. Dirty air filter.
   e. Low engine compression.
   f. Leaking vacuum line connection between the carburetor tuner and cylinder head.

14. Turn the engine off and remove the vacuum lines and adapters. Install the screws and washers into the vacuum ports in the cylinder heads. Make sure the screws are tight to prevent a vacuum leak. Replace any damaged washers.

15. Reverse the steps to install the previously removed parts.

16. Start the engine and set the idle speed (**Table 6**) with the throttle stop screw (**Figure 26**).

FUEL HOSE INSPECTION

Inspect the fuel hoses at the interval specified in **Table 1**.

WARNING
Some fuel may spill from the hoses, fuel filter and fuel pump when disconnecting fuel hoses to check or replace them. Because gasoline is extremely flammable and explosive, perform this

procedure away from all open flames (including appliance pilot lights) and sparks. Do not smoke or allow someone to smoke in the work area. Always work in a well-ventilated area. Wipe up any spills immediately.

1. Remove the left side cover (Chapter Fifteen).

2. Remove the fuel tank and air filter housing (Chapter Eight).

3. Inspect the fuel hoses for leaks, hardness, age deterioration or other damage. **Figure 35** shows the fuel hose routing from the fuel valve through the fuel filter to the fuel pump and the return hose leading to the carburetors. Follow these hoses to inspect them.

4. Replace damaged fuel hoses and weak or damaged hose clamps as required.

CAUTION
When replacing the fuel hoses, make sure to install the support springs over the hoses where used.

5. Install the air filter and fuel tank (Chapter Eight).

THROTTLE CABLE

Throttle Operation

Check the throttle operation at the interval specified in **Table 1**.

Check for smooth throttle operation from the fully closed to fully open positions. Check at various steering positions. The throttle grip must return to the fully closed position without any hesitation.

Check the throttle cables for damage, wear or deterioration. Make sure the throttle cables are not kinked at any place.

If the throttle does not return to the fully closed position smoothly and the cables do not appear to be damaged, lubricate the throttle cables as described in this section. If thc throttle still does not return properly, the cables are probably kinked or routed incorrectly. Replace damaged throttle cables.

Check free play at the throttle grip flange. The free play specification is 2-6 mm (1/8-1/4 in.). If adjustment is required, perform the following procedure in this section.

Lubrication

Inspect the throttle operation at the interval specified in **Table 1**. Lubricate the cables whenever the throttle becomes stiff and sluggish or fails to snap back after releasing it.

The main cause of cables breaking or becoming stiff is improper lubrication. Periodic lubrication assures long service life. Inspect the cables for fraying, and check the sheath for chafing. Replace any defective cables.

Because of their design, a cable lubricant tool cannot be mounted on the upper end of both throttle cables. To lubricate the cable at the upper end, use a can of graphite with a thin hollow tube. A cable lubricant tool can be mounted on the lower of the throttle cables.

> *CAUTION*
> *When servicing aftermarket cables, follow the manufacturer's cable lubrication requirements.*

1. Disconnect the upper throttle cable ends as follows:
   a. On VT750DC models, remove the throttle drum cover (**Figure 36**) and the cover mounting bracket (**Figure 37**).
   b. Remove the two screws (A, **Figure 38**) securing the lower throttle cable holder at the carburetor. Disconnect both cable ends from the carburetor throttle drum (B, **Figure 38**). Leave the lower part of the cables attached to the throttle cable holder.
   c. Remove the throttle housing and disconnect the upper throttle cable ends (**Figure 39**) as

described under *Handlebar* in Chapter Twelve.

NOTE
When using an aerosol type lubricant, cover the area around the nozzle and tube with a plastic bag.

2. Lubricate the cables. **Figure 40** shows a cable lube tool and a cable lubricant. Lubricate each cable until fluid exits through the end of the cable. Wipe up all excess lube from the end of the cable.

CAUTION
Do not use chain lube to lubricate control cables unless it is also advertised as a cable lube.

3. Lightly lubricate the upper cable ends with grease.

4. Installation is the reverse of removal. Note the following:

   a. Adjust the throttle cables by following the adjustment procedure described in this section.

WARNING
An improperly assembled and installed throttle grip assembly may cause the throttle to stick open. Failure to properly assemble and adjust the throttle cables and throttle grip could cause loss of steering control. Do not start or ride the motorcycle until the throttle grip is correctly installed and snaps back when released.

   b. Adjust the choke cable as described in this chapter.

Adjustment

Cable adjusters are provided at both ends of the pull cable. Minor cable adjustment is made at the upper adjuster. If this does not provide enough adjustment, continue by adjusting the lower adjuster.

WARNING
If the idle speed increases when the handlebar is turned, check the throttle cable routing. Correct this problem immediately. Do not ride the motorcycle in this unsafe condition.

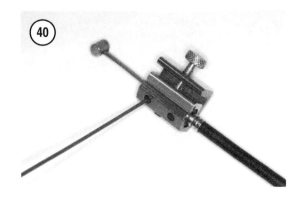

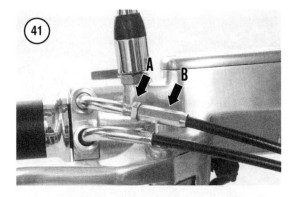

1. If minor adjustment is required, perform the following at the throttle grip:

   a. Loosen the locknut (A, **Figure 41**) and turn the upper adjuster (B) in or out to achieve 2-6 mm (5/64-1/4 in.) of free play rotation.

   b. Tighten the locknut and recheck the adjustment. If there is not enough cable adjustment, continue with Step 2.

2. If major adjustment is necessary, perform the following:

   a. On VT750DC models, remove the throttle drum cover (**Figure 36**) and the cover mounting bracket (**Figure 37**).

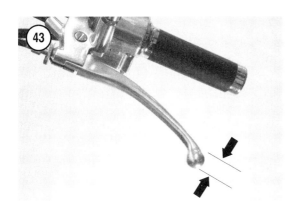

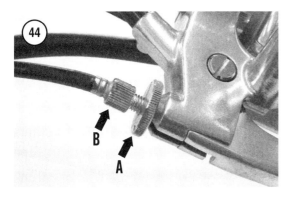

cable adjustment and routing. Do not ride the motorcycle in this unsafe condition.

7. Test ride the motorcycle, slowly at first, to make sure the throttle cables are operating correctly. Readjust if necessary.

3

CLUTCH CABLE ADJUSTMENT

Check clutch lever free play frequently and adjust to compensate for clutch cable stretching and clutch plate wear. Excessive clutch lever free play prevents the clutch from disengaging and causes clutch drag. Too little or no clutch lever free play does not allow the clutch to fully engage, causing clutch slippage. Both conditions cause unnecessary clutch wear. Transmission wear can also result from incorrect clutch adjustment.

1. Operate the clutch lever a few times. If the cable feels tight or dry, lubricate it as follows:
   a. Disconnect the upper clutch cable end as described in Chapter Twelve.
   b. Lubricate the cable as outlined under *Throttle Cable Lubrication* in this chapter.
   c. If the clutch lever pivot bolt feels tight or dry, remove, clean and lubricate it with grease as described under *Clutch Cable Replacement* in Chapter Six.

2. With the engine turned off, pull the clutch lever until resistance is felt, and then stop and measure free play at the end of the clutch lever (**Figure 43**). The clutch lever should have 10-20 mm (3/8-3/4 in.) free play.

3. Make minor adjustments at the clutch adjuster screw mounted at the clutch lever. Loosen the locknut (A, **Figure 44**) and turn the adjuster screw (B) as required to obtain the correct free play. Tighten the locknut and recheck the adjustment.

NOTE
If sufficient free play cannot be obtained at the hand lever or there is too much thread exposed on the clutch adjuster screw, use the adjuster at the opposite end of the clutch cable.

4. Loosen the lower clutch cable adjuster locknuts (**Figure 45**).

5. At the hand lever, loosen the locknut (A, **Figure 44**) and turn the adjuster screw (B) in to loosen the clutch cable all the way.

b. Loosen the cable locknut (A, **Figure 42**) and turn the lower adjuster (B) to achieve proper free play rotation at the throttle grip (**Figure 41**). Tighten the locknut securely.

c. Recheck free play. If necessary, readjust the upper adjuster as described in Step 1.

3. Operate the throttle a few times. The throttle grip should now be adjusted correctly. If not, the throttle cables may be stretched. Replace cables in this condition.

4. Reinstall all parts previously removed.

5. Open and release the throttle grip. Make sure it opens and closes (snaps back) without any binding or roughness. Then support the motorcycle and turn the handlebar from side to side, checking throttle operation at both steering lock positions.

6. Sit on the motorcycle and start the engine with the transmission in neutral. Turn the handlebars from lock-to-lock to check for idle speed variances due to improper cable adjustment, routing or damage.

WARNING
If idle speed increases when the handlebar is turned, recheck the throttle

6. At the lower clutch cable adjuster, pull the clutch cable forward and tighten the adjuster nuts (**Figure 45**) to lock the cable.

7. Turn the handlebar adjuster screw (B, **Figure 44**) as described in Step 3 and adjust the clutch cable. Tighten the adjuster locknut (A, **Figure 44**).

8. Tighten all locknuts.

9. Start the engine, pull the clutch lever in and shift the transmission into first gear. Check that the clutch does not drag or that the motorcycle does not stall. Slowly release the clutch lever while opening the throttle. The motorcycle should begin to move smoothly. If the clutch does not work correctly, turn the engine off and check the clutch adjustment. If the clutch does not work correctly, the clutch cable may be stretched or the friction plates are worn excessively.

SPEEDOMETER CABLE LUBRICATION

Refer to *Speedometer Gear and Cable* in Chapter Eleven.

ENGINE OIL AND FILTER

Engine Oil Level Check

Check the engine oil level with the dipstick mounted on the right crankcase cover.

1. Support the motorcycle on a stand so the seat is level.

2. Start the engine and let it idle for 2-3 minutes.

3. Shut off the engine and let the oil settle for 2-3 minutes.

> *CAUTION*
> *Do not check the oil level with the motorcycle on its sidestand; the oil flows away from the dipstick and causes a false reading.*

4. Remove the oil filler cap/dipstick (**Figure 46**), wipe the gauge and insert the dipstick *without* screwing it in.

5. Remove the oil filler cap/dipstick. The oil level should be between the upper and lower level marks (**Figure 47**).

6. If the oil level is near or below the lower level mark (**Figure 47**), add the recommended oil (**Table 3**) to correct the level. Add oil while checking the level to avoid overfilling.

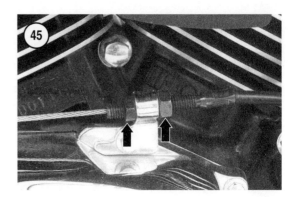

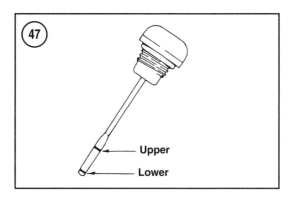

> *NOTE*
> *Refer to **Engine Oil Selection** in this section for additional information on oil.*

7. Inspect the O-ring on the oil filler cap/dipstick. Replace it if it is starting to deteriorate or harden.

8. Install the oil filler cap/dipstick (**Figure 46**) and tighten securely.

9. If the oil level is too high, do the following:

a. Remove the oil filler cap/dipstick (**Figure 46**) and draw out the excess oil using a syringe or suitable pump.

JASO CERTIFICATION LABEL

Sales company oil code number

OIL CLASSIFICATION:
MA: Designed for high-friction applications
MB: Designed for low-friction applications

API SERVICE SYMBOL

Oil classification

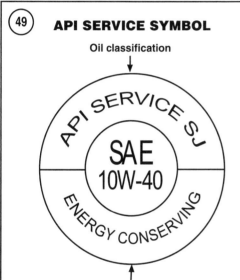

When ENERGY CONSERVING is listed in this part of the lable, the oil has demonstrated energy conserving properties in standard tests. Do not use ENERGY CONSERVING classified oil in motorcycle engines. Instead, look for this API service symbol.

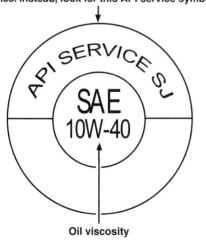

Oil viscosity

b. Recheck the oil level and adjust if necessary.

c. Install the oil filler cap/dipstick and tighten securely.

Engine Oil Selection

Regular oil and filter changes contribute more to engine longevity than any other maintenance. **Table 1** lists the recommended oil and filter change intervals. If the motorcycle is ridden infrequently consider a time interval schedule for changing the oil. Combustion acids formed by gasoline and water vapors can collect as sludge and contaminate the oil if the motorcycle is not ridden regularly or is used for only short trips. If a motorcycle is operated under dusty conditions, the oil gets dirty quicker and should be changed more frequently.

Because the engine oil lubricates the engine, clutch and transmission components, oil requirements for motorcycle engines are more demanding than for automobile engines. Oils specifically designed for motorcycles contain additives to prevent premature viscosity breakdown, protect the engine from oil oxidation resulting from higher engine operating temperatures and provide lubrication qualities designed for engines operating at higher rpm. Consider the following when selecting engine oil for the VT750 engine:

1. Do not use oil with oil additives or graphite or molybdenum additives. These may adversely affect clutch operation.

2. Do not use vegetable, non-detergent or castor-based racing oils.

3. The Japanese Automobile Standards Organization (JASO) has established an oil classification for motorcycle engines. JASO motorcycle specific oils are identified by the *JASO T 903 Standard*. The JASO label (**Figure 48**) appears on the oil container and identifies the two separate motorcycle oil classifications—MA and MB. Honda recommends the MA-classification oil for the VT750 models. JASO classified oil also uses the Society of Automotive Engineers (SAE) viscosity ratings.

4. When selecting an American Petroleum Institute (API) classified oil, use only an oil with an SG or higher classification that does not display the term *Energy Conserving* on the oil container circular API service label (**Figure 49**).

5. Use SAE 10W-40 weight oil. Use a lighter viscosity oil (10W-30) in cool climates and a heavier viscosity oil (20W-50) in warm or hot climates.

> *NOTE*
> *There are a number of ways to discard used oil safely. The easiest way is to pour it from the drain pan into a gallon plastic bleach, juice or milk container for disposal. Some service stations and oil retailers accept used oil for recycling. Do not discard oil in household trash or pour it onto the ground. Never add brake fluid, fork oil or any other type of petroleum-based fluid to any engine oil to be recycled.*

Engine Oil and Filter Change

1. Start the engine and run it until it is at normal operating temperature. Turn it off.

> *NOTE*
> *Warming the engine heats the oil so it flows freely and carries out contamination and sludge.*

2. Support the motorcycle on its sidestand when draining the engine oil. This ensures complete draining.

> *WARNING*
> *The engine, exhaust pipes and oil are hot. Work carefully when removing the oil drain bolt and oil filter to avoid contacting the oil or hot engine parts.*

3. Clean the area around the oil drain bolt and oil filter.

4. Place a clean drip pan under the crankcase and remove the oil drain bolt (**Figure 50**) and washer.

5. Remove the oil filler cap/dipstick (**Figure 46**) to help speed up the flow of oil. Allow the oil to drain completely.

6. To replace the oil filter, perform the following:

   a. Install a socket type oil filter wrench squarely onto the oil filter (**Figure 51**) and turn the filter counterclockwise until oil begins to run out, and then remove the oil filter.

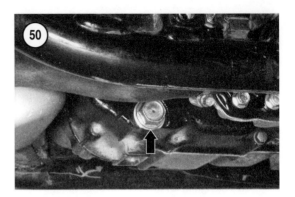

   b. Hold the filter over the drain pan and pour out any remaining oil. Place the old filter in a plastic bag and discard it properly.

   c. Carefully clean the oil filter sealing surface on the crankcase. Do not allow any dirt or other debris to enter the engine.

   d. Lubricate the rubber seal on the new filter with clean engine oil.

   e. Install the new oil filter onto the threaded fitting on the crankcase. Tighten the filter by hand until it contacts the crankcase. Then tighten an additional 3/4 turn. If using the oil filter socket, tighten the filter to 10 N•m (88 in.-lb.).

> *NOTE*
> *Overtightening the filter may cause it to leak.*

7. Replace the drain bolt gasket if it leaks or is damaged.

8. Install the oil drain bolt (**Figure 50**) and gasket and tighten to 30 N•m (22 ft.-lb.).

9. Support the motorcycle on a stand with the seat in a level position.

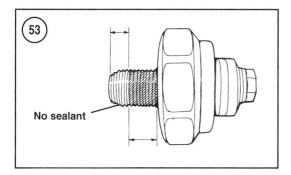

No sealant

10. Insert a funnel into the oil filler hole and fill the engine with the correct weight (**Table 3**) and quantity of oil (**Table 4**).

11. Remove the funnel and screw in the oil filler cap/dipstick and its O-ring (**Figure 46**).

NOTE
*If servicing a rebuilt engine, check the engine oil pressure as described under **Engine Oil Pressure Test** in this section.*

12. Start the engine and let it idle.

CAUTION
The oil pressure warning light should go out within 1-2 seconds. If it stays on, shut off the engine immediately and locate the problem. Do not run the engine with the oil pressure warning light on.

13. Check the oil filter and drain bolt for leaks.

14. Turn the engine off after 2-3 minutes and check the oil level as described in this section. Adjust the oil level if necessary.

WARNING
Prolonged contact with oil may cause skin cancer. Wash hands thoroughly

with soap and water after contacting engine oil.

Engine Oil Pressure Test

Check the engine oil pressure after reassembling the engine or when troubleshooting the lubrication system.

An oil pressure gauge and oil pressure adapter are required to test the oil pressure.

1. Connect a tachometer to the engine following the manufacturer's instructions.

2. Remove the drive sprocket cover. Refer to Chapter Eleven.

3. Check the engine oil level as described in this section. Add oil if necessary.

4. Start the engine and allow it to reach normal operating temperature. Turn the engine off.

5. Support the motorcycle on a stand so the seat is level.

6. Remove the rubber boot and disconnect the wire (A, **Figure 52**) from the oil pressure switch. Then loosen and remove the oil pressure switch (B, **Figure 52**).

7. Assemble the oil pressure adapter and gauge. Thread the oil pressure gauge adapter into the engine in place of the oil pressure switch. Make sure the fitting is tight to prevent leaks.

WARNING
Keep the gauge hose away from the exhaust pipe during this test. If the hose contacts the exhaust pipe, it may melt and spray hot oil.

8. Start the engine and let it idle.

9. Increase engine speed to 5500 rpm and read the oil pressure on the gauge. The oil pressure should be 530 kPa (77 psi) when the oil temperature is 80° C (176° F).

10. Allow the engine to return to idle, then shut it off and remove the test equipment.

11. If the oil pressure is lower or higher than specified, refer to *Engine Lubrication* in Chapter Two.

12. Install the oil pressure switch as follows:
   a. Clean the oil pressure switch and crankcase threads of all sealer and oil residue.
   b. Apply an RTV sealant to the oil pressure switch threads as shown in **Figure 53**. Do not

apply sealant within 3-5 mm (0.1-0.2 in.) from the end of the switch threads.

NOTE
Allow the RTV sealant to set for 10-15 minutes before installing the oil pressure switch.

c. Install the oil pressure switch and tighten to 12 N•m (106 in.-lb.).

d. Reconnect the wire onto the switch and cover the switch with its rubber boot.

13. Follow the sealant manufacturer's recommendations for drying time, then start the engine and check for leaks.

CAUTION
The oil pressure indicator should go out within 1-2 seconds. If it stays on, shut off the engine immediately and locate the problem. Do not run the engine with the oil pressure indicator on.

CAUTION
Do not overtighten the switch to correct an oil leak because it may strip the crankcase threads. If oil leaks from the switch after installing it, remove the switch and reclean the threads. Reseal and reinstall the switch.

14. Install the drive sprocket cover (Chapter Eleven).

15. Disconnect and remove the tachometer.

COOLING SYSTEM

Check, inspect and service the cooling system at the intervals specified in **Table 1**.

WARNING
When performing any service work on the engine or cooling system, never remove the radiator cap or coolant drain bolts, or disconnect any coolant hose while the engine and radiator are hot. Scalding fluid and steam may blow out under pressure and cause serious injury.

Coolant Selection

If adding coolant to the cooling system, use Pro Honda HP Coolant. This is a ready-to-use 50:50 antifreeze/purified, de-ionized water coolant blend. If mixing antifreeze and water, use a 50:50 mixture of distilled water and antifreeze that does not contain silicate inhibitors. Use only soft or distilled water. Never use tap or saltwater, as this damages engine parts. Distilled (or purified) water can be purchased at supermarkets or drug stores in gallon containers. Never use alcohol-based antifreeze.

CAUTION
Many antifreeze solutions contain silicate inhibitors to protect aluminum parts from corrosion damage. However, these silicate inhibitors can cause premature wear to water pump seals. When selecting an antifreeze, make sure it does not contain silicate inhibitors.

Coolant Test

WARNING
Do not remove the radiator cap when the engine is hot.

1. Remove the fuel tank (Chapter Eight).

2. On VT750C models, remove the steering covers (Chapter Fifteen).

3. Remove the radiator cap (**Figure 54**).

4. Test the specific gravity of the coolant with an antifreeze tester to ensure adequate temperature and corrosion protection. A 50:50 mixture is recommended. Never allow the mixture to become less than 40 percent antifreeze. Refer to *Coolant Selection* in this section.

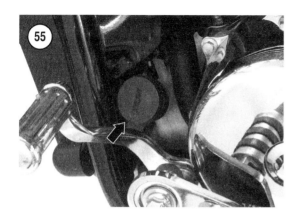

5. Reinstall the radiator cap (**Figure 54**).

6. Reverse Step 1 and Step 2.

Coolant Level

The coolant reserve tank is mounted between the radiator and the front of the engine.

1. Support the motorcycle on a stand so the seat is level.

2. Start the engine and allow it to idle until it reaches normal operating temperature. The engine must be running at idle speed when checking the coolant level.

3. The coolant level should be between the upper and lower level marks on the coolant reserve tank.

4. If necessary, add coolant as follows:

  a. Turn the engine off.

  b. Remove the coolant reserve tank cap (**Figure 55**) and add Pro Honda HP Coolant into the reserve tank (not the radiator) to bring the level to the upper mark. Refer to *Coolant Selection* in this section. Install the cap.

c. Inspect the cooling system for leaks as described in Chapter Ten.

Coolant Change

Drain and refill the cooling system at the interval listed in **Table 1**.

It is sometimes necessary to drain the cooling system when servicing the engine. If the coolant is still in good condition, it can be reused. Drain the coolant into a *clean* pan and pour the coolant into a container for storage.

> *WARNING*
> *Waste antifreeze is toxic and may never be discharged into storm sewers, septic systems, waterways or onto the ground. Place used antifreeze in the original container and dispose of it according to local regulations. Do not store coolant where it is accessible to children or pets.*

> *WARNING*
> *Do not remove the radiator cap (Figure 54) if the engine is hot. The coolant is very hot and is under pressure. Severe scalding results if hot coolant contacts skin.*

> *CAUTION*
> *Be careful not to spill antifreeze on painted surfaces as it damages the surface. Wash immediately with soapy water and rinse thoroughly.*

Perform the following procedure when the engine is *cold*:

1. Place the motorcycle on a stand so the seat is level.

2. Remove the fuel tank (Chapter Eight).

3. On VT750C models, remove the steering covers (Chapter Fifteen).

4. Remove the radiator cap (**Figure 54**).

> *NOTE*
> *Cut the top off a plastic gallon-size milk container and use the bottom of the container (Figure 56) to control the coolant as it drains from the water pump in Step 5.*

5. Place a drain pan under the coolant drain bolt. Remove the drain bolt (**Figure 57**) and washer and allow the coolant to drain into the pan.

6. Remove the rear cylinder coolant drain bolt and washer (**Figure 58**) and allow the coolant to drain.

7. Replace leaking or damaged sealing washers. Reinstall the drain bolts and sealing washers and tighten to 13 N•m (115 in.-lb.).

8. Use a siphon to remove coolant from the coolant reserve tank. Rinse the tank with clean water. Siphon this water from the tank.

CAUTION
Do not use a higher percentage of antifreeze-to-water solution than is recommended. A higher concentration of coolant decreases the performance of the cooling system.

9. Place a funnel in the radiator filler neck and slowly refill the radiator and engine with a 50:50 mixture of antifreeze and distilled water. Add the mixture slowly so it expels as much air as possible from the cooling system. Refer to *Coolant Selection* in this section before purchasing and mixing coolant. **Table 5** lists engine coolant capacity.

10. Fill the coolant reserve tank (**Figure 55**) to its upper level line.

WARNING
Do not start and run the motorcycle in an enclosed area. The exhaust gasses contain carbon monoxide, a colorless, odorless, poisonous gas. Carbon monoxide levels build quickly in a small enclosed area and can cause unconsciousness and death in a short time.

11. After filling the radiator, bleed the cooling system as follows:
   a. Start the engine and allow it to idle for 2-3 minutes.
   b. Snap the throttle a few times to bleed air from the cooling system. When the coolant level drops in the radiator, add coolant to bring the level to the bottom of the filler neck.
   c. When the radiator coolant level has stabilized, install the radiator cap (**Figure 54**).

12. Start the engine and let it run at idle speed until the engine reaches normal operating temperature. Make sure the coolant level in the coolant reserve

tank stabilizes at the correct level. Add coolant to the coolant reserve tank as necessary.

13. Test ride the motorcycle and readjust the coolant level in the reserve tank as required. Check the coolant drain bolts for leaks.

EMISSION CONTROL SYSTEMS INSPECTION

California models are equipped with secondary air supply and evaporative emission control systems. At the interval specified in **Table 1**, check all emission control hoses for deterioration, damage or loose connections. Replace any parts or hoses as required. Refer to the emission control sections in Chapter Eight for information on inspecting these systems.

BATTERY

The original equipment battery is a maintenance-free type. Maintenance-free batteries do not require periodic electrolyte inspection and water cannot be added. Refer to Chapter Nine for battery service, testing and replacement procedures.

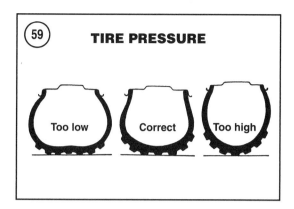

59 **TIRE PRESSURE**

Too low   Correct   Too high

TIRES AND WHEELS

Tire Pressure

Check and adjust the tire pressure to provide safe maximum tire life. Check tire pressure when the tires are *cold*. When the motorcycle is ridden, the tire temperature rises. Never release air pressure from a warm or hot tire to match the recommended tire pressure listed in **Table 2**; doing so may cause the tire to be underinflated. Use an accurate tire pressure gauge.

> *NOTE*
> *A loss of air pressure may be due to a loose or damaged valve core. Put a few drops of water on the top of the valve core. If the water bubbles, tighten the valve core and recheck. If air still leaks from the valve after tightening it, replace the tube.*

Tire Inspection

Inspect the tires periodically for excessive wear and damage. Inspect the tires for the following:
1. Deep cuts and embedded objects, such as nails and stones. If a nail or other object is in a tire, mark its location with a light crayon before removing it. This helps to locate the hole in the tube for repair. Refer to Chapter Eleven for tire changing and repair information.
2. Flat spots. Storing the motorcycle with one or both wheels on the ground can cause flat spots.
3. Sidewall cracks and other visual damage.
4. Separating plies.
5. Bulges.
6. Improper tire centering on rim.

7. Damaged tube stem.

Tire Wear Analysis

Analyze abnormal tire wear to determine the cause. Common causes are:

1. Incorrect tire pressure. This is the number one cause of abnormal tire wear. Compare the wear in the center of the contact patch with the wear at the edge of the contact patch (**Figure 59**). Check tire pressure and examine the tire tread. Note the following:

   a. If a tire shows excessive wear at the edge of the contact patch, but the wear at the center of the contact patch is normal, the tire has been underinflated. Underinflated tires cause the sidewalls to flex excessively. This causes higher tire temperatures, hard or imprecise steering and abnormal tire wear on the tire edges.

   b. If a tire shows excessive wear in the center of the contact patch, but wear at the edge of the contact patch in normal, the tire has been overinflated. Overinflated tires cause the tire to bulge in the center of the tread. This results in a hard ride and abnormal tire wear in the center of the tread. When a properly inflated tire hits a large bump in the road, it has a normal flex or give and is capable of absorbing much of the shock. However, an overinflated tire cannot flex or give and the tire casing (cord material) takes the shock. This weakens and breaks the tire cords and eventually causes tire failure.

> *NOTE*
> *Large amounts of high-speed riding on straight roads cause the tires to exhibit a similar wear pattern as described in substep b.*

2. Overloading.

3. Incorrect wheel alignment.

4. Incorrect wheel balance: The tire and wheel assembly should be balanced when installing a new tire.

5. Worn or damaged wheel bearings.

Tread Depth

Measure the tread depth (**Figure 60**) in the center of the tire using a small ruler or a tread depth gauge. Honda recommends replacing the original equipment tires before the center tread depth has worn to the following depth:

1. Front: 1.5 mm (0.06 in.).
2. Rear: 2.0 mm (0.08 in.).

Tires are also designed with tread wear indicators (**Figure 61**) that appear when a tire is worn out. When these are visible, the tire is no longer safe and must be replaced.

Wheel Bearing Inspection

Inspect the wheel bearings once a year and when the wheels are removed.

Front wheel

1. Support the motorcycle with the front wheel off the ground.
2. Hold the caliper housing from the outside and push it toward its brake disc. This pushes the pistons into the caliper and away from the disc.
3. Spin the front wheel while listening for any excessive wheel bearing noise. The wheel should turn freely. If there is any roughness or catching, the wheel bearings may be worn or damaged.
4. Apply the front brake to reposition the front brake pads in the caliper.
5. Have an assistant apply the front brake and then turn the handlebar to one side and hold securely in this position. Grasp the sides of the front tire 180° apart and try to move the tire from side to side. There should be no play. If play is detected, the wheel bearings may be worn.
6. Remove the stand from underneath the motorcycle. Sit on the motorcycle and apply the front brake. Then pump the front forks while trying to detect any play at the wheel bearings. If play is detected, the wheel bearings may be worn.

NOTE
When performing Step 6, play detected at the steering stem indicates loose or damaged steering bearings. Check these bearings as described in this chapter.

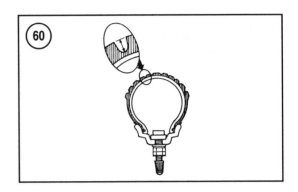

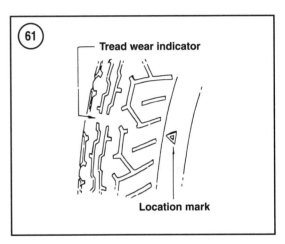

Tread wear indicator

Location mark

7. If necessary, remove the front wheel and inspect the wheel bearings as described in Chapter Eleven.

Rear wheel

Because of the drive chain and sprocket, it is harder to detect worn or damaged rear wheel bearings when the wheel is mounted on the motorcycle.

1. Support the motorcycle with the rear wheel off the ground.
2. Turn the rear brake adjuster counterclockwise to remove the brake shoes away from the brake drum.
3. Spin the rear wheel by hand. Listen for any excessive bearing noise that may indicate worn or damaged bearings.
4. Readjust the rear brake as described in this chapter.
5. Have an assistant apply the rear brake while steadying the motorcycle. Then grasp the back of the rear tire and try to move it sideways (parallel to the swing arm). If play is detected, determine if it is from the rear wheel bearings, swing arm bearings or both.

6. If necessary, remove the rear wheel and inspect the wheel bearings as described in Chapter Eleven.

7. If the rear wheel is removed from the swing arm, check the swing arm as follows:

    a. Remove the lower shock absorber mounting bolts (A, **Figure 62**) on both sides of the swing arm. Raise and support the shock absorbers with a piece of stiff wire.

    b. Grasp the back of the swing arm (B, **Figure 62**) and attempt to move it sideways (parallel to the ground).

    c. Raise and lower the swing arm by hand, while checking for any binding or roughness.

    d. If there is any questionable swing arm play, service the swing arm bearings as described in Chapter Thirteen.

8. Install the rear wheel (Chapter Eleven) if removed.

Spokes and Rim Inspection

Check the spokes and wheel runout at the intervals specified in **Table 1**. Refer to Chapter Eleven.

> *CAUTION*
> *Overtightening the spokes forces the wheel out of true and rounds off the nipple heads. Service the spokes as described in Chapter Eleven.*

STEERING BEARING INSPECTION

Inspect the steering bearing adjustment at the intervals specified in **Table 1**.

1. Support the motorcycle on a stand with the front wheel off the ground.

2. Hold onto the handlebars and move them from side to side. Note any binding or roughness.

3. Support the motorcycle so both wheels are on the ground.

4. Sit on the motorcycle and hold onto the handlebars. Apply the front brake lever and try to push the front fork forward. Try to detect any movement in the steering head area. If there is movement, adjust the bearings.

5. If any roughness, binding or looseness was detected when performing Step 2 or Step 4, service the steering bearings as described in Chapter Twelve.

FRONT SUSPENSION INSPECTION

The manufacturer does not provide a service interval for changing the front fork oil. Changing the fork oil on an annual basis is a typical recommendation. The fork sliders are not equipped with drain screws. Refer to Chapter Twelve for removal and disassembly procedures.

Inspect the front suspension at the interval specified in **Table 1**.

1. Use a soft, wet cloth to wipe the front fork tubes to remove any dirt, road tar and other debris. As this debris passes by the fork seals, it eventually damages the seals and causes them to leak.

2. Check the front fork for any leaks or damage.

3. Apply the front brake and pump the fork up and down vigorously. Check for smooth operation.

4. Make sure the upper and lower fork tube pinch bolts are tight.

5. Check that the handlebar mounting bolts are tight.

6. Make sure the front axle is tight.

> *CAUTION*
> *If any of the previously mentioned fasteners are loose, refer to Chapter Twelve for procedures and torque specifications.*

REAR SUSPENSION INSPECTION

Inspect the rear suspension at the interval specified in **Table 1**.

1. With both wheels on the ground, check the shock absorbers by bouncing on the seat several times.

2. Check the swing arm bearings as described under *Wheel Bearings* in this chapter.

3. Check the shock absorbers for oil leaks, loose mounting fasteners or other damage.

4. Check for loose or missing suspension fasteners.

5. Make sure the rear axle nut is tight.

6. To adjust the rear shock absorbers, refer to Chapter Thirteen.

> *CAUTION*
> *If any of the previously mentioned bolts and nuts are loose, refer to Chapter Thirteen for procedures and torque specifications.*

BRAKES

All models are equipped with a front disc brake and rear drum brake. Check both brake assemblies at the intervals specified in **Table 1**. Immediately inspect the brake components when their operating condition has changed.

Bleeding the front brake, servicing the brake components and replacing the brake pads and brake shoes are covered in Chapter Fourteen.

Brake System Inspection

Check the front and rear brake operation as follows:

1. Support the motorcycle on its sidestand.

2. Apply the front brake lever. Make sure it feels firm. If the lever feels soft or spongy, air has probably entered the system. Check the front brake hose and bleed the brake as described in Chapter Fourteen.

3. Support the motorcycle with the rear wheel off the ground. Spin the rear wheel and check for brake drag. However, because there is drag produced by the drive chain, it can be difficult to distinguish between the two. Apply the rear brake pedal. Make sure it feels firm. If necessary, check and adjust the rear brake as described in this section.

Front Brake Hose Inspection

Check the front brake hose between the master cylinder and brake caliper. If there are any leaks, tighten the bolt or hose and bleed the front brake as described in Chapter Fourteen. If this does not stop the leak or if a brake line is obviously damaged, cracked or chafed, replace the brake hose and bleed the system. Refer to Chapter Fourteen for brake system torque specifications.

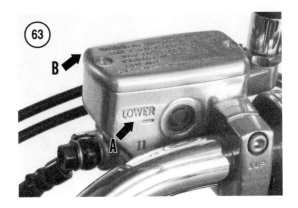

Brake Fluid Selection

Use DOT 4 brake fluid in the front master cylinder reservoir.

> *WARNING*
> *Use brake fluid clearly marked DOT 4. Others may cause brake failure. Do not intermix different brands or types of brake fluid as they may not be compatible. Do not intermix silicone based (DOT 5) brake fluid as it can cause brake component damage leading to brake system failure.*

> *CAUTION*
> *Handle brake fluid carefully. Do not spill it on painted or plastic surfaces, as it damages the surface. Wash the area immediately with soap and water and thoroughly rinse it off.*

Brake Fluid Change

Every time the reservoir cover is removed, a small amount of dirt and moisture enters the brake

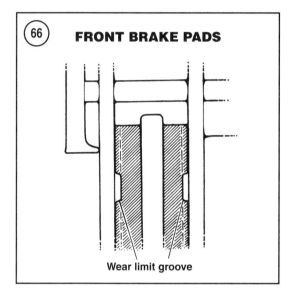

FRONT BRAKE PADS

Wear limit groove

63). If the brake fluid level is at or below the lower level line, continue with Step 3.

NOTE
If the reservoir is empty, air has entered the brake system. Bleed the front brake as described in Chapter Fourteen.

3. Wipe off the master cylinder cover and remove the cover screws. Then remove the cover (B, **Figure 63**), set plate and diaphragm.

4. Add fresh DOT 4 brake fluid to fill the reservoir to the level mark located inside the reservoir (**Figure 64**).

5. Install the diaphragm, set plate and cover (B, **Figure 63**). Install and tighten the cover screws. Check for seeping around the cover, indicating the reservoir was overfilled.

6. If the brake fluid level was low, check the brake pads for excessive wear as described in this section.

NOTE
A low brake fluid level usually indicates brake pad wear. As the pads wear (become thinner), the brake caliper pistons automatically extend farther out of their bores. As the caliper pistons move outward, the brake fluid level drops in the system. However, if the brake fluid level is low and the brake pads are not worn excessively, check the brake hose for leaks.

Front Brake Pad Wear Inspection

Inspect the front brake pads for wear at the intervals specified in **Table 1**.

1. Inspect the front pads through the top of the caliper (**Figure 65**) for uneven wear, oil contamination or other damage. Note the following:

  a. Binding or sticking caliper pistons or improper caliper bracket operation can cause uneven pad wear.

  b. A damaged left side fork seal allows oil to run down the fork tube and contaminate the brake pads and caliper housing. Always check the pads for contamination when a leaking fork seal is detected and replace the seal immediately.

  c. If there is no visible brake pad damage or contamination, perform Step 2.

fluid. The same thing happens if a leak occurs or when a brake hose is loosened. Dirt can clog the system and cause unnecessary wear. Water in the brake fluid vaporizes at high brake system temperatures, impairing the hydraulic action and reducing stopping ability. To maintain peak performance, change the brake fluid at the interval specified in **Table 1** or whenever the caliper or master cylinder is overhauled. To change brake fluid, follow the brake fluid draining and bleeding procedures in Chapter Fourteen.

Front Brake Fluid Level Check

1. Place the motorcycle on its sidestand. Turn the handlebar and level the front master cylinder.

2. The brake fluid level must be above the lower level line in the master cylinder window (A, **Figure**

2. Replace the brake pads as a set if either pad is worn to the bottom of the wear limit groove (**Figure 66**). Refer to Chapter Fourteen.

Front Brake Lever Adjustment

There is no front brake lever adjustment.

Front Brake Light Switch Adjustment

There is no front brake light switch adjustment.

Rear Brake Shoe Wear Inspection

1. Support the motorcycle on its sidestand.
2. Apply the rear brake pedal and hold it in place.
3. Check the brake arm arrow position. If the arrow mark on the brake arm (A, **Figure 67**) aligns with the fixed index mark on the brake panel (B) when the rear brake is applied, the rear brake shoes are excessively worn and require replacement. Replace the rear brake shoes as described in Chapter Fourteen.

Rear Brake Pedal Height

VT750C

1. Measure the pedal height from the top of the footpeg rubber to the top of the brake pedal rubber (**Figure 68**). The standard height is 50 mm (2.0 in.). If the height adjustment is incorrect, continue with Step 2.
2. Loosen the stopper bolt locknut (A, **Figure 69**) and turn the stopper bolt (B) in or out until the standard pedal height is reached. Tighten the locknut and recheck the pedal height.
3. If the pedal height adjustment was changed, check the rear brake pedal free play and the rear brake light switch adjustment as described in this section. Adjust if necessary.

VT750DC

Honda does not specify a brake pedal height for these models. Adjust the brake pedal height to suit rider preference.
1. Loosen the stopper bolt locknut (A, **Figure 69**) and turn the stopper bolt (B) in or out until the preferred pedal height is reached. Tighten the locknut and recheck the pedal height.

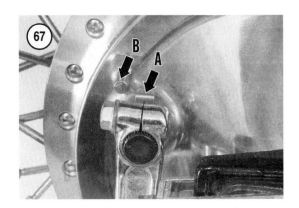

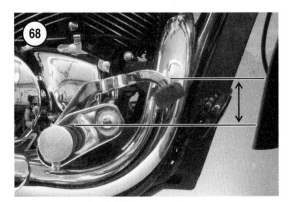

2. If the pedal height adjustment was changed, check the rear brake pedal free play and the rear brake light switch adjustment as described in this section. Adjust if necessary.

Rear Brake Pedal Free Play

1. Support the motorcycle on its sidestand.
2. Before checking and adjusting the free play, check the brake rod and brake arm assemblies for missing parts or damage.

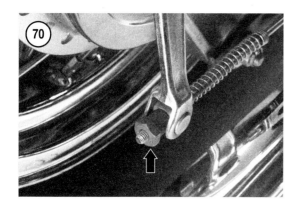

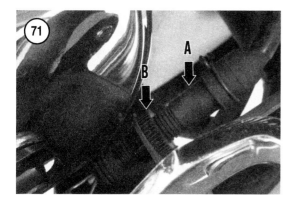

3. Depress the brake pedal (**Figure 68**) until resistance is felt at the pedal. The distance the brake pedal moved is rear brake free play. The correct free play measurement is 20-30 mm (3/4-1 1/4 in.). If out of specification, continue with Step 4.

4. Turn the rear brake rod adjusting nut (**Figure 70**) to adjust the rear brake free play. After turning the adjusting nut, seat the notch in the nut against the brake arm collar.

5. Apply the rear brake a few times, and recheck the free play. Then support the motorcycle with its rear wheel off the ground and spin the wheel, making sure it rotates freely. If there is any noticeable brake drag, the rear brake is adjusted too tightly. Readjust the brake pedal free play to the specifications in Step 3.

NOTE
If the rear brake pedal free play cannot be adjusted so there is no brake drag, the brake drum and brake shoe linings may be contaminated. Check and service the rear brake as described in Chapter Fourteen.

6. Check the rear brake light switch adjustment as described in the following section.

Rear Brake Light Switch Adjustment

Check the rear brake light switch adjustment at the intervals specified in **Table 1**.

NOTE
*Perform the **Rear Brake Pedal Height** and **Rear Brake Pedal Free Play** adjustments before checking and adjusting the rear brake light switch in this section.*

1. Turn the ignition switch on.

2. Depress the brake pedal (**Figure 68**). The brake light should come on just before the brake begins to work.

3. If the brake light comes on late, continue with Step 4.

CAUTION
Do not turn the switch body when adjusting the rear brake light switch. This damages the wires at the top of the switch. Hold the switch body and turn the adjusting nut.

4. Hold the brake light switch body (A, **Figure 71**) and turn the adjusting nut (B) as required to make the brake light come on earlier.

5. Recheck the rear brake light switch adjustment.

6. Turn the ignition switch off.

DRIVE CHAIN

Chain Lubrication

Lubricate the chain at the interval indicated in **Table 1**. A properly maintained chain provides maximum service life and reliability. Honda recommends SAE 80 or 90 gear oil or Pro Honda Chain Lube designed for O-ring chains.

On an O-ring chain, the chain lubrication applied in this procedure is used mainly to keep the O-rings pliable and to prevent the side plates and rollers from rusting. The chain is primarily lubricated by the lubricant enclosed within the chain by the O-rings (**Figure 72**).

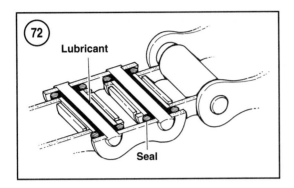

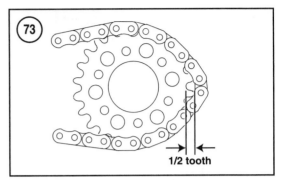

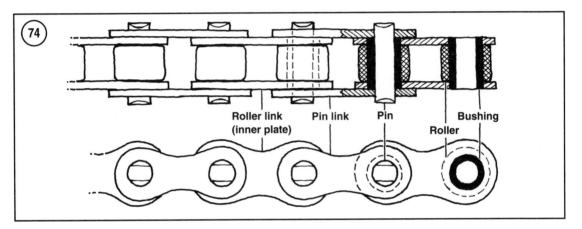

1. Ride the motorcycle a few miles to warm the drive chain. A warm chain increases lubricant penetration.

2. Support the motorcycle so the rear wheel clears the ground.

3. Oil the bottom chain run with SAE 80 or 90 gear oil or a commercial chain lubricant recommended for use on O-ring drive chains. Concentrate on getting the oil down between the side plates on both sides of the chain. Do not overlubricate.

CAUTION
Not all commercial chain lubricants are recommended for use on O-ring drive chains. Make sure it is formulated for O-ring chains.

4. Rotate the chain and continue until the entire chain has been lubricated.

5. Turn the rear wheel slowly and wipe off excess oil from the chain with a shop cloth. Also wipe off lubricant from the rear hub, wheel and tire.

Chain Cleaning and Inspection

Clean the drive chain after riding over dusty or sandy conditions.

CAUTION
All models are equipped with an O-ring drive chain. Clean the chain with kerosene only. Solvents and gasoline react with the rubber O-rings, causing them to swell. If this happens, replace the drive chain. The O-rings can also be damaged by high pressure washers, steam cleaning and stiff bristle brushes.

This section describes how to clean the drive chain while it is mounted on the motorcycle. To clean the chain off the motorcycle, remove it as described in Chapter Eleven.

1. Support the motorcycle on a stand with the rear wheel off the ground.

2. Place some stiff cardboard and a drain pan underneath the drive chain.

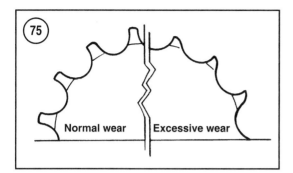

Normal wear | Excessive wear

2. Support the motorcycle on a stand with the rear wheel off the ground.

3. Turn the rear wheel and inspect the chain for missing or damaged O-rings.

4. At the rear sprocket, pull one of the links away from the driven sprocket. If the link pulls away more than 1/2 the height of the sprocket tooth (**Figure 73**), the chain is excessively worn. Also refer to *Chain Wear Inspection* in this section.

5. Inspect the inner plate chain faces (**Figure 74**). They should be polished on both sides. If they show considerable uneven wear on one side, the sprockets are not aligned properly. Excessive wear requires replacement of not only the drive chain but also the drive and driven sprockets.

6. Inspect the drive and driven sprockets for the following defects:

    a. Undercutting or sharp teeth (**Figure 75**).

    b. Broken teeth.

7. If excessive chain or sprocket wear is evident, replace the drive chain and both sprockets as a complete set. If only the drive chain is replaced, the worn sprockets cause rapid chain wear.

Chain Wear Inspection

A drive chain wear label is mounted on the left chain adjuster. Perform the following to determine chain wear:

1. Adjust the drive chain as described in this chapter.

2. If any part of the red zone (A, **Figure 76**) on the label aligns with the end of the swing arm (B) and the chain free play is correct, the drive chain is excessively worn and must be replaced. Replace the drive chain as described in Chapter Eleven.

Chain Adjustment

Check and adjust the drive chain at the interval specified in **Table 1**. If the motorcycle is operated at sustained high speeds or if it is repeatedly accelerated very hard, check the drive chain adjustment more often. The correct amount of drive chain free play, when pushed up midway on the lower chain run, is 15-35 mm (0.59-1.38 in.). Refer to **Figure 77**.

When adjusting the chain, check the free play at several places along its length by rotating the rear wheel. The chain rarely wears uniformly and therefore is tighter at some places. Measure the chain

CAUTION
Keep kerosene off the rear tire and other parts as much as possible.

NOTE
Wear rubber gloves when cleaning the drive chain in the following steps.

3. Soak a thick rag in kerosene, then wipe it against the section of chain that is exposed on the lower chain run. When this section of the chain is clean, turn the rear wheel to expose the next section and clean it. Repeat until the chain is clean. To remove stubborn dirt, scrub the rollers and side plates with a soft brush. Clean one section of the chain at a time.

4. Turn the rear wheel slowly and wipe the drive chain with a thick shop cloth.

5. Clean the rear swing arm, sprocket, chain guard, wheel and tire of all kerosene residue.

6. Lubricate the drive chain as described in this section.

Chain and Sprocket Inspection

Frequently check the chain and both sprockets for excessive wear and damage.

1. Clean the drive chain as described in this section.

free play halfway between the sprockets at the tightest place on the chain. Drive chain free play that exceeds 40 mm (1.57 in.) may damage the bottom of the frame.

1. Turn the engine off and shift the transmission into neutral.

2. Support the motorcycle on a stand with the rear wheel off the ground.

NOTE
As drive chains stretch and wear in use, the chain becomes tighter at one point. The chain must be checked and adjusted at its tightest point.

3. Turn the rear wheel slowly, then stop and check the chain tightness. Continue until its tightest point is located. Mark this spot with chalk and turn the wheel so the mark is located on the chain's lower run, midway between both sprockets.

NOTE
If the drive chain is kinked or feels tight, it may require cleaning and lubrication. Clean and lubricate the drive chain before measuring its free play.

4. Lower the motorcycle so the rear wheel is on the ground, and then support it on its sidestand.

5. With your thumb and forefinger, lift up and press down the chain at the center of the bottom chain run, measuring the distance the chain moves vertically (**Figure 77**). If necessary, adjust the chain as follows:

NOTE
When adjusting the drive chain, it is necessary to maintain rear wheel alignment. A misaligned rear wheel can cause poor handling and accelerate chain and sprocket wear. All models are equipped with alignment marks on the swing arm and the chain adjusters.

   a. Loosen the axle nut (A, **Figure 78**) on the right side.

   b. Turn both chain adjuster bolts (B, **Figure 78**) an equal number of turns to obtain the correct drive chain free play. Then check that the same index mark on each chain adjuster aligns with the swing arm index mark (C, **Figure 78**).

   c. When drive chain free play is correct, check the wheel alignment by sighting along the top of the drive chain from the rear sprocket. If neces-

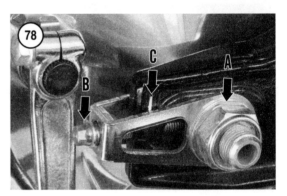

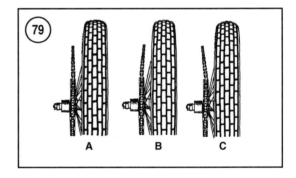

sary, remove the upper chain guard. The chain should leave the sprocket in a straight line (A, **Figure 79**). If the alignment is off (B and C, **Figure 79**), readjust.

   d. Tighten the rear axle nut (A, **Figure 78**) to 93 N•m (69 ft.-lb.).

   e. Recheck chain free play.

6. Check the chain wear indicator as described under *Chain Wear Inspection* in this section.

Swing Arm Slider Inspection

A slider installed on the left side of the swing arm (**Figure 80**) protects the swing arm from chain dam-

age. Inspect the slider frequently for wear or damage that would allow the chain to contact the swing arm. Replace the slider when it is worn to either one of the wear limit lines indicated by arrow marks on the slider. Replace the slider after removing the swing arm as described in Chapter Thirteen.

LIGHTS AND HORN

Headlight Aim

Check the headlight aim at the interval specified in **Table 1**. Refer to *Headlight* in Chapter Nine.

Lights and Horn Inspection

With the engine running, check the following:
1. Pull the front brake lever and check that the brake light comes on.
2. Push the rear brake pedal and check that the brake light comes on.
3. Move the dimmer switch up and down between the high and low positions, and check to see that both headlight elements are working.

4. Move the turn signal switch to the left position and then to the right position and check that all the turn signal lights are working.
5. Operate the horn button and make sure that both horns sound loudly.
6. If the horn or any light failed to work properly, refer to Chapter Nine.

SIDESTAND AND IGNITION CUT-OFF SWITCH INSPECTION

Check the sidestand and the ignition cut-off system operation at the interval specified in **Table 1**.
1. Operate the sidestand to check its movement and spring tension. Replace the spring if it is weak or damaged.
3. Lubricate the sidestand pivot bolt if necessary.
4. Check the sidestand ignition cut-off system as follows:
  a. Park the motorcycle so both wheels are on the ground.
  b. Sit on the motorcycle and raise the sidestand.
  c. Shift the transmission into neutral.
  d. Start the engine, then squeeze the clutch lever and shift the transmission into gear.
  e. Move the sidestand (**Figure 81**) down. When doing so, the engine should stop.
  f. If the engine did not stop as the sidestand was lowered, test the sidestand switch as described in Chapter Nine.

WARNING
Do not ride the motorcycle until the sidestand switch operates correctly. Riding the motorcycle with the sidestand down causes the rider to lose control when the sidestand contacts the ground.

FASTENER INSPECTION

Constant vibration can loosen many fasteners on a motorcycle.
1. Check the tightness of all exposed fasteners. Refer to the appropriate chapter for torque specifications.
2. Check that all hose clamps, cable stays and safety clips are properly installed. Replace missing or damaged items.

Table 1 MAINTENANCE AND LUBRICATION SCHEDULE[1]

Weekly/gas stop
  Check tire pressure cold; adjust to suit load and speed
  Check condition of tires
  Check brake fluid level; if low, check brakes for excessive wear
  Check brake operation
  Check throttle for smooth operation and return
  Check for smooth steering; must not be loose
  Check axle, suspension, controls and linkage fasteners; tighten if necessary
  Check engine oil level; add oil if necessary
  Check lights and horn operation
  Check brake stop switch operation
  Check coolant level
  Check for any abnormal engine noise and leaks

Every 500 miles (800 km)
  Check drive chain tension
  Lubricate drive chain

At initial 600 miles (10,000 km)
  Replace engine oil and filter
  Check valve clearance; adjust if necessary
  Check engine idle speed; adjust if necessary
  Check carburetor synchronization; adjust if necessary
  Check brake system
  Check clutch adjustment; adjust if necessary
  Check steering adjustment
  Check tightness of exposed chassis and engine fasteners
  Check tire and wheel condition

Every 4000 miles (6400 km)
  Check crankcase breather and clean if necessary[2]
  Check spark plugs, replace if necessary
  Check engine idle speed; adjust if necessary
  Check clutch adjustment; adjust if necessary
  Check brake fluid level
  Check front brake pads for wear; replace if necessary
  Check rear brake linings for wear; replace if necessary
  Check tire and wheel condition
  Check front and rear suspension

At 8000 miles (12,800 km); thereafter every 8000 miles (12,800 km)
  Check fuel hoses; replace if leaking or damaged
  Check choke (SE valve) operation; readjust cable if necessary or replace cable if damaged
  Check throttle operation and lubricate cables; readjust cable if necessary or replace cables if damaged
  Replace spark plugs
  Inspect valve clearance; adjust if necessary
  Replace engine oil and filter[3]
  Check carburetor synchronization; adjust if necessary
  Check coolant for contamination
  Check radiator and all coolant hoses for leaks.
  Check weep hole in bottom of water pump for coolant leakage; replace water pump if necessary
  Check front and rear brake system
  Check rear brake light switch adjustment
  Check steering adjustment
  Check headlight aim; adjust if necessary
  Check side stand operation and fastener tightness
  Check side stand ignition cut-off system operation; replace the side stand switch if necessary

Every 12,000 miles (19,200 km)
  Inspect the evaporative emission control system (California models)
(continued)

Table 1 MAINTENANCE AND LUBRICATION SCHEDULE[1] (continued)

Every 12,000 miles (19,200 km) (continued)
  Replace the air filter[4]
Every 12,000 miles (19,200 km) or every two years, whichever comes first:
  Replace brake fluid
  Replace coolant

1. Consider this schedule a guide to general maintenance and lubrication intervals. Harder than normal use and exposure to mud, water, and high humidity will require more frequent attention to most maintenance items.
2. Increase service intervals when riding at full throttle or in rain.
3. Every 8000 miles or 12 months.
4. Service more often when riding in wet or dusty conditions.

Table 2 TIRE INFLATION PRESSURE*

	Front psi (kPa)	Rear psi (kPa)
Rider	29 (200)	29 (200)
Maximum weight capacity	29 (200)	36 (250)

* The tire inflation pressures listed here are for original equipment tires. Aftermarket tires may require different inflation pressure. Refer to tire manufacturer's specifications.

Table 3 RECOMMENDED LUBRICANTS AND FUEL

Brake fluid	DOT 4
Control cables	Cable lubricant
Cooling system	Honda HP Coolant or equivalent[1]
Drive chain	Chain lubricant specified for O-ring use or No. 80-90 gear oil.
Engine oil	
Classification	
JASO T 903 standard classification	MA
API classification	SG or higher[2]
Viscosity classification	SAE 10W-40
Fork oil	Pro Honda Suspension Fluid SS-8 or equivalent 10 wt fork oil
Fuel	Unleaded gasoline with a pump octane number of 86 or higher[3]

1.Coolant must not contain silicate inhibitors as they can cause premature wear to the water pump seals. See text for further information.
2. API SG or higher classified oils not specified as ENERGY CONSERVING can be used. See text for additional information.

Table 4 ENGINE OIL CAPACITY

	Liters	U.S. qt.
Change engine oil only	2.2	2.32
Engine oil and filter change	2.4	2.54
Engine disassembly	2.9	3.06

Table 5 COOLANT CAPACITY

	Liters	U.S. qt.
Radiator and engine	1.75	1.85
Reserve tank	0.4	0.42

Table 6 MAINTENANCE SPECIFICATIONS

Brake pedal free play	20-30 mm (3/4-1 1/4 in.)
Brake pedal height	
VT750C	50 mm (2.0 in.) above top of footpeg
VT750DC	–
Carburetor synchronization	
Base carburetor	No. 1
Maximum vacuum difference	27 kPa (200 mm Hg 0.7 in. Hg)
Clutch lever free play	10-20 mm (3/8-3/4 in.)
Cylinder number	No. 1 (rear)
	No. 2 (front)
Drive chain free play adjustment	15-35 mm (0.59-1.38 in.)
Engine compression	1275 ± 98 kPa (185 ± 14 psi) @ 400 rpm
Engine idle speed	
2001-2003	1000 ± 100 rpm
2004-2005	
49-state/Canada	1000 ± 100 rpm
California	1200 ± 100 rpm
2006-on	1200 ± 100 rpm
Engine oil pressure	530 kPa (77 psi) @ 5500 rpm/80° C (176° F)
Firing order	Front (308°), rear (412°)
Ignition timing	
F mark	
VT750C	8° BTDC @ 1000 rpm
VT750DC	6° BTDC @ 1000 rpm
Spark plug gap	0.8-0.9 mm (0.031-0.035 in.)
Spark plug type	
NGK	
Standard	DPR8EA-9
Cold climate*	DPR7EA-9
Extended high speed riding	DPR9EA-9
Denso	
Standard	X24EPR-U9
Cold climate*	X22EPR-U9
Extended high speed riding	X2 EPR-U9
Valve clearance	
Intake	0.13-0.17 mm (0.005-0.007 in.)
Exhaust	0.18-0.22 mm (0.007-0.009 in.)
Throttle cable free play	2-6 mm (5/64-1/4 in.)

* Ambient temperature below 5° C (41° F).

Table 7 MAINTENANCE TORQUE SPECIFICATIONS

	N•m	in.-lb.	ft.-lb.
Coolant drain bolts			
Water pump and rear cylinder bolts	13	115	–
Crankshaft hole cap[1]	15	133	–
Oil drain bolt	30	–	22
Oil filter[2]	10	88	–
Oil pressure switch[3]	12	106	–
Rear axle nut[4]	93	–	69
Spark plug	14	124	–
		(continued)	

Table 7 MAINTENANCE TORQUE SPECIFICATIONS (continued)

	N•m	in.-lb.	ft.-lb.
Spoke nipples	4	35	–
Timing hole cap[1]			
VT750C	10	88	–
VT750DC	15	133	–
Vacuum plug	3	27	–
Valve adjusting screw locknut[5]	23	–	17

1. Lubricate threads with grease.
2. Lubricate O-ring with engine oil.
3. Apply silicone sealant to switch threads as described in text.
4. Interference type U-nut. Replace with same type nut.
5. Lubricate threads and flange surface with engine oil.

CHAPTER FOUR

ENGINE TOP END

This chapter provides engine top end service, overhaul and inspection procedures. Engine removal and installation is covered in Chapter Five. Clutch procedures are in Chapter Six and the transmission procedures are in Chapter Seven.

Before starting any work, review Chapter One.

Engine specifications are in **Tables 1-4** at the end of the chapter.

The engine is a liquid-cooled, four-stroke, V-twin with a single overhead camshaft in each cylinder head.

SERVICING THE ENGINE IN THE FRAME

The following components can be serviced with the engine installed in the frame:

1. Cylinder head covers.
2. Camshafts.
3. Cam chain tensioner and cam chains.
4. The front cylinder head on VT750C models.

CYLINDER HEAD COVERS

The front and rear cylinder head covers can be removed with the engine mounted in the frame.

Removal

Front

1. Drain the engine coolant (Chapter Three).
2. Remove the fuel tank (Chapter Eight).
3A. On VT750C models, perform the following:
    a. Remove the steering covers (Chapter Fifteen).
    b. Remove the air filter housing and air filter chamber (Chapter Eight).
    c. Remove the carburetors (Chapter Eight).
    d. Disconnect the spark plug caps.
    e. Remove the sub-air filter housing (A, **Figure 1**) from the cylinder head cover mounting bracket.
    f. Remove the bolts and the outer cover (B, **Figure 1**).
    g. Unbolt and remove the cylinder fins from the front cylinder.
    h. Remove the thermostat housing mounting bolt (**Figure 2**) and push the thermostat forward.
3B. On VT750DC models, perform the following:
    a. Remove the air filter housing (Chapter Eight).

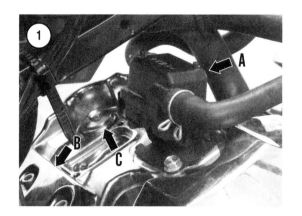

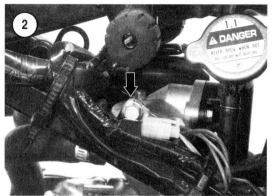

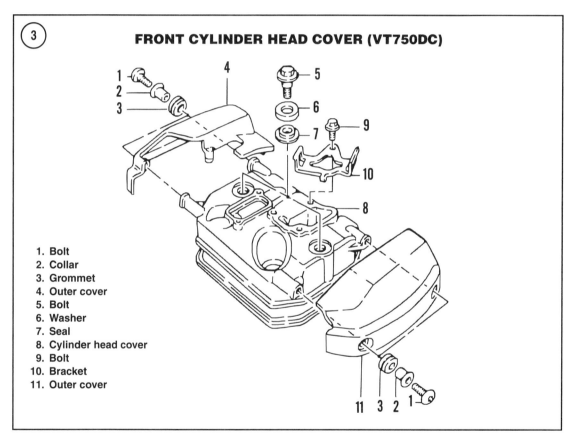

FRONT CYLINDER HEAD COVER (VT750DC)

1. Bolt
2. Collar
3. Grommet
4. Outer cover
5. Bolt
6. Washer
7. Seal
8. Cylinder head cover
9. Bolt
10. Bracket
11. Outer cover

b. Unbolt and remove the outer covers (**Figure 3**).

c. Disconnect the spark plug caps.

d. Unbolt and remove the cylinder fins from the front cylinder.

e. Remove the sub-air filter housing (A, **Figure 1**) from the cylinder head cover mounting bracket.

f. Remove the thermostat housing mounting bolt (**Figure 4**). Disconnect the coolant hoses from the thermostat.

4. Use compressed air to clean debris from the area around the cylinder head cover.

5. Remove the cylinder head cover retaining bolts, washers and rubber seals (C, **Figure 1**, typical).

6. Remove the cylinder head cover (**Figure 5**, typical) and gasket.

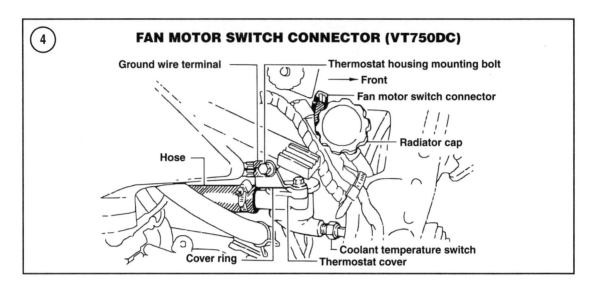

FAN MOTOR SWITCH CONNECTOR (VT750DC)

Ground wire terminal — Thermostat housing mounting bolt
→ Front
Fan motor switch connector
Radiator cap
Hose
Coolant temperature switch
Cover ring
Thermostat cover

Rear

1. Drain the engine coolant (Chapter Three).
2. Remove the fuel tank (Chapter Eight).
3A. On VT750C models, perform the following:
   a. Remove the air filter housing and air filter chamber (Chapter Eight).
   b. Remove the carburetors (Chapter Eight).
   c. Disconnect the spark plug caps.
   d. Unbolt and remove the breather cover (A, **Figure 6**).
   e. Remove the bolts, cable guide and the outer cover (B, **Figure 6**).
   f. Unbolt and remove the cylinder fins from the rear cylinder.
3B. On VT750DC models, perform the following:
   a. Remove the air filter housing (Chapter Eight).
   b. Unbolt and remove the outer covers (**Figure 3**).
   c. Disconnect the spark plug caps.
   d. Unbolt and remove the cylinder fins from the rear cylinder block.
   e. Remove the rear left spark plug wire clip from the frame.
   f. Disconnect the air supply hose from the breather cover, then unbolt and remove the breather cover (A, **Figure 6**).
4. Use compressed air to clean debris from the area around the cylinder head cover.
5. Remove the cylinder head cover retaining bolts, washers and rubber seals.

6. Remove the cylinder head cover (**Figure 7**) and gasket.

Installation

1. Remove all sealer residue from the cylinder head gasket surface.

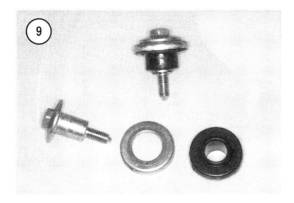

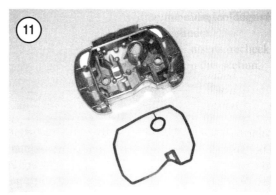

2. Fill the cylinder head oil pockets with engine oil (**Figure 8**).

3. Replace the cylinder head cover rubber seals (**Figure 9**) if damaged.

4. Lubricate the rubber washers with engine oil. Install a steel and rubber washer on each bolt (**Figure 9**).

5. Inspect the rubber gasket (**Figure 10**) around the perimeter of the cylinder head cover. Make sure the gasket is pliable and in good condition.

6. If necessary, replace the cylinder head cover gasket or reseal the original gasket as follows:

    a. Remove the old gasket (**Figure 11**) and clean the gasket groove around the perimeter of the cover and around the spark plug hole.

NOTE
In substep b, apply gasket sealer onto the side of the gasket that seats against the cylinder head cover. Do not apply gasket sealer to the side of the rubber gasket that mates to the cylinder head.

    b. Apply Gasgacinch, or a similar rubber adhesive, to the cylinder head cover grooves and upper side of the new gasket, following the sealant manufacturer's instructions.

    c. Install the gasket into the groove in the cylinder head cover (**Figure 10**). Make sure the gasket is seated in the cover groove with no gap.

7. Install the cylinder head cover onto the cylinder head. Confirm that the gasket seats squarely onto the cylinder head.

8. Install the cylinder head cover bolts, washers and seals. Tighten the bolts in a crossing pattern to 10 N•m (88 in.-lb.).

9. Reverse the removal steps to complete installation. Note the following:

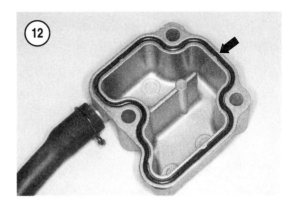

a. Replace the breather cover O-ring (**Figure 12**) if leaking or damaged. Lubricate the O-ring with engine oil and tighten the breather cover (A, **Figure 6**) mounting bolts to 12 N•m (106 in.-lb.).

b. Tighten the cylinder fin Allen bolts to 10 N•m (88 in.-lb.).

CAMSHAFTS

The camshafts can be serviced with the engine installed in the frame.

Camshaft Removal

This section describes removal of both camshafts. If it is only necessary to remove one camshaft, it is still necessary to remove both cylinder head covers to view the camshaft timing marks.

1. Disconnect the battery negative cable as described in Chapter Nine.

2. Support the motorcycle with a jackstand to position it upright. This makes it easier to view the flywheel timing marks when turning the engine over.

3. Remove both cylinder head covers as described in this chapter.

4. Remove the crankshaft and timing hole caps (**Figure 13**) from the left crankcase cover. The cover must be installed on the engine when viewing the flywheel timing marks.

5. Remove the spark plugs as described in Chapter Three. This makes it easier to turn the engine by hand. Cover the spark plug openings to prevent small items from falling into the engine.

6. Before removing the camshaft, inspect the cam chain for excessive wear as follows:

a. Measure the exposed length of cam chain tensioner wedge B as shown in **Figure 14**.

b. If the measurement is less than 6 mm (0.24 in.), the cam chain is excessively worn and must be replaced as described in this chapter.

c. Repeat for the opposite cam chain tensioner.

7. Remove the bolts, camshaft end holder (**Figure 15**) and dowel pins from both cylinder heads.

NOTE
In the following steps, always turn the crankshaft counterclockwise, as

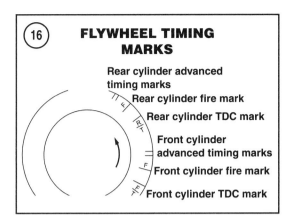

FLYWHEEL TIMING MARKS

Rear cylinder advanced timing marks

Rear cylinder fire mark

Rear cylinder TDC mark

Front cylinder advanced timing marks

Front cylinder fire mark

Front cylinder TDC mark

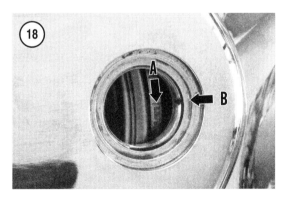

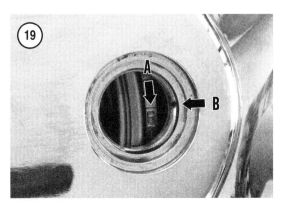

viewed from the left side of the motorcycle. The timing marks appear in the order shown in **Figure 16**. Use a 14-mm socket through the left crankcase cover to engage the flywheel bolt *(**Figure 17**)*.

NOTE
*Rotate the engine and check the front and rear camshaft and flywheel timing marks a few times before removing the camshafts. Confirm that the timing marks and camshaft positions are correct and note how the camshaft lobes are positioned when the engine is at TDC on its compression stroke. Refer to **Valve Adjustment** in Chapter Three.*

8A. When removing both camshafts or only the front cylinder camshaft, correctly position the front camshaft as follows:

a. When removing both camshafts, remove the front camshaft first.

b. Turn the crankshaft counterclockwise and align the *FT* mark on the flywheel with the index mark on the left crankcase cover (**Figure 18**).

c. Check that the front piston is at TDC on its compression stroke. Confirm by viewing the position of the camshaft lobes. The engine is on the compression stroke when all three cam lobes are facing down. If not, turn the crankshaft one full revolution (360°) counterclockwise and realign the *FT* mark. The piston should now be at its TDC position.

8B. When removing only the rear cylinder camshaft, correctly position the rear camshaft as follows:

a. Turn the crankshaft counterclockwise and align the *RT* mark on the flywheel with the index mark on the left crankcase cover (**Figure 19**).

b. Check that the piston is at TDC on its compression stroke. Confirm by viewing the position of the camshaft lobes. The engine is on the compression stroke when all three cam lobes are facing down. If not, turn the crankshaft one full revolution (360°) counterclockwise and realign the *RT* mark. The piston should now be at its TDC position.

9. Release the cam chain tensioner spring tension against the cam chain as follows:

  a. Refer to **Figure 20** to identify the A and B cam chain tensioner wedges.

  b. Cover the area around the cam chain tensioner to avoid dropping parts into the engine.

  c. Grab wedge B with a pair of pliers and pull it up, then push wedge A down with a screwdriver (**Figure 20**).

  d. Install a 2-mm pin through the hole in wedge B (**Figure 21**) to hold it in position and release spring tension against the cam chain.

10. Remove the exposed cam sprocket bolt (A, **Figure 22**). If necessary, hold the flywheel bolt to prevent the camshaft from turning.

11. Turn the crankshaft counterclockwise one full turn (360°) and remove the other cam sprocket bolt.

12. Slide the cam sprocket (B, **Figure 22**) off the camshaft flange. However, do not disconnect the sprocket from the cam chain at this time.

13. Using a crossing pattern, loosen and then remove the camshaft holder (A, **Figure 23**) nuts, bolts and single washer. Remove the oil guide plate (B, **Figure 23**).

14. Pull the camshaft holder (A, **Figure 23**) straight up to remove it from the cylinder head. Do not allow the dowel pins to fall into the engine.

15. Remove the dowel pins (A, **Figure 24**).

16. Secure the camshaft chain with a piece of wire.

17. Remove the camshaft (B, **Figure 24**) and sprocket.

NOTE
If both camshafts are to be removed, continue with Step 18 to remove the rear camshaft.

18. Hold the front cam chain to prevent it from binding on the drive sprocket and turn the crankshaft counterclockwise to align the *RT* mark on the flywheel with the index mark on the left crankcase cover (**Figure 19**). Check that the rear cylinder is at TDC on its compression stroke. Confirm by viewing the position of the camshaft lobes. The engine is on the compression stroke when all three cam lobes are facing down. If not, turn the crankshaft one full revolution (360°) counterclockwise and realign the *RT* mark. The piston should now be at its TDC position.

19. Repeat Steps 9-17 to remove the rear camshaft.

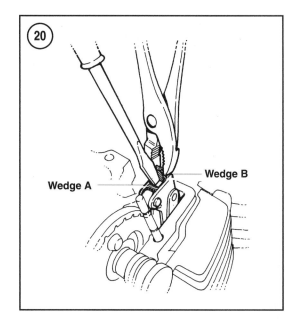
Wedge A — Wedge B

CAUTION
If the crankshaft must be rotated while one or both camshafts are removed, pull up on the cam chain(s) so it properly engages the crankshaft drive

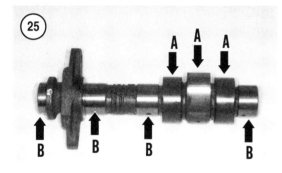

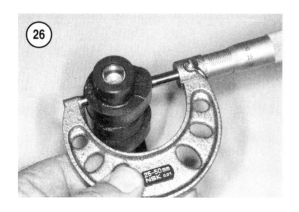

sprocket(s). Hold the chain taut on the drive sprocket while rotating the crankshaft. If this is not done, the cam chain could become kinked, which could damage the chain and drive sprocket.

Camshaft Inspection

When measuring the camshafts, compare the actual measurements to the specifications in **Table 2**. Replace worn or damaged parts as described in this section.

1. Before cleaning the camshafts, inspect the oil lubrication holes for contamination. Make sure these holes are clean and open.

2. Clean the camshafts in solvent and dry thoroughly. Flush the camshaft oil passages with solvent and compressed air.

3. Clean the camshaft and cam sprocket threads of all threadlock residue.

4. Check the cam lobes (A, **Figure 25**) for wear. The lobes should not be scored and the edges should be square. Replace the camshaft if the lobes are scored, worn or damaged.

5. Check the camshaft bearing journals (B, **Figure 25**) for wear or scoring. Replace the camshaft if the journals are scored, worn or damaged.

6. If the camshaft lobes or journals are excessively worn or damaged, check the journal surfaces in the cylinder head and in the camshaft holders. Refer to *Camshaft Holder Inspection* in this section.

7. Measure each cam lobe height (**Figure 26**) with a micrometer.

8. Measure each cam journal outside diameter (**Figure 27**) with a micrometer.

9. Support the camshaft journals on a set of V-blocks or crankshaft truing stand and measure

runout with a dial indicator (**Figure 28**). Note the following:

    a. If the runout is out of specification, replace the camshaft and measure the camshaft oil clearance as described in this section. If the clearance is out of specification, the camshaft holder and camshaft journals were damaged from the bent camshaft.

    b. If the camshaft was replaced, remeasure the camshaft oil clearance with the new camshaft.

10. Inspect the camshaft sprockets (**Figure 29**) for broken or chipped teeth. Also, inspect the cam chains and timing sprockets mounted on the crankshaft. Refer to *Cam Chain Tensioner and Cam Chain* in this chapter.

Camshaft Holders, Rocker Arms and Shafts

This section services the camshaft holders, rocker arms and shafts (**Figure 30**). Procedures for the front and rear assemblies are identical.

Disassembly

1. Before cleaning and disassembling the camshaft holder (**Figure 30**), inspect the oil lubrication holes for contamination. Small passages and holes in the camshaft holders provide lubrication for the holder, camshaft and cylinder journals. Make sure these passages and holes are clean and open.

> *CAUTION*
> *Infrequent oil and filter changes may be indicated if the camshaft holder passages are dirty. Contaminated oil passages can cause camshaft and journal failure.*

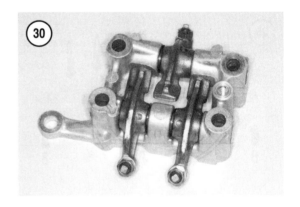

2. Clean the assembled camshaft holder assembly. Dry with compressed air.

> *CAUTION*
> *Identify the individual rocker arms so they can be reinstalled in their original operating positions.*

3. Refer to **Figure 31** and remove the rocker arm shafts, rocker arms and wave washers.

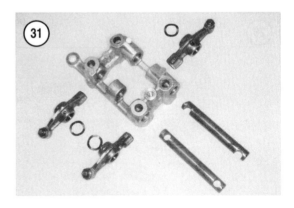

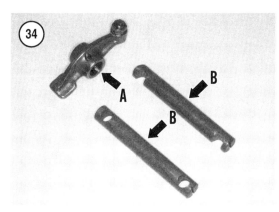

Camshaft holder inspection

1. Check the camshaft holder for stress cracks and other damage.

2. Check the camshaft bearing journals in the camshaft holders and cylinder head (**Figure 32**) for wear and scoring. If visual damage is present, replace the cylinder head and camshaft holder as a set. To determine operational clearance perform the

Camshaft Oil Clearance Measurement procedure in this section.

3. Check the camshaft holder mounting fasteners for damage.

4. Replace the wave washers (**Figure 31**) if damaged.

Rocker arms and shafts inspection

When measuring the rocker arm components in this section, compare the actual measurements to the specifications in **Table 2**. Replace parts that are out of specification or show damage as described in this section.

NOTE
Maintain the alignment of the rocker arm components when cleaning and inspecting the parts in this section.

1. Clean and dry the parts.

2. Inspect the rocker arm pad where it contacts the cam lobe and where the adjuster contacts the valve stem (**Figure 33**). Check the contact surfaces for flat spots, uneven wear and scoring.

3. Inspect the valve adjuster locknuts for rounding and other damage.

4. Inspect the rocker arm shafts for scoring, cracks or other damage.

5. Measure the rocker arm bore inside diameter (A, **Figure 34**).

6. Measure the rocker arm shaft outside diameter (B, **Figure 34**).

7. Calculate the rocker arm-to-rocker arm shaft clearance as follows:

    a. Subtract the rocker arm shaft outside diameter (Step 6) from the rocker arm bore inside diameter (Step 5).

    b. Replace the rocker arm and/or the rocker arm shaft if the clearance is out of specification.

Reassembly

1. Make sure the oil passages through the camshaft holder are clear.

2. Lubricate the valve adjuster threads and seating surfaces with engine oil.

3. If the rocker arms and shafts were not identified during disassembly, note the following:

a. The exhaust rocker arm pad (A, **Figure 35**) is larger than the pad on the intake rocker arms (B).

b. The intake rocker arm shaft (A, **Figure 36**) has a hole on each end.

c. The exhaust rocker arm shaft (B, **Figure 36**) has a groove on each end.

4. Lubricate the rocker arm shafts with molybdenum disulfide oil.

5. Install the rocker arms, wave washers and shafts as shown in **Figure 31**. Note the following:

a. Install the wave washers at the positions identified in A, **Figure 37**.

b. Align the holes in the intake shaft with the mounting bolt holes in the holder (B, **Figure 37**).

c. Align the grooves in the exhaust shaft with the mounting bolt holes in the holder (C, **Figure 37**).

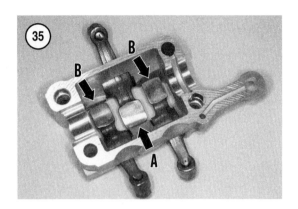

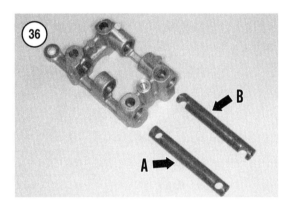

Camshaft Oil Clearance Measurement

This section describes how to measure the clearance between the camshaft and the camshaft holders and cylinder head journal using Plastigage (**Figure 38**). Plastigage is a material that flattens when pressure is applied to it. The marked bands on the envelope are used to measure the width of the flattened Plastigage. The camshaft and camshaft holder must be installed on the cylinder head when performing this procedure.

Plastigage is available from automotive parts stores in different clearance ranges.

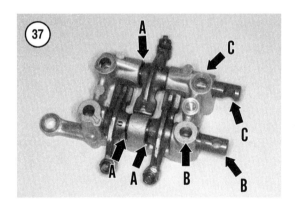

1. Wipe all oil residue from each cam bearing journal (camshafts, camshaft holders and cylinder head). These surfaces must be clean and dry.

2. The camshafts are identified by the F (front) and R (rear) cast marks indicated in **Figure 39**. Disregard all other camshaft marks.

3. Install the camshaft into the cylinder head. Position the cam lobes so the valves are not pressed open when the cam is installed. Refer to *Camshaft Installation* in this section.

4. Place a strip of Plastigage material on the top of each camshaft bearing journal (**Figure 40**), parallel to the cam.

5. Install and tighten the camshaft holder as described under *Camshaft Installation* in this section.

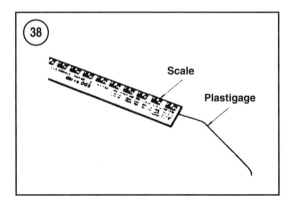

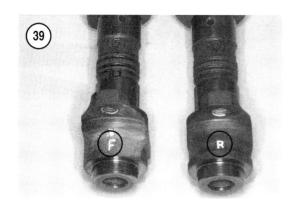

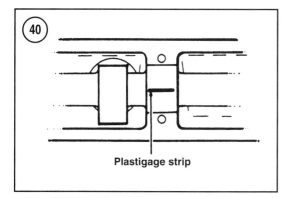

Plastigage strip

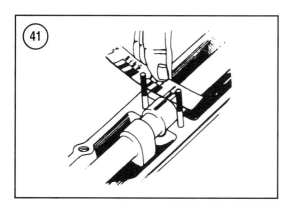

CAUTION
Do not rotate the camshafts with the
Plastigage in place.

CAUTION
Loosen the camshaft holder bolts as
described or the camshaft holder may
be damaged.

6. Loosen and remove the camshaft holder mounting bolts as described under *Camshaft Removal* in this section.

7. Remove the camshaft holder carefully, making sure the camshafts do not rotate. Do not drop the dowel pins into the engine.

8. Measure the widest portion of the flattened Plastigage according to the manufacturer's instructions (**Figure 41**) and compare to the camshaft oil clearance specification in **Table 2**. Note the following:

   a. If all the measurements are within specification, the cylinder head, camshaft and camshaft holder can be reused.

   b. If any measurement exceeds the service limit, replace the camshaft and recheck the oil clearance.

   c. If the new measurement exceeds the service limit with the new camshaft, replace the camshaft holder and cylinder head as a set.

9. Remove all Plastigage material from the camshafts, camshaft holders and cylinder head.

Camshaft Installation

1. Before installing the camshaft(s), note the following:

   a. Rotate the engine with a socket on the flywheel mounting bolt (**Figure 42**).

   b. Rotating the crankshaft 360° (1 turn) rotates the camshafts 180° (1/2 turn).

   c. Identify the camshafts by the F (front) and R (rear) flange marks identified in **Figure 39**. Disregard the letter marks found on the inside of the camshaft, between the sprocket flange and cam lobes.

   d. The front camshaft TDC index mark is adjacent to the camshaft's F identification mark. Refer to A, **Figure 43**.

   e. The rear camshaft TDC index mark is identified in B, **Figure 43**. Note that the TDC index mark is on the side of the camshaft *opposite* its R identification mark.

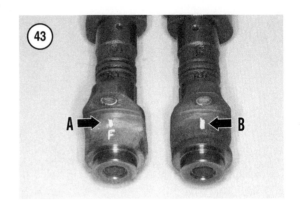

f. When the camshaft timing marks are facing up, the cam lobes face down.

g. If both camshafts were removed, install the front camshaft first, then the rear camshaft.

h. If only one camshaft was removed, remove the opposite cylinder head cover so the installed camshaft timing marks can be viewed.

i. Clean the cam sprocket bolts and camshaft threaded holes of all threadlock residue and oil. These threads must be clean and dry.

CAUTION
When rotating the crankshaft in the following steps, pull both cam chains outward to prevent them from jamming against the crankshaft drive sprockets. Doing so could damage the chains and sprockets.

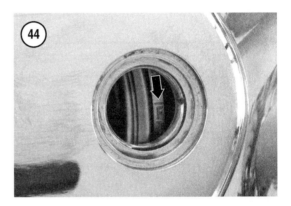

2A. If both camshafts were removed, perform the following:

a. Turn the crankshaft counterclockwise and align the *FT* mark on the flywheel (**Figure 44**) with the index mark on the left crankcase cover. Check that the piston is at TDC. If not, turn the crankshaft counterclockwise one full turn (360°) and realign the *FT* mark.

b. Go to Step 3 and install the front camshaft.

2B. If only the front camshaft was removed, perform the following:

a. Remove the rear camshaft end holder bolts, camshaft end holder and dowel pins.

b. Turn the crankshaft counterclockwise and align the *RT* mark on the flywheel (**Figure 45**) with the index mark on the left crankcase cover. Check the position of the rear camshaft TDC index mark (B, **Figure 43**).

c. If the TDC index mark is facing down, turn the crankshaft counterclockwise 52° and align the *FT* mark on the flywheel (**Figure 44**) with the index mark on the left crankcase cover. Go to Step 3 and install the front camshaft.

d. If the TDC index mark is facing up, turn the crankshaft counterclockwise 412° (360° + 52°) and align the *FT* mark on the flywheel (**Figure 44**) with the index mark on the left crankcase cover. Go to Step 3 and install the front camshaft.

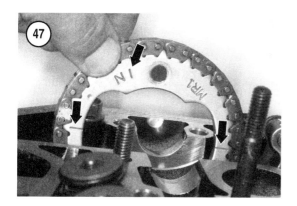

2C. If only the rear camshaft was removed, perform the following:

a. Remove the front camshaft end holder bolts, camshaft end holder and dowel pins.

b. Turn the crankshaft counterclockwise and align the *FT* mark on the flywheel with the index mark on the left crankcase cover (**Figure 44**). Check the position of the front camshaft TDC index mark (A, **Figure 43**).

c. If the TDC index mark is facing down, turn the crankshaft counterclockwise 668° (360° + 308°) and align the *RT* mark on the flywheel with the index mark on the left crankcase cover (**Figure 45**). Go to Step 3 and install the rear camshaft.

d. If the TDC index mark is facing up, turn the crankshaft counterclockwise 308° and align the *RT* mark on the flywheel with the index mark on the left crankcase cover (**Figure 45**). Go to Step 3 and install the rear camshaft.

NOTE
After setting the engine position as described in Step 2, perform Steps 3-17 to either install the front or rear camshaft.

3. Mesh the camshaft sprocket with the cam chain. The IN mark on the sprocket must face toward the *inside* of the engine and the sprocket timing marks must align with the cylinder head upper surface. Refer to **Figure 46** (front) or **Figure 47** (rear).

4. Apply molybdenum disulfide oil solution to the cylinder head camshaft journals, thrust surfaces and cam lobes.

5. Install the camshaft through the cam chain and cam sprocket with its TDC mark facing *up.* See **Figure 48** (front) or **Figure 49** (rear).

NOTE
*When the camshaft TDC mark is facing up, the camshaft lobes face down. Refer to **Figure 50** (front) and **Figure 51** (rear).*

6. Loosen the valve adjusting screw locknuts and the adjusting screws fully.

7. Lubricate the valve adjuster contact pads with molybdenum disulfide oil.

8. Install the camshaft holder dowel pins. Refer to **Figure 52** (front) or **Figure 53** (rear).

9. Install the camshaft holder over the camshaft and engage with the dowel pins. Refer to A, **Figure 54** (front) or A, **Figure 55** (rear).

10. Install the oil guide plate. Refer to B, **Figure 54** (front) or B, **Figure 55** (rear).

NOTE
In ***Figure 54*** *(front) and* ***Figure 55*** *(rear), callout C identifies the position of the single washer installed in Step 11.*

11. Install the camshaft holder bolts, washer and nuts. Tighten the bolts and nuts in two steps and in a crossing pattern to 23 N•m (17 ft.-lb.).

12. Slip the cam sprocket onto the camshaft flange. Check that the sprocket timing marks align with the cylinder head gasket surface and the camshaft TDC mark faces up. The exposed sprocket and camshaft bolt holes must also align. The alignment of these marks is critical because it establishes the cylinder's valve timing. Refer to **Figure 56** (front) or **Figure 57** (rear).

NOTE
The camshaft and sprocket mounting bolt threads must be clean and dry. Refer to Step 1.

13. Apply a medium strength threadlock onto the cam sprocket bolt threads.

14. Align the camshaft bolt holes with the holes in the cam sprocket. Install the first cam sprocket bolt and hand-tighten.

15. Turn the crankshaft counterclockwise 360°. Install the second cam sprocket bolt and tighten to 23 N•m (17 ft.-lb.).

16. Turn the crankshaft counterclockwise 360° and tighten the first cam sprocket bolt to 23 N•m (17 ft.-lb.).

17. Remove the 2-mm pin from the cam chain tensioner (**Figure 58**, typical). Spring tension should pull wedge B (**Figure 59**) into the tensioner.

18. If both camshafts were removed and the front camshaft was just installed, turn the crankshaft counterclockwise 308° and align the *RT* mark on the flywheel with the index mark on the left crankcase cover (**Figure 45**). Perform Steps 3-17 to install the rear camshaft.

19. Recheck the camshaft timing as follows:

    a. Turn the crankshaft counterclockwise and align the *FT* mark on the flywheel with the index mark on the left crankcase cover (**Figure 44**). Check that the piston is at TDC. This can be confirmed by observing the position of the cam lobes. When the front cylinder is at TDC, the cam lobes face down. If the cam lobes are facing up, turn the crankshaft counterclockwise one turn (360°) and realign the *FT* mark (**Figure 44**). The timing marks on the front camshaft sprocket must align with the cylinder head surface (**Figure 60**).

    b. Turn the crankshaft counterclockwise and align the *RT* mark on the flywheel with the index mark on the left crankcase cover (**Figure 45**). The timing marks on the rear camshaft sprocket must align with the cylinder head surface (**Figure 61**) and the cam lobes must be facing down.

CAUTION
The timing marks must align correctly at this time; otherwise, camshaft timing is incorrect. Do not proceed if the

camshaft sprocket timing marks are positioned incorrectly.

20. Adjust the valve clearance as described in Chapter Three.

21. Install the camshaft end holder dowel pins (A, **Figure 62**). Then install the camshaft end holder with its flat surface (B, **Figure 62**) facing in (toward camshaft).

22. Install the camshaft end holder bolts (**Figure 63**) and tighten to 10 N•m (88 in.-lb.).

23. Install the cylinder head covers as described in this chapter.

CAM CHAIN TENSIONER AND CAM CHAIN

The engine is equipped with a cam chain tensioner, chain guide and cam chain for each cylinder. The chain tensioner and cam chains can be removed with the engine mounted in the frame. Refer to *Cylinder Head* in this chapter to replace the chain guide.

Cam Chain Tensioner Removal/Inspection/Installation

Procedures required to remove the cam chain tensioner are the same for the front and rear cylinders.

1. Remove the camshaft as described in this chapter.

> *NOTE*
> *Do not remove the pin and release the tension spring when removing and inspecting the cam chain tensioner.*

2. Remove the cam chain tensioner mounting bolts (**Figure 64**), washers and tensioner (**Figure 65**). Discard the washers.

3. Remove the rubber guide (**Figure 66**) from the cylinder head.

4. Inspect the chain tensioner (**Figure 67**) for the following:

    a. Cracked or damaged tension spring.

    b. Worn or damaged tensioner guide.

5. Make sure the cam chain is properly meshed with the timing sprocket on the crankshaft.

6. Insert the rubber guide into the cylinder head chain tunnel as shown in **Figure 68**. Position the rubber guide so its top edge is flush with the cylinder head gasket surface (**Figure 66**).

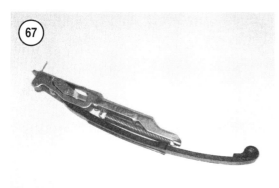

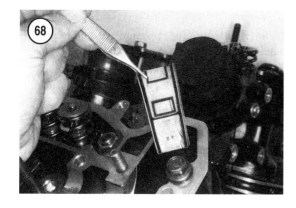

4

7. Install the cam chain tensioner (**Figure 65**) into position. Make sure the bottom of the tensioner seats into the lower pocket in the crankcase.

8. Install a new sealing washer onto each chain tensioner mounting bolt. Apply a medium-strength threadlock onto the bolt threads and tighten the bolts (**Figure 64**) to 10 N•m (88 in.-lb.).

9. Install the camshaft as described in this chapter.

Cam Chain Replacement

Continuous cam chains are used on all models. Do not cut the chains; replacement link components are not available.

NOTE
*Before removing the camshaft in Step 1, make sure to measure the cam chain tensioner wedge as described under **Camshaft Removal** in this chapter. Replace the cam chain if the measurement indicates a worn chain.*

1. Remove the camshaft as described in this chapter.

2. Drain the engine oil as described in Chapter Three.

3. To replace the front cam chain, remove the flywheel (Chapter Nine).

4. To replace the rear cam chain, remove the primary drive gear (Chapter Six).

5. Pry the guides away from the drive sprocket and remove the cam chain from the sprocket (**Figure 69**, typical). Pull the cam chain up through the chain tunnel and remove the chain.

NOTE
If there is not enough clearance to remove the chain from the sprocket, re-

move the cam chain tensioner as described in this section.

6. Install the cam chain by reversing these steps. Refill the engine with oil as described in Chapter Three.

Cam Chain Inspection

If the cam chain or chain guides are excessively worn, the cam chain tensioner may not be working properly. Inspect the cam chain tensioner as described in this section.

1. Clean and dry the chain.
2. Inspect the cam chain (**Figure 70**) for:
   a. Worn or damaged pins and rollers.
   b. Cracked or damaged side plates.
3. If the cam chain is excessively worn or damaged, inspect the drive (crankshaft) and driven (camshaft) sprockets for the same wear conditions. The driven sprocket can be replaced separately. An excessively worn or damaged drive sprocket requires crankshaft replacement.

CYLINDER HEAD

On VT750C models, the front cylinder head can be removed with the engine installed in the frame. The engine must be removed from the frame to service the rear cylinder head on the VT750C and both cylinder heads on the VT750DC.

Removal

1A. On VT750C front cylinder heads, perform the following:
   a. Remove the front camshaft as described in this chapter.
   b. Remove the exhaust system (Chapter Fifteen).
1B. On VT750C rear cylinder heads and VT750DC models, perform the following:
   a. Remove the engine from the frame (Chapter Five).
   b. Remove the camshaft as described in this chapter.
2. Remove the bolt, water pipe and O-ring from the cylinder head.

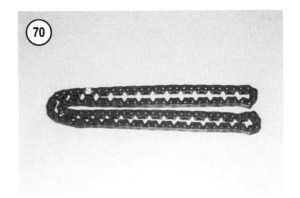

3. Remove the cam chain tensioner mounting bolts (**Figure 64**), washers and tensioner (**Figure 65**). Discard the washers.

4. Remove the rubber guide (**Figure 66**) from the cylinder head.

5. Remove the 6-mm bolt (A, **Figure 71**) from the chain tunnel.

6. In a crossing pattern and in several steps, loosen the 10-mm nuts (B, **Figure 71**) and the 8-mm bolts (C). Remove the nuts, bolts and washers.

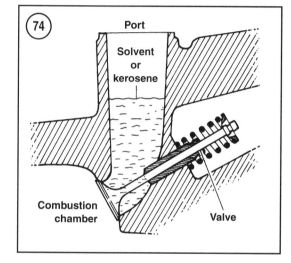

Port

Solvent or kerosene

Combustion chamber

Valve

7. Lift the cylinder head off the engine. If the cylinder head is tight, tap it with a plastic hammer to break its seal. Do not use a metal hammer or pry the head off.

8. Place the cylinder head on wooden blocks to avoid damaging the gasket surfaces.

9. Remove the cylinder head gasket (A, **Figure 72**) and the two dowel pins (B).

CAUTION
If the dowel pins are tight, do not remove them unless necessary. Stuck or rusted dowel pins are easily damaged during removal.

NOTE
After removing the cylinder head, check the top and bottom gasket surfaces for any indications of leakage. Also check the head and base gaskets for signs of leaking. A blown gasket could indicate possible cylinder head or cylinder warp or other damage.

10. Remove the chain guide (**Figure 73**).
11. Cover the cylinder and chain tunnel with a clean shop cloth.

Inspection

1. Before removing the valves for inspection, perform a solvent test to check the valve face-to-valve seat seal as follows:
   a. Support the cylinder head with the exhaust port facing up (**Figure 74**). Pour solvent or kerosene into the ports. Check the combustion chamber for fluid leaking past the exhaust valves. There should be no leaking past the seat in the combustion chamber.
   b. Repeat substep a for the intake valves.
   c. If fluid leaks into the combustion chamber it will be wet. This indicates the valve is not seating correctly.
   d. Check for a damaged valve stem, valve seat and/or face, or possibly a cracked combustion chamber.
2. Remove the spark plugs.
3. Remove all traces of gasket residue from the cylinder head (**Figure 75**) and cylinder gasket surfaces. Do not scratch the gasket surface. If the gasket residue is difficult to remove, place a solvent-soaked rag across the cylinder head gasket surface to soften the deposits.
4. Before removing the valves, remove all carbon deposits from the combustion chambers (**Figure 76**) with a wire brush. Take care not to damage the head, valves or spark plug threads.

CAUTION
Cleaning the combustion chambers with the valves removed can damage

the valve seat surfaces. A damaged or even slightly scratched valve seat causes poor valve seating.

5. Examine the spark plug threads in the cylinder head for damage. If damage is minor or if the threads are contaminated with carbon, use a spark plug thread tap to clean the threads following the manufacturer's instructions. If thread damage is excessive, repair the head by installing a steel thread insert.

CAUTION
When using a tap to clean spark plug threads, lubricate the tap with an aluminum tap cutting fluid or kerosene.

CAUTION
Aluminum spark plug threads are commonly damaged due to galling, cross threading and overtightening. To prevent galling, apply an antiseize compound on the plug threads before installation and do not overtighten. Do not lubricate the spark plug threads with engine oil.

6. Clean the entire head in solvent. Make sure the coolant passageways are clear.

NOTE
If the cylinder head was bead blasted, grit in small crevices can be difficult to remove. Any residual grit left in the engine contaminates the oil and causes premature wear. Repeatedly wash the cylinder head in a solution of hot soap and water to remove the debris.

7. Check for cracks in the combustion chamber (**Figure 76**) and exhaust. A cracked head must be replaced.
8. Examine the piston crowns. The crowns should show no signs of wear or damage. If the crown appears pecked or spongy-looking, check the spark plug, valves and combustion chamber for aluminum deposits. If these deposits are found, the cylinder is overheating.

CAUTION
Do not clean the piston crown while the piston is installed in the cylinder. Carbon scraped from the top of the piston may fall between the cylinder wall and piston and onto the piston rings. Because carbon grit is abra-

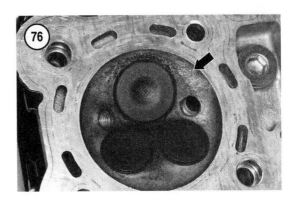

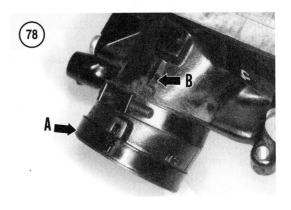

sive, premature cylinder, piston and ring wear occurs. If the piston crowns have heavy deposits of carbon, remove them as described in this chapter to clean them properly. Excessive carbon buildup on the piston crowns reduces piston cooling, raises engine compression and causes overheating.

9. Place a straightedge across the gasket surface at several points (**Figure 77**). Measure warp by inserting a feeler gauge between the straightedge and cylinder head at each location. Maximum allowable

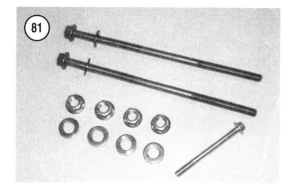

warp is listed in **Table 2**. If the warp exceeds this limit, the cylinder head must be resurfaced or replaced. Distortion or nicks in the cylinder head surface could cause an air leak and cause overheating.

10. Check the exhaust pipe studs for looseness or thread damage. Slight thread damage can be repaired with a thread file or die. If thread damage is excessive, replace the damaged stud(s) as described in Chapter One.

11. Service the intake tube (A, **Figure 78**) as follows:

a. Inspect the intake tube for cracks or other damage that would allow unfiltered air to enter the engine. On high mileage bikes, it is common to see surface cracks along the side of the tube. Make sure the cracks do not pass through the tube.

b. If necessary, loosen the hose clamp and remove the intake tube.

c. Install the intake tube by aligning the slot in the tube with the raised boss (B, **Figure 78**) on the cylinder head.

12. Check the valves and valve guides as described under *Valves and Valve Components* in this chapter.

Installation

1. Clean the cylinder head and cylinder gasket surfaces.

2. Position the cam chain inside the chain tunnel so it does not interfere with the cylinder head.

3. Install the chain guide (**Figure 73**) by aligning its tabs with the slots in the cylinder (**Figure 79**). Make sure the end of the guide seats into the pocket in the crankcase (**Figure 69**, typical).

4. If removed, install the two dowel pins (B, **Figure 72**).

5. Install a *new* cylinder head gasket (A, **Figure 72**) over the dowel pins and against the cylinder block. Make sure all holes align.

NOTE
The cylinder heads are not identical.
Each cylinder head contains either an
*F or R (**Figure 80**) identification mark.*

6. Install the cylinder head over the dowel pins and against the head gasket. Check that the cylinder head is sitting flush against the head gasket.

7. Pull on the cam chain and make sure it is properly engaged with the drive sprocket on the crankshaft.

8. Clean and dry the cylinder head fasteners (**Figure 81**). These fasteners must be free of debris. Dirt on the fastener threads or washers may affect bolt torque.

9. Lubricate the cylinder head 8-mm bolt threads with engine oil.

10. Lubricate all of the cylinder head bolt and nut seating surfaces with engine oil.

4

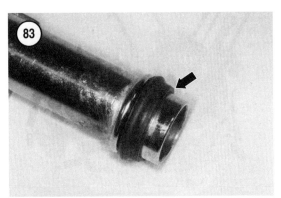

11. Install the fasteners and hand-tighten as follows:

    a. 10-mm nuts and washers (C, **Figure 71**).

    b. 8-mm bolts and washers (B, **Figure 71**).

    c. 6-mm bolt (A, **Figure 71**).

12. Tighten the 10-mm nuts and the 8-mm bolts sequentially (**Figure 82**) in two steps to 23 N•m (17 ft.-lb.).

13. Tighten the 10-mm nuts sequentially (**Figure 82**) to 47 N•m (35 ft.-lb.).

14. Tighten the 6-mm bolt to 12 N•m (106 in.-lb.).

15. Insert the rubber guide into the cylinder head chain tunnel as shown in **Figure 68**. Position the rubber guide so its top edge is flush with the cylinder head gasket surface (**Figure 66**).

16. Install the cam chain tensioner (**Figure 65**) into position. Make sure the bottom of the tensioner seats into the lower pocket in the crankcase.

17. Install a new sealing washer onto each chain tensioner mounting bolt. Apply a medium strength threadlock onto the bolt threads and tighten the bolts (**Figure 64**) to 10 N•m (88 in.-lb.).

18. Lubricate a new O-ring with coolant and install on the water pipe in the direction shown in **Figure 83**. Install the water pipe and secure with its mounting bolt (**Figure 84**).

19. Reverse Step 1 under *Removal* to complete installation.

20. Start the engine and check for leaks. While doing so, bleed the cooling system as described in Chapter Three.

VALVES AND VALVE COMPONENTS

Because of the number of special tools and the skills required to use them, it is general practice by those who do most of their own service to remove

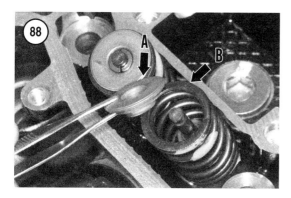

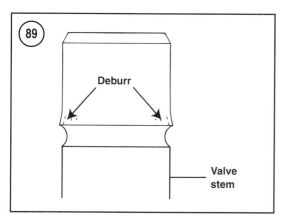

the cylinder heads and entrust valve service to a dealership or machine shop.

Valve Removal

Refer to **Figure 85**.

1. Remove the cylinder head as described in this chapter.

2. Install a valve spring compressor (**Figure 86**) squarely over the upper retainer with the other end of the tool placed against the valve head.

3. Tighten the valve spring compressor until the valve keepers separate. Lift the valve keepers out through the valve spring compressor with needlenose pliers or tweezers (**Figure 87**).

4. Gradually loosen the valve spring compressor and remove it from the head. Remove the spring retainer (A, **Figure 88**).

5. Remove the valve spring (B, **Figure 88**).

> *CAUTION*
> *Remove any burrs from the valve stem groove (**Figure 89**) before removing the valve; otherwise, the valve guide is damaged as the valve stem passes through it.*

6. Remove the valve (**Figure 90**) from its guide while rotating it slightly.

> *NOTE*
> *If a valve is difficult to remove, it may be bent, which causes it to stick in its valve guide. This condition requires valve and valve guide replacement.*

7. Pull the oil seal (**Figure 91**) off the valve guide and discard it.

8. Remove the spring seat (**Figure 92**).

9. Identify the parts (**Figure 85**) as they are removed so they can be reinstalled in their original position.

10. Repeat for the remaining intake and exhaust valves.

NOTE
Do not remove the valve guides unless they require replacement.

Valve Inspection

Valve components

Refer to the troubleshooting chart in **Figure 93** when performing valve inspection procedures in this section. When measuring the valves and valve components, compare the actual measurements to the specifications in **Table 2**. Replace parts that are damaged or out of specification as described in this section. Maintain the alignment of the valve components to ensure installation in their original location.

1. Clean the valve components in solvent. Do not damage the valve seating surface.

2. Inspect the valve face (**Figure 94**) for burning, pitting or other signs of wear. Unevenness of the valve face is an indication that the valve is not serviceable. If the wear on a valve is too extensive to be corrected by hand-lapping the valve into its seat, replace the valve. The face on the valve cannot be ground. Replace the valve if defective.

3. Inspect the valve stems for wear and roughness. Check the valve keeper grooves for damage.

4. Measure each valve stem's outside diameter with a micrometer (**Figure 95**). Note the following:

   a. If a valve stem is out of specification, discard the valve.

   b. If a valve stem is within specification, record the measurement to use it to determine the valve stem-to-guide clearance in Step 7.

NOTE
Honda recommends reaming the valve guides to remove any carbon buildup before checking and measuring the guides. For the home mechanic it is more practical to remove carbon and varnish from the valve guides with a stiff spiral wire brush. Then clean the valve guides with sol-

vent to wash out all particles, and dry with compressed air.

5. Insert each valve into its respective valve guide and move it up and down by hand. The valve should move smoothly.

6. Measure each valve guide inside diameter with a small hole gauge and record the measurements. Note the following:

NOTE
Because valve guides wear unevenly (oval shape), measure each guide at different positions. Use the largest bore diameter measurement when determining its size.

   a. If a valve guide is out of specification, replace it as described in this section.

   b. If a valve guide is within specification, record the measurement to use it to determine the valve stem-to-guide clearance in Step 7.

7. Subtract the measurement made in Step 4 from the measurement made in Step 6 to determine the valve stem-to-guide clearance. Note the following:

   a. If the clearance is out of specification, determine if a new guide would bring the clearance within specification.

   b. If the clearance would be out of specification with a new guide, replace the valve and guide as a set.

8. Inspect the valve springs as follows:

   a. Inspect each spring for any cracks or other visual damage.

   b. Use a square and check the spring for distortion or tilt (**Figure 96**). Tilt should be minimal.

   c. Measure the free length of each valve spring with a vernier caliper (**Figure 97**).

   d. Replace defective springs.

(93)   **VALVE TROUBLESHOOTING**

4

| Excessive valve deposits |

Check:
- Worn valve guide
- Carbon buildup from incorrect tuning
- Carbon buildup from incorrect fuel delivery operation
- Dirty or gummed fuel
- Dirty engine oil

| Valve sticking |

Check:
- Worn valve guide
- Bent valve stem
- Deposits collected on valve stem
- Valve burning or overheating

| Valve burning |

Check:
- Valve sticking
- Cylinder head warped
- Valve seat distorted
- Valve clearance incorrect
- Incorrect valve spring
- Valve spring worn
- Worn valve seat
- Carbon buildup in engine
- Ignition or fuel delivery malfunction

| Valve seat/face wear |

Check:
- Valve burning
- Incorrect valve clearance
- Abrasive material on valve face and seat

| Valve damage |

Check:
- Valve burning
- Incorrectly installed or serviced valve guides
- Incorrect valve clearance
- Incorrect valve, spring seat and retainer assembly
- Detonation caused by incorrect ignition and/or fuel delivery malfunction

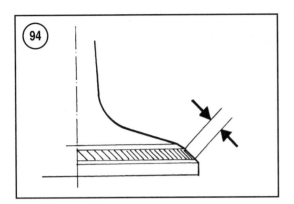

9. Check the valve keepers. If they are in good condition, they may be reused; replace in pairs as necessary.

10. Inspect the spring retainer and spring seat for damage.

11. Inspect the valve seats as described in this section.

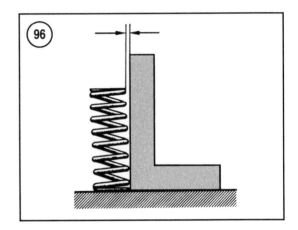

Valve seat

The most accurate method for checking the valve seal is to use a marking compound (machinist's dye), available from auto parts and tool stores. Use marking compound to locate high or irregular spots when checking or making close fits. Follow the manufacturer's directions.

> *NOTE*
> *Because of the close operating tolerances within the valve assembly, the valve stem and guide must be within tolerance; otherwise the inspection results will be inaccurate.*

1. Remove the valves as described in this section.

2. Clean the valve seat in the cylinder head and valve mating areas with contact cleaner.

3. Thoroughly clean all carbon deposits from the valve face with solvent and dry thoroughly.

4. Spread a thin layer of marking compound evenly on the valve face.

5. Slowly insert the valve into its guide and tap the valve against its seat several times (**Figure 98**) without spinning it.

6. Remove the valve and examine the impression left by the marking compound. If the impression (on the valve or in the cylinder head) is not even and continuous, and the valve seat width (**Figure 99**) is not within

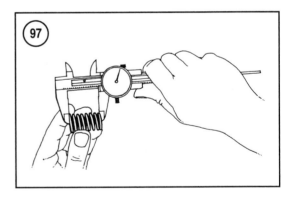

the specified tolerance listed in **Table 2**, the valve seat in the cylinder head must be reconditioned.

7. Closely examine the valve seat in the cylinder head (**Figure 100**). It should be smooth and even with a polished seating surface.

8. If the valve seat is not in good condition, recondition the valve seat as described in this section.

9. Repeat for the other valves.

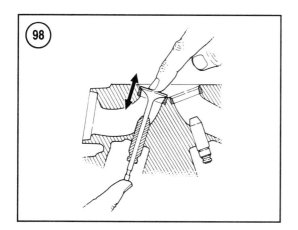

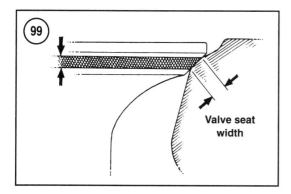

Valve seat
width

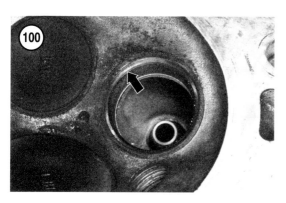

Valve Guide Replacement

Tools

The following Honda tools (or equivalents) are required to remove and install the valve guides.
1. Valve guide driver:
  a. Intake: 5.5 mm.
  b. Exhaust: 6.6 mm.
2. Valve guide reamer:
  a. Intake: 5.5 mm.
  b. Exhaust: 6.6 mm.

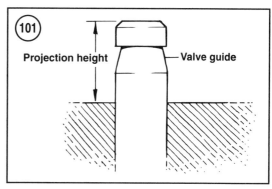

Projection height — Valve guide

Procedure

Read the entire procedure before beginning and have the required tools ready. It is necessary to work quickly when working with hot/cold components.
1. Remove all the valves and valve guide seals from the cylinder head.
2. Place the new valve guides in the freezer for approximately one hour before heating the cylinder head. Chilling them slightly reduces the outside diameter, while the cylinder is lightly larger due to heat expansion. This makes valve guide installation much easier. One at a time remove the guides as needed.

NOTE
Flangeless valve guides are used. Step 3 confirms that the original guides were installed to the height specified in **Table 2**.

3. Measure the valve guide projection height above the cylinder head surface (**Figure 101**) with a vernier caliper. Record the projection height for each valve guide. Compare to the specification in **Table 2**.
4. Place the cylinder head on a hot plate and heat to 130-140° C (275-290° F). Do not exceed 150° C (300° F). Monitor the temperature with heat sticks, which are available at welding supply stores.

WARNING
Wear welding gloves or similar insulated gloves when handling the head. The cylinder head is very hot.

CAUTION
Do not heat the cylinder head with a torch. Never bring a flame into contact with the cylinder head or valve guide. The direct heat damages the case hardening of the valve guide and may warp the cylinder head.

5. Remove the head from the hot plate. Place the head on wooden blocks with the combustion chamber facing *up*.

6. From the combustion chamber side of the head, drive out the valve guide with the valve guide remover (**Figure 102**). Quickly repeat this step for each guide to be replaced. Reheat the head as required. Discard the valve guides after removing them.

> *CAUTION*
> *Do not attempt to remove the valve guides if the head is not hot enough. Doing so may damage the valve guide bore in the cylinder head and require replacement of the head.*

7. Allow the head to cool.

8. Inspect and clean the valve guide bores. Check for cracks or any scoring along the bore wall.

9. Reheat the cylinder head as described in Step 4. Remove it from the hot plate and install it onto the wooden blocks with the valve spring side facing *up*.

10. Remove one new valve guide, either intake or exhaust, from the freezer.

11. Align the valve guide in the bore. Using the valve guide driver tool and hammer, drive in the valve guide (**Figure 103**) until the projection height of the valve guide is within the specification in **Table 2** (**Figure 101**).

12. Repeat to install the remaining valve guides.

13. Allow the head to cool to room temperature.

14. Ream each valve guide as follows:
   a. Place the head on wooden blocks with the combustion chamber facing *up*. The guides are reamed from this side.
   b. Coat the valve guide and valve guide reamer with cutting oil.
   c. Rotate the reamer clockwise into the valve guide (**Figure 104**).

> *CAUTION*
> *Always rotate the reamer **clockwise** through the entire length of the guide, both when reaming the guide and when removing the reamer. Rotating the reamer counterclockwise reverses the cut and damages (enlarges) the valve guide bore.*

> *CAUTION*
> *Do not allow the reamer to tilt. Keep the tool square to the hole and apply*

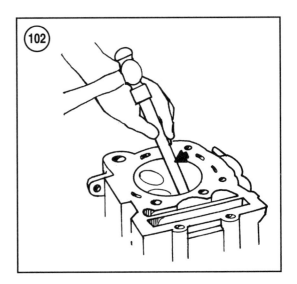

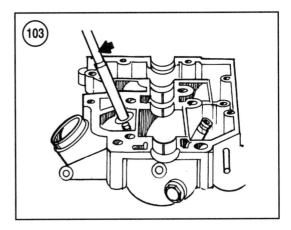

even pressure and twisting motion during the entire operation.

   d. Slowly rotate the reamer through the guide, while periodically adding cutting oil.
   e. As the end of the reamer passes through the valve guide, maintain the clockwise motion and work the reamer back out of the guide while continuing to add cutting oil.
   f. Clean the reamer of all chips and relubricate with cutting oil before starting on the next guide. Repeat for each guide as required.

15. Thoroughly clean the cylinder head and all valve components in solvent, and then with detergent and hot water to remove all cutting residue. Rinse in cold water. Dry with compressed air.

16. Measure the valve guide inside diameter with a small hole gauge. The measurement must be within the specification listed in **Table 2**.

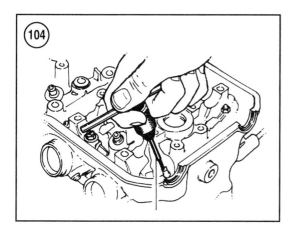

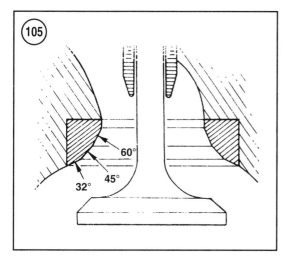

17. Apply engine oil to the valve guides to prevent rust.

18. Lubricate a valve stem with engine oil and pass it through each valve guide, verifying that it moves without any roughness or binding.

19. Reface the valve seats as described under *Valve Seat Reconditioning* in this section.

Valve Seat Reconditioning

Tools

To cut the cylinder head valve seats the following tools are required:

1. Valve seat cutters (**Figure 105**). See a Honda dealership.

2. A vernier caliper.

3. Gear-marking compound.

4. Valve lapping tool.

Procedure

> *NOTE*
> *Follow the manufacturer's instructions when using valve facing equipment.*

Before reconditioning the valve seats, inspect and measure them as described under *Inspection* in this section.

1. Carefully rotate and insert the solid pilot into the valve guide. Be sure the pilot is correctly seated.

2. Install the 45° cutter and cutter holder onto the solid pilot.

> *CAUTION*
> *Work slowly and make light cuts. Overcutting the valve seats recedes the valves into the cylinder head, reducing the valve adjustment range. If cutting is excessive, the ability to set the valve adjustment may be lost. This condition requires cylinder head replacement.*

3. Using the 45° cutter, de-scale and clean the valve seat with one or two turns.

4. If the seat is still pitted or burned, turn the 45° cutter additional turns until the surface is clean.

5. Measure the valve seat width with a vernier caliper (**Figure 99**). Record the measurement to use as a reference point when performing the following.

> *CAUTION*
> *The 32° cutter removes material quickly. Work carefully and check the progress often.*

6. Install the 32° cutter onto the solid pilot and lightly cut the seat to remove 1/4 of the existing valve seat (**Figure 106**).

7. Install the 60° cutter onto the solid pilot and lightly cut the seat to remove 1/4 of the existing valve seat (**Figure 107**).

8. Measure the valve seat width with a vernier caliper (**Figure 99**). Then fit the 45° cutter onto the solid pilot and cut the valve seat to the specified width (**Figure 108**) listed in **Table 2**.

9. When the valve seat width is correct, check valve seating as follows:

    a. Clean the valve seat with contact cleaner.

    b. Spread a thin layer of marking compound evenly on the valve face.

c. Slowly insert the valve into its guide.

d. Support the valve with two fingers (**Figure 98**) and tap the valve up and down in the cylinder head several times. Do not rotate the valve or a false reading results.

e. Remove the valve and examine the impression left by the marking compound.

f. Measure the valve seat width as shown in **Figure 99**. Refer to **Figure 2** for specified valve width.

g. The valve contact should be approximately in the center of the valve seat area.

10. If the contact area is too high on the valve or if it is too wide, use the 32° cutter and remove a portion of the top area of the valve seat material to lower and narrow the contact area on the valve (**Figure 109**).

11. If the contact area is too low on the valve or too wide, use the 60° cutter and remove a portion of the lower area of the valve seat material to raise and narrow the contact area on the valve (**Figure 109**).

12. After the desired valve seat position and width is obtained, use the 45° cutter to lightly clean off any burrs that may have been caused by previous cuts.

13. When the contact area is correct, lap the valve as described in this chapter.

14. Repeat Steps 1-13 for all remaining valve seats.

15. Thoroughly clean the cylinder head and all valve components in solvent, and then with detergent and hot water. Rinse in cold water and dry with compressed air. Apply a light coat of clean engine oil to all non-aluminum surfaces to prevent rust.

Valve Lapping

Valve lapping can restore the valve seat without machining if the amount of wear or distortion is not too great.

Perform this procedure after determining that the valve seat width and outside diameter are within specifications. A valve lapping tool and compound are required.

1. Smear a light coating of fine grade valve lapping compound on the valve face seating surface.

2. Insert the valve into the head.

3. Wet the suction cup of the lapping stick and stick it onto the head of the valve. Spin the tool in both directions while pressing it against the valve seat and lap the valve to the seat. Every 5 to 10 seconds, lift and rotate the valve 180° in the valve seat. Continue

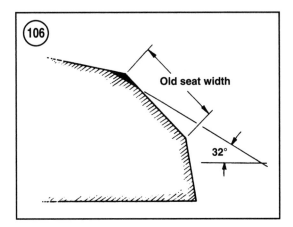

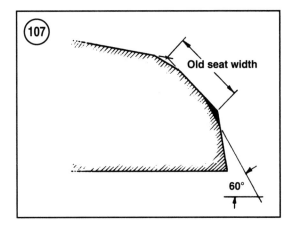

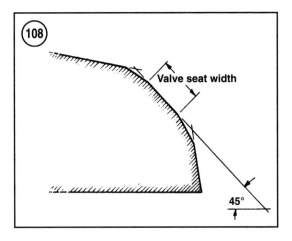

until the gasket surfaces on the valve and seat are smooth and equal in size.

4. Closely examine the valve seat width in the cylinder head (**Figure 99**). It should be smooth and even with a polished seating ring.

5. Repeat Steps 1-4 for the other valves.

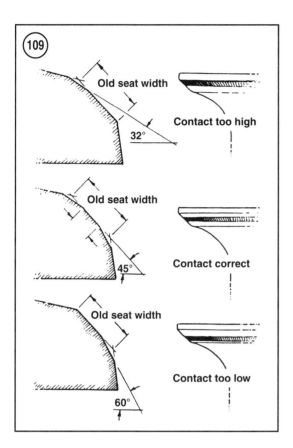

6. Thoroughly clean the cylinder head and all valve components in solvent, and then with detergent and hot water. Rinse in cold water and dry with compressed air. Apply a light coat of clean engine oil to all non-aluminum surfaces to prevent rust.

CAUTION
Any compound left on the valves or in the cylinder head causes wear to the engine components.

7. Install the valve assemblies as described in this chapter.

8. Perform a solvent test as described under *Cylinder Head, Inspection* in this chapter. There should be no leaks past the seat. If leaks occur, the combustion chamber appears wet. If fluid leaks past any of the seats, disassemble that valve assembly and repeat the lapping procedure until there are no leaks.

9. After cleaning the cylinder head and valve components in detergent and hot water, apply a light coat of engine oil onto all bare metal surfaces to prevent rust formation.

Valve Installation

Install the valves in their original locations. Refer to **Figure 110**.

1. Install the spring seat with its shoulder facing up (**Figure 111**).

2. Lubricate the inside of a *new* oil seal with engine oil. Push the seal straight down the valve guide until it snaps into the groove in the top of the guide (**Figure 112**). Check that the oil seal is centered and seats squarely on top of the guide. If the seal is cocked to one side, oil will leak past the seal during engine operation.

NOTE
The oil seals must be replaced when-
ever the valves are removed. Also, if a
new seal was installed and then re-
moved, do not reuse it.

3. Install the valve as follows:

a. Coat a valve stem with molybdenum oil solution.

NOTE
Molybdenum oil solution is a 50:50
mixture of engine oil and molybde-
num disulfide grease.

b. Install the valve partway into its guide.
Slowly turn the valve as it enters the valve
stem seal and continue turning it until the
valve is installed all the way.

c. Make sure the valve moves up and down
smoothly.

4. Install the valve spring (A, **Figure 113**) with its
closer wound coils facing the cylinder head.

5. Install the spring retainer (B, **Figure 113**) on top
of the valve spring.

CAUTION
To avoid loss of spring tension, do not
compress the spring any more than
necessary when installing the valve
keepers.

6. Compress the valve spring with a valve spring
compressor tool and install the valve keepers. Make
sure the keepers fit into the rounded groove in the
valve stem (**Figure 114**).

7. Gently tap the upper retainer with a plastic hammer to ensure the keepers (**Figure 115**) are properly
seated.

8. Repeat Steps 1-7 for the remaining valves.

9. After installing the cylinder head, camshaft and
camshaft holders on the engine, check and adjust
the valve clearance as described in Chapter Three.

CYLINDER

Service procedures for the front and rear cylinders are the same.

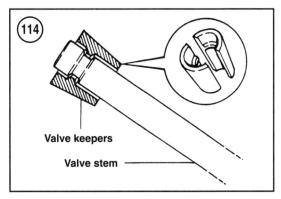

Valve keepers

Valve stem

Removal

CAUTION
When it is necessary to rotate the
crankshaft, pull up the cam chains so
they cannot bind internally.

1. Remove the engine from the frame (Chapter
Five).

2. Remove the cylinder head as described in this
chapter.

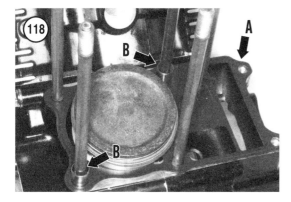

3. Remove the clips (**Figure 116**) from the water pipe.

4. Slide the water pipe either toward the front or rear cylinder (**Figure 117**).

5. Loosen the cylinder by tapping around the perimeter with a rubber or plastic mallet.

6. Pull the cylinder straight up and off the crankcase.

7. Remove and discard the base gasket (A, **Figure 118**).

8. Remove the dowel pins (B, **Figure 118**).

9. Slide a length of plastic hose down two of the cylinder studs and rest the piston and rings against them (**Figure 119**).

10. Cover the piston and crankcase opening.

11. Remove the water pipe (**Figure 120**) and discard both O-rings (**Figure 121**).

Inspection

When measuring the cylinder in this section, compare the actual measurements to the specifications in **Table 3**. Service the cylinder if it is out of specification or shows damage as described in this section.

1. Soak the cylinder surfaces in solvent, then carefully remove gasket material from the top and bottom mating surfaces with a scraper. Do not nick or gouge the gasket surfaces or leaks result.

2. Wash the cylinder in solvent. Dry with compressed air.

3. Check the dowel pin holes for cracks or other damage.

4. Place a straight edge across the upper cylinder surface. Insert a flat feeler gauge between the straight edge and the cylinder at different locations and check for warp (**Figure 122**).

5. Measure the cylinder bore with a bore gauge or inside micrometer at the points shown in **Figure 123**. Measure in line with the piston pin and 90° to the pin. Use the largest measurement to determine cylinder bore. If the taper or out-of-round is greater than specifications, bore the cylinder oversize and install a new piston and rings.

6. Determine piston-to-cylinder clearance as described in *Piston Clearance* in this chapter.

7. If the cylinder is not worn past the service limit, check the bore for scratches or gouges. The bore still may require boring and reconditioning.

8. After the cylinder has been serviced, clean the cylinder as follows:

> *CAUTION*
> *A combination of soap and hot water is the only solution that completely cleans cylinder walls. Solvent and kerosene cannot wash fine grit out of cylinder crevices. Any grit left in the cylinder acts as a grinding compound and causes premature wear to the new rings.*

   a. Wash the cylinder bore in hot soapy water.

   b. Also wash out any fine grit material from the cooling passages surrounding the cylinder.

   c. After washing the cylinder, wipe the cylinder wall with a clean white cloth. It should *not* show any traces of grit or debris. If the rag is the slightest bit dirty, the wall is not thoroughly cleaned and must be washed again.

   d. When the cylinder is clean, lubricate the liner with clean engine oil to prevent rust.

Water Joint (Front Cylinder)

A water joint (**Figure 124**) is installed on the front cylinder.

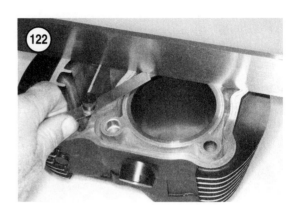

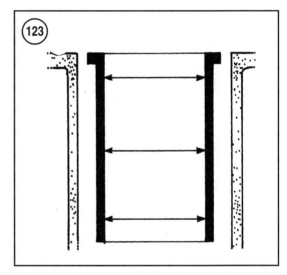

1. Inspect the water joint for leaks or damage.

2. If necessary, remove the bolts and install a new O-ring between the water joint and cylinder. Tighten the bolts securely.

Installation

> *NOTE*
> *The front and rear cylinders are not identical. The front cylinder is equipped with a water joint (**Figure 124**). The water passage opening on the rear cylinder is blocked off.*

> *CAUTION*
> *When rotating the crankshaft, pull up the cam chains so they cannot bind internally.*

1. Make sure all crankcase and cylinder gasket surfaces are clean and dry.

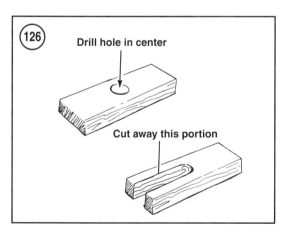

Drill hole in center

Cut away this portion

2. If removed, install the piston as described in this chapter.

CAUTION
Make sure to install and secure the piston pin circlips.

3. Lubricate the water pipe O-rings with coolant and install them onto the pipe grooves shown in **Figure 121**.

4. Install the water pipe into the cylinder (**Figure 120**). It does not matter which cylinder.

NOTE
The water pipe cannot be installed when both cylinders are installed on the engine.

5. Install the dowel pins (B, **Figure 118**) into the crankcase.
6. Install a new base gasket (A, **Figure 118**). Make sure all holes align.
7. Install a piston holding fixture (A, **Figure 125**) under the piston.

NOTE
*To fabricate a wooden piston holding fixture from a piece of scrap wood, re-fer to the example in **Figure 126**.*

8. Lubricate the cylinder wall, piston and rings with engine oil. Liberally lubricate the oil control rings to fill them with oil.
9. Stagger the piston ring end gaps evenly around the piston circumference. They must not align.

NOTE
*The cylinder can be installed with or without a piston ring compressor (B, **Figure 125**).*

10A. Without piston ring compressor— Align the cylinder with cylinder studs and lower it onto the piston. Compress each piston ring by hand as it enters the cylinder. Push the cylinder down until it bottoms on the piston holding fixture.
10B. With piston ring compressor—Lubricate the parts of the piston ring compressor that contact the piston rings with clean engine oil. Install the compressor so it covers all three rings (B, **Figure 125**). Tap the top of the cylinder evenly to push the cylinder over the rings and piston. Push the cylinder down until the ring compressor bottoms on the piston holding fixture. Remove the ring compressor.
11. Remove the piston holding fixture and push the cylinder down into place over the dowel pins and against the base gasket.
12. Install a length of hose over one of the cylinder studs and secure it with a nut (**Figure 127**). The hose holds the cylinder in place when the crankshaft is turned over in the following steps.
13. Have an assistant pull up on both cam chains, then rotate the crankshaft counterclockwise. The

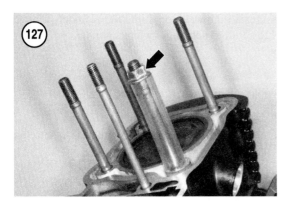

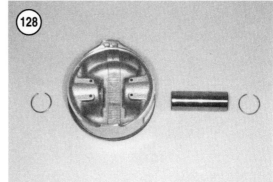

piston must move up and down in the bore with no binding or roughness. If there is any interference, a piston ring may have broken during cylinder installation.

14. Make sure the water pipe (**Figure 120**) is installed in one of the cylinders.

15. Repeat these steps to install the other cylinder.

16. Slide the water pipe (**Figure 117**) into the opposite cylinder and secure with the two clips (**Figure 116**). Make sure the clips seat in the grooves completely.

17. Install the cylinder heads as described in this chapter.

18. Install the engine into the frame (Chapter Five).

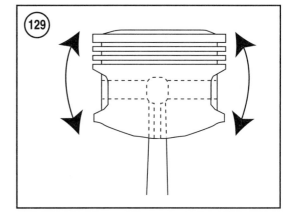

PISTON AND PISTON RINGS

Refer to **Figure 128** when servicing the piston and rings. Procedures for the front and rear piston are the same.

Piston Removal

CAUTION
When it is necessary to rotate the crankshaft, pull up the cam chains so they cannot bind internally. Protect the pistons so they are not damaged when retracting into the crankcase.

1. Remove the cylinder as described in this chapter.

2. Mark the top of the piston with an identification letter (F or R) and a directional arrow pointing toward the front of the engine.

3. Block off the crankcase below the piston with a clean shop cloth to prevent the piston pin circlips from falling into the crankcase.

4. Before removing the piston, hold the rod and rock the piston (**Figure 129**). Any rocking motion (do not confuse with the normal sliding motion) indicates wear on the piston pin, rod bushing, pin bore or a combination of all three.

5. Support the piston with a piston holder fixture, then install two plastic hoses over the cylinder studs to protect the piston rings (**Figure 130**) when removing the circlips and piston pin.

6. Remove the piston circlips (**Figure 131**).

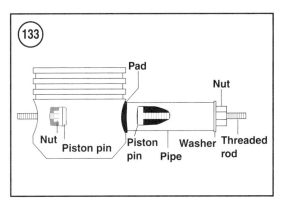

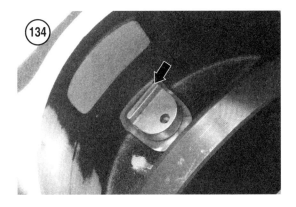

NOTE
The operating clearance between the piston pin and pin bore is such that the piston pin can be removed and installed by hand. However, problems such as varnish on the piston pin, a burred pin bore or circlip groove, or a damaged piston can make it difficult to remove the piston pin.

7. Push the piston pin (**Figure 132**) out of the piston by hand. If the pin is tight, use a homemade tool (**Figure 133**) to remove it. Do not drive the piston pin out because this may damage the piston pin, connecting rod or piston. Heat can also be used to ease removal. Heat the piston crown (and not the side of the piston) with a heat gun.

8. Lift the piston off the connecting rod.

9. Remove the oil jet (**Figure 134**) and its O-ring from the crankcase.

10. Inspect the piston as described in this section.

Piston Inspection

1. Remove the piston rings as described in this section.

2. Soak the piston in solvent to soften the carbon deposits.

3. Clean the carbon from the piston crown with a soft scraper or wire wheel mounted in a drill. A thick carbon buildup reduces piston cooling and causes detonation and piston damage. Relabel the piston as soon as it is cleaned.

CAUTION
Do not wire brush the piston skirt.

4. After cleaning the piston, examine the crown. The crown must show no signs of wear or damage. If the crown appears pecked or spongy-looking, also check the spark plugs, valves and combustion chamber for aluminum deposits. If these deposits are found, the engine is overheating.

5. Examine each ring groove for burrs, dented edges or other damage. Pay particular attention to the top compression ring groove (A, **Figure 135**) as it usually wears more than the others. Because the oil rings are bathed in oil, these rings and grooves wear little compared to compression rings and their grooves. If there is evidence of oil ring groove wear or if the oil ring is tight and difficult to remove, the

piston skirt may have collapsed due to excessive heat. Replace the piston.

6. Clean the oil control holes (A, **Figure 136**) in the piston.

7. Check the piston skirt (B, **Figure 136**) for cracks or other damage. If the piston shows signs of partial seizure (bits of aluminum built up on the piston skirt), replace the piston.

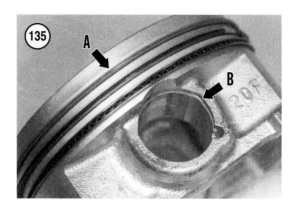

> *NOTE*
> *If the piston skirt is worn or scuffed unevenly from side-to-side, the connecting rod may be bent or twisted.*

8. Check the piston circlip grooves (B, **Figure 135**) for wear, cracks or other damage.

9. Measure piston-to-cylinder clearance as described under *Piston Clearance* in this section.

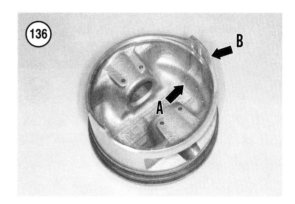

Piston Pin Inspection

When measuring the piston pin, compare the actual measurements to the specifications in **Table 3**. Replace the piston pin if out of specification or if it shows damage as described in this section.

1. Clean and dry the piston pin.

2. Inspect the piston pin for chrome flaking or cracks.

3. Oil the piston pin and install it in the piston. Slowly rotate the piston pin and check for tightness or excessive play (**Figure 137**).

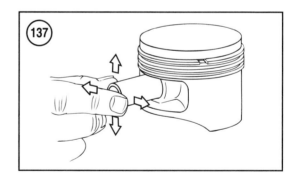

4. Lubricate the piston pin and install it (**Figure 138**) in the connecting rod. Slowly rotate the piston pin and check for radial play.

5. Measure the piston pin bore inside diameter (A, **Figure 139**).

6. Measure the piston pin outside diameter (B, **Figure 139**).

7. Subtract the measurement made in Step 5 from the measurement made in Step 6. The difference is the piston-to-piston pin clearance.

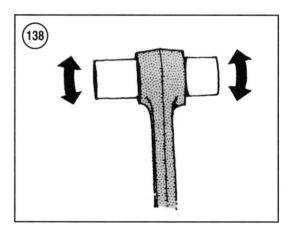

Connecting Rod Small End Inspection

1. Inspect the connecting rod small end for cracks or heat damage.

2. Measure the connecting rod small end inside diameter. Check this against the dimension in **Table 3**. If out of specification, replace the crankshaft as described in Chapter Five.

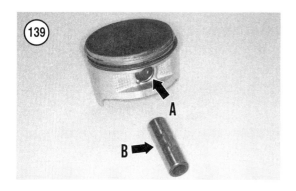

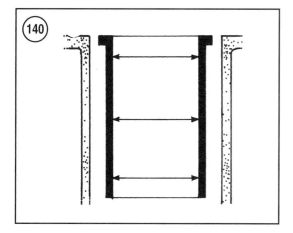

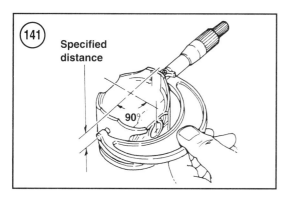

Specified
distance

90°

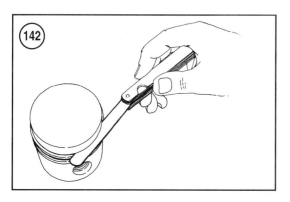

Piston Clearance

1. Make sure the piston skirt and cylinder walls are clean and dry.

2. Measure the cylinder bore with a bore gauge or inside micrometer at the points shown in **Figure 140**. Measure in line with the piston pin and 90° to the pin. Use the largest measurement to determine cylinder bore diameter. If the cylinder bore is out of specification, replace the piston and bore the cylinder oversize. If the cylinder bore is within specification, continue with Step 3.

3. Measure the piston diameter with a micrometer at a right angle to the piston pin bore. Measure up 7-17 mm (0.3-0.7 in.) from the bottom edge of the piston skirt (**Figure 141**).

4. Subtract the piston diameter from the largest bore diameter. The difference is piston-to-cylinder clearance. If clearance exceeds the service limit in **Table 3**, determine if the piston, cylinder or both are worn. If necessary, take the cylinder to a dealership that can bore the cylinder to accept an oversize piston.

Piston Ring Inspection and Removal

A 3-ring type piston and ring assembly is used (**Figure 135**). The top and second rings are compression rings. The lower ring is an oil control ring assembly (consisting of two ring rails and a spacer).

When measuring the piston rings in this section, compare the actual measurements to the specifications in **Table 3**. Replace the piston rings as a set if out of specification or if they show damage as described in this section.

1. Measure the side clearance of each ring in its groove with a flat feeler gauge (**Figure 142**):

   a. If the clearance is greater than specified, replace the rings. If the clearance is still excessive with new rings, replace the piston.

   b. If the clearance is too small, check the ring and ring groove for carbon and oil residue. Carefully clean the ring without removing any metal from its surface. Clean the piston ring groove as described in this section.

WARNING
The edges of all piston rings are very sharp. Be careful when handling them to avoid cut fingers.

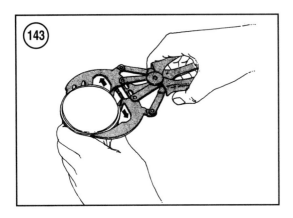

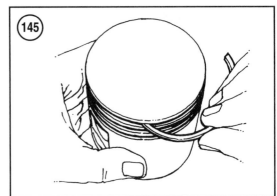

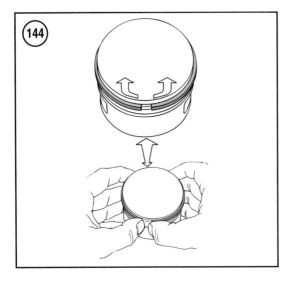

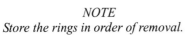

NOTE
Store the rings in order of removal.

2. Remove the compression rings with a ring expander tool (**Figure 143**) or spread the ring ends by
hand (**Figure 144**).

3. Remove the oil ring assembly by first removing
the upper and then the lower ring rails. Remove the
spacer.

4. Remove carbon and oil residues from the piston
ring grooves (**Figure 145**) with a broken piston ring
(if available). Do not remove aluminum material
from the ring grooves as this increases the side
clearance.

5. Inspect the ring grooves for burrs, nicks or broken
or cracked lands. Replace the piston if necessary.

6. Check the end gap of each ring. Inserting the ring
into the bottom of the cylinder bore and square it
with the cylinder wall by pushing it with the piston
(**Figure 146**). Measure the end gap with a feeler

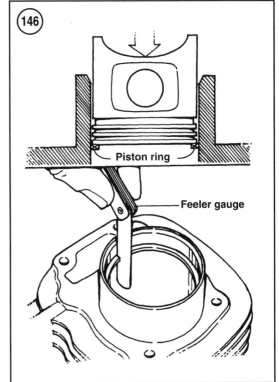

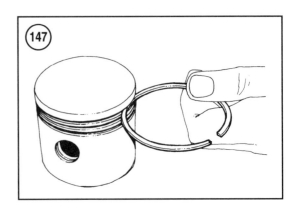

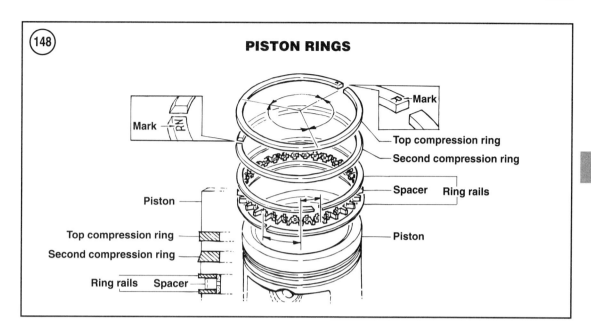

PISTON RINGS

Mark

Mark — RN

Top compression ring

Second compression ring

Spacer — Ring rails

Piston

Piston

Top compression ring

Second compression ring

Ring rails   Spacer

4

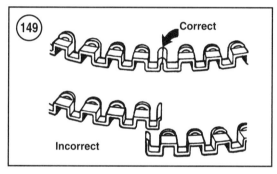

Correct

Incorrect

gauge (**Figure 146**). Replace the rings if the gap is too large. If the gap on the new ring is smaller than specified, hold a small file in a vise. Grip the ends of the ring with your fingers and slowly enlarge the gap.

NOTE
When measuring the oil control ring end gap, measure the upper and lower ring rail end gaps only. Do not measure the spacer.

7. Roll each compression ring around its piston groove (**Figure 147**) to measure the ring-to-ring groove clearance and to check for binding. Repair minor binding with a fine-cut file.

Piston Ring Installation

1. When installing new piston rings, hone or deglaze the cylinder wall. This helps the new rings to

seat in the cylinder. If necessary, refer this service to a Honda dealership. After honing, measure the end gap of each ring and compare to the dimensions in **Table 3**.

NOTE
If the cylinder was honed or deglazed, clean the cylinder as described under **Cylinder, Inspection** *in this chapter.*

2. Clean and dry the piston and rings.

3. Install the piston rings as follows:

   a. Install the oil ring assembly into the bottom ring groove. Install the spacer first, and then the bottom and top ring rails (**Figure 148**). Make sure the ends of the spacer butt together (**Figure 149**). They should not overlap. If reassembling used parts, install the ring rails in their original positions.

   b. Install the compression rings with a ring expander tool (**Figure 143**) or by spreading the ring ends by hand (**Figure 144**).

   c. Install the second or middle compression ring with the RN mark facing up. This ring has a slight taper (**Figure 148**).

   d. Install the top compression ring with the R mark facing up.

4. Make sure the rings are seated completely in their grooves all the way around the piston and that the end gaps are distributed around the piston as

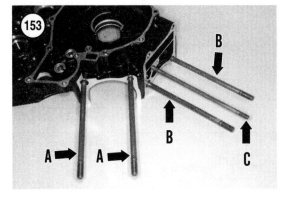

shown in **Figure 148**. To prevent combustion from escaping past them, the ring gaps must not align.

5. If new parts were installed, follow the *Engine Break-In* procedure in Chapter Five.

Oil Jet Inspection

1. Inspect the oil jet (**Figure 150**) for any debris that may be clogging the oil holes. If the engine suffered any type of lubrication failure, it is safer to replace the oil jets than attempt to clean the original jets.

2. Lubricate a new O-ring (**Figure 150**) and install it in the oil jet groove.

Piston Installation

> *CAUTION*
> *When it is necessary to rotate the crankshaft, pull up the cam chains so they cannot bind internally. Protect the pistons so they are not damaged when retracting into the crankcase.*

1. Make sure the crankcase gasket surface is clean.

2. Lubricate the oil jet O-ring with clean engine oil, then install the jet into the crankcase (**Figure 134**) until it bottoms.

3. Install the piston rings onto the piston as described in this section.

4. Coat the connecting rod small end, piston pin and piston with engine oil.

5. Use the plastic hoses and piston fixture to support the piston and protect the piston rings as described under *Piston Removal*.

6. Slide the piston pin into the piston until its end is flush with the piston pin boss.

7. Place the piston over the connecting rod so the IN mark on the piston crown (A, **Figure 151**) faces toward the intake side of the engine.

8. Line up the piston pin with the hole in the connecting rod. Push the piston pin (B, **Figure 151**) through the connecting rod and into the other side of the piston. Center the piston pin in the piston.

9. Block off the crankcase below the piston with a clean shop cloth to prevent the piston pin circlips from falling into the crankcase.

10. Install *new* piston pin circlips (**Figure 152**) in both ends of the piston pin boss. Make sure they seat in the piston grooves completely.

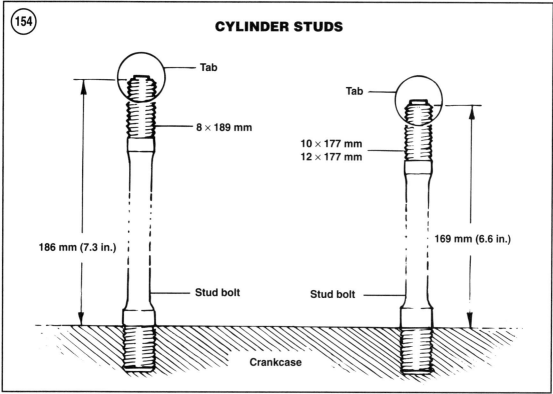

CAUTION
Do not align the piston pin circlip end gap with the cut out in the piston.

11. Install the cylinder as described in this chapter.

CYLINDER STUD REPLACEMENT

Figure 153 shows the cylinder studs with the crankcase halves disassembled. The studs can be serviced without splitting the crankcase. Refer to Chapter One for general information on replacing studs.

1. Check for loose, bent or damaged studs. Retighten or replace damaged studs.

2. Remove the stud.

3. Clean the threaded hole in the crankcase. Check for any debris or damaged threads.

4. Install the studs with the tab side of the stud (**Figure 154**) facing up. Lubricate the threads on the opposite end of the stud with clean engine oil. Do not use a threadlock.

5. Install the studs to the following dimensions (**Figure 154**):

   a. 12 × 177 mm (A, **Figure 153**): 169 mm (6.6 in.).

   b. 10 × 177 mm (B, **Figure 153**): 169 mm (6.6 in.).

   c. 8 × 189 mm (C, **Figure 153**): 186 mm (7.3 in.).

Tables 1-4 begin on the following page.

Table 1 GENERAL ENGINE SPECIFICATIONS

Bore and stroke	79.0 x 76.0 mm (3.11 x 2.99 in.)
Compression ratio	9.0:1
Cylinder alignment	52° V-Twin
Displacement	745 cc (45.4 cu.-in.)
Engine firing order	Front (308°), rear (412°)
Valve timing	
Intake valve	
Opens	0° BTDC @ 1 mm (0.04 in.) lift
Closes	20° ABDC @ 1 mm (0.4 in.) lift
Exhaust	
Opens	30° BBDC @ 1 mm (0.04 in.) lift
Closes	0° ATDC @ 1 mm (0.04 in.) lift

Table 2 CYLINDER HEAD AND VALVES SERVICE SPECIFICATIONS

	New mm (in.)	Service limit mm (in.)
Cylinder head warp limit	–	0.10 (0.004)
Camshaft		
Lobe height		
Intake		
VT750C	38.381 (1.5111)	38.10 (1.500)
VT750DC	37.188-37.348 (1.4641-1.4704)	37.16 (1.463)
Exhaust		
VT750C	38.407 (1.5121)	38.20 (1.504)
VT750DC	37.605-37.765 (1.4805-1.4868)	37.58 (1.480)
Journal outside diameter	21.959-21.980 (0.8645-0.8654)	21.90 (0.862)
Oil clearance	0.050-0.111 (0.0020-0.0044)	0.13 (0.005)
Runout	–	0.05 (0.002)
Rocker arm and shaft		
Rocker arm bore inside diameter	12.000-12.018 (0.4724-0.4731)	12.05 (0.474)
Rocker arm shaft outside diameter	11.966-11.984 (0.4711-0.4718)	11.83 (0.466)
Rocker arm-to-rocker arm shaft clearance	0.016-0.052 (0.0006-0.0020)	0.07 (0.003)
Valve		
Valve stem outside diameter		
Intake	5.475-5.490 (0.2156-0.2161)	5.45 (0.215)
Exhaust	6.555-6.570 (0.2580-0.2587)	6.55 (0.258)
Valve guide inside diameter		
Intake	5.500-5.512 (0.2165-0.2170)	5.56 (0.219)
Exhaust	6.600-6.615 (0.2598-0.2604)	6.65 (0.262)
	(continued)	

Table 2 CYLINDER HEAD AND VALVES SERVICE SPECIFICATIONS (continued)

	New mm (in.)	Service limit mm (in.)
Exhaust (continued)		
Valve stem-to-guide clearance		
Intake	0.010-0.037 (0.0004-0.0015)	0.10 (0.004)
Exhaust	0.030-0.060 (0.12-0.0024)	0.11 (0.004)
Valve guide projection above cylinder head		
Intake	19.5 (0.77)	–
Exhaust	18.0 (0.71)	–
Valve seat width	0.90-1.10 (0.035-0.043)	1.5 (0.06)
Valve spring free length		
Intake	42.14 (1.659)	40.58 (1.598)
Exhaust	42.83 (1.686)	41.25 (1.624)

Table 3 PISTON, RINGS AND BORE SPECIFICATIONS

	New mm (in.)	Service limit mm (in.)
Connecting rod small end inside diameter	18.016-18.034 (0.7093-0.7100)	18.07 (0.711)
Connecting rod-to-piston pin clearance	0.016-0.040 (0.0006-0.0016)	0.06 (0.002)
Cylinder		
Bore inside diameter	79.000-79-015 (3.1102-3.1108)	79.10 (3.114)
Out-of-round	–	0.06 (0.002)
Taper	–	0.06 (0.002)
Warp limit	–	0.10 (0.004)
Piston-to-cylinder clearance	0.010-0.045 (0.0004-0.0018)	0.10 (0.004)
Piston		
Outside diameter*	78.97-78.99 (3.109-3.110)	78.90 (3.106)
Piston pin bore inside diameter	18.002-18.008 (0.7087-0.7090)	18.05 (0.711)
Piston pin		
Outside diameter	17.994-18.000 (0.7084-0.7087)	17.98 (0.708)
Piston-to-piston pin clearance	0.002-0.014 (0.0001-0.0006)	0.04 (0.002)
Piston rings		
Ring-to-ring groove clearance		
Top ring	0.025-0.055 (0.0010-.0022)	0.08 (0.003)
Second ring	0.015-0.045 (0.006-0.0018)	0.07 (0.003)

(continued)

Table 3 PISTON, RINGS AND BORE SPECIFICATIONS (continued)

	New mm (in.)	Service limit mm (in.)
Piston rings (continued)		
Piston ring end gap		
Top ring		
VT750C		
1998-2000	0.20-0.35 (0.008-0.014)	0.5 (0.02)
Piston ring end gap		
Top ring		
VT750C (continued)		
2001-on	0.15-0.25 (0.006-0.010)	0.4 (0.02)
VT750DC	0.15-0.25 (0.006-0.010)	0.4 (0.02)
Second ring		
VT750C		
1998-2000	0.35-0.50 (0.014-0.020)	0.7 (0.03)
2001-on	0.25-0.40 (0.010-0.016)	0.6 (0.02)
VT750DC	0.25-0.40 (0.010-0.016)	0.6 (0.02)
Oil ring (side rails)	0.20-0.80 (0.008-0.031)	1.0 (0.04)
Piston ring marks		
Top ring	R	
Second ring	RN	
*See text for piston measuring point.		

Table 4 ENGINE TOP END TORQUE SPECIFICATIONS

	N•m	in.-lb.	ft.-lb.
Air filter housing stay mounting bolt	13	115	–
Breather cover mounting bolts	12	106	–
Cam chain tensioner mounting bolts	10	88	–
Cam sprocket bolts[1]	23	–	17
Camshaft end holder bolts	10	88	–
Camshaft holder			
8-mm bolts	23	–	17
8-mm nuts	23	–	17
Cylinder head cover bolts	10	88	–
Cylinder head fasteners[2, 3]			
6-mm bolt	12	106	–
8-mm boit	23	–	17
10-mm nut	47	–	35
Cylinder head fin Allen bolts	10	88	–
EVAP air injection reed valve cover bolt	5	44	–

1. Apply a medium strength threadlock to bolt threads.
2. Lubricate fastener threads and flange surfaces with engine oil.
3. Refer to text procedure.

CHAPTER FIVE

ENGINE LOWER END

This chapter provides service procedures for lower end components. These include the crankcase, crankshaft, connecting rods and oil pump. This chapter also includes removal and installation procedures for the transmission and internal shift mechanism assemblies. However, service procedures for these components are described in Chapter Seven.

References to the left and right sides refer to the position of the parts as viewed by the rider sitting on the seat facing forward, not how the engine may sit on the workbench.

Refer to **Tables 1-6** at the end of this chapter for specifications and bearing selection information.

SHOP CLEANLINESS

Before removing and disassembling the engine, clean the engine and frame with a degreaser. The disassembly job is easier and there is a lower chance of dirt entering the assemblies. Keep the work environment as clean as possible. Store parts and assemblies in well-marked plastic bags and containers. Keep reconditioned parts wrapped until they are installed.

CAUTION
Do not allow the degreaser to contact the O-ring drive chain because it causes the O-rings to swell, permanently damaging the chain. Cover the O-ring chain before cleaning the motorcycle.

SERVICING ENGINE IN FRAME

The frame is an excellent holding fixture, especially for breaking loose stubborn bolts and nuts.

1. The following components can be serviced with the engine mounted in the frame:
   a. Alternator and starter clutch.
   b. Camshafts.
   c. Carburetors.
   d. Clutch, primary drive and external shift linkage.
   e. Front cylinder head and cylinder on VT750C models.
   f. Ignition pulse generator.
   g. Starter.
2. The following components require engine removal for service:

a. On VT750C models, the rear cylinder head, cylinder and piston.

b. On VT750DC models, the front and rear cylinder heads, cylinders and pistons.

c. Crankshaft and connecting rods.

d. Oil pump.

e. Transmission and internal shift mechanism.

f. Water pump.

ENGINE

Tools

1. The Honda pivot locknut wrench is required to loosen the swing arm adjusting bolt locknut. The tool is also required to tighten the locknut to the torque specification during installation. Refer to *Rear Swing Arm* in Chapter Thirteen for information on this tool.

2. Because the swing arm pivot shaft passes through the engine, it is helpful to control both the swing arm and frame with separate jacks when removing the engine (which requires a separate jack also). This section shows engine removal and installation using three jacks.

Removal

This procedure describes the steps to remove the complete engine assembly. If desired, remove the sub-assemblies attached to the crankcase while the engine is still in the frame.

1. Support the bike securely.

2. If possible, perform a compression test (Chapter Three) and leakdown test (Chapter Two) before dismantling the engine.

3. Drain the engine oil and remove the oil filter (Chapter Three).

4. Drain the coolant (Chapter Three).

5. Remove the engine side covers (Chapter Fifteen).

6. Disconnect the negative battery cable (Chapter Nine).

7. Remove the fuel tank (Chapter Eight).

8. On VT750C models, remove the steering covers (Chapter Fifteen).

9. Remove the exhaust system (Chapter Fifteen).

10. Remove the air box and carburetors (Chapter Eight).

11. Remove the sub-air filter (Chapter Eight).

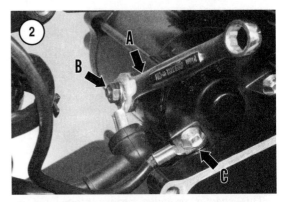

12. Disconnect the coolant hose from the cylinder head water pipes. Then remove the bolt, water pipe and O-ring from each cylinder head (**Figure 1**).

13. If the engine is going to be removed with the cylinder head covers installed on the engine, remove the following as described in Chapter Four under *Cylinder Head Covers*:

a. Crankcase breather cover.

b. Outer covers.

c. Cylinder cooling fins.

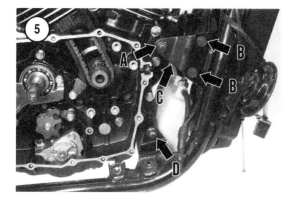

14A. On VT750C models, remove the right footpeg and rear brake pedal assembly.

14B. On VT750DC models, remove the shift pedal and brake rod assembly.

15. Disconnect the clutch cable from the engine (Chapter Six).

16. Remove the engine sprocket and drive chain (Chapter Eleven).

17. Disconnect the spark plug caps.

18. Disconnect the starter cable as follows:

   a. Hold the inner nut with a wrench (A, **Figure 2**) and remove the outer nut (B) to disconnect the cable.

   b. Holding the inner nut prevents the terminal bolt from turning and damaging the insulator installed on the inside of the starter.

19. Disconnect the following electrical connectors:

NOTE
Use tape and a marking pen to identify the position of any clamps or guides used to route and secure connectors and wires before disconnecting them.

   a. Engine ground cable (C, **Figure 2**).

   b. Oil pressure connector.

   c. Neutral switch connector.

   d. Sidestand switch connector.

   e. Alternator connector.

   f. Ignition pulse generator connector.

20A. On VT750C models, disconnect the lower radiator hose at the radiator or disconnect the hose at the water pump (**Figure 3**).

20B. On VT750DC models, perform the following:

   a. Remove the thermostat housing (Chapter Ten).

   b. Disconnect the lower hose at the water pump (**Figure 3**).

21. If the engine requires disassembly, remove the following sub-assemblies:

   a. Alternator (Chapter Nine).

   b. Starter (Chapter Nine).

   c. Clutch (Chapter Six).

   d. Primary drive gear (Chapter Six).

   e. External shift mechanism (Chapter Six).

22. Move all electrical wires, harnesses and hoses out of the way. Disconnect any electrical connector or hose that could interfere with engine removal.

23. Wrap the right side of the frame with pieces of rubber cut from an old inner tube. Secure these with plastic tie wraps. These protect the frame from scratches when removing and installing the engine.

24. Place a floor jack (A, **Figure 4**) underneath the engine. Place a thick wooden block on the jack to protect the engine. Adjust this jack as required to relieve pressure on the engine when removing the engine mounting bolts in the following steps.

25. Support the rear center frame member (B, **Figure 4**) and swing arm (C) with separate jacks.

NOTE
Identify the collars when removing them in the following steps.

26. On the engine front upper mounting bracket, perform the following:

   a. Remove the engine front upper mounting nut (A, **Figure 5**), bolt and collar.

   b. Remove the engine front bracket bolts (B, **Figure 5**) and bracket (C).

27. Remove the engine lower mounting nut (D, **Figure 5**), bolt and two collars.

28. Remove the engine rear mounting nut (**Figure 6**) and bolt.

29. Remove the engine rear bracket bolts (A, **Figure 7**) and bracket (B).

30. Remove the rear swing arm pivot shaft:

    a. Remove the swing arm pivot shaft covers.

    b. Remove the pivot shaft nut (A, **Figure 8**).

    c. Hold the pivot shaft with an 8-mm hex socket (A, **Figure 9**), then loosen and remove the pivot shaft locknut with the special tool (B).

NOTE
Make sure the jack is positioned correctly against the engine. Adjust the jack used at the frame and swing as required to maintain alignment of these components when removing the pivot shaft in the next step.

NOTE
When the pivot shaft is removed, the swing arm loosens.

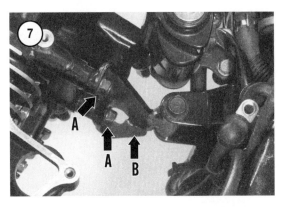

    d. Turn the pivot shaft (**Figure 10**) to loosen the swing arm adjusting bolt. Continue until the adjusting bolt (A, **Figure 11**) is positioned flush with the inside of the frame. Then remove the pivot shaft from the engine.

WARNING
Remove the engine with the help of one or more assistants.

31. Remove the engine from the right side.

32. Push the pivot shaft back through the frame and swing arm.

33. Clean and inspect the frame and all exposed hardware, hoses and wiring. Check for cracks and damage, particularly at welded joints.

Installation

Installation is the reverse of removal. Follow the installation and tightening sequence described. Do not tighten any of the engine mounting fasteners until they all have been installed.

1. Spray the engine bolts with a rust inhibitor. Do not lubricate the bolt threads.

2. Secure the frame and swing arm with separate jacks (**Figure 12**) and adjust them so the pivot shaft can be removed and installed without force.

3. Remove the swing arm adjusting bolt (A, **Figure 13**) from the frame. Clean the pivot shaft locknut, adjusting bolt and frame threads of all grease and

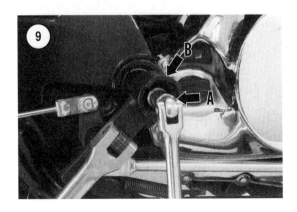

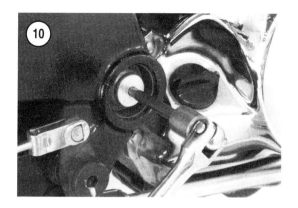

5

oil. These threads must clean and dry when the pivot shaft assembly is tightened.

4. Reinstall the swing arm adjusting bolt (A, **Figure 13**) so it does not extend past the inside of the frame bore.

5. Route the drive chain around the swing arm (B, **Figure 13**).

6. Make sure the collar (C, **Figure 13**) is installed through the left side of the swing arm and contacts the frame.

7. Check the swing arm alignment with the frame.

> *NOTE*
> *Make sure the water pump is installed on the engine. The water pump cannot be installed with the engine installed in the frame.*

8. Lubricate the pivot shaft with grease.

9. Position the engine into the frame and align the frame, swing arm and engine pivot shaft holes. Support the engine with the jack.

10. Install the pivot shaft (B, **Figure 11**) through the adjusting bolt, frame and engine from the right side. Turn the pivot shaft until its hex shoulder engages with and seats flush against the swing arm adjusting bolt socket bore. **Figure 14** shows proper installation.

> *NOTE*
> *The threads on the swing arm pivot shaft, pivot shaft adjusting bolt and all engine mounting fasteners must be free of oil when tightened. Refer to **Swing Arm Installation** in Chapter Thirteen.*

11. Install the pivot shaft locknut and tighten the pivot shaft assembly as described in Chapter Thirteen under *Swing Arm Installation*.

12. Install the engine rear bracket (B, **Figure 7**) and bolts (A). Tighten the bolts fingertight.

13. Install the engine rear mounting bolt (from the left side) and nut (**Figure 6**). Tighten the nut fingertight.

14. Install the two collars, the engine front lower mounting bolt (from the left side) and nut (D, **Figure 5**). Tighten the nut fingertight.

15. Install the engine front upper mounting bracket as follows:

   a. Install the bracket (C, **Figure 5**) and the bracket bolts (B).

   b. Install the collar, the engine front upper mounting bolt (from the left side) and nut (A, **Figure 5**). Tighten the nut fingertight.

16. Tighten the engine fasteners in the following order:

   a. Engine front upper mounting nut (A, **Figure 5**): 54 N•m (40 ft.-lb.).

   b. Engine front lower mounting nut (D, **Figure 5**): 54 N•m (40 ft.-lb.).

   c. Engine rear mounting nut (**Figure 6**): 54 N•m (40 ft.-lb.).

   d. Engine front bracket bolts (B, **Figure 5**): 26 N•m (20 ft.-lb.).

   e. Engine rear bracket bolts (A, **Figure 7**): 26 N•m (20 ft.-lb.).

17. Assemble the engine by reversing Steps 3-22 of engine removal. Note the following:

   a. Fill the engine with the recommended type and quantity of engine oil and coolant, as described in Chapter Three.

   b. Adjust the drive chain as described in Chapter Three.

   c. Check throttle operation.

   d. If the engine top-end was rebuilt, perform a compression check. Record the results for future reference.

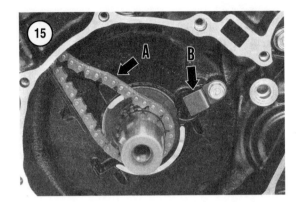

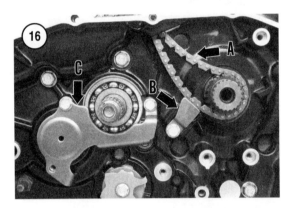

CRANKCASE

The following procedures detail the disassembly and reassembly of the crankcase. When the two halves of the crankcase are disassembled or split, the crankshaft, transmission and oil pump can be removed for inspection and repair.

The crankcase is made in two halves of precision die cast aluminum alloy. To avoid damage, do not hammer or pry on any of the interior or exterior projected walls. These areas are easily damaged. The cases are split vertically down the centerline of the connecting rods. The crankcase is assembled without a gasket; only gasket sealer is used. Dowel pins align the crankcase halves where they are bolted together. The crankcase halves are sold separately and select fitted to the crankshaft.

Tools

The tool requirements vary depending on the type of work to be performed. The engine can be disas-

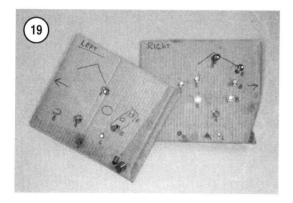

sembled and the crankshaft removed and installed without special tools. Special tools are required when replacing the crankcase bearings.

To protect the cases during the service procedures, support them on wooden blocks and thick pieces of rubber (old car floor mats) placed across the workbench.

Disassembly

As components are removed, keep each part/assembly separated from the other components. Keep seals and O-rings oriented with their respective parts to help with inspection, new parts identification and reassembly.

Remember that the right and left side of the engine relates to the engine as it sits in the frame, not as it may sit on the workbench.

1. Remove the engine from the frame as described in this chapter.

2. Remove all engine assemblies as described in this chapter and other related chapters.

3. Remove the countershaft seal plate (B, **Figure 8**).

4. Remove the front (A, **Figure 15**) and rear (A, **Figure 16**) cam chains.

NOTE
Do not remove the cam chain set plates (B, Figure 15 and B, Figure 16) unless necessary.

5. Remove the mainshaft bearing set plate (C, **Figure 16**).

6. If the cam plate was not removed, shift the transmission to align the cam plate with the crankcase half as shown in **Figure 17**.

CAUTION
The cam plate position must be maintained during crankcase separation; otherwise, the cam plate will damage the crankcase half.

7. Place the engine on wooden blocks with the left side facing up (**Figure 18**).

NOTE
To ensure the crankcase bolts are correctly located during assembly, make an outline of the left and right crankcase shapes on a piece of cardboard. Punch holes in the cardboard at the same locations as the bolts. As each bolt is removed from the crankcase, place the bolt in its respective hole. See Figure 19.

8. Perform the following at the left crankcase (**Figure 18**):

   a. Loosen and remove the 6-mm bolts (A, **Figure 18**).

   b. Working in a crossing pattern, loosen the 8-mm bolts (B, **Figure 18**) in several steps, then remove them.

9. Turn the engine over with the right side (**Figure 20**) facing up. Perform the following:

   a. Loosen and remove the 6-mm bolts (A, **Figure 20**).

   b. Working in a crossing pattern, loosen the 8-mm bolts (B, **Figure 20**) in several steps, then remove them.

10. Remove the right crankcase half from the left crankcase as follows:

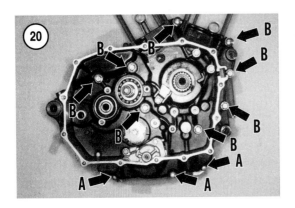

CAUTION
*During crankcase separation, check that the cam plate is aligned with the crankcase half (**Figure 17**).*

CAUTION
Do not hammer or pry on areas of the engine cases that are not reinforced. Never pry between case halves. Doing so may cause oil leaks, requiring replacement of the crankcase.

a. Locate the tabbed pry points around the mating surfaces of the crankcase. The tabs are cast into the case.

b. Using a soft mallet, alternately tap on the ends of the transmission shafts, shift drum and crankshaft, while carefully prying in small increments at the *pry* points. Work slowly and separate the halves equally. Do not allow the halves to bind. If binding occurs, reseat the halves and start again.

c. Slowly raise and remove the right crankcase (**Figure 20**).

d. Locate the outer washer installed on the countershaft (A, **Figure 21**). Reinstall it if it came off with the right crankcase.

e. Remove the two dowel pins (B, **Figure 21**).

11. Remove the oil pump as follows:

a. Remove the bolt (C, **Figure 21**) and relief pipe (D).

b. Remove the oil relief valve and O-ring (**Figure 22**).

c. Remove the two bolts (A, **Figure 23**) and the oil pump (B). Store and seal the oil pump in a plastic bag.

d. Remove the two collars and O-rings (A, **Figure 24**) and dowel pin (B).

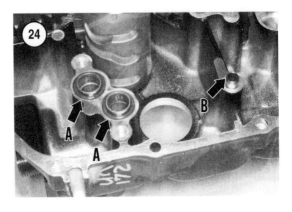

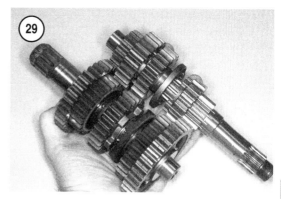

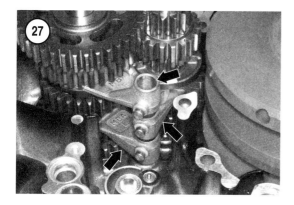

e. Locate the two external seals (**Figure 25**) installed on the oil pipe. Reinstall them back onto the pipe if they came off with either crankcase half.

12. Remove the transmission assembly from the left case half as follows:

NOTE
If the engine was experiencing shifting problems, examine the transmission assembly before removing it. Look for excessive wear or damaged parts. Spin the countershaft and turn the shift drum by hand to shift the transmission. Check the movement and operation of each shift fork and sliding gear. Look for hard shifting and incomplete gear dog engagement. Check also for seized gears and bushings.

NOTE
When removing the transmission, the gears on both ends of the countershaft are not secured with snap rings and can slide off. Hold these lower gears as the transmission is removed.

a. Remove the shift fork shaft (A, **Figure 26**).
b. Pivot the shift forks away from the shift drum and remove the shift drum (B, **Figure 26**).
c. Remove the shift forks (**Figure 27**).

NOTE
*The countershaft and mainshaft (**Figure 28**) are removed at the same time.*

d. Hold the crankcase upright, then tap the end of the countershaft and remove both transmission shafts (**Figure 29**).

    e. Service the transmission as described in Chapter Seven.

13. Lift and remove the crankshaft (**Figure 30**) from the case half.

> *CAUTION*
> *Use extreme care when servicing the crankshaft. Store the crankshaft in a manner that eliminates exposure to dirt and impact damage. Place the crankshaft on the workbench so it cannot roll off. If the crankshaft is damaged due to impact, it may affect the alignment and require service.*

14. Inspect the crankcase, crankshaft, connecting rods and oil pump as described in this chapter.

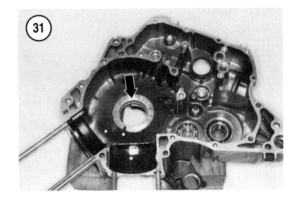

Inspection

1. Remove all sealer residue from the gasket surfaces.
2. Remove the oil seals as described in this chapter.
3. Clean the crankcase halves with solvent.
4. Using clean solvent, flush each bearing.
5. Dry the case halves with compressed air.

> *WARNING*
> *When drying a bearing with compressed air, do not allow the inner bearing race to rotate. The air can spin the bearing at excessive speed, possibly causing the bearing to destruct.*

6. Blow through each oil passage with compressed air.
7. Lightly oil the engine bearings before inspecting their conditions. A dry bearing exhibits more sound and looseness than a properly lubricated bearing.
8. Inspect the bearings for roughness, pitting, galling and play. Replace any bearing that is not in good condition. Always replace the opposite bearing at the same time. When inspecting the clutch push lever bearing, insert the push lever into the bearing and check for roughness. Refer to this chapter for bearing replacement.
9. Inspect the cases for fractures around all mounting and bearing bosses, stiffening ribs and threaded holes. If repair is required, have a dealership or machine shop that is experienced in the repairs of precision aluminum castings inspect the crankcase.

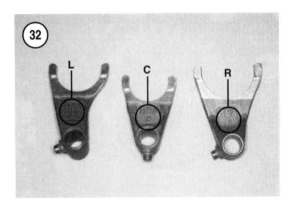

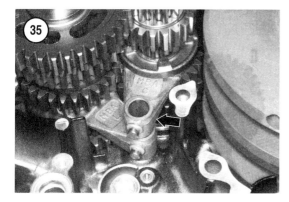

10. Check all threaded holes for damage or buildup. Clean threads with the correct size metric tap. Lubricate the tap with kerosene or aluminum tap fluid.

11. Retighten or replace the cylinder studs. Refer to *Cylinder Stud Replacement* in Chapter Four.

Assembly

1. Before assembly:
   a. Make sure all new O-rings, seals and sealant are on hand. Lubricate all O-rings with engine oil as they are installed.
   b. Grease the lip of each seal to prevent damage to the seals.
   c. Lubricate all surfaces of the transmission assembly and the crankshaft assembly with engine oil. Apply engine oil to all bearings.

2. Support the left crankcase half on wooden blocks.

3. Lubricate the main bearing surfaces (**Figure 31**) with molybdenum disulfide grease.

4. Carefully install the crankshaft into the left crankcase so the tapered (flywheel) end faces the left crankcase. Position the connecting rods into their respective cylinder openings at the same time. See **Figure 30**.

5. Install the transmission as follows:
   a. Lubricate all rotating and sliding surfaces with engine oil.
   b. Mesh the two shafts together (**Figure 29**) and install them into the left crankcase (**Figure 28**).

6. Install the shift forks, shift drum and shift shaft as follows:
   a. Each shift fork can be identified by its letter mark (**Figure 32**)—L (left shift fork), C (center shift fork) and R (right shift fork). Install the shift forks with these marks facing up (toward the right crankcase half).
   b. Lift the mainshaft fourth gear (A, **Figure 33**) and the countershaft fifth gear (B) and install the L shift fork (**Figure 34**) into the countershaft fifth gear groove.
   c. Install the C shift fork (**Figure 35**) into the mainshaft fourth gear groove.
   d. Install the R shift fork (**Figure 36**) into the countershaft third gear groove.
   e. Pivot the shift forks so that they do not contact the shift drum, then install the shift drum (**Figure 37**).

5

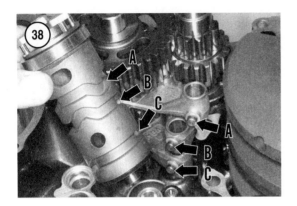

f. Pivot the shift forks so the pins on the shift
   forks properly engage the grooves in the shift
   drum. Match the callout letters in **Figure 38**
   to identify the shift forks with their proper
   shift drum groove.

g. Install the shift fork shaft—shoulder end facing up—through the three shift forks (**Figure
   39**). When properly installed, the shaft bottoms solidly against the left crankcase.

h. Spin the transmission shafts and turn the shift
   drum by hand to check transmission operation.
   Check that each fork travels through its operating groove in the shift drum and bottoms
   against both ends. Observe the shift forks as the
   transmission is shifted into the different gears.

> *NOTE*
> *It is difficult to identify the different
> gear positions when turning the shift
> drum without the stopper lever in-
> stalled on the engine. Substep h does
> show whether the shift forks can move
> through their complete operational
> range.*

7. Install the oil pump as follows:

   a. If a new oil pump is being installed or the ex-
      isting oil pump was cleaned in solvent, the oil
      pump must be primed. Pour fresh engine oil
      into one of the openings in the oil pump. Ro-
      tate the pump shaft several times by hand to
      make sure the rotors are coated with oil.

   b. Install the O-rings, oil strainer and oil pipe
      onto the oil pump (**Figure 40**) as described
      under *Oil Pump* in this chapter.

   c. Install the dowel pin (A, **Figure 41**).

   d. Lubricate two new O-rings with engine oil.
      Install the collars and O-rings (B, **Figure 41**).

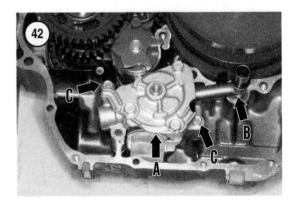

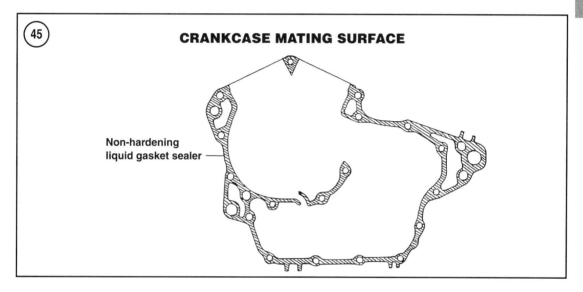

CRANKCASE MATING SURFACE

Non-hardening
liquid gasket sealer

e. Install the oil pump (A, **Figure 42**) over the dowel pin and collars, while inserting the oil pipe (B) into the crankcase.

f. Install the oil pump mounting bolts (C, **Figure 42**) and tighten securely.

g. Lubricate the O-ring on the pressure relief valve with engine oil. Then install the valve (**Figure 43**) into the pump.

h. Install the oil relief pipe (A, **Figure 44**) and tighten the mounting bolt (B) securely.

8. Clean the crankcase mating surfaces with an aerosol electrical contact cleaner. Allow the cleaner to evaporate before applying gasket sealant.

9. Clean the two dowel pins, then install them into the left crankcase (C, **Figure 44**).

10. Make sure the washer (D, **Figure 44**) is installed on the countershaft.

11. Apply a nonhardening, liquid gasket sealant to the right and left crankcase mating surfaces as shown in **Figure 45**. Observe the sealant manufac-

turer's instructions. Do not get any on the bearings or in the oil passageways.

NOTE
Some acceptable sealants are ThreeBond Liquid Gasket 1104 and Yamabond 4 (part No. ACC-YAMAB-ON-D4). Many sealants have a shelf life of one year, starting when a new tube is first opened. For best results, date the tube to avoid using old sealant.

12. Make sure the connecting rods are positioned as shown in **Figure 30**.

13. Install the right crankcase onto the left crankcase. Make sure there are no gaps between the crankcase halves.

CAUTION
Throughout the tightening process, occasionally turn the crankshaft and countershaft. If there is any binding,

stop. *Take the crankcase apart and find the trouble. Usually it is an incorrectly installed gear or an incorrectly installed dowel pin.*

14. Install the right crankcase 8-mm and 6-mm mounting bolts. Tighten the 8-mm bolts (A, **Figure 46**) in a crossing pattern and in two steps to 23 N•m (17 ft.-lb.). Tighten the 6-mm bolts (B, **Figure 46**) securely.

15. Install the left crankcase 8-mm and 6-mm mounting bolts. Tighten the 8-mm bolts (A, **Figure 47**) in a crossing pattern and in two steps to 23 N•m (17 ft.-lb.). Tighten the 6-mm bolts (B, **Figure 47**) securely.

16. Turn the crankshaft and both transmission shafts. If there is binding, separate the cases to determine the cause.

17. Check the transmission for proper shifting as follows:

   a. Install the stopper lever assembly as shown in A, **Figure 48**.

   b. Turn the cam plate (B, **Figure 48**) while turning the mainshaft and align its raised ramp with the stopper lever roller (C). This is the transmission's *neutral* position. The mainshaft and countershaft should turn freely of one another.

   c. Turn the mainshaft while turning the cam plate *counterclockwise*. Stop when the stopper lever seats between the ramps of the shift drum stopper. The transmission is in first gear. The mainshaft and countershaft should be meshed together.

   d. Turn the shift drum stopper *clockwise*. Turn the cam plate past neutral, then place the stopper lever between the ramps to check the remaining gears for proper engagement. The mainshaft and countershaft should mesh (turn together) whenever the transmission is in gear.

   e. Remove the shift drum stopper and stopper lever when the check is completed. If the transmission did not engage properly, disassemble the crankcase and inspect the transmission for proper assembly or damaged parts.

18. Apply a medium strength threadlock onto the mainshaft bearing set plate mounting bolt threads. Install the set plate (A, **Figure 49**) and tighten the bolts securely.

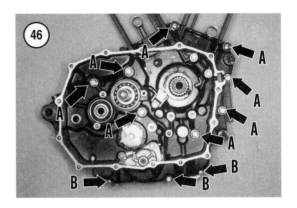

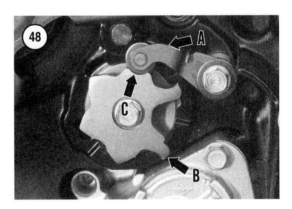

19. Install the front and rear cam chains (B, **Figure 49**).

20. If a cam chain set plate (C, **Figure 49**) was removed, apply a medium strength threadlock onto the bolt threads. Install the set plate and tighten the bolt securely.

21. Apply a medium strength threadlock onto the countershaft oil seal plate mounting bolts. Install the plate and tighten the bolts securely.

22. Reverse Step 1 and Step 2 under *Disassembly* to complete installation.

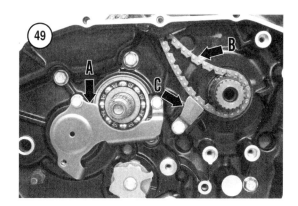

CRANKCASE SEAL AND BEARING REPLACEMENT

Refer to Chapter One for general bearing removal and installation techniques.

Refer to this section for removal and installation techniques unique to this engine.

Seal Replacement

When servicing the crankcase halves, replace the countershaft and shift shaft seals (**Figure 50**).

CAUTION
Do not allow the pry tool to contact the seal bore when removing the seal. It may gouge the bore and cause the new seal to leak.

1. Pry out the old seal with a seal puller, wide-blade screwdriver or tire iron (**Figure 51**). Place a folded shop cloth under the tool to prevent damage to the case.
2. If a new bearing will be installed, replace the bearing before installing the new seal.
3. Clean the seal bore. Sand or file any raised grooves in the bore surface and clean thoroughly.
4. Pack grease into the lip of the new seal.
5. Place the seal in the bore, with the closed side of the seal facing out. The seal must be square to the bore.
6. Install the new seal with a seal driver until its outer edge is even with the top of the bore.

CAUTION
When driving seals, the driver must fit at the perimeter of the seal. If the driver presses toward the center of the seal, the seal can distort and the internal garter spring can become dislodged, causing the seal to leak.

Bearing Replacement

This section covers the transmission bearings installed in both crankcase halves. Refer to *Crankshaft* in this chapter for the crankshaft main bearings installed in both crankcase halves.

1. When replacing crankcase bearings, note the following:
   a. Identify and record the size code of each bearing before it is removed from the case. This eliminates confusion when installing the bearings in their correct bores.
   b. Record the orientation of each bearing in its bore. Note if the size code faces toward the inside or outside of the case.
   c. Use a hydraulic press or a set of bearing drivers to remove and install bearings. Bearings can also be removed and installed using heat, as described in Chapter One.
   d. Bearings that are only accessible from one side of the case are removed with a blind bearing puller. The puller is fitted through the bearing, then expanded to grip the back-side of the bearing (**Figure 52**).

5

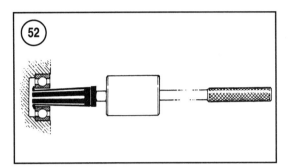

2. The following identifies the *left* crankcase bearings.

    a. Countershaft bearing (A, **Figure 53**).

    b. Mainshaft bearing (B, **Figure 53**).

3. The following identifies the *right* crankcase bearings.

    a. Countershaft bearing (A, **Figure 54**).

    b. Mainshaft bearing (B, **Figure 54**).

CRANKSHAFT

Removal/Installation

Remove and install the crankshaft as described under *Crankcase* in this chapter.

Inspection

Carefully handle the crankshaft assembly during inspection.

1. Clean the crankshaft and connecting rods thoroughly with solvent. Clean the crankshaft oil passageways with compressed air. Dry the crankshaft with compressed air, then lubricate all bearing surfaces with a light coat of engine oil.

2. Inspect each crankshaft main journal (**Figure 55**) for scratches, ridges, scoring, nicks or heat discoloration. Very small nicks and scratches may be removed with crocus cloth. Anything more serious must be referred to a machine shop.

3. To determine main journal wear, perform the *Main Bearing Inspection* in this section.

4. Inspect the crankshaft splines, flywheel taper and drive gears for damage.

5. Measure crankshaft runout with the crankshaft mounted on a set of V-blocks. Rotate the crankshaft two full turns with a dial gauge contacting the left main bearing journal at the distance indicated in

Figure 56. If the runout exceeds the service limit in **Table 1**, replace the crankshaft.

Main Bearing Inspection

The crankcase is equipped with insert-type main bearings (A, **Figure 57**) in each crankcase half. The main bearing inserts cannot be replaced. If excessively worn or damaged, the crankcase half must be replaced. Do not remove the inserts when inspecting them in the following steps.

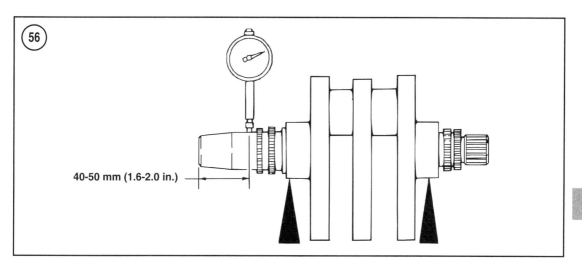

40-50 mm (1.6-2.0 in.)

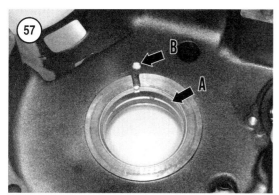

a. Measure the inside diameter of the bearing insert with a bore gauge or inside micrometer (**Figure 58**).

b. Measure the crankshaft main bearing journal outside diameter with a micrometer (**Figure 59**).

c. Subtract the main bearing journal outside diameter from the bearing insert inside diameter to determine the main journal oil clearance. If the main bearing journal oil clearance exceeds the service limit in **Table 1**, replace the crankcase.

Crankcase and Crankshaft Selection

The crankcase and crankshaft are select fitted. A letter stamped on the inside of each crankcase half (B, **Figure 57**) is the size code for the main bearing inside diameter. A number stamped on each crankshaft web (**Figure 60**) is the size code for the main bearing journal outside diameter. If a code on either

1. Inspect the inside surface of each bearing insert (A, **Figure 57**) for excessive wear, bluish or burned appearance, flaking and scoring. If the insert is questionable, replace the crankcase half.

2. Clean the crankshaft main bearing journal (**Figure 55**) and crankcase bearing insert (A, **Figure 57**) surfaces.

3. Measure the main bearing clearance by performing the following steps:

part is undecipherable, refer selection to a Honda dealership.

1. Record the main journal outside diameter code number (1 or 2) on the crankshaft web (**Figure 60**).

2. Record the main journal bearing inside diameter code (A or B) on the crankcase half (B, **Figure 57**).

3. Refer to **Table 2** to cross-reference the codes. Where a YES is indicated in the table, a match is made.

CONNECTING RODS

Removal/Installation

1. Separate the crankcase and remove the crankshaft assembly as described under *Crankcase* in this chapter.

2. Measure the connecting rod side clearance with a feeler gauge between the connecting rod and crankshaft machined surfaces (**Figure 61**). Compare to the connecting rod side clearance service limit in **Table 1**. Measure each connecting rod. If the measurement is out of specification, replace the connecting rod as described in this section. Recheck the clearance with the new rod.

3. Remove the nuts securing the connecting rod caps and remove the caps (**Figure 62**).

4. Carefully remove the connecting rod from the crankshaft. Mark the rod, bearing and cap to show its correct cylinder and crankpin position for reassembly (**Figure 63**).

5. Remove and identify each bearing insert (**Figure 64**) as to its upper or lower position.

6. Clean these parts and the crankshaft in solvent and dry with compressed air.

7. Inspect the connecting rods and bearings as described in this section.

8. If new bearing inserts are being installed, check the bearing clearance as described in this chapter.

9. Wipe off any oil from the bearing inserts, connecting rod and cap contact surfaces. No lint or debris should be on the contact surfaces when installing the inserts.

10. Install the bearing inserts into each connecting rod and cap (**Figure 64**). Make sure they are locked in place correctly (**Figure 65**).

CAUTION
If the old bearing inserts are reused,
they must be installed in their original

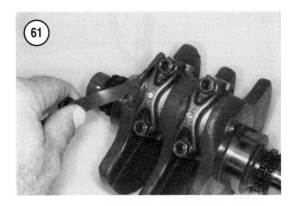

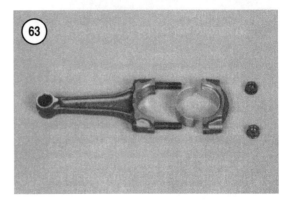

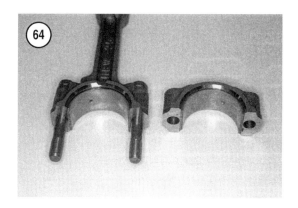

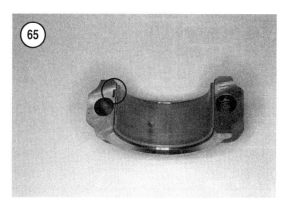

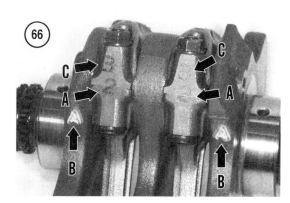

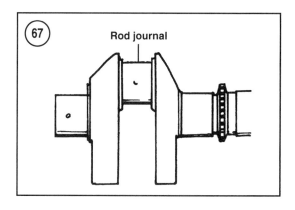

Rod journal

positions (Step 4 and Step 5); other-wise, engine damage may occur.

11. Apply molybdenum disulfide grease to the bearing inserts and crank pin bearing thrust surfaces.

12. Install the connecting rod onto the crankshaft so it is facing in its original position, as noted during Step 4.

13. Match the code number on the end of the cap with the mark on the rod (A, **Figure 66**) and install the cap.

CAUTION
The fine threads used on the connecting rod studs and cap nuts are easily damaged. Start the nuts carefully by hand.

14. Lubricate the bearing cap nut threads and seating surfaces with engine oil and install the cap nuts (**Figure 62**). Tighten the cap nuts in several steps to 33 N•m (24 ft.-lb.).

15. Rotate the connecting rod several times to check there is no binding or roughness.

16. Repeat for the other connecting rod.

Connecting Rod Inspection

1. Remove and identify the connecting rods from the crankshaft as described in this section.

2. Clean the connecting rods and inserts in solvent and dry with compressed air.

3. Carefully inspect each rod journal on the crankshaft for scratches, ridges, scoring and other damage.

4. Inspect each bearing insert (**Figure 64**) for evidence of wear, abrasion and scoring. They are reusable if in good condition.

5. Measure the rod journal (**Figure 67**) with a micrometer and check for out-of-roundness and taper.

6. Check each connecting rod big end for signs of seizure, bearing or connecting rod damage.

7. Check each connecting rod small end (**Figure 68**) for signs of excessive heat (blue coloration) or other damage.

8. Measure the inside diameter of the small end of the connecting rod with an inside micrometer or small hole gauge. Replace the connecting rod if the small end inside diameter exceeds the service limit specified in **Table 1**.

9. If all of the parts are within specification and do not show any type of visible damage, check the connecting rod bearing clearance as described in this section.

Connecting Rod Bearing

Clearance measurement

1. Clean any oil from the bearing insert and crankpin surfaces.
2. Place a strip of Plastigage (**Figure 68**) over each rod bearing journal parallel to the crankshaft as shown in **Figure 69**. Do not place the Plastigage material over an oil hole in the crankshaft.

> *NOTE*
> *Do not rotate the connecting rod on the crankshaft while the Plastigage strips are in place.*

3. Install the bearing inserts into each connecting rod and cap. Make sure they are locked in place correctly (**Figure 65**).

> *NOTE*
> *Make sure the bearing inserts are installed in their original mounting positions.*

4. Install the connecting rod onto the crankshaft so it is facing in its original position.
5. Match the code number on the end of the cap with the mark on the rod (A, **Figure 66**) and install the cap.
6. Lubricate the bearing cap nut threads and seating surfaces with engine oil and install the cap nuts (**Figure 62**). Tighten the cap nuts in several steps to 33 N•m (24 ft.-lb.).
7. Remove the rod cap nuts and rod cap.
8. Measure the width of the flattened Plastigage (**Figure 69**) following the manufacturer's instructions. Measure both ends of the Plastigage strip.
   a. A difference of 0.025 mm (0.001 in.) or more indicates a tapered journal. Confirm the measurement using a micrometer.
   b. If the connecting rod bearing clearance exceeds the service limit in **Table 1**, select new bearings as described in this section.
9. Remove all of the Plastigage material from the crankshaft journals and connecting rod caps.

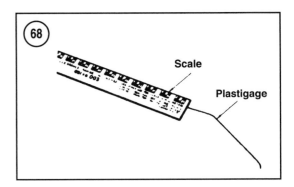

Scale

Plastigage

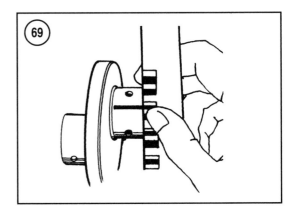

10. If the bearing clearance is greater than specified, go to the next section to select the new bearings.

Selection

A code number stamped on the side of each connecting rod and cap (A, **Figure 66**) is used to identify the connecting rod inside diameter. Half of the number is stamped on the rod and the other half is stamped on the cap. A code letter stamped on each crankshaft web (B, **Figure 66**) is used to identify the rod journal outside diameter.

> *NOTE*
> *If a code on either part is undecipherable, refer selection to a Honda dealership.*

1. Measure the rod journal outside diameter (**Figure 67**) with a micrometer. If the measurement is within the tolerances stated for each rod journal outside diameter code letter in **Table 3**, the new bearing can be selected by color code; continue with Step 2. If a dimension exceeds the tolerances in **Ta-**

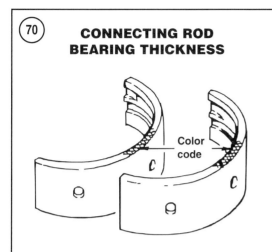

CONNECTING ROD BEARING THICKNESS

Color code

Code letter	Color code	Beraing insert thickness
A	Blu	1.495-1.499 mm (0.0589-0.0590 in.)
B	Blk	1.491-1.495 mm (0.0587-0.0589 in.)
C	Brn	1.487-1.491 mm (0.0585-0.0587 in.)

ble 3, the crankshaft is worn and should be referred to a Honda dealership for further inspection.

2. Record the connecting rod inside diameter code number (1 or 2) on the rod and cap (A, **Figure 66**).

3. Record the rod journal outside diameter code letter (A or B) on the crankshaft web (B, **Figure 66**).

4. Select new bearings by cross-referencing the journal outside diameter code letter (B, **Figure 66**) in the horizontal column of **Table 3** to the connecting rod inside diameter code number (A, **Figure 66**) in the vertical column. Where the two columns intersect, the new bearing insert color is indicated.

Figure 70 identifies the different bearing colors and thicknesses.

5. After installing the new bearing inserts, recheck the bearing clearance as described in this section.

Connecting Rod and Crankshaft Selection

The connecting rods are matched to the crankshaft according to the weight of the connecting rod. A code letter stamped on the side of each connecting rod cap (C, **Figure 66**) is used to identify the connecting rod weight. A code letter stamped on the side of each crankshaft weight (**Figure 71**) is used to identify the crankshaft weight.

When replacing a connecting rod, replace it with the same weight code found on the original rod (C, **Figure 66**). If the same weight code is unavailable, perform the following:

1. To select replacement connecting rods:

   a. Record the connecting rod weight code (A, B or C) on each rod cap (C, **Figure 66**).

   b. Select a new connecting rod by cross-referencing the connecting rod code letters (A, **Figure 66**) in the vertical and horizontal columns of **Table 4**. Where the two columns intersect with a 0 mark, a match is made.

2. To select a replacement crankshaft weight, note the following:

   a. Select a L crankshaft weight if the front and rear connecting rods are marked with code A (*) in **Table 4**.

   b. Select a R crankshaft weight if the front and rear connecting rods are marked with Code C (**) in **Table 4**.

   c. Select a no code crankshaft weight when the two previous examples are not present in **Table 4**.

OIL PUMP

Removal/Installation

Remove and install the oil pump as described under *Crankcase* in this chapter.

Disassembly

Refer to **Figure 72**.

1. Remove the oil pipe, O-ring and seals (A, **Figure 73**).

5

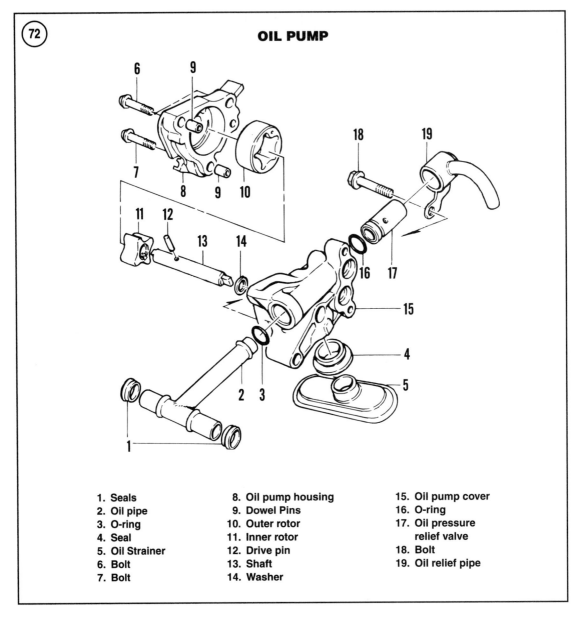

OIL PUMP

72

1. Seals
2. Oil pipe
3. O-ring
4. Seal
5. Oil Strainer
6. Bolt
7. Bolt
8. Oil pump housing
9. Dowel Pins
10. Outer rotor
11. Inner rotor
12. Drive pin
13. Shaft
14. Washer
15. Oil pump cover
16. O-ring
17. Oil pressure
    relief valve
18. Bolt
19. Oil relief pipe

2. Remove the oil strainer and seal (B, **Figure 73**) from the oil pump housing.

3. Note the following before disassembling the oil pump:

   a. Different length bolts are used to secure the oil pump. Identify the bolts for reassembly.

   b. The outer rotor may have a punch mark to help identify its installation position in the pump. Record whether the mark is facing up or down so the rotor can be installed facing in its original position.

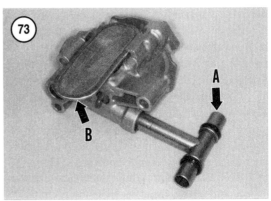

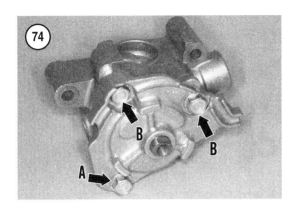

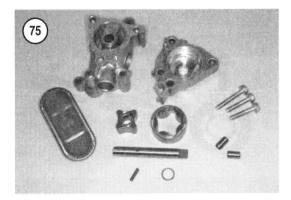

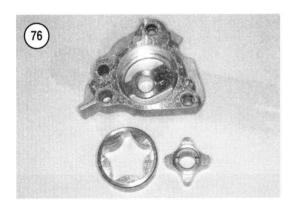

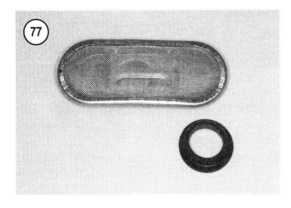

4. Remove the three mounting bolts (A and B, **Figure 74**) and disassemble the oil pump assembly. Refer to **Figure 75**.

Inspection

When measuring the oil pump components in this section, compare the actual measurements to the new and service limit specifications in **Table 5**. If any measurement is out of specification or if any component shows visual damage, the entire oil pump assembly must be replaced. Replacement parts are not available for the oil pump.

1. Clean and dry all parts.

2. Inspect the outer cover and housing for cracks.

3. Check the rotor and housing bore (**Figure 76**) for deep scratches and wear.

4. Inspect the strainer screen (**Figure 77**) for broken areas. Replace if damaged or if it cannot be thoroughly cleaned.

5. Inspect the shaft, pin and washer for cracks or other damage.

6. Inspect the relief pipe and replace if damaged.

7. Install the outer rotor into the pump housing with its punch mark facing in its original position (up or down).

8. Install the inner rotor into the pump housing with its pin groove facing out.

9. Measure the axial clearance between the rotors and pump housing with a straightedge and flat feeler gauge (**Figure 78**).

10. Install the pin into the shaft and install the shaft and pin into the inner rotor.

11. Measure the tip clearance between the inner and outer rotors with a flat feeler gauge (**Figure 79**).

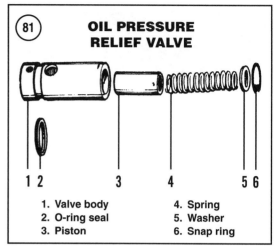

OIL PRESSURE RELIEF VALVE

1 2   3   4   5 6

1. Valve body   4. Spring
2. O-ring seal   5. Washer
3. Piston   6. Snap ring

12. Measure the side clearance between the outer rotor and housing bore with a flat feeler gauge (**Figure 80**).

13. Inspect the oil pressure relief valve (**Figure 81**) as described in this section.

    a. Remove and discard the O-ring (**Figure 82**).

    b. Remove the snap ring and disassemble the oil pressure relief valve assembly.

    c. Clean and dry all parts.

    d. Inspect the valve bore and piston outside diameter for scratches or wear. Replace if damaged.

    e. Inspect the spring for cracks, distortion or other damage. Replace the spring if any damage is noted.

    f. Make sure the holes in the valve body are not clogged.

    g. Install the piston, spring, washer and snap ring. Make sure the snap ring seats in the groove completely.

    h. Install a new O-ring (**Figure 82**) into the valve body groove.

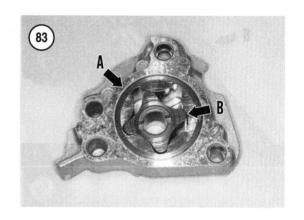

Assembly

1. Lubricate the rotors, shaft and washer with engine oil, then place the parts on a clean, lint-free cloth until reassembly.

2. Install the outer rotor (A, **Figure 83**) into the pump housing with its punch mark facing in its original mounting direction.

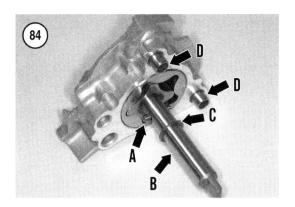

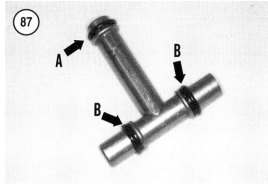

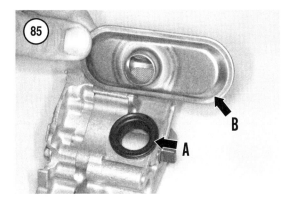

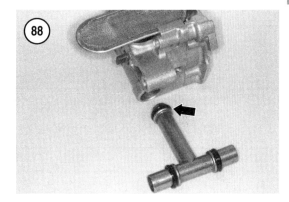

5

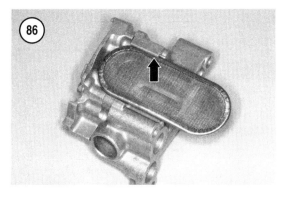

3. Install the inner rotor into the pump housing with its pin groove facing out (B, **Figure 83**).

4. Install the pin into the shaft (A, **Figure 84**), then install the shaft (B) and pin into the inner rotor.

5. Install the washer (C, **Figure 84**) over the shaft and seat it against the inner rotor.

6. Install the two dowel pins (D, **Figure 84**) into the housing.

7. Lubricate the shaft with engine oil.

8. Install the cover over the shaft and against the pump housing.

NOTE
The threads on the mounting bolts and in the oil pump cover must be clean and dry.

9. Install the 6 × 37-mm bolt (A, **Figure 74**) and the two 6 × 29-mm bolts (B). Tighten the bolts to 13 N•m (115 in.-lb.).

10. Turn the shaft and make sure the oil pump turns freely with no binding.

11. Lubricate a new seal with engine oil and install it into the oil pump (A, **Figure 85**).

12. Install the oil strainer (B, **Figure 85**) into the seal. Align the oil strainer with the groove on the pump housing (**Figure 86**). Because the sides of the strainer are offset, the strainer only fits one way against the groove.

13. Lubricate the new oil pipe O-ring and seals with engine oil. Install the O-ring (A, **Figure 87**) onto the long arm of the pipe. Install the two seals with their larger ends facing out (B, **Figure 87**).

14. Insert the long arm of the oil pipe (**Figure 88**) into the oil pump. Refer to A, **Figure 73**.

15. Install the oil pump as described under *Crankcase* in this chapter.

Table 1 CRANKSHAFT SPECIFICATIONS

	New mm (in.)	Service limit mm (in.)
Crankshaft runout	–	0.03 (0.001)
Connecting rod bearing clearance measurement	0.028-0.052 (0.0011-0.0020)	0.07 (0.003)
Connecting rod side clearance	0.05-0.20 (0.002-0.008)	0.30 (0.012)
Connecting rod small end inside diameter	18.016-18.034 (0.7093-0.7100)	18.17 (0.711)
Main journal oil clearance	0.030-0.046 (0.0012-0.0018)	0.07 (0.003)

Table 2 CRANKCASE/CRANKSHAFT SELECTION

Crankcase main journal bearing inside diameter code	Crankshaft main journal outside diameter code	
	1	2
A	Yes	No
B	No	Yes

Table 3 CONNECTING ROD BEARING SELECTION

Connecting rod inside diameter code number and dimension	Connecting rod journal outside diameter code letter and dimension	
	A 39.982-39.990 (1.5741-1.5744)	B 39.974-39.981 (1.5738-1.5741)
Number 1 43.000-43.007 (1.6929-1.6932)	C (brown)	B (black)
Number 2 43.008-43.016 (1.6932-1.6935)	B (black)	A (blue)

Table 4 CONNECTING ROD/CRANKSHAFT SELECTION

Rear connecting rod weight code	Front connecting rod weight code		
	A	B	C
A	*	0	0
B	0	0	0
C	0	0	**

Table 5 OIL PUMP SPECIFICATIONS

	New mm (in.)	Service limit mm (in.)
Axial clearance	0.15-0.22 (0.006-0.009)	0.35 (0.014)
Side clearance	0.02-0.07 (0.001-0.003)	0.10 (0.004)
Tip clearance	0.15 (0.006)	0.20 (0.008)

Table 6 ENGINE LOWER END TORQUE SPECIFICATIONS

	N•m	in.-lb.	ft.-lb.
Connecting rod bearing cap nuts*	33	–	24
Crankcase 8-mm bolt	23	–	17
Engine mounting fasteners			
Engine front bracket bolts	26	–	19
Engine front upper and lower mounting nuts	54	–	40
Engine rear bracket bolts	26	–	19
Engine rear mounting nut	54	–	40
Neutral switch	12	106	–
Oil pump assembly bolts	13	115	–
Shift pedal pinch bolt	12	106	–

* Lubricate threads and seating surface with engine oil.

5

CHAPTER SIX

CLUTCH AND EXTERNAL SHIFT MECHANISM

This chapter describes service procedures for the right crankcase components. All these components can be serviced with the engine mounted in the frame.

1. Clutch cable.
2. Right crankcase cover.
3. Clutch release lever.
4. Clutch.
5. Primary drive gear.
6. External shift mechanism.

Read this chapter before attempting repairs to the clutch and other components in the right crankcase cover. Become familiar with the procedures, photos and illustrations to understand the skill and equipment required. Refer to Chapter One for tool usage and service methods.

Clutch specifications are located in **Table 1**. **Table 1** and **Table 2** are located at the end of this chapter.

Most of the torque specifications in this chapter call for clean and dry fastener threads. Do not lubricate threads unless specified in the text.

The inspection procedures in this chapter help to detect parts that are excessively worn or damaged. However, it is also important to inspect the parts during their removal and disassembly, especially when troubleshooting a problem area. Look for loose fasteners, incorrect adjustments, binding, rough turning and abnormal wear marks or patterns. Locating these types of problems can help prevent future operating problems.

CLUTCH CABLE REPLACEMENT

1. Remove the fuel tank (Chapter Eight).
2. Hold the new cable up to the old cable and compare them. Make sure the length of the cable and both cable ends are correct.
3. Lubricate the new clutch cable as described in Chapter Three.
4. Loosen the clutch cable adjuster locknut (A, **Figure 1**) and adjuster (B) at the handlebar.
5. Loosen the clutch cable adjuster nuts (A, **Figure 2**) and disconnect the cable from the release arm (B).

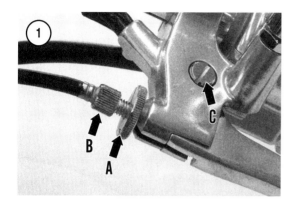

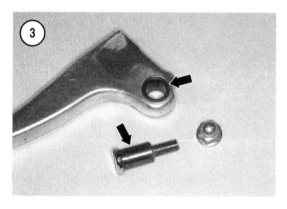

6. Tie a piece of heavy string to the lower end of the old cable. Cut the string to a length that is longer than the new clutch cable.

7. Tie the lower end of the string to a frame or engine component.

NOTE
It may be necessary to detach cable clamps or guides when replacing the cable.

8. Remove the old clutch cable by pulling it from the top (upper cable end). Continue until the cable is

removed from the frame, leaving the attached piece of string in its mounting position.

9. Untie the string from the old cable and discard the old cable.

10. Tie the string onto the bottom end of the new clutch cable.

11. Slowly pull the string and cable to install the cable along the path of the original clutch cable. Continue until the new cable is correctly routed beside the engine and through the frame. Untie and remove the string.

12. Visually check the entire length of the clutch cable. Make sure there are no kinks or sharp bends. Reroute the cable if necessary.

13. Lubricate the clutch hand lever bore and pivot bolt before attaching the cable:

   a. Remove the nut, clutch pivot bolt (C, **Figure 1**) and lever.

   b. Clean and dry the pivot bolt and clutch lever bore. Inspect the operating areas (**Figure 3**) for excessive wear or damage.

   c. Clean the recess in the clutch perch of all old grease.

   d. Lubricate the pivot bolt with grease and reinstall the lever, pivot bolt and nut. Tighten the pivot bolt. Hold the pivot bolt and tighten the nut. Operate the clutch lever to make sure there is no binding.

14. Connect the upper cable end to the clutch lever.

15. Reattach the lower end of the clutch cable as shown in **Figure 2**.

16. Adjust the clutch cable as described in Chapter Three.

RIGHT CRANKCASE COVER

Removal/Installation

NOTE
If the right crankcase cover is being removed to troubleshoot the clutch or other engine related problem, drain the oil into a clean container so it can be examined for debris and small, broken parts.

1. Drain the engine oil (Chapter Three).

2. Remove the exhaust system (Chapter Fifteen).

3. Remove the right footpeg and rear brake pedal (Chapter Fourteen).

4. Clean the right crankcase cover and the area around the cover to prevent dirt from entering the engine.

5. Loosen the clutch cable adjuster locknut (A, **Figure 1**) and adjuster (B) at the handlebar.

NOTE
Different length bolts are used to retain the right crankcase cover. Note the length and location of the bolts during removal.

6. Loosen the clutch cable adjuster nuts (A, **Figure 2**) and disconnect the cable from the release arm (B).

7. Remove the bolts securing the crankcase cover (**Figure 4**) to the engine. If necessary, lightly tap the cover to loosen it from the engine. Do not pry the cover off.

8. Remove the dowel pins (**Figure 5**).

9A. On 1998-2000 models, remove and discard the gasket. Remove all gasket residue from the crankcase and cover surfaces.

9B. On 2001-on models, remove all sealer residue from the crankcase and cover surfaces.

10. Installation is the reverse of removal. Note the following:

  a. Make sure the ignition pulse generator grommet (**Figure 6**) is positioned firmly into the crankcase notch.

  b. Clean the cover and crankcase mating surfaces. On 2001-on models, clean the crankcase bolt holes of all oil.

  c. On 1998-2000 models, install a new gasket.

  d. On 2001-on models, apply a gasket sealer to the crankcase cover gasket surface.

  e. Make sure the pushrod (**Figure 7**) is in place. Operate the clutch release lever by hand. The pushrod should move freely and return under spring pressure.

  f. Tighten the right crankcase cover mounting bolts in a crisscross pattern and in several steps.

NOTE
On 2001-on models, allow the gasket sealer to set before filling the engine with oil. Refer to the manufacturer's recommendations.

  g. Refill the engine with the recommended type and quantity of oil as described in Chapter Three.

  h. Adjust the clutch (Chapter Three).

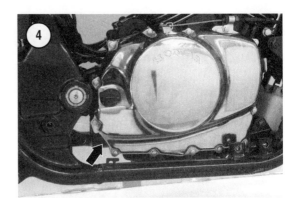

CLUTCH RELEASE LEVER

The clutch release lever is mounted in the right crankcase cover. The assembly consists of the clutch release lever, pushrod and return spring. The clutch cable and clutch lever at the handlebar are part of the system and are covered under *Clutch Cable Replacement* in this chapter.

Clutch disengagement is accomplished via the clutch release lever assembly. The clutch cable is attached between the clutch lever at the handlebar and the clutch release lever at the engine. Operating the

eration than other clutch release designs. Make sure all parts are installed correctly and in good condition to prevent additional pressure requirements.

1. Remove the right crankcase cover as described in this chapter.
2. Remove the pushrod (**Figure 7**).
3. Remove the snap ring (A, **Figure 8**), return spring (B) and slide the clutch release lever from the cover.
4. Remove and discard the seal from the end of the lever operating bore.
5. Remove any burrs or roughness from the release lever and pushrod operating areas. These areas must be smooth.
6. Reinstall the release lever and turn it by hand. If there is any binding or roughness, inspect the release lever and the needle bearings for damage.
7. Both bearings must be a tight fit in their bore. If one or both bearings are loose, replace the right crankcase cover. To replace the needle bearings, refer to *Basic Service Methods* in Chapter One.
8. If the seal was leaking, inspect the seal operating area at the top of the release lever. If wear grooves are visible, replace the lever.
9. Lubricate the lips of a new seal with grease. Install the seal with its closed side facing out.
10. Lubricate the needle bearings with engine oil.
11. Install the release lever. Hook the lower end of the spring into the hole in the lever. Hook the upper end against the cover boss as shown in C, **Figure 8**.
12. Install the snap ring into the lever groove (A, **Figure 8**). Make sure it seats in the groove completely.
13. Turn the release lever so the flat surface on the lever is visible through the pushrod hole (**Figure 9**). Lubricate the pushrod with oil and install it in the hole (**Figure 7**).
14. Reinstall the right crankcase cover as described in this chapter.

CLUTCH

The clutch is a multi-plate type that operates immersed in the engine oil supply. The clutch assembly consists of a housing, pressure plate and clutch hub (**Figure 10**). A set of friction and steel clutch plates are alternately locked to the two parts. The gear-driven clutch housing is mounted on the transmission mainshaft. The housing receives power from the primary drive gear mounted on the crankshaft. The housing then transfers the power via the

clutch lever causes the release lever to rotate. This forces the pushrod against the pressure plate, thereby compressing the clutch springs and releasing the clutch plates where they can rotate freely. This system requires routine adjustment (Chapter Three) to compensate for cable stretch and clutch disc wear.

Removal/Inspection/Installation

NOTE
This type of clutch release lever assembly requires more pressure during op-

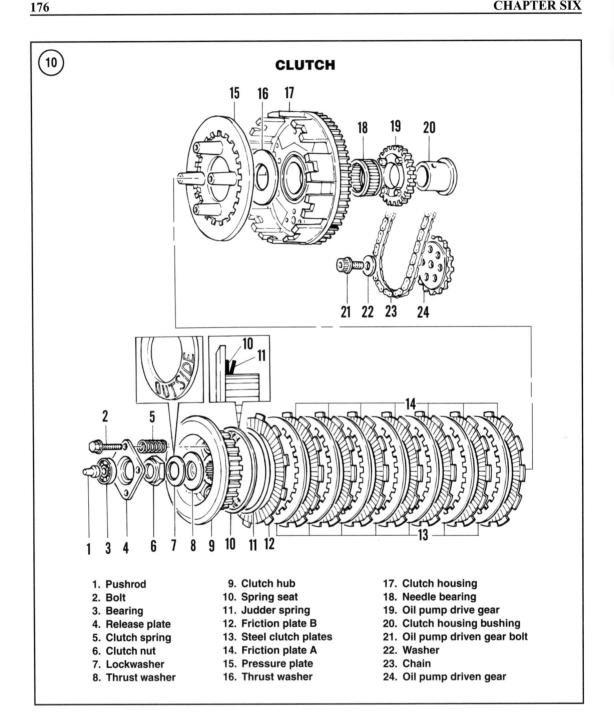

CLUTCH

1. Pushrod
2. Bolt
3. Bearing
4. Release plate
5. Clutch spring
6. Clutch nut
7. Lockwasher
8. Thrust washer
9. Clutch hub
10. Spring seat
11. Judder spring
12. Friction plate B
13. Steel clutch plates
14. Friction plate A
15. Pressure plate
16. Thrust washer
17. Clutch housing
18. Needle bearing
19. Oil pump drive gear
20. Clutch housing bushing
21. Oil pump driven gear bolt
22. Washer
23. Chain
24. Oil pump driven gear

friction plates to the steel clutch plates locked to the clutch hub. The clutch hub is splined to the mainshaft and powers the transmission. The clutch plates are engaged by springs and disengaged by the cable-actuated release lever assembly.

When troubleshooting the clutch, visually inspect the clutch assembly before removing it.

Clutch Nut
Removal/Installation

The pressure plate is installed inside the clutch housing. This requires the clutch hub, clutch plates and pressure plate to be assembled inside the clutch housing when loosening and tightening the clutch nut. To remove/install the clutch nut, the clutch as-

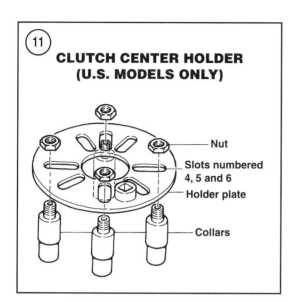

a. After removing the release plate (4, **Figure 10**) and bearing, reinstall the clutch springs (5) and secure them in place with a flat washer and their original mounting bolts (2). This is done to hold the friction and steel clutch plates together and prevent them from turning separately when pressure is applied to the clutch nut.

b. Lock the clutch housing to the primary drive gear with a small holding gear (**Figure 12**). Refer to *Primary Drive Gear* in this chapter.

c. Loosen or tighten the clutch nut as required. Remove the small holding gear. However, if the clutch plates turn when attempting to loosen or tighten the clutch nut, install additional clutch springs, washers and bolts. If the clutch continues to turn, this method will not work. Instead, use the Honda tool.

2. The clutch nut (6, **Figure 10**) is staked to a notch in the mainshaft. Purchase a new nut for reassembly.

Clutch Removal/Disassembly

Refer to **Figure 10**.

1. Remove the right crankcase cover as described in this chapter.

2. Using a crisscross pattern, gradually and evenly loosen the clutch spring bolts (A, **Figure 13**).

3. Remove the release plate and bearing (B, **Figure 13**) and clutch springs.

4. Using a hand grinder with a small grinding stone, carefully grind the staked portion of the clutch nut (**Figure 14**) to *weaken* it. Do not grind through the nut or the mainshaft will be damaged.

5. Lock the clutch and loosen the clutch nut using one of the methods described under *Clutch Nut Re-*

sembly must be held by one of the following methods:

1A. Honda clutch center holder. Refer to **Figure 11**.

1B. An alternative method to the special tool is the following:

moval/Installation in this section. **Figure 15** shows the Honda tool installed over the pressure plate.

6. Remove the clutch nut, lockwasher and flat washer.

> *NOTE*
> *To remove the clutch plate assembly without disturbing its alignment, install a clutch spring, flat washer and clutch spring bolt as shown in A, **Figure 16**.*

7. Refer to **Figure 10** and remove the clutch hub, clutch plate assembly and pressure plate (B, **Figure 16**). Note the judder spring (11, **Figure 10**) and spring seat (10) alignment before removing them.

8. Remove the thrust washer (**Figure 17**).

9. Loosen the oil pump driven sprocket bolt (A, **Figure 18**) if the sprocket is removed.

10. Align the primary drive gear and sub-gear teeth with a screwdriver and remove the clutch housing (**Figure 19**).

> *NOTE*
> *Continue with Step 11 if removing the oil pump sprocket assembly.*

11. Remove the oil pump driven sprocket bolt and washer (A, **Figure 20**).

12. Remove the drive and driven sprockets and chain (B, **Figure 20**) as a set.

13. Remove the clutch housing bushing (**Figure 21**).

14. Inspect all parts as described in this section.

Clutch Inspection

Always replace steel clutch plates, friction plates or clutch springs as a set if individual components

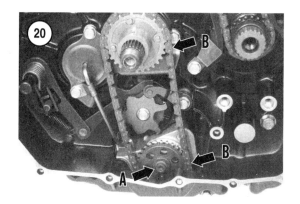

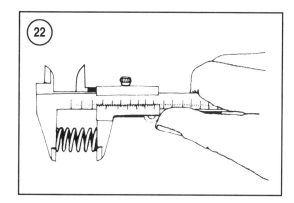

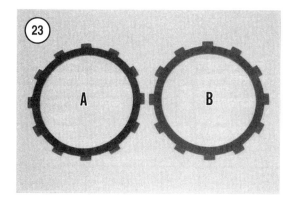

6

do not meet specifications (**Table 1**). If parts show other signs of wear or damage, replace them, regardless of their specifications. Individual parts that operate together or against each other must be inspected for the same wear and damage. When the damage on one part is more apparent than on the other part, replace both parts to prevent premature wear.

1. Clean and dry all parts.

2. Inspect the clutch springs for cracks and heat damage (blue discoloration).

3. Measure the free length of each clutch spring (**Figure 22**). To maintain even clutch pressure and maximum performance, replace all springs as a set if any one is not within the specified tolerance.

4. Inspect each friction plate (**Figure 23**) as follows:

   a. The friction material on the friction plates is bonded to an aluminum plate for warp resistance and durability. Inspect the friction material for excessive or uneven wear, cracks and other damage.

   b. The tabs on the friction plates operate along the grooves in the clutch housing. Inspect the tabs for rough spots, notches or other damage. The tabs must slide smoothly in the clutch housing grooves; otherwise, clutch drag results.

   c. Measure the thickness of each friction plate (**Figure 24**). Measure at different locations around the plates. Note that the width specifications for friction plates A (quantity 7) and friction plate B (quantity 1) are different. Friction plate B (B, **Figure 23**) has a larger inside diameter than friction plates A (A, **Figure 23**).

5. Inspect each steel clutch plate (**Figure 25**) as follows:

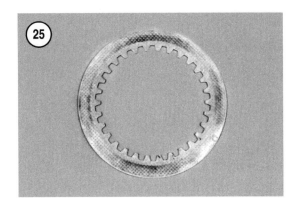

  a. Inspect the steel clutch plates for cracks, damage or color change. Overheated steel clutch plates have a blue discoloration.

  b. Check the steel clutch plates for an oil glaze buildup. Remove by lightly sanding both sides of each plate with 400 grit sandpaper placed on a surface plate or piece of glass.

  c. The steel clutch plate's inner teeth mesh with the clutch hub splines. Inspect the teeth for rough spots or other damage. The teeth must slide smoothly on the splines; otherwise, clutch drag results.

  d. Place each steel clutch plate on a flat surface, such as a piece of glass, and check for warp with a feeler gauge (**Figure 26**). If any plate is warped more than specified, replace the entire set of steel clutch plates. Do not replace only one or two plates, as clutch operation will be unsatisfactory.

6. Inspect the spring seat and judder spring for roughness and cracks. Lay them on a flat surface and check for warp.

7. Check the clutch housing as follows:

  a. Inspect the clutch housing slots (A, **Figure 27**) for notches, grooves or other damage. Repair minor damage with a file. If damage is excessive, replace the clutch housing. The slots must be smooth so the friction plates can move smoothly when the clutch is released.

> *NOTE*
> *Filing the clutch housing slots is only a temporary fix because removing metal from the sides of the slots provides more room for the plates to move around and start wearing new grooves.*

  b. Check the clutch housing needle bearing (A, **Figure 28**) for scoring, cracks, pitting or other damage. If damage is noted, replace the needle bearing as described in this section.

  c. Check the primary driven gear (B, **Figure 28**) for excessive wear, pitting, chipped gear teeth or other damage.

  d. Hold the clutch housing and turn the primary driven gear (B, **Figure 28**). Replace the clutch housing if there is any free play.

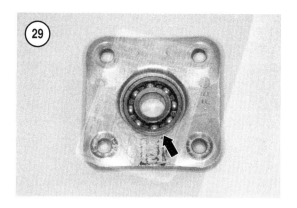

e. Inspect the pin holes (C, **Figure 28**) in which the oil pump drive sprocket pins operate. Replace the clutch housing if these holes are cracked, enlarged or otherwise damaged.

8. Inspect the clutch hub as follows:

a. Inspect the outer splines (B, **Figure 27**) for rough spots, grooves or other damage. Repair minor damage with a file or oil stone. If the damage is excessive, replace the clutch hub. The splines must smooth so the steel clutch plates can move smoothly when the clutch is released.

b. Check the plate surface for cracks and other damage.

9. Check the pressure plate (15, **Figure 10**) as follows:

a. Inspect for damaged spring towers.

b. Inspect the plate surface area for cracks, grooves and other damage.

10. Inspect the release plate bearing (**Figure 29**). Turn the bearing inner race and check for any roughness, catching or binding. Replace the bearing if there is damage. The outer bearing race should fit in the plate bore without any play. The bearing, however, can be replaced. Replace the bearing if necessary.

11. Inspect the clutch housing bushing (A, **Figure 30**). Replace the bushing if it is galled or shows other damage. Measure the bushing inside and outside diameters. Replace the bushing if either measurement is out of specification.

12. Inspect the oil pump drive (B, **Figure 30**) and driven sprockets for the following conditions:

a. Worn or damaged pins.

b. Chipped or missing gear teeth.

c. Measure the oil pump drive sprocket inside diameter.

13. Inspect the links on the oil pump drive chain. If any are worn or damaged or there are any cracks along the chain, replace the chain and both sprockets.

14. Measure the mainshaft outside diameter at the clutch housing bushing operating area (**Figure 31**). If out of specification, disassemble the crankcase (Chapter five) and replace the mainshaft (Chapter Seven).

Clutch Housing Needle Bearing Replacement

The clutch housing needle bearing (A, **Figure 32**) can be replaced with a press.

1. Measure the clearance between the bottom of the bearing and the bearing bore surface (B, **Figure 32**). The correct clearance measurement is 1.0 mm (0.03 in.).

2. Support the clutch housing in a press (**Figure 33**).

3. Press the needle bearing out through the bottom of the clutch housing. Discard the bearing.

4. Inspect the bearing bore for gouges and other damage.

5. Support the clutch housing in a press (**Figure 33**).

6. Install the new needle bearing squarely into the top of the bore with its manufacturer's marks facing up.

7. Press the needle bearing into the bore until the distance, measured from the bottom of the bearing to the bearing bore outer surface (B, **Figure 32**), is 1.0 mm (0.03 in.).

8. Lubricate the needle bearing with engine oil. Then fit the clutch housing bushing into the bearing. Make sure the bushing enters and turns easily in the bearing. If there is any roughness or binding, the bearing may have been damaged during installation.

9. If the new bearing does not fit tightly in its bore, replace the clutch housing assembly.

Clutch Assembly/Installation

Refer to **Figure 10**.

> *NOTE*
> *If removed, install the external shift mechanism, oil pipe and primary drive gear before installing the clutch.*

1. Lubricate all clutch parts and the mainshaft with engine oil before reassembly. Do not lubricate the clutch nut threads.

2. Install the clutch housing bushing (**Figure 34**) onto the mainshaft.

3. Install the oil pump drive sprocket (A, **Figure 35**) with its pins facing out.

4. Install the drive chain and the oil pump driven sprocket (B, **Figure 35**):

   a. Install the oil pump driven sprocket with its IN mark (**Figure 36**) facing in (toward the engine).

   b. Align the flat surfaces on the driven sprocket and oil pump drive shaft.

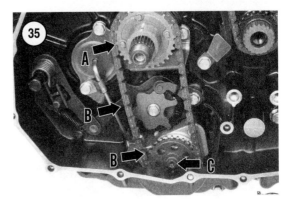

c. Mesh the drive chain with the driven and driven sprockets.

5. Clean the oil pump driven sprocket bolt and oil pump shaft threads with contact cleaner and allow to dry.

6. Apply a medium strength threadlock onto the oil pump driven sprocket bolt threads. Install the bolt (C, **Figure 35**) and washer and tighten finger-tight.

NOTE
Tighten the bolt to the specification after the clutch housing is installed.

7. Install the clutch housing as follows:

   a. Align the holes in the clutch housing (A, **Figure 37**) with the pins (B) on the oil pump drive sprocket.

NOTE
The primary driven gear, mounted on the clutch housing, meshes with the primary drive gear mounted on the crankshaft. The primary drive gear is an antibacklash type consisting of a fixed inner gear and a spring-loaded outer gear. Because these two gears are off-set (teeth do not align), the outer primary drive gear must be pried forward to align its gear teeth when installing the clutch housing.

   b. Install the clutch housing over the mainshaft. Pry the outer primary drive gear forward with a screwdriver (**Figure 19**), then push the clutch housing to mesh the primary drive and driven gears.

   c. Turn the oil pump driven gear (**Figure 38**) to align the pins and holes described in substep A, and push the clutch housing (A, **Figure 39**) on all the way.

8. Hold the clutch housing and tighten the oil pump driven gear bolt (B, **Figure 39**) to 15 N•m (11 ft.-lb.).

9. Install the thrust washer (**Figure 40**).

NOTE
Lubricate the contact surfaces of the friction plates and steel clutch plates with clean engine oil before assembly.

10. Assemble the friction plates, steel clutch plates, clutch hub and pressure plate as follows:

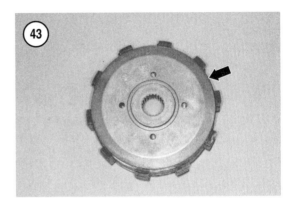

a. Install friction plate B (**Figure 41**) onto the clutch hub. The inside diameter of friction plate B is larger than the inside diameter of each of the other seven friction plates (**Figure 23**).

b. Install the spring seat and judder spring as shown in **Figure 10**.

NOTE
The steel clutch plates are stamped during manufacturing and have one flat side and one chamfered side. Install all of the steel clutch plates with the flat side facing in the same direction (either in or out).

c. Install a steel clutch plate next to friction plate B.

d. Install a friction plate A, then continue to install a steel clutch plate, a friction plate A and alternate them until all are installed (**Figure 10**). The last item installed is a friction plate (**Figure 42**).

e. Install the pressure plate (**Figure 43**) and seat it against the friction plate. Make sure the splines on the friction plate align with the clutch hub splines.

f. Align all of the tabs on friction plate A as shown in A, **Figure 44**.

g. Turn and offset the tabs on friction plate B as shown in B, **Figure 44**.

h. Install a clutch spring, flat washer and clutch spring bolt (C, **Figure 44**) to keep the assembly together during installation.

11. Install the clutch hub assembly over the mainshaft and into the clutch housing (**Figure 45**). Align and install friction plate B into the grooves in the clutch housing (**Figure 46**).

6

12. Install the thrust washer (8, **Figure 10**) and lockwasher (9). Install the lockwasher with its OUT SIDE mark facing out (**Figure 47**).

13. Lubricate the clutch nut threads with engine oil, then install it with its shoulder side facing out (**Figure 48**). Tighten the locknut finger-tight.

14. Remove the bolt, washer and clutch spring (**Figure 48**) installed previously.

15. Use the same tool arrangement used in Step 5 of *Removal/Disassembly* and tighten the clutch nut (**Figure 49**) to 128 N•m (94 ft.-lb.).

CAUTION
*In Step 16, stake the locknut into the groove in the mainshaft. Do **not** stake the locknut against any other part of the mainshaft.*

16. Use a punch and stake a portion of the clutch nut shoulder into the groove in the mainshaft (**Figure 50**).

17. Install the clutch springs, release plate (A, **Figure 51**) (bearing side facing out) and bolts (B).

18. Tighten the clutch spring bolts (B, **Figure 51**) securely in several steps and in a crisscross pattern until tight. Then tighten to 12 N•m (106 in.-lb.).

> *CAUTION*
> *If loosened, make sure the oil pump driven sprocket mounting bolt was tightened as described in Step 8 of this procedure.*

19. Install the pushrod and right crankcase cover as described in this chapter.

20. Shift the transmission into neutral and start the engine. After the engine warms up, pull the clutch in and shift the transmission into first gear. Note the following:

   a. If the clutch makes a loud grinding and spinning noise immediately after the engine is started and then stops, either the engine oil level is low or the new friction plates were not lubricated with oil.

   b. If the bike jumps forward and stalls or creeps with the transmission in gear and the clutch pulled in, recheck the clutch adjustment. If the clutch does not adjust properly, either the clutch cable or the friction plates are excessively worn. Replace them.

   c. If the clutch adjustment is correct but the clutch is not working correctly, the clutch may have been assembled incorrectly or there is a broken part in the clutch. Disassemble the clutch as described in this chapter and inspect the parts.

PRIMARY DRIVE GEAR

The primary drive gear is mounted on the crankshaft and positioned behind the ignition pulse generator rotor. The primary drive gear assembly is an antibacklash type consisting of a fixed inner gear and a spring-loaded outer gear.

Removal/Disassembly

1. Remove the right crankcase cover as described in this chapter.

2. Remove the ignition pulse generator mounting bolts (A, **Figure 52**), then remove the grommets (B) from the crankcase.

3. To prevent crankshaft rotation when performing the next step, use one of the following methods:

a. Place a small section of gear (**Figure 53**) in mesh with the primary drive and driven gears.

> *NOTE*
> *The section of gear shown in **Figure 53** was cut from a discarded transmission gear using a Dremel and cut-off wheel.*

b. Place a soft copper washer or penny into mesh with the gears.

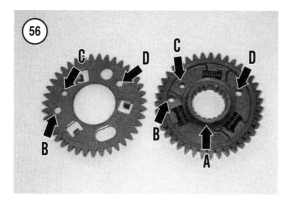

CAUTION
Do not hold the gears with metal washers or screwdrivers. This could chip or break a gear tooth.

4. Loosen the primary drive gear bolt (**Figure 53**). Remove the tool used to mesh the gears.
5. Remove the clutch as described in this chapter.

NOTE
The primary drive gear is a subassembly and may come apart during removal.

6. Remove the primary drive gear bolt and washer (A, **Figure 54**), ignition pulse generator rotor (B) and primary drive gear assembly (C).
7. Disassemble the primary drive gear (**Figure 55**).

Inspection

1. Clean and dry all parts.
2. Inspect the subgear (A, **Figure 55**) for:
    a. Broken or chipped teeth.
    b. Worn or damaged spring lugs.
3. Inspect the friction spring (B, **Figure 55**) for cracks and fatigue.
4. Inspect the primary drive gear (C, **Figure 55**) for:
    a. Broken or chipped teeth.
    b. Worn or damaged splines.
    c. Damaged spring grooves.
5. Check the primary drive gear springs (D, **Figure 55**) for cracks and fatigue.

Reassembly/Installation

1. Install the three springs into the primary drive gear (D, **Figure 55**).
2. Install the friction spring onto the primary drive gear with its concave side facing up (A, **Figure 56**).
3. Install the subgear onto the primary drive gear by aligning the three holes (B, C and D, **Figure 56**) in each gear. Position the spring lugs on the subgear against the three springs. Refer to **Figure 57**.
4. Install the primary drive gear assembly by aligning the wide groove in the gear with the wide spline on the crankshaft (**Figure 58**).
5. Install the ignition pulse generator by aligning the wide groove in the generator with the wide spline on the crankshaft (**Figure 59**).

6. Lubricate the primary drive gear bolt threads and seating surface with engine oil.

7. Install the bolt and washer (A, **Figure 54**) and tighten hand-tight.

8. Install the clutch as described in this chapter.

9. Lock the crankshaft with the same tool used during removal. Place the tool between the primary drive and driven gears as shown in **Figure 60**.

10. Tighten the primary drive gear bolt to 88 N•m (65 ft.-lb.).

11. Remove the gear holder (**Figure 60**).

12. Install the ignition pulse generator:

   a. Clean the threads on the ignition pulse generator bolts and mating threaded holes of any oil and threadlock residue.

   b. Apply a medium strength threadlock onto the ignition pulse generator bolt threads.

   c. Install the ignition pulse generator and tighten the mounting bolts to 12 N•m (106 N•m).

   d. Reinstall the ignition pulse generator wire harness grommets into the crankcase.

13. Install the right crankcase cover as described in this chapter.

EXTERNAL SHIFT MECHANISM

The external shift mechanism consists of the shift pedal and linkage, shift shaft, stopper arm assembly and cam plate assembly (**Figure 61**). These parts can be removed with the engine mounted in the frame. Access to the shift drum and shift forks requires removing the engine and splitting the crankcase (Chapter Five).

Shift Pedal and Linkage
Removal/Installation

1. Remove the drive sprocket cover (Chapter Eleven).

2. Remove the pinch bolt and slide the shift arm (A, **Figure 62**) off the shift shaft.

NOTE
If the shift pedal is tight, check the splines for bending or other damage.

3A. On VT750C models, remove the bolts and the left footpeg assembly (B, **Figure 62**). Remove the pivot bolt and pedal/linkage arm from the left footpeg.

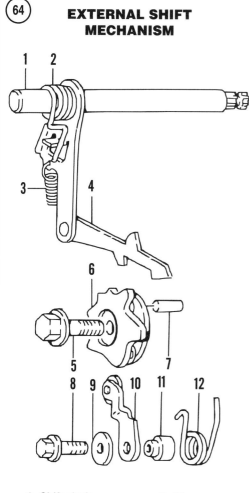

EXTERNAL SHIFT MECHANISM

1.	Shift shaft	7.	Pin
2.	Return spring	8.	Bolt
3.	Tension spring	9.	Washer
4.	Shift pawl	10.	Stopper arm
5.	Bolt	11.	Bushing
6.	Cam plate	12.	Return spring

3B. On VT750DC models, remove the pivot bolt, cap nut and shift pedal/linkage arm from the frame.

4. Clean the pivot bolt and the pivot bore in the shift pedal.

5. Inspect the pivot bolt and shift pedal bore for damage.

6. Installation is the reverse of removal. Note the following:

    a. Lubricate the pivot bolt with a waterproof grease.

    b. Tighten the shift pedal pivot bolt to 34 N•m (25 ft.-lb.).

    c. On VT750C models, tighten the left footpeg mounting bolts to 26 N•m (19 ft.-lb.).

    d. Tighten shift arm pinch bolt to 12 N•m (106 in.-lb.).

    e. Check the shift pedal position and operation.

Shift Linkage Adjustment

The shift pedal is connected to the shift arm with an adjustable linkage rod. Turning the linkage rod changes the shift pedal's height position, moving it closer to or farther away from your foot.

1. Loosen the locknut (**Figure 63**) at each end of the shift linkage rod.

2. Turn the linkage rod to raise or lower the shift pedal. Hold the linkage rod with a pair of locking pliers and tighten both locknuts.

3. Recheck the pedal position.

Shift Mechanism

Removal

Refer to **Figure 64**.

1. Remove the right crankcase cover and clutch as described in this chapter.

> *NOTE*
> *If troubleshooting a shifting problem, inspect the external shift mechanism before removing it. Refer to **Gearshift Linkage** in Chapter Two.*

2. Remove the pinch bolt and slide the shift arm (A, **Figure 62**) off the shift shaft.

3. Remove the drive sprocket cover as described in Chapter Eleven.

4. Remove the bolt (A, **Figure 65**) and pull the oil pipe (B) and its O-ring out of the bearing bracket and oil pump.

5. Lift the shift pawl (C, **Figure 65**) and remove the shift shaft (D) from the crankcase.

6. Remove the bolt and washer (A, **Figure 66**), stopper arm (B), bushing and return spring.

7. Remove the bolt (C, **Figure 66**), cam plate (D) and dowel pin (7, **Figure 64**).

8. Inspect the components as described in this section.

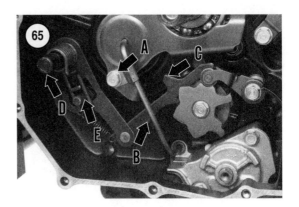

Inspection

Worn or damaged shift linkage components cause missed shifts and wear to the transmission gears, shift forks and shift drum. Replace parts that show excessive wear or damage.

1. Clean and dry the parts. Remove all threadlock residue from the cam plate mounting bolt threads.

2. Inspect the shift shaft assembly (**Figure 67**) as follows:

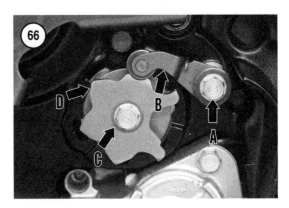

   a. Inspect the splines for damage.

   b. Inspect the shaft for straightness.

   c. Inspect the return spring (A, **Figure 67**) for wear and fatigue cracks.

   d. Inspect the shift pawl (B, **Figure 67**) for excessive wear or damage.

   e. Make sure the return spring seats in the shift pawl grooves (C, **Figure 67**).

   f. Inspect the tension spring (D, **Figure 67**) for damage.

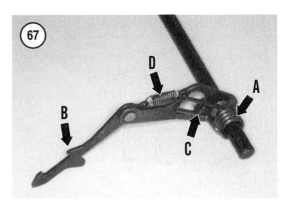

3. Check the stopper arm (**Figure 68**) assembly for:

   a. Weak or damaged spring. Check spring for cracks.

   b. Bent, cracked or damaged stopper arm. Check roller for flat spots.

   c. Damaged stopper arm pivot bolt.

4. Check the cam plate (6, **Figure 64**) as follows:

   a. Inspect the ramps in the front side of the cam for wear and damage. If the sides of the ramps are rounded or damaged, the stopper arm roller can slip and the transmission will jump out of gear.

   b. Inspect the detents in the rear side of the cam plate. The detents must not be worn or shifting will be incorrect.

5. Clean and dry the oil pipe (**Figure 69**).

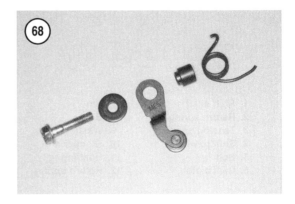

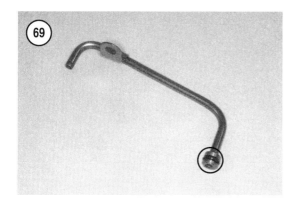

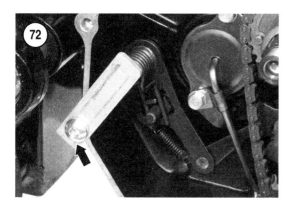

Installation

1. Install the cam plate as follows:
   a. Insert the pin into the shift drum hole and then align the hole in the cam plate with the pin and install the cam plate (D, **Figure 66**).
   b. Apply a medium strength threadlock onto the cam plate bolt threads and install the bolt. Tighten the bolt (C, **Figure 66**) securely.

2. Install the stopper arm assembly (**Figure 68**) as follows:
   a. Assemble the stopper arm as shown in **Figure 70**.
   b. Install the stopper arm as shown in B, **Figure 66**. Finger-tighten the stopper arm pivot bolt. Make sure the spring is aligned around the bolt and against the crankcase.
   c. Pry the stopper arm up with a screwdriver (**Figure 71**), and then release it. When properly installed, the stopper arm moves and returns under spring tension. If the stopper arm does not move, the spring is pinched against the pivot bolt. Loosen the bolt and center the stopper arm on the bolt's shoulder. Tighten the bolt (A, **Figure 66**) securely.

3. Install the shift shaft as follows:
   a. Clean the shift shaft oil seal with a rag, and then lubricate the seal lips with grease.
   b. Slide the shaft slowly through the engine and seal, and engage the return spring with the spring pin (E, **Figure 65**) while aligning the shift pawl (C) with the cam plate.

4. Install the shift pedal and secure it with its pinch bolt.

5. Support the bike with the rear wheel off the ground and check the shifting as follows:
   a. Mount a plate across the crankcase to hold the shift shaft in position (**Figure 72**).
   b. Slowly turn the rear wheel and shift the transmission into first gear, then shift to neutral and the remaining forward gears.

> *NOTE*
> **Figure 73** *shows the cam plate in neutral.*

   c. If the shift shaft moves and then locks in place, the return spring (E, **Figure 65**) may not be centered on the spring pin.
   d. If the transmission over-shifts, check for an incorrectly assembled stopper arm assembly.

e. If the transmission does not shift properly, check for an incorrectly installed shift shaft return spring. Check the shift lever assembly.
f. Remove the plate.

6. Lubricate a new O-ring with engine oil and install it on the oil pipe (**Figure 69**).
7. Install the oil pipe upper end into the bearing bracket and the lower end into the oil pump (B, **Figure 65**). Install and tighten the bolt (A, **Figure 65**) securely.
8. Reverse Steps 1-3 under *Removal*. Tighten the shift arm pinch bolt to 12 N•m (106 in.-lb.).

73

Table 1 CLUTCH SPECIFICATIONS

	New mm (in.)	Service limit mm (in.)
Clutch housing bushing		
Inside diameter	21.991-22.016 (0.8658-0.8668)	22.03 (0.867)
Outside diameter	29.994-30.007 (1.1809-1.1814)	29.98 (1.180)
Clutch spring free length	45.5 (1.79)	43.9 (1.73)
Friction plate thickness		
Plate A	2.62-2.78 (0.103-0.107)	2.3 (0.09)
Plate B	2.92-3.08 (0.115-0.121)	2.6 (0.10)
Mainshaft outside diameter at clutch housing bushing	21.967-21.980 (0.8648-0.8654)	21.95 (0.864)
Oil pump drive sprocket inside diameter	30.025-30.145 (1.1821-1.1868)	30.15 (1.187)
Steel clutch plate warp	–	0.30 (0.012)

Table 2 CLUTCH TORQUE SPECIFICATIONS

	N•m	in.-lb.	ft.-lb.
Clutch nut[1,2]	128	–	94
Clutch spring bolts	12	106	–
Gearshift return spring pin	23	–	17
Ignition pulse generator mounting bolts[3]	12	106	–
Left footpeg mounting bolts			
VT750C	26	–	19
Oil pump driven gear bolt[3]	15	–	11
Primary drive gear bolt[1]	88	–	65
Shift arm pinch bolt	12	106	–
Shift pedal pivot bolt	34	–	25

1. Lubricate threads and flange surface with engine oil.
2. Stake nut as described in text.
3. Apply a medium strength threadlock onto bolt threads.

CHAPTER SEVEN

TRANSMISSION AND INTERNAL SHIFT MECHANISM

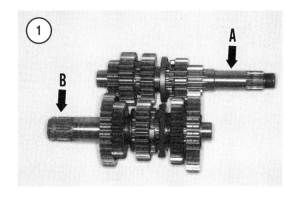

This chapter describes disassembly and reassembly of the transmission shafts and internal shift mechanism. Remove the engine and separate the crankcase halves to service these components as described in Chapter Five.

Table 1 lists transmission gear ratios. Service specifications are listed in **Tables 2-4**. **Tables 1-4** are at the end of the chapter.

TRANSMISSION OPERATION

The engine is equipped with a 5-speed constant-mesh transmission. The gears on the mainshaft (A, **Figure 1**) are meshed with the gears on the countershaft (B). Each pair of meshed gears represents one gear ratio. For each pair of gears, one

of the gears is splined to its shaft, while the other gear freewheels on its shaft.

Next to each freewheeling gear is a gear that is splined to the shaft. Each splined gear can slide on the shaft and lock onto the freewheeling gear, making that gear ratio active. Any time the transmission is in gear, one pair of meshed gears are locked to their shafts and that gear ratio is selected. All other meshed gears are freewheeling, making those ratios inoperative.

To engage and disengage the various gear ratios, the splined gears are moved by shift forks. The shift forks are guided by grooves in the shift drum, which is operated by a shift pedal and linkage assembly. As the bike is upshifted and downshifted, the shift drum rotates and guides the forks to engage and disengage pairs of gears on the transmission shafts.

TRANSMISSION

Troubleshooting

Refer to Chapter Two.

Removal/Installation

The engine crankcase must be split to remove the transmission and shift assemblies (**Figure 2**). Refer to *Crankcase* in Chapter Five.

Service Notes

1. Clean and dry the transmission shafts and gears before disassembling them.

2. As the transmission shafts are disassembled, store the individual parts in a divided container, or make an identification mark on each part to indicate orientation.

> *NOTE*
> *Heavy duty marking pens, such as those made by Speedry, work well when marking and identifying gears and other metal parts. These pens can be purchased in different colors at tool and bearing supply stores.*

3. Install *new* snap rings during reassembly. The snap rings fatigue and distort when they are removed. Do not reuse them, although they may appear to be in good condition.

4. To install new snap rings without distorting them, use the following technique:

   a. Open the new snap ring with a pair of snap ring pliers while holding the back of the snap ring with a pair of pliers (**Figure 3**).

   b. Slide the snap ring down the shaft and seat it into its correct groove.

   c. This technique can also be used to remove the snap rings from a shaft once they are free from their grooves.

Mainshaft

Refer to **Figure 4**.

Disassembly

Remove the parts from the mainshaft in the order below.

> *NOTE*
> *Organize the parts as they are removed as shown in* **Figure 5**.

1. Remove second gear.
2. Remove fifth gear.
3. Remove the fifth gear bushing.
4. Remove the spline washer and snap ring.
5. Remove fourth gear.
6. Remove the snap ring and spline washer.
7. Remove third gear.

8. Remove the third gear bushing and thrust washer.

> *NOTE*
> *First gear is an integral part of the mainshaft.*

9. Inspect the mainshaft assembly as described under *Inspection* in this section.

Assembly

Before beginning assembly, have two *new* snap rings on hand. Throughout the procedure, the orientation of parts is made in relationship to first gear (A, **Figure 6**), which is part of the mainshaft.

> *CAUTION*
> *The snap rings and washers used on the transmission shafts are stamped types. One edge is rounded, while the other is sharp. The side with the sharp edge, referred to as the flat side, must be installed so the flat side always faces away from the part producing the thrust (**Figure 7**). The sharp edge prevents the snap ring from rolling*

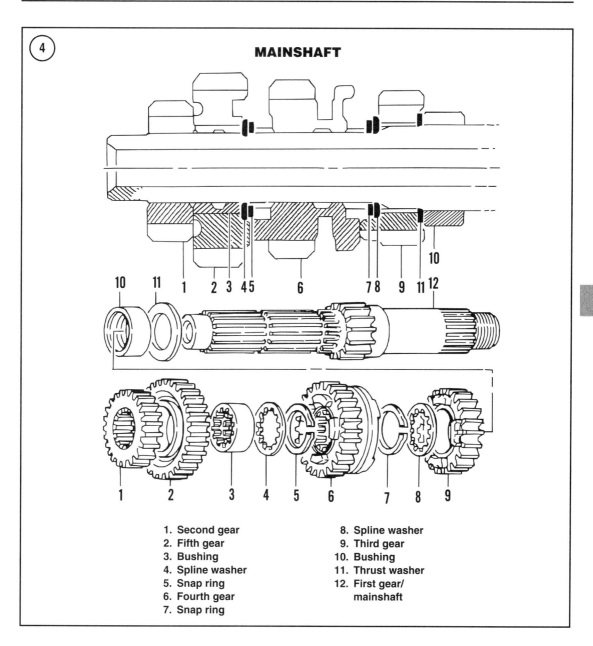

④ MAINSHAFT

1. Second gear
2. Fifth gear
3. Bushing
4. Spline washer
5. Snap ring
6. Fourth gear
7. Snap ring
8. Spline washer
9. Third gear
10. Bushing
11. Thrust washer
12. First gear/ mainshaft

7

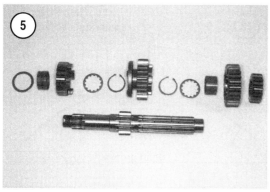

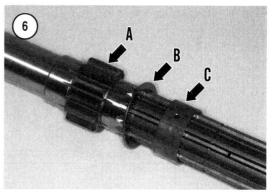

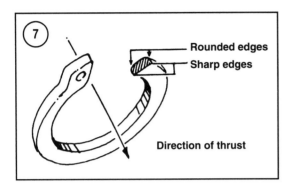

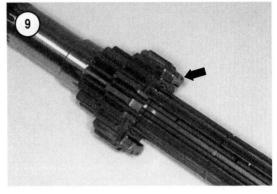

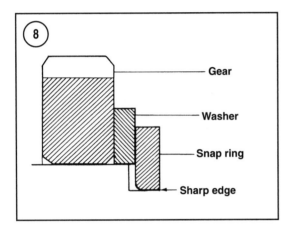

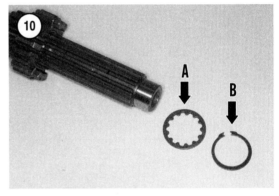

out of its groove when thrust is ap-plied (Figure 8).

1. Clean and dry all parts before assembly. Lubricate all parts with engine oil.

2. Install the thrust washer (B, **Figure 6**) with its flat side facing away from first gear.

3. Install the third gear bushing (C, **Figure 6**) and seat it against the thrust washer.

4. Install third gear (**Figure 9**) so the gear dogs face *away* from first gear.

5. Install the spline washer (A, **Figure 10**) and *new* snap ring (B) onto the shaft. The flat side of both parts must face *away* from first gear. The snap ring must seat in the groove in the shaft.

> *CAUTION*
> *Install the snap ring so its ends align with a groove in the splines (Figure 11 and Figure 12).*

6. Install fourth gear (A, **Figure 13**) so the gear dogs face *away* from first gear. Align the oil hole in the gear (B, **Figure 13**) with the oil hole in the shaft (C).

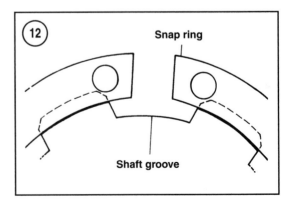

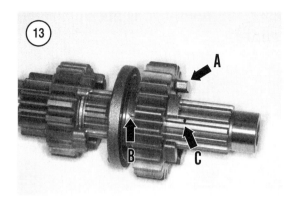

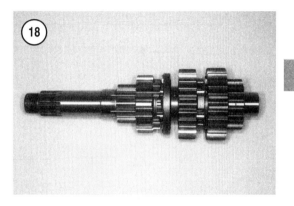

7

7. Install a *new* snap ring (A, **Figure 14**) and spline washer (B) onto the shaft. The flat sides of both parts must face *toward* first gear. The snap ring must seat in the groove in the shaft.

> *CAUTION*
> *Install the snap ring so its ends align with a groove in the splines (**Figure 12**).*

8. Install the spline bushing (A, **Figure 15**) and seat it against the spline washer. Align the oil hole in the bushing with the oil hole in the shaft.

9. Install fifth gear (B, **Figure 15**) so the gear dogs face *toward* first gear. Refer to **Figure 16**.

10. Install second gear (**Figure 17**) and seat it against fifth gear. Both sides of second gear are symmetrical and can be installed either way. If the gear was marked before removal, install it facing in its original position.

11. Refer to **Figure 18** for the correct placement of the mainshaft gears.

12. Wrap a heavy rubber band around the end of the shaft to prevent parts from sliding off the shaft.

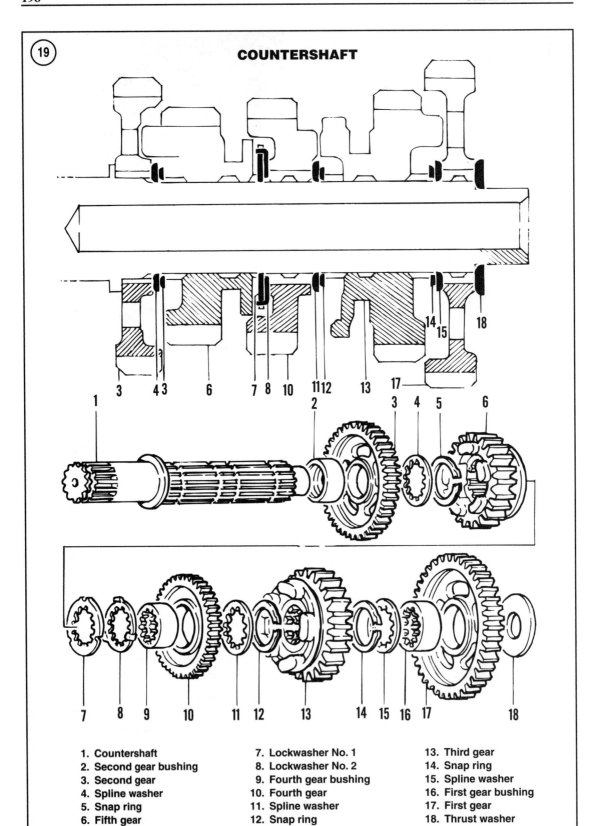

COUNTERSHAFT

1. Countershaft
2. Second gear bushing
3. Second gear
4. Spline washer
5. Snap ring
6. Fifth gear
7. Lockwasher No. 1
8. Lockwasher No. 2
9. Fourth gear bushing
10. Fourth gear
11. Spline washer
12. Snap ring
13. Third gear
14. Snap ring
15. Spline washer
16. First gear bushing
17. First gear
18. Thrust washer

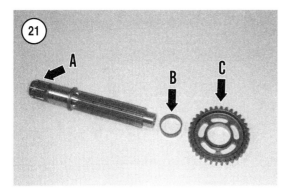

Wrap and store the assembly until it is ready for installation into the crankcase.

Countershaft

Refer to **Figure 19**.

Disassembly

Remove the parts from the countershaft in the order below.

NOTE
Organize the parts as they are removed as shown in Figure 20.

1. Remove the thrust washer.
2. Remove first gear and first gear bushing.
3. Remove the spline washer and snap ring.
4. Remove third gear.
5. Remove the snap ring and spline washer.
6. Remove fourth gear and fourth gear bushing.
7. Remove lockwasher No. 2 and lockwasher No. 1.
8. Remove fifth gear.
9. Remove the snap ring and spline washer.
10. Remove second gear and second gear bushing.

Assembly

Before beginning assembly, have three *new* snap rings on hand. Throughout the procedure, the orientation of many parts is made in relationship to the splined end of the countershaft (A, **Figure 21**).

CAUTION
The snap rings and washers used on the transmission shafts are stamped types. One edge is rounded, while the other is sharp. The side with the sharp edge, referred to as the flat side, must be installed so the flat side always faces away from the part producing the thrust (Figure 7). The sharp edge prevents the snap ring from rolling out of its groove when thrust is applied (Figure 8).

1. Clean and dry all parts before assembly. Lubricate all parts with engine oil.
2. Install the second gear bushing (B, **Figure 21**) and seat it against the shaft shoulder.
3. Install second gear (C, **Figure 21**) so the side with the deeper shoulder (**Figure 22**) faces *away* from the splined end.
4. Install the spline washer (A, **Figure 23**) and a *new* snap ring (B) onto the shaft. The flat sides of both parts must face *away* from the splined end. The snap ring must seat in the groove in the shaft.

CAUTION
Install the snap ring so its ends align with a groove in the splines (Figure 24).

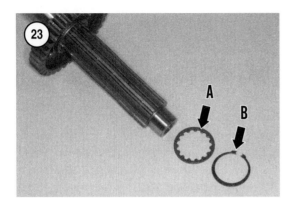

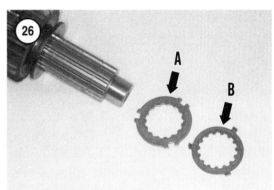

5. Install fifth gear (**Figure 25**) so the gear dogs face *toward* the splined end.

6. Install and lock lockwasher No. 1 (A, **Figure 26**) and lockwasher No. 2 (B) as follows:

  a. Install lockwasher No. 1 (A, **Figure 27**). Rotate the lockwasher in either direction so the tangs on the lockwasher engage the raised grooves in the countershaft.

  b. Install lockwasher No. 2 (B, **Figure 27**) by aligning its bent tabs with the slots in lockwasher No. 1.

  c. Lockwasher No. 2 must engage and seat flush against lockwasher No. 1 (**Figure 28**).

7. Install the fourth gear bushing (**Figure 29**) and seat it against the lockwasher assembly.

8. Install fourth gear over its bushing (**Figure 30**) so the gear dogs face *away* from the splined end.

9. Install the spline washer (A, **Figure 31**) and a *new* snap ring (B) onto the shaft. The flat sides of both parts must face *away* from the splined end. The snap ring must seat in the groove in the shaft.

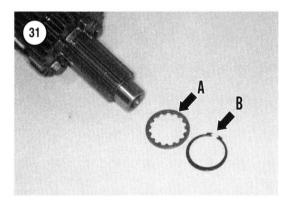

CAUTION
*Install the snap ring so its ends align with a groove in the splines (**Figure 32**).*

10. Install third gear (A, **Figure 33**), so its slider groove (B) faces *toward* the splined end.

11. Install a *new* snap ring (A, **Figure 34**) and spline washer (B) onto the shaft. The flat sides of both parts must face *toward* the splined end. The snap ring must seat in the groove in the shaft.

CAUTION
*Install the snap ring so its ends align with a groove in the splines (**Figure 34**).*

12. Install the first gear bushing (C, **Figure 34**) and seat it against the spline washer.

13. Install first gear (A, **Figure 35**) so its narrower shoulder recess faces away from the splined end.

14. Install the thrust washer (B, **Figure 35**) and seat against first gear. The flat side of the washer must face *away* from the splined end.

15. Refer to **Figure 36** for the correct placement of the countershaft gears.

16. Wrap a heavy rubber band around both ends of the shaft to prevent parts from sliding off the shaft. Wrap and store the assembly until it is ready for installation into the crankcase.

Inspection

When measuring the transmission components in this section, compare the actual measurements to the specifications in **Table 2** and **Table 3**. Replace parts that are worn or damaged.

> *NOTE*
> *Maintain the alignment of the transmission components when cleaning and inspecting the parts in this section.*

1. Inspect the mainshaft (**Figure 37**) and countershaft (**Figure 38**) for:
   a. Worn or damaged splines.
   b. Missing, broken or chipped first gear teeth (mainshaft).
   c. Worn or damaged bearing surfaces.
   d. Cracked or rounded-off snap ring grooves.
2. Measure the mainshaft outside diameter at its third gear operating position (**Figure 37**).
3. Measure the countershaft outside diameter at the second gear operating positions (**Figure 38**).
4. Check each gear for excessive wear, burrs, pitting, or chipped or missing teeth. Check the splines on sliding gears and the bore on stationary gears for excessive wear or damage.

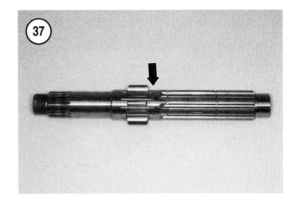

5. To check stationary gears for wear, install them and their bushings, on their correct shafts and in their original operating positions. If necessary, use the old snap rings to secure them in place. Spin the gear by hand. The gear should turn smoothly. A rough turning gear indicates heat damage. Check for a dark blue color or galling on the operating surfaces. Rocking indicates excessive wear, either to the gear, bushing or shaft.

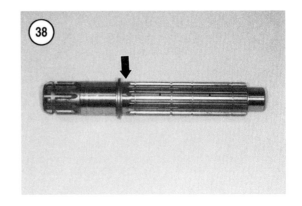

6. To check the sliding gears, install them on their correct shafts and in their original operating positions. The gear should slide back and forth without any binding or excessive play.
7. Check the gear dogs and dog slots (**Figure 39**) on the gears for excessive wear, rounding, cracks or other damage. Any wear on the dogs and mating slots should be uniform. If the dogs are not worn

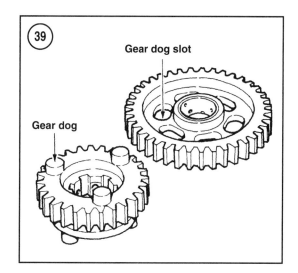

Gear dog slot

Gear dog

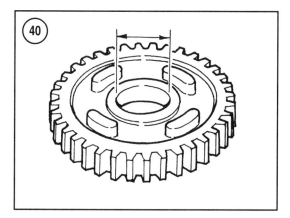

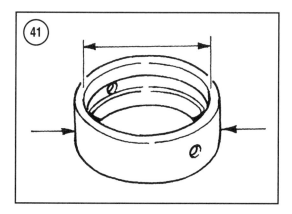

both directions. If damage is evident, also inspect the condition of the shift forks, as described in this chapter.

NOTE
The side of the gear dogs that carries the engine load wears and eventually becomes rounded. The unloaded side of the dogs remain unworn. Rounded dogs cause the transmission to jump out of gear.

9. Check for worn or damaged shift fork grooves. Check the gear groove and its mating shift fork.

10. Measure the mainshaft third and fifth gear inside diameters. Refer to **Figure 40**.

11. Measure the countershaft first, second and fourth gear inside diameters. Refer to **Figure 40**.

12. Check the bushings for:

   a. Excessively worn or damaged bearing surface.

   b. Worn or damaged splines.

   c. Cracked or scored gear bore.

13. Measure the mainshaft third and fifth gear bushing outside diameters. Also measure the third gear bushing inside diameter (**Figure 41**).

14. Measure the countershaft first, second and fourth gear bushing outside diameters. Also measure the second gear bushing inside diameter (**Figure 41**).

15. Using the measurements recorded in the previous steps, determine the bushing-to-shaft and gear-to-bushing clearances specified in **Table 2** (mainshaft) and **Table 3** (countershaft). Replace worn parts to correct any clearance not within specification.

NOTE
Replace defective gears and their mating gears at the same time, though they may not show equal wear or damage.

16. Inspect the spline washers. The teeth in the washer should be uniform.

17. Inspect the thrust washers. The washers should be smooth and show no signs of wear or heat damage (bluing).

evenly, the remaining dogs are overstressed and could fail.

8. Check engaging gears by installing both gears on their respective shafts and in their original operating positions, then twist the gears together to engage the dogs. Check for positive engagement in

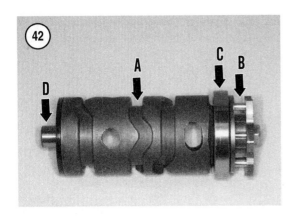

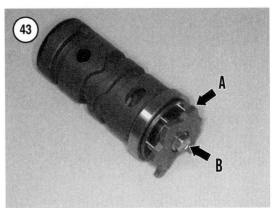

INTERNAL SHIFT MECHANISM

As the transmission is upshifted and downshifted, the shift drum and fork assembly engages and disengages pairs of gears on the transmission shafts. Gear shifting is controlled by the shift forks, which are guided by cam grooves in the shift drum.

It is important that the shift drum grooves, shift forks and mating gear grooves be in good condition. Too much wear between the parts causes unreliable and poor engagement of the gears. This can lead to premature wear of the gear dogs and other parts.

Shift Drum Inspection

1. Clean and dry the shift drum.
2. Check the shift drum for wear and damage as follows:
   a. The shift drum grooves (A, **Figure 42**) should be a uniform width. Worn grooves can prevent complete gear engagement, which can cause rough shifting and allow the transmission to disengage.
   b. Check for damaged pins (B, **Figure 42**).
   c. Spin the ball bearing (C, **Figure 42**) by hand. Replace the bearing if there is any excessive noise or the bearing turns roughly.
   d. Check the left side journal (D, **Figure 42**). The journal surface must not be worn or show overheating discoloration due to lack of lubrication. Measure the shift drum journal outside diameter. Replace the shift drum if the measurement is equal to or less than the service limit in **Table 4**.
   e. The cam plate (A, **Figure 43**) should be uniform in appearance. Check the ramp surfaces for uneven wear and damage.

   f. If necessary, refer to Step 3 to service the shift drum assembly.
3. Overhaul the shift drum as follows:
   a. Secure the shift drum with a holder and remove the bolt (B, **Figure 43**).
   b. Remove the shift drum segment (with pins), dowel pin and bearing.
   c. Replace damaged parts.
   d. Remove all threadlock residue from the bolt and shift drum threads.
   e. Install the four pins into the cam plate holes.
   f. Install the bearing onto the shift drum.
   g. Install the dowel pin into the shift drum hole.
   h. Install the cam plate by aligning is hole with the dowel pin.
   i. Apply a medium strength threadlock onto the cam plate mounting bolt threads. Install the bolt and tighten securely.

Shift Fork and Shaft Inspection

Table 4 lists new and service limit specifications for the shift forks and shift fork shaft. Replace the shift forks and shaft if out of specification or if they show damage as described in this section.
1. Inspect each shift fork for signs of wear or damage. Examine the shift forks where they contact the gear (A, **Figure 44**). These surfaces must be smooth with no signs of excessive wear, bending, cracks, heat discoloration or other damage.
2. Check each shift fork for arc-shaped wear or burn marks. These marks indicate a bent shift fork.
3. The guide pin (B, **Figure 44**) should be symmetrical and not flat on the sides.
4. Check the shift fork shafts for bending or other damage. Install each shift fork on its shaft and slide

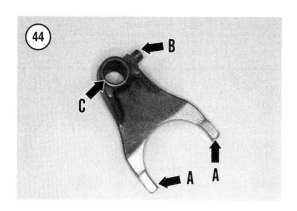

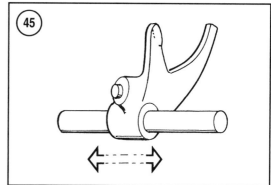

it back and forth. Each shift fork must slide smoothly with no binding or tight spots. If any fork binds, check the shaft for bending.

5. Measure the thickness of each shift fork claw (A, **Figure 44**).

6. Measure the inside diameter (C, **Figure 44**) of each shift fork.
7. Slide each shift fork (**Figure 45**) along the shaft and check for any binding or roughness.
8. Inspect the shift fork shaft for wear and damage. Measure the shaft diameter.

Table 1   TRANSMISSION SPECIFICATIONS

Transmission type	5-speed, constant mesh
Shift pattern	1-N-2-3-4-5
Primary reduction	1.667 (65/39)
Final reduction ratio	
VT750C	2.412 (41/17)
VT750DC	2.471 (42/17)
Gear ratios	
First gear	3.167 (38/12)
Second gear	2.000 (34/17)
Third gear	1.500 (30/20)
Fourth gear	1.174 (27/23)
Fifth gear	1.042 (25/24)

Table 2   MAINSHAFT SERVICE SPECIFICATIONS

	New mm (in.)	Service limit mm (in.)
Bushing inside diameter		
Third gear	25.000-25.021 (0.9843-0.9851)	25.04 (0.986)
Bushing outside diameter		
Third and fifth gear	27.959-27.980 (1.1007-1.1016)	27.94 (1.100)
Bushing-to-shaft clearance		
Third gear	0.007-0.049 (0.0003-0.0019)	0.08 (0.003)
	(continued)	

Table 2 MAINSHAFT SERVICE SPECIFICATIONS (continued)

	New mm (in.)	Service limit mm (in.)
Gear inside diameter		
Third and fifth gear	28.000-28.021 (1.1024-1.1032)	28.04 (1.104)
Gear-to-bushing clearance		
Third and fifth gear	0.020-0.062 (0.0008-0.0024)	0.10 (0.004)
Mainshaft outside diameter		
Third gear position	24.972-24.993 (0.9831-0.9840)	24.95 (0.982)

Table 3 COUNTERSHAFT SERVICE SPECIFICATIONS

	New mm (in.)	Service limit mm (in.)
Bushing inside diameter		
Second gear	27.995-28.016 (1.1021-1.1030)	28.04 (1.104)
Bushing outside diameter		
First, second and fourth gear	30.950-30.975 (1.2185-1.2195)	30.93 (1.218)
Bushing-to-shaft clearance		
Second gear	0.015-0.049 (0.0006-0.0019)	0.08 (0.003)
Gear inside diameter		
First, second and fourth gear	31.000-31.025 (1.2204-1.2215)	31.05 (1.222)
Gear-to-bushing clearance		
First, second and fourth gear	0.025-0.075 (0.0010-0.0030)	0.11 (0.004)
Countershaft outside diameter		
Second gear position	27.967-27.980 (1.1011-1.1016)	27.95 (1.100)

Table 4 SHIFT FORK AND SHIFT SHAFT SERVICE SPECIFICATIONS

	New mm (in.)	Service limit mm (in.)
Shift drum outside diameter (at left journal)	11.966-11.984 (0.4711-0.4718)	11.94 (0.470)
Shift fork claw thickness	5.93-6.00 (0.233-0.236)	5.6 (0.22)
Shift fork inside diameter	13.000-13.021 (0.5118-0.5126)	13.04 (0.513)
Shift fork shaft outside diameter	12.966-12.984 (0.5105-0.5112)	12.90 (0.508)

CHAPTER EIGHT

FUEL AND EMISSION CONTROL SYSTEMS

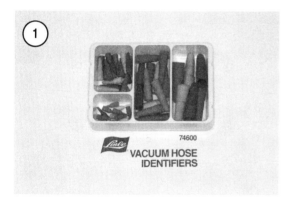

This chapter includes service procedures for the fuel and emission control systems. Refer to Chapter Three for air filter service.

Carburetor specifications are listed in **Table 1**. **Tables 1-3** are at the end of this chapter.

FUEL SYSTEM PRECAUTIONS

The fuel system consists of a fuel tank, shutoff valve, fuel pump and fuel filter, two Keihin constant velocity carburetors and air filter.

Because of the explosive and flammable conditions that exist around gasoline, always observe the following:

1. Disconnect the negative battery cable before working on the fuel system.

2. Gasoline dripping onto a hot engine component may cause a fire. Always allow the engine to cool completely before working on any fuel system component.

3. Wipe up spilled gasoline immediately with dry rags. Store the rags in a suitable metal container until they can be cleaned or disposed of.

4. Do not service any fuel system component while in the vicinity of open flames, sparks or while anyone is smoking next to the motorcycle.

5. Always have a fire extinguisher nearby when working on the fuel system.

FUEL HOSE IDENTIFICATION

The fuel system uses a number of fuel and vacuum hoses. To allow easier reassembly, develop a system to identify the hoses before disconnecting them. Make tags with strips of masking tape and a fine point permanent-marking pen. There are also a number of aftermarket hose identification kits, such as the Lisle Vacuum Hose Identifiers (part No. 74600) shown in **Figure 1**. This kit consists of 48 color-coded hose fittings in 1/8-to-1/2 in. sizes. Automotive and aftermarket parts suppliers carry this kit or similar equivalents.

AIR FILTER HOUSING

Air filter service is described in Chapter Three. The following section describes air filter housing removal and installation.

Removal/Installation

The air filter housing can be removed as an assembly.

1. Refer to *Fuel Hose Identification* in this chapter.
2. Remove the fuel tank as described in this chapter.
3. Remove the air filter housing mounting bolts (**Figure 2**).
4. Loosen the air filter housing-to-air filter chamber hose clamp (**Figure 3**).
5. Remove the air filter housing.
6. Cover the air filter chamber and air filter openings with a plastic bag.
7. Installation is the reverse of removal. Note the following:

   a. Lubricate the air filter housing inner mating hose surface with grease as shown in **Figure 4**.
   b. Align the boss on the air filter housing (A, **Figure 5**) with the grommet in the front cylinder head fin (B).
   c. Tighten the air filter housing bolts (**Figure 2**) securely.
   d. Tighten the air filter housing-to-air chamber hose clamp (**Figure 3**) securely.

AIR FILTER CHAMBER

The air filter chamber connects the air filter housing to the carburetors.

Removal/Installation

1. Remove the air filter housing as described in this chapter.

> *NOTE*
> *The air filter chamber is a snug fit between the frame and carburetors. Using compressed air (Step 2) helps to clean the area and prevent dirt and other abrasive dust from falling into the carburetors.*

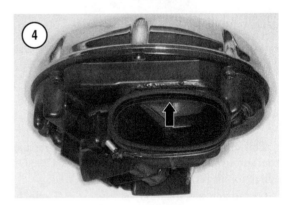

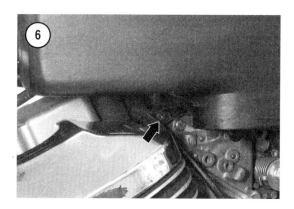

2. Clean the air filter chamber and the area where it connects to the carburetors with compressed air.

3. Loosen the air filter chamber-to-carburetor clamp screws. Refer to **Figure 6** and **Figure 7**.

4. Disconnect the crankcase breather tube (**Figure 8**) from the air filter chamber.

5. Remove the air filter chamber (**Figure 9**).

6. Check each hose for alignment and looseness that may have occurred during removal.

7. Check the air filter chamber for any dirt or debris. Clean the chamber and hoses if necessary.

8. Installation is the reverse of removal. Note the following:

   a. Make sure the hoses seal tightly against the air chamber. Reseal the hoses with a rubber sealant (Permatex Black Rubber Sealant [part No. RS-9] or an equivalent) and align the index mark on each hose with the marks on the air chamber.

   b. Position the hose clamps within their guides on the hoses.

   c. After installing the air filter chamber, check each hose connection at the air filter chamber. Due to the tight fit between the frame and engine, it is easy to knock a hose off the air filter chamber when installing it.

   d. Tighten the hose clamps securely.

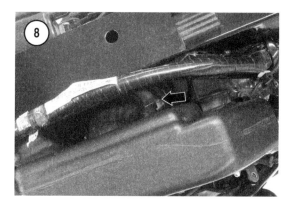

SUB-AIR FILTER ELEMENT

The sub-air filter housing is mounted on top of the front cylinder head cover (**Figure 10**).

Filter Cleaning

The filter can be serviced with its housing mounted on the motorcycle.

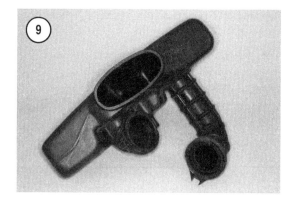

1. Remove the fuel tank as described in this chapter.

2A. On VT750C models, remove the steering covers (Chapter Fifteen).

2B. On VT750DC models, remove the front cylinder left overhead cover.

3. Disconnect the front cylinder left side spark plug cap.

4. Lift the sub-air filter housing cover (**Figure 10**) and remove the filter (**Figure 11**).

5. Inspect the filter and replace if deteriorated or damaged.

6. Clean the filter in a high flash solvent and allow to dry.

7. Soak the filter in SAE 80-90 weight gear oil. Squeeze the filter to remove excess oil.

8. Installation is the reverse of removal. Make sure the cover snaps fully onto the housing.

Housing Removal/Installation

1. Remove the fuel tank as described in this chapter.

2A. On VT750C models, remove the steering covers (Chapter Fifteen).

2B. On VT750DC models, remove the front cylinder left overhead cover.

3. Disconnect the front cylinder left side spark plug cap.

4. Disconnect the two hoses from the cover (**Figure 10**).

5. Lift the sub-air filter housing cover to disconnect its lock tabs from the filter housing.

6. Remove the sub-air filter housing assembly.

7. Installation is the reverse of removal. Make sure the cover snaps fully onto the housing.

CARBURETOR OPERATION

Understanding the function of each of the carburetor components and their relationships to one another is a valuable aid for pinpointing carburetor trouble.

The carburetor's purpose is to supply and atomize fuel and mix it in correct proportions with air that is drawn in through the air intake. At the primary throttle opening (idle), a small amount of fuel is siphoned through the pilot jet by the incoming air. As the throttle is opened further, the air stream begins to siphon fuel through the main jet and needle jet. The tapered needle increases the effective flow

capacity of the needle jet as it is lifted, in that it occupies less of the area of the jet.

At full throttle the carburetor venturi is fully open and the needle is lifted far enough to permit the main jet to flow at full capacity.

The choke circuit is a bystarter system in which the choke lever opens a choke valve and needle rather than closing a butterfly in the venturi area as on many carburetors. In the open position, the pilot jet discharges a stream of fuel into the carburetor venturi, enriching the mixture when the engine is cold.

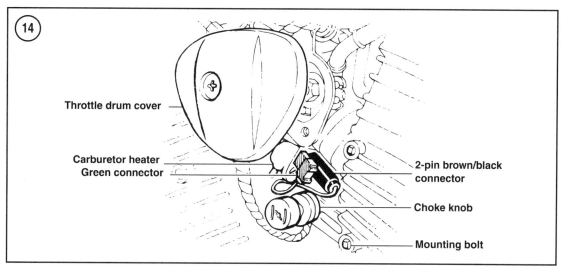

Throttle drum cover

Carburetor heater
Green connector

2-pin brown/black
connector

Choke knob

Mounting bolt

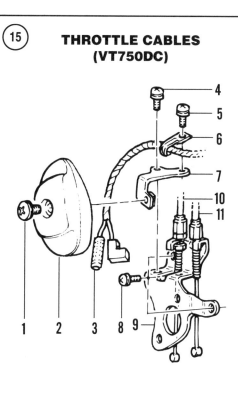

THROTTLE CABLES (VT750DC)

1. Screw
2. Throttle drum cover
3. Carburetor heater wiring harness
4. Screw
5. Screw
6. Carburetor heater harness wire clamp
7. Throttle drum cover bracket
8. Screw
9. Throttle cable holder
10. Pull cable
11. Return cable

CARBURETOR SERVICE

The rear cylinder carburetor (No. 1) is mounted on the left side of the motorcycle; the front carburetor (No. 2) is mounted on the right side.

Carburetor Removal

1. Refer to *Fuel Hose Identification* in this chapter.
2. Remove the left side cover (Chapter Fifteen).
3. Remove the following as described in this chapter:
   a. Fuel tank.
   b. Air filter housing.
   c. Air filter chamber.
4. Connect a hose (A, **Figure 12**) to the drain nozzle on the bottom of the rear carburetor. Loosen the drain screw (B, **Figure 12**) and drain the fuel into a clean container. Close the drain screw and remove the hose.
5. Repeat Step 4 for the front carburetor.
6A. On VT750C models, perform the following:
   a. Remove the two screws (A, **Figure 13**) securing the throttle cable holder to the carburetor.
   b. Disconnect the throttle cables (B, **Figure 13**) from the throttle drum on the carburetor. Leave the cables attached to the throttle cable holder.
6B. On VT750DC models, perform the following:
   a. Remove the screw and the throttle drum cover (**Figure 14**).
   b. Remove the screw and the carburetor heater harness wire clamp (6, **Figure 15**).

8

c. Remove the screw and the throttle drum cover bracket (7, **Figure 15**).

d. Remove the three screws and the throttle cable holder (9, **Figure 15**).

e. Disconnect the throttle cables from the throttle drum on the carburetor (B, **Figure 13**). Leave the cables attached to the throttle cable holder.

7. Disconnect the clamp (**Figure 16**) securing the fuel hose to the frame.

8. Disconnect the fuel hose (**Figure 17**) from the joint leading to the fuel pump.

9. Loosen the front and rear carburetor upper intake tube hose clamps (**Figure 18**, typical). Do not loosen the lower clamps that secure the intake tube to the cylinder heads.

10A. On VT750C models, perform the following:

a. Disconnect the rear cylinder left side spark plug cap (A, **Figure 19**).

b. Remove the bolts and the rear cylinder left side fin (B, **Figure 19**) and the choke knob (C).

10B. On VT750DC models, perform the following:

a. Remove the bolt and the choke knob (**Figure 14**).

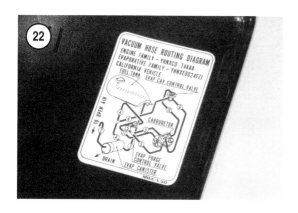

b. Disconnect the carburetor heater electrical connectors from the each carburetor (**Figure 14**).

11. Disconnect the sub-air filter hose from each carburetor. Refer to **Figure 20** (front carburetor) and **Figure 21** (rear carburetor).

12. On California models, perform the following:

a. Refer to *Evaporative Emission Control System (California Models)* in this chapter to identify the EVAP CAV control valve and EVAP purge control valve hoses.

b. Refer to the emission control hose diagram (**Figure 22**) on the left side cover when identifying and disconnecting hoses in the following steps.

c. Label and disconnect the hoses at the EVAP CAV control valve (**Figure 23**). Do not disconnect the air vent hose from the bottom of the valve.

d. Disconnect the two carburetor hoses at the charcoal canister tee-joint (**Figure 24**).

e. Disconnect the No. 11 hose from the charcoal canister (**Figure 25**). The opposite end of this hose connects to the rear cylinder carburetor.

NOTE
Before removing the carburetors, note how the choke cable routes around the carburetors and exits the left side of the motorcycle.

13. Pry each carburetor, one at a time, from the intake manifolds. When both carburetors are free, pull them toward the right side (**Figure 26**).

14. Push the carburetor assembly forward and locate the tee-joint connecting the main fuel hose to the individual fuel hoses attached at the carburetors. Disconnect both carburetor fuel hoses (**Figure 27**)

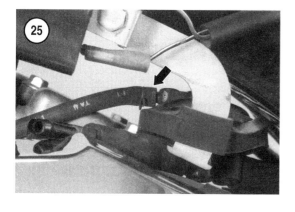

from the tee-connection. The rear carburetor fuel hose is equipped with a metal spring for additional strength and protection. Pull the rear cylinder carburetor fuel hose forward (**Figure 28**) so it clears the intake tube when the carburetor is removed.

15. Remove the carburetor assembly from the right side.

16. Plug the intake tubes to prevent dirt and small objects from falling into the cylinder heads.

17. Installation is the reverse of removal. Note the following:

    a. Adjust the throttle cables (Chapter Thirteen).

    b. Check and adjust the carburetor idle speed and synchronization (Chapter Three).

    c. Adjust the choke and check the choke cable operation (Chapter Three).

18. After installing the fuel tank and turning on the fuel valve, check the carburetors for any fuel leaks. Repair any leak before starting the engine.

> *WARNING*
> *Do not ride the motorcycle until the throttle cables are adjusted properly.*

Air Cut-Off Valve
Removal/Installation

During deceleration when the throttle is released, the fuel mixture becomes lean. This is a condition that can cause backfiring and popping in the exhaust pipe. To prevent this, a vacuum operated air cut-off valve is mounted on each carburetor. Each valve assembly contains a spring-loaded diaphragm installed inside a sealed chamber. The shaft on the end of the diaphragm operates in the carburetor pilot air passageway. A separate carburetor passageway aligns with the hole in the diaphragm cover to supply vacuum to operate the valve.

When the throttle is released, vacuum in the air-cut off valve chamber increases enough to overcome the spring pressure applied against the diaphragm. This allows the diaphragm's shaft to move outward and close the pilot jet air passageway and richen the air/fuel mixture. During acceleration, the vacuum decreases and the spring pressure once again operates against the diaphragm to open the pilot air passageway.

The air cut-off valves can be removed without disassembling the carburetors.

Refer to **Figure 29**.

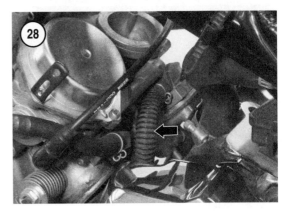

1. Remove the carburetor as described in this chapter.

2. Remove the air cut-off valve cover screws, and then remove the retainer (A, **Figure 30**), cover (B) spring (A, **Figure 31**), diaphragm (B) and O-ring (C).

3. Inspect the spring (**Figure 32**) for weakness or damage.

4. Inspect the cover (**Figure 32**) for corrosion or damage. Clean the cover passageway with compressed air.

5. Inspect the diaphragm (**Figure 32**) for soft spots, deterioration or other damage.

6. Inspect the diaphragm shaft for grooves, wear or damage.

7. Replace the O-ring if deteriorated or damaged.

8. Check the vacuum passageway in the carburetor for dirt or other debris.

9. Replace excessively worn or damaged parts.

10. Install the O-ring (C, **Figure 31**) with its flat side facing the carburetor body. Refer to **Figure 29**.

11. Install the diaphragm and seat it into the carburetor groove as shown in B, **Figure 31**.

CARBURETOR

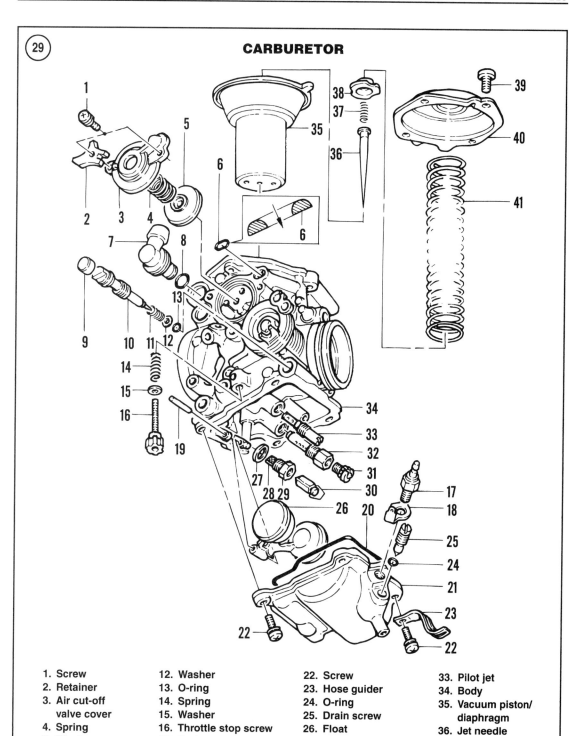

1. Screw
2. Retainer
3. Air cut-off valve cover
4. Spring
5. Diaphragm
6. O-ring
7. Hose joint
8. O-ring
9. Plug
10. Pilot screw
11. Spring
12. Washer
13. O-ring
14. Spring
15. Washer
16. Throttle stop screw
17. Carburetor heater (VT750DC)
18. Ground terminal/ sealing washer
19. Float pin
20. O-ring
21. Float bowl
22. Screw
23. Hose guider
24. O-ring
25. Drain screw
26. Float
27. Gasket
28. Screen
29. Float valve seat
30. Float valve
31. Main jet
32. Needle jet holder
33. Pilot jet
34. Body
35. Vacuum piston/ diaphragm
36. Jet needle
37. Spring
38. Holder
39. Screw
40. Vacuum chamber cover
41. Spring

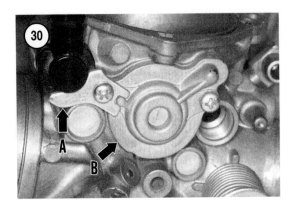

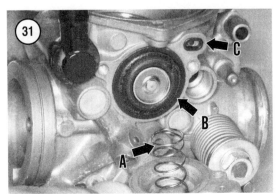

12. Install the spring and seat it into the cover (A, **Figure 31**) and then install the cover (B, **Figure 30**) and retainer (A). Secure it with its mounting screws.

13. Repeat these steps for the other air-cut off valve assembly.

Carburetor Disassembly

The carburetors are jointed together (**Figure 29**). However, all internal carburetor parts can be serviced without separating the carburetors. If the carburetor body must be cleaned internally or if the hose joints or O-rings must be replaced, separate the carburetors as described in this section.

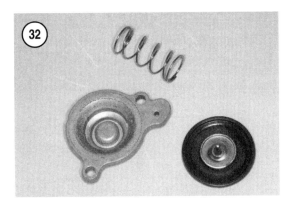

> *NOTE*
> *The photographs in the following procedure show a carburetor assembly from a California model. The number of hoses and their fitting locations vary for carburetors found on other models.*

> *NOTE*
> *Do not interchange parts between the front and rear carburetors. Keep both carburetors and their parts separate when servicing them.*

1. Make a diagram of the hoses and their routing on the carburetors, then remove them. Refer to **Figure 33**, typical.

2. Loosen the choke cable locknut (**Figure 34**) and remove the choke valve assembly (**Figure 35**).

3. Repeat Step 3 for the other carburetor and remove the choke cable from the carburetor assembly.

4. Remove the air cut-off valve as described in this section.

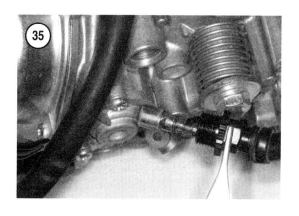

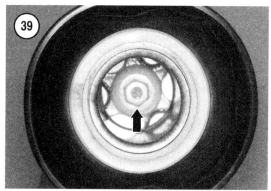

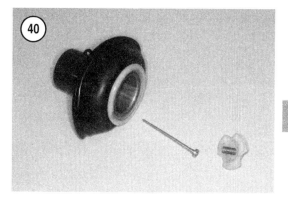

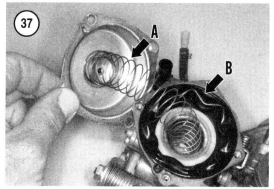

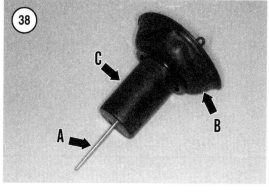

NOTE
Before removing the vacuum chamber cover, lift the vacuum piston with a finger, then release it. It should move up the bore smoothly and then drop slowly with no binding or roughness. If there is any noticeable drag, the spring installed inside the vacuum chamber may be broken or was installed incorrectly.

5. Remove the vacuum chamber cover screws and cover (**Figure 36**).

6. Remove the spring (A, **Figure 37**) and the vacuum piston/diaphragm (B).

7. To remove the jet needle (A, **Figure 38**) from the vacuum piston/diaphragm, perform the following:

   a. Insert a Phillips screwdriver into the vacuum piston cavity and turn the holder (**Figure 39**) 1/4 turn counterclockwise to unlock it from the tangs within the piston cavity.

   b. Remove the holder, spring and jet needle (**Figure 40**).

NOTE
*Compare the jet needle assembly with the parts in **Figure 29**. Any additional*

shims or spacers may indicate an af-termarket jet kit installed by a previous owner.

8. Remove the float bowl mounting screws, float bowl (**Figure 41**) and O-ring. Inspect the float bowl for dirt and other contamination.

9. Remove the float pin (A, **Figure 42**), float (B) and float valve (**Figure 43**).

10. Remove the float valve seat and gasket (**Figure 44**).

11. Remove the main jet (**Figure 45**).

12. Remove the needle jet holder (**Figure 46**).

> *NOTE*
> *The needle jet is pressed into the carburetor and cannot be removed.*

13. Remove the pilot jet (**Figure 47**).

14. If necessary, separate the carburetor assemblies as described in this section

> *NOTE*
> *Further disassembly is not recommended. If the throttle plate and shaft are damaged, the carburetor body must be replaced.*

Carburetor
Cleaning and Inspection

> *WARNING*
> *Wear safety goggles when cleaning the carburetors.*

1. A gasket kit is available from Honda and includes the following replacement parts identified in **Figure 29**: No. 13, 20, 24 and 28. If a gasket kit is used, discard all parts replaced in the kit. A separate gasket kit is required for each carburetor.

> *NOTE*
> *Replace all O-rings upon assembly. O-rings tend to become hardened after prolonged use and exposure to heat and lose their ability to seal properly.*

2. Before cleaning the parts in a dip-type carburetor cleaner or with an aerosol carburetor cleaner, note the following:

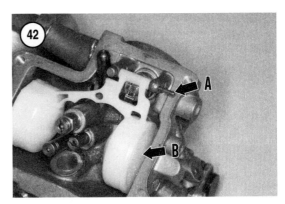

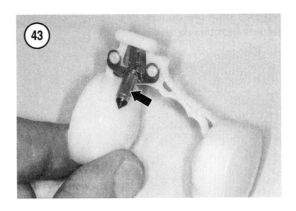

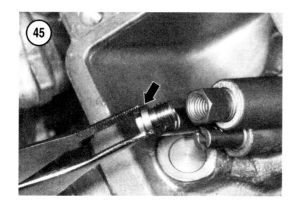

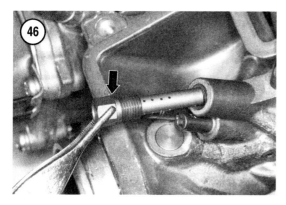

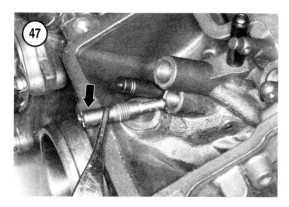

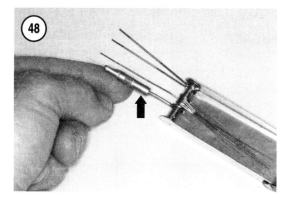

a. Remove the O-ring, drain screw and O-ring, and carburetor heater (V750DC models) from the float bowl.

b. Remove the pilot screws as described in this section.

c. All parts, except the carburetor body, rubber and plastic parts, can be cleaned with carburetor cleaner.

NOTE
When using a dip-type carburetor cleaner, the parts are placed in a small basket and immersed in the container. Follow the manufacturer's directions for immersion time.

3. After soaking the parts, rinse them in warm water and blow dry with compressed air. Blow out the jets with compressed air.

4. Visually inspect the main jet, pilot jet and needle jet bores for contamination. Hold the part with pliers and blow out the bore with compressed air. If the bore is still plugged, soak the part in carburetor cleaner. Dry and clean again with compressed air. If the bore is still plugged, either replace the part or try to clean it with a piece of wire or a drill bit. The pilot jet is the most difficult part to clean because its bore is the smallest. Before starting, first examine the same part in the other carburetor. If its bore is not plugged, find a cleaning tool that can pass through it. The K&L Carb Cleaner Wire Set (part No. 35-3498 [**Figure 48**]) includes a number of different size probes designed for cleaning jets and passageways.

CAUTION
When using a carburetor cleaning tool, wire or drill bit to clean jets and other carburetor passages, work carefully to avoid gouging or enlarging the bore. Doing so can alter the air/fuel mixture.

5. Clean the carburetor housing with compressed air. Operate the throttle shaft to check for binding or damage. Then try to move the throttle shaft back and forth. If there is any play, the throttle shaft and shaft bores are worn. This requires replacement of the carburetor body.

6. Make sure all openings in the carburetor body are clear. Clean them out if they are plugged, and then clean with compressed air.

7. If any part of the float valve and seat is damaged, it must be replaced as an assembly. Inspect the assembly as follows:

    a. Inspect the end of the float valve (A, **Figure 49**) and float valve seat for wear or damage. If the float valve is excessively worn or damaged, replace the valve and seat assembly.

    b. Lightly press on the spring-loaded pin in the float valve. The pin should easily move in and out of the valve. If it is varnished with fuel residue, replace the float valve and seat assembly.

    c. Clean and inspect the float valve seat screen (B, **Figure 49**) and replace if damaged. The screen can be replaced separately (it is included in the carburetor gasket kit).

8. Inspect the float valve sealing washer (C, **Figure 49**) for damage that would allow it to leak.

NOTE

*A worn float valve and seat assembly causes engine flooding. If there is any doubt about the condition of these parts, replace them as a set (27, 28,29 and 30, **Figure 29**).*

9. Inspect the main jet, needle jet holder and pilot jet for thread damage.

10. Inspect the jet needle (A, **Figure 38**) for excessive wear at the tip or other damage on the needle.

11. Check the diaphragm (B, **Figure 38**) for tearing, soft spots, pin holes, age deterioration or other damage.

12. Check the vacuum piston (C, **Figure 38**) for nicks, scoring or damage. Install the vacuum piston/diaphragm into the carburetor body and move it up and down in the bore. The vacuum piston should move smoothly with no binding or excessive play.

13. Inspect the jet needle spring and holder (**Figure 40**) for corrosion or damage.

14. Submerge the float in water and check for leakage. Replace the float if water or fuel is detected inside the float.

15. On VT750DC models, a carburetor heater is installed in each float bowl. Test the carburetor heater as described in this chapter.

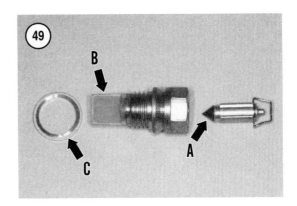

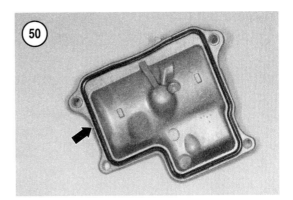

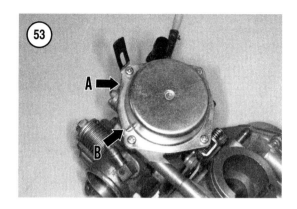

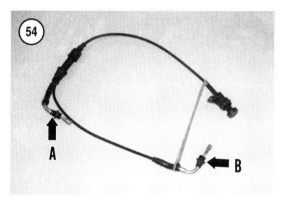

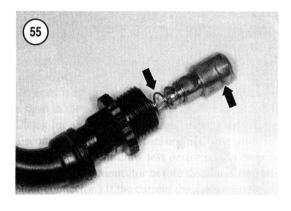

Carburetor Assembly

1. If the pilot screw was removed, install it as described under *Pilot Screw Removal/Installation* in this section.

2. Install and tighten the pilot jet (**Figure 47**).

3. Install and tighten the needle jet holder (**Figure 46**).

4. Hold the needle jet holder, and then install and tighten the main jet (**Figure 45**).

5. Install the sealing washer (C, **Figure 49**) onto the float valve seat. Install and tighten the seat.

6. Hook the float valve onto the float (**Figure 43**), and then install the float (B, **Figure 42**) and secure with the float pin (A).

7. Measure the float height as described under *Carburetor Adjustment* in this chapter.

8. If removed, install the O-ring (**Figure 50**) into the float bowl groove.

9. Align the float bowl with the carburetor body and install the float bowl (**Figure 41**). Install and tighten the float bowl mounting screws securely.

10. Install the needle jet assembly (**Figure 40**) as follows:

    a. Install the needle jet into the vacuum piston.

    b. Install the spring onto the holder, and then install the holder into the vacuum piston.

    c. Press and turn the holder (**Figure 39**) 1/4 turn clockwise to lock it in place.

11. Install the vacuum piston/diaphragm into the carburetor. Align the diaphragm tab with the cavity in the carburetor housing (**Figure 51**).

12. Lift the vacuum piston (from the bottom) and seat the diaphragm lip (**Figure 52**) into the groove in the top of the carburetor housing.

13. Install the spring (A, **Figure 37**) into the vacuum piston.

14. Align the shoulder on the inside of the vacuum chamber cover with the spring. Install the cover (A, **Figure 53**). Align the diaphragm tab with the concave part of the cover (B, **Figure 53**) when installing the cover.

15. Install and tighten the vacuum chamber cover screws securely.

NOTE
Lift the vacuum piston with a finger, then release it. If the piston moves roughly, the spring installed inside the vacuum chamber was incorrectly installed.

16. If the carburetors were separated, assemble them as described in this section.

17. Referring to the notes made during disassembly, install the fuel and vacuum hoses onto the carburetors.

18. Install the choke cable assembly (**Figure 54**) as follows:

    a. If removed, install the spring and choke valve onto the end of each cable (**Figure 55**).

    b. Install the short choke cable end (A, **Figure 54**) into the rear carburetor (**Figure 56**) and

8

the long cable end (B, **Figure 54**) into the front carburetor (**Figure 57**).

c. Insert the choke valve into the carburetor bore and tighten the cable nut (**Figure 58**) securely.

d. Operate the choke knob to make sure the choke valves move smoothly in the carburetor bores.

19. Install the air cut-off valve as described in this section.

Carburetor
Separation/Assembly

The carburetors are joined together by two screws. All internal carburetor parts can be replaced without separating the carburetors. If the carburetors must be cleaned internally or the synchronization springs replaced, separate the carburetors.

Refer to **Figure 59** (VT750C) or **Figure 60** (VT750DC).

1. Loosen the synchronization screw (**Figure 61**) to remove all tension from the screw.

NOTE
The carburetor assembly screws are secured tightly. Wrap the carburetors with a thick towel. Loosen the screws with a hand impact driver and the correct size Phillips bit.

2. Loosen and remove the two carburetor assembly screws (**Figure 62** and **Figure 63**).
3. Separate the carburetors while removing the thrust spring and synchronization spring.
4. Service the carburetors as described in this chapter.
5. Clean the two springs in solvent. Check the springs for cracks, flat spots and other damage. Replace if necessary.
6. Assemble by reversing these disassembly steps, while noting the following.
7. Install the thrust spring and synchronization spring and join the two carburetors as shown in **Figure 59** or **Figure 60**.
8. Check that there is no clearance or gap where the two carburetor housings join together and install and tighten the screws (**Figure 62** and **Figure 63**) gradually, first one screw and then the other until they are both tight.

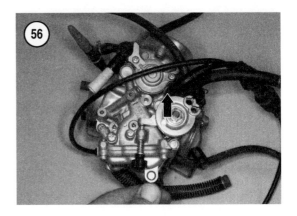

9. Open the throttle with the throttle drum (A, **Figure 64**) and release it. The throttle should return smoothly with no drag.

10. Turn the throttle stop screw (B, **Figure 64**) to align the throttle valve with the edge of the by-pass hole (**Figure 65**) in the No. 1 (rear) carburetor.

11. Turn the synchronization screw (**Figure 61**) to align the throttle valve with the edge of the by-pass hole (**Figure 66**) in the No. 2 (front) carburetor.

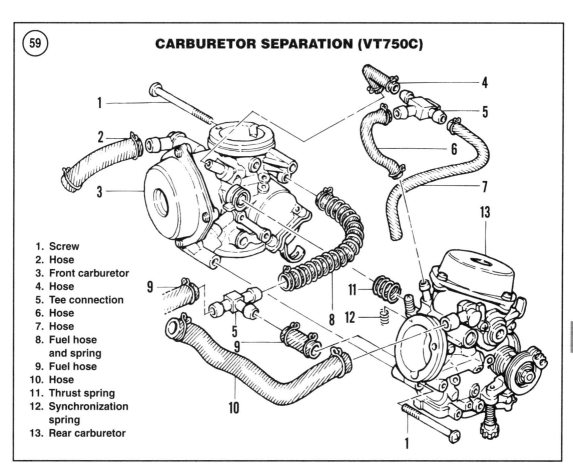

CARBURETOR SEPARATION (VT750C)

1. Screw
2. Hose
3. Front carburetor
4. Hose
5. Tee connection
6. Hose
7. Hose
8. Fuel hose and spring
9. Fuel hose
10. Hose
11. Thrust spring
12. Synchronization spring
13. Rear carburetor

8

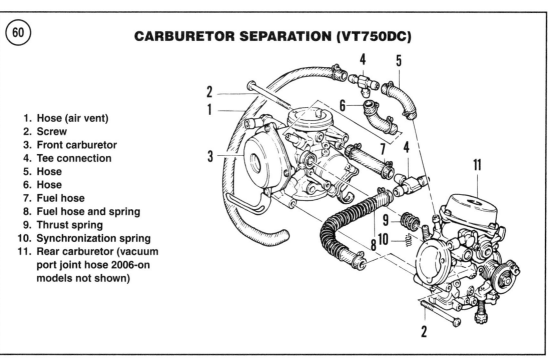

CARBURETOR SEPARATION (VT750DC)

1. Hose (air vent)
2. Screw
3. Front carburetor
4. Tee connection
5. Hose
6. Hose
7. Fuel hose
8. Fuel hose and spring
9. Thrust spring
10. Synchronization spring
11. Rear carburetor (vacuum port joint hose 2006-on models not shown)

12. Rotate the throttle drum (A, **Figure 64**) to make sure each throttle valve opens and closes correctly.

13. If the throttle drum does not move smoothly or return properly, recheck all previous steps until the problem is solved.

14. Check carburetor synchronization after installing the carburetors onto the motorcycle. Refer to Chapter Three.

Pilot Screw
Removal and Installation

The pilot screw bores are sealed with an aluminum plug (**Figure 67**) to prevent routine adjustment. The pilot screws do not require adjustment unless the carburetors are overhauled, the pilot screws are incorrectly adjusted, the pilot screws require replacement or to adjust them when installing a jet kit.

1. Use a small center punch and hammer to center punch the middle of the plug (**Figure 67**).

2. Install a drill stop 3 mm (1/8 in.) from the end of a 5/32-inch drill bit (**Figure 68**).

> *CAUTION*
> *If tape is used as a drill stop, use it as a visual guide only. The tape will not stop the drill bit from drilling deeper into the plug.*

3. Drill a hole into the plug until the drill stop contacts the plug. If a drill stop is not used, do not drill too deeply. The pilot screw is difficult to remove if the head is damaged.

4. Thread a sheet metal screw into the drilled hole. Continue to turn the screw until the plug starts to turn with the screw.

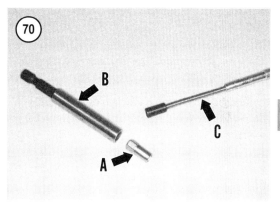

8

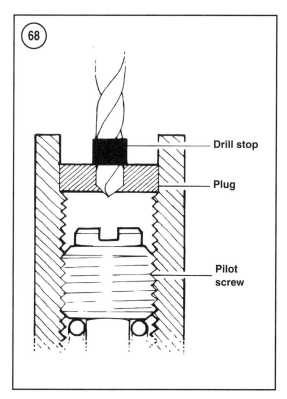

5. Remove the plug and screw with a pair of pliers (**Figure 69**) and blow away all metal shavings from the area.

> *CAUTION*
> *The pointed end of the pilot screw can break off if the screw is tightened against the carburetor seat. Seat the screw as described in Step 6.*

> *NOTE*
> *If the pilot screw uses a D-shaped head, a D-shaped driver head tool is required to remove and install the screw. An inexpensive tool can be assembled by mounting a Motion Pro D-shaped 1/4-inch hex drive bit (part No. 08-0242 [A, **Figure 70**]) on any standard driver (B) that accepts 1/4-inch hex-shaped bits. Honda also offers a D-shaped pilot screw wrench (C, **Figure 70**).*

6. Screw the pilot screw in until it *lightly* seats while counting and recording the number of turns.

Reinstall the pilot screw to the same position during assembly.

NOTE
Identify the pilot screws so they can be reinstalled in their original carburetor.

7. Remove the pilot screw, spring, washer and O-ring. If the O-ring stayed inside the carburetor, remove it with a piece of bent wire. Make sure to remove the O-ring so its condition can be checked.
8. Inspect the pilot screw for a worn or damaged tip. Replace if damaged.

NOTE
If one pilot screw is damaged, both pilot screws must be replaced at the same time.

9. Replace the O-ring if cracked or damaged.
10. Slide the spring, washer and O-ring onto the pilot screw.

NOTE
Install used pilot screws into their original carburetor.

11. Screw the pilot screw into the carburetor until it *lightly* seats. Back it out the number of turns noted during disassembly.

NOTE
Do not install new plugs until after the carburetor has been installed on the motorcycle and the carburetor adjusted.

12. Repeat these steps for the other carburetor.
13. If new pilot screws were installed, adjust the pilot screws as described under *Carburetor Adjustment* in this chapter.
14. Drive in new pilot screw plugs until their outer surface is recessed 1 mm (0.04 in.) into the pilot screw bore.

CARBURETOR ADJUSTMENT

Float Level

The carburetors must be removed and partially disassembled for this adjustment.
1. Remove the carburetors as described in this chapter.

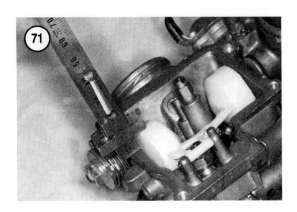

2. Remove the screws securing the float bowls to the main bodies and remove them.
3. Hold the carburetor assembly so the float arm is just touching the float needle. Use a float level gauge (Honda part No. 07401-0010001 or equivalent) and measure the distance from the carburetor body to the float (**Figure 71**). Position the measurement tool in line with the main jet. The float level is listed in **Table 1**. If the measurement is incorrect, note the following:
   a. On some floats, the float arm lip is not adjustable. If the float level is incorrect on this type of float, replace the float.
   b. If the float arm lip is adjustable, bend it to correct the float level. Install the float and recheck the float level adjustment.

NOTE
If the float level is too high (low fuel level), the result is a lean air/fuel mixture. If it is too low (high fuel level), the mixture is too rich.

4. Install the float bowl as described under *Carburetor Assembly* in this chapter.
5. Reassemble and install the carburetors as described in this chapter.

Needle Jet

The needle jet is non-adjustable.

Pilot Screw
(Idle Drop Procedure)

1. The pilot screws are preset. Adjustment is not necessary except under the following conditions:
   a. The carburetors have been overhauled.

b. The pilot screws were replaced.

c. The carburetor is being adjusted for high altitude (see procedure in following section).

d. An aftermarket jet kit was installed.

2. Check the air filter and replace if necessary (Chapter Three).

3. Check carburetor synchronization and adjust if necessary (Chapter Three).

4. Remove the pilot screw plugs (A, **Figure 72**) as described in this chapter.

CAUTION
*Seat the pilot screw **lightly** in Step 5 or the screw tip can break off into the pilot screw bore.*

NOTE
*If the pilot screws use D-shaped heads, a D-shaped driver head tool is required. An inexpensive tool can be assembled by mounting a Motion Pro D-shaped 1/4-inch hex drive bit (part No. 08-0242 [A, **Figure 70**]) on any standard driver (B) that accepts 1/4-inch hex-shaped bits. Honda also offers a D-shaped pilot screw wrench (C, **Figure 70**).*

5. Carefully turn the pilot screw on each carburetor in until they *lightly* seat and then back them out the number of turns (initial opening) listed in **Table 1**.

6. Start the engine and let it reach normal operating temperature. Approximately 10-15 minutes of stop-and-go riding is sufficient.

7. Turn the engine off and support it on its sidestand.

8. Connect a portable tachometer (that can register a change of 50 rpm or less) to the engine following the manufacturer's instructions.

9. Start the engine and turn the throttle stop screw (B, **Figure 72**) in or out to achieve the specified idle speed (**Table 1**).

10. Read the tachometer scale and turn each pilot screw out 1/2 turn from the initial setting in Step 5. If the engine speed increases by 50 rpm or more, turn each pilot screw out by an additional 1/2 turn at a time until the engine speed does not increase.

11. Turn the throttle stop screw (B, **Figure 72**) in or out to achieve the idle speed specification.

12. Turn the rear cylinder pilot screw clockwise until the engine speed drops 50 rpm.

13. Turn the pilot screw on the rear cylinder counterclockwise 1 turn (VT750C) or 1/2 turn (VT750DC) from the position obtained in Step 11.

14. Turn the throttle stop screw (B, **Figure 72**) in or out to achieve the idle speed specification.

15. Repeat Steps 11-13 for the front cylinder carburetor pilot screw.

16. Turn the engine off and disconnect the portable tachometer.

17. Test ride the motorcycle. Throttle response from idle should be without any hesitation.

18. Drive in new pilot screw plugs until their outer surface is recessed 1 mm (0.04 in.) into the pilot screw bore.

High Elevation

If the motorcycle is ridden for a sustained period at high elevation above 2000 m (6500 ft.), readjust the carburetors to improve performance and decrease emissions.

NOTE
Honda technicians place a Vehicle Emission Control Information update label on the inside of the left side cover when the carburetors have been adjusted for high altitude. Before adjusting the carburetors on an unfamiliar motorcycle, check for this label.

1. Remove each pilot screw plug (A, **Figure 72**) as described in this chapter.

2. Start the engine and let it reach normal operating temperature. Approximately 10-15 minutes of stop-and-go riding is sufficient.

NOTE
If the pilot screws use D-shaped heads, a D-shaped driver head tool is

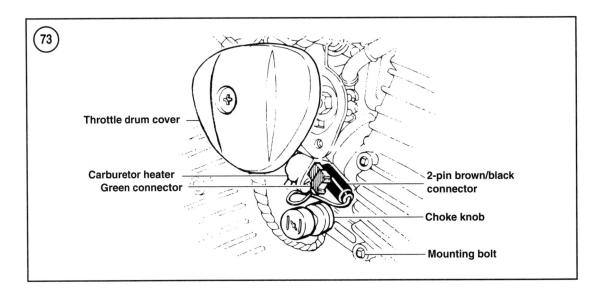

(73)

Throttle drum cover

Carburetor heater
Green connector

2-pin brown/black
connector

Choke knob

Mounting bolt

required. An inexpensive tool can be
assembled by mounting a Motion Pro
D-shaped 1/4-inch hex drive bit (part
No. 08-0242 [A, **Figure 70**]) on any
standard driver (B) that can accept
1/4-inch hex-shaped bits. Honda also
offers a D-shaped pilot screw wrench
(C, **Figure 70**).

3. Turn each pilot screw *clockwise* 1/2 turn.

4. Turn the throttle stop screw (B, **Figure 72**) in or
out again to achieve the specified idle speed (**Table
1**).

5. Drive in new limiter caps until their outer surface is recessed 1 mm (0.04 in.) into the pilot screw
bore.

6. When the motorcycle is returned to elevations
below 2000 m (6500 ft.), adjust the pilot screws to
their original position and reset the idle speed to the
specified rpm. Make sure to make these adjustments with the motorcycle at a lower altitude and
with the engine at its normal operating temperature.

CAUTION
Adjust the carburetors for the eleva-
tion that the motorcycle is primarily
operated in. Operating the motorcy-
cle at altitudes lower than 1500 m
(5000 ft.) with the carburetors ad-
justed for high altitude may cause the
engine to idle roughly and stall.
Overheating may also cause engine
damage.

CARBURETOR HEATER AND AIR
TEMPERATURE SWITCH
(VT750DC)

Each carburetor is equipped with a heater element (**Figure 73**) designed to improve engine starting in cold weather.

Carburetor Heater Circuit Test

This section tests the carburetor heater circuit.

1. Remove the seat (Chapter Fifteen).

2. Remove the air filter housing as described in this
chapter.

3. Disconnect the air temperature switch black
2-pin connector at the switch (**Figure 74**).

4. Disconnect the carburetor heater brown/black
wire connector on the bottom of each float bowl
(**Figure 73**).

5. Check for continuity in the brown/black wire between the air temperature switch black 2-pin connector and each carburetor heater brown/black wire
connector terminal. There should be continuity. If
there is no continuity, check the brown/black wire
for an open circuit.

6. Check for voltage in the heater circuit. Turn the
ignition switch on and measure the voltage between
the black/brown wire (+) in the air temperature
switch black 2-pin connector and each carburetor
heater green wire terminal (–). There should be battery voltage.

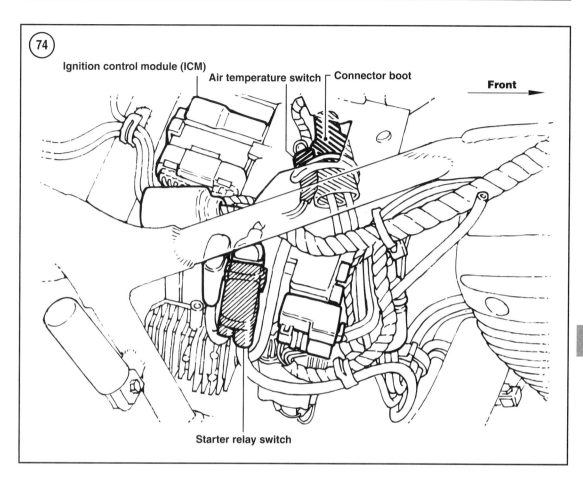

(74)

Ignition control module (ICM)

Air temperature switch ┌ Connector boot

Front

Starter relay switch

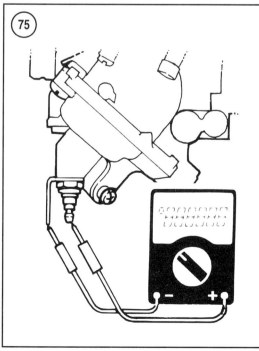

(75)

a. If there is no battery voltage, check the heater circuit wires for an open circuit.

b. If there is battery voltage, the carburetor heater circuit is working correctly. Test the carburetor heater(s) and air temperature switch as described in this section to determine the faulty part.

7. Reverse Steps 1-4.

Carburetor Heater Test

1. Disconnect the carburetor heater connectors on the bottom of each float bowl (**Figure 73**).

2. Switch an ohmmeter to the R × 1 scale. Measure the resistance between the carburetor heater terminals (**Figure 75**). Replace the carburetor heater if the resistance is not within the range specified in **Table 1**.

3. If necessary, replace the switch as described in this section.

4. Reconnect the switch connectors.

8

Carburetor Heater
Removal/Installation

1. Drain the carburetors as described under *Carburetor Removal/Installation* in this chapter.
2. Disconnect the two connectors from the carburetor heater on the bottom of the float bowl (**Figure 73**).
3. Unscrew and remove the carburetor heater and the ground terminal from the bottom of the float bowl.
4. Installation is the reverse of removal. Note the following:
   a. Clean the ground terminal with a stiff brush or sandpaper.
   b. Install the ground terminal with its terminal end facing out.
   c. Tighten the carburetor heater securely.

Air Temperature Switch
Testing and Replacement

1. Remove the seat (Chapter Fifteen).
2. Remove the air filter housing as described in this chapter.
3. Disconnect the air temperature switch black 2-pin connector at the switch and remove the switch (**Figure 74**).
4. Fill a beaker or pan with cold water (colder than 7° C [45° F]) and place it on a stove or hot plate.
5. Suspend a thermometer in the water (**Figure 76**). Use a thermometer that is rated higher than 20° C (68° F).
6. Suspend the air temperature switch in the container (**Figure 76**). Connect an ohmmeter across the switch terminals (**Figure 76**).

> *NOTE*
> *The thermometer and air temperature switch must not touch the side or bottom of the container during this test. If either does, the test results are inaccurate.*

7. Observe the switch operation as follows:
   a. When the temperature is below 7° C (45° F), the switch should be on (continuity).
   b. Gradually heat the water. When the thermometer reads between 7° C (45° F) and 20° C (68° F), the switch can be on (continuity) or off (no continuity).

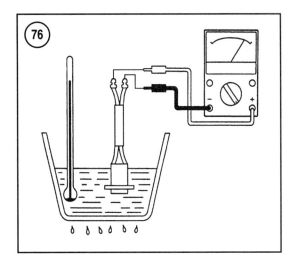

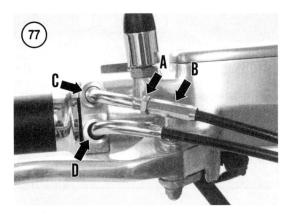

   c. When the temperature is above 20° C (68° F), the switch should turn off (no continuity).
8. Replace the air temperature switch if the test results are not within specifications.
9. Reverse Steps 1-3 to install the switch.

THROTTLE CABLE REPLACEMENT

> *NOTE*
> *There are two throttle cables. One is the pull cable (accelerate) and the other is the return cable (decelerate). These cables must be reinstalled in the correct position on the carburetor and connected to the correct position on the throttle grip pulley.*

1. Lubricate the new cables (Chapter Three) and set them aside until installation.
2. Remove the fuel tank as described in this chapter.

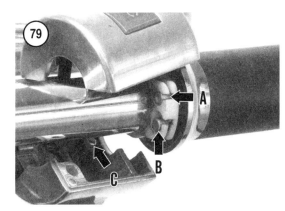

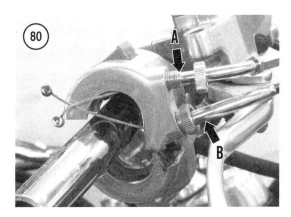

3. Note the routing of both cables from the throttle grip to the carburetors. Record this information on a piece of paper for proper installation. Identify each cable's mounting position at the handlebar and carburetor for proper installation.

4. At the throttle grip, loosen the locknut (A, **Figure 77**) and turn the adjuster (B) all the way in to obtain maximum slack in the pull cable.

5. Loosen the pull (C, **Figure 77**) and return (D) cable nuts at the throttle housing.

6. Loosen the pull cable (A, **Figure 78**) and return cable (B) locknuts at the carburetor. Disconnect the cables from the throttle drum.

7. Remove the two handlebar switch/throttle housing screws and separate the switch housing from around the handlebar.

8. Disconnect the pull (A, **Figure 79**) and return (B) cable ends from the throttle grip. Remove the pull (A, **Figure 80**) and return (B) cables from the throttle housing.

9. Remove any cable clamps or plastic ties from the cables.

10. Tie a piece of heavy string to the lower end of both cables. Cut the string to a length that is longer than the new cables.

11. Tie the lower end of both strings to a frame or engine component.

12. Remove one cable by pulling it from the top (upper cable end). Continue until the cable is removed from the frame, leaving the attached piece of string in its mounting position.

13. Repeat to remove the other cable.

14. Untie the string from the old cable and discard the old cable.

15. Tie the string onto the bottom end of the new cable.

16. Slowly pull the string and cable to install the cable along the path of the original cable. Continue until the new cable is correctly routed beside the engine and through the frame. Untie and remove the string.

17. Repeat to install the other cable.

18. Visually check the entire length of both cables. Make sure there are no kinks or sharp bends. Reroute the cables if necessary.

19. Connect the pull throttle cable (C, **Figure 77**) as follows:

    a. Connect the pull throttle cable into the upper hole (A, **Figure 80**) in the throttle housing and into the upper hole in the throttle grip (A, **Figure 79**).

    b. Attach the pull throttle cable into the lower portion of the throttle drum (A, **Figure 78**).

20. Connect the return throttle cable (D, **Figure 77**) as follows:

    a. Connect the return throttle cable into the lower hole (B, **Figure 80**) in the throttle housing and into the lower hole in the throttle grip (B, **Figure 79**).

8

b. Attach the return throttle cable into the upper portion of the throttle drum (B, **Figure 78**).

21. Install and tighten the right side switch housing as follows:

a. Align the switch housing locating pin (C, **Figure 79**) with the hole in the handlebar and close the switch halves around the handlebar. Try to twist the switch. It must not turn.

b. Install the front and rear switch housing screws and tighten securely.

22. Secure the throttle cables with the cable clamps or plastic ties in their original positions.

23. Install the fuel tank as described in this chapter.

24. Operate the throttle grip and make sure the carburetor linkage is operating correctly with no binding. If operation is incorrect or if there is binding, carefully check that the cables are attached correctly and that there are no tight bends in the cables.

25. Adjust the throttle cables as described in Chapter Three.

WARNING
An improperly adjusted or incorrectly routed throttle cable can cause the throttle to hang open. This could cause loss of control. Do not ride the motorcycle until throttle cable operation is correct.

26. Start the engine and let it idle. Turn the handlebar from side to side and listen to the engine speed. Make sure the idle speed does not increase. If it does, the throttle cables are adjusted incorrectly or the throttle cables are improperly routed. Find and correct the source of the problem before riding.

27. Test ride the motorcycle slowly at first and make sure the throttle is operating correctly.

CHOKE CABLE REPLACEMENT

The choke cable is constructed as one cable at the control end that actuates two cables, which operate the choke valve in each carburetor.

NOTE
Standard practice on these models is to remove the carburetors first, then to disconnect and remove the choke cable from the carburetors. However, if the choke valve nuts can be loosened from the carburetors, the choke cable can be removed without having

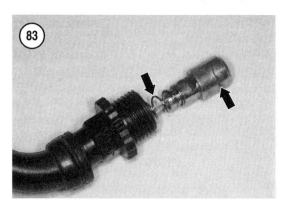

to remove the carburetors. Attempt this method first before removing the carburetors.

Carburetors Installed

This procedure describes choke cable removal with the carburetors mounted on the engine.

1. Remove the left side cover (Chapter Fifteen).

2. Remove the following as described in this chapter:

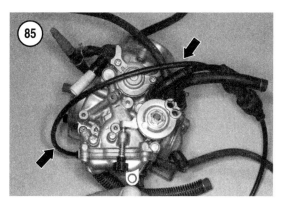

a. Fuel tank.
b. Air filter housing.
c. Air filter chamber.

3. Remove the bolt securing the choke knob bracket to the rear cylinder (**Figure 81**).

4. Draw a diagram of the choke cable routing, from the choke knob to where the cable separates and connects to both carburetors.

5. Loosen the choke cable locknut (**Figure 82**) and remove the choke valve assembly from the carburetor. Remove the valve and spring (**Figure 83**) from the end of the cable.

NOTE
*It may be easier to loosen the nut by turning the knurled part of the cable nut (**Figure 84**) with a pair of needle nose pliers.*

6. Repeat at the other carburetor.

7. Carefully remove the choke cable from around the carburetors and through the frame.

8. Install the new choke cable assembly, following the original path recorded in Step 4.

9. Reconnect the choke cables to the carburetors as follows:
  a. Install the spring and hook the choke valve onto the cable (**Figure 83**).
  b. Insert the choke valve into the carburetor and tighten the choke valve nut until it contacts the carburetor housing (**Figure 82**). Tighten securely.
  c. Repeat for the other cable end and carburetor.

10. Operate the choke knob and make sure the choke valves operate correctly. If the operation is incorrect or there is binding, check that the cables are routed and attached correctly. Make sure the cables work correctly before adjusting the choke.

11. Reverse Steps 1-3.

12. Check the choke cable operation as described in Chapter Three.

Carburetors Removed

If the choke cables cannot be disconnected from the carburetors with the carburetors installed, replace the choke cable as follows:

1. Remove the carburetors as described in this chapter.

2. Draw a diagram of the choke cable routing around the carburetor (**Figure 85**).

3. Loosen the choke cable locknut (**Figure 84**) and remove the choke valve assembly.

4. Repeat Step 3 for the other carburetor and remove the choke cable assembly. Remove the valve and spring (**Figure 83**) from the end of the cable.

5. Repeat for the other cable end.

6. Installation is the reverse of removal. Note the following:
  a. If removed, install the spring and choke valve onto the end of each cable (**Figure 83**).
  b. Install the short choke cable end into the rear carburetor (**Figure 85**) and the long cable end into the front carburetor (**Figure 86**).

c. Insert the choke valves into the carburetor bores and tighten the nut (**Figure 84**) securely.

FUEL FILTER

The fuel filter (A, **Figure 87**) is connected into the fuel line between the fuel tank and fuel pump. A restricted fuel filter lowers the fuel pressure, a condition that causes a number of engine drivability problems. These include difficult starting, engine hesitation during acceleration and surging at high speed. While there is no recommended fuel filter replacement interval, inspect the fuel filter at the same time the fuel hoses are inspected (refer to Chapter Three intervals). While the fuel filter is plastic, contaminants are not always visible. If a restricted fuel filter is suspected, check the fuel pump flow rate as described in this chapter.

Removal/Installation

1. Refer to *Fuel System Precautions* in this chapter before removing the fuel filter.
2. Turn the fuel valve off (B, **Figure 87**, typical).
3. Disconnect the negative battery cable at the battery (Chapter Nine).
4. Place a rag underneath the fuel filter.
5. Disconnect the lower fuel hose at the fuel filter (A, **Figure 87**) and allow the fuel to drain onto the rag. Dispose of the rag properly. Disconnect the upper hose and remove the fuel filter.
6. Transfer the rubber damper onto the new fuel filter.
7. Installation is the reverse of removal. Note the following:
   a. Replace weak or damaged fuel hose clamps.
   b. Install the fuel filter with its arrow mark facing down (toward the fuel pump).
   c. Reconnect the hoses onto the fuel filter, and then secure each hose with its metal hose clamp.
   d. Turn the fuel valve and ignition switch on and check the fuel hoses for leaks.

FUEL PUMP

Fuel Pump System Test

1. Check if the fuel pump runs:

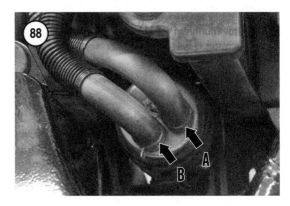

a. Remove the left side cover (Chapter Fifteen).
b. Turn the engine stop switch to RUN.
c. Turn the ignition switch on, but do not start the engine. You should hear the fuel pump run for two seconds. If the fuel pump ran, perform the *Fuel Pump Flow Test* in this section. If the fuel pump did not run, continue with Step 2.

NOTE
A timer function in the fuel cut-off relay allows the fuel pump to run for two seconds when the ignition switch is turned on. This allows the fuel pump to fill the carburetor float bowls with fuel.

NOTE
The ignition system primary circuit controls the fuel cut-off relay. When performing voltage tests with the ignition switch turned on in this section, set the engine stop switch to RUN.

2. Turn the ignition switch off.
3. Remove the right side cover (Chapter Fifteen).

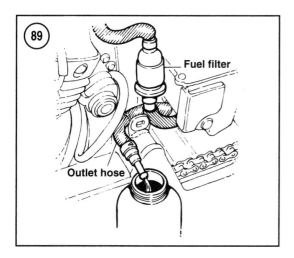

NOTE
*Refer to **Electrical Component Location** in Chapter Nine to locate the fuel cut-off relay and fuel pump connector called out in this procedure.*

4A. On VT750C models, disconnect the 3-pin fuel cut-off relay connector.

4B. On VT750DC models, perform the following:

   a. Remove the fuse box from its mounting position and set it aside.

   b. Disconnect the 3-pin fuel cut-off relay connector.

5. Turn the ignition switch on and measure voltage between the fuel cut-off relay harness side connector black terminal and an engine ground. The voltmeter should read battery voltage. Turn the ignition switch off.

   a. No battery voltage: Check the black wire for an open circuit or a contaminated or damaged connector. If good, check the ignition system sub-fuse, fuse contacts and the ignition switch (Chapter Nine).

   b. Battery voltage present: Go to Step 6.

6. Check for continuity on the black/blue wire between the 3-pin fuel cut-off relay harness side connector and ground. There should be continuity.

   a. Continuity: Go to Step 7.

   b. No continuity: Go to Step 8.

7. Disconnect the ignition control module (ICM) electrical connector.

8. Check for continuity on the yellow/blue wire between the fuel cut-off relay and the ignition control module (ICM) harness side connectors. There should be continuity. Reconnect the ICM connector.

   a. Continuity: Replace the fuel cut-off relay as described in this chapter.

   b. No continuity: Go to Step 9.

9. Disconnect the 2-pin fuel pump connector.

10. Connect a jumper wire between the 3-pin fuel cut-off relay harness side connector black and black/blue terminals. Turn the ignition switch on and measure voltage between the 2-pin fuel pump harness side connector green and black/blue terminals. There should be battery voltage. Turn the ignition switch off and disconnect the jumper wire.

   a. No battery voltage: Check the black/blue and green wires for an open circuit or a contaminated or damaged connector.

   b. Battery voltage present: Replace the fuel pump as described in this chapter.

11. Reconnect the fuel pump and fuel cut-off relay connector terminals. Reposition the fuse box on VT750DC models.

12. Install the right side cover.

Fuel Cut-Off Relay
Replacement

1. Remove the left side cover (Chapter Fifteen).

2. Disconnect the electrical connector from the fuel cut-off relay. Refer to *Electrical Component Location* in Chapter Nine to locate the fuel cut-off relay.

3. Remove the fuel cut-off relay and replace it.

4. Install by reversing these removal steps.

Fuel Pump Flow Test

1. Refer to *Fuel System Precautions* in this chapter.

2. Remove the left and right side covers (Chapter Fifteen).

NOTE
*Refer to **Electrical Component Location** in Chapter Nine to locate the fuel cut-off relay and fuel pump connector called out in this procedure.*

3. Disconnect the 3-pin fuel cut-off relay connector. Connect a jumper wire between the harness side connector black and black/blue terminals.

4. Disconnect the fuel pump outlet hose at the hose joint (C, **Figure 87**). Make sure this hose is connected to the outlet nozzle at the fuel pump (A, **Figure 88**). Place the outlet hose into a plastic graduated beaker (**Figure 89**).

5. Turn the fuel valve on.

6. Have an assistant turn the ignition switch on and allow fuel to run out of the fuel hose and into the graduated beaker for 5 seconds, and then turn the ignition switch off.

7. Multiply the amount of fuel in the beaker by 12 (12 × 5 = 60 seconds). This gives the fuel pump flow capacity for one minute.

8. Refer to **Table 2** for the fuel flow capacity specification.

9. If the fuel pump does not deliver the specified amount of fuel, replace the fuel pump as described in this section.

10. Pour the fuel from the beaker back into the fuel tank.

11. Reconnect the fuel outlet hose (A, **Figure 88**) to the hose joint (C, **Figure 87**). Secure the hose with its clamp.

12. Disconnect the jumper wire, and then reconnect the fuel cut-off relay connector at the relay.

13. Start the engine and allow it to idle. Inspect the fuel hose for leaks.

> *WARNING*
> *Repair any fuel leaks before riding the motorcycle.*

14. Install the left and right side covers.

Fuel Pump Replacement

1. Turn the fuel valve off.

2. Remove the left and right side covers (Chapter Fifteen).

3. Disconnect the fuel pump 2-pin connector. Refer to *Electrical Component Location* in Chapter Nine for fuel pump connector locations. Disconnect the pump wire harness from the band strap.

4. Note how the fuel pump is aligned in its rubber mounting damper so it can be installed with the hose nozzles facing in their original position.

5. Disconnect the outlet (A, **Figure 88**) and inlet (B) hoses at the fuel pump.

6. Disconnect the breather hose at the fuel pump (**Figure 90**).

7. Before installing the new pump, inspect the fuel hoses and the breather hose for cracks, soft spots or other damage and replace if necessary.

8. Replace the hose clamps if weak or damaged.

9. Clean the hose ends before reconnecting them.

10. Transfer the rubber mounting damper onto the new fuel pump. Position the pump so the breather hose nozzle is positioned facing in its original direction and position.

> *WARNING*
> *Some fuel remains in the old fuel pump. Properly store the pump until it can be discarded.*

11. Secure the rubber mounting damper onto the frame brackets.

12. Reconnect the breather hose (**Figure 90**) and secure it with its clamp.

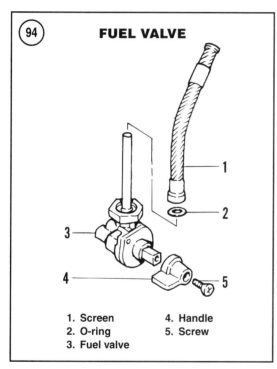

FUEL VALVE

1. Screen
2. O-ring
3. Fuel valve
4. Handle
5. Screw

13. Reconnect the outlet (A, **Figure 88**) and inlet (B) hoses at the fuel pump. Secure each hose with its clamp.

NOTE
The inlet nozzle on the fuel pump is identified with an IN or INLET mark.

14. Reconnect the fuel pump 2-pin connector. Secure the wire harness with the band strap.
15. Turn the fuel valve on. Turn the engine stop switch to RUN and turn the ignition switch on. The pump should run for approximately 2 seconds then stop. Check for fuel leaks. Start the engine and check again for fuel leaks. Turn the engine off.
16. Install the left and right side covers.

FUEL TANK

Removal/Installation

1. Refer to *Fuel System Precautions* in this chapter.
2. Disconnect the battery negative cable as described in Chapter Nine.
3. On models where the speedometer is mounted on the fuel tank, remove the speedometer assembly (Chapter Nine).
4. Turn the fuel valve off (A, **Figure 91**) and disconnect the fuel hose (B). Plug the end of the hose.
5. Remove the fuel tank mounting bolt (**Figure 92**).
6. Perform the following:
   a. Lift the rear of the tank and secure it with a wooden block.
   b. On 49-State and Canada models, disconnect the fuel tank breather hose (**Figure 93**) on the bottom of the fuel tank.
   c. On California models, disconnect the air vent hose (**Figure 93**) on the bottom of the fuel tank.
7. Remove the fuel tank.
8. Installation is the reverse of removal. Note the following:
   a. Replace missing or damaged fuel tank dampers.
   b. Tighten the fuel tank mounting bolt (**Figure 92**) to 19 N•m (14 ft.-lb.).
   c. After completing installation, turn the fuel valve on and check for leaks.

Fuel Valve Replacement

1. Refer to *Fuel System Precautions* in this chapter.
2. Disconnect the battery negative cable as described in Chapter Nine.
3. Turn the fuel valve off (A, **Figure 91**) and disconnect the fuel hose (B).
4. Connect a separate hose onto the fuel valve and insert the other end of the hose in a container suitable for gasoline storage. Turn the fuel valve on and drain the tank. Turn the fuel valve off and disconnect the hose.
5. Remove the fuel tank as described in this section.
6. Place the fuel tank with the fuel valve facing up.
7. Loosen the fuel valve nut and remove the fuel valve.
8. Remove the screen and O-ring (**Figure 94**) from the fuel valve. Discard the O-ring.

8

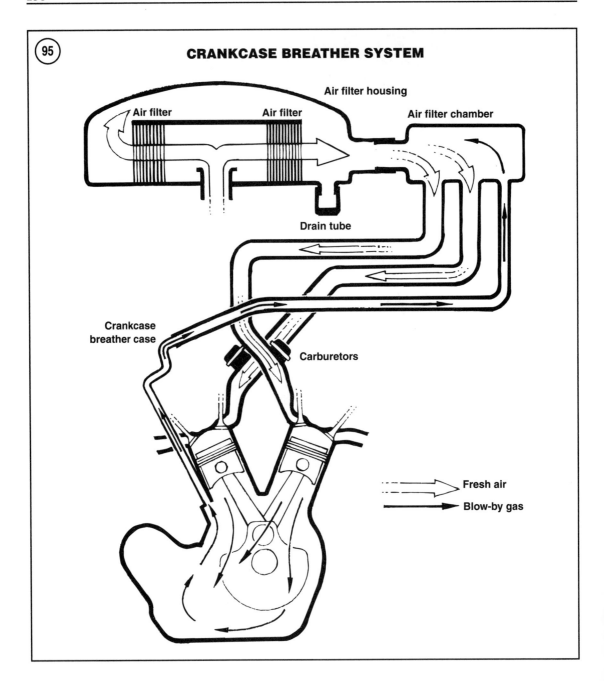

CRANKCASE BREATHER SYSTEM

Air filter housing

Air filter

Air filter

Air filter chamber

Drain tube

Crankcase
breather case

Carburetors

Fresh air

Blow-by gas

9. Clean the screen. Replace the screen if it cannot be cleaned.

10. Installation is the reverse of removal. Note the following:

  a. Install a new O-ring.

  b. Tighten the fuel valve nut to 34 N•m (25 ft.-lb.).

  c. Pour a small amount of fuel into the tank and check for leaks. Do not overtighten the fuel valve nut to stop a leak.

CRANKCASE BREATHER SYSTEM

The engine is equipped with a closed crankcase breather system (**Figure 95**). The system draws blow-by gasses from the crankcase and recirculates them into the combustion chamber to be burned.

Liquid residues collect in the crankcase breather drain tube. These must be emptied at periodic intervals. Refer to *Crankcase Breather Inspection* in Chapter Three for service intervals and procedures.

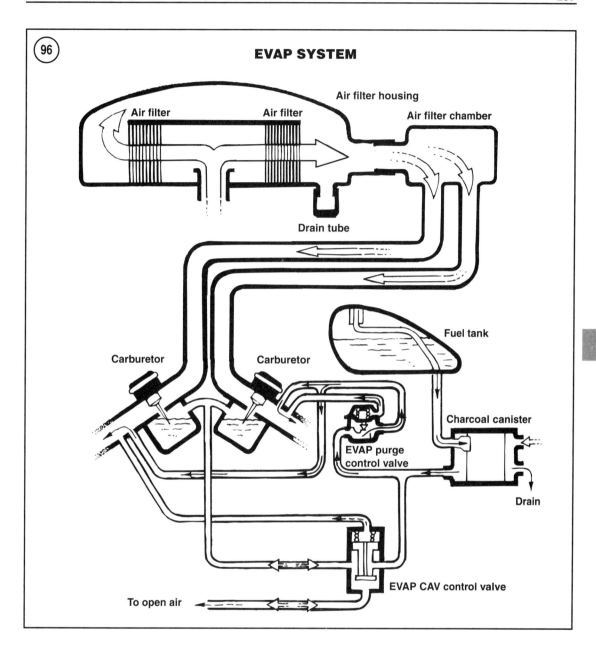

EVAP SYSTEM

EVAPORATIVE EMISSION CONTROL SYSTEM (CALIFORNIA MODELS)

An evaporative emission control system (EVAP) is installed on all models sold in California (**Figure 96**). When the engine is not running, fuel vapors in the fuel tank and both carburetors are routed and stored in a charcoal canister. When the engine is running, these vapors are drawn through an EVAP purge control valve and into the carburetors to be burned. Make sure all hose clamps are tight. Check all hoses for deterioration and replace as necessary.

Labels

Emission control labels are attached to the inside of the left side cover. The motorcycle emission control information label (A, **Figure 97**) lists tune-up information. The vacuum hose routing diagram label (B, **Figure 97**) shows a schematic of the emission control system (2001-2003 California models). This decal is useful when identifying hoses used in the emission control system.

Emission control system hoses are labeled with identification numbers that correspond with the numbers listed on the vacuum hose routing diagram label (B, **Figure 97**). If these identification numbers have deteriorated or the original hose was replaced, identify the hoses and their fittings for proper installation. Refer to *Fuel Hose Identification* in this chapter.

A Vehicle Emission Control Information Update Label is used when the carburetors have been adjusted for high altitude operation. Refer to *Carburetor Adjustment* in this chapter.

Charcoal Canister
Removal/Installation

The charcoal canister (A, **Figure 98**) is mounted on the vertical frame rail, between the engine and swing arm.

1. Disconnect the No. 1 hose (B, **Figure 98**) from the canister.

2. Disconnect the No. 4 hose (C, **Figure 98**) from the canister.

3. Remove the mounting bolts and the charcoal canister (A, **Figure 98**).

4. Installation is the reverse of these steps.

Evaporative Emission (EVAP)
Purge Control Valve

Removal/installation

Refer to **Figure 99** (VT750C) or **Figure 100** (VT750DC) to identify the hose fittings called out in this procedure.

1. Remove the fuel tank as described in this chapter.

2. Pull the EVAP purge control valve (A, **Figure 101**, typical) off its mounting stay.

3. Disconnect the following hoses from the EVAP purge control valve:

    a. No. 4 hose.

    b. No. 5 hose.

    c. No. 11 hose.

4. Reverse these steps to install the EVAP purge control valve.

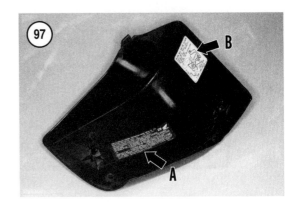

Testing

If the engine is difficult to restart when hot, test the EVAP purge control valve as follows. Refer to **Figure 99** (VT750C) or **Figure 100** (VT750DC) to identify the hose fittings called out in this procedure.

A hand-operated vacuum pump and pressure pump are required during this test.

1. Remove the EVAP purge control valve as described in this section.

2. Connect a vacuum pump to the No. 5 hose fitting and apply 33 kPa (9.8 in.) HG of vacuum. The vacuum should hold. If the vacuum does not hold, replace the EVAP purge control valve.

3. Disconnect the vacuum pump.

4. Connect the vacuum pump to the No. 11 hose fitting and apply 33 kPa (9.8 in.) HG of vacuum. The vacuum should hold. If the vacuum does not hold, replace the EVAP purge control valve. If the vacuum held, leave the vacuum pump connected to the No. 11 hose fitting and continue with Step 5

5. Connect a pressure pump to the No. 4 hose fitting.

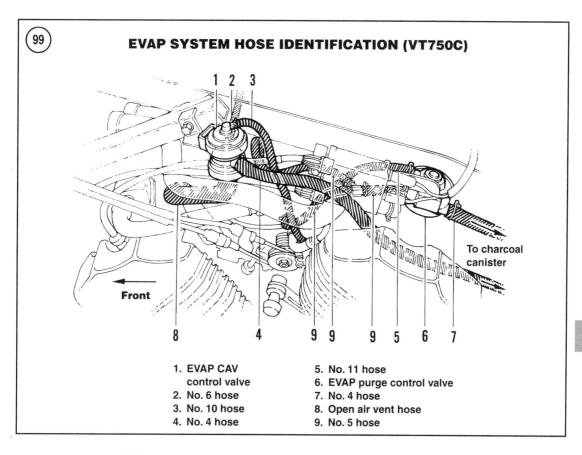

EVAP SYSTEM HOSE IDENTIFICATION (VT750C)

1 2 3

To charcoal canister

Front

8   4   9 9   9 5   6   7

1. EVAP CAV
   control valve
2. No. 6 hose
3. No. 10 hose
4. No. 4 hose

5. No. 11 hose
6. EVAP purge control valve
7. No. 4 hose
8. Open air vent hose
9. No. 5 hose

CAUTION
Using air from a high-pressure source damages the EVAP purge control valve. Use a hand-operated pressure pump.

6. Apply 33 kPa (9.8 in.) HG of vacuum to the No. 11 hose fitting, and then pump air through the No. 4 hose fitting. When doing so, air should flow through the No. 5 hose fitting. If air did not flow through the No. 5 hose fitting, replace the EVAP purge control valve.

7. Disconnect the vacuum and pressure pumps.

8. Install the EVAP purge control valve as described in this chapter.

Evaporative Emission Carburetor Air Vent (EVAP CAV) Control Valve

Removal/Installation

Refer to **Figure 99** (VT750C) or **Figure 100** (VT750DC) to identify the hose fittings called out in this procedure.

1. Remove the fuel tank as described in this chapter.

2. Pull the EVAP CAV control valve (B, **Figure 101**, typical) off its mounting stay.

3. Disconnect the following hoses from the EVAP CAV control valve:
   a. No. 4 hose.
   b. No. 6 hose.
   c. No. 10 hose.
   d. Open air vent hose.

4. Reverse these steps to install the EVAP CAV control valve.

Testing

Refer to **Figure 99** (VT750C) or **Figure 100** (VT750DC) to identify the hose fittings called out in this procedure.

A hand-operated vacuum pump and pressure pump are required during this test.

1. Remove the EVAP CAV control valve as described in this section.

2. Connect a vacuum pump to the No. 10 hose fitting and apply 33 kPa (9.8 in.) HG of vacuum. The

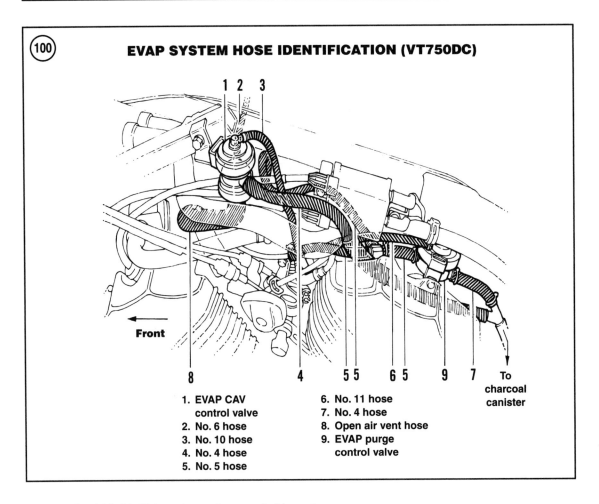

EVAP SYSTEM HOSE IDENTIFICATION (VT750DC)

1 2 3

Front

8   4   5 5   6 5   9   7   To
                                                      charcoal
                                                      canister

1. EVAP CAV   6. No. 11 hose
   control valve   7. No. 4 hose
2. No. 6 hose   8. Open air vent hose
3. No. 10 hose   9. EVAP purge
4. No. 4 hose   control valve
5. No. 5 hose

vacuum should hold. If the vacuum does not hold, replace the EVAP CAV control valve.

3. Disconnect the vacuum pump.

4. Connect the vacuum pump to air vent hose fitting and apply 33 kPa (9.8 in.) HG of vacuum. The vacuum should hold. If the vacuum does not hold, replace the EVAP CAV control valve.

CAUTION
Using air from a high-pressure source in Step 5 damages the EVAP purge control valve. Use a hand-operated pressure pump.

5. Remove the vacuum pump and reconnect it to the No. 10 hose fitting. Connect a pressure pump to the air vent hose fitting.

6. Apply vacuum to the No. 10 hose fitting, and then pump air through the air vent hose fitting. Air must flow through the valve and exit through the No. 6 hose fitting.

7. Plug the No. 6 hose fitting. Apply vacuum to the No. 10 hose fitting while pumping air through the air vent hose fitting. The air pressure pumped through the air vent hose fitting should hold steady.

8. Disconnect the vacuum and pressure pumps.

9. Replace the EVAP CAV control valve if it failed any one of these tests.

10. Install the EVAP CAV control valve as described in this section.

Table 1 CARBURETOR SPECIFICATIONS

Throttle bore	34 mm (1.3 in.)
Identification number	
VT750C	
49-state	
1998	VDFFG
1999-on	VDFFJ
California	
1998	VDFEB
1999-on	VDFEC
Canada	
1998	VDFFG
1999-on	VDFFJ
VT750DC	
49-state and Canada	VDF2D
California	
2001-2003	VDF2C
2004-on	VDF2F
Idle speed	
2001-2003	1000 ± 100 rpm
2004-2005	
49-state/Canada	1000 ± 100 rpm
California	1200 ± 100 rpm
2006-on	1200 ± 100 rpm
Idle drop procedure	
Pilot screw initial opening	
VT750C	2 1/4 turns out
VT750DC	2 3/8 turns out
Pilot screw final opening	
VT750C	1 turn out
VT750DC	1/2 turn out
Main jet	
Front	105
Rear	
VT750C	110
VT750DC	108
Pilot jet	40
Float level	7.0 mm (0.28 in.)
Carburetor heater	
VT750DC*	
Air temperature switch	
Below 7° C (45° F)	Continuity (switch on)
Above 20° C (68° F)	No continuity (switch off)
Heater resistance*	13-15 ohms

*Test must be made at an ambient temperature of 20° C (68° F). Do not test when the engine or component is hot.

Table 2 FUEL PUMP SPECIFICATIONS

Fuel pump flow capacity	Minimum 900 cc (30.4 U.S. oz.) per minute

Table 3   FUEL SYSTEM TORQUE SPECIFICATIONS

	N•m	in.-lb.	ft.-lb.
Air filter housing cover bolt	2	18	–
Fuel tank mounting bolt	19	–	14
Fuel valve nut	34	–	25

CHAPTER NINE

ELECTRICAL SYSTEM

This chapter contains service and test procedures for the following components:

1. Battery.
2. Charging system.
3. Ignition system.
4. Starting system.
5. Lighting system.
6. Electrical components.
7. Switches.
8. Fuses.

Tables 1-10 are at the end of this chapter.

ELECTRICAL COMPONENT REPLACEMENT

Most motorcycle dealerships and parts suppliers do not accept the return of any electrical part. If you cannot determine the exact cause of any electrical system malfunction, have a Honda dealership retest that specific system to verify your test results. If you purchase a new electrical component(s), install it, and then find that the system still does not work properly, you will probably not be able to return the unit for a refund.

Consider any test result carefully before replacing a component that tests only *slightly* out of speci-

fication, especially resistance. A number of variables can affect test results dramatically. These include the testing meter's internal circuitry, ambient temperatures and conditions under which the motorcycle has been operated. All instructions and specifications have been checked for accuracy; however, successful test results depend largely upon individual accuracy.

ELECTRICAL CONNECTORS

The Honda VT750 is equipped with numerous electrical components, connectors and wiring harnesses. Corrosion-causing moisture can enter these electrical connectors and cause poor electrical connections which can lead to component failure. Troubleshooting an electrical circuit with one or more corroded electrical connectors can be time-consuming and frustrating.

When reconnecting electrical connectors, pack them in a dielectric grease compound. Dielectric grease is specially formulated for sealing and waterproofing electrical connections without interfering with current flow. Do not use a substitute that may interfere with the current flow within the electrical connector. Do not use silicone sealant.

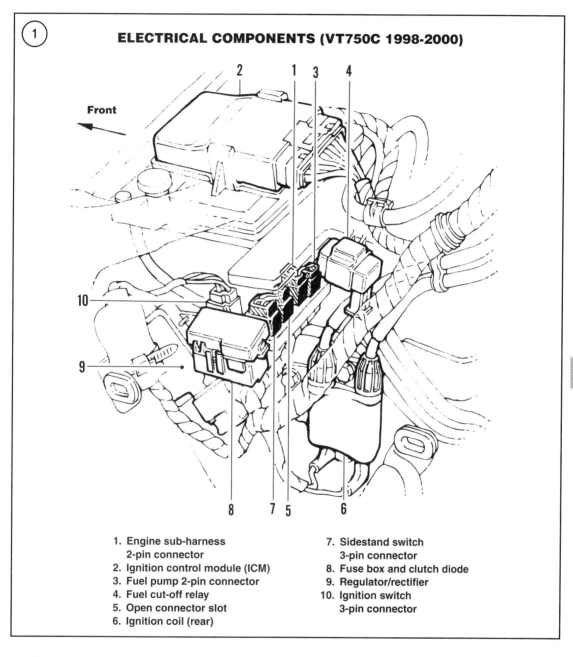

ELECTRICAL COMPONENTS (VT750C 1998-2000)

Front

1. Engine sub-harness
   2-pin connector
2. Ignition control module (ICM)
3. Fuel pump 2-pin connector
4. Fuel cut-off relay
5. Open connector slot
6. Ignition coil (rear)
7. Sidestand switch
   3-pin connector
8. Fuse box and clutch diode
9. Regulator/rectifier
10. Ignition switch
    3-pin connector

After cleaning both the male and female connectors, make sure they are thoroughly dry. Apply dielectric grease to the interior of one of the connectors before connecting the two connector halves. After the connector is fully packed, wipe the exterior of all excessive compound.

Clean and seal all electrical connectors every time they are unplugged. This may prevent a breakdown on the road and save time if troubleshooting is required.

ELECTRICAL COMPONENT LOCATION

This section identifies electrical components installed behind either the left or right side cover. When necessary, use the wiring harness color codes identified on the applicable wiring diagram at the end of this manual to confirm the proper electrical part is being serviced.

1. 1998-2000 VT750C: **Figure 1**.
2. 2001-on VT750C: **Figure 2**.

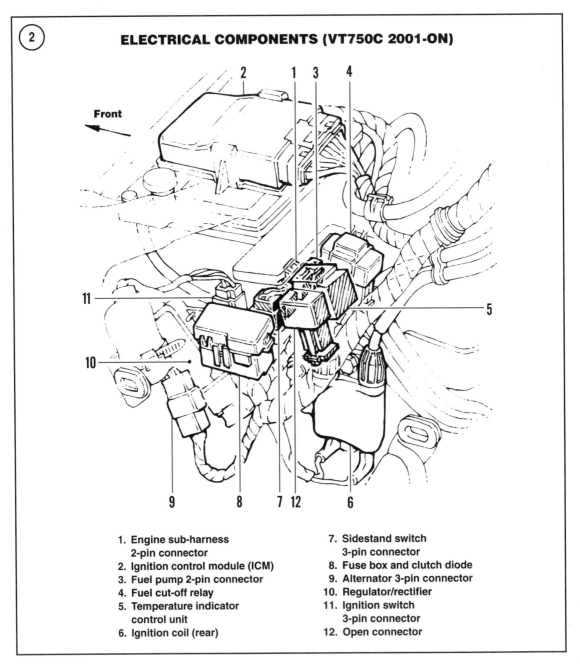

2

ELECTRICAL COMPONENTS (VT750C 2001-ON)

Front

1. Engine sub-harness
   2-pin connector
2. Ignition control module (ICM)
3. Fuel pump 2-pin connector
4. Fuel cut-off relay
5. Temperature indicator
   control unit
6. Ignition coil (rear)
7. Sidestand switch
   3-pin connector
8. Fuse box and clutch diode
9. Alternator 3-pin connector
10. Regulator/rectifier
11. Ignition switch
    3-pin connector
12. Open connector

3. 2001-on VT750DC: **Figure 3**.

BATTERY

A sealed, maintenance-free battery is installed on all VT750 models. The battery electrolyte level cannot be serviced. When replacing the battery, use a sealed type. Do not install a non-sealed battery. Never remove the sealing cap from the top of the battery. The battery does not require periodic electrolyte inspection or refilling. See **Table 1** for battery specifications.

To prevent accidental shorts that could blow a fuse when working on the electrical system, always disconnect the negative battery cable from the battery.

WARNING
Although the battery is a sealed type,
protect your eyes, skin and clothing.

③ **ELECTRICAL COMPONENTS (VT750DC)**

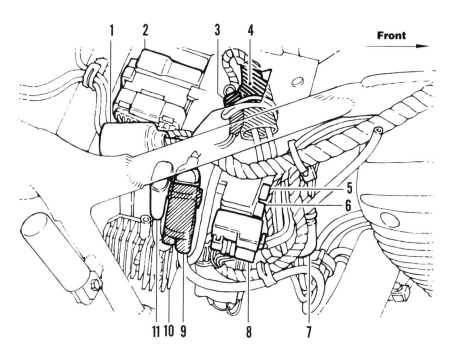

Front

9

1. Connector pouch (brake/taillight and rear turn signal connector)
2. Ignition control module (ICM)
3. Air temperature switch
4. Connector pouch (regulator/rectifier 2-pin and 3-pin connectors)
5. Turn signal relay
6. Fuel cut-off relay
7. Connector pouch (fuel pump 2-pin connector, ignition switch 3-pin connector, neutral and oil pressure switch 2-pin connector and sidestand switch 2-pin connector)
8. Fuse box and clutch diode
9. Starter relay switch and main fuse
10. Regulator/rectifier
11. Positive battery cable

Electrolyte is corrosive and can cause burns and permanent injury. The battery case may be cracked and leaking electrolyte. If electrolyte gets into your eyes, flush your eyes thoroughly with clean, running water and get immediate medical attention. Always wear safety goggles when servicing the battery.

WARNING
While batteries are being charged, highly explosive hydrogen gas forms in each cell. Some of this gas escapes through a vent opening and may form an explosive atmosphere in and around the battery. This condition can

persist for several hours. Sparks, an open flame or a lighted cigarette can ignite the gas, causing an internal battery explosion and possible serious injury.

NOTE
Recycle the old battery. When replacing the old battery, turn in the old battery at that time. The lead plates and the plastic case can be recycled. Most motorcycle dealerships accept old batteries in trade when purchasing a new one. Never place an old battery in household trash; it is illegal in most states to place any acid or lead (heavy metal) contents in landfills.

Safety Precautions

Take the following precautions to prevent an explosion:

1. Do not smoke or permit any open flame near any battery that is being charged or that has been recently charged.

2. Do not disconnect live circuits at the battery. A spark usually occurs when a live circuit is broken.

3. Use caution when connecting or disconnecting a battery charger. Make sure the power switch is off before making or breaking connections. Poor connections are a common cause of electrical arcs, which cause explosions.

4. Keep children and pets away from the charging equipment and battery.

Removal/Installation

The battery is installed in the battery box, underneath the seat.

1. Read *Safety Precautions* in this section.

2. On models with an electronic tripmeter, turn the ignition switch on and record the tripmeter and tripmeter reset mileage numbers. These numbers erase when the battery is disconnected.

3. Turn the ignition switch off.

4. Remove the seat (Chapter Fifteen).

5. Remove the ignition control model (ICM) from the battery case cover. Refer to *Ignition Control Module* in this chapter. Set the ICM aside without disconnecting its connectors.

6. Remove the screw(s) and the battery case cover.

7. Disconnect the negative battery lead (A, **Figure 4** [VT750C] or **Figure 5** [VT750DC]), then the positive lead (B, **Figure 4** [VT750C] or **Figure 5** [VT750DC]), from the battery terminals.

8. Remove the battery.

9. Move the ICM back into position to remove stress on the wiring harness.

10. After servicing the battery, install it by reversing these removal steps while noting the following:

   a. Always connect the positive cable first, then the negative cable.

> *CAUTION*
> *Make sure the battery cables are connected to their proper terminals. Connecting the battery backward reverses the polarity and damages components in the electrical system. When install-*

> *ing a replacement battery, confirm that the negative cable is connected to the negative battery terminal.*

   b. Coat the battery leads with dielectric grease or petroleum jelly.

Cleaning/Inspection

The battery electrolyte level cannot be serviced. *Never* remove the sealing bar cap from the top of the battery (**Figure 6**). The battery does not require periodic electrolyte inspection or refilling.

1. Read *Safety Precautions* in this section.

2. Remove the battery from the motorcycle as described in this section. Do not clean the battery while it is mounted in the motorcycle.

3. Clean the battery case (**Figure 6**) with a solution of warm water and baking soda. Rinse thoroughly with clean water.

4. Inspect the physical condition of the battery. Look for bulges or cracks in the case, leaking electrolyte or corrosion buildup.

5. Check the battery terminal bolts, spacers and nuts for corrosion and damage. Clean parts with a solution of baking soda and water and rinse thoroughly. Replace if damaged.

6. Check the battery cable clamps for corrosion and damage. If corrosion is minor, clean the battery cable clamps with a stiff brush. Replace excessively worn or damaged cables.

Voltage Test

Use a digital voltmeter to test the battery while it is mounted on the motorcycle. Refer to **Table 1** and

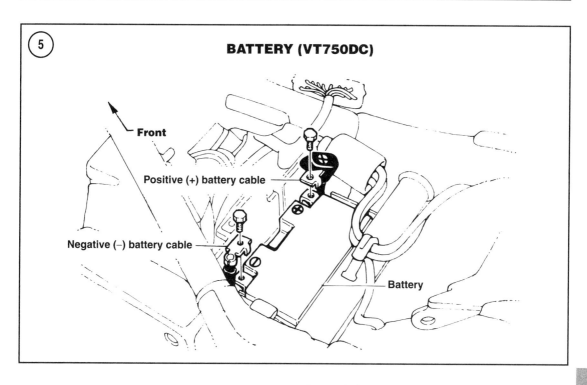

5

BATTERY (VT750DC)

Front

Positive (+) battery cable

Negative (–) battery cable

Battery

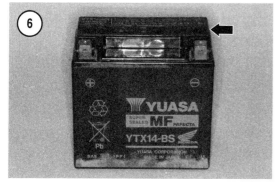

6

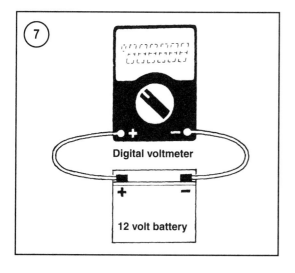

7

Digital voltmeter

12 volt battery

9

Table 2 for battery voltage readings for maintenance-free batteries.

1. Read *Safety Precautions* in this section.

> *NOTE*
> *To prevent false test readings, do not test the battery if the battery terminals are corroded. Remove and clean the battery and terminals as described in this chapter, then reinstall it.*

2. Connect a digital voltmeter between the battery negative and positive leads (**Figure 7**). Then locate the voltage reading in **Table 2** to determine the battery state of charge. Note the following:

  a. If the battery voltage is 12.8-13.0 volts, the battery is fully charged.

  b. If the battery voltage is below 12.3-12.5 volts, the battery is undercharged and requires charging. Refer to **Table 2** for charging time.

3. If the battery is undercharged, recharge it as described in this section. Test the charging system as described under *Charging System* in this chapter.

Load Test

A battery load test or capacity performed with a load tester is the most accurate way to determine battery condition. A battery load tester places an electrical load on the battery to determine if it can provide current while maintaining the minimum required voltage. **Figure 8** shows the BatteryMate electronic battery tester available from Motion Pro.

A battery load test procedure varies depending on the type of tester. Use the following guidelines to supplement the manufacturer's instructions:

1. Remove the battery as described in this section.
2. Inspect the battery case for any leaks or damage. Do not test the battery if the case is damaged.
3. Clean the battery terminals.

NOTE
*Do **not** charge the battery before performing a load test unless otherwise specified by the tester manufacturer. The battery must be tested in its current operating condition for the results to be accurate.*

4. Connect the load tester to the battery terminals—red lead to the positive terminal and the black lead to the negative terminal.
5. Determine the correct amount of load to apply to the battery. Refer to the manufacturer's instructions, plus the following:

   a. Refer to **Table 1** for battery capacity. VT750C models use a 12-volt/14 amp hour battery. VT750DC models use a 12-volt/12 amp hour battery.

   b. The amount of load to use is determined by the original capacity of the battery. This is measured in cold cranking amperes (CCA) or in the amp/hour rating. For the VT750C, the correct load to apply is three times the amp/hour rating (14 amps × 3 = 42 amps). For the VT750DC, the correct load to apply is three times the amp/hour rating (12 amps × 3 = 36 amps).

6. Test the battery and determine the results following the manufacturer's instructions. Refer to **Figure 9**, typical.
7. It the battery fails the load test, recharge the battery and retest. If the battery fails the load test again, replace the battery.
8. If a battery load tester is not available, use a digital voltmeter to perform a quick low-amperage load test. Refer to Step 9 and Step 10.
9. Connect a digital voltmeter between the battery negative and positive leads (**Figure 7**).

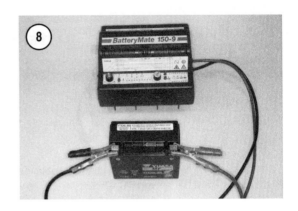

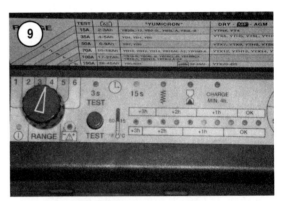

10. Turn the ignition switch on and make sure the headlight is on. The voltmeter should read at least 11.5 volts.

   a. Yes. The battery is charged.

   b. No. The battery requires charging.

Charging

Refer to *New Battery Setup* in this section if the battery is new.

To recharge a maintenance-free battery, a digital voltmeter and a charger (**Figure 10**) with an adjustable or automatically variable amperage output are required. If this equipment is not available, have the battery charged by a shop with the proper equipment. Excessive voltage and amperage from an unregulated charger can damage the battery and shorten service life.

The battery should only self-discharge approximately one percent of its given capacity each day. If a battery not in use, without any loads connected, loses its charge within one week after charging, the battery is defective.

If the motorcycle is not used for long periods, an automatic battery charger with variable voltage and amperage outputs is recommended for optimum battery service life.

> **WARNING**
> *During the charging process, highly explosive hydrogen gas is released from the battery. Charge the battery only in a well-ventilated area away from any open flames (including pilot lights on home gas appliances). Do not allow any smoking in the area. Never check the charge of the battery by connecting screwdriver blades or other metal objects between the terminals; the resulting spark can ignite the hydrogen gas.*

> **CAUTION**
> *Always remove the battery from the motorcycle before connecting the battery charger. Never recharge a battery in the frame; corrosive gasses emitted during the charging process will damage surfaces.*

1. Remove the battery as described in this section.

2. Measure the battery voltage as described under *Voltage Test* in this section.

   a. Locate the voltage reading in **Table 2** to determine the battery state of charge and the amount of charge time required.

   b. For example, if the voltage reading is 12.3 volts, the battery state of charge is between 50 and 75 percent. The battery needs to be charged for approximately 5-11 hours.

> **NOTE**
> *If the voltage reading is 11.5 volts or less, internal resistance in the battery may prevent it from recovering when following normal charging attempts. When a battery's state of charge is 25 percent or less (**Table 2**), it is necessary to increase the charging voltage of the battery by applying a low current rate to allow the battery to recover. This requires an adjustable battery charger with a separate amp and volt meter. However, some battery chargers can do this automatically. The OptiMate III Battery Optimiser (**Figure 10**) can automatically diagnose and recover deep-discharged batteries. The OptiMate III can also be used to charge and maintain batteries during all normal battery service without overcharging or overheating the battery. Refer to the charger manufacturer's instructions and specifications for making this test.*

3. Clean the battery terminals and case.

4. Connect the positive (+) charger lead to the positive battery terminal and the negative (–) charger lead to the negative battery terminal.

5. Charge the battery following the manufacturer's instructions. Set the charger at 12 volts and switch it on. Charge the battery at a slow charge rate of 1/10 its given capacity. To determine the current output in amps, divide the battery amp hour capacity by 10. Refer to **Table 1**.

> **CAUTION**
> *When using an adjustable battery charger, follow the manufacturer's instructions. Do not use a larger output battery charger or increase the charge rate on an adjustable battery charger to reduce charging time. Doing so can cause permanent battery damage.*

6. After the battery has been charged for 4-5 hours, turn the charger off, disconnect the leads and allow the battery to sit for a minimum of 30 minutes. Then check the battery with a digital voltmeter. A fully charged battery reads 12.8 volts or higher 30 minutes after taken off the charger. If the battery read-

ing is between 12.5 and 12.8 volts, it may require additional charging.

Battery Storage

When the motorcycle is ridden infrequently or put in storage for an extended amount of time, the battery must be periodically charged to ensure it is capable of working correctly when returned to service. Use an automatic battery charger with variable voltage and amperage outputs (**Figure 10**).

1. Remove the battery as described in this chapter.
2. Clean the battery and terminals with a solution of baking soda and water.
3. Inspect the battery case for any cracks, leaks or bulging. Replace the battery if the case is leaking or damaged.
4. Clean the battery box in the motorcycle.
5. Charge the battery to 100 percent. Store the battery in a cool dry place. Continue to charge the battery once a month when stored in temperatures below 16° C (60° F) and every two weeks when stored in temperatures above 16° C (60° F).

New Battery Setup

When installing a new battery, it is necessary to fill and charge the battery. Follow the battery manufacturer's instructions while observing the following guidelines when activating a new battery:

WARNING
Safety goggles must be worn when servicing and handling the battery in this section.

CAUTION
A new battery must be fully charged before installation. Failure to do so reduces the life of the battery. Using a new battery without an initial charge causes permanent battery damage. That is, the battery never is able to hold more than an 80 percent charge. Charging a new battery after it has been used does not bring its charge to 100 percent. When purchasing a new battery from a dealership or parts store, verify its charge status. If necessary, have them perform the initial or booster charge before accepting the battery.

1. Use the electrolyte that comes with the battery. Do not use an electrolyte from a common container.
2. Fill the battery using all the electrolyte included with the battery kit.
3. Allow the battery to sit for one hour. This allows the plates to absorb the electrolyte for optimum performance.
4. Loosely install the sealing cap over the battery filling holes.
5. Charge the battery following the manufacturer's instructions. Wait 30 minutes and test the battery as described under *Voltage Test* in this section. If the battery charge is 12.8 volts or higher, the battery is considered fully charged. If the battery charge reads 12.7 volts or less, repeat the charging process. When the battery charge reads 12.8 volts 30 minutes after charging, go to Step 6.
6. Press the sealing cap firmly to seal each of the battery fill holes. Make sure the cap seats flush into the battery.

CAUTION
Never remove the sealing cap or add electrolyte to the battery.

CHARGING SYSTEM

The charging system supplies power to operate the engine and electrical system components and keeps the battery charged. The charging system consists of the battery, alternator and a voltage regulator/rectifier. A 30-amp fuse protects the circuit. Refer to the appropriate wiring diagram at the end of this manual.

Alternating current generated by the alternator is rectified to direct current. The voltage regulator maintains constant voltage to the battery and additional electrical loads (such as lights or ignition) despite variations in engine speed and load.

Troubleshooting

Because the charging system is not equipped with an indicator system (light or gauge), slow engine cranking or short bulb life may be the first indicator of a charging system problem.

1. A fully charged battery is required to accurately test the charging system. Perform the battery load test as described under *Battery* in this chapter. If the battery is damaged or worn out, the charging system

may not be at fault. Use the correct wiring diagram at the end of this manual to identify and locate the appropriate connectors.

2. Once a repair has been made, repeat the *Charging Voltage Test* in this section to confirm the charging system is working correctly.

Battery discharging

If the battery is dead or the regulated voltage readings recorded in the *Charging Voltage Test* in this section were too low, perform the steps in the order listed below.

1. Check all the connections. Make sure they are tight and free of corrosion.

2. Perform the *Charging Voltage Test* in this section. If the regulated voltage reading is correct, go to Step 3. If the regulated voltage is too low, go to Step 5. If the regulated voltage is too high, refer to *Battery Overcharging* in this section.

3. Perform the *Current Draw Test* as described in section. If the current draw is acceptable, the battery is probably faulty. Perform the battery load test as described under *Battery* in this chapter. If the draw is high, continue with Step 4.

4. Disconnect the regulator/rectifier connector (**Figure 1-3**) and repeat the *Current Draw Test* described in Step 3. If the current draw is acceptable, the regulator/rectifier is faulty. Replace the regulator/rectifier as described in this section and retest. If the draw is high, the problem is probably caused by a short in the wiring or the ignition switch is faulty. Check for a short circuit in the charging system by disconnecting the connectors one at a time while repeating the current draw test performed in Step 3. (Reconnect the connector before disconnecting another connector.) If the current draw returns to normal when a connector is disconnected, the circuit is shorting to ground. If a short circuit cannot be located, test the ignition switch as described in Chapter Nine.

5. Check the battery charge circuit as described under *Wiring Harness Test* in this section. If there is battery voltage, go to Step 6. If not, check the red/white wire between the starter relay switch and regulator/rectifier for an open circuit. Then check the circuit connectors for dirty or damaged terminals.

6. Check the charge coil circuit and stator coil resistance as described under *Stator Coil and Left*

Crankcase Cover in this chapter. If the stator coil tests correctly, replace the regulator/rectifier as described in this section. If not, check the yellow wires between the alternator and regulator/rectifier for an open circuit. Then check the connectors for dirty or damaged terminals.

Battery overcharging

If the regulated voltage is too high, perform this test in the order listed below:

1. Perform the *Charging Voltage Test* in this section. If the regulated voltage reading is correct, replace the battery and retest. If not, the regulated voltage is too high. Go to Step 2.

2. Perform the ground circuit test as described under *Wiring Harness Test* in this section. If continuity is present, check the regulator/rectifier connector for dirty or loose-fitting terminals. If the battery continues to overcharge after cleaning or repairing these connectors, replace the regulator/rectifier. If there is no continuity, check for dirty or loose-fitting terminals. Then check for an open circuit in the wiring harness.

Current Draw Test

A short circuit increases current draw or leakage and drains the battery. Perform this test before troubleshooting the charging system or performing the charging voltage test to determine if the current draw is normal or excessive. If the battery discharges because of a short, the charging system may not be at fault.

> *NOTE*
> *When installing electrical accessories, do not wire them into a live circuit where they stay on all the time. Refer to the accessory manufacturer's instructions.*

1. Turn the ignition switch off.

2. Disconnect the negative battery cable as described under *Battery Removal/Installation* in this chapter.

> *CAUTION*
> *Before connecting the ammeter into the circuit, set the meter to its highest amperage scale. This prevents a large*

current flow from damaging the meter or blowing the meter's fuse.

3. Connect an ammeter between the negative battery cable and the negative battery terminal (**Figure 11**). Do *not* turn the ignition switch on once this connection is made.

4. Switch the ammeter to its lowest scale and note the reading. The maximum current draw is 1.0 mA or less. A current draw that exceeds 1.0 mA must be found and repaired.

5. If the current draw is excessive, consider the following probable causes:

    a. Damaged battery.

    b. Faulty voltage regulator/rectifier.

    c. Short circuit in the system.

    d. Loose, dirty or faulty electrical connectors.

    e. After market electrical accessories added to the electrical system.

6. To find the short circuit that is causing the current draw, refer to the wiring diagram at the end of this manual. Then disconnect different electrical connectors one by one while monitoring the ammeter. When the current draw returns to an acceptable level, the faulty circuit is indicated. Test the circuit further to find the problem.

7. Disconnect the ammeter.

8. Reconnect the negative battery cable.

Charging Voltage Test

This procedure tests the charging system regulated voltage. It does not measure maximum charging system output.

To obtain accurate test results, the battery must be fully charged (13.0-13.2 volts).

1. Start and run the engine until it reaches normal operating temperature, then turn the engine off.

2. Connect a digital voltmeter to the battery terminals as shown in **Figure 7**. To prevent a short, make sure the voltmeter leads attach firmly to the battery terminals. On VT750DC models, record the voltage reading.

CAUTION
Do not disconnect either battery cable when making this test. Doing so may damage the voltmeter or electrical accessories.

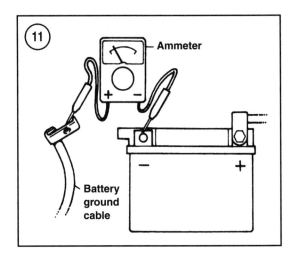

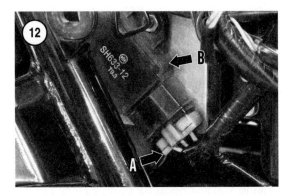

3A. On VT750C models, start the engine and allow it to idle. Turn the headlight to LO beam. Gradually increase engine speed to 4000 rpm and read the voltage indicated on the voltmeter. The voltmeter should read 14-15 volts.

3B. On VT750DC models. start the engine and allow it to idle. Turn the headlight to HI beam. Gradually increase engine speed to 5000 rpm and read the voltage indicated on the voltmeter. The voltmeter should show a reading greater than the measured battery voltage recorded in Step 2 and less than 15.5 volts.

NOTE
*If the battery is often discharged, but the charging voltage tested normal during Step 3, the battery may be damaged. Perform a battery load-test as described under **Battery** in this chapter.*

4. If the voltage reading is incorrect, perform the *Wiring Harness Test* in this section, while noting the following:

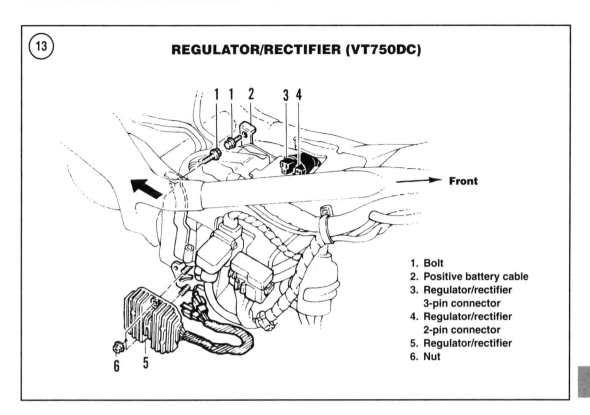

REGULATOR/RECTIFIER (VT750DC)

1. Bolt
2. Positive battery cable
3. Regulator/rectifier
   3-pin connector
4. Regulator/rectifier
   2-pin connector
5. Regulator/rectifier
6. Nut

Front

a. If the charging voltage is too low, check for an open or short circuit in the charging system wiring harness, an open or short in the alternator, high resistance in the alternator-to-battery cable or a damaged regulator/rectifier.

b. If the charging voltage is too high, check for a poor regulator/rectifier ground, damaged regulator/rectifier or a damaged battery.

Wiring Harness Test

This procedure tests the integrity of the wires and connectors attached to the regulator/rectifier.

1A. On VT750C models, perform the following:

a. Remove the left side cover (Chapter Fifteen).

b. Disconnect the 5-pin connector (A, **Figure 12**, typical) at the regulator/rectifier.

1B. On VT750DC models, perform the following:

a. Remove the seat and the right side cover (Chapter Fifteen).

b. Disconnect the 2-pin regulator/rectifier connector (**Figure 13**).

2. Check for loose or corroded terminals in the regulator/rectifier and wiring harness side connectors.

NOTE
Make all of the tests on the wiring harness connector side, not on the regulator/rectifier connector side.

3. Check the battery charge circuit as follows:

a. Connect a voltmeter between the red/white wire (+) and a good engine ground (–).

b. The voltmeter should read battery voltage at all times (ignition switch on or off).

c. If there is no voltage, check the red/white wire for an open circuit.

d. Disconnect the voltmeter leads.

4. Check the ground circuit as follows:

a. Connect the ohmmeter between the green wire and a good engine ground.

b. The ohmmeter should read continuity.

c. If there is no continuity, check the green wire for an open circuit.

5. Check the charge coil circuit and stator coil resistance as described under *Stator Coil and Left Crankcase Cover* in this chapter.

6. Reverse Step 1A or Step 1B.

Regulator/Rectifier
Removal/Installation

1A. On VT750C models, perform the following:
   a. Remove the left side cover (Chapter Fifteen).
   b. Disconnect the 5-pin connector (A, **Figure 12**, typical) at the regulator/rectifier.
   c. Remove the nuts and the regulator/rectifier (B, **Figure 12**).
1B. On VT750DC models, perform the following:
   a. Remove the seat and the right side cover (Chapter Fifteen).
   b. Disconnect the 2-pin and 3-pin regulator/rectifier connectors (**Figure 13**).
   c. Remove the battery case mounting bolts and push the battery box rearward to expose the regulator/rectifier mounting nuts.
   d. Remove the regulator/rectifier mounting nuts and the regulator/rectifier unit.
2. Installation is the reverse of removal.

STATOR COIL AND LEFT
CRANKCASE COVER

The stator coil is mounted inside the left crankcase cover.

Left Crankcase Cover
Removal/Installation

1. Remove the seat (Chapter Fifteen).
2. On VT750C models, remove the right side cover (Chapter Fifteen).
3. Follow the wiring harness from the left crankcase cover to the alternator electrical connector. Then disconnect the alternator 3-pin connector. Refer to **Figure 14** (VT750C) or **Figure 13** (VT750DC).
4. Remove the drive sprocket cover. Refer to *Drive and Driven Sprockets* in Chapter Eleven.
5. On VT750C models, remove the left footpeg and shift pedal/linkage assembly. Refer to *External Shift Mechanism* in Chapter Six.
6. Note the wiring harness clamps and routing position around the left crankcase cover.
7. Place a clean drain pan underneath the left crankcase cover.

NOTE
Some engine oil will drain out when the left crankcase cover is removed.

NOTE
*Two different length crankcase cover mounting bolts are used. The bolt indicated in A, **Figure 15** is longer than the other bolts.*

8. Remove the bolts securing the crankcase cover (**Figure 15**, typical) to the engine. If necessary, lightly tap the cover to loosen it from the engine. Do not pry the cover off.
9. Remove the dowel pins (**Figure 16**).
10A. On 1998-2000 models, remove and discard the gasket. Remove all gasket residue from the crankcase and cover surfaces.
10B. On 2001-on models, remove all sealer residue from the crankcase and cover surfaces.
11. If necessary, service the stator coil as described in this section.
12. Do not clean the cover or stator coils in solvent. Wipe the cover with a clean rag.

NOTE
If the cover is contaminated with oil sludge, remove the stator coil as described in the following procedure and then clean the cover.

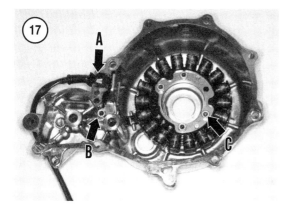

13. Installation is the reverse of removal. Note the following:

a. Make sure the grommet (A, **Figure 17**) on the stator coil wiring harness is positioned firmly into the crankcase notch.

b. Clean the cover and crankcase mating surfaces. On 2001-on models, spray the crankcase bolt holes with an aerosol cleaner to remove all oil residue.

c. On 1998-2000 models, install a new gasket.

d. On 2001-on models, apply a gasket sealer to the crankcase cover gasket surface.

e. The bolt indicated in A, **Figure 15** is longer than the other crankcase cover mounting bolts.

f. Tighten the left crankcase cover mounting bolts in a crisscross pattern and in several steps.

NOTE
On 2001-on models, allow the gasket sealer to set before adding engine oil to the crankcase. Refer to the manufacturer's recommendations.

g. Make sure the electrical connector is free of corrosion. Check the wiring harness routing.

h. Check the engine oil level (Chapter Three) and add oil as required.

Stator Coil Resistance Test

The stator coil is mounted inside the left crankcase side cover (**Figure 17**). The stator coil can be tested while mounted on the engine.

1. Remove the seat (Chapter Fifteen).

2. On VT750C models, remove the right side cover (Chapter Fifteen).

3. Follow the wiring harness from the left crankcase cover to the alternator electrical connector. Then disconnect the alternator 3-pin connector. Refer to **Figure 14** (VT750C) or **Figure 13** (VT750DC).

4. Measure the resistance between each yellow wire on the alternator side of the connector. **Table 3** lists the specified stator coil resistance.

5. Replace the stator if any resistance reading is incorrect.

6. Check for continuity from each yellow stator wire to ground. Replace the stator coil if any yellow terminal has continuity to ground. Continuity indicates a short within the stator coil winding.

NOTE
Before replacing the stator assembly, check the electrical wires to and within the electrical connector for any opens or poor connections.

7. If the stator coil (**Figure 17**) fails either of these tests, replace it as described in this section.

8. Make sure the electrical connector is secure and corrosion free.

Stator Coil Removal/Installation

1. Remove the left crankcase cover as described in this section.

2. Remove the bolt and wire holder (B, **Figure 17**).

3. Remove the stator coil mounting bolts (C, **Figure 17**).

4. Pull the rubber plug out of the cover and remove the stator coil.

5. Clean and dry the left crankcase cover. Clean the stator coil mounting bolt holes of all threadlock residue.

6. Installation is the revere of removal. Note the following:

    a. Apply a medium strength threadlock onto all the stator coil mounting bolts (C, **Figure 17**) and tighten to 12 N•m (106 in.-lb.).

    b. Apply Gasgacinch or an RTV sealer to the wiring harness rubber plug, and then insert the plug into the cover notch (A, **Figure 17**).

    c. Install the wire holder (A, **Figure 18**) over the wire harness. Position the lower part of the wire holder against the stop (B, **Figure 18**) in the crankcase cover. Apply a medium strength threadlock onto the wire holder mounting bolt (C, **Figure 18**) and tighten to 12 N•m (106 in.-lb.).

FLYWHEEL, STARTER CLUTCH AND STARTER REDUCTION GEARS

The flywheel (alternator rotor) is mounted on the left end of the crankshaft. The starter clutch is mounted on the back of the flywheel. The starter reduction gears can be removed without having to remove the flywheel.

Tools

The following tools or their equivalents are required to remove the flywheel (alternator rotor):

1. Flywheel puller, Motion Pro part No. 08-074 (A, **Figure 19**) or Honda part No. 07733-002000 or 07933-328001.

2. Honda flywheel holder, Honda part No. 07725-0040000 (B, **Figure 19**).

Flywheel Removal

1. Remove the left crankcase cover as described in this chapter.

2. Remove the starter idler gear and shaft (A, **Figure 20**) and the reduction gear and shaft (B).

NOTE
The flywheel mounting bolt has ***left-hand*** *threads.*

3. Hold the flywheel with a holding tool (A, **Figure 21**) and turn the flywheel mounting bolt (B) *clockwise* to loosen it. Remove the flywheel bolt and washer.

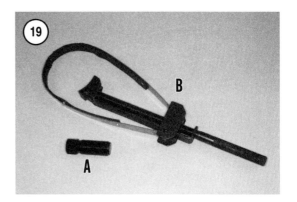

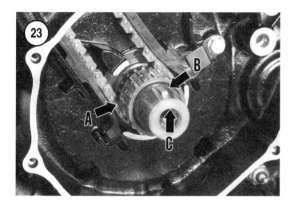

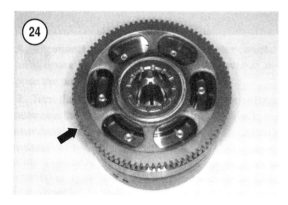

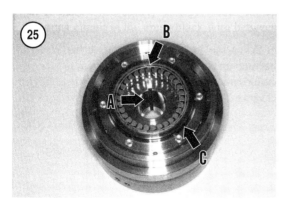

4. Screw the flywheel puller (**Figure 22**) into the flywheel.

CAUTION
Do not try to remove the flywheel without the correct puller. Any attempt to do so may damage the flywheel and crankshaft.

CAUTION
If normal flywheel removal attempts fail, do not force the puller. Excessive force strips the flywheel threads, causing expensive damage. Take the engine to a dealership for flywheel removal.

5. Hold the flywheel with the flywheel holder and gradually tighten the flywheel puller (**Figure 22**) until the flywheel pops off the crankshaft taper. Remove the flywheel while also holding onto the starter driven gear

6. Remove the needle bearing (A, **Figure 23**).

7. Do not remove the Woodruff key (B, **Figure 23**) from the crankshaft unless it is loose. If it is loose, check both the crankshaft keyway and Woodruff key for damage.

8. Remove the holder and puller from the flywheel.

9. Remove the starter driven gear (**Figure 24**) from the starter clutch.

Flywheel/Starter Clutch Inspection

1. Clean the flywheel/starter clutch assembly and the starter gears in solvent and dry with compressed air.

2. Check the flywheel for cracks or breaks.

WARNING
Replace a cracked or chipped flywheel. A damaged flywheel can fly apart at high engine speeds, throwing metal fragments into the engine. Do not repair a damaged flywheel.

3. Check the flywheel tapered bore and the crankshaft taper for pitting and other damage.

4. Inspect the flywheel keyway (A, **Figure 25**) for damage.

5. Inspect the starter clutch assembly as follows:
   a. Inspect the one-way clutch roller cage (B, **Figure 25**) for overheating, pitting or flaking.

9

If damaged, replace the starter clutch as described in this section.

b. Inspect the starter reduction gear for damaged gear teeth (A, **Figure 26**). Then inspect the needle bearing (B, **Figure 26**) and starter clutch (C) operating surfaces for pitting, cracks and other damage.

c. Measure the starter driven gear inside (B, **Figure 26**) and outside diameters (C) and compare to the specifications in **Table 4**. Replace the gear if any measurement is out of specification.

d. Inspect the needle bearing for damage. Check the cage for cracks or areas where the needles can fall out. Check the needles for flat spots, pitting and other damage.

e. If there is no visible damage, perform Step 6 to check the starter clutch operation.

6. Insert the starter driven gear (**Figure 24**) into the starter clutch. Hold the flywheel and try to turn the gear clockwise and then counterclockwise. The gear should only turn *counterclockwise* (**Figure 27**). If the gear turns clockwise, replace the starter clutch as described in this section.

7. Inspect the starter reduction gears and shafts (**Figure 28**) for:

a. Broken or chipped gear teeth.

b. Worn or scored gear bores.

c. Pitted or damaged shaft surfaces.

8. Inspect the flywheel mounting bolt and washer for damage. Both parts are made of hardened material. Replace only with Honda OEM parts.

Flywheel Installation

1. Lubricate the starter reduction gear shoulder with engine oil, and then install the gear into the starter clutch (**Figure 24**).

2. Degrease the crankshaft outer taper and the flywheel inner taper with aerosol parts cleaner. Allow both tapers to dry before installing the flywheel.

3. Lubricate the needle bearing with engine oil and install it onto the crankshaft (A, **Figure 23**). Reclean the crankshaft taper if necessary.

4. If removed, install the Woodruff key (B, **Figure 23**) into the crankshaft keyway.

5. Place a paint mark on the end of the crankshaft in-line with the crankshaft keyway (C, **Figure 23**). This serves as a visual aid to help align the flywheel keyway with the Woodruff key during installation.

6. Align the flywheel keyway with the Woodruff key and install the flywheel. The paint mark on the crankshaft should align with the flywheel keyway (**Figure 29**).

NOTE
Shine a flashlight through the flywheel bore to visually make sure the Woodruff key is installed in its keyway.

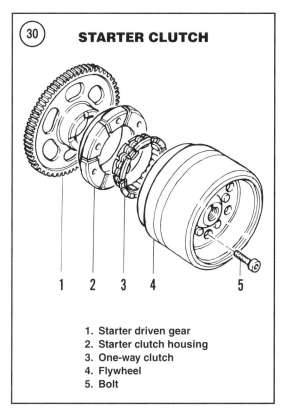

STARTER CLUTCH

1. Starter driven gear
2. Starter clutch housing
3. One-way clutch
4. Flywheel
5. Bolt

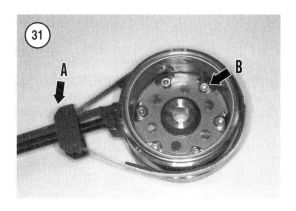

NOTE
*The flywheel bolt has **left-hand** threads.*

7. Lubricate the flywheel bolt threads and washer with engine oil.

8. Install the flywheel mounting bolt by turning it *counterclockwise*.

9. Hold the flywheel with the flywheel holder and tighten the flywheel mounting bolt (B, **Figure 21**) to 127 N•m (94 ft.-lb.).

10. Lubricate both starter gear bores and shafts (**Figure 28**) with engine oil.

11. Install the starter reduction gear (A, **Figure 28**) and the starter idler gear (B) as shown in **Figure 20**. Install the starter idler gear (A, **Figure 20**) with its OUT mark facing out. Then install both shafts until they bottom. Refer to **Figure 28** to identify the length of each shaft with its appropriate gear.

12. Install the left crankcase cover as described in this chapter.

Starter Clutch Disassembly/Assembly

The starter clutch (**Figure 30**) can be inspected while assembled and installed on the flywheel. Do not remove the starter clutch unless replacement is necessary.

1. Inspect the starter clutch as described in this section.

2. Secure the flywheel with the flywheel holder (A, **Figure 31**) used to remove the flywheel. Remove the Torx bolts (B, **Figure 31**) securing the starter clutch assembly to the flywheel. Remove the starter clutch housing (C, **Figure 25**) from the flywheel.

3. Remove the one-way clutch from the starter clutch housing and discard it.

4. Clean and dry all parts. Remove all thread sealer residue from the Torx bolts and starter clutch housing threads.

5. Measure the starter clutch housing (2, **Figure 30**) inside diameter and compare to the dimensions in **Table 4**. Replace the starter clutch housing if the bore is too large.

6. Install the new one-way clutch into the starter clutch housing in the direction shown in **Figure 30**.

7. Install the starter clutch housing (C, **Figure 25**) onto the flywheel.

8. Apply a medium strength threadlock onto the threads of each Torx bolt and tighten to 29 N•m (21 ft.-lb.).

9

IGNITION SYSTEM TROUBLESHOOTING

Peak Voltage Tests and Equipment

> *WARNING*
> *High voltage is present during igni-*
> *tion system operation. Do not touch*
> *ignition components, wires or test*
> *leads while cranking or running the*
> *engine.*

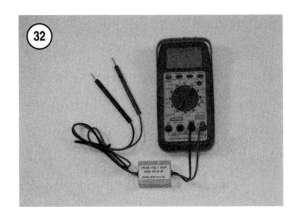

Peak voltage tests check the voltage output of the ignition coils and pulse generator at normal cranking speed. These tests make it possible to accurately test the voltage output under operating conditions.

The peak voltage specifications listed in **Table 5** are minimum values. If the measured voltage meets or exceeds the specification, the test results are satisfactory. In some cases, the voltage may greatly exceed the minimum specification.

To check peak voltage, a peak voltage tester is required. One of the following testers or an equivalent, can be used to perform peak voltage tests described in this section. Refer to the manufacturer's instructions when using these tools.

1. Honda Peak voltage adapter (part No. 07HGJ-0020100). This tool must be used in combination with a digital multimeter with a minimum impedance of 10M ohms/DCV. A meter with a lower impedance does not display accurate measurements. Refer to **Figure 32**.
2. Ignition Mate (Motion Pro part No. 08-0193). Refer to **Figure 33**.

Preliminary Checks

Before testing the ignition system, make the following checks:
1. Make sure the battery is fully charged and in good condition. A weak battery causes a slow engine cranking speed.
2. Perform the *Spark Test* in Chapter Two. If a crisp, blue spark is noted, the ignition system is working correctly. Test each spark plug and note the following:
   a. If there is no spark at both spark plugs, check for a disconnected or contaminated connector or a damaged ignition switch or engine stop switch. Test each switch as described in this chapter.
   b. If the spark test shows there is no spark at one coil group (front or rear cylinder), switch the ignition coils and repeat the spark test. If the inoperative cylinder now has spark, the original ignition coil is defective. Replace it and retest. However, if the inoperative cylinder still does not have spark, check the ignition coil wires for an open circuit.
   c. Also check for fouled or damaged spark plugs, loose spark plugs caps or water in the spark plugs caps.
3. If the problem has not been found and the spark plugs, plug caps and all electrical system connectors are in good working order, the problem is probably due to a defective switch or ignition system component. Perform the peak voltage tests in this section to locate the damaged component.

Ignition Coil Signal Peak Voltage Test

This test requires a peak voltage tester as described under *Peak Voltage Tests and Equipment* in this section. Refer to **Figure 34** for test results.
1. Check the battery to make sure it is fully charged and in good condition. A weak battery causes a slow engine cranking speed and inaccurate peak voltage tests results.
2. Remove the seat (Chapter Fifteen).
3. Remove the fuel tank (Chapter Eight).
4. Check engine compression as described in Chapter Three. If the compression is low in one or both cylinders, the following test results will be inaccurate.
5. Check all of the ignition component electrical connectors and wiring harnesses. Make sure the connectors are clean and properly connected.

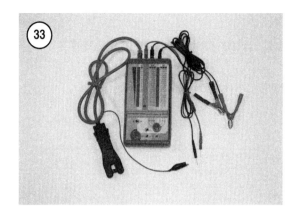

6. Disconnect each spark plug cap. Then connect a new spark plug to each plug cap and ground the plug against the cylinder head. Do not remove the spark plugs installed in the cylinder heads. These must remain in the cylinder heads.

7. If using the Honda peak voltage adapter, connect it to the multimeter as shown in **Figure 32**.

NOTE
*If using the Ignition Mate (**Figure 33**) tester or a similar peak voltage tester, follow its manufacturer's instructions for connecting the tester to the ignition coil.*

NOTE
Do not disconnect the ignition coil primary connectors when performing Step 8.

8. Locate the ignition coil to be checked. Connect the peak voltage test leads to the ignition coil terminals (**Figure 35**) as follows:

NOTE
*Refer to **Ignition Coils** in this chapter to identify the ignition coils.*

  a. Front cylinder ignition coil: Connect the positive test lead to the blue/yellow terminal and the negative test lead to ground.

  b. Rear cylinder ignition coil: Connect the positive test lead to the yellow/blue connector terminal and the negative test lead to ground.

9. Shift the transmission into neutral.

10. Turn the ignition switch on and the engine stop switch to RUN.

11. Read the voltage and note the following:

  a. If there is no battery voltage or the voltage reading is low, refer to the test results in **Figure 34**. Perform the steps in order to find the problem.

  b. If the battery voltage reading is correct, continue with Step 12.

WARNING
High voltage is present during ignition system operation. Do not touch spark plugs, ignition components, connectors or test leads while cranking the engine.

12. Press the starter button while reading the meter.

13. Release the starter button, and then connect the test lead to the other ignition coil primary lead and repeat Step 12.

14. Turn the ignition switch off and interpret the test results as follows:

NOTE
*All peak voltage specifications are **minimum** voltages. As long as the measured voltage meets or exceeds the specification, consider the test results satisfactory. On some components, the voltage may greatly exceed the minimum specification.*

  a. The minimum ignition coil peak voltage reading is 100 volts minimum.

  b. The individual peak voltage reading recorded for each ignition coil can vary as long as the voltage readings are higher than the specified minimum value.

  c. If the peak voltage reading for one or both ignition coils is less than 100 volts, refer to the test results in **Figure 34**. Perform the steps in order to find the problem.

15. Disconnect the test leads.

16. Remove the spark plugs from the plug caps, and then reconnect the plug caps onto the spark plugs installed in the cylinder head.

17. Reverse Step 2 and Step 3 to complete installation.

Ignition Pulse Generator Peak Voltage Test

This test requires a peak voltage tester as described under *Peak Voltage Tests and Equipment* in this section. Refer to **Figure 36** for test results.

(34)

IGNITION COIL PRIMARY PEAK VOLTAGE TROUBLESHOOTING

NOTE:
Initial voltage is the recorded battery voltage before cranking the engine with the starter.

| No peak voltage. | Check the following in order:
1. Damaged engine stop switch.
2. Open circuit in the black/white wire between the engine stop switch and ignition coil.
3. Poorly connected connectors or an open circuit in the ignition coil primary circuit.
4. Damaged ignition control module (ICM) when all of the above are normal. |

| Peak voltage reading is normal, but there is no spark. | Check the following in order:
1. Open circuit in the ignition coil ground or power circuits.
2. Damaged ignition coil.
3. Loose spark plug cap.
4. Damaged spark plug wire. |

| Initial voltage is normal, but drops to 2-4 volts when engine is cranked. | Check the following in order:
1. Incorrect peak voltage adapter connections.
2. Cranking speed is too low. Perform the starter voltage drop tests in this chapter to check for voltage drop when attempting to start engine.
3. No battery voltage between the black ignition control module (ICM) connector and an engine ground. Check also for a loose or contaminated ICM connector.
4. Poorly connected connectors or an open circuit in the ignition control module (ICM) green wire.
5. Poorly connected connectors or an open circuit in the yellow/blue or blue/yellow wires between the ignition control module (ICM) and the ignition coils.
6. Short circuit in ignition coil primary circuit.
7. Damaged neutral switch.
8. Damaged sidestand switch. |

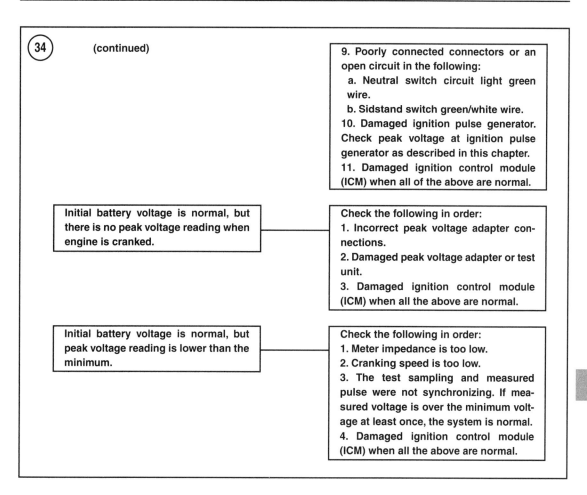

34 (continued)

9. Poorly connected connectors or an open circuit in the following:
  a. Neutral switch circuit light green wire.
  b. Sidstand switch green/white wire.
10. Damaged ignition pulse generator. Check peak voltage at ignition pulse generator as described in this chapter.
11. Damaged ignition control module (ICM) when all of the above are normal.

Initial battery voltage is normal, but there is no peak voltage reading when engine is cranked.

Check the following in order:
1. Incorrect peak voltage adapter connections.
2. Damaged peak voltage adapter or test unit.
3. Damaged ignition control module (ICM) when all the above are normal.

Initial battery voltage is normal, but peak voltage reading is lower than the minimum.

Check the following in order:
1. Meter impedance is too low.
2. Cranking speed is too low.
3. The test sampling and measured pulse were not synchronizing. If measured voltage is over the minimum voltage at least once, the system is normal.
4. Damaged ignition control module (ICM) when all the above are normal.

9

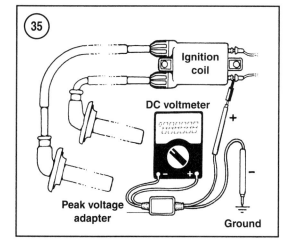

35

Ignition coil

DC voltmeter

Peak voltage adapter

Ground

1. Check the battery to make sure it is fully charged and in good condition. A weak battery causes a slow engine cranking speed and inaccurate peak voltage tests results.

2. Remove the seat (Chapter Fifteen).

3. Check engine compression as described in Chapter Three. If the compression is low in one or both cylinders, the following test results will be inaccurate.

4. Check all of the ignition component electrical connectors and wiring harnesses. Make sure the connectors are clean and properly connected.

5. Disconnect the ICM connector. Refer to *Ignition Control Module* (ICM) in this chapter to identify the connector.

6. If using the Honda peak voltage adapter, connect it to the multimeter as shown in **Figure 32**.

NOTE
*If using the Ignition Mate (**Figure 33**) tester or a similar peak voltage tester, follow its manufacturer's instructions for connecting the tester to the ignition coil.*

7. Connect the peak voltage positive test lead to the white/yellow connector terminal and the negative

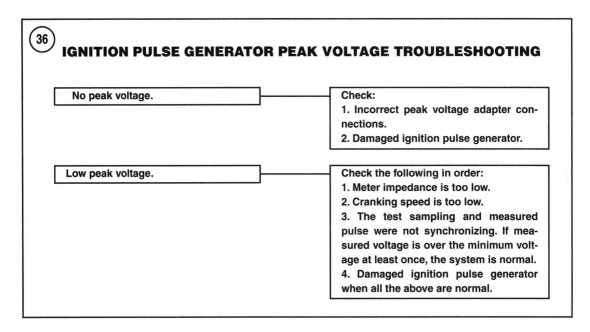

test lead to the yellow connector terminal (**Figure 37**).

NOTE
*Visually identify the wire colors/terminals at the wire harness connector. The wire color/terminal position in your connector may differ from the terminals identified in **Figure 37**.*

8. Shift the transmission into neutral.

9. Turn the ignition switch on and the engine stop switch to RUN.

WARNING
High voltage is present during ignition system operation. Do not touch spark plugs, ignition components, connectors or test leads while cranking the engine.

10. Press the starter button while reading the meter. The meter should indicate a minimum peak voltage reading of 0.7 volts DC. If the reading is less than this, continue with Step 11.

NOTE
*All peak voltage specifications are **minimum** voltages. If the measured voltage meets or exceeds the specification, consider the test results satisfactory. On some components, the*

voltage may greatly exceed the minimum specification.

11. Measure the peak voltage at the ignition pulse generator connector:

a. Turn the ignition switch off.

b. Remove the fuel tank (Chapter Eight).

c. Disconnect the ignition pulse generator 2-pin red connector.

NOTE
*Refer to **Ignition Pulse Generator** in this chapter to locate the connector.*

d. Connect the peak voltage positive test lead to the white/yellow connector terminal and the negative test lead to the yellow connector terminal (**Figure 38**).

NOTE
Connect the test leads to the ignition pulse generator side connector terminals, not to the wire harness connector terminals.

e. Turn the ignition switch on and the engine stop switch to RUN.

f. Press the starter button while reading the meter. The meter should indicate a minimum peak voltage reading of 0.7 volts DC. If the reading is now correct, check the yellow wire between the ignition pulse generator and the

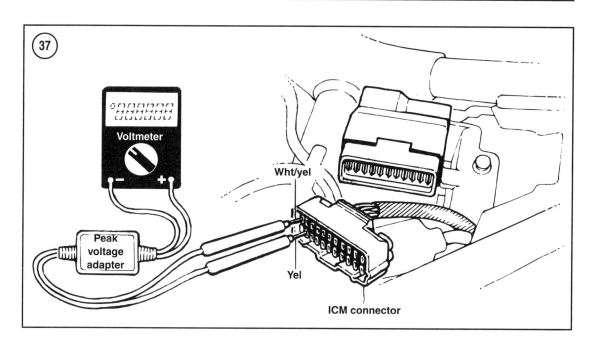

Voltmeter

Wht/yel

Peak
voltage
adapter

Yel

ICM connector

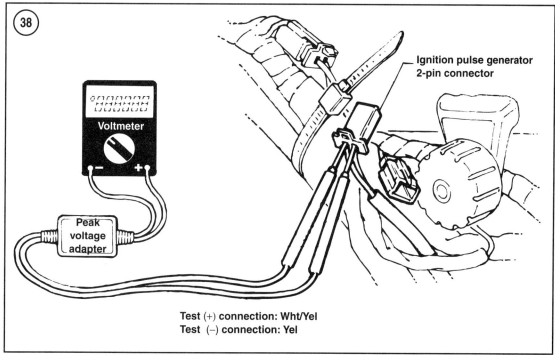

Voltmeter

Ignition pulse generator
2-pin connector

Peak
voltage
adapter

Test (+) connection: Wht/Yel
Test (−) connection: Yel

ICM connector for an open or short circuit. Then check the white/yellow wire between the ignition pulse generator and the ICM connector. At the same time, check the connectors for loose terminals or contamination. If the reading is still incorrect, refer to the test results in **Figure 36**.

12. Install the previously removed parts to complete assembly.

IGNITION COILS

Refer to **Figure 39** and **Figure 40**.

Removal/Installation

1. Turn the ignition switch off.
2. To remove the front cylinder ignition coil, remove the fuel tank (Chapter Eight).
3. To remove the rear cylinder ignition coil, remove the right side cover (Chapter Fifteen).
4. Identify the secondary wires (plug wires) and the two primary coil wires at the ignition coil. Refer to **Figure 41** (front cylinder ignition coil) or **Figure 42** (rear cylinder ignition coil). Note the routing of the secondary wires from the coil to the spark plugs. Remove the band clips used to support the rear cylinder ignition coil secondary wires.
5. Disconnect the spark plug caps from the spark plugs. Note the routing of each plug wire.
6. Disconnect the ignition coil primary connectors at the ignition coil.
7. Remove the mounting bolts and ignition coil. Note any spacers where used.
8. Installation is the reverse of removal. Reconnect the primary connectors at the ignition coils as follows:

    a. Front coil black terminal: black/white wire.
    b. Front coil green terminal: blue/yellow wire.
    c. Rear coil black terminal: black/white wire.
    d. Rear coil green terminal: yellow/blue wire.

IGNITION PULSE GENERATOR

The ignition pulse generator is mounted behind the right crankcase housing.

Removal/Installation

1. Remove the fuel tank (Chapter Eight).
2. Disconnect the ignition pulse generator 2-pin connector (**Figure 43**, typical).
3. Remove the right crankcase cover (Chapter Six).
4. Remove the two bolts (A, **Figure 44**) and then pull the rubber grommets (B) from the crankcase.
5. Remove the ignition pulse generator.
6. Installation is the reverse of removal. Note the following:

    a. Clean the threads on the ignition pulse generator bolts and mating threaded holes of any oil and threadlock residue.
    b. Apply a medium strength threadlock onto the ignition pulse generator bolt threads.

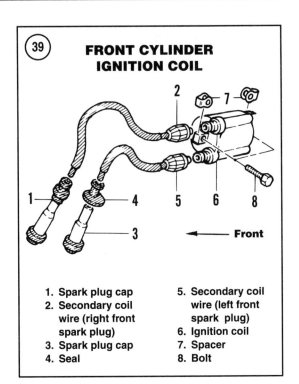

39 FRONT CYLINDER IGNITION COIL

1. Spark plug cap
2. Secondary coil wire (right front spark plug)
3. Spark plug cap
4. Seal
5. Secondary coil wire (left front spark plug)
6. Ignition coil
7. Spacer
8. Bolt

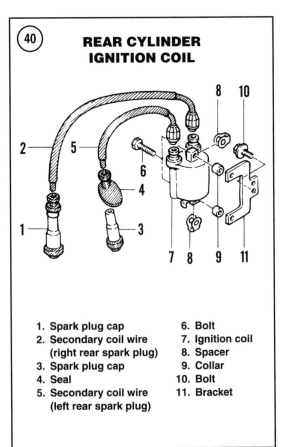

40 REAR CYLINDER IGNITION COIL

1. Spark plug cap
2. Secondary coil wire (right rear spark plug)
3. Spark plug cap
4. Seal
5. Secondary coil wire (left rear spark plug)
6. Bolt
7. Ignition coil
8. Spacer
9. Collar
10. Bolt
11. Bracket

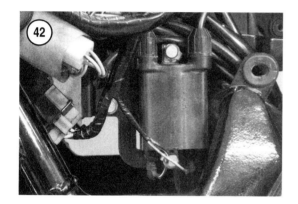

c. Install the ignition pulse generator and tighten the mounting bolts (A, **Figure 44**) to 12 N•m (106 in.-lb.).

d. Reinstall the wire harness grommets into the crankcase.

IGNITION PULSE GENERATOR ROTOR

Removal/Installation

Remove and install the ignition pulse generator rotor. Refer to *Primary Drive Gear* in Chapter Six. Disregard the information for camshaft removal.

IGNITION CONTROL MODULE (ICM)

The ignition control module is mounted underneath the seat.

Removal/Installation

1. Remove the seat (Chapter Fifteen).

2. Remove the ICM (**Figure 45**, typical) from the battery case cover.

3. Disconnect the connector at the ICM.

4. Installation is the reverse of removal.

IGNITION TIMING

Refer to *Ignition Timing* in Chapter Three.

STARTING SYSTEM
TROUBLESHOOTING

The starting system consists of the battery, starter, starter relay switch, start button, starter mechanism and related wiring.

When the ignition is turned on and the start button is pushed, current is transmitted from the battery to the starter relay switch. When the relay is activated, it activates the starter solenoid that mechanically engages the starter with the engine.

A starting system problem may be electrical or mechanical. The *Engine Will Not Start* procedure in Chapter Two lists general troubleshooting procedures to help isolate starting problems.

1. If troubleshooting a starting system problem, check the following before proceeding with more in-depth testing:

   a. Make sure the battery is fully charged and has passed a battery load test.

   b. Make sure the battery cables are the proper size and length. Replace damaged or undersized cables.

   c. Make sure all electrical connections are clean and tight. High resistance caused from dirty or loose connections can affect voltage and current levels.

   d. Make sure the wiring harness is in good condition, with no worn or frayed insulation or lose harness sockets.

   e. Make sure the fuel tank is filled with an adequate supply of fresh gasoline.

   f. Make sure the spark plugs are in good condition and properly gapped.

   g. Make sure the ignition system is working correctly.

2. If the starter does not turn over, perform these quick tests to isolate the problem:

   a. Turn the ignition switch on and shift the transmission into neutral. The headlight should come on. If not, check the main fuse and appropriate subfuse. Refer to *Fuses* in this chapter. If the fuses are good, check the battery.

   b. If the headlight came on, push the starter button to start the engine. The solenoid should click. If not, the problem is in the wiring to the solenoid, ignition switch or the solenoid is faulty.

   c. If the solenoid did click but the starter did not turn the engine over, the problem may be due to excessive voltage drop in the starter circuit or the starter is damaged. This could be due to worn brushes or a shorted commutator. The problem can also be in the starter drive system or engine.

3. If the problem is traced to the starter circuit, refer to the *Symptom-Based Tests* procedure in this section and perform the procedure that matches the starting problem.

Voltage Drop Tests

A voltage drop test measures the voltage drop (or difference in voltage) in a circuit between the power source and destination to locate poor electrical connections that may test normal during a resistance test.

Before performing *Symptom-Based Tests* in this section, perform the voltage drop tests in this procedure. These steps check the starting circuit from the battery to the starter to find weak or damaged electrical components that may be causing the problem.

1. A voltmeter that can read in millivolts (mV) (1/1000 of a volt) is required to test voltage drop.

2. Remove the seat and the right side cover (Chapter Fifteen).

3. Turn the fuel valve off.

4. Disconnect the fuel pump electrical connector. Refer to *Fuel Pump* in Chapter Eight.

5. Disconnect each spark plug cap but do not remove the spark plugs because they must remain in the cylinder heads. Install a grounding tool into each spark plug cap. Refer to *Basic Tools* in Chapter One. This step prevents the engine from starting while also protecting the ignition system.

CAUTION
When checking voltage drop, do not operate the starter for more than five seconds at a time. Wait approximately 10 seconds between starting attempts. Position the voltmeter so it can be easily read when operating the starter button.

NOTE
When connecting the voltmeter test lead to the starter terminal, connect it to the terminal bolt threads and not to the cable or cable nut. When connecting the test lead to the battery terminal, connect it to the battery terminal (post) and not to the end of the cable

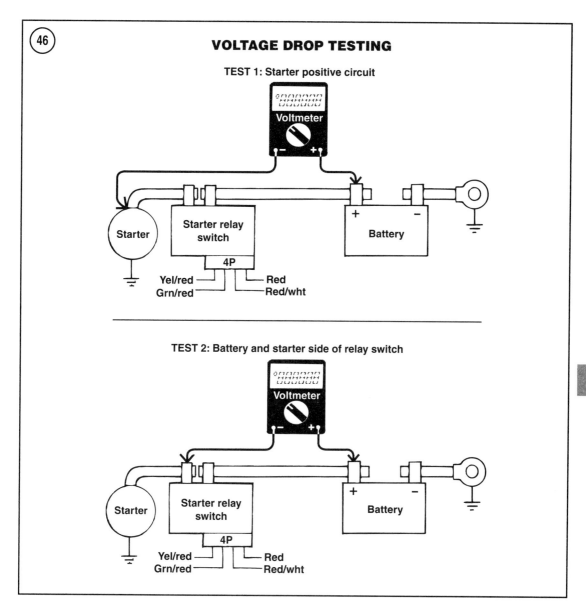

VOLTAGE DROP TESTING

TEST 1: Starter positive circuit

TEST 2: Battery and starter side of relay switch

or the cable bolt. The voltmeter read-ings are then taken directly off the starter and battery terminals to iden-tify problems between the terminal and cable connection.

6. Test the positive side of the starter circuit (**Figure 46**) as follows:

   a. Connect the voltmeter positive lead across the battery positive terminal.

   b. Connect the voltmeter negative lead across the starter terminal. The voltmeter should read battery voltage.

   c. Turn the ignition switch on and press the starter button while reading the voltmeter. The voltmeter shows the difference in voltage between the two test points. A voltage drop of more than 0.5 volts indicates a faulty connec-tion or excessive resistance in the starting cir-cuit. A voltmeter reading of 12 volts indicates an open circuit. If the voltage reading exceeds 0.5 volts, continue with Step 7. If the voltage reading is 0.5 volts or less, go to Step 9 to check the negative (ground side).

7. Test the voltage drop between the battery and the starter side of the relay switch as follows:

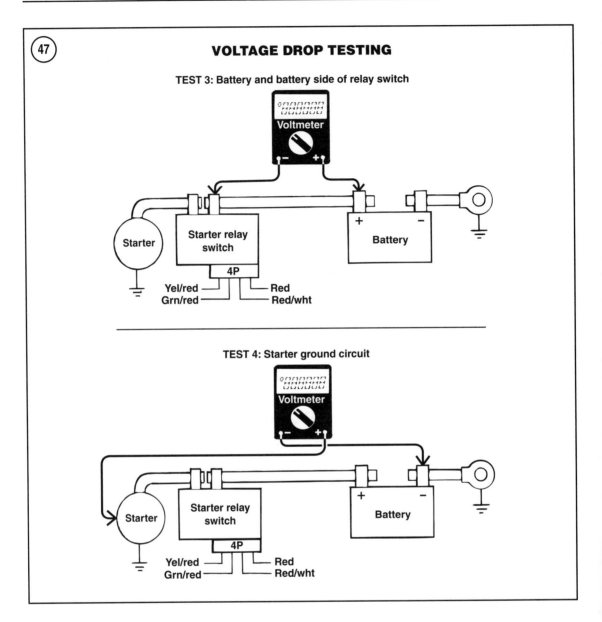

VOLTAGE DROP TESTING

TEST 3: Battery and battery side of relay switch

TEST 4: Starter ground circuit

a. Connect the voltmeter positive lead across the battery positive terminal.

b. Connect the voltmeter negative lead across the relay switch starter side terminal (**Figure 46**). The voltmeter should read battery voltage.

c. Turn the ignition switch on and press the starter button while reading the voltmeter. The voltmeter shows the difference in voltage between the two test points. A voltage drop of more than 0.2 volts indicates a faulty connection or excessive resistance between the battery terminal and the starter terminal on the relay switch.

8. Test the voltage drop between the battery and the battery side of the relay switch as follows:

a. Connect the voltmeter positive lead across the battery positive terminal.

b. Connect the voltmeter negative lead across the relay switch battery side terminal (**Figure 47**). The voltmeter should read approximately 0 volts.

c. Turn the ignition switch on and press the starter button while reading the voltmeter. The voltmeter shows the difference in voltage between the two test points. A voltage drop of more than 0.2 volts indicates a faulty connection or excessive resistance between the battery terminal and the battery terminal on the relay switch.

9. Test the negative (ground) side of the starter circuit (**Figure 47**) as follows:

 a. Connect the voltmeter negative lead across the battery negative terminal.

 b. Connect the voltmeter positive lead against the starter housing.

 c. With the voltmeter connected as described, it should read 0 volts.

 d. Turn the ignition switch on and press the starter button while reading the voltmeter. The voltmeter should read 0 volts. A voltage drop of more than 0.3 volts indicates high resistance in the ground circuit. If it does, check the ground connections between the meter leads. Then check the starter mounting bolts for looseness or contamination.

NOTE
Step 9 can be repeated to check any ground circuit in the starting circuit. Leave the negative lead connected to the battery and connect the positive lead to the ground in question.

10. If the problem is not found, refer to *Symptom-Based Tests* in this section.

11. Reconnect the fuel pump electrical connector.

12. Remove the grounding plugs and reconnect the spark plug caps.

Symptom-Based Tests

The following symptom related sections are:

1. Starter spins slowly.
2. Starter relay switch clicks but engine does not turn over.
3. Starter operates but engine does not turn over.
4. Starter does not spin.
5. Starter spins with the transmission in neutral but does not turn with the transmission in gear with the clutch lever pulled in and the sidestand up.

CAUTION
Never operate the starter for more than 5 seconds at a time. Allow the starter to cool 10 seconds before reusing it. Failing to allow the starter to cool after continuous starting attempts can damage the starter.

Starter spins slowly

If the starter operates but does not turn the engine over at normal speed, check the following:

1. Test the battery as described in this chapter.
2. Check for the following:

 a. Loose or corroded battery terminals.
 b. Loose or corroded battery ground cable.
 c. Loose starter cable.

3. If the battery is fully charged and passes a load test and the cables are in good condition, the starter may be faulty. Remove, disassemble and bench test the starter as described in this chapter.

Starter relay switch clicks but engine does not turn over

1. Test the battery as described in this chapter.
2. Perform the voltage drop tests described in this section. Confirm all connections are clean and tight.
3. Damaged starter idle gear.
4. Damaged starter reduction gear.
5. Crankshaft cannot turn over because of mechanical failure.

Starter operates but engine does not turn over

1. If the starter was just overhauled, it may have been assembled incorrectly and is turning backward.
2. Check for a damaged starter clutch as described in this chapter.

Starter does not spin

1. Check for a blown main or subfuse as described in this chapter. If the fuses are good, continue with Step 2.
2. Check the starter cable for an open circuit or dirty or loose-fitting terminals. Perform the voltage drop tests as described in this section. Repair any dirty, loose fitting or damaged connectors or wiring.
3. Check the 4-pin starter relay connector (**Figure 48**) for dirty or loose-fitting terminals. Clean and repair as required. Reconnect the connector and continue with Step 4.
4. Check the starter relay switch as follows. Turn the ignition switch on and push the starter button while listening for a click at the starter relay. Turn the ignition switch off and note the following:

9

a. If the starter relay clicks, continue with Step 5.

b. If there was no click, go to Step 6.

> *CAUTION*
> *Because of the large amount of current that flows from the battery to the starter in Step 5, use a large diameter cable when making the connection. To avoid damaging the starter, do not leave the battery connected for more than 10 seconds.*

5. Remove the starter from the motorcycle as described this chapter. Using an auxiliary battery, apply battery voltage directly to the starter terminal (**Figure 49**) and ground the cover. The starter should turn when battery voltage is directly applied.

   a. If the starter did not turn, disassemble and inspect the starter as described in this chapter. Test the starter components and replace worn or damaged parts as required.

   b. If the starter turned, check for loose or damaged starter cables. If the cables are good, remove and test the starter relay switch as described in this chapter. Replace the starter relay switch if necessary.

   c. Reinstall the starter.

6. Check the starter relay switch ground circuit for continuity as described under *Starter Relay Switch Testing* in this chapter. There should be continuity.

   a. If there is continuity, continue with Step 7.

   b. If there is no continuity, check for a loose or damaged connector or an open circuit in the wiring harness. If these items are good, test the following items as described in this chapter: sidestand switch, neutral switch, clutch switch diode.

   c. Reconnect the starter relay switch electrical connector.

7. Check the starter relay for voltage as described under *Starter Relay Switch* in this chapter. There should be voltage when the ignition switch is on and the starter button is pushed.

   a. If there is battery voltage, continue with Step 8.

   b. If there is no battery voltage, check for a blown main or subfuse. If the fuses are good, check for an open circuit in the wiring harness or for dirty or loose-fitting terminals. If the wiring and connectors are in good condition,

check for a faulty ignition and/or starter switch as described in this chapter.

8. Perform the starter relay switch operational check as described under *Starter Relay Switch* in this chapter.

   a. If the starter relay switch is normal, check for dirty or loose-fitting terminals in its connector block.

   b. If the starter relay switch is faulty, replace it and retest.

Starter works with the transmission in neutral but does not turn with the transmission in gear with the clutch lever pulled in and the sidestand up

1. On VT750C models, turn the ignition switch on and move the sidestand up and down while watching the sidestand switch indicator light.

   a. If the indicator light works properly, continue with Step 2.

   b. If the indicator light does not work, check for a blown bulb, damaged sidestand switch or an open circuit in the wiring harness.

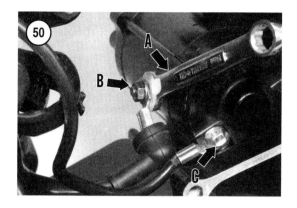

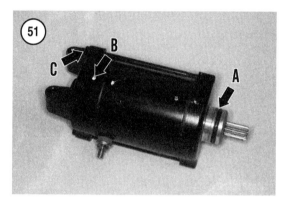

2. Test the clutch switch as described in this chapter

    a. If the clutch switch is good, perform Step 3.

    b. If the clutch switch is defective, replace the switch and retest.

3. Test the sidestand switch as described in this chapter.

    a. If the sidestand switch is good, perform Step 4.

    b. If the sidestand switch is defective, replace the switch and retest.

4. Check for an open circuit in the wiring harness. Check for loose or damaged electrical connector.

WARNING
Before riding the motorcycle, make sure the sidestand switch and its indicator light (on VT750C models) work properly. Riding the motorcycle with the sidestand down can cause loss of control.

STARTER

CAUTION
Do not operate the starter for more than five seconds at a time. Wait approximately 10 seconds between starting attempts.

Removal/Installation

1. Disconnect the negative battery cable at the battery as described in this chapter.
2. Remove the left and right side covers (Chapter Fifteen).

NOTE
The insulator described in Step 3 cannot be purchased separately. If this part is damaged, the starter must be replaced, or a salvage starter located.

3. Disconnect the starter cable. Hold the inner nut with a wrench (A, **Figure 50**) and remove the starter cable nut (B) to disconnect the cable. Holding the inner nut prevents the terminal bolt from turning and damaging the insulator installed on the inside of the starter.
4. Remove the mounting bolts and ground cable (C, **Figure 50**).
5. Pull the starter toward the right side to disconnect it from the starter drive mechanism. Then remove the starter. If the exhaust pipes are installed on the motorcycle, remove the starter from the left side.
6. Install by reversing these removal steps, plus the following:

    a. Lubricate the starter O-ring (A, **Figure 51**) with engine oil.

    b. Remove all corrosion from the starter cables.

    c. Tighten the starter mounting bolts to 29 N•m (21 ft.-lb.).

    d. Hold the inner nut and tighten the starter cable nut to 10 N•m (88 in.-lb.).

    e. Fit the rubber cover securely over the starter cable. Replace the cover if damaged.

    f. Start the engine to make sure the starter works correctly.

Disassembly

Refer to **Figure 52**.

9

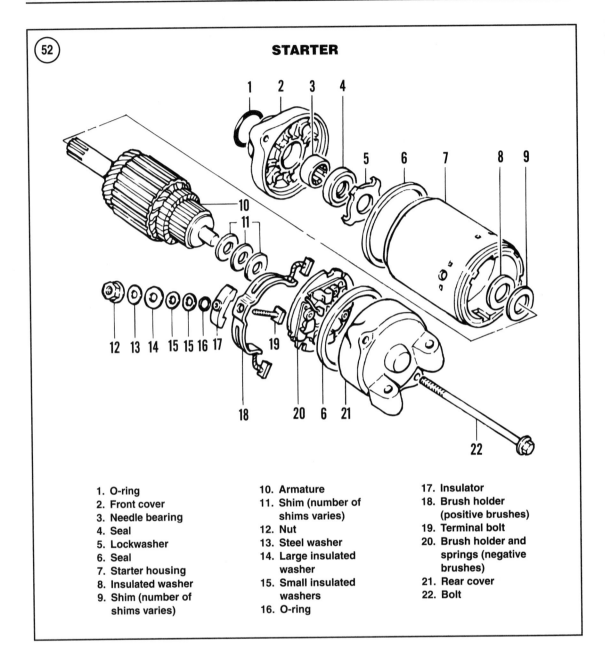

STARTER

1. O-ring
2. Front cover
3. Needle bearing
4. Seal
5. Lockwasher
6. Seal
7. Starter housing
8. Insulated washer
9. Shim (number of shims varies)
10. Armature
11. Shim (number of shims varies)
12. Nut
13. Steel washer
14. Large insulated washer
15. Small insulated washers
16. O-ring
17. Insulator
18. Brush holder (positive brushes)
19. Terminal bolt
20. Brush holder and springs (negative brushes)
21. Rear cover
22. Bolt

1. Find the alignment marks across the armature housing and both end covers. If necessary, scribe or paint the marks (B, **Figure 51**) to identify them.
2. Remove the bolts (C, **Figure 51**).

NOTE
The number of shims used in each starter varies. The shims and washers must be reinstalled in their correct order and number. Failing to install the correct number of shims and washers may increase armature end play and
cause the starter to draw excessive current. Record the thickness and alignment of each shim and washer removed during disassembly.

NOTE
If disassembling the starter to only check brush condition, remove only the rear cover. The brushes can be inspected and the cover installed if further disassembly is not required.

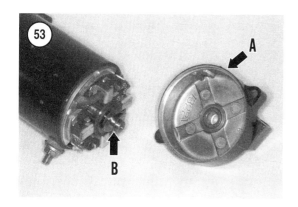

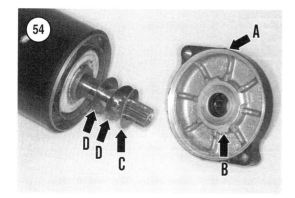

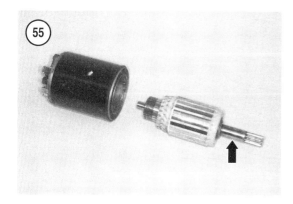

*When doing so, locate and reinstall
the shims onto the armature shaft.*

3. Remove the rear cover (A, **Figure 53**) and shims
(B).

4. Remove the front cover (A, **Figure 54**) and the
lockwasher (B).

NOTE
*Do not remove the seal from the front
cover. It is not available as a replacement part.*

5. Remove the insulated washer (C, **Figure 54**) and
shim(s) (D).

6. Remove the armature (**Figure 55**) from the
housing.

7. Before removing the brush holder, test the
brushes and terminal bolt as follows:

NOTE
*The positive brushes have insulated
leads.*

a. Check for continuity between the starter terminal and each positive brush (**Figure 56**).
There should be continuity. If there is no continuity, replace the positive brush holder during reassembly.

b. Check for continuity between the cable terminal and starter housing (**Figure 57**). There
should be no continuity. If there is continuity,
check for damaged, missing or improperly installed insulators. Note the alignment of the
installed insulators when removing them.

c. Check for continuity between the positive and
negative brushes (**Figure 58**). There should be
no continuity. If there is continuity, check the
positive brush wires for damaged insulation

9

sleeves. The insulation sleeves must be installed through the negative brush holder so
the positive brush wires cannot short out.

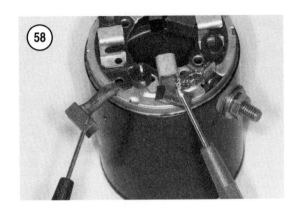

8. Remove the terminal nut and remove the steel
washer, insulators and O-ring (**Figure 59**).

9. Remove the negative brush holder (A, **Figure
60**), terminal bolt (B) and positive brush holder (C).

10. Remove the insulator (17, **Figure 52**).

11. Clean all grease, dirt and carbon from the armature, starter housing and end covers.

Inspection

If any starter component (other than O-rings and
brush sets) is excessively worn or damaged, the
starter must be replaced as an assembly. Individual
replacement parts are not available.

> *NOTE*
> *Before purchasing a new starter, try
> to find a replacement starter through
> a motorcycle wrecking yard. If you
> cannot locate an identical starter,
> look for a starter that is similar in de-
> sign. The internal part needed may
> be identical or similar.*

1. The internal parts in a used starter are often contaminated with carbon and copper dust released
from the brushes and commutator. Because a starter
can be damaged from improper cleaning, note the
following:

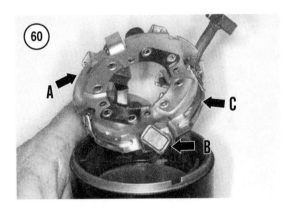

   a. Clean all parts (except the armature, starter
   housing and insulated washers) in solvent.
   Use a rag lightly damped with solvent to wipe
   off the armature, insulated washers and the
   starter housing (inside and outside).

   b. Use a fine grade sandpaper to clean the
   brushes. Do not use emery cloth because its
   fibers may insulate the brushes.

   c. Use only crocus cloth to clean the commutator. Do not use emery cloth or sandpaper. Any
   abrasive material left on or embedded in the
   commutator may cause excessive brush wear.
   Do not leave any debris on or between the
   commutator bars.

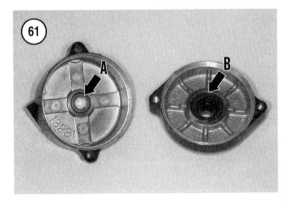

2. Replace the starter housing O-rings (6, **Figure
52**) if damaged.

3. Inspect the bushing (A, **Figure 61**) in the rear
cover for wear or damage.

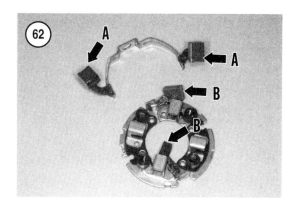

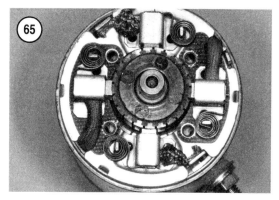

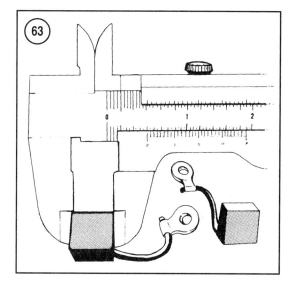

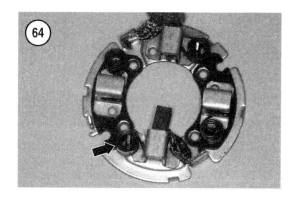

4. Inspect the seal and needle bearing (A, **Figure 61**) in the front cover for damage. Do not remove the seal to check the bearing.

NOTE
The bushing, seal and bearing used in the end covers are not available separately.

5. Check the lockwasher, shims and insulated washers for damage.

6. Inspect the brushes (A and B, **Figure 62**) as follows:

    a. Inspect each brush for cracks and other damage.

    b. Inspect the insulation on the positive brushes (B, **Figure 62**) for tearing and other damage.

    c. Check each brush where it is fixed to its holder (A or B, **Figure 62**).

    d. Measure the length of each brush (**Figure 63**). If the length of any one brush is less than the service limit (**Table 6**), replace both brush holders (**Figure 62**) as a set. Replacement brushes are permanently fixed to the holders. Soldering is not required.

7. Inspect the brush springs (**Figure 64**) for weakness or damage. Even though a spring tension measurement is not available, compare spring tension using a spring scale as follows:

    a. Assemble the negative brush holder, brushes and commutator as described under *Assembly* in this section. Refer to **Figure 65**.

    b. Support the starter in a vise with soft jaws.

    c. Hook a spring scale to the exposed part of the spring as shown in **Figure 66**.

    d. Pull the spring scale and record the spring tension measurement the moment the spring lifts off the brush.

    e. Repeat for each spring. If there is any noticeable difference in tension measurements, replace the negative brush holder and springs as a set.

8. Inspect the armature (A, **Figure 67**):

    a. Inspect both shafts for scoring and other damage.

    b. Inspect the windings for obvious damage.

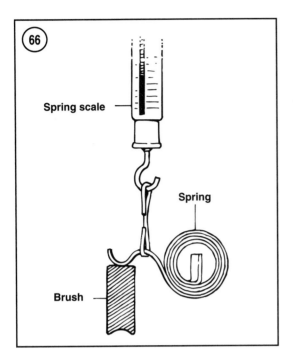

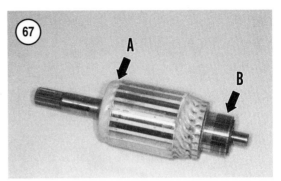

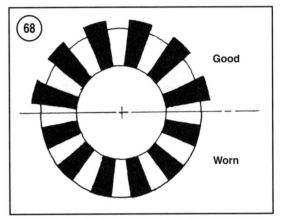

c. To check the armature for a short circuit, have it tested on a growler. Refer this service to a Honda dealership or an automotive electrical repair shop.

9. Inspect the commutator (B, **Figure 67**):

a. Inspect the commutator bars for visual damage.

b. Clean the commutator surface as described in Step 1.

c. The mica must be below the surface of the copper bars. On a worn commutator the mica and copper bars may be worn to the same level (**Figure 68**).

d. If the mica level is too high or if its shape is too narrow or V-shaped, undercut the mica with a hacksaw blade (**Figure 69**).

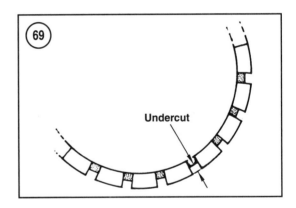

e. Inspect the commutator copper bars for discoloration. If a pair of bars are discolored, grounded armature coils are indicated.

f. Check for continuity across all adjacent pairs of commutator bars (**Figure 70**). There should be continuity across all pairs of bars. If an open circuit exists between a pair of bars, replace the starter.

g. Check for continuity between the armature shaft and each commutator bar (**Figure 71**). There should be no continuity. If there is continuity, replace the starter.

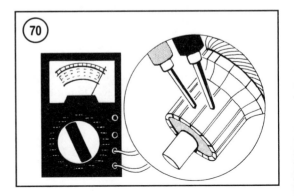

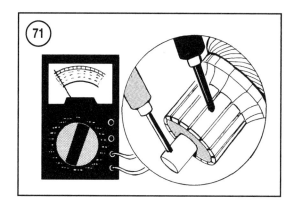

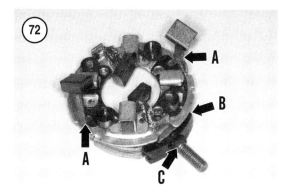

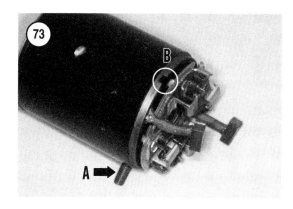

h. Check for continuity between the armature coil core and each commutator bar. There should be no continuity. If there is continuity, replace the starter.

10. Inspect the starter housing for cracks or other damage. Then inspect for loose, chipped or damaged magnets.

Assembly

1. Assemble the positive (A, **Figure 62**) and negative (B) brush holders as follows:
   a. Install the insulated brush wires through the two notches in the negative brush holder as shown in A, **Figure 72**.
   b. Install the terminal bolt through the brush holder, and then install the insulator (B, **Figure 72**) and O-ring (C).

2. Install the terminal bolt through the hole in the starter housing (A, **Figure 73**) while aligning the tab on the negative brush holder with the notch in the starter housing (B). Align the insulator (17, **Figure 52**) with the notch in the starter housing bracket.

CAUTION
In the next step, reinstall all parts in the order described. This is essential to insulate the positive brushes from the case.

3. Install the two small insulators (15, **Figure 52**), large insulator (14), steel washer (13) and nut (12) to secure the terminal bolt to the starter housing.

4. Perform the two continuity checks described in Step 7 of *Disassembly* in this section to check the positive brushes and terminal bolt for proper installation.

5. Install the brushes into their holders as follows:
   a. Cut a plastic tie into four separate pieces, each approximately 20 mm long.
   b. Hold the springs against their holders with the plastic strips (**Figure 74**). This allows the commutator to pass under the brushes with no tension placed against the brushes.
   c. Install the brushes into their holders (**Figure 75**).

CAUTION
In Step 6, magnetic force pulls the armature against the coils inside the starter housing. Hold the armature

tightly when installing it to avoid damaging the coils or brushes.

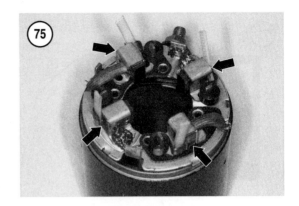

6. Install the armature (**Figure 55**) into the starter housing. Then remove the plastic ties (**Figure 76**) to release the brush springs and allow them to push the brushes against the commutator. Check that each brush seats squarely against the commutator (**Figure 65**).

7. Install the shims (B, **Figure 53**) onto the armature shaft.

8. Install the O-ring onto the commutator side of the starter housing.

9. Apply a thin coat of grease onto the armature shaft.

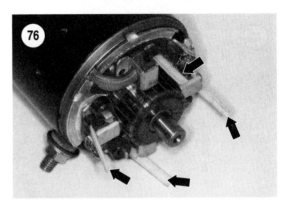

10. Align the groove in the rear cover (A, **Figure 77**) with the raised tab on the negative brush holder (B) and install the rear cover.

11. Install the O-ring onto the front side of the starter housing.

12. Lubricate the front cover oil seal lips and bearing (B, **Figure 61**) with grease.

13. Refer to **Figure 54** and install the front cover as follows:

 a. Install the steel shims (D, **Figure 54**) onto the armature shaft. The number of shims on the starter may differ from the shims.

 b. Install the insulator (C, **Figure 54**) and seat against the shims.

 c. Install the lockwasher (**Figure 78**) onto the front cover.

 d. Align the front cover tabs with the lockwasher tabs and install the front cover. Then check that the index marks on the starter case and both covers align (B, **Figure 51**).

14. Install the starter bolts (C, **Figure 51**) and tighten securely.

NOTE
If one or both bolts do not pass through the starter, the end covers and/or negative brush holder are installed incorrectly.

15. Lubricate the O-ring with grease and install it into the front cover groove.

16. Hold the starter and turn the armature shaft by hand. The armature should turn with some resistance, but should not bind or lockup. If the armature does not turn properly, disassemble the starter and check the shim, insulated washer and lockwasher alignment.

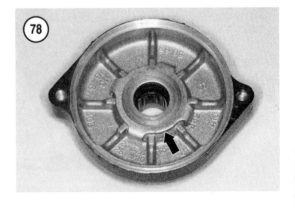

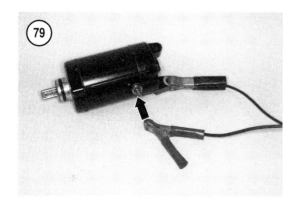

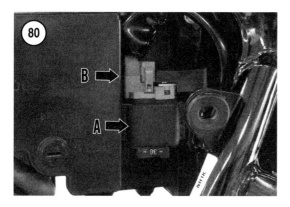

17. Use an auxiliary battery and apply battery voltage directly to the starter terminal and ground the cover (**Figure 79**). The starter should turn when battery voltage is directly applied. If the starter does not turn, disassemble and inspect the starter as described in this section.

STARTER RELAY SWITCH

The starter relay switch is mounted behind either the left (VT750C [A, **Figure 80**]) or right

(VT750DC [**Figure 81**]) side cover. The 30-amp main fuse is located in the connector holder (B, **Figure 80**) plugged into the starter relay switch.

Testing

1. Refer to *Starting System Troubleshooting* in this chapter to test the starting circuit. If the problem has been isolated to the starter relay switch, perform the following test.
2. Remove the left (VT750C) or right (VT750DC) side cover (Chapter Fifteen).
3. Shift the transmission into neutral.
4. Turn the ignition switch on and press the starter button. The starter relay should click.
   a. Yes. The starter relay switch is working correctly.
   b. No. Continue with Step 5.
5. Disconnect the starter relay switch electrical connector (B, **Figure 80**). Repair any dirty, loose fitting or damaged terminals. If the wiring is in good condition, leave the connector disconnected and continue with Step 6.
6. Ground circuit connection test: Shift the transmission into neutral. Check for continuity between the starter relay switch connector green/red wire and ground. There should be continuity or a slight resistance reading.

NOTE
Normally the ohmmeter reads 0 ohms when making a ground test. However, because of the diode placed in the circuit, it is normal for the ohmmeter to show a slight resistance reading.

   a. Continuity: Go to Step 7.
   b. No continuity: Repair the open circuit in the green/red wire between the starter relay switch connector and the left handlebar switch connector.
7. Starter relay switch voltage check: Reconnect the starter relay switch electrical connector (B, **Figure 80**). Turn the ignition switch on and measure voltage between the starter relay switch yellow/red wire at the starter relay switch connector (B, **Figure 80**) and ground when pressing the starter button. There should be battery voltage.
   a. Battery voltage: Go to Step 8.
   b. No battery voltage: Repair the open in the yellow/red wire between the starter/relay

switch connector and the engine stop switch in the right-handlebar switch connector.

8. Bench test the starter relay switch as follows:

a. Remove the starter relay switch as described in this section. Clean the switch electrical contacts (**Figure 82**).

b. Connect test leads across the two large leads on the starter relay switch (**Figure 83**). There should be no continuity.

c. If there is continuity, replace the starter relay switch.

d. If there is no continuity, leave the ohmmeter connected to the switch and continue with substep e.

e. Connect the positive lead from a fully charged 12 volt battery to the starter relay switch yellow/red wire terminal and the negative battery lead to the green/red wire terminal (**Figure 83**). There should be continuity.

f. If there is no continuity, replace the starter relay switch.

g. If there is continuity, the starter relay switch is operational. Reinstall the starter relay switch and perform the *Voltage Drop Tests* in this chapter to test the integrity of the wires and cables in the starting circuit.

9. Install all parts previously removed.

Removal/Installation

1. Remove the left (VT750C) or right (VT750DC) side cover (Chapter Fifteen).

2. Disconnect the negative battery lead as described in this chapter.

3. Disconnect the starter relay switch electrical connector (B, **Figure 80**) at the switch.

4. Disconnect the battery and starter cable leads (**Figure 84**) at the starter relay switch.

5. Remove the starter relay switch from the frame.

6. Installation is the reverse of removal. Note the following:

a. Clean the battery and starter cable leads before connecting them to the relay.

b. Make sure to install the cover firmly over the two cable leads at the starter relay switch.

c. Install the 30-amp fuse into the new starter relay switch socket.

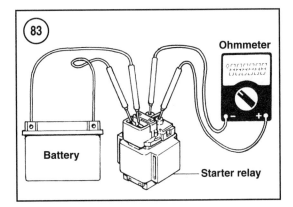

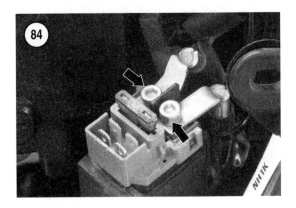

CLUTCH DIODE

The clutch diode is part of the starter circuit and is wired between the clutch switch and neutral switch. The diode prevents the flow of current from the neutral switch back through the clutch switch.

Suspect a faulty clutch diode if the neutral light comes on when the transmission is in gear and the clutch is disengaged. Also, look for a dirty or loose clutch diode connection if the starter does not operate when the transmission is in neutral.

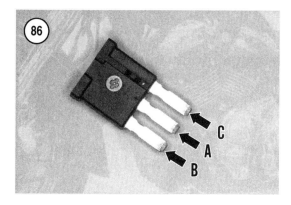

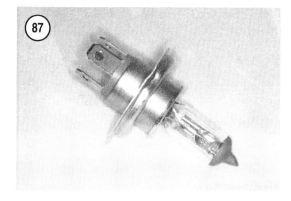

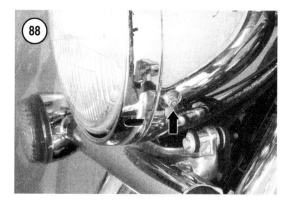

Testing/Replacement

1. Remove the left (VT750C) or right (VT750DC) side cover (Chapter Fifteen).
2. Open the fuse box cover and remove the diode (**Figure 85**) from the fuse box.
3. Set an ohmmeter to the R × 1 scale.
4. Connect an ohmmeter test lead to the A terminal (**Figure 86**). Then touch the opposite ohmmeter test lead to the B and then the C terminals. Reverse the first test lead attached to the A terminal and check continuity in the opposite direction at the B, then the C terminals. Each pair should have continuity in one direction and no continuity when the test leads are reversed.
5. Replace the diode if it fails this test.
6. Install the diode by aligning the raised tab on the diode with the slot in the fuse box.

LIGHTING SYSTEM

See **Table 7** for bulb specifications. Always use the correct wattage bulb. Using the wrong size bulb gives a dim light or causes the bulb to burn out prematurely. Some models use LED's to illuminate certain indicators.

Headlight Lens Removal/Installation (Bulb Replacement)

A quartz-halogen bulb is installed inside the headlight lens assembly. The bulb and lens can be replaced separately.

> *WARNING*
> *If the headlight just burned out or it was just turned off it is hot! Do not touch the bulb until it cools off.*

> *CAUTION*
> *All models use a quartz-halogen bulb (Figure 87). Because traces of oil on the glass reduce the life of the bulb, do not touch the bulb glass. Clean any oil or other chemicals from the bulb glass with an alcohol-moistened cloth.*

1. Remove the two outer bolts and collars (**Figure 88**) and remove the headlight from the housing.
2. Disconnect the electrical connector at the bulb and remove the headlight assembly.

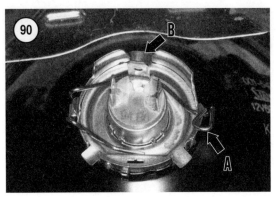

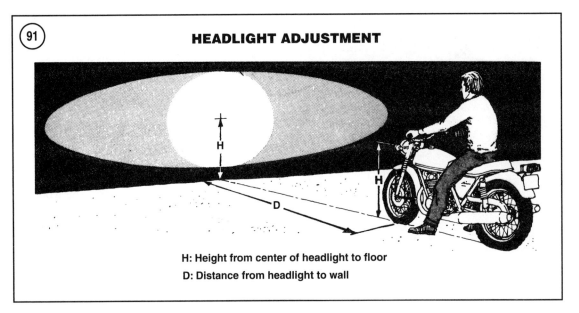

HEADLIGHT ADJUSTMENT

H: Height from center of headlight to floor
D: Distance from headlight to wall

3. Remove the dust cover (A, **Figure 89**) from around the bulb.

4. Unhook the bulb retainer (A, **Figure 90**) and remove the bulb (B).

5. Install the bulb and headlight lens by reversing these removal steps, while noting the following:

   a. Align the tabs on the bulb with the notches in the bulb holder and install the bulb.

   b. Install the dust cover with its TOP mark (B, **Figure 89**) at the top of the housing. Make sure the dust cover fits tightly around the bulb and against the lens.

   c. Hook the tab at the top of the lens with the retainer at the top of the headlight housing, and then pivot the lens into the housing and install the collars and two mounting bolts.

   d. Turn the ignition switch on and check the headlight operation. If necessary, refer to *Headlight Adjustment* in this section.

Headlight Adjustment

Adjust the headlight according to the motor vehicle regulations in your area, or use the following procedure as a guide:

1. Park the motorcycle on a level surface 7.6 m (25 ft.) from a wall.

2. Check tire inflation pressure (Chapter Three).

3. Draw a horizontal line on the wall the same height as the center of the headlight (**Figure 91**).

4. Have an assistant (with the same approximate weight as the primary rider) sit on the seat.

5. Turn the ignition switch on and the light switch to HIGH beam. Turn the handlebars so they point

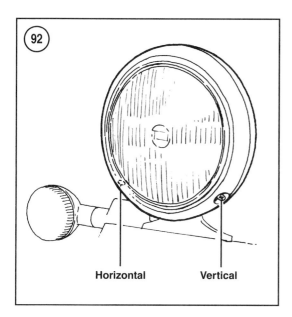

Horizontal   Vertical

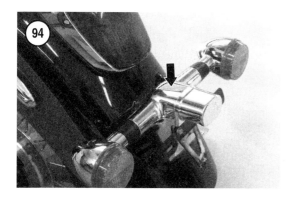

straight ahead and the beam is centered with the horizontal mark on the wall.

6. Check the headlight beam alignment. The broad, flat pattern of light (main beam of light) must be centered on the horizontal light with an equal area of light above and below the line (**Figure 91**).

7. Check the headlight beam lateral alignment. With the front wheel pointed straight ahead, there should be an equal area of light to the left and right of center.

8. If the beam is incorrect, adjust it as follows:
   a. To adjust the headlight horizontally, turn the screw on the right side of the headlight (**Figure 92**).
   b. To adjust the headlight vertically, turn the screw on the left side of the headlight (**Figure 92**).

Taillight/Brake Light/Turn Signal Bulb Replacement

1. Remove the screws, lens and gasket.
2. Replace the gasket if damaged.
3. Push the bulb in and turn it counterclockwise to remove it (**Figure 93**, typical).
4. Install the new bulb and lens by reversing these steps. Do not overtighten the screws as the lens may crack.

License Plate Light Bulb Replacement (VT750C)

1. Remove the screws from underneath the license light cover and remove the cover (**Figure 94**).
2. Remove the nuts (A, **Figure 95**), cover (B) and lens.
3. Push the bulb (**Figure 96**) in and turn it counterclockwise to remove it.
4. Install the new bulb and lens by reversing these steps.

Indicator Bulb Replacement
(1998-2000 VT750C, CD and CD2)

High beam, neutral and turn signal bulbs

These bulbs are mounted in the upper steering bridge (**Figure 97**).

1. Remove the lens (A, **Figure 98**) from the socket and lower the socket (B) from the bridge.
2. Remove the bulb from the socket.
3. Installation is the reverse of removal.

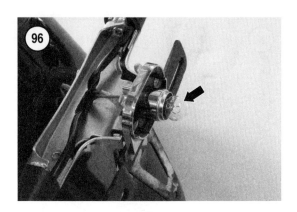

Speedometer housing bulb

The speedometer is equipped with a single bulb to light the speedometer unit. An LED unit installed in the speedometer unit illuminates the sidestand, coolant temperature and low oil pressure indicators. The LED unit is an integral part of the speedometer and cannot be replaced separately.

1. Disconnect the speedometer cable (A, **Figure 99**) from the housing.
2. Remove the cover screws (B, **Figure 99**) and lower the cover (C) away from the housing.
3. Remove the holder (**Figure 100**) and replace the bulb (**Figure 101**).
4. Installation is the reverse of removal.

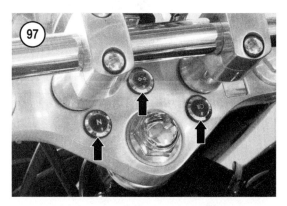

Indicator Bulb Replacement
(2001-on VT750CD, CD2, CD3 and C3)

High beam, neutral and turn signal bulbs

These bulbs are mounted in the upper steering bridge (**Figure 97**).

1. Remove the lens (A, **Figure 98**) from the socket and lower the socket (B) from the bridge.
2. Remove the bulb from the socket.
3. Installation is the reverse of removal.

Speedometer and speedometer cover bulbs

The speedometer is equipped with a single bulb to light the speedometer unit. Individual bulbs are mounted in the speedometer cover to illuminate the sidestand, coolant temperature and low oil pressure indicators.

1. Remove the speedometer as described in this chapter.
2. Remove the lens from the socket and remove the socket from the speedometer cover.

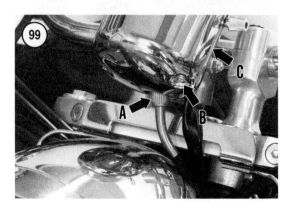

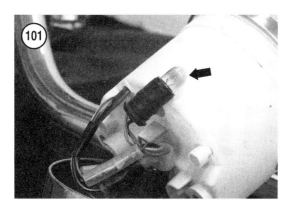

3. Remove the bulb from the socket.

4. Installation is the reverse or removal.

Indicator Lights (VT750DC)

The indicator lights are mounted in the speedometer unit and illuminated by LED's. The LED's are not replaceable. If an indicator fails to operate, perform the *Power/Ground Circuit Check* under *Speedometer/Speed Sensor (VT750DC)* in this chapter.

HEADLIGHT HOUSING

Removal/Installation

1. Remove the headlight lens as described in this chapter.

2. Disconnect the connectors mounted inside the headlight housing. Refer to **Figure 102**, typical.

3. Note how the wire harness clamps are installed and routed inside the headlight housing.

4. Identify the group of wires and the speedometer housing holes they are installed through.

5A. On VT750C models, remove the bolts (**Figure 103**) installed inside the headlight housing and remove the housing.

5B. On VT750DC models, remove the nuts and bolts securing the headlight housing to the mounting bracket and remove the housing.

6. Installation is the reverse of removal. Note the following:

    a. Turn the ignition switch on and check the operation of all switches and indicators.

    b. Check the headlight adjustment as described in this chapter.

SPEEDOMETER ASSEMBLY (1998-2000 VT750C, CD2)

Removal/Installation

1. Remove the headlight lens as described in this chapter.

2. Disconnect the speedometer connector located inside the headlight housing.

3. Disconnect the speedometer cable (A, **Figure 104**).

4A. To remove the speedometer and housing, remove the speedometer mounting nut and bolt (B,
Figure 104) and the speedometer assembly (C)
with its wiring harness.

4B. To remove the speedometer only, remove the
speedometer housing screws (B, **Figure 99**) and the
speedometer unit with its wiring harness.

5. Installation is the reverse of removal.

6. Check all meter functions after installation.

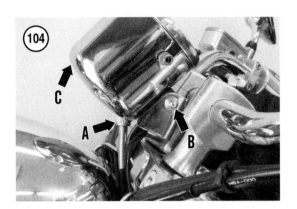

SPEEDOMETER/SPEED SENSOR
(2001-ON VT750CD, CD2, CD3 AND C3)

Troubleshooting

If the speedometer or tripmeter/odometer operates incorrectly, refer to the procedure that most
closely matches the operating condition and perform the troubleshooting steps in order.

Speedometer or odometer/tripmeter failure

If either the speedometer or odometer/tripmeter
work correctly but the other meter does not, replace
the speedometer assembly as described in this section.

Speedometer and odometer/tripmeter failure

1. When making the following tests, note the following:
   a. Make all voltage checks on the wiring har-
      ness side connectors, not on the speedometer
      or speed sensor side connector.
   b. Turn the ignition switch off after making each
      voltage test.

2. Check the battery charge as described under *Battery* in this chapter. If the battery is good, continue
with Step 3.

3. Check for a blown main or subfuse as described
under *Fuses* in this chapter.

4. Remove the speedometer as described in this
section.

5. Check the black 9-pin speedometer connectors
(**Figure 105**) for dirty, loose or damaged connector
terminals and wires.

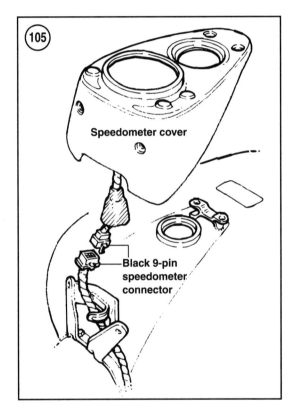

Speedometer cover

Black 9-pin
speedometer
connector

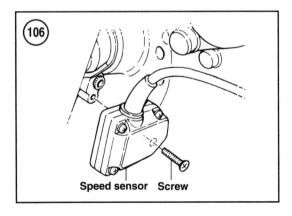

Speed sensor   Screw

Speed sensor

6. Remove the screw and the speedometer sensor (**Figure 106**).

7. Turn the ignition switch on and measure voltage between the black/yellow (+) and green/black (–) terminals in the black 9-pin connector while turning the speed sensor with a screwdriver (**Figure 107**). The voltmeter should alternately read between 0-5 volts.

    a. Yes. Continue with Step 8.

    b. No. Go to Step 9.

8. Reconnect the black 9-pin speedometer connector (**Figure 105**). Turn the speedometer over to expose the terminals on the speedometer.

9. Turn the ignition switch on and measure voltage between the black/brown (+) and green/black (–) speedometer terminals. There should be battery voltage.

    a. If there is battery voltage, the speedometer is damaged. Replace the speedometer and re-test.

    b. If there is no battery voltage, check for an open circuit in the green/black wire between the speedometer and speed sensor. Then check for an open circuit in the black/brown wire between the speedometer and the speed sensor.

10. Remove the headlight lens as described in this chapter.

11. Disconnect the white 3-pin speed sensor connector located inside the speedometer housing.

12. Turn the ignition switch on and measure voltage between the white 3-speed sensor black/brown

connector terminal and ground. There should be battery voltage.

    a. If there is no battery voltage, check for an open circuit in the black/brown wire.

    b. If there is battery voltage, continue with Step 13.

13. Turn the ignition switch off.

14. Check for continuity between the speed sensor green/black wire terminal and ground. There should be continuity.

    a. If there is no continuity, repair the open circuit in the green/black wire.

    b. If there is continuity, continue with Step 15.

15. Check for continuity between the speedometer and fuse box pink wire. There should be continuity.

    a. If there is no continuity, repair the open circuit in the pink wire.

    b. If there is continuity, replace the speed sensor as described in this chapter.

16. Install all parts previously removed.

Large speedometer error

If the speedometer accuracy has changed, perform the following steps in order.

1. Remove and test the speed sensor as described in this section. If the speed sensor is good, continue with Step 2.

2. Remove the speedometer as described in this section.

3. Check the black 9-pin speedometer connectors (**Figure 105**) for dirty, loose or damaged connector terminals and wires.

4. Turn the ignition switch on and measure voltage between the black/brown (+) and green/black (−) terminals in the black 9-pin connector. There should be battery voltage.

   a. If there is battery voltage, the speedometer is damaged. Replace the speedometer and re-test.

   b. If there is no battery voltage, check for an open circuit in the green/black wire between the speedometer and speed sensor. Then check for an open circuit in the black/brown wire between the speedometer and the speed sensor.

5. Install all parts previously removed.

Speed Sensor Operational Check/Replacement

1. Remove the speed sensor mounting screw and speed sensor (**Figure 106**).

2. Turn the speed sensor with a screwdriver (**Figure 107**). Replace the speed sensor if it does not turn smoothly.

3. To replace the speedometer sensor:

   a. Note the speed sensor wire harness routing from the speed sensor to the headlight housing.

   b. Remove the headlight lens as described in this chapter.

   c. Disconnect the speed sensor white 3-pin connector and remove the speed sensor.

4. Installation is the reverse of removal.

Speedometer Removal/Installation

The speedometer is mounted on the fuel tank.

> *WARNING*
> *Because fuel vapors are released during this procedure, read the Warning at the beginning of Chapter Eight.*

1. Turn the fuel valve off.

2. Remove the rear fuel tank mounting bolt and lift the fuel tank to access the black 9-pin speedometer connector.

3. Remove the speedometer housing mounting bolts, collars and grommets (**Figure 108**).

4. Disconnect the black 9-pin speedometer connector (**Figure 105**).

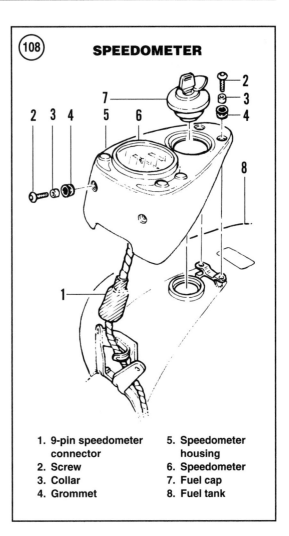

108 SPEEDOMETER

1. 9-pin speedometer connector	5. Speedometer housing
2. Screw	6. Speedometer
3. Collar	7. Fuel cap
4. Grommet	8. Fuel tank

5. Remove the fuel cap.

6. Remove the speedometer housing from the fuel tank.

7. Reinstall the fuel cap.

8. Label and then disconnect the indicator bulb holders, headlight bulb holder and tripmeter reset button from the back of the speedometer cover.

9. Remove the screws and remove the speedometer from the speedometer housing.

10. Installation is the reverse of removal. Note the following:

   a. Turn the fuel valve on and check the fuel hose for leaks.

   b. Tighten the rear fuel tank mounting bolt to 19 N•m (14 ft.-lb.).

   c. Check the operation of all indicator bulbs.

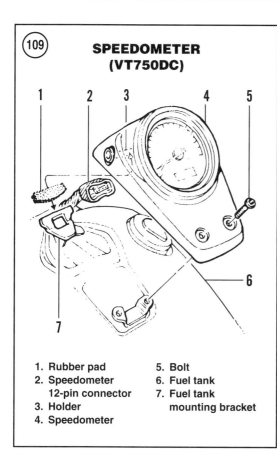

SPEEDOMETER (VT750DC)

1. Rubber pad
2. Speedometer
   12-pin connector
3. Holder
4. Speedometer
5. Bolt
6. Fuel tank
7. Fuel tank
   mounting bracket

SPEEDOMETER/SPEED SENSOR (VT750DC)

Troubleshooting

Perform this test if the odometer/tripmeter does not work correctly.

When making the following tests, turn the ignition switch off after making each voltage test.

1. Check the battery charge as described under *Battery* in this chapter. If the battery is good, continue with Step 2.

2. Check for a blown main or subfuse as described under *Fuses* in this chapter.

3. Perform the *Power/Ground Circuit Check* in this section. If all of the test results are correct, continue with Step 4.

4. Remove the speedometer as described in this section.

5. Remove the screw and the speedometer sensor (**Figure 106**).

6. Check the 12-pin speedometer connector (2, **Figure 109**) for dirty, loose or damaged connector terminals and wires.

7. Turn the ignition switch on and measure voltage between the black/yellow (+) and green/black (–) terminals in the 12-pin connector while turning the speed sensor with a screwdriver (**Figure 107**). The voltmeter should alternately read between 0-5 volts.

   a. Yes. Check the speed sensor operation as described in this section. If the speed sensor turns correctly, replace the speedometer as described in this section.

   b. No. Check for an open circuit in the black/yellow wire. If the wire is good, check the speed sensor as described in this section.

8. Install all parts previously removed.

Power/Ground Circuit Check

1. Remove the speedometer as described in this section.

NOTE
Perform the following tests at the speedometer 12-pin connector (2, Figure 109).

2. Check the power input circuit as follows:

   a. Connect a voltmeter between the black/brown wire and a good engine ground.

   b. Turn the ignition switch on. There should be battery voltage with the ignition switch on.

   c. If there is no voltage, check for a blown meter subfuse. If the subfuse is good, check the black/brown wire between the speedometer and fuse box for an open circuit.

   d. Turn the ignition switch off and disconnect the voltmeter leads.

3. Check the back-up voltage circuit as follows:

   a. Connect a voltmeter between the pink wire and a good engine ground.

   b. There should be battery voltage at all times (ignition switch on or off).

   c. If there is no voltage, check for a blown odometer subfuse. If the subfuse is good, check the pink wire between the speedometer and fuse box for an open circuit.

   d. Turn the ignition switch off and disconnect the voltmeter leads.

4. Check the ground circuit as follows:

   a. Switch an ohmmeter to R × 1.

9

b. Connect the ohmmeter between the green wire and a good engine ground.

c. The ohmmeter must read continuity.

d. If there is no continuity, check the green wire for an open circuit.

5. Check the sensor ground circuit as follows:

a. Switch an ohmmeter to R × 1.

b. Connect the ohmmeter between the green/black wire and a good engine ground.

c. The ohmmeter must read continuity.

d. If there is no continuity, check the green/black wire between the speedometer and speed sensor for an open circuit.

**Speed Sensor
(Circuit Test)**

This section tests just the speed sensor circuit.

1. Remove the headlight lens as described in this chapter.

2. Locate the speed sensor 3-pin connector in the headlight housing. It has a green/black, black/yellow and black/brown wire. Do not disconnect the connector.

3. Turn the ignition switch on and measure voltage between the black/brown (+) and green/black (–) wires in the speed sensor 3-pin connector. There should be battery voltage.

a. Yes. Continue with Step 4.

b. No. Check for an open circuit in the black/brown and green/black wires.

4. Turn the ignition switch off and disconnect the voltmeter leads.

5. Remove the speed sensor from the wheel as described in this section. Do not disconnect the speed sensor 3-pin connector.

6. Turn the ignition switch on and measure voltage between the black/yellow (+) and green/black (–) 3-pin speed sensor connector wires while turning the speed sensor with a screwdriver (**Figure 107**). The voltmeter should alternately read between 0-5 volts.

a. Yes. The speed sensor circuit is good. Check the speed sensor operation as described in this section. If the speed sensor turns correctly, replace the speedometer as described in this section.

b. No. Check for an open circuit in the black/yellow wire. If the wire is good, check the speed sensor as described in this section.

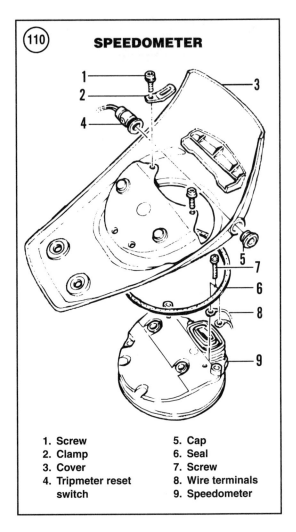

110 **SPEEDOMETER**

1. Screw	5. Cap
2. Clamp	6. Seal
3. Cover	7. Screw
4. Tripmeter reset switch	8. Wire terminals
	9. Speedometer

7. Turn the ignition switch off.

8. Install all parts previously removed.

**Speed Sensor Operational
Check/Replacement**

1. Remove the speed sensor mounting screw and speed sensor (**Figure 106**).

2. Turn the speed sensor with a screwdriver (**Figure 107**). Replace the speed sensor if it does not turn smoothly.

3. To replace the speedometer sensor:

a. Note the speed sensor wire harness routing from the speed sensor to the headlight housing.

b. Remove the headlight lens as described in this chapter.

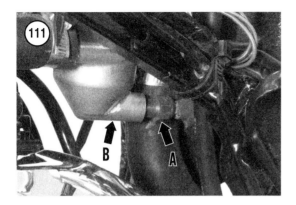

c. Disconnect the speed sensor black 3-pin connector and remove the speed sensor.

4. Installation is the reverse of removal.

Speedometer
Removal/Installation

Refer to **Figure 109**.

1. Remove the two speedometer cover bolts and slide the speedometer forward.

2. Disconnect the speedometer 12-pin connector.

3. Installation is the reverse of removal. Note the following:

a. Reconnect the speedometer 12-pin connector. Position the connector dust cover into the groove in the meter.

b. Install the rubber pad into the fuel tank mounting bracket.

c. Install the speedometer by aligning the meter cover holder with the rubber pad.

d. Tighten the speedometer cover bolts to 10 N•m (88 in.-lb.).

Speedometer
Disassembly/Reassembly

Refer to **Figure 110**.

1. Remove the speedometer as described in this section.

2. Remove the two tripmeter terminals screws and disconnect the terminals.

3. Remove the two speedometer mounting screws and clamp.

4. Remove the cap and tripmeter reset switch.

5. Installation is the reverse of removal.

COOLANT TEMPERATURE CIRCUIT
TROUBLESHOOTING
(1998-2000 VT750C)

The coolant temperature switch (A, **Figure 111**) is mounted in the thermostat housing.

Coolant Temperature Indicator
Does Not Come On

1. Turn the ignition switch on and lower the sidestand. The sidestand indicator and oil pressure indicator should come on.

a. Yes. Continue with Step 2.

b. No. Check for a blown subfuse (meter). If the subfuse is good, go to Step 4.

2. Remove the left steering cover (Chapter Fifteen).

3. Disconnect the coolant temperature switch connector at the switch (A, **Figure 111**). Connect a jumper wire between the coolant temperature switch connector and ground. Turn the ignition switch on. The coolant temperature indicator should come on.

a. Yes. The coolant temperature switch is defective. Replace the switch as described in this chapter.

b. No. Check the green/blue wire between the coolant temperature switch and the speedometer for an open circuit.

4. Remove the headlight lens as described in this chapter.

5. Disconnect the black 6-pin headlight connector located inside the headlight housing.

6. Turn the ignition switch ON and measure voltage between the black/brown (+) and green/blue (−) wires in the harness side of the 6-pin connector. There should be battery voltage.

a. Yes. Replace the speedometer.

b. No. Check the wire harness for an open circuit in the black/brown wire between the speedometer and fuse box. Then check for an open circuit in the green/blue wire between speedometer and coolant temperature switch.

7. Install all parts previously removed.

**Coolant Temperature Indicator
Does Not Turn Off**

1. Remove the headlight lens as described in this chapter.
2. Disconnect the black 6-pin headlight connector located inside the headlight housing.
3. Switch an ohmmeter to R × 1.
4. Check for continuity between the green/blue wire in the harness side of the 6-pin connector and ground. There should be continuity.
   a. If there is continuity, check for an open circuit in the green/blue wire between the connector and the coolant temperature switch.
   b. If there is no continuity, test the coolant temperature switch as described in this chapter.

**COOLANT TEMPERATURE CIRCUIT
TROUBLESHOOTING
(2001-ON VT750C)**

The coolant temperature switch is mounted in the thermostat housing (B, **Figure 111**).

Circuit Test

1. Park the motorcycle on its sidestand.
2. Turn the ignition switch on. The coolant temperature indicator should come on for a few seconds and then turn off.
   a. Yes. The circuit is good.
   b. No. The indicator did not come on. Refer to *Indicator off* in this section.
   c. No. The indicator came on but did not turn off. Refer to *Indicator on* in this section.

Indicator off

1. Remove the right side cover (Chapter Fifteen).
2. Disconnect the temperature indicator control unit from its 4-pin connector and turn the ignition switch on. The coolant temperature indicator should come on.
   a. No. Continue with Step 3.
   b. Yes. Go to Step 4.
3. Check for continuity between the green/blue wire in the harness side of the 4-pin connector and ground. There should be continuity.
   a. If there is continuity, check for a blown coolant temperature indicator bulb as described

under *Lighting System* in this chapter. Check the bulb socket for contamination.
   b. If there is no continuity, check for an open circuit in the green/blue wire.
4. Turn the ignition switch on and measure voltage between the black/brown (+) and green (–) wires in the harness side of the 4-pin connector. There should be battery voltage.
   a. Yes. Replace the temperature indicator control unit.
   b. No. Check for an open circuit in the black/brown wire between the 4-pin connector and the speedometer.
5. Install all parts previously removed.

Indicator on

1. Remove the right side cover (Chapter Fifteen).
2. Disconnect the temperature indicator control unit from its 4-pin connector and turn the ignition switch on. The coolant temperature indicator should come on.
   a. Yes. Continue with Step 3.
   b. No. Go to Step 4.
3. Check for an open circuit in the green/blue wire between the 4-pin connector and the coolant temperature bulb connector in the speedometer housing. If the circuit is working correctly, test the coolant temperature switch as described in this chapter.
4. Plug the temperature indicator control unit into its 4-pin connector. Turn the ignition switch on. The coolant temperature bulb should come on.
   a. If the bulb came on but did not turn off, replace the temperature indicator control unit.
   b. If the bulb comes on for a few seconds and then turns off, replace the coolant temperature switch as described in this chapter.
5. Install all parts previously removed.

**COOLANT TEMPERATURE CIRCUIT
TROUBLESHOOTING
(VT750DC)**

Circuit Test

The coolant temperature indicator does not come on until the engine is overheating. To see if the indicator is working correctly, perform the following test.

1. Separate light emitting diodes (LED) in the speedometer provide information for the engine temperature, neutral position, high beam, turn signal and low oil pressure. Check the operation of these indicators and note the following:

    a. If none of the indicators perform correctly, perform the *Power/Ground Circuit Check* listed under *Speedometer/Speed Sensor (VT750DC)* in this chapter.

    b. If all of the indicators work correctly but you suspect that the temperature indicator is not working correctly or want to check its operation, continue with Step 2.

2. Disconnect the coolant temperature switch connector at the switch (A, **Figure 111**). Connect a jumper wire between the coolant temperature switch connector and ground. Turn the ignition switch on. The coolant temperature indicator should come on.

    a. Yes. The coolant indicator and circuit is working correctly. If necessary, test the coolant temperature switch as described in this chapter.

    b. No. Check the green/blue wire between the coolant temperature switch and the speedometer for an open circuit. If the green/blue wire is good, replace the speedometer.

Coolant Temperature Indicator Comes On When the Engine is Cold

1. Park the motorcycle on its sidestand.

2. Disconnect the coolant temperature switch connector at the switch (A, **Figure 111**). Connect a jumper wire between the coolant temperature switch connector and ground. Turn the ignition switch on. The coolant temperature indicator should come on.

    a. Yes. Test the coolant temperature switch as described in this chapter.

    b. No. Check the green/blue wire between the coolant temperature switch and the speedometer for a short circuit. If the green/blue wire is good, replace the speedometer.

COOLANT TEMPERATURE SWITCH TESTING AND REPLACEMENT

The coolant temperature switch threads into the thermostat housing (B, **Figure 111**) and controls

current flow to the coolant temperature indicator according to coolant temperature. When the coolant temperature is below approximately 108° C (252° F), the switch is open (no continuity). The indicator is off. When the coolant temperature increases to 112-118° C (259-270° F), the switch closes (continuity) and the indicator is on, indicating an overheating condition.

CAUTION
The coolant temperature switch can be damaged if dropped. Handle the switch carefully during service and testing.

Removal/Installation

1. On VT750C models, remove the steering cover (Chapter Fifteen).

2. Drain the engine coolant (Chapter Three).

3. Disconnect the coolant temperature switch connector at the switch (A, **Figure 111**) and remove the switch.

4. Installation is the reverse of removal. Note the following:

    a. Clean the switch and thermostat housing threads of all sealant residue.

    b. Apply an electrically conductive water-resistant sealer to the threads on the switch. Do not apply sealant to the sensing element.

    c. Install the coolant temperature switch and tighten to the torque specification in **Table 10**.

    d. Allow the thread sealer to set before filling the radiator with coolant. Refer to the manufacturer's recommendations.

    a. Fill and bleed the cooling system (Chapter Three).

Testing

1. Remove the coolant temperature switch (A, **Figure 111**) from the thermostat housing as described in this section.

2. Fill a beaker or pan with a 50/50 mixture of antifreeze and water, and place it on a stove or hot plate.

3. Position the switch so the temperature sensing element and the threaded portion of the switch body are submerged as shown in A, **Figure 112**. Maintain

a distance of 40 mm (1.57 in.) from the switch threads to the bottom of the pan.

NOTE
The switch and thermometer must not touch the container sides or bottom. If either does, it causes a false reading.

4. Place a thermometer (B, **Figure 112**) in the pan (rated higher than the test temperature).
5. Attach one ohmmeter lead to the switch lead and the other lead to the switch body (A, **Figure 112**). The ohmmeter should indicate no continuity (open circuit). If the ohmmeter reads continuity, the switch is shorted and must be replaced. If the switch is open, continue with Step 6.
6. Test the switch as follows:
   a. Gradually heat the water.
   b. When the temperature reaches 112-118° C (259-270° F), the switch should read continuity (closed circuit). Maintain this temperature for three minutes.
   c. Gradually reduce the heat.
   d. When the temperature lowers to approximately 108° C (252° F), the ohmmeter should indicate no continuity (open circuit).
7. Replace the coolant temperature switch if it failed to operate as described in Step 5 or Step 6.
8. Install the switch as described in this section.

FAN MOTOR SWITCH

The fan motor switch is mounted on the bottom, left side of the radiator (**Figure 113**). It controls the radiator fan according to engine coolant temperature.

Testing

When troubleshooting the fan motor switch, first check the fan motor subfuse. Clean any corrosion from the electrical terminals on the fan motor switch. If these items are good, refer to the appropriate symptom-based section.

Fan motor does not stop

1. Turn the ignition switch off and disconnect the fan motor switch connector (**Figure 113**). Turn the ignition switch on again and note the operation of the fan motor.

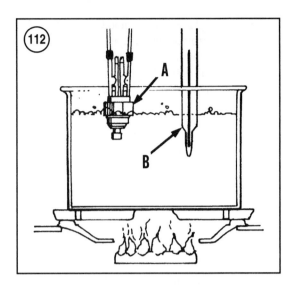

2. If the fan motor stops, replace the fan motor switch as described in this section.
3. If the fan motor did not stop, check for a short circuit in the black wire between the fan motor switch and fan motor.

Fan motor does not start

1. Check for a blown subfuse. If the fuse is good, continue with Step 2.
2. Start the engine and warm it up to normal operating temperature.
3. Disconnect the connector at the fan motor switch (**Figure 113**).
4. Connect a jumper wire between the fan motor switch connector and ground. Then turn the ignition switch on. The fan motor should run.
   a. If the fan motor runs, continue with Step 5
   b. If the fan motor did not run, go to Step 6.
5. Check the connector at the fan motor switch for a dirty or loose fitting terminal. If the connector is good, replace the fan motor switch and retest.
6. Remove the fuel tank (Chapter Eight).
7. Disconnect the black 2-pin fan motor switch connector located in the wiring harness above the front cylinder head cover.
8. Turn the ignition switch on and measure voltage between blue/black (+) and green (–) wires in the harness side of the 2-pin connector. There should be battery voltage.
   a. If there is battery voltage, the fan motor is damaged. Replace the fan motor (Chapter Ten).

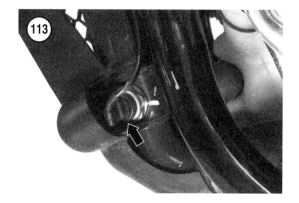

b. If there is no battery voltage, check for an open circuit in the blue/black wire between the 2-pin connector and the fuse box. If the wire is good, continue with Step 9.

9. Check for the following conditions:

a. Dirty or damaged wiring between the ignition switch and fuse box.

b. Damaged ignition switch. Test the ignition switch as described in this chapter.

Replacement

1. Drain the cooling system (Chapter Three).

2. Remove the upper radiator mounting bolt. Then carefully pull the radiator cover away from the fan motor switch (**Figure 113**).

3. Disconnect the electrical connector at the fan motor switch.

4. Remove the fan motor switch and O-ring.

5. Install a new O-ring onto the fan motor switch.

6. Install the fan motor switch and tighten to 18 N•m (13 ft.-lb.).

7. Tighten the upper radiator mounting bolt.

8. Fill and bleed the cooling system (Chapter Three).

OIL PRESSURE INDICATOR AND OIL PRESSURE SWITCH

Troubleshooting

When the ignition switch is turned on, the oil pressure indicator comes on and remains on until the engine is started. When the engine is started, the oil pressure rises and the oil pressure indicator turns off (usually within 1-2 seconds). If the indicator fails to operate as specified, perform the test that matches the indicator's operating condition.

NOTE
Make sure the oil level (Chapter Three) is correct before making the following tests.

Oil pressure indicator does not come on when ignition switch is turned on

1. Check the engine oil level (Chapter Three).

2. Remove the drive sprocket cover as described in Chapter Eleven.

3. Disconnect the wire at the oil pressure switch (**Figure 114**).

4. Ground the oil pressure switch wire with a jumper wire.

5. Turn the ignition switch on. The oil pressure indicator light should come on.

a. Yes. Replace the oil pressure switch and retest.

b. No. Check the blue/red wire between the oil pressure switch and speedometer for an open circuit.

6. Reverse Step 2 and Step 3 to complete installation

Oil pressure indicator stays on when engine is running

1. Turn the engine off and check the engine oil level (Chapter Three).

2. Remove the drive sprocket cover as described in Chapter Eleven.

3. Disconnect the wire at the oil pressure switch (**Figure 114**).

4. Check for continuity between the oil pressure switch wire and ground. There should be no continuity.

    a. If there is no continuity, check the oil pressure. Refer to *Engine Oil and Filter* in Chapter Three. If the oil pressure is normal, replace the oil pressure switch.

    b. If there is continuity, check the blue/red wire between the oil pressure switch and speedometer for an open circuit.

> *CAUTION*
> *Do not ride the motorcycle until the problem is corrected. Low oil pressure damages the engine.*

5. Reverse Step 2 and Step 3 to complete installation.

Oil Pressure Switch Replacement

1. Remove the drive sprocket cover as described in Chapter Eleven.
2. Disconnect the wire at the oil pressure switch (**Figure 114**).
3. Loosen and remove the oil pressure switch.
4. Clean the oil pressure switch and crankcase threads of all sealer and oil residue.
5. Apply an RTV sealant to the oil pressure switch threads as shown in **Figure 115**. Do not apply sealant within 3-5 mm (0.1-0.2 in.) from the end of the switch threads.

> *NOTE*
> *Allow the RTV sealer to set for 10-15 minutes before installing the oil pressure switch.*

6. Install the oil pressure switch and tighten to 12 N•m (106 in.-lb.).
7. Reconnect the wire onto the switch and cover the switch with its rubber boot.
8. Follow the sealer manufacturer's recommendations for drying time, and then start the engine and check for leaks.

> *NOTE*
> *The oil pressure indicator should go out within 1-2 seconds after starting the engine. If it stays on, shut off the engine immediately and locate the*

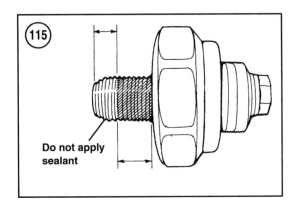

Do not apply sealant

problem. *Do not run the engine with the oil pressure indicator on.*

> *CAUTION*
> *Do not overtighten the switch to correct an oil leak, as this may strip the crankcase threads. If oil leaks from the switch after installing it, remove the switch and reclean the threads. Reseal and reinstall the switch.*

9. Reverse Step 1 and Step 2 to complete installation.

NEUTRAL INDICATOR AND NEUTRAL SWITCH

Circuit Test

1. Shift the transmission into neutral and turn the ignition switch on. The neutral indicator should come on.

    a. Yes. The system is normal.

    b. No. Go to Step 2.

2. Remove the drive sprocket cover as described in Chapter Eleven.

3. Disconnect the wire at the neutral switch (**Figure 116**).

4. Check for continuity between the terminal on the neutral switch and ground. There should be continuity with the transmission in *neutral* and no continuity with the transmission in *any gear.*

    a. If the switch fails either of these tests, replace the neutral switch.

    b. If the switch is good, continue with Step 5.

5. Check for an open circuit in the following wires:

    a. Light green/red wire between the speedometer and diode.

    b. Light green wire between the neutral switch and diode.

6. Reverse Step 2 and Step 3 to complete installation.

Replacement

1. Remove the drive sprocket cover as described in Chapter Eleven.

2. Disconnect the wire at the neutral switch (**Figure 116**).

3. Remove the neutral switch and sealing washer (**Figure 117**).

4. Install the neutral switch with a new sealing washer and tighten to 12 N•m (106 in.-lb.).

5. Reverse Step 1 and Step 2.

SIDESTAND SWITCH

The sidestand switch is part of the ignition cut-off system. This is a safety system designed to prevent the motorcycle from being ridden when the sidestand is down. When the sidestand is down, the engine only starts when the transmission is in neutral. When the sidestand is up, the engine can be started in neutral or in gear when the clutch lever is pulled in. If the engine is started with the transmission in neutral and the sidestand down, the engine cuts off if the transmission is shifted into gear before the sidestand is raised.

Testing

A problem in the sidestand switch circuit can prevent the engine from starting or can cause the engine to cut-out.

1. Remove the right side cover (Chapter Fifteen).

2A. On VT750C models, disconnect the green 3-pin sidestand switch connector. Refer to *Electrical Component Location* in this chapter.

2B. On VT750DC models, disconnect the green 2-pin sidestand switch connector. Refer to *Electrical Component Location* in this chapter.

> *NOTE*
> *Switch an ohmmeter to R × 1 when testing the switch in Step 3. Make the test on the switch side of the connector, not on the harness side.*

3A. On VT750C models, test the sidestand switch as follows:

    a. Check for continuity between the 3-pin connector yellow/black and green terminals. There should be continuity with the sidestand down (**Figure 118**) and no continuity with the sidestand up.

    b. Check for continuity between the 3-pin connector green/white and green terminals. There should be continuity with the sidestand up and no continuity with the sidestand down (**Figure 118**).

3B. On VT750DC models, test the sidestand switch
as follows:

   a. Check for continuity between the 2-pin con-
     nector green/white and green terminals.

   b. There should be continuity with the sidestand
     up and no continuity with the sidestand down
     (**Figure 118**).

4. Replace the sidestand switch if it did not test as
described in Step 3.

5. Reverse Step 1 and Step 2.

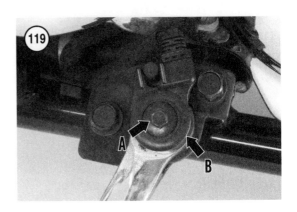

Replacement

The sidestand switch is mounted on the sidestand
mounting bracket.

1. Support the bike on a stand so the sidestand can
be serviced.

2. Remove the drive sprocket cover as described in
Chapter Eleven.

3. Remove the right side cover (Chapter Fifteen).

> *NOTE*
> *Note the sidestand switch wiring har-*
> *ness routing before removing the*
> *switch in this section.*

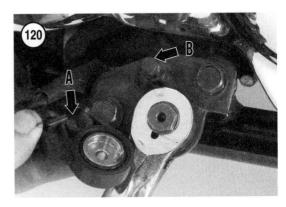

4A. On VT750C models, disconnect the green
3-pin sidestand switch connector. Refer to *Electrical Component Location* in this chapter.

4B. On VT750DC models, disconnect the green
2-pin sidestand switch connector. Refer to *Electrical Component Location* in this chapter.

5. Remove the bolt (A, **Figure 119**) and sidestand
switch (B).

6. Clean the switch mounting area on the sidestand.

7. Install the sidestand switch by aligning the notch
(A, **Figure 120**) in the switch with the pin (B) on the
mounting bracket.

8. Install a *new* sidestand switch mounting bolt and
tighten to 10 N•m (88 in.-lb.).

9. Reverse Steps 1-4 to complete installation.

10. Remove the motorcycle from the stand. Shift
the transmission into neutral and start the engine.
Shift the transmission into first gear and lower the
sidestand. The engine should turn off.

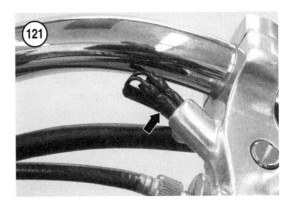

CLUTCH SWITCH

The clutch switch is mounted inside the clutch lever housing.

Testing/Replacement

1. Disconnect the two electrical connectors at the
clutch switch (**Figure 121**).

2. Connect ohmmeter leads across the two clutch
switch terminals (**Figure 122**).

3. Read the ohmmeter scale while operating the
clutch lever. Note the following:

   a. There must be continuity with the clutch lever
     pulled in and no continuity with the lever re-
     leased.

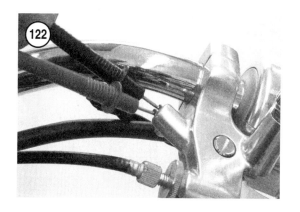

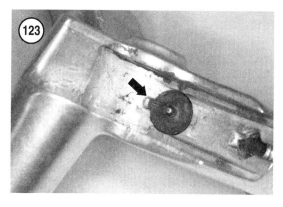

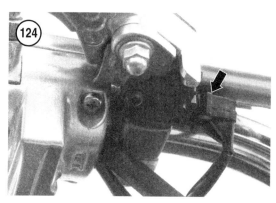

b. Replace the clutch switch if it fails to operate as described.

4. Replace the clutch switch as follows:

a. Disconnect the clutch cable from the clutch lever at the handlebar.

b. Remove the nut, pivot bolt and clutch lever.

c. Gently push the clutch switch out of the housing.

d. Install the clutch switch by aligning the tab on the switch with the notch in the housing (**Fig-**

ure 123). Push the switch into the housing until it bottoms.

5. Clean the clutch lever pivot bolt and clutch lever bore, then lubricate with grease.

6. Install the clutch lever and pivot bolt. Tighten the pivot bolt securely, then the nut.

7. Reconnect the clutch cable and adjust the clutch (Chapter Three).

8. Reconnect the electrical connectors at the switch.

FRONT BRAKE LIGHT SWITCH

The front brake light switch is mounted on the bottom of the front master cylinder.

Testing/Replacement

1. Disconnect the connectors from the switch terminals (**Figure 124**).

2. Check for continuity between the switch terminals. There should be continuity with the brake lever applied and no continuity with the brake lever released. Replace the switch if faulty.

3. Replace the switch by removing the screw and switch.

4. Installation is the reverse of removal.

5. Make sure all connectors are plugged tightly into the switch.

6. Turn the ignition switch on and operate the front brake lever to check the rear brake light.

> *WARNING*
> *Do not ride the motorcycle until the rear brake light works correctly.*

REAR BRAKE LIGHT SWITCH

The rear brake light switch is mounted on the rear brake pedal assembly.

Testing/Replacement

1A. On VT750C models, perform the following:

a. Remove the fuel tank (Chapter Eight).

b. Locate and disconnect the rear brake light switch black 2-pin connector mounted in the connector pouch underneath the left-front fuel tank rubber damper. The connector con-

9

tains two wires—black/brown and green/yellow.

1B. On VT750DC models, perform the following:

a. Remove the radiator mounting bolt and pull the radiator grill forward.

b. Disconnect the rear brake light switch black 2-pin connector. The connector contains two wires—black/brown and green/yellow.

2. Check for continuity between the switch terminals. There should be no continuity with the brake pedal released and continuity with the brake pedal applied. Replace the switch if faulty.

3. To replace the switch:

a. Disconnect the spring and remove the switch and spring (**Figure 125**).

b. Remove the spring and connect it onto the new switch.

c. Install the switch onto its mounting bracket and reconnect the spring.

4. Installation is the reverse of removal.

5. Adjust the rear brake light switch (Chapter Three).

WARNING
Do not ride the motorcycle until the rear brake light works correctly.

IGNITION SWITCH

The ignition switch is mounted on the left side of the motorcycle.

Testing/Replacement

NOTE
*Refer to **Electrical Component Location** in this chapter for the ignition switch connector location.*

1A. On VT750C models, perform the following:

a. Remove the seat and the left side cover (Chapter Fifteen).

b. Disconnect the ignition switch 3-pin connector.

1B. On VT750DC models, perform the following:

a. Remove the right side cover (Chapter Fifteen).

b. Disconnect the ignition switch 3-pin connector.

2. Test the ignition switch as described under *Switch Continuity Test* in this chapter. Refer to the

wiring diagram at the end of this manual for the ignition switch continuity diagram. Replace the switch if faulty.

NOTE
Purchase new ignition switch break-off bolts when ordering the switch.

3. Remove the ignition switch as follows:

a. Disconnect the band from the ignition switch wiring harness, if used.

b. Remove the screw and switch cover (**Figure 126**).

c. Center punch each of the two break-off bolts. Then drill the bolt heads (**Figure 127**) off the bolt shanks with a hand drill. Remove the switch and the rubber damper.

d. Remove the remaining threaded bolt shanks from the ignition switch mounting bracket and discard them.

4. Install the ignition switch as follows:

a. Secure the rubber damper and ignition switch with two new break-off bolts. Tighten the bolts hand-tight. Then install the key to make sure it turns freely.

b. Tighten the bolt heads until they twist off.

c. Record the new key number in the *Quick Reference Data* section at the front of this manual.

5. Reverse to complete installation.

HANDLEBAR SWITCH

The left handlebar switch housing (**Figure 128**) includes the headlight dimmer switch, turn signal switch and horn button.

The right handlebar switch housing (**Figure 129**) includes the engine stop switch and the starter switch.

Testing/Replacement

1. Remove the headlight lens as described in this chapter.

2. Trace the switch wiring harness from the switch assembly to the connectors in the headlight housing and disconnect them. Refer to **Figure 128** or **Figure 129**. Refer to the appropriate wiring diagram at the end of this manual to identify the connectors and wire colors for each switch.

3. Test the switch as described under *Switch Continuity Test* in this chapter. Note the following:

    a. If the continuity test shows a faulty switch, continue with Step 4 to replace the switch assembly.

    b. If the switch is okay, reconnect the connectors and install the headlight lens.

4. Note how the switch wiring harness is routed from the switch to the headlight housing. Then carefully pull the wiring harness and connectors from the headlight housing.

5. Remove the left (**Figure 128**) and right (**Figure 129**) side handlebar switches from the handlebars as described in Chapter Twelve.

6. Installation is the reverse of removal. Check each switch function for proper operation.

> *WARNING*
> *Do not ride the motorcycle until each switch works properly.*

SWITCH CONTINUITY TEST

Test the switches for continuity using an ohmmeter or a self-powered test light at the switch connector by operating the switch in each of its operating positions. Compare the results with its switch operation diagram. For example, **Figure 130** shows a continuity diagram for the ignition switch. The horizontal line indicates which terminals should show continuity when the switch in that position. Continuing with the example, in the on position there should be continuity between all three terminals. When the switch is off, there should be no continuity between any of the terminals.

1. Refer to the appropriate switch procedure in this chapter to access the switch connectors. Some switches do not use a continuity diagram for testing. Instead, follow the procedure in its appropriate section.

2. Check the subfuse as described under *Fuses* in this chapter.

3. Check the battery as described under *Battery* in this chapter. Charge the battery to the correct state of charge, if required.

4. Disconnect the negative battery cable at the battery if the switch connectors are not disconnected from the circuit.

CAUTION
Do not attempt to start the engine with the battery disconnected.

5. When separating two connectors, pull on the connector housings and not the wires.

6. After locating a defective circuit, check the connectors to make sure they are clean and properly connected. Check all wires going into a connector housing to make sure each wire is properly positioned and that the wire end is not loose.

7. Before disconnecting two connectors, check them for any locking tabs or arms that must be pushed or opened. If two connectors are difficult to separate, do not force them because damage may occur.

8. When reconnecting electrical connector halves, push them together until they click or snap into place.

9. If the switch is operating erratically, the contacts may be oily, dirty or corroded. Disassemble the switch housing as described in this section to access the switch contacts. Clean the contacts as required.

10. If a switch or button does not perform properly, replace the switch as described in its appropriate section.

TURN SIGNAL RELAY

On VT750C models, the turn signal relay (**Figure 131**) is mounted in the headlight housing.

On VT750DC models, the turn signal relay is mounted in the connector block behind the right side cover. Refer to *Electrical Component Location* in this chapter.

Testing/Replacement

1. If both turn signals do not work, test the turn signal relay as described in this section. If only one bulb or individual side does not work, check for a blown bulb or a disconnected turn signal connector.

(130) **IGNITION SWITCH**

	FAN	IG	BAT 1
ON	●————	●————	————●
OFF			
LOCK			
Color	blue/orange	red/black	red

(131)

2A. On VT750C models, remove the headlight lens as described in this chapter and disconnect the turn signal relay (**Figure 131**).

2B. On VT750DC models, remove the right side cover (Chapter Fifteen) and disconnect the turn signal relay.

3. Check for loose, bent or corroded turn signal relay terminals. Then check the socket terminals in the connector or relay box for corrosion or damage.

4. Connect a jumper wire between the black/brown wire and gray wire in the 3-pin turn signal relay connector (**Figure 132**). Turn the ignition switch on and operate the turn signal switch. The turn signal should light and stay on. Turn the turn signal off and the ignition switch off. Disconnect the jumper wire.

    a. If the light did not come on, check for an open circuit in the black/brown and gray wires.

    b. If the light came on, continue with Step 5.

5. Check for continuity between the green terminal in the turn signal switch connector and a good ground. There should be continuity.

    a. If there is no continuity, check the green wire for an open circuit.

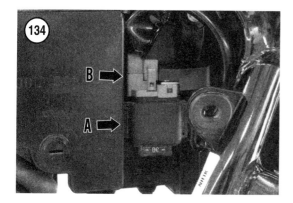

b. If there is continuity, replace the turn signal relay.

6. Installation is the reverse of removal. Install the turn signal relay, turn the ignition switch on and check the turn signal operation.

HORN

The horn is an important safety device and must be kept in good working order.

Removal/Installation

1. Disconnect the electrical connectors from the horn (**Figure 133**).
2. Remove the bolt and the horn assembly.
3. Install by reversing these removal steps. Make sure the electrical connections are secure and corrosion-free.
4. Check the horn operation. If the horn does not work properly, test the horn as described in this section.

> *WARNING*
> *Do not ride the bike until the horn works properly.*

Testing

1. Disconnect the electrical connectors from the horn.
2. Connect a 12-volt battery across the horn terminals. The horn must sound loudly. If not, replace the horn.

FUSES

Whenever a fuse blows, determine the cause before replacing the fuse. Usually, the trouble is a short circuit in the wiring. Worn-through insulation or a short to ground from a disconnected or damaged wire may cause this.

> *CAUTION*
> *If replacing a fuse, make sure the ignition switch is turned off. This lessens the chance of a short circuit.*

> *CAUTION*
> *Never substitute any metal object for a fuse. Never use a higher amperage fuse than specified. A circuit overload could cause a fire and the complete loss of the motorcycle.*

Main Fuse

The main fuse is mounted on the starter relay switch. On VT750C models, the starter relay switch (A, **Figure 134**) is mounted behind the left side cover. On VT750DC models, the starter relay switch (A, **Figure 135**) is mounted behind the right side cover. Perform the following to check or replace the main fuse.

9

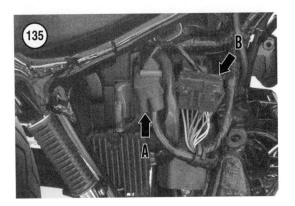

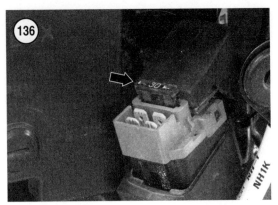

1. Turn the ignition switch off.
2. Remove the left (VT750DC) or right (VT750C) side cover. Refer to Chapter Fifteen.
3. Disconnect the electrical connector (B, **Figure 134**) from the starter relay switch.
4. Remove the main fuse (**Figure 136**) and inspect it. Replace the fuse if blown (**Figure 137**).

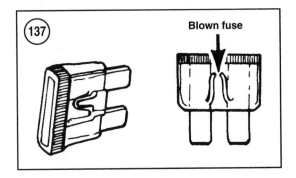

> *NOTE*
> *A spare 30-amp fuse is stored in the bottom of the starter relay switch rubber holder.*

5. Reconnect the starter relay switch connector.
6. Reinstall the side cover.

**Fuse Box
(Subfuses)**

All of the subfuses are mounted inside the fuse box located behind the right side cover. Refer to **Figure 138** (VT750C) or B, **Figure 135** (VT750DC). To identify an individual fuse and its amperage, refer to the printed information on the fuse box cover (**Figure 139**) and **Table 9**.

1. Turn the ignition switch off.
2. Remove the right side cover (Chapter Fifteen).
3. Open the fuse box cover.
4. Remove and inspect the fuse. Replace the fuse if it has blown (**Figure 137**).
5. Close and secure the fuse box cover.
6. Install the right side cover.

WIRING DIAGRAMS

Color wiring diagrams for all models are located at the end of this manual.

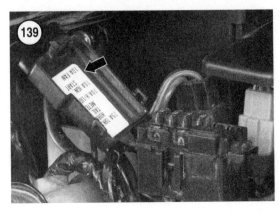

Table 1 BATTERY SPECIFICATIONS

Type	Maintenance-free (sealed)*
Capacity	
VT750C	12 volts, 14 amp hour
VT750DC	12 volts, 12 amp hour
Current draw (leakage)	1.0 mA maximum
Voltage (at 20° C [68° F])	
Fully charged	13.0-13.2 volts
Needs charging	Below 12.3-12.5 volts
Charging current	
Normal	
VT750C	1.4 amps × 5-10 hours
VT750DC	1.2 amps × 5-10 hours
Quick	
VT750C	6.0 amps × 1 hour
VT750DC	5.5 amps × 1 hour

* A maintenance-free battery is installed on all models. Because this type of battery requires a high-voltage charging system, do not install a standard type battery.

Table 2 MAINTENANCE-FREE BATTERY VOLTAGE READINGS AND BATTERY STATE OF CHARGE

Voltage reading	State of charge	Service Required	Charging Time*
12.8-13.0	100%	None	None
12.5-12.8	75-100%	May require small charge	3-6 hours
12.0-12.5	50-75%	Charging required	5-11 hours
11.5-12.0	25-50%	Charging required	Approximately 13 hours
11.5 volts or less	0-25%	Charging required	20 hours

* Charging times can vary. Charging times listed in table are for a constant current charger set at the standard amperage rating listed on battery.

Table 3 ALTERNATOR AND CHARGING SYSTEM SPECIFICATIONS

Alternator	
Type	Triple phase
Charging system output	
VT750C	345 watts @ 5000 rpm
VT750DC	333 watts @ 5000 rpm
Charging voltage test (regulated voltage)	See text
Stator coil resistance*	
VT750C	0.1-0.3 ohms
VT750DC	0.1-1.0 ohms

* Test must be made at an ambient temperature of 20° C (68°F). Do not test when the engine or component is hot.

Table 4 STARTER CLUTCH SPECIFICATIONS

	New mm (in.)	Service limit mm (in.)
Starter clutch housing inside diameter	74.414-74.440 (2.9297-2.9307)	74.46 (2.931)
Starter driven gear		
Inside diameter	40.000-40.021 (1.5748-1.5756)	40.10 (1.579)
Outside diameter	57.749-57.768 (2.2736-2.2743)	57.73 (2.273)

Table 5 IGNITION SYSTEM SPECIFICATIONS

Ignition coil primary peak voltage	100 volts minimum
Ignition pulse generator peak voltage	0.7 volts minimum

Table 6 STARTING SYSTEM SPECIFICATIONS

Starter brush length	
New	12.5 mm (0.49 in.)
Service limit	6.5 mm (0.26 in.)

Table 7 BULB SPECIFICATIONS

Item	Specification
Brake/taillight	
VT750C	32/3CP
VT750DC	21/5W
Front turn signal/running light	21/5W
Headlight (HI/Low beam)	60/55W
License light	
VT750C	4CP
VT750DC	–
Rear turn signal light	21W
Speedometer light	
VT750C	
1998-2000	3.4W
2000-on	1.7W
Indicators	
VT750C	
High beam indicator	3.4W
Neutral indicator	3.4W
Oil indicator	3.4W
Side stand indicator	3.4W
Temperature indicator	3.4W
Turn signal indicator	3.4W
VT750DC	
High beam indicator	LED
Instrument light	LED
Neutral indicator	LED
Oil pressure indicator	LED
Temperature indicator	LED

Table 8 SENSOR TEST SPECIFICATIONS

Coolant temperature switch	
Starts to close (ON)	112-118° C (259-270° F)
Starts to open (OFF)	Below 108° C (252° F)
Fan motor switch	
Starts to close (ON)	98-102° C (208-216° F)
Starts to open (OFF)	93-97° C (199-207° F)

Table 9 FUSE SPECIFICATIONS

Type	Specification
Main fuse	30A
Subfuses	
Fan motor	10A
Headlight	10A
Ignition/starter	10A
Turn signal/front and rear brake/meter	15 A

Table 10 ELECTRICAL SYSTEM TORQUE SPECIFICATIONS

	N•m	in.-lb.	ft.-lb.
Battery case cover screw			
VT750C	10	88	–
VT750DC	9	80	–
Coolant temperature switch[2]			
VT750C	12	106	
VT750DC	8	71	–
Crankshaft hole cap[1]	15	–	11
Fan motor switch	18	–	13
Flywheel mounting bolt[2]	127	–	94
Fuel tank mounting bolt	19	–	14
Horn mounting bolt	21	–	15
Ignition pulse generator mounting bolts[3]	12	106	–
Ignition switch	See text		
Neutral switch	12	106	–
Oil pressure switch[4]	12	106	–
Sidestand switch mounting bolt	10	88	–
Speedometer cover bolts	10	88	–
Starter cable nut	10	88	–
Starter mounting bolts	29	–	21
Starter clutch Torx mounting bolts[3]	29	–	21
Stator coil mounting bolts	12	106	–
Stator wire holder mounting bolt	12	106	–
Timing hole cap[1]	15	–	11

1. Lubricate threads with grease.
2. Lubricate bolt threads and flange surface with engine oil.
3. Apply a medium strength threadlock onto fastener threads.
4. Apply RTV to switch threads as described in text

9

CHAPTER TEN

COOLING SYSTEM

This chapter describes repair and replacement of cooling system components. **Table 1** and **Table 2** at the end of this chapter list cooling system specifications. For routine maintenance of the system, refer to Chapter Three. The water pump requires no routine maintenance and is replaced as a complete unit if defective.

The pressurized cooling system consists of the radiator, water pump, thermostat, electric cooling fan and a coolant reserve tank.

> *WARNING*
> *Do not remove the radiator cap (**Figure 1**) or any cooling system component that is under pressure when the engine is hot. The coolant is very hot and under pressure. Excessive scalding could result if the coolant touches skin. The cooling system must be cool before removing or disconnecting any system component.*

> *CAUTION*
> *Do not reuse the old coolant because it deteriorates with use. Do not operate the cooling system with only distilled water (even if freezing temperatures are not expected). The antifreeze inhibits internal engine corrosion and provides lubrication of moving parts in the water pump.*

TEMPERATURE WARNING SYSTEM

A coolant temperature indicator is located on the face of the speedometer. If the coolant temperature is above a preset level when the ignition switch is on, the indicator light on the speedometer face illuminates.

During normal operation the radiator fan does not operate constantly. It turns on when the temperature increases to a specified temperature. Problems in the cooling system can cause the engine to overheat. Conditions that do not have anything to do with the cooling system or engine can also cause overheating. These include riding in areas of high ambient temperatures, continuous stop-and-go traffic and when climbing in foothill and mountain areas. Because the VT750 is not equipped with a temperature gauge, the engine temperature cannot be monitored. The coolant temperature indicator coming on may be the first indicator that the engine is overheating. If this happens, park in a safe spot and turn the engine off. Steam coming from the engine or a part in the cooling system indicates a leak. Do not touch the engine or parts of the cooling system until the engine cools down. Determine the cause of the overheating before operating the motorcycle. Refer to *Engine Overheating* in Chapter Two for additional information.

COOLING SYSTEM INSPECTION

1. If steam is observed at the muffler after the engine has sufficiently warmed up, a head gasket might be damaged. If enough coolant leaks into a cylinder(s), the cylinders could hydrolock. This would prevent the engine from being turned over. Coolant may also be present in the engine oil. If the oil visible on the dipstick is foamy or milky-looking, there is coolant in the oil. If so, correct the problem before returning the motorcycle to service.

2. Refer to *Cooling System* in Chapter Three to check the coolant level.

3. Check the radiator for clogged or damaged fins.

4. Check the radiator for loose or missing mounting bolts.

5. Check all coolant hoses for cracks or damage. With the engine cold, squeeze the hoses by hand. If a hose collapses easily, it is damaged and must be replaced. Make sure the hose clamps are tight, but not so tight that they cut the hoses. Refer to *Hoses* in this section.

6. Make sure the overflow tube is connected to the radiator (next to the radiator cap) and is not clogged or damaged.

7. To check the cooling system for leaks, pressure test it as described in this section.

Hoses

After removing any cooling system component, inspect the adjoining hose(s) to determine if replacement is necessary. Hoses deteriorate with age and should be inspected carefully for conditions that may cause them to fail. Loss of coolant causes the engine to overheat, and spray from a leaking hose can injure the rider. A collapsed hose prevents coolant circulation and causes overheating. Observe the following when servicing hoses:

1. Refer to **Figure 2** for a diagram of the engine cooling hoses.

2. Make sure the cooling system is cool before removing any coolant hose or component.

3. Use original equipment replacement hoses; they are formed to a specific shape and dimension for correct fit.

4. Loosen the hose clamps on the hose that is to be replaced. Slide the clamps back off the component fittings.

5. Before disconnecting a formed hose, look for a paint mark on the end of the hose. This mark usually aligns with a raised boss on the connecting part to ensure the hose is properly installed.

CAUTION
Do not use excessive force when attempting to remove a stubborn hose. Also use caution when attempting to loosen hoses with hose pliers. The aluminum radiator and water pump hose joints are easily damaged.

6. Twist the hose to release it from the joint. If the hose is difficult to break loose, insert a small screwdriver between the hose and joint and spray WD-40 or a similar lubricant into the opening. Carefully twist the hose to break it loose.

NOTE
Remove all lubricant residue from the hose and hose fitting before reinstalling the hose.

7. Examine the fittings for cracks or other damage. Repair or replace as necessary. If the fitting is good, use a wire brush and clean off any hose residue that may have transferred to the fitting. Wipe clean with a cloth.

8. Inspect the hose clamps for rust and corrosion and replace if necessary.

9. If a hose is difficult to install on the joint, soak the end in hot water to make it more pliable. Do not use any lubricant when installing hoses.

10. Formed hoses must be properly installed. Refer to Step 5.

11. With the hose correctly installed, position and tighten the clamp securely. Position the clamp head so it is accessible for future removal and does not contact other parts.

10

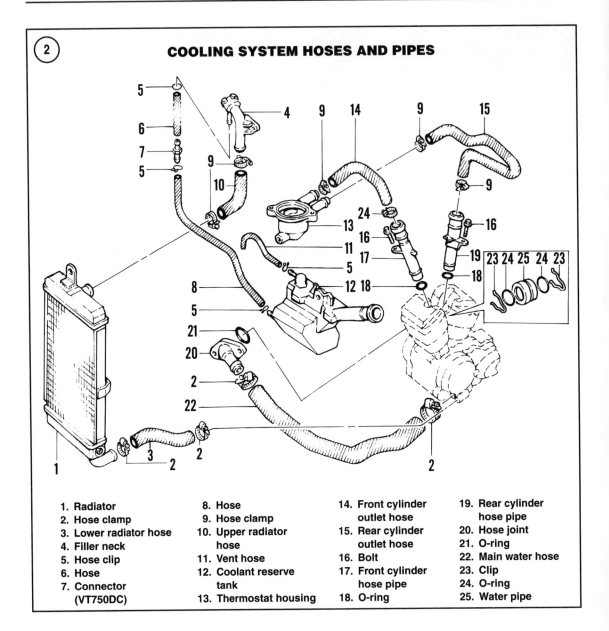

② **COOLING SYSTEM HOSES AND PIPES**

1. Radiator	8. Hose	14. Front cylinder	19. Rear cylinder
2. Hose clamp	9. Hose clamp	outlet hose	hose pipe
3. Lower radiator hose	10. Upper radiator	15. Rear cylinder	20. Hose joint
4. Filler neck	hose	outlet hose	21. O-ring
5. Hose clip	11. Vent hose	16. Bolt	22. Main water hose
6. Hose	12. Coolant reserve	17. Front cylinder	23. Clip
7. Connector	tank	hose pipe	24. O-ring
(VT750DC)	13. Thermostat housing	18. O-ring	25. Water pipe

Pressure Test

This test simulates the integrity of the cooling system under engine running conditions by placing pressure on the hoses, gaskets and seals. Perform this test whenever troubleshooting a cooling system leak. The test is performed when the engine is cold. Use a hand pump tester to pressurize the system.

WARNING
Never remove the radiator cap (Figure 1), coolant drain plugs or disconnect any coolant hose while the *engine and radiator are hot. Scalding fluid and steam may be blown out under pressure and cause serious injury.*

1. Remove the fuel tank (Chapter Eight).
2. On VT750C models, remove the steering covers (Chapter Fifteen).
3. With the engine cold, remove the radiator cap (**Figure 1**).
4. Add coolant to the radiator to bring the level up to the filler neck.
5. Check the rubber washers on the radiator cap (**Figure 3**). Replace the cap if the washers show

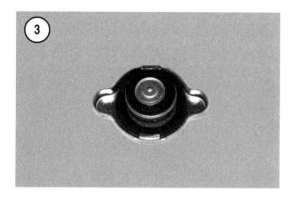

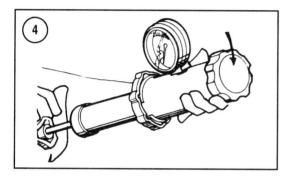

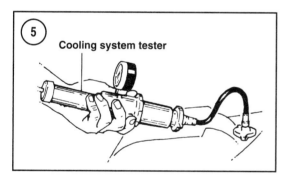

Cooling system tester

signs of deterioration, cracking or other damage. If the radiator cap is good, perform Step 6.

CAUTION
Do not exceed 137 kPa (20 psi) or the cooling system components may be damaged.

6. Lubricate the rubber washer on the bottom of the radiator cap with coolant and install it on a cooling system pressure tester (**Figure 4**, typical). Apply 108-137 kPa (16-20 psi) and check for a pressure drop. Replace the cap if it cannot hold this pressure.
7. Mount the pressure tester onto the thermostat housing filler neck (**Figure 5**, typical) and pressure test the cooling system to 108-137 kPa (16-20 psi).

If the system cannot hold this pressure, check for a coolant leak:
    a. Radiator cap. If the radiator cap passed the pressure test in Step 6 but is now leaking, inspect the thermostat filler neck and cap mounting flange for damage.
    b. Leaking or damaged coolant hoses.
    c. Damaged or deteriorated O-rings installed in coolant hose connectors. Refer to **Figure 2**.
    d. Damaged water pump mechanical seal. Refer to *Water Pump* in this chapter and inspect the weep hole.
    e. Water pump leakage.
    f. Loose coolant drain bolt(s).
    g. Warped cylinder head or cylinder mating surfaces.

NOTE
*If the test pressure drops rapidly, but there are no visible coolant leaks, coolant may be leaking into one of the cylinder heads. Refer to **Engine Compression Test** in Chapter Three.*

8. Check all cooling system hoses for damage or deterioration. Replace any questionable hose. Make sure all hose clamps are tight.
9. Remove the tester and install the radiator cap.
10. Reverse Step 1 and Step 2.

RADIATOR

Removal/Installation

Refer to **Figure 6**.
1. Disconnect the negative battery cable (Chapter Nine).
2. Remove the fuel tank (Chapter Eight).
3. On VT750C models, remove the steering covers (Chapter Fifteen).
4. Drain the cooling system (Chapter Three).
5. Disconnect the fan motor switch connector. **Figure 7** shows the connector used on VT750C models. On VT750DC models, the connector is mounted on the right side of the frame, near the radiator cap.

NOTE
*The radiator grill (**Figure 8**) cannot be removed until after the radiator is removed from the frame.*

10

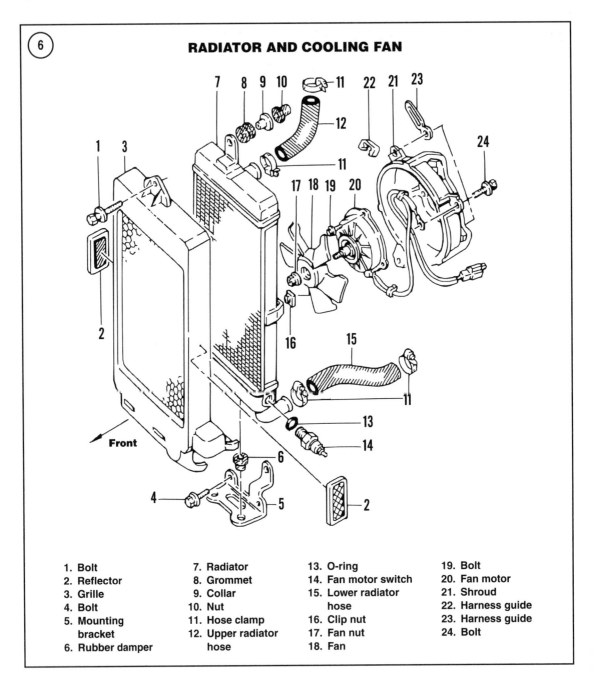

RADIATOR AND COOLING FAN

1. Bolt	7. Radiator	13. O-ring	19. Bolt
2. Reflector	8. Grommet	14. Fan motor switch	20. Fan motor
3. Grille	9. Collar	15. Lower radiator	21. Shroud
4. Bolt	10. Nut	hose	22. Harness guide
5. Mounting	11. Hose clamp	16. Clip nut	23. Harness guide
bracket	12. Upper radiator	17. Fan nut	24. Bolt
6. Rubber damper	hose	18. Fan	

6. Disconnect the lower radiator hose (**Figure 9**) at the radiator.

7. Remove the upper radiator mounting bolt and washer. Then pull the radiator (A, **Figure 10**) out slightly and disconnect the upper radiator hose (B) at the radiator.

8. Lift the radiator to disconnect its lower rubber dampers from the mounting bracket. Remove the radiator with the front grill and cooling fan.

9. Installation is the reverse of removal. Note the following:

    a. Check the radiator hoses for damage that may have occurred during radiator removal.

    b. Replace missing or damaged rubber dampers and grommets.

    c. Refill and bleed the cooling system (Chapter Three).

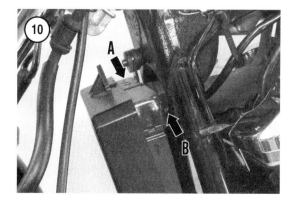

d. After starting the engine, check the coolant hoses for leaks.

Inspection

1. Flush off the exterior of the radiator with a garden hose on low pressure. Spray the front and back sides to remove all debris. Carefully use a whisk broom or stiff paint brush to remove any stubborn dirt.

CAUTION
Do not press too hard or the cooling fins and tubes may be damaged.

2. Carefully straighten out any bent cooling fins with a broad-tipped screwdriver or putty knife.
3. Check for cracks or leaks (usually a moss-green colored residue) at the filler neck, the inlet and outlet hose fittings and the upper and lower tank seams.
4. If paint has been worn off in any area of the radiator, repaint with a quality black spray paint. This helps prolong the radiator life by cutting down on oxidation from the outside. Do not apply too much paint to the cooling fin area as this cuts down on the cooling capabilities of the radiator.
5. Replace the lower mounting bracket rubber dampers if damaged.
6. Inspect the rubber seals on the radiator cap. Replace the cap if they are hardened or starting to deteriorate.

COOLING FAN

Removal/Installation

Refer to **Figure 6**.
1. Remove the radiator as described in this chapter.
2. Disconnect the fan motor switch connector. Then remove the wire from the clamps on the radiator.
3. Remove the fan mounting bolts and ground wire, and then remove the fan.
4. To separate the fan from the fan motor:
    a. Remove the nut and the cooling fan.
    b. Remove the bolts and the fan motor from the shroud.
5. Installation is the reverse of removal. Note the following:
    a. Install the cooling fan onto the fan motor shaft by aligning the flat surfaces. Install and tighten the fan motor to 3 N•m (26 in.-lb.).

COOLANT RESERVE TANK AND THERMOSTAT

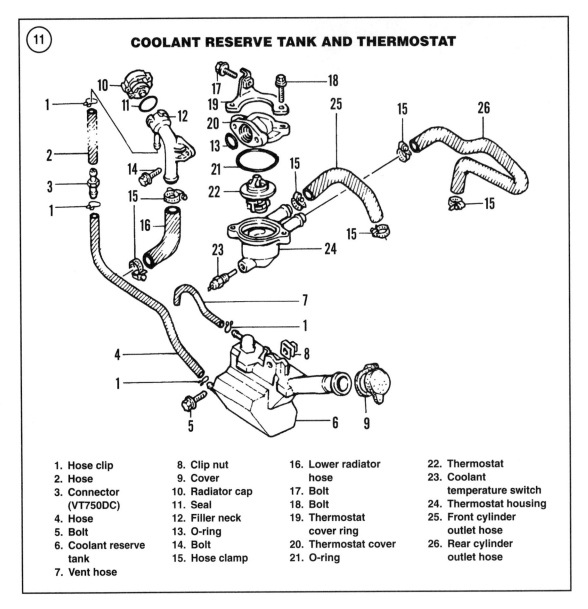

1. Hose clip	8. Clip nut	16. Lower radiator	22. Thermostat
2. Hose	9. Cover	hose	23. Coolant
3. Connector	10. Radiator cap	17. Bolt	temperature switch
(VT750DC)	11. Seal	18. Bolt	24. Thermostat housing
4. Hose	12. Filler neck	19. Thermostat	25. Front cylinder
5. Bolt	13. O-ring	cover ring	outlet hose
6. Coolant reserve	14. Bolt	20. Thermostat cover	26. Rear cylinder
tank	15. Hose clamp	21. O-ring	outlet hose
7. Vent hose			

b. Check the wire harness routing.

Testing

Refer to *Fan Motor Switch* in Chapter Nine to test the fan motor and its related circuit.

COOLANT RESERVE TANK

Removal/Installation

Refer to **Figure 11**.

1. Remove the radiator as described in this chapter.

2. Disconnect the hose from the bottom of the coolant reserve tank and drain the coolant from the tank.

3. Remove the mounting bolt and the coolant reserve tank.

4. Flush the reserve tank with clean water. Check the tank for cracks or other damage.

5. Install the coolant reserve tank by reversing these steps.

6. Fill the reserve tank as described under *Coolant Change* in Chapter Three.

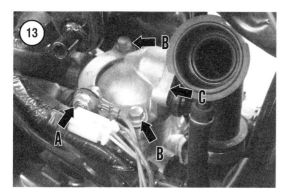

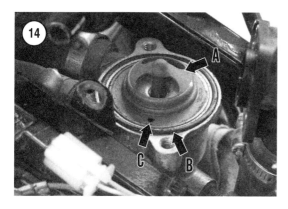

THERMOSTAT

The thermostat is a temperature sensitive valve used to control the flow of coolant into the radiator. When the engine is cold, the thermostat is closed and coolant bypasses the radiator. This helps the engine warm up quickly. When the engine reaches operating temperature, the thermostat opens and coolant flows between the engine and radiator. The thermostat can be removed without removing the thermostat housing or disconnecting any coolant hoses. Refer to **Figure 11** when servicing the thermostat and thermostat housing in this section.

Removal/Installation

The thermostat can be removed without having to remove the thermostat housing or disconnect any coolant hoses.

1. Remove the fuel tank (Chapter Eight).
2A. On VT750C models, remove the steering covers (Chapter Fifteen).
2B. On VT750DC models, remove the following:
    a. Air cleaner housing (Chapter Eight).
    b. Sub-air filter housing (Chapter Eight).
    c. Front cylinder right overhead cover.
3. Drain the cooling system until the coolant level is below the thermostat housing or drain all the coolant as described in Chapter Three.
4. Place a rag underneath the thermostat to catch any residue coolant spilled from the thermostat housing.

NOTE
Make sure the front cylinder head spark plugs and spark plug caps are installed to prevent coolant from entering the cylinder.

5A. On VT750C models, perform the following:
    a. Remove the mounting bolts and pull the filler neck (**Figure 12**) away from the thermostat. Remove and discard the O-ring (13, **Figure 11**).
    b. Remove the bolt (A, **Figure 13**) securing the ground wire terminal and thermostat cover ring to the frame.
    c. Remove the thermostat cover mounting bolts (B, **Figure 13**), cover ring and cover (C).
    d. Remove the thermostat (A, **Figure 14**).
    e. Remove and discard the O-ring (B, **Figure 14**).
5B. On VT750DC models, perform the following:
    a. Remove the thermostat housing mounting bolt and ground wire terminal (**Figure 15**).
    b. Remove the thermostat cover mounting bolts, cover ring and cover (**Figure 15**).
    c. Remove the thermostat (A, **Figure 14**).
    d. Remove and discard the O-ring (B, **Figure 14**).
6. Rinse the thermostat with clean water.
7. Inspect the thermostat (**Figure 16**) for damage. Make sure the spring has not sagged or broken.
8. Inspect the thermostat valve and valve seat for any gaps, which indicates a stuck thermostat.
9. If necessary, test the thermostat as described in this section.
10. Clean the thermostat housing, O-ring groove and all mating surfaces.

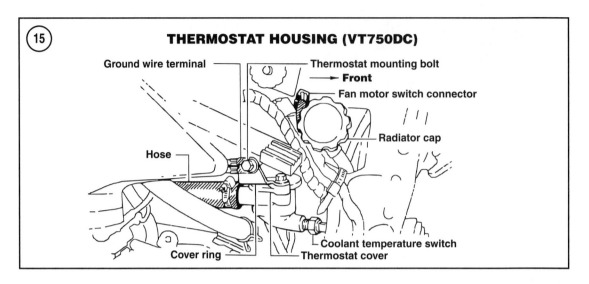

THERMOSTAT HOUSING (VT750DC)

(15)

Ground wire terminal — Thermostat mounting bolt
→ Front
Fan motor switch connector
Radiator cap
Hose
Coolant temperature switch
Cover ring — Thermostat cover

11. Installation is the reverse of removal. Note the following:

   a. Install the thermostat by aligning its support arm (A, **Figure 17**) with the housing groove (B). The vent hole (C, **Figure 14**) on the thermostat flange must be facing up.

   b. Install a new O-ring (B, **Figure 14**).

   c. Tighten the thermostat housing bolts to 9 N•m (80 in.-lb.).

   d. On VT750C models, install a new O-ring onto the thermostat filler neck shoulder. Tighten the thermostat filler neck bolts to 9 N•m (80 in.-lb.).

   e. Fill and bleed the cooling system (Chapter Three). Check for coolant leaks.

Testing

A stuck thermostat causes the engine to warm up slowly (when stuck open) or causes overheating (stuck partially or fully closed). Check by starting the engine (when cold) and allow it to warm to normal operating temperature. During this time, carefully touch the top radiator hose (10, **Figure 2**). If the hose becomes hot quickly, the thermostat is probably stuck open. This condition causes the engine to run colder for a longer period. If the hose gradually warms and then becomes hot, the thermostat is probably operating correctly. However, if the upper hose and radiator do not feel hot after the engine has run long enough to warm to normal operating temperature, the thermostat is probably stuck

(16)

(17)

closed and is blocking coolant flow through the radiator. This condition causes the engine to overheat.

Test the thermostat to ensure proper operation as follows:

1. Support the thermostat and a thermometer (rated higher than the test temperature) in a pan of water (**Figure 18**). The thermostat and thermometer must not touch the sides or bottom of the pan or a false reading results.

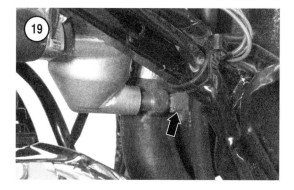

2. Gradually heat the water and continue to gently stir the water until it reaches 80-84° C (176-183° F). At this temperature, the thermostat valve should start to open.

3. At 95° C (203° F), the minimum valve lift should be 8 mm (0.31 in.).

NOTE
Valve operation is sometimes sluggish. It may take 3-5 minutes for the valve to operate properly.

4. If the valve fails to operate at the listed temperatures or if the valve lift is below minimum at the specified temperature, replace the thermostat. Al-

ways replace the thermostat with one of the same temperature rating.

THERMOSTAT HOUSING

The thermostat housing contains the thermostat, filler neck and serves as a hose manifold (**Figure 11**). Hoses route the coolant from the cylinders to the manifold, while a bypass hose directs coolant to the water pump when the thermostat is closed. The coolant temperature switch is mounted on the thermostat housing.

Removal/Installation

1. Drain the cooling system (Chapter Three).
2. Remove the fuel tank (Chapter Eight).
3. Remove the air filter housing (Chapter Eight).
4. On VT750DC models, remove the following:
   a. Sub-air filter housing (Chapter Eight).
   b. Front cylinder right overhead cover.
5. Disconnect the electrical connector at the coolant temperature switch (**Figure 19**).
6. Remove the thermostat housing mounting bolt and disconnect the ground wire terminal. Refer to A, **Figure 13** (VT750C) or **Figure 15** (VT750DC).
7. Disconnect the coolant hoses at the thermostat housing (**Figure 11**).
8. Remove the thermostat housing.
9. Installation is the reverse of removal. Note the following:
   a. The radiator hoses are formed and must be installed properly. Refer to **Figure 2** and **Figure 11**.
   b. Refill the cooling system with the recommended type and quantity of coolant (Chapter Three).

Coolant Temperature Switch

Refer to *Coolant Temperature Switch Testing and Replacement* in Chapter Nine to test and service the switch.

WATER PUMP

The water pump is mounted on the bottom, left side of the engine (**Figure 20**). The engine must be removed from the frame to replace the water pump.

10

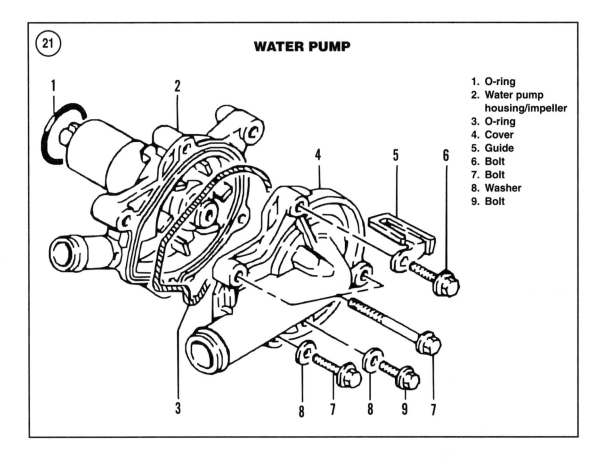

WATER PUMP

1. O-ring
2. Water pump housing/impeller
3. O-ring
4. Cover
5. Guide
6. Bolt
7. Bolt
8. Washer
9. Bolt

The water pump is sold as a complete unit only. If any component is damaged, the entire water pump assembly must be replaced. The two water pump O-rings (1 and 3, **Figure 21**) can be replaced separately.

Mechanical Seal Inspection

An inspection or weep hole (**Figure 22**) is built into the bottom of the water pump. When coolant leaks from the hole, the mechanical seal in the water pump is damaged and must be replaced.

> *NOTE*
> *Figure 22 shows the inspection hole with the water pump removed for clarity.*

1. Check for signs of coolant or coolant stains on the bottom of the water pump. If there is coolant in this area, first check the condition of the two hoses and hose clamps mounted on the water pump. Check the hose clamps for tightness.

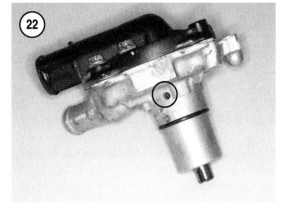

> *NOTE*
> *Because the engine must be removed from the frame to replace the water pump, make sure the coolant leak is from the pump inspection hole and not from a leaking or damaged hose.*

2. Clean up any spilled coolant so it does not contact the rear tire.

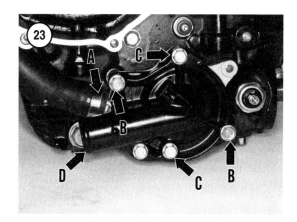

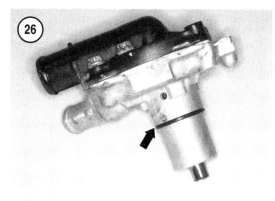

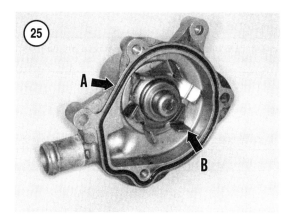

Removal/Installation

Refer to **Figure 21**.

1. Remove the engine from the frame (Chapter Five).

2. Disconnect the coolant hose (A, **Figure 23**) at the water pump.

3. Remove the water pump mounting bolts (B, **Figure 23**) and cover bolts (C). Then remove the cover (D, **Figure 23**).

> *NOTE*
> *To remove the water pump without removing the cover, remove only the mounting bolts (B, Figure 23).*

4. Remove the water pump housing (**Figure 24**).

5. Remove the internal (A, **Figure 25**) and external (**Figure 26**) O-rings and discard them.

6. Inspect the water pump as described in this section.

7. Install the water pump by reversing these steps. Note the following:

   a. Install a new external O-ring (**Figure 26**) onto the pump body. Lubricate the O-ring with engine oil.

   b. Lubricate the new internal O-ring with engine oil and install it into the water pump groove (A, **Figure 25**).

   c. Install the water pump body by aligning the slot in the end of the water pump shaft (A, **Figure 27**) with the notch in the end of the oil pump shaft (B).

   d. Install the hose (A, **Figure 23**) by aligning the paint mark on the hose with the raised boss on the water pump. Tighten the hose clamp securely.

   e. Install the water pump cover, bolts and mounting bolts. Tighten the bolts to 13 N•m (115 in.-lb.).

   f. Install the engine in the frame (Chapter Five).

10

Inspection

1. Replace the water pump if there is engine oil in the pump. This indicates that the seal mounted over the pump shaft is damaged.

2. Check the impeller blades (B, **Figure 25**) for corrosion or damage. If the corrosion buildup on the blades is minor, clean the blades. If the corrosion is excessive or if the blades are cracked or broken, replace the water pump assembly.

3. Turn the impeller shaft and check the pump bearing for excessive noise or roughness. If the bearing operation is rough or abnormal, replace the water pump assembly.

Table 1 COOLING SYSTEM SPECIFICATIONS

Coolant	
Standard concentration	50% mixture coolant and purified water
Type	Honda HP coolant or an equivalent*
Coolant capacity	
Radiator and engine	1.75L (1.85 U.S. qt.)
Reserve tank	0.4L (0.42 U.S. qt.)
Thermostat	
Begins to open	80-84° C (176-183° F)
Fully open	95° C (203° F)
Valve lift (minimum)	8 mm (0.3 in.)

* Use a high quality ethylene coolant that does not contain silicate inhibitors as they can cause premature wear to the water pump seals and block radiator passages.

Table 2 COOLING SYSTEM TORQUE SPECIFICATIONS

	N•m	in.-lb.
Cooling fan nut	3	26
Fan motor bolt	3	26
Thermostat filler neck bolt	9	80
Thermostat cover bolts	9	80
Water pump cover and mounting bolts	13	115

WHEELS, TIRES AND DRIVE CHAIN

This chapter describes repair and maintenance for the front and rear wheels, hubs, tires, sprockets and drive chain. Routine maintenance procedures for these components are in Chapter Three.

Tables 1-5 are at the end of this chapter.

MOTORCYCLE LIFT

Many procedures in this chapter require lifting either the front or rear wheel off the ground. Because the VT750 is not equipped with a centerstand, a separate jack or lift stand is required. The K&L MC450 Center Jack is a scissors jack (**Figure 1**)

that can be placed under the motorcycle to lift either the front or rear wheel. When using the MC450 center jack, have an assistant sit onto the motorcycle and center it upright. Place a block of wood across the jack and position the jack underneath the front part of the engine or the rear part of the frame. Operate the jack and lift the motorcycle until the front or rear wheel just clears the ground. The K&L Center Jack can be ordered through most motorcycle dealerships.

> *WARNING*
> *Regardless of the type of jack or stand used to lift a motorcycle, make sure the motorcycle is properly supported before walking away from it.*

FRONT WHEEL

Removal

1. Support the motorcycle securely with the front wheel off the ground.

2A. On speed sensor equipped models, remove the screw and speed sensor (**Figure 2**).

2B. On all other models, remove the screw and disconnect the speedometer cable (**Figure 3**).

3. On the right fork tube, loosen the axle pinch bolts (A, **Figure 4**), and then loosen and remove the front axle nut or bolt (B).

4. On the left fork tube, loosen the axle pinch bolts (A, **Figure 5**), and then remove the axle (B).

5. Pull the wheel forward and remove the speedometer gear housing (**Figure 6**) and collar (**Figure 7**).

> *NOTE*
> *Do not operate the front brake lever while the wheel is removed. Insert a spacer block between the pads until the wheel is installed. This prevents the caliper pistons from extending if the lever is operated.*

6. Inspect the front wheel as described in this chapter.

Installation

1. Clean the front axle, collar and the axle bolt or nut.

2. Check the axle bearing surfaces on both fork tubes and the axle for burrs and nicks. Smooth with a file.

3. Apply a light coat of grease to the axle and collar. Do not lubricate the axle threads. These threads must be free of oil and grease when the axle bolt or nut is tightened.

4. Remove the spacer block from between the brake pads.

5. Install the collar (**Figure 7**) into the right side of the wheel. The shoulder side of the collar must face out.

6. Install the speedometer gear housing by aligning the arms in the housing (**Figure 8**) with the slots in the retainer. Refer to **Figure 6**.

7. Carefully insert the disc between the brake pads, then install the front axle from the left side. Position the raised arm on the speedometer gear housing against the backside of the stopper on the left fork tube (**Figure 9**).

8. Install the axle bolt (B, **Figure 4**) or nut finger-tight.

> *CAUTION*
> *The front axle and pinch bolt tightening sequence in Steps 9-12 correctly*

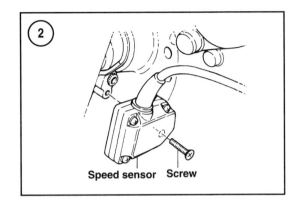
Speed sensor   Screw

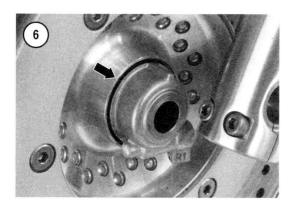

seats the front axle so both sliders are positioned parallel with each other. Fork misalignment can cause premature seal and bushing wear, increase the wear against the slider, reduce fork performance and cause steering problems.

9. Hold the axle and tighten the axle bolt or nut to 59 N•m (44 ft.-lb.). Make sure the groove on the axle (**Figure 10**) aligns with the outer edge of the fork tube axle bore as shown in (C, **Figure 5**).

10. Pump the front brake lever to reposition the brake pads against the brake disc.

11. Remove the motorcycle from the stand so the front wheel is on the ground. Apply the front brake, then compress and release the front suspension several times to center the axle in the slider axle bores. Compress the fork as far as possible. Check that the fork legs are parallel.

12. Tighten the left (A, **Figure 5**) and right (A, **Figure 4**) side front axle pinch bolts to 22 N•m (16 ft.-lb.).

13A. On speed sensor equipped models, install the speed sensor and tighten the screw securely (**Figure 2**).

13B. On all other models, install the speedometer cable (**Figure 3**) by aligning the slot in the end of the cable with the tab in the speedometer gear housing. Install and tighten the screw securely.

Inspection

1. Inspect the seals (A, **Figure 11**) for wear, hardness, cracks or other damage. If necessary, replace the seals as described under *Front and Rear Hubs* in this chapter.

2. Inspect the bearings on both sides of the wheel for:

    a. Roughness. Turn each bearing inner race (B, **Figure 11**) by hand and check for smooth, quiet operation.

    b. Radial and axial play (**Figure 12**). Try to push the bearing in and out to check for axial play. Slight play is normal. Try to push the bearing up and down to check for radial play. Any radial play should be difficult to feel. If play is easily felt, the bearing is worn out. Always replace bearings as a set. Refer to *Front and Rear Hubs* in this chapter.

3. Clean the axle and collar in solvent to remove all grease and dirt. Make sure the axle contact surfaces are clean.

4. Service the speedometer gear housing as described in this chapter.

5. Check the axle for straightness with a set of V-blocks and dial indicator. Refer to **Table 2** for maximum axle runout. Actual runout is one-half of the gauge reading. Do not straighten a bent axle.

6. Check the brake disc bolts for tightness. To service the brake disc, refer to Chapter Fourteen.

7. Refer to *Wheel Service* in this chapter for inspecting and truing the rim.

SPEEDOMETER GEAR AND CABLE

Periodically inspect and lubricate the speedometer drive gear and cable (if so equipped).

NOTE
*For models equipped with a speed sensor (**Figure 2**), refer to Chapter Nine for testing and replacement.*

Speedometer Gear
Inspection/Lubrication

1. Remove the front wheel as described in this chapter.

2. Remove the drive gear (**Figure 13**) and both washers (**Figure 14**) from the housing.

3. Clean and dry all parts.

4. Inspect the drive gear teeth for breakage or other damage. Check the slots on the top of the gear for cracks or other damage that would cause inaccurate speedometer readings. Replace the drive gear if necessary.

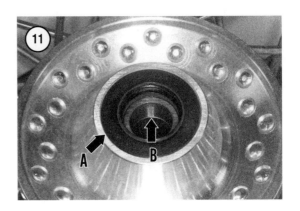

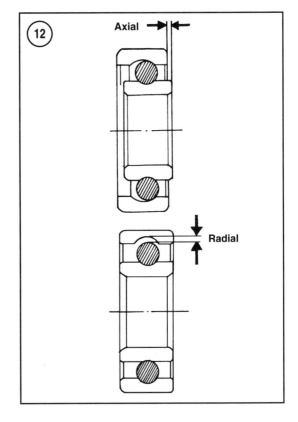

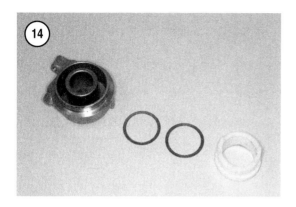

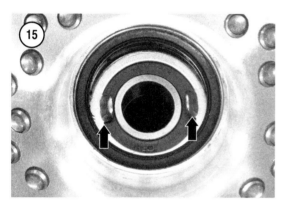

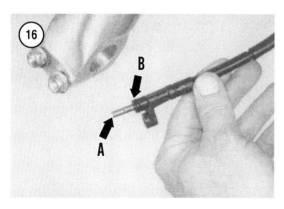

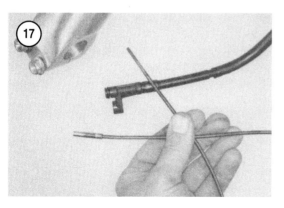

5. Check the washers for cracks, excessive thrust wear or other damage.

6. Check the gear shoulder in the speedometer housing for cracks or other damage.

7. Lubricate the gear and both washers with a high-temperature grease, and then install the washers (**Figure 14**) and drive gear (**Figure 13**).

8. Inspect the retainer (**Figure 15**) in the left side of the front wheel that engages with the drive gear. Check the tabs for cracks or breakage. If necessary, replace the retainer as described under *Front and Rear Hubs* in this chapter.

9. Install the front wheel as described in this chapter.

Speedometer Cable Lubrication

1. Remove the screw and disconnect the speedometer cable (**Figure 3**) from the front wheel.

2. Pull the speedometer cable (A, **Figure 16**) out of its housing.

3. Wipe the cable (**Figure 17**) with a rag soaked in solvent.

4. Inspect the cable for any broken cable strands or other damage. Check both cable ends for damage.

5. Lubricate the cable with a waterproof grease.

6. Install the cable into its housing, making sure its upper end engages with the square drive hole in the speedometer.

7. Lubricate the cable housing O-ring (B, **Figure 16**) with grease.

8. Reconnect the speedometer cable (**Figure 3**) at the front wheel and secure with the screw.

REAR WHEEL

Removal

> *NOTE*
> *On models with the tall rear fender, the rear of the motorcycle must be raised considerably to provide clearance for removing and installing the rear wheel (**Figure 18**). Before beginning this procedure, make sure the jack can support the motorcycle at the required height. An alternative is to remove the rear fender as described in Chapter Fifteen.*

11

1. Support the motorcycle with the rear wheel off the ground.

2. Remove the adjusting nut (A, **Figure 19**), collar and spring.

3. Remove the brake rod nut (B, **Figure 19**), flat washer and rubber cushion. Then remove the brake stopper arm pivot bolt.

4. Remove the axle nut and washer (A, **Figure 20**).

5. Loosen the drive chain adjuster bolts (B, **Figure 20**) on both sides of the swing arm and push the wheel forward to obtain maximum chain slack.

6. Remove the rear axle partway and remove the right side collar (**Figure 21**).

7. Remove the axle from the left side of the wheel and allow the wheel to drop down. Remove the drive chain from around the driven sprocket.

CAUTION
The axle should slide out of the wheel without any excessive force. If the axle is tight, tap it out with an aluminum or brass rod. Do not use a steel rod or punch as it may damage the threads on the end of the axle.

NOTE
The driven sprocket is mounted on a separate housing (driven flange) that can fall out when removing the wheel from the swing arm.

8. Remove the left side collar (**Figure 22**).

9. Remove the brake panel (**Figure 23**) from the rear hub.

WARNING
When handling the rear brake assembly, do not inhale brake dust as it may contain asbestos, which can cause lung injury and cancer. Wear a disposable face mask and wash hands thoroughly after completing the work. Wet down the brake dust on brake components before storing or working on them. Secure and dispose of all brake dust and cleaning materials properly. Do not use compressed air to blow off brake parts.

10. Remove and service the driven flange (A, **Figure 24**) as described in this chapter.

11. Inspect the rear wheel as described in this section.

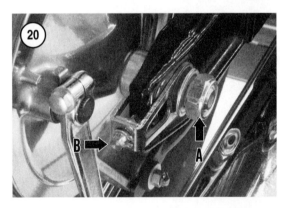

5. Lubricate the seal lip (B, **Figure 24**) with a waterproof grease.

6. Install the brake panel (**Figure 23**) into the brake drum.

7. Install the left collar (**Figure 22**) into the seal.

8. Install the wheel through the swing arm with the driven sprocket on the left side. Install the drive chain around the driven sprocket.

9. If using a scissors-jack, lower the motorcycle around the wheel and align the swing arm and rear wheel axle holes.

10. From the left side, install the axle partway through the swing arm, left collar and wheel.

11. Install the right collar (**Figure 21**), then install the axle until it bottoms against the left side. Clean grease from the axle threads.

12. Install the washer and axle nut (A, **Figure 20**).

13. Install the bolt through the brake panel and install the brake stopper arm over it. Then install the rubber cushion, flat washer and nut (B, **Figure 19**). Tighten the nut to 20 N•m (15 ft.-lb.). Install a new cotter pin through the pivot bolt and bend its arms over to lock it.

14. Install the brake adjusting rod through the brake arm, then install the spring, collar and adjusting nut (A, **Figure 19**).

15. Adjust the drive chain as described in Chapter Three.

16. Tighten the rear axle nut (A, **Figure 20**) to 93 N•m (69 ft.-lb.).

17. Adjust the rear brake as described in Chapter Three.

18. After the wheel is completely installed, rotate it several times to make sure it rotates freely.

> *WARNING*
> *Do not ride the motorcycle until you are sure the brakes are operating properly.*

Inspection

1. Inspect the bearings on both sides of the wheel. Check both bearings for:
   a. Roughness. Turn each bearing inner race (A, **Figure 25**) by hand and check for smooth, quiet operation.
   b. Radial and axial play (**Figure 12**). Try to push the bearing in and out to check for axial play. Slight play is normal. Try to push the bearing up and down to check for radial play. Any ra-

Installation

1. Clean the rear axle, collars and axle nut.

2. Check the axle bearing surfaces for burrs and nicks. Smooth with a file.

3. Apply a light coat of grease to the axle and collars. Do not lubricate the axle threads. These threads must be free of oil and grease when the axle nut is tightened.

4. If removed, install the driven flange assembly (A, **Figure 24**) as described in this chapter.

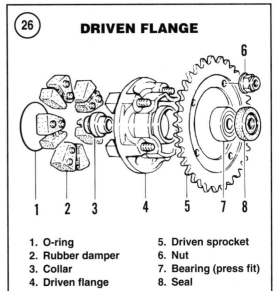

DRIVEN FLANGE

1. O-ring
2. Rubber damper
3. Collar
4. Driven flange
5. Driven sprocket
6. Nut
7. Bearing (press fit)
8. Seal

dial play should be difficult to feel. If play is easily felt, the bearing is worn out. Always replace bearings as a set. Refer to *Front and Rear Hubs* in this chapter.

2. Clean the axle and collars in solvent to remove all grease and dirt. Make sure the axle contact surfaces are clean.

3. Service the driven flange as described in this section.

4. Check the axle for straightness with a set of V-blocks and dial indicator. Refer to **Table 2** for maximum axle runout. Actual runout is one-half of the gauge reading. Do not straighten a bent axle.

5. Check the brake drum as described in Chapter Fourteen.

DRIVEN FLANGE

The driven flange (**Figure 26**) connects the driven sprocket to the rear wheel. The driven flange housing is equipped with an oil seal, ball bearing and collar. Wedge-shaped rubber shock dampers installed in the driven flange absorb some of the shock that results from torque changes during acceleration and braking.

Removal/Installation

1. Remove the rear wheel as described in this chapter.

2. Pull the driven flange assembly (A, **Figure 24**) out of the wheel hub.

3. Remove the rubber dampers (**Figure 27**) from the rear hub.

4. Remove the O-ring (A, **Figure 28**) from the hub groove.

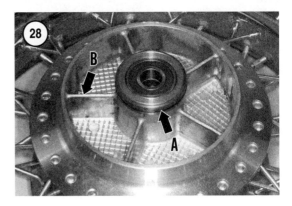

5. Inspect the driven flange assembly as described in this section.

6. Install by reversing these removal steps. Lubricate the O-ring with grease. Do not lubricate the rubber dampers.

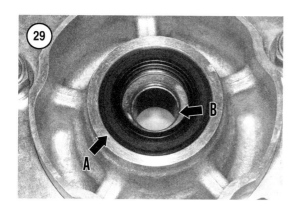

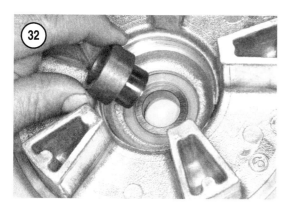

NOTE
If the driven flange is difficult to install, do not lubricate the rubber dampers with oil or grease. Instead, tap the driven flange into the wheel with a rubber hammer and a block of wood, working alternately around the driven flange to prevent if from binding in the wheel.

Inspection

Replace parts that show excessive wear or damage as described in this section.
1. Visually inspect the rubber dampers (**Figure 27**) for signs of damage or deterioration. Replace the dampers as a set.
2. Inspect the driven flange housing and rear hub brackets (B, **Figure 28**) for cracks or other damage.
3. Wipe the seal (A, **Figure 29**) with a rag and inspect it for excessive wear or damage.
4. Turn the bearing inner race (B, **Figure 29**) by hand. The bearing should turn smoothly with no roughness, binding or excessive noise. There should be no excessive axial or radial play (**Figure 12**). Replace the bearing if it has an excess amount of play or if there is visible damage.
5. Check that the bearing fits tightly in its mounting bore. If the bearing is a loose fit, the driven flange is probably damaged and should be replaced.
6. Inspect the driven sprocket as described in this chapter.

Seal and Bearing Replacement

1. Pry the seal (**Figure 30**) out of the mounting bore with a wide-blade screwdriver. Support the screwdriver with a rag to avoid damaging the mounting bore.
2. Remove any burrs created during seal removal. Use an emery cloth to remove only metal that is raised. Do not enlarge the mounting bore.
3. Tap the collar out of the bearing with a socket (**Figure 31**). Refer to **Figure 32**.
4. To remove the bearing, do the following:
   a. Support the driven flange on wooden blocks with its sprocket side facing down.
   b. Place a bearing driver or socket on the bearing's inner race, then drive or press the bearing (**Figure 33**) out of the driven flange.
   c. Discard the bearing.

11

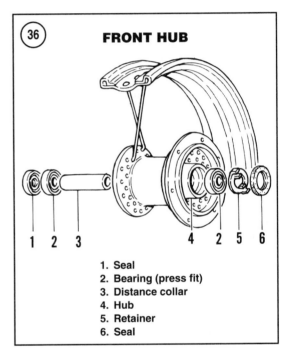

FRONT HUB

1. Seal
2. Bearing (press fit)
3. Distance collar
4. Hub
5. Retainer
6. Seal

5. Blow any debris out of the housing.

6. Inspect the bearing mounting bore for any cracks, burrs or other damage.

7. Install the collar into the new bearing as follows:
   a. Support the bearing (A, **Figure 34**) on a wooden block with its manufacturer's marks facing down.
   b. Drive the collar (B, **Figure 34**) into the bearing.

8. Install the new bearing as follows:
   a. Support the driven flange with its sprocket side facing up.
   b. Center the bearing in its mounting bore with the collar side facing down.
   c. Tap or press (**Figure 35**) the bearing squarely into place by applying pressure against the bearing's outer race. Do not tap on the inner race or the bearing might be damaged. Install the bearing until it bottoms in its mounting bore.

9. Install the new seal as follows:
   a. Pack the seal lips with grease.
   b. Position the seal in the driven flange mounting bore with its closed side facing out.
   c. Use a suitable tool to drive the seal into its mounting bore. Install the oil seal until it is

flush with the top mounting bore surface or when it bottoms out against the bearing's outer race (B, **Figure 29**).

FRONT AND REAR HUBS

Each hub contains two wheel bearings and a distance collar. Seals are also installed in both sides of the front hub. A brake disc is mounted onto the front hub. Refer to **Figure 36** (front) or **Figure 37** (rear) when servicing the front and rear hubs in this section.

Procedures for servicing the front and rear hubs are essentially the same. Where differences occur, they are described in the procedure.

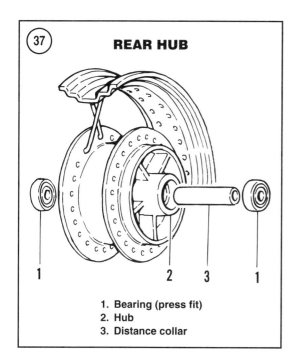

REAR HUB

1. Bearing (press fit)
2. Hub
3. Distance collar

Refer to *Basic Service Methods* in Chapter One for typical bearing procedures and information.

Preliminary Inspection

Initially inspect the bearings with the wheels installed on the motorcycle. With the wheels installed, leverage can be applied to the bearings to detect wear. In addition, the wheels can be spun to listen for roughness in the bearings. Use the following procedure to check the bearings while the wheels are installed. If the wheels must be removed, inspect the bearings as described under *Bearing Replacement* in this section.

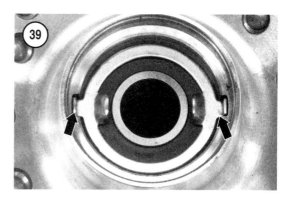

1. Support the motorcycle with the wheel off the ground. The axle nut must be tight.
2. Grasp the wheel with both hands, 180° apart. Rock the wheel up and down and side to side to check for radial and axial play. Have an assistant apply the brake while the test is repeated. Play is detected in excessively worn bearings, although the wheel is locked.
3. Spin the wheel and listen for bearing noise. A grinding or catching noise indicates worn bearings.
4. If damage is evident, replace the bearings as a set. Always install new seals in the front hub.

CAUTION
Do not remove the wheel bearings to check their condition. If the bearings are removed, they must be replaced.

Seal Replacement
(Front Wheel)

Seals protect the bearings from dirt and moisture contamination. Always install new seals when replacing bearings.

CAUTION
In the following procedure, do not allow the wheel to rest on the brake disc. Support the wheel on wooden blocks.

1. Pry the seals out of the hub with a seal puller, tire iron or wide-blade screwdriver (**Figure 38**). Place a shop cloth under the tool to protect the hub from damage.
2. On the left side of the wheel, remove the retainer (**Figure 39**).

NOTE
If necessary, replace the bearings before installing the seals.

11

3. Clean the seal bore.

4. Inspect unshielded bearings for proper lubrication. If necessary, clean and repack the bearings while installed in the hub.

5. On the left side, install the retainer by aligning its raised arms with the two notches in the hub (**Figure 39**).

6. Pack grease into the lip of the new seal.

7. Place the seal in the bore with the closed side of the seal facing out. The seal must be square in the bore

8. Use a seal driver or socket to install the seal in the bore. Install the seal until it is flush with the top of the hub bore surface. Refer to **Figure 40** (left side) and **Figure 41** (right side).

> *CAUTION*
> *When installing the seals, the edge of the driver must fit at the perimeter of the seal. If the driver outside diameter is significantly smaller than that of the seal, the driver presses against the center of the seal and damages it.*

Bearing Replacement Tools

The wheel bearings are installed with a slight press fit and can be removed with or without special tools. The tools described in this section prevent damage to the hub bore.

1. Motion Pro Bearing Remover Set (**Figure 42**)—This tool uses a remover head (split collet) that can be wedged against the inner bearing race. The bearing can then be driven from the hub using a driver rod (**Figure 43**). The set includes the following remover head sizes: 10, 12, 15, 17, 20 and 25 mm and two driver rods. The remover heads and driver rods can also be purchased separately. To do so, select the 20 mm remover head and the large driver rod. The complete bearing remover set or the individual sizes can be ordered through most motorcycle dealerships.

2. Wheel bearing removal with common shop tools—This method requires a propane torch, driver and hammer to remove the bearings.

Removal

This section describes removal of the wheel bearings from the front (**Figure 36**) and rear (**Figure 37**) hubs. If the bearings are intact, one of the removal

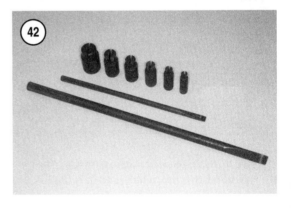

methods described in this section may be used. To remove a bearing where the inner race assembly has fallen out, refer to Step 4.

> *CAUTION*
> *In the following procedure, do not allow the front wheel to rest on the brake disc. Support the wheel with wooden blocks.*

1. Remove the seals as described in this section.

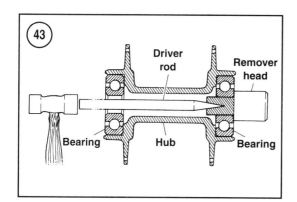

2. Examine the wheel bearings for excessive damage, especially the inner race. If the inner race of one bearing is damaged, remove the other bearing first. If both bearings are damaged, select the bearing with the least amount of damage and remove it first. On rusted and damaged bearings, applying pressure against the inner race can cause the inner race to pop out, leaving the outer race in the hub.

WARNING
Wear safety glasses when removing the bearings in the following steps.

NOTE
Step 3 describes two methods of removing the wheel bearings. Step 3A requires the use of the Motion Pro Bearing Remover Set. Step 3B describes steps on how to remove the bearings with common hand tools.

3A. Remove the wheel bearings with the Motion Pro Bearing Remover Set (**Figure 42**) as follows:
  a. Select the correct size remover head tool and insert it into one of the hub bearings (**Figure 44**).
  b. From the opposite side of the hub, insert the driver into the slot in the backside of the remover head. Position the hub with the remover head tool resting against a solid surface and strike the driver to wedge it firmly in the remover head (**Figure 43**).
  c. Position the hub so the remover head is free to move and the driver can be struck again.
  d. Strike the driver (**Figure 45**) as required to force the bearing (**Figure 46**) from the hub. Then release the driver from the remover head and remove the first bearing and distance collar.
  e. Repeat the procedure to remove the opposite bearing.

3B. Remove the wheel bearings with a hammer, drift and propane torch as follows:

WARNING
This procedure requires the use of a propane torch to heat the hub. Work in a well-ventilated area away from combustible materials. Wear protective clothing, including eye protection and insulated gloves. Refer to Chapter One.

a. Clean all lubricants from the hub.

b. Heat the hub around the bearing to be removed. Work the torch in a circular motion around the hub, taking care not to hold the torch in one area. Turn the wheel over and remove the bearing as described in the following steps.

c. Tilt the distance collar away from one side of the bearing with a long driver (**Figure 47**).

CAUTION
Do not damage the distance collar when removing the bearing. If there is not enough room to tilt the distance collar away from the bearing, grind a clearance groove in the driver to allow it to contact the bearing while clearing the distance collar.

CAUTION
The bearing must be removed evenly to prevent it from binding into and damaging the hub bearing bore. Reheat the hub as required.

d. Tap around the inner bearing race to remove the bearing. Make several passes until the bearing is removed evenly from the hub. Do not allow the bearing to bind in the bore.

e. Remove the distance collar from the hub.

f. Turn the hub over and heat the opposite side.

g. Drive out the opposite bearing using a large socket or bearing driver placed on the bearing's outer race.

h. Inspect the distance collar for burrs created during removal. Remove burrs with a file.

4. When damaged wheel bearings remain in use, the inner race can break apart, leaving the outer race pressed in the hub. Removal is difficult because only a small part of the race is accessible above the hub's shoulder, leaving little material to drive against. To remove a bearing's outer race under these conditions, first heat the hub evenly with a propane torch. Drive out the outer race with a driver and hammer. It may be necessary to grind a clearance tip on the end of the driver, to avoid damaging the hub bore. Check before heating the hub. Remove the race evenly by applying force at different points around the race. Do not allow the race to bind in its bore. After removing the race, inspect the hub mounting bore for cracks or other damage.

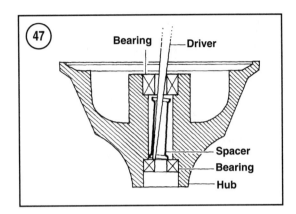

Inspection

1. Clean and dry the interior of the hub.

2. Check the hub bearing bore for cracks or other damage. If a bearing fits loosely in the hub bore (no longer a press fit), replace the hub.

3. Inspect the distance collar for corrosion and damage. Clean the bore of all corrosion and other debris. Check the ends for cracks or other damage. Do not try to repair the distance collar by cutting or grinding its end surfaces as this shortens the distance collar. Replace the distance collar if one or both ends are damaged.

CAUTION
The distance collar operates against both wheel bearing inner races to prevent them from moving inward when the axle is tightened. If a distance collar is too short or if it is not installed, the inner bearing races move inward and bind on the axle when the axle nut is tightened. This can damage the bearings and the bearing bores in the hub.

Installation

1. Before installing the new bearings and seals, note the following:

a. Install both bearings with their closed sides facing out. If a bearing is sealed on both sides, install the bearing with its manufacturer's marks facing out. If a shield is installed on one side of the bearing, the shield faces out.

b. Apply waterproof grease to bearings that are not lubricated by the manufacturer or that are not sealed on both sides. Work the grease into the cavities between the balls and races.

c. Always support the bottom side of the hub, near the bore when installing bearings.

WARNING
This procedure requires the use of a propane torch to heat the hub. Work in a well-ventilated area away from combustible materials. Wear protective clothing, including eye protection and insulated gloves.

2. Heat the hub around the bearing bore with a propane torch.

3. Place the first bearing squarely against the bore opening with its closed side facing out.

4. Place a driver or socket over the bearing (**Figure 48**). The driver should seat against the bearing's outer race. Drive the bearing into the hub until it bottoms.

5. Turn the hub over and install the distance collar.

6. Position the opposite bearing squarely against the bore opening and drive the bearing partway into the bearing bore. Make sure the distance collar is centered in the hub. If not, install the axle through the hub to align the distance collar with the bearing. Then remove the axle and continue installing the bearing until it bottoms.

7. Insert the axle though the hub and turn it by hand. Check for any roughness or binding, indicating bearing damage.

NOTE
If the axle does not go in, the distance collar is not aligned correctly with one of the bearings.

8. Install the seals as previously described.

WHEEL SERVICE

Component Condition

Inspect the wheels regularly for lateral (side-to-side) and radial (up-and-down) runout, even spoke tension and visible rim damage. When a wheel has a noticeable wobble, it is out of true. This is usually caused by loose spokes, but it can be caused by a damaged hub or rim.

Truing a wheel corrects the lateral and radial runout to bring the wheel back into specification. The condition of the individual wheel components affects the ability to successfully true the wheel. Note the following:

1. Spoke condition—Do not true a wheel with bent or damaged spokes. Doing so places an excessive amount of tension on the spokes, hub and rim. Overtightening the spoke may damage the spoke nipple hole in the hub or rim. It can also cause the spokes to be drawn through the rim and possibly puncture the tube. Inspect for and replace damaged spokes.

2. Nipple condition—When truing the wheels the nipples must turn freely on the spoke. However, corroded and rusted spoke threads are common and difficult to adjust. Spray a penetrating liquid onto the nipple and allow sufficient time for it to penetrate before trying to turn the nipples. Turn the spoke wrench in both directions and continue to apply penetrating liquid. If the spoke wrench rounds off the nipple, it is necessary to remove the tire from the rim and cut the spoke(s) out of the wheel.

3. Rim condition—Minor rim runout can be corrected by truing the wheel. However, do not correct rim damage by overtightening the spokes. Inspect the rims for cracks, flat spots or dents. Check the spoke holes for cracks or elongation. Replace damaged rims and hubs.

Wheel Truing Preliminaries

Before checking the runout and truing the wheel, note the following:

1. Make sure the wheel bearings are in good condition.

2. Check each spoke hole on both sides of the hub for cracks.

3. Check runout by mounting a pointer against the fork or swing arm and slowly rotating the wheel. A truing stand can also be used.

11

4. Use the correct size spoke wrench. Using the wrong type of tool or incorrect size spoke wrench may round off the spoke nipples, making adjustment difficult.

Tightening Loose Spokes

This section describes steps for checking and tightening loose spokes without affecting the wheel runout. When many spokes are loose and the wheel is running out of true, refer to *Wheel Truing Procedure* in this section.

1. Support the wheel so it can turn freely.

2. Spokes can be checked for looseness by one of three ways:

    a. Spoke torque wrench: A number of different spoke torque wrenches are available. When using a spoke torque wrench, the correct torque specification is 4 N•m (35 in.-lb.).

    b. Hand check: Grasp and squeeze two spokes where they cross (**Figure 49**). Loose spokes can be flexed by hand. Tight spokes feel stiff with little noticeable movement. Tighten the spokes until the tension between the different spoke groups feels the same.

    c. Spoke tone: Tapping a spoke causes it to vibrate and produce sound waves. Loose and tight spokes produce different sounds or tones. A tight spoke rings. A loose spoke has a soft or dull ring. Tap each spoke with a spoke wrench or screwdriver (**Figure 50**) to identify loose spokes.

3. Check the spokes using one of the methods described in Step 2. If there are loose spokes, spin the wheel and note the following:

    a. If the wheel is running true, continue with Step 4 to tighten the loose spokes.

    b. If the wheel is running out of true, go to *Wheel Truing Procedure* to measure runout and to true the wheel.

4. Use tape and divide the rim into four equally spaced sections. Number the sections as shown in **Figure 51**.

5. Start by tightening the loose spokes in Section 1, then in sections 2, 3 and 4. Do not turn each spoke more than 1/4 to 1/2 turn at a time. Doing so overtightens the spokes and brings the wheel out of true. Work slowly while checking spoke tightness. Continue until all the spokes are tightened evenly.

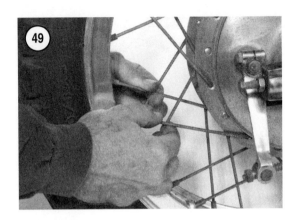

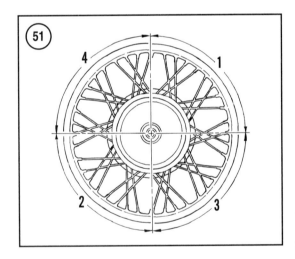

NOTE
If the spokes are hard to turn, spray penetrating oil into the top of the nipple. Wipe excess oil from the rim.

6. When all of the spokes are tightened evenly, spin the wheel. If there is any noticeable runout, true the wheel as described in the following procedure.

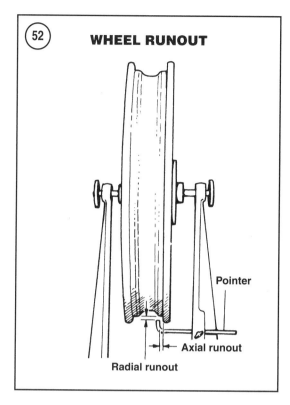

(52) **WHEEL RUNOUT**

Pointer

Axial runout

Radial runout

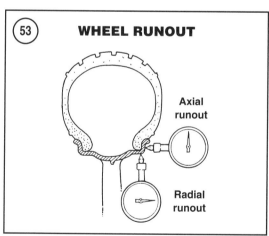

(53) **WHEEL RUNOUT**

Axial runout

Radial runout

Wheel Truing Procedure

Table 1 lists axial (side-to-side) and radial (up-and-down) runout specifications.

1. Clean the rim, spokes and nipples.

2. Position a pointer against the rim as shown in **Figure 52**. If the tire is mounted on the rim, position the pointer as shown in **Figure 53**.

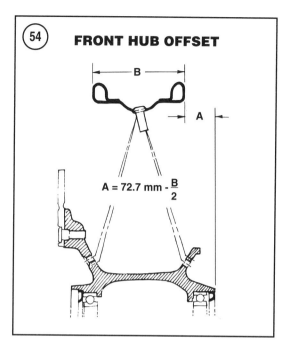

(54) **FRONT HUB OFFSET**

B

A

$$A = 72.7 \text{ mm} - \frac{B}{2}$$

3. Spin the wheel slowly and check the axial and radial runout. If the rim is out of adjustment, continue with Step 4.

> *NOTE*
> *It is normal for the rim to jump at the point where the rim was welded together. Also small cuts and dings in the rim affect the runout reading, especially when using a dial indicator.*

4. Spray penetrating oil into the top of each nipple. Wipe excess oil from the rim.

> *NOTE*
> *If the runout is minimal, the tire can be left on the rim. However, if the runout is excessive or if the rim must be centered with the hub (Step 5), remove the tire from the rim.*

5. If there are a large number of loose spokes or if some or all of the spokes were replaced, check the hub to rim offset as shown in **Figure 54** (front) or **Figure 55** (rear). If necessary, reposition the hub when truing the wheel.

6. Lateral runout adjustment: If the side-to-side runout is out of specification, adjust the wheel. For example, to pull the rim to the left side (**Figure 56**), tighten the spokes on the left side of the hub (at the runout point) and loosen the adjacent spokes on the

right side of the hub. Always loosen and tighten the spokes in equal number of turns.

NOTE
Determining the number of spokes to loosen and tighten depends on how far the runout is out of adjustment. Loosen two or three spokes, then tighten the opposite two or three spokes. If the runout is excessive and affects a greater area along the rim, loosen and tighten a greater number of spokes.

7. Radial runout adjustment: If the up and down runout is out of specification, the hub is not centered in the rim. Draw the high point of the rim toward the centerline of the wheel by tightening the spokes in the area of the high point and loosening the spokes on the side opposite the high point (**Figure 57**). Tighten the spokes in equal amounts to prevent distortion.

NOTE
Alternate between checking and adjusting axial and radial runout. Remember, changing spoke tension on one side of the rim affects the tension on the other side of the rim.

8. After truing the wheel, seat each spoke in the hub by tapping it with a flat nose punch and hammer. Then recheck the spoke tension and wheel runout. Readjust if necessary as described under *Tightening Loose Spokes* in this section.

9. Check the ends of the spokes where they are threaded in the nipples. Grind off any ends that protrude through the nipples to prevent them from puncturing the tube.

TIRE SAFETY

Tire wear and performance are greatly affected by tire pressure. Have a good tire gauge on hand and make a habit of frequent pressure checks. Refer to Chapter Three.

Follow a sensible break-in period when running on new tires. New tires exhibit significantly less adhesion ability. Do not subject a new tire to hard corning, hard acceleration or hard braking for the first 100 miles (160 km). If possible, find a large,

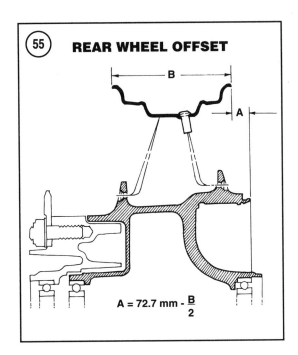

(55) **REAR WHEEL OFFSET**

$$A = 72.7 \text{ mm} - \frac{B}{2}$$

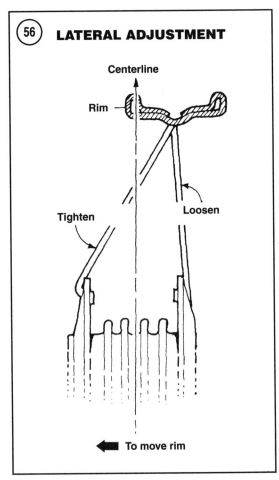

(56) **LATERAL ADJUSTMENT**

Centerline

Rim

Loosen

Tighten

To move rim

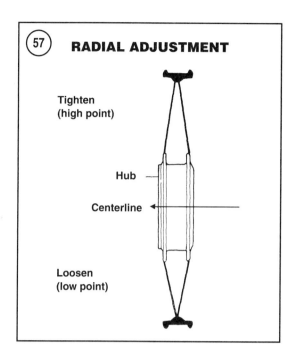

RADIAL ADJUSTMENT

Tighten
(high point)

Hub

Centerline

Loosen
(low point)

raised platform. A popular item used
by many home mechanics is a metal
drum. Before placing the wheel on a
drum, cover the drum edge with a
length of garden hose, split length-
wise and secured in place with plastic
ties. When changing the front tire at
ground level, support the wheel on
two wooden blocks to prevent the
brake disc from contacting the floor.

NOTE
Warming the tire makes it softer and
more pliable. Place the tire and wheel
assembly in the sun or in a completely
closed automobile. Place the new tire
in the same location.

1. Remove the valve core and deflate the tire.
2. Press the entire bead on both sides of the tire into
the center of the rim. If necessary, step on the sidewall, and not the rim, to break the bead. Check that
the beads are free on both sides of the rim.
3. Lubricate the beads on both sides of the tire with
soapy water or a tire lubricant.

NOTE
Use rim protectors (**Figure 58**) or insert scraps of leather between the tire
iron and the rim to protect the rim
from damage.

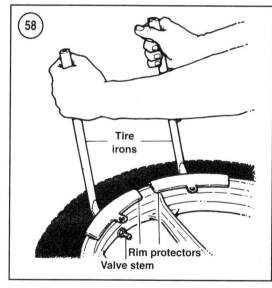

Tire
irons

Rim protectors
Valve stem

deserted parking area and scuff in the new tires
without having to ride in traffic.

4. Insert the first tire iron under the bead on the opposite side of the valve stem. Force the bead into the
center of the rim, and then pry the bead over the rim
with the tire iron (**Figure 59**).
5. Insert a second tire iron next to the first to hold the
bead over the rim (**Figure 60**). While holding the tire
with one tire iron, work around the tire with the second tire iron, prying the tire over the rim and working

TIRE CHANGING

Removal

NOTE
It is easier to replace tires when the
wheel is mounted on some type of

11

in small bites of one to two inches at a time. Be careful not to pinch the inner tube with the tire irons.

> *CAUTION*
> *If it is difficult to pry the bead over the rim with the second tire iron, stop and make sure the bottom bead was broken from the rim. Excessive force splits and tears the tire bead and causes permanent tire damage.*

> *CAUTION*
> *If the tube is being removed to fix a flat, identify the tube's installed position in the tire immediately after removing it to help locate the foreign object in the tire.*

6. When the upper bead is free of the rim, remove the inner tube from the tire (**Figure 61**).

7. Stand the tire upright and pry the second tire bead (**Figure 62**) over the rim. Then peel the tire off the rim by hand. If necessary, use a second tire iron.

Inspection

1. Inspect the tire for damage. If the tube was leaking air, pump air into it to locate the leak. Then place the tube on top of the tire, facing in its original position, to help locate the object in the tire. Remove the object and check the tire for damage.

> *NOTE*
> *Cracks in the inner tire liner can pinch and damage the tube. If the tube is leaking air, but there are no foreign objects in the tire, spread the tire and check the inner liner for cracks.*

2. Run a rag through the inside of the tire to locate any protruding objects. Do not use bare hands.

> *WARNING*
> *Carefully consider whether a tire should be replaced. If there is any doubt about the condition of the existing tire, replace it with a new one. Do not take a chance on a tire failure at any speed.*

3. If any one of the following is observed, replace the tire with a new one:

    a. A noticeable puncture or split.

    b. A scratch or split on the sidewall or along the inner liner.

    c. Any type of ply separation.

    d. Tread separation or abnormal wear pattern.

    e. Tread depth of less than the minimum value specified in **Table 1** for original equipment tires. The minimum depth on aftermarket tires may vary. Refer to the tire manufacturer's information.

    f. Scratches on either sealing bead.

    g. The cord is cut in any place.

    h. Flat spots in the tread from skidding.

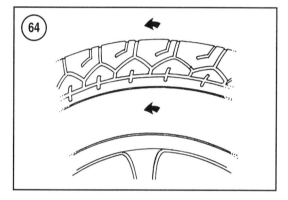

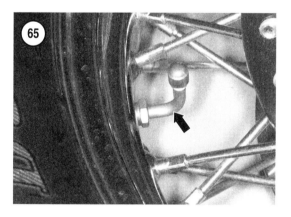

i. Any abnormality in the inner liner.

4. If the tire can be reused, clean and dry the inside of the tire with compressed air.

5. Remove the rim strap from the center of the rim. Replace if damaged.

6. Use a brush to clean dirt, rust and rubber from the inside of the rim.

7. Inspect the spokes (**Figure 63**) for rust and corrosion. Then check for any spoke ends that protrude above the nipple head and into the center of the rim.

Grind or file the exposed part of the spoke flush with the nipple.

8. Check the valve stem hole in the rim for any roughness or cuts that could damage the valve stem. Remove any roughness with a file.

9. Mount the wheel onto a truing stand and check runout before mounting the tire.

10. If possible, install a new tube. If not, inflate the original tube to make sure it was not punctured during tire removal. However, discard the tube if it has been previously patched or if it appears balancing liquids were introduced into the tube. Check the inner nut on the valve stem to make sure it is tight. Check the area around the valve stem for cracks and other weak spots.

Installation

NOTE
Installation is easier if the tire is pliable. This can be achieved by warming the tire in the sun or inside an enclosed automobile.

1. Install the rim band around the rim by aligning the hole in the band with the hole in the rim.
2. When installing the tire on the rim, make sure the correct tire, either front or rear, is installed on the correct wheel. Also install the tire with the direction arrow facing the normal direction of wheel rotation (**Figure 64**).

CAUTION
Use a tire lubricant when installing the tire over the rim and when seating the beads. Use a commercial tire lubricant, if available. Plain or soapy water can also be used. Do not use Teflon and WD-40 aerosol spray lubes and other petroleum chemicals as a tire lubricant. These lubricants stay on the tire beads without drying out and can cause the tire to slip on the rim and damage the valve stem. Some chemicals also damage the rubber.

NOTE
*The rear tire uses an angled valve stem (**Figure 65**) that must face toward the right side of the wheel when installed. When installing the rear tire, begin by positioning the wheel with the brake drum side facing up.*

3. Sprinkle the tube with talcum powder and install it into the tire (**Figure 66**). The powder minimizes tube chafing and helps the tube distribute itself when inflated.

4. Inflate the tube to shape it against the tire. Then bleed most of the air from the tube. Too much air makes tire installation difficult and too little air increases the chance of pinching the tube.

5. Most tires are marked with a colored spot near the bead that indicates a lighter point on the tire. Align this spot with the valve stem hole in the rim (**Figure 67**).

6. Lubricate the lower bead. Then start pushing the lower bead over the rim while inserting the air valve through the hole in the rim (**Figure 68**). Install the nut onto the valve stem to prevent the stem from sliding back into the tire.

7. Continue to push the lower bead over the rim by hand-fitting it as much as possible. The last part of the bead is the most difficult to install. If necessary, grasp the spokes to steady the wheel and push the front part of the tire toward the inside of the rim with your knees. This may provide additional room at the back of the bead to help with its installation. If it is necessary to use a tire lever, use it carefully to avoid pinching the tube or tearing the tire bead.

8. When the lower bead is installed over the rim, turn the wheel over and check that the tube is not pinched between the bead and rim. If so, carefully push the tube back into the center of the tire by hand.

9. Turn the wheel back over and lift the upper bead to check the tube. Make sure the tube is laying evenly around the tire. If necessary, inflate the tube to remove any wrinkles, then bleed most of the air from the tube.

10. Turn the tire so the air valve is straight up (front tire) or angled as shown in **Figure 65** (rear tire). Also, check that the tire weight mark identified in Step 5 aligns with the valve stem hole in the rim (**Figure 67**).

NOTE
Properly aligning the tire weight mark with the valve stem hole helps to reduce the amount of weight required to balance the tire.

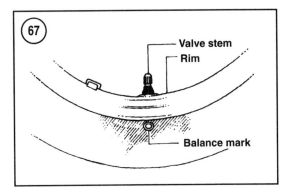

NOTE
*Do not use excessive force when using the tire irons to install the upper tire bead. Instead, use your knees to push the front part of the tire (the part closest to you) toward the inside of the rim and to keep the lower bead positioned in the **center** of the rim. Forcing the tire irons between the upper bead and rim because the lower bead is not properly positioned can damage the rim, cut the tire bead and pinch the tube.*

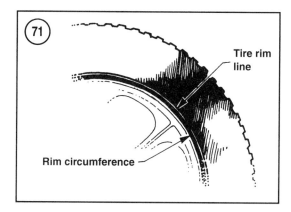

Tire rim line

Rim circumference

11. Lubricate the upper tire bead, and then start installation opposite the valve stem (**Figure 69**). If necessary, relubricate the bead. Use the tire irons to pry the remaining section of bead over the rim (**Figure 70**). Remember to keep the lower bead positioned in the center of the rim when installing the upper bead.

12. When both beads are installed over the rim, perform the following:

a. Check the bead for uniform fit on both sides of the tire.

b. Check both sides of the tire for any part of the tube that is pinched between the tire bead and rim. Lift the tire and carefully push the tube back into the tire.

c. Turn the tire so the air valve is straight up and the tire weight mark (**Figure 67**) aligns with the valve stem hole.

> *WARNING*
> *Special care must be taken when inflating the tire and seating the tire beads in the next step. Never exceed 300 kPa (43.5 psi) inflation pressure because the tire could burst, causing injury. If the tire does not seat at the recommended pressure, do not continue by overinflating the tire. Doing so could cause the tire to burst and cause injury. Deflate the tire and repeat the procedure. The safest way to inflate the tire is to use a clamp-on air chuck and a remote air gauge/inflator. Wear safety glasses and stand as far away from the tire as possible. Never stand directly over a tire while inflating it.*

13. Lubricate both beads. Use a clamp-on air chuck and inflate the tire to seat the beads on the rim. Do not exceed 43.5 psi (300 kPa).

14. After inflating the tire, check to see that the beads are fully seated and that the rim lines are the same distance from the rim all the way around the tire (**Figure 71**). If not, deflate the tire and repeat the procedure.

15. When the beads are correctly seated, deflate the tire (but do not break the tire beads). Inflate the tire again to help stretch the tube and seat it fully against the tire. Set the tire to the required tire pressure listed in **Table 3**. Tighten the outer valve stem nut (**Figure 72**) and the valve stem cap.

16. Balance the tire and wheel assembly as described in this chapter.

WHEEL BALANCE

A wheel that is not balanced is unsafe because it seriously affects the steering and handling of the motorcycle. Depending on the degree of unbalance and the speed of the motorcycle, anything from a mild vibration to a violent shimmy may occur, which may result in loss of control. An imbalanced wheel also causes abnormal tire wear.

11

Motorcycle wheels can be checked for balance either statically (single plane balance) or dynamically (dual plane balance). This section describes how to static balance the wheels using a wheel balancing stand. To obtain a higher degree of accuracy, take both wheels to a dealership and have them balanced with a two plane computer dynamic wheel balancer. This machine spins the wheel to accurately detect any imbalance.

Balance weights are used to balance the wheel and are attached to the spokes (**Figure 73**). Weight kits are available from motorcycle dealerships.

The wheel must be able to rotate freely when checking wheel balance. Because excessively worn or damaged wheel bearings affect the accuracy of this procedure, check the wheel bearings as described in this chapter. Also confirm that the tire balance mark, a paint mark on the tire, is aligned with the valve stem (**Figure 67**).

NOTE
Leave the brake disc mounted on the front wheel when checking and adjusting wheel balance.

1. Remove the wheel as described in this chapter.
2. Clean the seals and inspect the wheel bearings as described in this chapter.
3. Clean the tire, rim and spokes. Remove any stones or pebbles stuck in the tire tread.
4A. Mount the front wheel (with brake disc attached) on a balance stand (**Figure 74**).
4B. Mount the rear wheel (with driven flange assembly and sprocket) on a balance stand (**Figure 74**).

NOTE
To check the original balance of the wheel, leave the original weights attached to the spokes.

5. Spin the wheel by hand and let it coast to a stop. Mark the tire at its bottom point with chalk.
6. Spin the wheel several more times. If the same spot on the tire stops at the bottom each time, the wheel is out of balance. This is the heaviest part of the tire. When an unbalanced wheel is spun, it always comes to rest with the heaviest spot at the bottom.
7. Attach a test weight to the wheel at the point opposite the heaviest spot and spin the wheel again.
8. Experiment with different weights until the wheel, when spun, comes to rest at a different posi-

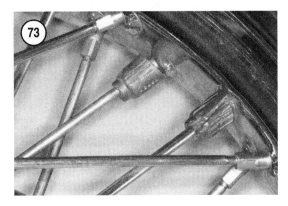

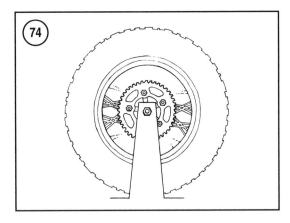

tion each time. When a wheel is correctly balanced, the weight of the tire and wheel assembly is distributed equally around the wheel.

9. Remove the test weight and install the correct size weight or weights to the rim. Crimp the weight tightly against the spoke and nipple (**Figure 73**).

NOTE
Do not exceed 60 grams (2.1 oz.) to the front wheel or 70 grams (2.5 oz.) to the rear wheel. If a wheel requires

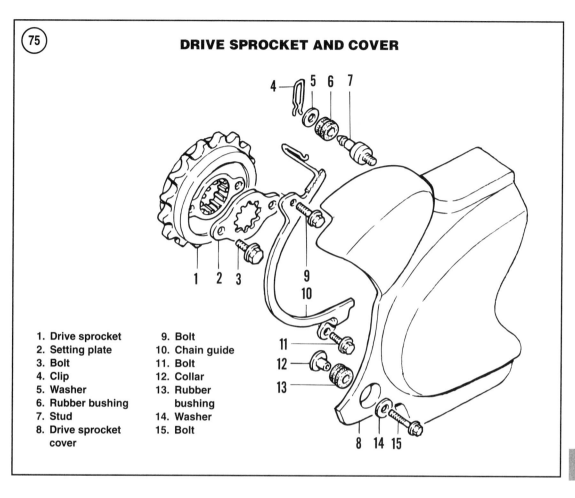

DRIVE SPROCKET AND COVER

1. Drive sprocket
2. Setting plate
3. Bolt
4. Clip
5. Washer
6. Rubber bushing
7. Stud
8. Drive sprocket cover
9. Bolt
10. Chain guide
11. Bolt
12. Collar
13. Rubber bushing
14. Washer
15. Bolt

an excessive amount of weight, make sure the weight mark on the tire aligns with the valve stem.

10. Record the weight, number and position of the weights in the maintenance log at the end of the manual. Then, if the motorcycle experiences a handling or vibration problem in the future, check for any missing balance weights as previously recorded.

11. Install the wheel as described in this chapter.

DRIVE AND DRIVEN SPROCKETS

This section describes service procedures on replacing the drive (front) and driven (rear) sprockets. Refer to **Table 4** for the sprocket sizes.

Inspection

Refer to *Drive Chain* in Chapter Three.

Drive Sprocket Removal

Refer to **Figure 75**.

1. Support the motorcycle with the rear wheel off the ground.
2. Remove the drive sprocket cover as follows:
   a. From the top, inside of the drive sprocket cover, remove the clip and washer (**Figure 76**).
   b. Remove the bolt and washer from the outside of the cover (A, **Figure 77**).
   c. Remove the drive sprocket cover (B, **Figure 77**). Locate the collar (12, **Figure 75**), installed on the inside of the cover to prevent its loss.
3. Loosen the rear axle nut (A, **Figure 78**).

4. Loosen the chain adjuster bolts (B, **Figure 78**) and push the rear wheel forward until maximum chain slack is obtained.

5. Remove the pinch bolt (A, **Figure 79**) and the gearshift arm (B).

6. Remove the drive sprocket mounting bolts (C, **Figure 79**). Turn and remove the setting plate (D) from the countershaft.

7. Slide the drive sprocket (E, **Figure 79**) off the countershaft and remove it from the drive chain.

8. If necessary, unbolt and remove the chain guide (A, **Figure 80**). Remove the wiring harness from the holder (B, **Figure 80**) at the top of the guide.

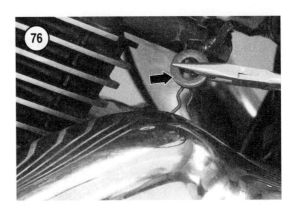

Drive Sprocket Installation

1. If removed, install the chain guide (A, **Figure 80**) and tighten its mounting bolts to 12 N•m (106 in.-lb.). Secure the wiring harness in the holder (B).

2. Install the drive chain onto the drive sprocket with its manufacturer's marks facing out. Then install the drive sprocket (E, **Figure 79**) onto the countershaft.

3. Install the setting plate (D, **Figure 79**) over the countershaft, and then turn and align its bolt holes with the two holes in the drive sprocket.

4. Install the drive sprocket bolts (C, **Figure 79**) and tighten to 10 N•m (88 in.-lb.).

5. Install the gearshift arm onto the shift shaft by aligning the slot in the arm with the punch mark on the shaft (**Figure 81**).

6. Install the gearshift arm pinch bolt (A, **Figure 79**) and tighten to 12 N•m (106 in.-lb.).

7. If removed, install the collar (12, **Figure 75**) into the bushing in the cover.

8. Install the drive sprocket cover (B, **Figure 77**), washer and mounting bolt (A). Tighten the mounting bolt to 12 N•m (106 in.-lb.).

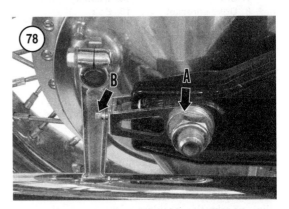

9. Install the washer and clip (**Figure 76**) onto the upper drive sprocket cover stud. After installing the clip, turn it clockwise behind the cover.

10. Adjust the drive chain and tighten the rear axle nut as described in Chapter Three.

Driven Sprocket
Removal/Installation

The driven sprocket is mounted onto the driven flange.

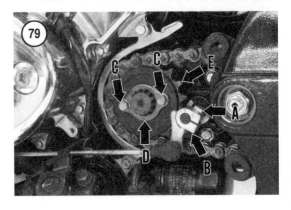

1. Support the motorcycle on a stand with the rear wheel off the ground.

2. Have an assistant apply the rear brake, and then loosen the driven sprocket nuts.

3. Remove the rear wheel as described in this chapter.

4. Remove the driven sprocket nuts and sprocket (**Figure 82**).

5. Installation is the reverse for removal. Note the following:

a. Install the driven sprocket with its stamped sprocket number side facing out.
b. Replace damaged sprocket nuts.
c. Tighten the driven sprocket nuts to 88 N•m (65 ft.-lb.).

DRIVE CHAIN

Refer to **Table 4** for drive chain specifications. Refer to *Drive Chain* in Chapter Three for routine drive chain inspection and lubrication procedures.

This section describes how to replace the drive chain with the swing arm mounted on the motorcycle.

Removal/Installation

To remove the drive chain without disconnecting it, perform the following:

1. Remove the swing arm as described in Chapter Thirteen.

2. Remove the drive sprocket as described in this chapter.

3. Remove the drive chain.

4. Installation is the reverse of removal.

Replacement

All models use an O-ring type drive chain with a staked master link (**Figure 83**). The drive chain can be replaced with the swing arm mounted on the motorcycle. The following section describes chain replacement using the Motion Pro Jumbo Chain Tool (part No. 08-0135 [**Figure 84**]). This and other tools like it can break roller chains up to No. 630 and rivet chain sizes up to No. 530. Always follow the manufacturer's instructions provided with the tool. Use the following steps to supplement the instructions provided with the chain tool.

1. Support the motorcycle with the rear wheel off the ground.

2. Loosen the rear axle nut (A, **Figure 78**).

3. Loosen the chain adjuster bolts (B, **Figure 78**) and push the rear wheel forward until maximum chain slack is obtained.

4. Assemble the extractor bolt onto the body bolt. Turn the extractor bolt until its pins are withdrawn into the pin guide chain tool, following the manufacturer's instructions.

11

5. Turn the chain to locate the crimped pin ends on the master link (**Figure 85**). Break the chain at this point.

> *NOTE*
> *When using a smaller chain breaker, grind the staked heads off the master link before attempting to break the chain.*

6. Install the chain tool across the master link, and then operate the tool and push the connecting link out of the side plate to break the chain. Remove the side plate, connecting the link and O-rings (**Figure 83**) and discard them.

> *WARNING*
> *Discard the connecting link, side plate and O-rings after removing them. Never reuse these parts because they could cause the chain to come apart and lock the rear wheel, causing a serious accident.*

> *NOTE*
> *Do not remove the old drive chain. Use it to pull the new chain around the drive sprocket.*

7. If installing a new drive chain, count the links of the new chain and if necessary, cut the chain to length as described under *Cutting A Drive Chain to Length* in this section. See **Table 4** for the original equipment chain sizes and lengths.

8. Connect the new chain to the old chain and pull the new chain around the drive sprocket, swing arm and driven sprocket. Disconnect the old chain and discard it.

> *NOTE*
> *Always install the drive chain around the swing arm before connecting and staking the master link.*

9. Assemble the new master link as follows:
   a. Install an O-ring on each connecting link pin (**Figure 83**).
   b. Insert the connecting link through the inside of the chain and connect both chain ends together.
   c. Install the remaining two O-rings (**Figure 83**) onto the connecting link pins.
   d. Install the side plate (**Figure 83**) with its identification mark facing out (away from chain).

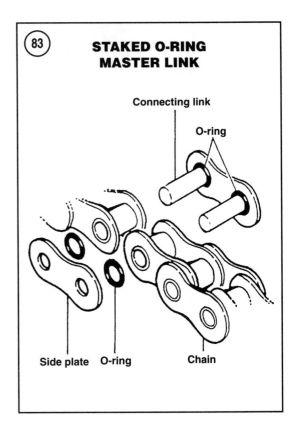

STAKED O-RING MASTER LINK

Connecting link

O-ring

Side plate   O-ring   Chain

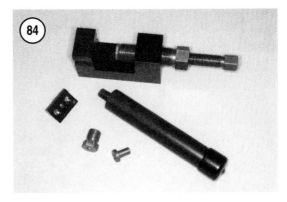

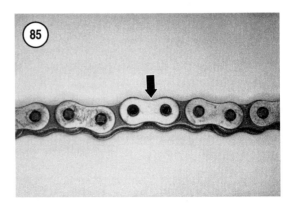

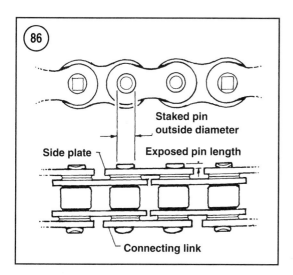

86

Staked pin
outside diameter

Side plate

Exposed pin length

Connecting link

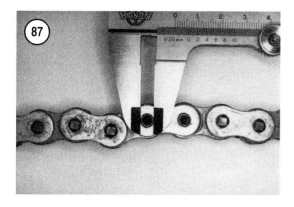

87

10. Stake each connecting link pin as follows:

NOTE
The master link specifications referred to in the following steps and listed in Table 4 are for the original equipment DID and RK drive chains installed on the VT750. If installing a different drive chain, refer to its manufacturer's specifications.

a. Measure the height of the exposed pin length from the outer side plate surface to the top of the connecting link (**Figure 86**). Refer to **Table 4** for the exposed pin length measurement. If the height measurement is incorrect, readjust the side plate's height position on the connecting link.

b. Assemble the chain tool onto the master link and carefully stake each connecting link pin end to the diameter (**Figure 86**) specified in **Table 4**. Work carefully and do not exceed

the specified outside diameter measurement. Measure with a vernier caliper (**Figure 87**).

NOTE
If the diameter of one pin end is out of specification, remove and discard the master link. Then install a new master link assembly.

11. Remove the chain tool and inspect the master link for any cracks or other damage. Check the staked area for cracks. Make sure the master link O-rings were not crushed. If there are any cracks on the staked link surfaces or other damage, remove the master link and install a new one.

12. If there are no cracks, pivot the chain ends where they hook onto the master link. Each chain end must pivot freely. Compare by pivoting other links of the chain. If one or both drive chain ends cannot pivot on the master link, the chain is too tight. Remove and install a *new* master link assembly.

WARNING
An incorrectly installed master link may cause the chain to come apart and lock the rear wheel, causing a serious accident. If the tools to safely rivet the chain together are not available, take it to a Honda dealership. Do not ride the motorcycle unless absolutely sure the master link is installed correctly.

13. Adjust the drive chain and tighten the rear axle nut as described in Chapter Three.

Cutting A Drive Chain To Length

Table 4 lists the correct number of chain links required for original equipment gearing. If the replacement drive chain is too long, cut it to length as follows.

1. Stretch the new chain on a workbench. Set the master link aside for now.

2. If installing a new chain over original gearing, rcfcr to **Tablc 4** for the correct number of links for the new chain. If sprocket sizes were changed, install the new chain over both sprockets, with the rear wheel moved forward to determine the correct number of links to remove. Make a chalk mark on the two chain pins to be cut. Count the chain links

11

one more time or check the chain length before cutting.

WARNING
Using a hand or bench grinder as described in Step 3 causes flying particles. Do not operate a grinding tool without proper eye protection.

3A. If using a chain breaker, use it to break the drive chain.

3B. If not using a chain tool, cut the chain as follows:

a. Grind the head of two pins flush with the face of the side plate with a grinder or suitable grinding tool.

b. Press the side plate out of the chain with a chain breaker. Support the chain carefully while doing this. If the pins are still tight, grind more material from the end of the pins and then try again.

c. Remove the side plate and push out the connecting link.

4. Install the new drive chain as described in this section.

Table 1 TIRE AND WHEEL SPECIFICATIONS

Tire size	
Front	
VT750C	120/90-17 64S
VT750DC	110/80-19 59S
Rear	
VT750C	170/80-15 M/C 77S
VT750DC	160/80-15 M/C 74S
Tire brands	
Front	
VT750C	Bridgestone G701
	Dunlop D404F
VT750DC	Bridgestone G515G
	Dunlop F24
Rear	
VT750C	Bridgestone G702
	Dunlop D404
VT750DC	Bridgestone G702
	Dunlop K425G
Minimum tire tread depth	1.5 mm (0.06 in.)

Table 2 WHEEL AND AXLE SERVICE SPECIFICATIONS

	Service Limit mm (in.)
Axle runout	0.20 (0.008)
Wheel runout	
Axial (side-to-side)	2.0 (0.08)
Radial (up-and-down)	2.0 (0.08)

Table 3 TIRE INFLATION PRESSURE

	Front psi (kpa)	Rear psi (kPa)
Up to 90 kg (200 lbs. Load)	29 (200)	29 (200)
Maximum weight capacity	29 (200)	36 (250)

Table 4 DRIVE CHAIN SPECIFICATIONS

Chain type	
VT750C	DID 525 V8
	RK 525 SM0Z5
VT750DC	RK SM0Z5
Master link	
Exposed pin length	1.2-1.4 mm (0.05-0.06 in.)
Staked pin diameter	5.50-5.80 mm (0.217-0.228 in.)
Number of links	
VT750C	122
VT750DC	
2001-2003	124
2004-on	122
Sprockets	
Number of teeth	
Drive sprocket	17
Driven sprocket	
VT750C	41
VT750DC	42

Table 5 WHEELS AND SPROCKET TORQUE SPECIFICATIONS

	N•m	in.-lb.	ft.-lb.
Chain guide bolts	12	106	–
Drive sprocket bolts	10	88	–
Drive sprocket cover bolt	12	106	–
Driven sprocket nuts	88	–	65
Front axle bolt or nut	59	–	44
Front axle pinch bolt	22	–	16
Gearshift arm pinch bolt	12	106	–
Rear axle nut	93	–	69
Rear brake stopper arm nut	20	–	15
Spokes	4	35	–

11

CHAPTER TWELVE

.

FRONT SUSPENSION AND STEERING

This chapter describes procedures for the repair and maintenance of the handlebar, front fork and steering components. Refer to Chapter Eleven for front wheel and tire service.

Front suspension and steering specifications are listed in **Tables 1-3** at the end of the chapter.

> *WARNING*
> *Replace all fasteners used on the front suspension and steering components with parts of the same type. Do not use a replacement part of lesser quality or substitute design. This may affect the performance of the system or cause failure of the part, which may lead to loss of control of the bike. The torque values specified must be used during installation to ensure proper retention of these parts.*

HANDLEBAR

Removal

1. Cover the fuel tank with a thick blanket to protect it from scratches and other damage.
2. Remove the left and right side mirrors.

3. Disconnect the clutch switch electrical connectors at the clutch switch (**Figure 1**).
4. Disconnect the clutch cable at the lever, if necessary.
5. Remove the two clutch lever bracket mounting bolts and remove the clutch bracket holder (A, **Figure 2**) and lever bracket.
6. Remove the two left handlebar switch housing screws (B, **Figure 2**). Then remove the end adapter (A, **Figure 3**) and separate the switch housing from around the handlebar.
7. Disconnect the front brake light switch connectors at the switch (**Figure 4**).

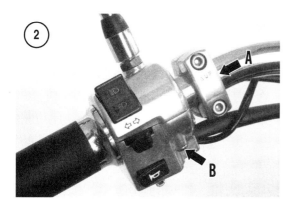

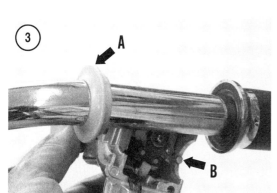

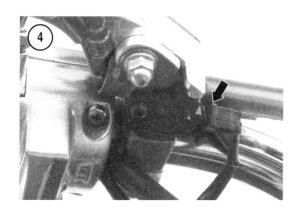

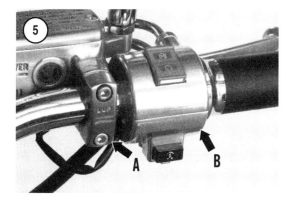

8. Remove the two master cylinder holder bolts and remove the holder and front master cylinder (A, **Figure 5**). Support the master cylinder upright so air does not enter the hydraulic system.

9. Remove the two right side handlebar switch housing screws and separate the switch housing (B, **Figure 5**) from around the handlebar.

10. Disconnect the throttle cables (A, **Figure 6**) from the throttle grip and slide the throttle grip off the handlebar.

NOTE
If the throttle cables are tight at the throttle grip and cannot be disconnected, disconnect them at the carburetor first. Refer to Chapter Eight.

11. If the handlebar lower holders (**Figure 7**) are going to be removed, loosen the lower holder mounting nuts while the handlebar is still mounted in place.

12. Remove the handlebar upper holder bolt caps, bolts and holders (**Figure 8**).

13. Remove the handlebar.

12

14. To remove the handlebar lower holders (**Figure 9**), perform the following:

   a. Identify the holders so they can be installed facing in their original direction.

   b. Remove the holder mounting nut from under the upper steering bracket, and then remove the bolt.

   c. Remove the handlebar lower holders and bushings.

   d. Repeat the procedure for the remaining lower holder.

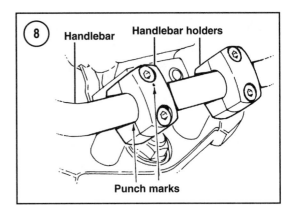

Installation

1. Clean and inspect the handlebar holders and bolts.

2. If removed, install the handlebar lower holders as follows:

   a. Install the bushings and the handlebar lower holder.

   b. Install the mounting bolt and nut and tighten finger-tight.

3. Install the handlebar as follows:

   a. Place the handlebar onto the lower holders.

   b. Install the upper holders with their punch marks facing forward (**Figure 8**).

   c. Install the handlebar holder mounting bolts and tighten finger-tight.

   d. Position the handlebar so the punch mark on the handlebar aligns with the gap between the holders as shown in **Figure 9**.

   e. Tighten the front handlebar holder bolts, and then the rear bolts to 23 N•m (17 ft.-lb.). Check there is not at gap at the front of the holders. The gap must be at the rear of the holders.

   f. Install the bolt caps.

4. If the handlebar lower holders were removed, tighten the mounting nuts as specified in **Table 3**.

5. Clean the inside of the throttle grip and the right side of the handlebar of all old grease. Relubricate lightly with grease. Lubricate the holes in the throttle grip with grease.

6. Install the right side handlebar switch housing as follows:

   a. Reconnect the two throttle cables (A, **Figure 6**) to the throttle grip.

   b. Align the switch housing locating pin (B, **Figure 6**) with the hole in the handlebar and

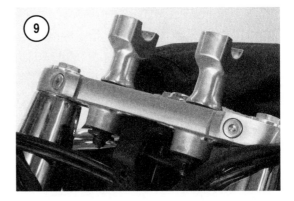

close the switch halves (B, **Figure 5**) around the handlebar and throttle grip.

   c. Install the front and rear switch housing screws and tighten securely.

7. Install the master cylinder as follows:

   a. Clean the handlebar, master cylinder and clamp mating surfaces.

   b. Mount the master cylinder onto the handlebar. Install its clamp (A, **Figure 5**) and both mounting bolts. Install the clamp with the UP mark facing up (A, **Figure 10**).

   c. Align the master cylinder and clamp mating halves with the punch mark (B, **Figure 10**) on the handlebar. Tighten the upper master cylinder clamp bolt first, and then the lower bolt to 12 N•m (106 in.-lb.).

8. Reconnect the front brake light switch connectors at the switch (**Figure 4**).

9. Install the left side handlebar switch housing as follows:

   a. Align the switch housing locating pin (B, **Figure 3**) with the hole in the handlebar and close the switch halves around the handlebar.

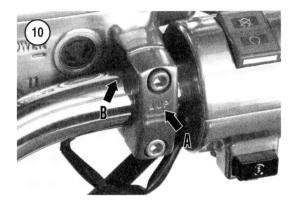

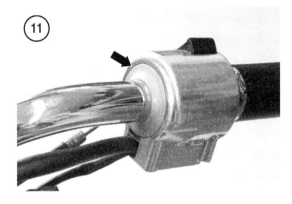

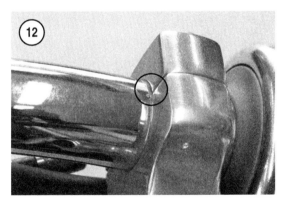

b. Slide the end adapter into the switch recess (**Figure 11**).

c. Install the front and rear switch housing screw. Tighten the front screw, then the rear screw securely.

10. Install the clutch lever brackct as follows:

a. Clean the handlebar, clutch lever bracket and holder mating surfaces.

b. Mount the clutch lever bracket onto the handlebar, and then install its clamp (A, **Figure**

2) and both mounting bolts. Install the clamp with the UP mark facing up.

c. Align the end of the clutch lever bracket with the punch mark on the handlebar (**Figure 12**). Then tighten the upper holder bolt first, and then the lower bolt securely.

d. Reconnect the electrical connectors at the clutch switch (**Figure 1**).

11. Install, adjust and tighten the mirrors.

12. If the throttle cable adjusters were loosened, adjust the throttle cables as described in Chapter Three.

13. If the clutch cable was disconnected, adjust the clutch as described in Chapter Three.

14. If air entered the front master cylinder brake line, bleed the front brake as described in Chapter Fourteen.

15. After all assemblies are installed, test each one to make sure it operates correctly. Correct any problem at this time.

WARNING
An improperly installed throttle grip assembly may cause the throttle to stick open. Failure to properly assemble and adjust the throttle cables and throttle grip could cause steering control loss. Do not start or ride the motorcycle until the throttle grip is installed correctly and snaps back when released.

12

HANDLEBAR GRIPS AND WEIGHTS

Inspection

The handlebar grips must be secured tightly to the left handlebar and to the throttle grip (right side). Replace cut or damaged grips because water may enter between the grip and its mounting surface and cause the grip to slip. This could cause a loss of steering control. Replace the handlebar grips as described in the following procedure.

Replacement

1A. On the left hand grip, remove the clutch holder and left handlebar switch as described under *Handlebar* in this chapter.

1B. On the right hand grip, remove the throttle grip as described under *Handlebar* in this chapter.

2. Measure the distance from the inside of the right grip to the cable flange on the throttle sleeve (**Figure 13**). This gap must be maintained to prevent the grip from contacting the switch housing.

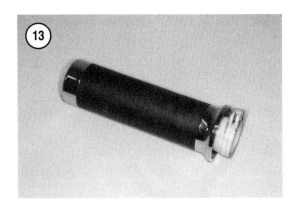

> *CAUTION*
> *If reusing the hand grips, remove them carefully to avoid damaging them.*

3. Insert a thin blade screwdriver between the grip and handlebar or throttle sleeve and spray electrical contact cleaner into the open gap (**Figure 14**). Quickly turn the grip to break the cement bond and slide it off (**Figure 15**).

4. If reusing the grips, use an electrical contact cleaner to remove all cement residue from inside the grips.

> *WARNING*
> *If the original hand grips are torn or damaged, install new grips.*

5. Remove all sealant residue from the handlebar or throttle sleeve.

6. To replace the handlebar weight, perform the following:

 a. Squeeze the lock arms on the end of the handlebar weight (**Figure 16**) and pull the weight assembly from the handlebar. Refer to **Figure 17**.

 b. Inspect the handlebar weight for damage. Replace if necessary.

 c. Slide the handlebar weight into the handlebar with the lock arms facing out (**Figure 17**).

 d. Position the weight so the lock arms spring out and lock into the holes in the handlebar (**Figure 18**).

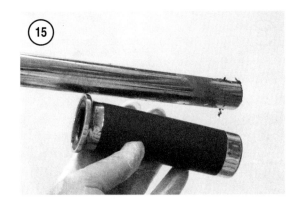

7. Install the left handlebar switch (**Figure 19**) before installing the grip. This prevents the grip from being installed too far onto the handlebar.

> *WARNING*
> *When using a grip cement in the next step, follow the manufacturer's instructions for application and drying time.*

8. Apply Honda Grip Cement, ThreeBond Griplock or an equivalent grip cement onto the left side of the handlebar or onto the outside of the throttle sleeve. Install the grip as follows:

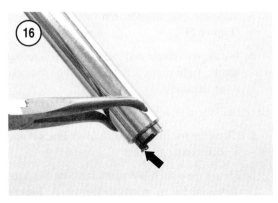

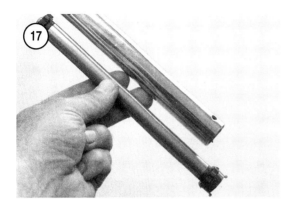

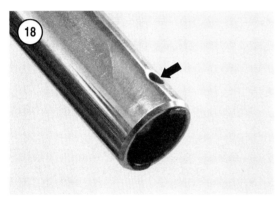

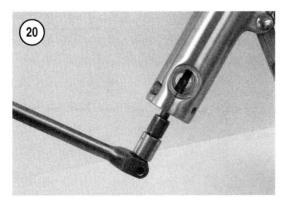

a. Install the grip with the chrome end cap installed on the grip.
b. Install the left side grip until it almost contacts the left switch housing. When the grip is positioned correctly, remove the left switch housing and clean excess cement from the end of the grip, handlebar and left switch housing.
c. Install the right side grip onto the throttle sleeve to the dimension recorded in Step 2. Wipe off all excess cement.

WARNING
Do not ride the motorcycle until the appropriate amount of drying time has elapsed; otherwise, the grip could move or slide off the handlebar or throttle sleeve and cause a loss of control. Refer to the drying time recommendations listed on the cement container or tube.

WARNING
Loose or damaged hand grips can slide off and cause loss of steering control. Make sure the hand grips are correctly installed and cemented in place before operating the motorcycle.

FRONT FORK

The following sections describe complete service and adjustment of the front fork. To prevent damaging the fork when servicing it, note the following:
1. To avoid rounding off the shoulders on the fork caps, use a 6-point socket when loosening and tightening the fork caps.
2. Do not overtighten the fork tube pinch bolts because this can damage the fork bridge threads and fork tubes. Always use the torque specifications listed.
3. The fork tubes and sliders are easily scratched. Handle them carefully during all service procedures.
4. Use a metal plate (as described in the text) to hold the fork tubes in a vise.

Removal

1. Remove the front wheel (Chapter Eleven).
2. If the fork is going to be disassembled, loosen, but do not remove, the Allen bolt in the bottom of each fork tube (**Figure 20**).

12

3. Remove the bolt (A, **Figure 21**) securing the front brake hose to the front fender.

NOTE
Do not remove the brake hose banjo bolt when removing the brake caliper.

4. Remove the bolts (B, **Figure 21**) and the front brake caliper. Support the caliper with a piece of stiff wire.

5. Unbolt and remove the front fender.

6. Loosen the top fork tube pinch bolt (A, **Figure 22**).

7. If the fork tube is going to be disassembled, loosen, but do not remove, the fork cap (B, **Figure 22**).

8A. On VT750DC models, perform the following:

   a. Remove the bolt, collar and turn signal light from the fork tube (**Figure 23**).

   b. Support the turn signal assembly with a piece of stiff wire.

8B. On models with fork covers, perform the following:

   a. Remove the top fork bridge as described in this chapter.

   b. Remove the bolt and the upper fork cover (**Figure 24**). Locate the upper O-ring installed in the fork cover.

NOTE
The bushing removed in substep c has two different inside diameters. The smaller inside diameter faces up.

   c. Mark the top of the bushing (A, **Figure 25**) so it can be installed facing in its original mounting position. Remove it from the fork tube.

   d. Measure the distance from the lower fork bridge to the top of the fork tube.

9. While supporting the fork tube, loosen the lower fork tube pinch bolts (B, **Figure 25**) and remove the fork tube.

NOTE
Rust and corrosion buildup around the fork tube and steering stem clamp surfaces can lock the fork tube in place. Support the fork tube and spray the top area of each clamp with a penetrating oil.

10. Remove the other fork tube.

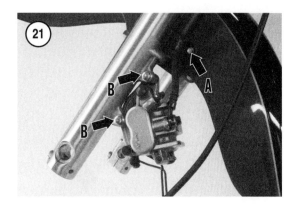

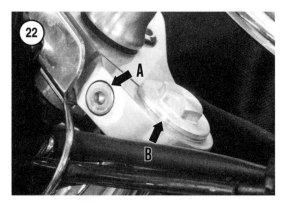

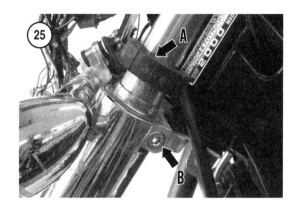

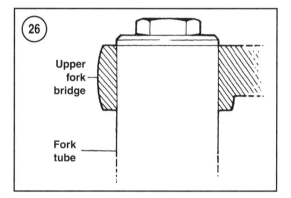

Upper fork bridge

Fork tube

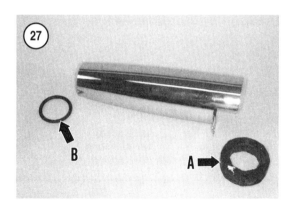

B

A

Installation

1. Clean the fork tube pinch bolts and fork bridge threads.

2A. On models without fork covers, perform the following:

   a. Slide the fork tube through the lower and upper fork bridges. Position the fork so the top of the fork tube is flush with the top bridge surface (**Figure 26**). Tighten the lower fork tube pinch bolt to 49 N•m (36 ft.-lb.).

   b. Tighten the fork cap to 22 N•m (16 ft.-lb.).

   c. Tighten the upper fork tube pinch bolt to 26 N•m (19 ft.-lb.).

   d. On VT750DC models, install the front turn signal assembly (**Figure 23**). Position the assembly and tighten the mounting bolt securely.

2B. On models with fork covers, perform the following:

   a. Slide the fork tube through the lower fork cover and lower fork bridge. Position the fork tube to the height position recorded during removal and tighten the lower fork tube pinch bolt. The bolt is tightened to its final torque later in this step.

   b. Install the lower bushing (A, **Figure 27**) into the upper fork cover (**Figure 28**) with its smaller inside diameter side facing up. This should be the side of the bushing previously identified during removal.

   c. Install the upper fork cover over the fork tube (**Figure 24**).

   d. Install the O-ring (B, **Figure 27**) down the fork tube until it is 5.0 mm (0.20 in. [maximum]) below the upper surface of the upper fork cover (**Figure 29**).

   e. Tighten the upper fork cover mounting bolts securely.

12

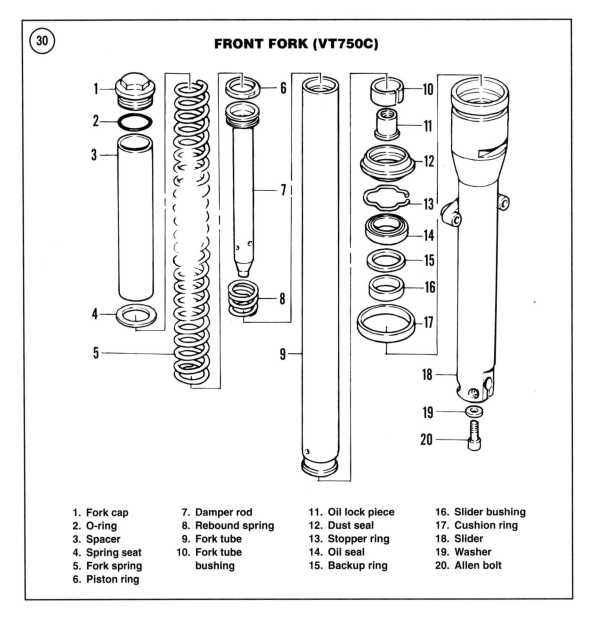

FRONT FORK (VT750C)

1. Fork cap	7. Damper rod	11. Oil lock piece	16. Slider bushing
2. O-ring	8. Rebound spring	12. Dust seal	17. Cushion ring
3. Spacer	9. Fork tube	13. Stopper ring	18. Slider
4. Spring seat	10. Fork tube	14. Oil seal	19. Washer
5. Fork spring	bushing	15. Backup ring	20. Allen bolt
6. Piston ring			

f. Install the top fork bridge as described in this chapter.

g. Loosen the lower fork tube pinch bolt and position the fork so the top of the fork tube is flush with the top bridge surface (**Figure 26**). Tighten the bottom fork tube pinch bolt (B, **Figure 25**) to 49 N•m (36 ft.-lb.).

h. Tighten the fork cap (B, **Figure 22**) to 22 N•m (16 ft.-lb.).

i. Tighten the upper fork tube pinch bolt (A, **Figure 22**) to 26 N•m (19 ft.-lb.).

NOTE
Make sure any cables or wiring harnesses are routed correctly around the fork tubes. Refer to the notes made before removing the fork tubes.

3. Install the front fender.

4. Secure the front brake hose to the front fender. Tighten the mounting bolt securely.

5. Install the front brake caliper using two new mounting bolts (B, **Figure 21**). Tighten the bolts to 30 N•m (22 ft.-lb.).

6. Install the front wheel (Chapter Eleven).

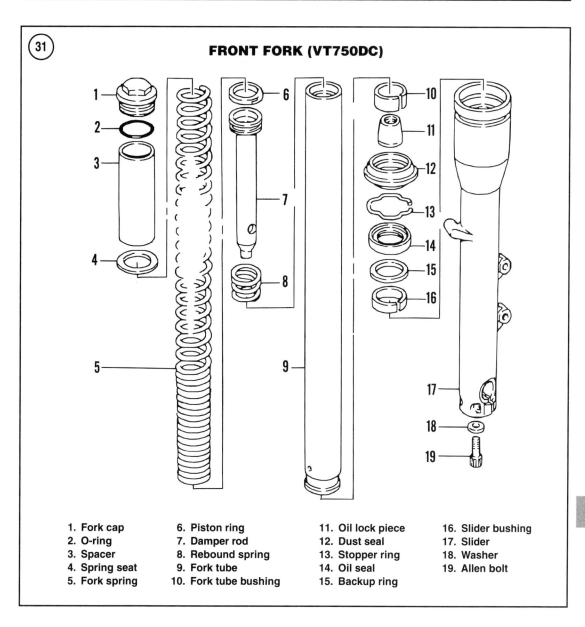

FRONT FORK (VT750DC)

1. Fork cap
2. O-ring
3. Spacer
4. Spring seat
5. Fork spring
6. Piston ring
7. Damper rod
8. Rebound spring
9. Fork tube
10. Fork tube bushing
11. Oil lock piece
12. Dust seal
13. Stopper ring
14. Oil seal
15. Backup ring
16. Slider bushing
17. Slider
18. Washer
19. Allen bolt

WARNING
After installing the front wheel, operate the front brake lever to reposition the caliper pistons. If the brake lever feels spongy, bleed the brakes as described in Chapter Fourteen.

Disassembly

This section describes complete disassembly of the fork tubes. If only changing the fork oil and/or setting the oil level, begin at Step 1 and follow the required steps listed in the text.

Refer to **Figure 30** (VT750C) or **Figure 31** (VT750DC).

1. Remove the fork tube as described in this chapter.

2. Bolt a flat metal plate onto the fork tube and clamp the metal plate (**Figure 32**) in a vise to support the fork tube when loosening and tightening the fork tube Allen bolt.

NOTE
If only changing the fork oil and/or setting the oil level, disregard the

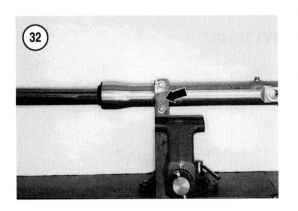

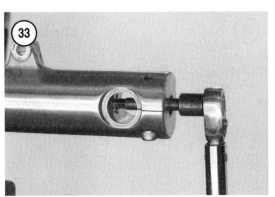

steps pertaining to loosening the fork tube Allen bolt in Step 3.

NOTE
Disregard Step 3 if the fork tube Allen bolt was loosened during fork removal.

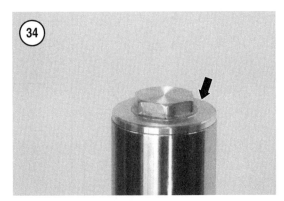

NOTE
When loosening the Allen bolt in the bottom of the fork tube, leave the fork assembled until the Allen bolt is loosened. The internal spring pressure against the damper rod helps hold it in place as the Allen bolt is being loosened.

3. Loosen the fork tube Allen bolt as follows:

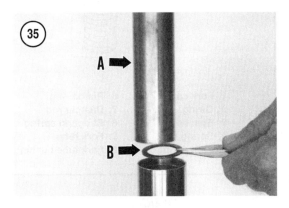

   a. Clean the recess in the top of the bolt of all dirt and debris.

   b. Have an assistant compress the fork tube assembly as much as possible and hold it compressed against the damper rod. Then loosen, but do not remove, the fork tube Allen bolt (**Figure 33**).

WARNING
Be careful when removing the fork cap because the spring is under pressure. Protect eyes and face accordingly.

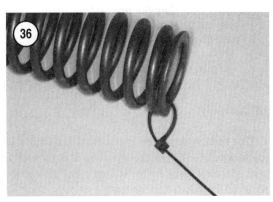

4. Slowly unscrew and remove the fork cap (**Figure 34**) and its O-ring.

5. Remove the spacer (A, **Figure 35**), spring seat (B) and fork spring. Place a plastic tie (**Figure 36**) on the top of the fork spring to identify its upper end.

6. Turn the fork tube over a drain pan and pour out the fork oil by operating the fork tube several times.

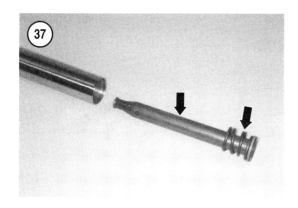

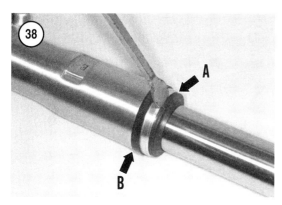

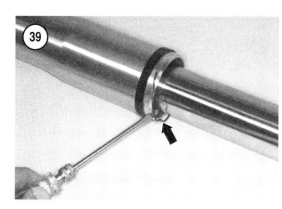

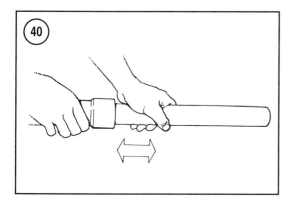

NOTE
*If only changing the fork oil and/or setting the oil level, go to the **Oil Adjustment** procedure at the end of this section. If disassembling the fork, continue with Step 7.*

7. Remove the Allen bolt, previously loosened, and the washer from the base of the slider. Discard the washer.

8. Turn the fork over and slide out the damper rod and rebound spring (**Figure 37**).

CAUTION
Do not use excessive force when removing the dust seal in Step 9.

9. Carefully pry the seal out of the slider with a suitable tool. Move the tool around the seal in small increments. It is easy to scratch and damage the slider at the top of the dust seal bore. When selecting a starting point, choose the side facing into the wheel.

10. Pry the dust seal (A, **Figure 38**) out of the slider and slide it off the fork tube.

NOTE
*On models so equipped, do not remove or damage the cushion ring (B, **Figure 38**) installed in the top of the slider.*

11. Slip the tip of a small screwdriver behind the stopper ring and carefully pry the ring out of the slider groove (**Figure 39**) and remove it from the fork tube.

NOTE
A pressed-in bushing in the slider and a bushing on the fork tube keep the slider and fork tube from separating. To remove the fork tube from the slider, use these parts as a slide hammer as described in Step 12.

12. Hold the fork tube and pull hard on the slider, using quick in-and-out strokes (**Figure 40**). Doing so withdraws the oil seal, backup ring and guide bushing from the slider. Refer to **Figure 41**.

13. Remove the slider and pour any remaining oil in the oil pan.

14. Remove the oil lock piece from the slider if it did not come out in Step 12 (A, **Figure 42**, typical).

12

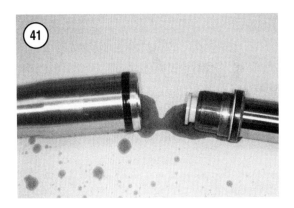

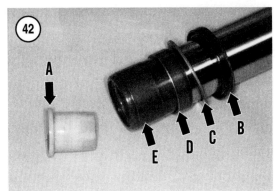

15. Slide off the oil seal (B, **Figure 42**), backup ring (C) and slider bushing (D) from the fork tube. Discard the dust seal and oil seal.

NOTE
Do not remove the fork tube bushing (E, Figure 42) unless it is going to be replaced. Inspect it as described in this section.

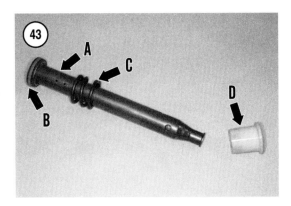

Inspection

When measuring the fork components, compare the actual measurements to the specifications in **Table 2**. Replace worn or damaged parts as described in this section.

1. Thoroughly clean all parts in solvent and dry them. Remove all threadlocking compound from the fork damper and Allen bolt threads.

2. Check the fork tube for wear or scratches. Check the chrome for flaking or other damage that could damage the oil seal.

3. Check the fork tube for straightness. Place the fork tube on V-blocks and measure runout with a dial indicator. If the runout is excessive (**Table 2**), replace the fork tube.

4. Check the slider for dents or exterior damage. Check the stopper ring groove for cracks or damage. Check the oil seal mounting bore for dents or other damage.

5. Inspect the damper rod (A, **Figure 43**) for straightness, damage or roughness. Check for galling, deep scores or excessive wear. Check the threads for damage.

6. Inspect the piston ring (B, **Figure 43**) on the end of the damper rod for wear or damage. Replace if necessary.

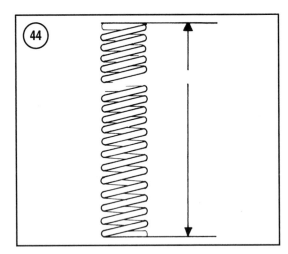

7. Inspect the rebound spring (C, **Figure 43**) on the damper rod for cracks or other damage.

8. Inspect the oil lock assembly (D, **Figure 43**) for wear or damage.

9. Measure the free length of the fork spring (**Figure 44**) with a tape measure. Replace the spring if it is too short (**Table 2**). Replace the springs as a set if they are unequal in length.

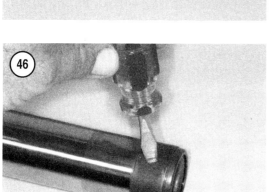

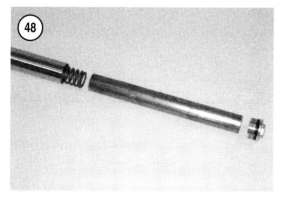

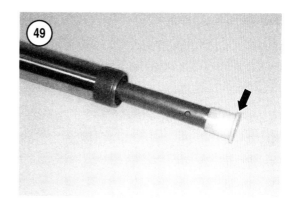

10. Inspect the slider and fork tube bushings for scoring, wear or damage. Check for discoloration and material coating damage. If the coating is worn off so that the base material is showing on approximately 3/4 of the total surface, the bushing is excessively worn. Replace both bushings (**Figure 45**) as a set.

11. To replace the fork tube bushing, pry its slot open with a screwdriver (**Figure 46**) and slide it off the fork tube. Clean the groove on the bottom of the fork tube, and then install the new bushing until it seats fully in the groove (**Figure 47**).

12. Replace the fork cap O-ring if damaged or leaking.

Assembly

Refer to **Figure 30** (VT750C) or **Figure 31** (VT750DC) for this procedure.

1. Before assembling the parts, make sure there is no solvent left in the slider or on any part.

2. Coat all parts, except the Allen bolt and damper rod threads with new fork oil before installation.

3. Install the rebound spring onto the damper rod and slide the damper rod assembly through the fork tube (**Figure 37**).

4. Temporarily install the fork spring, spacer and fork cap (**Figure 48**) to apply tension against the damper rod.

5. Install the oil lock piece onto the end of the damper rod. Refer to **Figure 49** (VT750C) or **Figure 50** (VT750DC).

NOTE
On VT750C models, the shoulder on the oil lock piece must face toward the end of the damper rod.

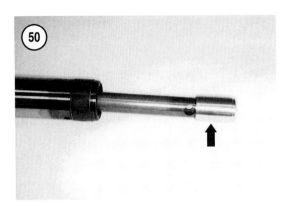

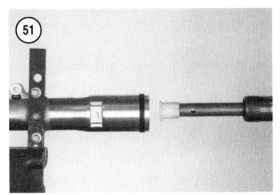

6. Mount the slider in a vise by attaching a piece of metal to the fender mounting holes.

7. Carefully install the fork tube and the damper rod into the slider (**Figure 51**) until the oil lock piece bottoms against the bottom of the slider.

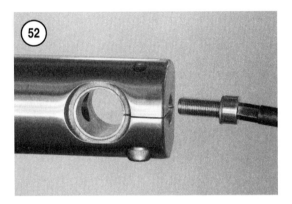

8. Install a new washer onto the Allen bolt.

9. Install a medium strength threadlock onto the fork tube Allen bolt threads and thread the Allen bolt into the bottom of the damper rod (**Figure 52**). Tighten until the damper rod starts to turn. Have an assistant compress the fork tube as much as possible and tighten the fork tube Allen bolt (**Figure 33**) to 29 N•m (21 ft.-lb.).

10. Remove the fork cap, spacer and fork spring.

11. Using the same piece of metal to hold the fork assembly, position the slider in the vise so the fork tube faces straight up.

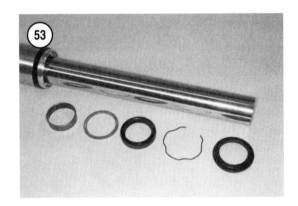

12. **Figure 53** shows the alignment of the bushing and seal assembly.

13. Install the fork slider bushing and backup ring as follows:

    a. Slide the bushing (A, **Figure 54**) and backup ring (B) down the fork tube. Install the backup ring with its chamfered side facing down and set it on top of the bushing.

    b. Use a fork oil seal driver (**Figure 55**) to drive the bushing into the fork slider until it bottoms out into the recess in the slider. The knocking sound made by the driver changes when the bushing bottoms out.

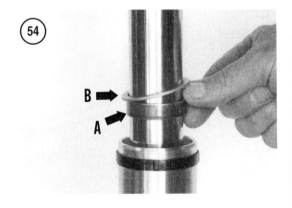

NOTE
*Motion Pro fork oil seal drivers (**Figure 55**) or an equivalent can be purchased from aftermarket suppliers. To select a driver, first measure the outside diameter of one fork tube.*

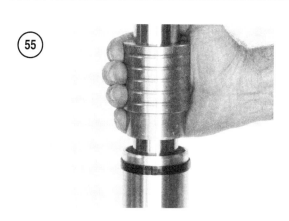

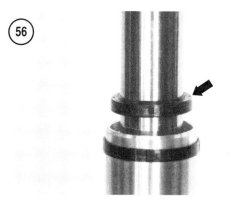

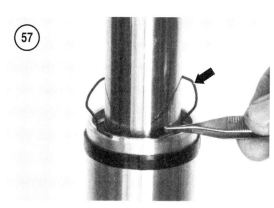

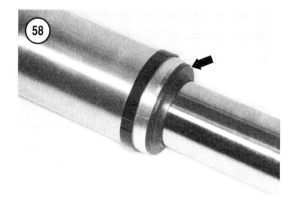

> *CAUTION*
> *To avoid damaging the fork seal and dust seal when installing them over the top of the fork tube, place a plastic bag over the fork tube and coat it thoroughly with fork oil.*

14. Install a new fork seal as follows:
    a. Lubricate the seal lips with fork oil.
    b. Install the seal (**Figure 56**) over the fork tube with its manufacturer's name and size code facing up. Slide it down the fork tube and center it into the top of the slider until its outer surface is flush with the slider's outer bore surface.
    c. Drive the oil seal into the slider with the same tool (**Figure 55**) used in Step 13.
    d. Continue to install the seal until the groove in the slider can be seen above the top surface of the seal.

15. Slide the stopper ring (**Figure 57**) over the fork tube and install it into the groove in the slider. Make sure that the stopper ring is completely seated in the slider groove.

> *NOTE*
> *If the stopper ring cannot seat completely into the slider groove, the seal is not installed far enough into the slider.*

16. Slide the dust seal down the fork tube and seat it into the slider (**Figure 58**).

17. Fill the fork with oil and set the oil level as described under *Oil Adjustment* in this section.

18. Install the fork spring (**Figure 59**) as follows:
    a. On VT750C models, the original spring is not directional and either end can be inserted first. If an aftermarket spring was installed, install it facing in its original position. If a plastic tie

was used to identify the spring, install the spring with the plastic tie end facing up. Cut and remove the plastic tie from the fork tube.

    b. On VT750DC models, install the spring with its closer wound springs facing down (**Figure 31**).

19. Install the spring seat (A, **Figure 60**) and spacer (B).

20. Install a new O-ring onto the fork cap, if needed.

21. Lubricate the fork cap O-ring with fork oil. Install the fork cap (**Figure 39**) hand tight at this time.

> *NOTE*
> *The fork cap is tightened completely after the fork tube is installed onto the motorcycle.*

Oil Adjustment

This section describes steps on filling the fork with oil and setting the oil level.

See **Table 2** for the recommended type of fork oil.

1. Remove the fork spring and drain the fork tube as described under *Disassembly* in this section.

2. Push the fork tube down and bottom it out against the slider. Support the slider so it cannot tip over.

3. Slowly pour the recommended type of fork oil into the fork.

> *NOTE*
> *As oil replaces air during the bleeding procedure, the oil level in the fork drops. Continue to add oil to maintain a high oil level in the fork. When bleeding the fork tube, do not be concerned with maintaining or achieving the proper oil capacity. Setting the oil level determines the actual amount of oil used in each fork tube.*

4. Hold the slider with one hand and slowly extend the fork tube. Repeat until the fork tube moves smoothly with the same amount of tension through the compression and rebound travel strokes. Then stop with the fork tube bottomed out.

5. Set the fork tube aside for approximately five minutes to allow any suspended air bubbles in the oil to surface.

6. Set the oil level (**Figure 61**) as follows:

    a. Make sure the fork tube is bottomed against the slider and placed in a vertical position.

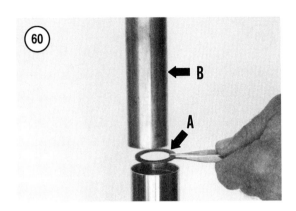

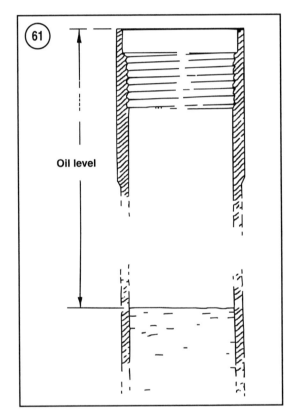

Oil level

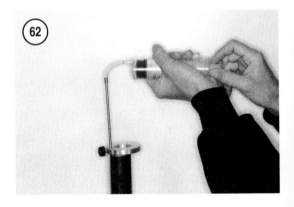

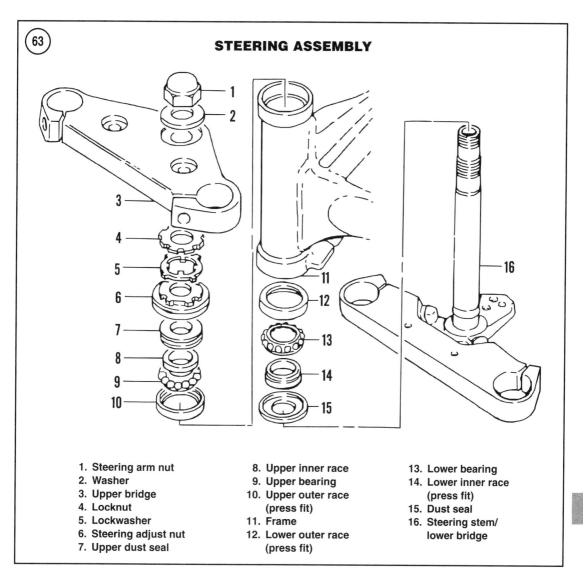

63 **STEERING ASSEMBLY**

1. Steering arm nut
2. Washer
3. Upper bridge
4. Locknut
5. Lockwasher
6. Steering adjust nut
7. Upper dust seal
8. Upper inner race
9. Upper bearing
10. Upper outer race (press fit)
11. Frame
12. Lower outer race (press fit)
13. Lower bearing
14. Lower inner race (press fit)
15. Dust seal
16. Steering stem/ lower bridge

12

b. Use an oil level gauge (**Figure 62**) and set the oil level to the specification listed in **Table 2**.

c. Remove the oil level gauge.

7. Complete fork assembly as described under *Assembly* in this section.

STEERING HEAD AND STEM

The steering head (**Figure 63**) uses retainer-type steel bearings. Each bearing consists of the inner race, outer race and bearing. The bearings can be lifted out of their operating positions after removing the steering stem. Do not remove the lower inner race (pressed onto the steering stem) or the outer bearing races (pressed into the frame) unless they are to be replaced.

Regular maintenance consists of steering inspection, adjustment and bearing lubrication. When the steering cannot be adjusted correctly, the bearings may require replacement. To determine bearing condition, the steering assembly must be removed and inspected. Inspect the steering adjustment and lubricate the bearings at the intervals listed in the maintenance schedule (Chapter Three).

This section describes complete service and adjustment procedures for the steering head assembly.

Tools

A Honda steering stem socket (part No. 07916-3710100 or equivalent) and a spring scale are required to adjust the steering stem/bearing. These tools are shown in the appropriate procedure.

Refer to *Steering Head Bearing Race Replacement* and *Steering Stem Bearing Race Replacement* in this chapter for bearing race replacement procedures and special tools.

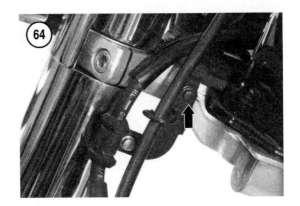

Troubleshooting

Before removing the steering assembly to troubleshoot a steering complaint, refer to *Front Steering and Suspension* in Chapter Two. Refer to the topic that most identifies the problem and check the items listed as possible causes.

Removal

Refer to **Figure 63**.

1. Remove the handlebar as described in this chapter.

2. Remove the headlight housing (Chapter Nine).

3. Remove the speedometer if mounted on the upper fork bridge (Chapter Nine).

4. On VT750C models, identify and remove the indicator bulb holders mounted in the upper bridge.

5. Remove the bolt and brake hose clamp from the steering stem (**Figure 64**).

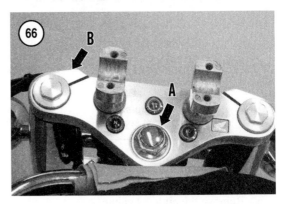

> *NOTE*
> *At this point there should be no cables, hoses or wiring harnesses interfering with the movement of the steering stem. Check by turning the steering stem. If so, reposition the item so the steering stem can move with no interference.*

6. Before loosening the steering stem nut, check the steering adjustment as described under *Steering Bearing Preload Check* in this chapter.

7. Remove the front wheel (Chapter Eleven).

8. Loosen the upper fork tube pinch bolts (**Figure 65**).

9. Remove the steering stem nut and washer (A, **Figure 66**).

10. Remove the upper bridge (B, **Figure 66**). Refer to **Figure 67**.

11. Remove the fork tubes as described in this chapter.

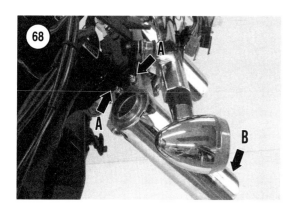

12. On models with chrome fork covers, remove the mounting bolts (A, **Figure 68**) and the lower fork covers (B).

13. On VT750C models, perform the following:

  a. Remove the headlight stay with the lower light bar attached (**Figure 69**) by pulling the wiring harness and connectors through the large hole in the mounting bracket.

  b. Remove the mounting bolt and the steering stem cover (**Figure 70**). Locate the rubber dampers installed in the cover.

14. Pry the lockwasher tabs (A, **Figure 71**) away from the locknut grooves. Remove the locknut (B, **Figure 71**) and lockwasher (A). Install a new lockwasher during reassembly.

NOTE
Before loosening the steering adjust nut, turn the steering stem from lock-to-lock to check the steering adjustment.

15. Loosen the steering adjust nut (**Figure 72**) with the Honda steering stem socket (part No. 07916-3710100 or equivalent), a fabricated tool made from a piece of pipe or deep socket or a spanner wrench.

NOTE
Support the weight of the steering stem assembly while removing the steering adjust nut, or the assembly will drop out of the steering head.

16. Support the steering stem and remove the following:

  a. Steering adjust nut (**Figure 73**).

  b. Dust seal (**Figure 74**).

12

c. Lower the steering stem and remove it and the lower bearing assembly (**Figure 75**) from the frame.

d. Upper inner race and bearing assembly (**Figure 76**).

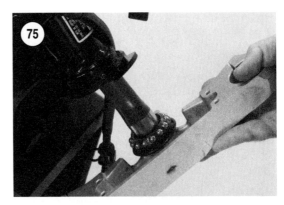

NOTE
The upper outer race, lower outer race and lower inner race are installed with a press fit. Only remove these parts when replacing the bearing assembly.

Inspection

Replace parts that show excessive wear or damage as described in this section.

WARNING
Improper repair of a damaged frame and/or steering components can cause the loss of steering control. If there is apparent frame, steering stem or fork bridge damage, consult with a Honda dealership or qualified frame shop for professional inspection and possible repair.

1. Clean and dry all parts. Make certain the cleaning solution is compatible with the rubber dust seals.

2. Check the frame for cracks and fractures.

3. Inspect the steering stem nut, locknut and steering adjust nut for excessive wear or damage.

4. Inspect the upper dust seal for tearing, deterioration or other damage.

5. Check the steering stem (**Figure 77**) for:

a. Cracked or bent stem.

b. Damaged lower bridge.

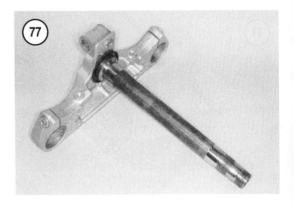

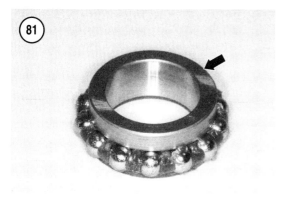

c. Damaged threads.

6. Check the upper bridge for cracks or other damage. Replace if necessary.

7. Inspect the bearing assemblies as follows:

    a. Inspect the bearing races for wear, pitting, cracks or other damage. To replace the outer bearing races, refer to *Steering Head Bearing Race Replacement* in this chapter. To replace the lower inner bearing race, refer to *Steering Stem Bearing Race Replacement* in this chapter.

    b. Inspect the upper and lower bearings (**Figure 78**) for dents, pitting, excessive wear, corrosion, retainer damage or discoloration.

    c. Replace the upper and lower bearing assemblies at the same time.

NOTE
*Each bearing assembly consists of the bearing and an inner and outer race (**Figure 63**). Always replace the bearings in upper and lower sets.*

8. When reusing bearings, clean them thoroughly with a bearing degreaser and dry thoroughly. Repack each bearing with grease.

Assembly and Adjustment

1. Make sure the upper and lower outer bearing races are properly seated in the steering head. Then lubricate each bearing race with grease.

2. Thoroughly lubricate each bearing (**Figure 78**) with grease.

3. Lubricate the upper dust seal (bottom side) with grease and set it aside until installation.

4. Lower bearing:

    a. Lubricate the lower outer bearing race and dust seal lip (**Figure 79**) with grease.

    b. Install the lower steering bearing (**Figure 80**) onto the lower inner bearing race.

5. Upper bearing:

    a. Lubricate the upper inner bearing race with grease.

    b. Install the upper inner race into its bearing (**Figure 81**).

    c. Install the upper bearing and its inner race into the outer race in the steering head (**Figure 76**).

6. Install the steering stem (**Figure 75**) into the steering head and through the upper bearing race

12

and hold in place. Make sure the lower bearing is centered inside the lower outer race.

7. Install the upper dust seal (**Figure 74**) and seat it over the bearing assembly.

> *NOTE*
> *The steering stem, steering stem nut and steering adjust nut threads must be clean for accurate tightening of these fasteners. Any dirt, grease or other residue on the threads can affect the steering stem tightening torque and bearing preload adjustment.*

8. Lubricate the steering adjust nut threads with oil and thread it onto the steering stem (**Figure 73**). Tighten finger-tight.

9. Tighten the steering adjust nut (**Figure 73**) as follows:

   a. Use the Honda steering stem socket or equivalent to seat the bearings in the following steps. Refer to *Tools* in this section.

> *NOTE*
> *If the Honda tool is not available, use a spanner wrench and torque wrench (Figure 82) to seat the bearings. Refer to **Torque Wrench Adapters** in Chapter One for information.*

   b. Tighten the steering adjust nut (**Figure 72**) to 21 N•m (15 ft.-lb.).

   c. Turn the steering stem from lock-to-lock five times to seat the bearings. The steering stem must pivot smoothly. Retighten the steering adjust nut to 21 N•m (15 ft.-lb.).

> *NOTE*
> *If the steering stem does not pivot smoothly, one or both bearing assemblies may be damaged. Remove the steering stem and inspect the bearings.*

> *NOTE*
> *Do not continue with Step 10 until the steering stem turns correctly. If there is any excessive play or roughness, recheck the steering adjustment.*

10. Align the tabs of a *new* lockwasher with the grooves in the steering adjust nut and install the lockwasher (**Figure 83**). The outer two tabs bend into the locknut grooves.

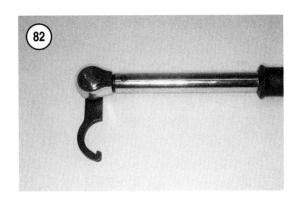

> *CAUTION*
> *Never reinstall a used lockwasher because the tabs may break off, making the lockwasher ineffective.*

11. Install and tighten the locknut as follows:

   a. Install the locknut (B, **Figure 71**) and tighten finger-tight.

   b. Hold the steering adjust nut to keep it from turning and tighten the locknut approximately 1/4 turn (90°) to align its grooves with the outer lockwasher tabs.

   c. Bend the outer lockwasher tabs (A, **Figure 71**) up into the locknut grooves.

12A. On VT750DC models, perform the following:

   a. Install the upper bridge, washer and steering stem nut.

   b. Install the fork tubes through both fork bridges and tighten the bolts temporarily to hold the tubes in place. The pinch bolts will be tightened to their final torque later in this step.

   c. Tighten the steering stem nut to 103 N•m (76 ft.-lb.).

   d. Go to Step 13 to check the steering adjustment.

   e. When the steering adjustment is correct, position the fork tubes and tighten the upper and lower pinch bolts as described under *Front Fork* in this chapter.

12B. On all other models, perform the following:

   a. Install the stem cover (**Figure 70**) onto the lower bridge and secure with the right side mounting bolt. The left bolt is installed later in this procedure. Install the two rubber dampers into the cover.

   b. Install the wiring harness and connectors through the headlight stay and install the

headlight stay (**Figure 69**) by inserting its two pins into the rubber dampers in the stem cover.

c. On models with chrome fork covers, install the rubber dampers into the lower fork covers. Then install the lower fork covers (B, **Figure 68**) and secure with the mounting bolts (A).

d. Install the fork tubes (and upper fork covers, if so equipped) as described in this chapter.

e. Check that the headlight stay lower pins are installed in the lower fork bridge rubber dampers.

f. Install the upper fork bridge over the fork tubes. Align the upper pins on the headlight stay with the two rubber dampers in the bottom of the upper fork bridge.

g. Install the steering stem nut and washer. Tighten the steering stem nut to 103 N•m (76 ft.-lb.).

h. Go to Step 13 to check the steering adjustment.

i. When the steering adjustment is correct, position the fork tubes and tighten the upper and lower pinch bolts as described under *Front Fork* in this chapter.

13. Turn the steering stem lock-to-lock. Make sure it moves smoothly. There must be no play or binding. Note the following:

a. If the steering stem turns correctly, continue with Step 14.

b. If the steering stem is too loose or tight, remove the steering stem nut, washer and upper bridge. Then readjust the steering adjust nut. Repeat until the steering play feels correct. Damaged bearings and races can also cause tightness.

CAUTION
If the steering adjustment is too loose, the steering becomes unstable and causes front wheel wobble. If the steering adjustment is too tight, the bearings eventually score or notch the races. The steering then becomes sluggish as the damaged bearings and races operate against each other. Both conditions hamper steering performance.

NOTE
Arriving at the proper steering adjustment usually comes down to the steering effort required to turn the handlebar. The number of attempts required to arrive at the correct steering adjustment (feel) can vary considerably.

14. Mount the brake hose clamp to the steering stem and tighten its mounting bolt securely.

15. Install the front wheel, brake caliper and front fender as described under *Front Fork* in this chapter.

16. Install the speedometer, if removed. Refer to Chapter Nine.

17. Install the headlight housing (Chapter Nine).

18. On VT750C models, install the indicator bulb holders into the upper bridge.

19. Install the handlebar as described in this chapter.

20. Perform the *Steering Bearing Preload Check* in this chapter.

NOTE
The steering bearing preload check measures the amount of weight required to move the steering stem. This check confirms whether the steering adjustment is correct.

WARNING
Do not ride the motorcycle until all the controls and brakes work properly.

STEERING BEARING PRELOAD CHECK

Proper steering bearing preload is important because it controls bearing play and steering control. If the preload is too loose, excessive play in the

12

steering allows the wheel to wobble, which causes side-to-side movement or oscillation of the handlebars. A wobble may occur at all speeds or start and then stop at certain speeds. The condition can be difficult to troubleshoot. If the preload is too tight, the bearings and races suffer unnecessary wear and cause stiff and uneven steering, requiring the rider to make a greater steering effort when turning the handlebars. Dry or damaged bearings can cause similar conditions.

Check the steering head for looseness at the intervals specified in Chapter Three or whenever the following symptoms or conditions exist:

1. The handlebars vibrate more than normal.
2. The front fork makes a clicking or clunking noise when the front brake is applied.
3. The steering feels tight or slow.
4. The motorcycle does not steer straight on level road surfaces.

Inspection

When installing the steering stem assembly, the steering bearings are preloaded (bearing placed under pressure) by carefully tightening the steering adjust nut and the steering stem nut. When the bearings are lubricated and correctly preloaded, the bearings should not move out of alignment. To check bearing preload, Honda specifies the use of a spring scale attached to one of the fork tubes. This method measures the amount of weight required to move the steering stem with the front end assembled and the front wheel off the ground. When measuring bearing preload with a spring scale, the steering stem must be free to turn without interference from cables, hoses or wiring harnesses.

> *NOTE*
> *This procedure must be performed with the front fork and front wheel mounted on the motorcycle.*

1. Support the motorcycle so it is sitting level with the front wheel off the ground.
2. Turn the steering stem side to side. There should be no interference or drag from a cable, wire harness or the front brake hose when the steering stem is rotated. If there still is interference, reposition or remove the affecting part as required.

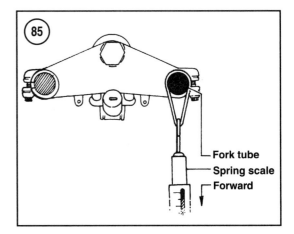

Fork tube
Spring scale
Forward

3. Attach a plastic zip tie onto one of the fork tubes between the fork bridges. Then attach a spring scale onto the zip tie (**Figure 84**).

4. Center the wheel. Position the spring scale at a 90° angle with the steering stem (**Figure 85**). Pull the spring scale and note the reading on the scale when the steering stem begins to turn. This reading is steering stem bearing preload. Refer to **Table 1** for the correct steering preload reading.

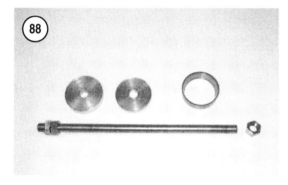

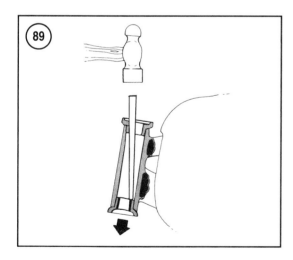

5. If the preload reading is incorrect, adjust the steering assembly as described under *Steering Head and Stem, Assembly and Adjustment* in this chapter. Perform the adjustment with the front fork and front wheel mounted on the motorcycle.

WARNING
Do not ride the motorcycle until the horn, cables and brakes all work properly.

STEERING HEAD BEARING RACE REPLACEMENT

The steering head bearing races (**Figure 86** and **Figure 87**) are pressed into the frame's steering head. The bearing races should only be removed when new races are installed.

A threaded rod and disc tool (**Figure 88**) will be used to install the races. When properly used, this tool exerts even pressure around the race. One disc is sized to fit the outer diameter of the races, while the other disc is slightly larger than the diameter of the steering head. This tool is shown in the following procedure.

CAUTION
The following procedure describes simple home techniques to remove the bearing races. If removal is difficult, do not chance damage to the frame or new bearing races. Have the task performed by a Honda dealership or a qualified specialist.

Replace both bearing races and bearings at the same time.

CAUTION
If binding occurs when removing or installing the bearing races, stop and release tension from the bearing race. Check the tool alignment to make sure the bearing race is moving evenly in its mounting bore. Otherwise, the bearing race may gouge the frame mounting bore and cause permanent damage.

1. Chill the new bearing races in a freezer for a few hours to shrink the outer diameter of the race as much as possible.

2. Insert a drift into the steering head and position it on the edge of the lower race (**Figure 89**). Carefully drive out the race. To prevent binding, make several passes around the perimeter of the race. Repeat the procedure to remove the upper race.

3. Clean the race bores in the frame and check for damage.

4. To install the upper race, do the following:

   a. Place the new upper race (**Figure 90**) squarely into the mounting bore opening with its bearing side facing out.

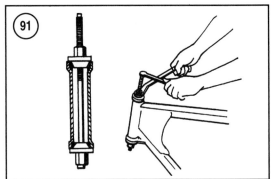

b. Assemble the threaded rod tool as shown in **Figure 91**.

CAUTION
If there is any binding when installing the bearing races in the following steps, stop and release all tension from the bearing race. Check the tool alignment to make sure the bearing race is moving evenly in its mounting bore. Otherwise, the bearing race may gouge the frame mounting bore and cause permanent damage.

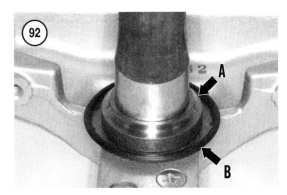

c. Hold the lower nut and tighten the upper nut to draw the race into the frame tube. Continue until the race bottoms out in its mounting bore. Remove the puller assembly and inspect the bearing race. It must seat fully and squarely in the frame tube (**Figure 86**).

CAUTION
Do not allow the installer shaft to contact the bearing race.

5. Reverse the tool and repeat Step 4 to install the lower race (**Figure 87**). Insert the threaded rod tool carefully through the frame to avoid scratching the upper bearing race.
6. Lubricate the upper and lower bearing races with grease.

STEERING STEM BEARING RACE REPLACEMENT

The lower inner race (A, **Figure 92**) is a press fit on the steering stem. Replace the lower dust seal (B, **Figure 92**) when replacing the lower inner race.
1. Thread the steering stem nut onto the steering stem (**Figure 93**).

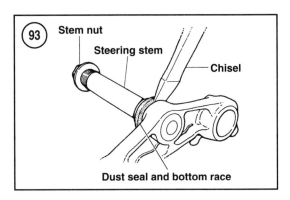

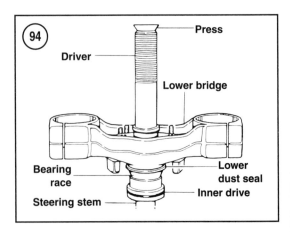

NOTE
Installing the steering stem nut as described in Step 1 helps prevent damaging the steering stem threads when removing the lower inner bearing race.

WARNING
Striking a chisel with a hammer can cause flying chips. Wear safety glasses in Step 2 to prevent eye injury.

2. Remove the lower inner bearing race and dust seal with a chisel as shown in **Figure 93**. To prevent damaging the steering stem, remove the bearing race evenly. Apply pressure against the bearing race a little at a time and at different points around the bearing.

3. Discard the lower inner bearing race and dust seal.

4. Clean the steering stem with solvent and dry thoroughly.

5. Inspect the steering stem race surface for cracks or other damage. Replace the steering stem if necessary.

6. Install a new lower dust seal (B, **Figure 92**) over the steering stem.

7. Slide the new lower inner bearing race with the bearing surface facing up onto the steering stem until it stops.

8. Install the steering stem in a press. Support the bottom of the steering stem with a bearing driver or piece of round metal. Then install a bearing driver (**Figure 94**) over the steering stem and seat it against the inner bearing race inside shoulder. Do not allow the bearing driver to contact the bearing race surface.

9. Press the lower inner race onto the steering stem until it bottoms.

10. Remove the steering stem from the press.

11. Lubricate the bearing race (A, **Figure 92**) and dust seal (B) with grease.

Table 1 STEERING AND FRONT SUSPENSION SPECIFICATIONS

Front axle travel	
VT750C	140 mm (5.5 in.)
VT750DC	108 mm (4.3 in.)
Front axle runout limit	0.20 mm (0.008 in.)
Steering	
Caster angle	
VT750C	33° 50 minutes
VT750DC	34° 00 minutes
Trail length	
VT750C	157 mm (6.2 in.)
VT750DC	152 mm (6.0 in.)
Steering stem bearing preload	0.43-1.04 kg (0.95-2.30 lbs.)

Table 2 FRONT FORK SERVICE SPECIFICATIONS

Fork tube runout limit	0.20 mm (0.008 in.)
Fork oil capacity	
VT750C	511.5-516.5 ml
	(16.96-17.12 U.S. oz.)
VT750DC	470.5-475.5 ml
	(15.92-16.08 U.S. oz.)
Fork oil level	
VT750C	108 mm (4.3 in.)
VT750DC	124 mm (4.9 in.)
Fork oil type	Pro-Honda Suspension Fluid SS-8 or 10 wt. fork oil

(continued)

12

Table 2 FRONT FORK SERVICE SPECIFICATIONS (continued)

Spring free length	
VT750C	
New	303.4 mm (11.94 in.)
Service limit	297.3 mm (11.70 in.)
VT750DC	
New	492.4 mm (19.39 in.)
Service limit	482.5 mm (19.00 in.)

Table 3 FRONT SUSPENSION AND STEERING TORQUE SPECIFICATIONS

	N•m	in.-lb.	ft.-lb.
Fork cap	22	–	16
Fork tube Allen bolts[1]	29	–	21
Fork tube pinch bolts			
Upper	26	–	19
Lower	49	–	36
Front brake caliper mounting bolts	30	–	22
Front master cylinder clamp bolts	12	106	–
Handlebar holder			
Upper holder bolts	23	–	17
Lower holder nuts			
VT750C	26	–	19
VT750DC	23	–	17
Steering stem nut[2]	103	–	76

1. Apply a medium strength threadlock onto fastener threads.
2. See text for adjustment procedure.

CHAPTER THIRTEEN

REAR SUSPENSION

This chapter contains repair and replacement procedures for the rear shock absorbers and rear swing arm. Rear wheel, hub and tire service are covered in Chapter Eleven.

Specifications for the rear suspension are listed in **Table 1** and **Table 2** at the end of this chapter.

SHOCK ABSORBER

The shocks are sealed units. Do not attempt to replace the shock spring or disassemble the shock in any way. Service is limited to shock adjustment and replacing the shock mount dampers installed in each end of the shock absorber.

Adjustment

Each shock absorber is equipped with a five-position spring preload adjuster. This adjustment allows the rider to change the ride height at the rear of the motorcycle to compensate for different rider weights, loads and road conditions. The softest setting is No. 1 and the stiffest setting is No. 5. The standard setting is No. 2. Adjust the shock absorbers to best suit different load and riding conditions.

For example, if the weight added to the motorcycle causes the rear end to sag excessively, bottoming and reduced cornering clearances may become a problem. These conditions reduce the ride performance and may make the motorcycle unstable under certain conditions.

A cam type preload adjuster is mounted on the bottom of the shock absorber. Notches machined into the adjuster form an adjustable cam. The depth of the cam's notch determines the spring preload adjustment (**Figure 1**). Turning the adjuster moves the cam against a fixed stop on the shock body. As a cam notch rides over and engages with the stop, the spring preload has changed one position. Moving the cam up increases the spring preload. Moving the cam down decreases the spring preload. On some models, a chrome cover hides the spring and preload adjuster. A label (**Figure 2**) attached to the bottom of the shock absorber identifies the different spring preload positions.

> *NOTE*
> *Spring preload is the amount the spring is initially compressed. Changing the preload does not make the spring stiffer or softer. It simply in-*

13

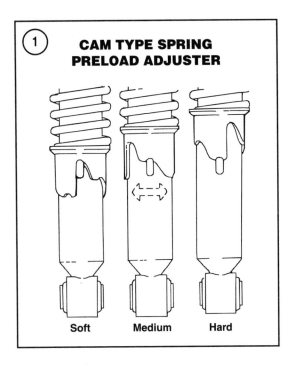

CAM TYPE SPRING PRELOAD ADJUSTER

Soft   Medium   Hard

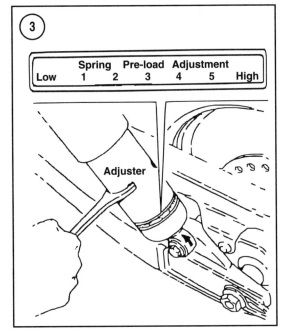

	Spring	Pre-load	Adjustment			
Low	1	2	3	4	5	High

Adjuster

creases or decreases the beginning spring load, which either raises or lowers the ride height.

1. Remove the tool kit and assemble the spanner wrench and its extension bar.

CAUTION
Always adjust the shock absorber in single increment numbers. For example, if the shock is in position No. 2 and it is necessary to adjust the spring to position No. 5, turn the adjuster to the No., 3, No. 4 and then to position No. 5. Do not turn the adjuster directly from the No. 2 to the No. 5 position without stopping at the other adjustment numbers or the adjuster may be damaged.

2. Using the pin spanner, adjust the shock absorber to the desired adjustment position. Refer to **Figure 3** (VT750C) or **Figure 4** (VT750DC).

3. Adjust the other shock to the same setting.

WARNING
Both shock absorbers must be adjusted to the same preload number; otherwise, an unstable riding condition may result.

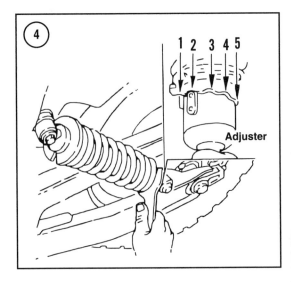

1 2 3 4 5

Adjuster

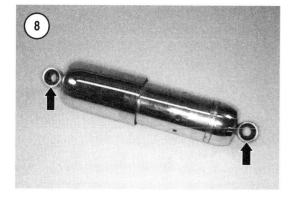

Removal/Installation

1. Support the bike on a workstand so the rear wheel clears the ground.

2. Remove the upper and lower mounting bolts and washers. Refer to **Figure 5** (VT750C) or **Figure 6** (VT750DC). Remove the shock absorber.

3. Inspect the shock absorber as described in this section.

4. Installation is the reverse of removal. Note the following:

    a. On VT750C models, install the shock absorber with the arrow mark on the lower shock mount facing forward (**Figure 7**).

    b. Tighten the shock absorber mounting bolts to 26 N•m (19 ft.-lb.).

    c. Check that both shock absorbers are adjusted to the same preload position as described in this section.

Inspection

Do not attempt to remove the shock spring or disassemble the shock absorber.

1. Inspect the shock absorber (**Figure 8**) for oil leaks or other damage. Replace the shock absorber if it is leaking.

2. Inspect the upper and lower shock dampers (**Figure 8**) for excessive wear, age deterioration or other damage. Replace the shock dampers as follows:

    a. Support the shock in a press.

    b. Press out the old bushing.

    c. Clean the bushing bore for all rubber residue. Inspect the bore for cracks and other damage.

    d. Press in the new bushing until both sides are flush with the bushing bore.

REAR SWING ARM

This section describes complete service for the swing arm (**Figure 9**).

Tools

A Honda swing arm pivot locknut wrench is required to loosen and tighten the swing arm pivot shaft locknut. This tool is shown in the text and can be ordered through a Honda dealership. Do not service the swing arm without this tool.

13

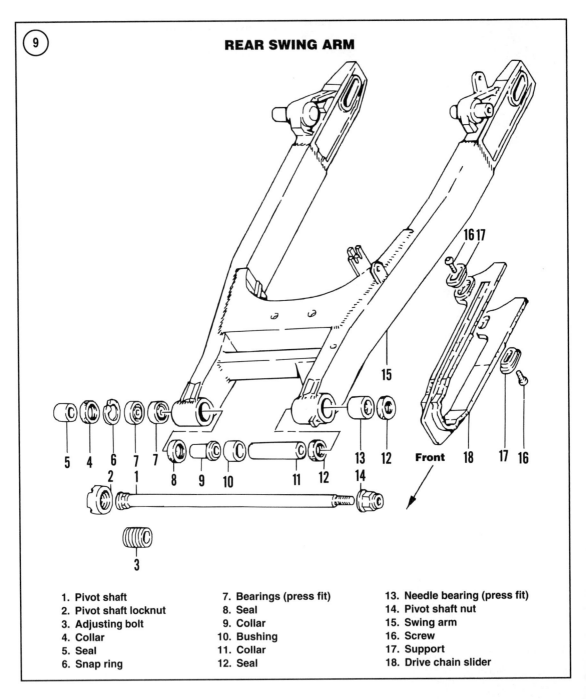

REAR SWING ARM

1. Pivot shaft
2. Pivot shaft locknut
3. Adjusting bolt
4. Collar
5. Seal
6. Snap ring
7. Bearings (press fit)
8. Seal
9. Collar
10. Bushing
11. Collar
12. Seal
13. Needle bearing (press fit)
14. Pivot shaft nut
15. Swing arm
16. Screw
17. Support
18. Drive chain slider

Removal

1. Remove the exhaust system (Chapter Fifteen).

2. Remove the rear wheel (Chapter Eleven).

3. Remove the shock absorbers (A, **Figure 10**) as described in this chapter.

4. Remove the chain guard (B, **Figure 10**).

NOTE
Have an assistant steady the bike when performing Step 5.

5. Grasp the rear end of the swing arm and try to move it from side to side in a horizontal arc. There must be no noticeable side play. Then grasp the rear of the swing arm again and pivot it up and down through

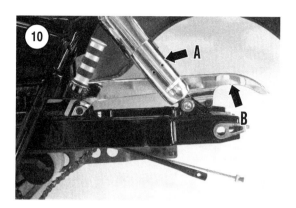

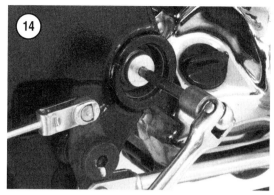

its full travel. The swing arm must pivot smoothly with no roughness or binding. If play is evident and the pivot bolts are tightened correctly, inspect the swing arm bearings for excessive wear or damage.

> *NOTE*
> *The condition of the swing arm bearings can greatly affect the handling of the motorcycle. Worn bearings can cause wheel hop, pulling to one side under acceleration and pulling to the other side during braking. Replace damaged bearings as required.*

6. Remove the left and right side swing arm pivot caps (**Figure 11**).

7. On the left side, remove the pivot shaft nut (**Figure 12**).

8. On the right side, hold the pivot shaft with an 8-mm hex socket (A, **Figure 13**), then loosen and remove the pivot shaft locknut with the Honda pivot locknut wrench (B).

> *NOTE*
> *Male splines on the pivot shaft (1, **Figure 9**) engage with female splines on the adjusting bolt (3). Before attempting to remove the pivot shaft, turn it as described in Step 9 to loosen the adjusting bolt and move it away from the swing arm. When the adjusting bolt is positioned correctly, the pivot shaft can be removed. If the pivot shaft is removed first, the adjusting bolt will continue to apply pressure against the swing arm, making it difficult to remove the swing arm.*

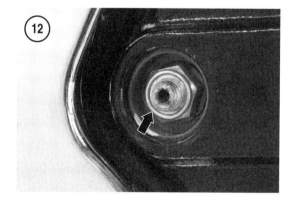

9. Turn the pivot shaft (**Figure 14**) without removing it to loosen and turn the adjusting bolt away

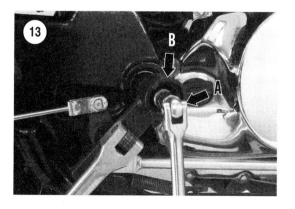

13

from the swing arm. Continue until the adjusting bolt (A, **Figure 15**) is positioned flush with the inside of the frame (**Figure 16**). Then remove the pivot shaft (B, **Figure 15**) from the right side and pull the swing arm from the engine and frame.

NOTE
*If the left side of the swing arm is difficult to remove, the engine is misaligned in the frame and causing the left collar to bind between the frame and engine. **Figure 17** shows the collar positioned against the frame and engine with the swing arm removed for clarity. To remove the swing arm without damaging the collar, loosen all of the engine mounting fasteners (Chapter Five). The swing arm should then be easy to remove. Do not tighten the engine mounting fasteners until after the swing is reinstalled back into the frame. The correct installation sequence is covered during the **Installation** procedure at the end of this section.*

10A. Locate and remove the collars installed on each side of the swing arm (**Figure 9**).

10B. If the swing arm bearings are not going to be serviced, tie a plastic bag around each end of the swing arm. This protects the bearings and prevents the loss of the collars.

Inspection

Refer to **Figure 9**.

1. Clean and dry the swing arm and its components.

2. Replace the drive chain slider (**Figure 18**) if excessively worn or damaged. Secure the screws with a medium strength threadlock.

3. Different size seals (**Figure 19**) are used in the swing arm. Mark the original seals and use them to identify the new seals during reassembly.

4. Remove the collars and seals (**Figure 19**) from the swing arm.

5. Inspect the swing arm bearings as follows:

   a. Turn each ball bearing inner race (A, **Figure 20**) by hand. Use the collar to turn the inner bearing and check its condition. Replace both bearings if there is any excessive play or roughness.

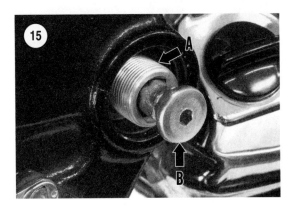

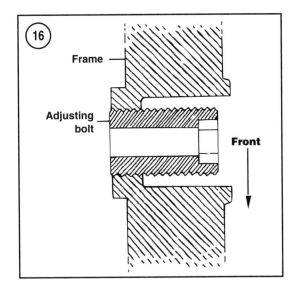

   b. Inspect the needle bearing rollers (**Figure 21**) for wear, pitting or rust. Install the collar into the needle bearing and rotate the collar. The collar must turn smoothly without excessive play or roughness.

   c. If bearing damage is noted, inspect the collar for damage.

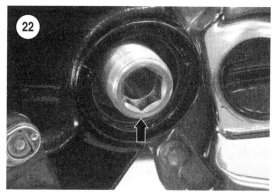

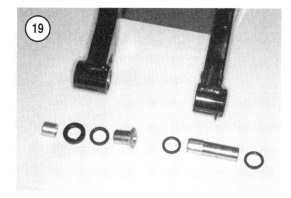

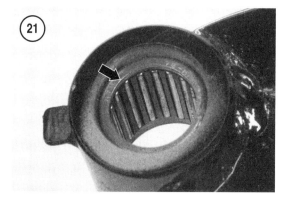

d. Replace and lubricate any worn or damaged bearing as described in this section. Remember to replace both ball bearings as a set.

6. If the original bearings are to be reused, perform the following:

a. Clean the needle bearing (**Figure 21**) in the left side of the swing arm with solvent and dry with compressed air. Pack the bearing with grease.

b. It is more difficult to service the two ball bearings (A, **Figure 20**) installed in the right side of the swing arm. If the grease does not look contaminated or dry, wipe the outer race of each bearing with a clean rag. Then use the tip of a grease gun to pack the bearings with as much grease as possible. Wipe up any excess grease from the bore surface. Otherwise, clean the bearings with solvent and try to force as much grease into the bearings as possible. Check that the snap ring was not dislodged from its groove in the swing arm.

7. Install the new seals (**Figure 19**) as follows:

a. Pack the lip of each new seal with grease.

b. Use the marks made on the original seals to help identify the new seals. Then install the seals with their flat side facing out.

8. Check the pivot shaft for straightness with V-blocks and a dial indicator. Replace the pivot shaft if there is any runout.

9. Remove the adjusting bolt (**Figure 22**) from the frame. Clean the adjusting bolt and frame threads of all dirt and grease. Inspect the threads for damage.

Bearing Replacement

Do not remove the swing arm bearings unless they must be replaced.

Ball bearings

Replace both ball bearings (7, **Figure 9**) as a set.

1. Chill the new bearings in a freezer for a few hours to shrink the outer diameter of the bearings as much as possible.

2. Remove the snap ring (B, **Figure 20**) from the groove in the swing arm.

3. Support the right side bearing bore in a press as shown in **Figure 23**.

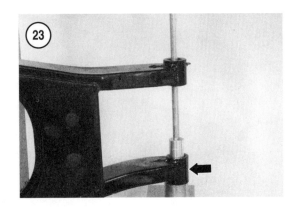

> *CAUTION*
> *Do not support any other part of the swing arm or it will be damaged when pressure is applied to the bearings.*

4. Press the ball bearings (**Figure 23**) out of the swing arm and discard them.

5. Clean the bearing bore and snap ring groove. Check for damage.

6. Install the new bearings with their manufacturer's marks facing out.

7. Pack each bearing with grease.

8. Support the right side of the swing arm in a press as shown in **Figure 24**.

9. Press in the inner bearing until it bottoms against the bore shoulder.

10. Check that the bearing is properly seated. Turn the inner race by hand. It should turn smoothly.

11. Use the same setup and install the outer bearing until it bottoms against the inner bearing. Repeat Step 10 to check the bearing.

12. Install the snap ring (B, **Figure 20**) into the groove with its flat side facing out. Make sure the snap ring seats in the groove completely.

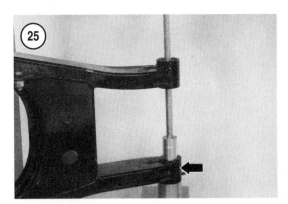

Needle bearing

1. Chill the new bearing in a freezer for a few hours to shrink the outer diameter of the bearing as much as possible.

2. Support the left side bearing bore in a press as shown in **Figure 25**.

> *CAUTION*
> *Do not support any other part of the swing arm or it will be damaged when pressure is applied to the bearing.*

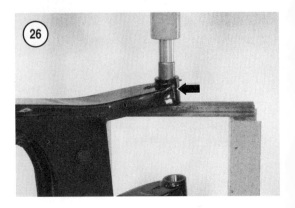

3. Press the needle bearing out of the swing arm and discard it.

4. Clean the bearing bore. Check for damage.

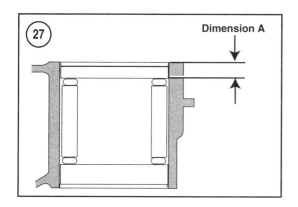

27

Dimension A

28

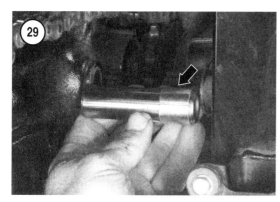

29

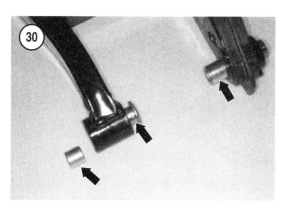

30

5. Install the new bearing with its manufacturer's marks facing out.

6. Pack the area between the bearing rollers with grease.

7. Support the left side of the swing arm in a press as shown in **Figure 26**.

8. Press the needle bearing into the bore until its outer surface is 4.0 mm (0.16 in.) below the outer swing arm bore surface as shown in Dimension A, **Figure 27**.

9. Check the bearing for damage.

Installation

1. Clean and lubricate the bearings and seals as described in this section.

2. Make sure the adjusting bolt threads in the frame, and the threads on the pivot shaft, adjusting bolt, pivot shaft locknut and pivot nut are clean and dry.

3. Tie the drive chain to the frame with its upper run positioned above the swing arm pivot hole (**Figure 28**).

4. Thread the adjusting bolt into the frame (**Figure 22**). Do not thread the adjusting bolt so it extends past the inside of the frame (**Figure 16**).

5. Before installing the swing arm, fit the right side collar between the engine and frame as shown in **Figure 29**. If there is room to install the collar, the engine is positioned correctly in the frame. However, if the collar cannot be installed, the engine is misaligned in the frame. If not previously done during swing arm removal, loosen all the engine mounting fasteners (Chapter Five). The swing arm and engine fasteners will be tightened at the same time to ensure proper alignment.

6. Lubricate the pivot shaft with grease and set aside until installation.

7. Install the collars into the swing arm:
   a. Install the bushing (10, **Figure 9**) onto the collar (11).
   b. Lubricate the collars with grease and install them into the swing arm (**Figure 30**).

8. Position the swing arm into the frame and align with the frame and engine. From the right side of the frame, install the pivot shaft (**Figure 31**) through the adjusting bolt, engine and frame mounting holes.

9. Turn the pivot shaft to engage it flush against the adjusting bolt as shown in **Figure 32**.

13

10. Turn the pivot shaft until the adjusting bolt contacts the swing arm. Then tighten the adjusting bolt by turning the pivot shaft (**Figure 33**) to 25 N•m (18 ft.-lb.). Make sure the swing arm pivots smoothly.

11. Install the right side pivot shaft locknut and tighten with the Honda pivot locknut wrench as follows:

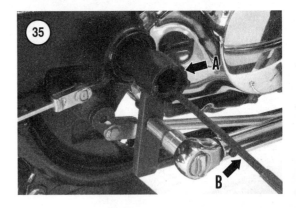

   a. Install the pivot shaft locknut (**Figure 34**) and tighten finger-tight.

NOTE
*Mount the Honda pivot locknut wrench onto the torque wrench at a right angle as shown in **Figure 35**. If the locknut wrench is mounted so it lengthens the torque wrench, the torque reading on the wrench does not equal the actual torque applied to the locknut. Refer to **Torque Adapters** in Chapter One for more information.*

   b. Hold the pivot shaft with an 8-mm Allen wrench (B, **Figure 35**) and use the Honda tool (A) to tighten the pivot shaft locknut to 64 N•m (47 ft.-lb.).

c. Move the swing arm. If the swing arm is tight or loose, loosen the locknut and retighten.

12. Tighten the pivot shaft nut (**Figure 36**) to 88 N•m (65 ft.-lb.).

13. Move the swing arm up and down and check for smooth movement. If the swing arm is tight or loose, the fasteners were tightened either in the wrong order or to the incorrect torque specification. Loosen the fasteners and retighten in orer.

14. If the engine mounting fasteners were loosened, tighten them as described in Chapter Five.

15. Install the left and right side swing arm pivot caps.

16. Install the chain guard (B, **Figure 10**).

17. Install the shock absorbers (A, **Figure 10**) as described in this chapter.

18. Install the rear wheel (Chapter Eleven).

19. Install the exhaust system (Chapter Fifteen).

Table 1 REAR SUSPENSION SPECIFICATIONS

Rear axle travel	
VT750C	90 mm (3.5 in.)
VT750DC	80 mm (3.1 in.)
Shock absorber standard preload adjuster setting	Second position

Table 2 REAR SUSPENSION TORQUE SPECIFICATION

	N•m	ft.-lb.
Pivot shaft adjusting bolt	25	18
Pivot shaft locknut	64	47
Pivot shaft nut	88	65
Rear shock absorber mounting bolts	26	19

13

CHAPTER FOURTEEN

BRAKES

This chapter covers service, repair and replacement procedures for the front disc brake and rear drum brake. Routine brake inspection and adjustment procedures are in Chapter Three. The front and rear brake units are critical to riding performance and safety. Inspect the front and rear brakes frequently and repair any problem immediately.

Brake specifications are located in **Tables 1-3** at the end of this chapter.

BRAKE FLUID SELECTION

When adding brake fluid, use DOT 4 brake fluid from a sealed container. DOT 4 brake fluid is glycol-based and draws moisture, which greatly reduces its ability to perform correctly. It is a good idea to purchase brake fluid in small containers and discard any small leftover quantities. Do not store a container of brake fluid with less than 1/4 of the fluid remaining.

> *CAUTION*
> *Do not intermix DOT 5 (silicone-based) brake fluid, as it can cause brake system failure.*

PREVENTING BRAKE FLUID DAMAGE

Many of the procedures in this chapter require handling brake fluid. Be careful not to spill any fluid, as it stains or damages most surfaces. To prevent brake fluid damage, note the following:

1. Before performing any procedure in which there is the possibility of brake fluid contacting the motorcycle, cover the area with a large piece of plastic. It only takes a few drops of brake fluid to damage an expensive part.

2. Before handling brake fluid or working on the brake system, fill a small container with soap and water and keep it close to the motorcycle while working. If brake fluid contacts the motorcycle, clean the area and rinse it thoroughly.

3. To help control the flow of brake fluid when filling the reservoirs, punch a small hole into the seal of a new container next to the edge of the pour spout.

BRAKE SERVICE

When working on the brake system, the work area and all tools must be clean. Any tiny particles of dirt or debris in the caliper assembly or master cylinder can damage the components and prevent the system from functioning properly.

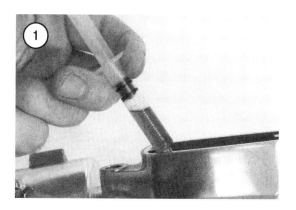

Consider the following when servicing the disc brakes.

WARNING
*Whenever working on the brake system, do **not** inhale brake dust. Do **not** use compressed air to blow off brake parts. It may contain asbestos, which can cause lung injury and cancer. Wear a face mask that meets OHSA requirements for trapping asbestos particles, and wash hands and forearms thoroughly after completing the work. Wet down the brake dust on brake components before working on the brake system. Secure and dispose of all brake dust and cleaning materials properly.*

1. DOT 4 brake fluid damages plastic, painted and plated surfaces.

2. Always keep the master cylinder reservoir and brake fluid containers closed to prevent dust or moisture from entering. This contaminates the brake fluid and can cause brake failure.

3. Handle the brake components carefully when servicing them. Use only DOT 4 brake fluid or isopropyl alcohol to wash rubber parts in the brake system. Never allow any petroleum-based cleaner to contact any of the rubber parts. These chemicals cause the rubber to swell, requiring their replacement.

4. Do not allow any grease or oil to contact the brake pads or brake shoes.

5. When cleaning the brake components, wear rubber gloves to keep brake fluid off skin.

6. Whenever loosening any brake hose banjo bolt, the brake system is opened. The system must be bled to remove air bubbles. Also, if the brake feels spongy, this usually means there are air bubbles in the system. Bleed the brakes as described in this chapter.

WARNING
Never reuse brake fluid (line fluid expelled during brake bleeding). Contaminated brake fluid can cause brake failure. Dispose of used brake fluid safely.

FRONT BRAKE PADS

There is no recommended mileage interval for changing the brake pads. Pad wear depends greatly on riding habits and the condition of the brake system. As the brake pads wear, the brake fluid level drops in the reservoir and automatically adjusts for wear.

The brake pads can be replaced with the brake caliper mounted on the motorcycle.

Always replace both front brake pads at the same time. Never use one new brake pad with a used brake pad in a caliper because it causes an unbalanced braking condition.

Inspection

Inspect the front brake pads as described in Chapter Three.

Replacement

1. Review the *Brake Service* information in the preceding section.

2. Turn the front wheel to level the master cylinder. Remove the front master cylinder cover, set plate and diaphragm and use a syringe (**Figure 1**) to remove and discard about 50 percent of the fluid from the reservoir. This prevents the master cylinder from overflowing when the caliper pistons are compressed for pad reinstallation. Do *not* drain the reservoir to the point where the outlet holes in the bottom of the reservoir are exposed to air. Air enters the system and the system has to be bled.

CAUTION
Do not allow the master cylinder reservoir to overflow when performing Step 3. Brake fluid damages most surfaces it contacts.

14

3. Hold the caliper housing from the outside and push it toward its brake disc. This pushes the pistons into the caliper to make room for the new brake pads. Reinstall the diaphragm, set plate and cover removed in Step 1.

> *NOTE*
> *The pistons should move smoothly when compressing them in Step 3. If not, check the caliper for sticking pistons or damaged caliper bores, pistons and seals. Repair requires overhaul of the brake caliper assembly. Also note that road debris collected on the exposed part of the pistons can tear the seals as the pistons pass through them.*

4. Remove the pad pin plug (A, **Figure 2**) and loosen the pad pin (B).
5. Remove the pad pin and both brake pads (**Figure 3**).
6. Make sure the pad spring (**Figure 4**) is in good condition and installed inside the caliper. Replace the pad spring if damaged.
7. Inspect the pad pin (A, **Figure 5**) for excessive wear, corrosion or damage. Remove corrosion and dirt from the pad pin surface. A dirty or damaged pad pin surface prevents the brake pads from sliding properly and results in brake drag and overheating of the brake disc.

8. Inspect the brake pads (B, **Figure 5**) as follows:
   a. Inspect the friction material for light surface dirt, grease and oil contamination. Remove light contamination with sandpaper. If the contamination has penetrated the surface, replace the brake pads.
   b. Inspect the brake pads for excessive wear or damage. Replace the brake pads when the friction material is worn to the wear indicator line (**Figure 6**) on the pad.
   c. Inspect the brake pads for uneven wear. If one pad is worn more than the other, the caliper may be binding on one or both pin bolts.
   d. Check the shim (**Figure 7**) on the backside of the inner pad for rust, corrosion and damage. Make sure the shim fits tightly on the pad.

> *NOTE*
> *If brake fluid is leaking from around the pistons, overhaul the brake caliper as described in this chapter.*

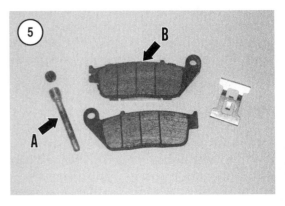

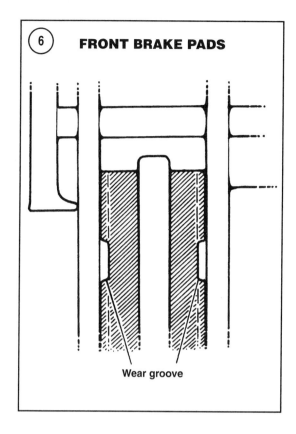

⑥ **FRONT BRAKE PADS**

Wear groove

⑦

⑧

9. Service the brake disc as follows:

   a. Use brake cleaner and a fine-grade emery cloth to remove road debris and brake pad residue from the brake disc. Clean both sides of the disc.

> *NOTE*
> *Cleaning the brake disc is especially important if changing brake pad compounds. Some compounds are not compatible with each other.*

   b. Check the brake disc for wear as described in this chapter.

10. Install the brake pads into the caliper (**Figure 3**) so the friction material on both brake pads faces toward the brake disc. Install the pad with the shim on the inside. Insert the extended arm on the end of each pad into the pad retainer in the caliper bracket (**Figure 8**).

11. Push both brake pads against the pad spring and install the pad pin (B, **Figure 2**) through the brake caliper and brake pad holes. Tighten the pad pin finger-tight.

12. Tighten the pad pin (B, **Figure 2**) to 18 N•m (13 ft.-lb.).

13. Install the pad pin plug (A, **Figure 2**) and tighten to 3 N•m (26 in.-lb.).

14. Pump the front brake lever to correctly seat the pads against the disc and then check the brake fluid level in the reservoir. If necessary, add new DOT 4 brake fluid (Chapter Three).

> *WARNING*
> *Do not ride the motorcycle until the brakes operate correctly.*

15. Bed the pads in gradually for the first two to three days of riding by using only light pressure as much as possible. Immediate hard application glazes the new friction pads and greatly reduces their effectiveness.

FRONT CALIPER

Removal/Installation

Refer to **Figure 9**.

1. If the caliper is going to be removed from the motorcycle, perform the following:

14

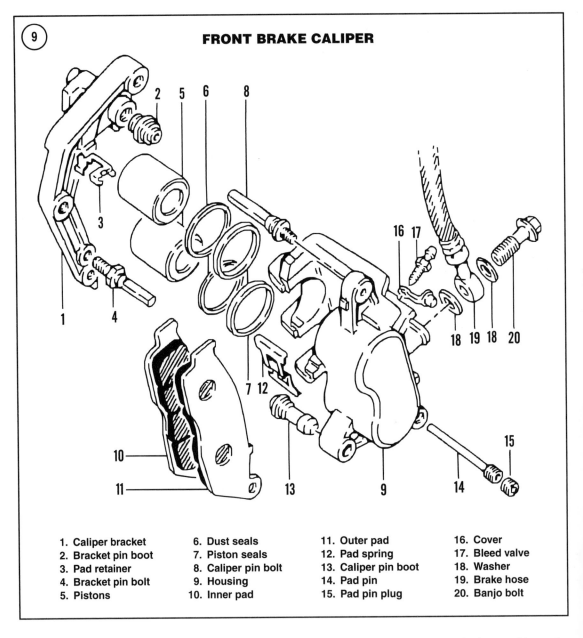

⑨ **FRONT BRAKE CALIPER**

1. Caliper bracket	6. Dust seals	11. Outer pad	16. Cover
2. Bracket pin boot	7. Piston seals	12. Pad spring	17. Bleed valve
3. Pad retainer	8. Caliper pin bolt	13. Caliper pin boot	18. Washer
4. Bracket pin bolt	9. Housing	14. Pad pin	19. Brake hose
5. Pistons	10. Inner pad	15. Pad pin plug	20. Banjo bolt

a. Remove the brake pads as described in this chapter to prevent their contamination from contact with brake fluid.

b. Drain the brake fluid as described in this chapter.

2. Remove the brake hose banjo bolt and the two washers at the caliper (A, **Figure 10**). Place the loose end of the hose in a plastic bag to prevent leakage and hose contamination.

3. Remove the two brake caliper mounting bolts (B, **Figure 10**) and lift the caliper off the brake disc.

Remove the brake hose from the hose guide on the caliper.

4. If the brake hose was not disconnected at the caliper, insert a spacer block between the brake pads and support the caliper with a wire hook.

NOTE
The spacer block prevents the pistons from being forced out of the caliper if the front brake is applied while the brake caliper is removed from the brake disc.

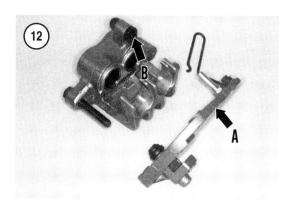

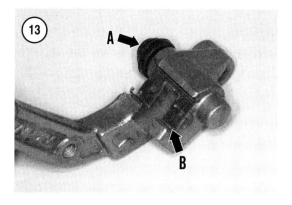

5. If necessary, service the brake caliper as described in this chapter.

6. Installation is the reverse of removal. Note the following:

  a. Install the caliper assembly over the brake disc. If the pads are installed in the caliper, be careful not to damage their leading edge.

  b. Install two new brake caliper mounting bolts (B, **Figure 10**) and tighten to 30 N•m (22 ft.-lb.). Install the brake hose into the brake hose guide on the caliper.

  c. Place a new washer on each side of each brake hose (A, **Figure 10**.). Then thread the banjo bolt into the caliper and tighten to 34 N•m (25 ft.-lb.).

  d. If removed, install the brake pads as described in this chapter.

  e. If the brake hose was disconnected or it is necessary to do so, bleed the front brake as described in this chapter.

  f. Pump the front brake lever to seat the pads against the brake disc.

Disassembly

Refer to **Figure 9**.

1. Remove the brake pads and brake caliper as described in this chapter.

2. Remove the pad spring (**Figure 11**).

3. Slide the caliper bracket (A, **Figure 12**) from the caliper housing.

4. Remove the caliper pin boot (B, **Figure 12**).

5. Remove the bracket pin boot (A, **Figure 13**) and pad retainer (B).

6. Remove the pistons as follows:

> *WARNING*
> *Be careful when using compressed air. The pistons, dirt or brake fluid can fly from the caliper at great speed and cause injury. Compressed air forces the pistons out of the caliper under considerable force. Do not cushion the pistons by hand, as injury could result. Wear safety eyewear and shop gloves and apply compressed air gradually. Do not use high pressure air.*

  a. Identify the pistons by marking their inner bores with a black marker so they can be reinstalled in their original cylinders.

b. Place the caliper on a workbench with the pistons facing down. Place a thick towel between the pistons and workbench. Make sure there is enough space underneath the caliper for the pistons to be removed completely.

c. Tighten the bleed screw.

d. Blow the pistons out with compressed air directed into the hydraulic fluid hose (**Figure 14**).

e. Remove the pistons (**Figure 15**).

7. Remove the dust seals (A, **Figure 16**) and piston seals (B) and discard them.

8. Remove the bleed screw and its cover from the caliper.

Inspection

When measuring the brake caliper components, compare the actual measurements to the specifications in **Table 1**. Replace worn or damaged parts as described in this section.

1. Clean and dry the caliper assembly as follows:

a. Handle the brake components carefully when servicing them.

b. Use only DOT 4 brake fluid or isopropyl alcohol to wash rubber parts in the brake system. Never allow any petroleum-based cleaner to contact the rubber parts. These chemicals cause the rubber to swell, which requires their replacement.

c. Clean the dust and piston seal grooves carefully to avoid damaging the caliper bore. Use a small pick or brush to clean the grooves. If a hard varnish residue has built up in the grooves, soak the caliper in solvent to help soften the residue. Then wash the caliper in soapy water and rinse completely.

d. If alcohol or solvent was used to clean the caliper, blow dry with compressed air.

e. Check the fluid passages to make sure they are clean and dry.

f. After cleaning the parts, place them on a clean lint-free cloth until reassembly.

> *CAUTION*
> *Do not get any oil or grease onto any of the brake caliper components. These chemicals cause the rubber parts in the brake system to swell, permanently damaging them.*

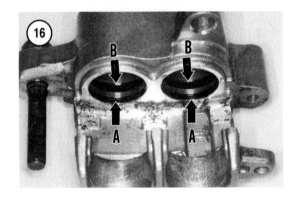

2. Check each cylinder bore for corrosion, deep scratches and other wear marks. Do not hone the cylinder bores.

3. Measure the caliper cylinder bore diameters (A, **Figure 17**).

4. Inspect the pistons for pitting, corrosion, cracks or other damage.

5. Measure each piston outside diameter (B, **Figure 17**).

6. Clean the bleed screw with compressed air. Check the valve threads for damage. Replace the dust cap if it is missing or damaged.

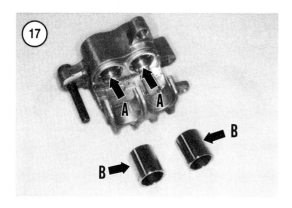

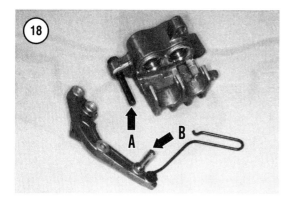

7. Clean the banjo bolt with compressed air.

8. Inspect the caliper, bracket pin bolts and pin boots as follows:

NOTE
The brake calipers are of a floating design. Pin bolts mounted on the caliper housing and caliber bracket allow the brake caliper to slide or float during piston movement. Pin boots installed over each bolt help control caliper movement by preventing excessive bolt vibration and play and to prevent dirt from damaging the bolt operating surfaces. Grooved or damaged pin bolts prevent caliper movement. This condition causes brake pads to wear unevenly, causing brake drag and overheating of the brake disc and brake fluid. The pin bolts and pin boots must be maintained to provide proper brake operation.

 a. Inspect the pin boots for age deterioration and damage.

 b. Inspect the pin bolts (A and B, **Figure 18**) for excessive wear, uneven wear (steps) and

other damage. Replace damaged pin bolts as required.

9. When reinstalling or replacing damaged pin bolts, apply a medium strength threadlock onto the bolt threads and tighten as follows:

 a. Caliper pin bolt (A, **Figure 18**): 27 N•m (20 ft.-lb.).

 b. Bracket pin bolt (B, **Figure 18**): 13 N•m (115 in.-lb.).

Assembly

Use new DOT 4 brake fluid when lubricating the parts in the following steps.

NOTE
A brake caliper rebuild kit for the VT750 is available from K&L Supply and can be ordered through most Honda dealerships. The kit contains all of the necessary components to rebuild the brake caliper.

1. Install and tighten the bleed screw.

2. Soak the new piston and dust seals in new brake fluid.

3. Lubricate the pistons and cylinder bores with brake fluid. Check that the surfaces are free of dust and other particles.

NOTE
The piston seals are thicker than the dust seals.

4. Install a *new* piston seal (B, **Figure 16**) into each inner cylinder bore groove.

5. Install a *new* dust seal (A, **Figure 16**) into each outer cylinder bore groove.

NOTE
Make sure each seal fits squarely in its groove.

6. Install each piston into its respective caliper bore with its open side facing out (**Figure 19**). To prevent the pistons from damaging the seals, turn them into the bore by hand.

7. Apply silicone brake grease to the inside of the pin boots and along the pin bolts. Install the small boot onto the caliper bracket (A, **Figure 13**), and the large boot through the caliper housing (B, **Figure 12**).

14

8. Install the brake pad retainer (B, **Figure 13**) onto the caliper bracket. Make sure it fits tightly.

9. Align and install the caliper bracket over the caliper housing (**Figure 20**).

10. Install the pad spring (**Figure 11**).

11. Install the brake caliper and brake pads as described in this chapter.

FRONT MASTER CYLINDER

Read the information listed under *Brake Service* in this chapter before servicing the front master cylinder.

Removal/Installation

1. Remove the rear view mirror from the master cylinder.

2. Cover the fuel tank and front fender to prevent damage from brake fluid contact.

> *CAUTION*
> *Wash brake fluid off any surface immediately because it damages the finish. Use soapy water and rinse completely.*

3. Clean the top of the master cylinder of all dirt and debris.

4. Turn the handlebar so the master cylinder reservoir is level. Remove the master cylinder cover, set plate and diaphragm. Empty the brake fluid reservoir with a syringe (**Figure 1**).

5. Disconnect the brake light switch connectors (A, **Figure 21**) at the switch.

6. Remove the banjo bolt (B, **Figure 21**) and the two washers securing the brake hose to the master cylinder. Cover the open end of the hose with a plastic bag to prevent leakage and hose contamination.

7. Remove the bolts and clamp (**Figure 22**) securing the master cylinder to the handlebar and remove the master cylinder.

8. If necessary, service the master cylinder as described in this chapter.

9. Clean the handlebar, master cylinder and clamp mating surfaces.

10. Installation is the reverse of removal. Note the following:

   a. Mount the master cylinder onto the handlebar and align the upper master cylinder and clamp mating surfaces with the punch mark on the handlebar.

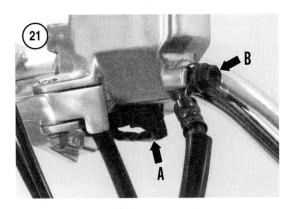

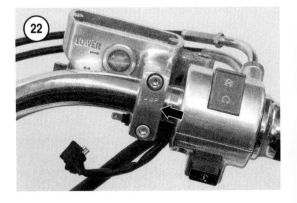

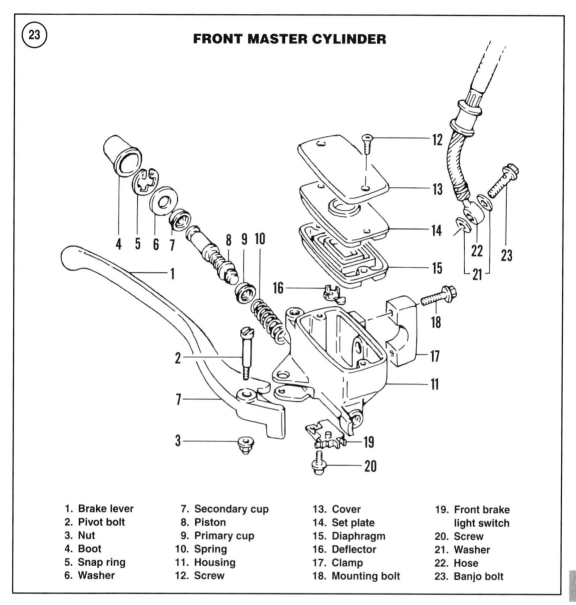

FRONT MASTER CYLINDER

1. Brake lever	7. Secondary cup	13. Cover	19. Front brake
2. Pivot bolt	8. Piston	14. Set plate	light switch
3. Nut	9. Primary cup	15. Diaphragm	20. Screw
4. Boot	10. Spring	16. Deflector	21. Washer
5. Snap ring	11. Housing	17. Clamp	22. Hose
6. Washer	12. Screw	18. Mounting bolt	23. Banjo bolt

14

b. Install the clamp (**Figure 22**) with its UP mark facing up and secure with the mounting bolts. Tighten the upper clamp bolt first, and then the lower clamp bolt to 12 N•m (106 in.-lb.). Check that there is a gap at the bottom of the clamp.

c. Secure the brake hose to the master cylinder with the banjo bolt (B, **Figure 21**) and two *new* washers. Install a new washer on each side of the brake hose. Position the brake hose arm against the master cylinder bracket as shown in **Figure 21** and tighten the banjo bolt to 34 N•m (25 ft.-lb.).

d. Bleed the front brake as described in this chapter.

e. Turn the ignition switch on and make sure the brake light comes on when operating the front brake lever.

Disassembly

Refer to **Figure 23**.

1. Remove the master cylinder as described in this chapter.

2. If not already removed, remove the master cylinder cover, set plate and diaphragm.

3. Remove the screw and the brake light switch (A, **Figure 24**).

4. Remove the nut (B, **Figure 24**), pivot bolt and front brake lever.

5. Remove the boot (**Figure 25**) from the groove in the end of the piston.

> *NOTE*
> *If brake fluid is leaking from the piston bore, the piston cups are worn or damaged. Replace the piston assembly.*

> *NOTE*
> *To aid in the removal and installation of the master cylinder snap ring, thread a bolt and nut into the brake hose port and secure the bolt in a vise (Figure 26).*

6. Compress the piston and remove the snap ring (**Figure 27**) from the groove in the master cylinder.

7. Remove the piston assembly (**Figure 28**) from the master cylinder bore. Do not remove the primary and secondary cups from the piston.

8. Remove the deflector (**Figure 29**) from the reservoir.

Inspection

When measuring the master cylinder components, compare the actual measurements to the specifications in **Table 1**. Replace worn or damaged parts as described in this section.

1. Clean and dry the master cylinder assembly as follows:

   a. Handle the brake components carefully when servicing them.

   b. Use only DOT 4 brake fluid or isopropyl alcohol to wash rubber parts in the brake system. Never allow any petroleum-based cleaner to contact the rubber parts. These chemicals cause the rubber to swell, which requires their replacement.

   c. Clean the master cylinder snap ring groove carefully. Use a small pick or brush to clean the groove. If a hard varnish residue has built up in the groove, soak the master cylinder in solvent to help soften the residue. Then wash in soapy water and rinse completely.

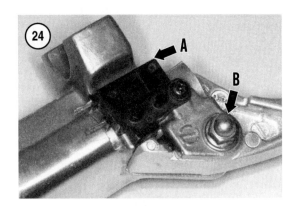
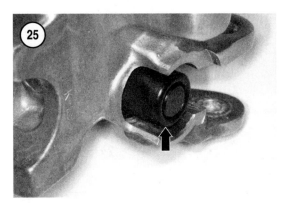

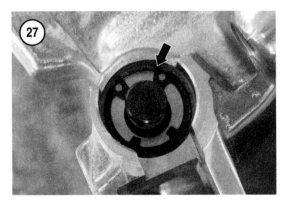

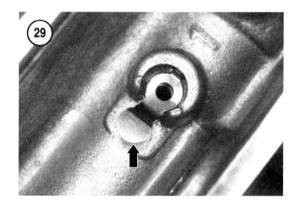

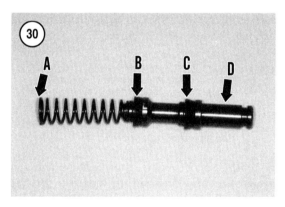

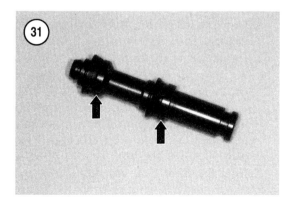

d. Blow the master cylinder dry with compressed air.

e. Place cleaned parts on a clean lint-free cloth until reassembly.

WARNING
Do not get any oil or grease onto any of the components. These chemicals cause the rubber parts in the brake system to swell, permanently damaging them.

CAUTION
Do not remove the primary and secondary cups from the piston assembly for cleaning or inspection purposes. The cups are not available separately and must be replaced along with the new piston and spring as an assembly.

2. Check the piston assembly for the following defects:

a. Broken, distorted or collapsed piston return spring (A, **Figure 30**).

b. Worn, cracked, damaged or swollen primary (B, **Figure 30**) and secondary cups (C).

c. Scratched or damaged piston (D, **Figure 30**).

d. Worn or damaged boot.

e. If any of these parts are worn or damaged, replace the piston assembly.

3. Measure the piston outside diameter at the two points indicated in **Figure 31**.

4. To assemble a new piston assembly, perform the following:

NOTE
A master cylinder rebuild kit for the VT750 is available from K&L Supply and can be ordered through most Honda dealerships. The kit contains all of the necessary components to rebuild the master cylinder.

a. If replacing the piston, install the new primary and secondary cups onto the piston. Use the original piston assembly (**Figure 30**) as a reference when installing the new cups onto the piston.

NOTE
On the K&L master cylinder rebuild kit, the secondary piston is installed on the piston. It is only necessary to install the primary cup.

b. Before installing the new piston cups, lubricate them with brake fluid.

c. Clean the new piston in brake fluid.

d. Install the secondary cup (C, **Figure 30**), and then the primary cup (B) onto the piston.

5. Inspect the master cylinder bore. Replace the master cylinder if its bore is corroded or damaged. Do not hone the master cylinder bore to remove scratches or other damage.

6. Inspect the threads in the master cylinder body. If damaged, clean with a suitable size metric tap or replace the master cylinder assembly.

7. Inspect the fluid viewing port for fluid leakage. If leakage has occurred, replace the master cylinder body.

8. Inspect the hand lever pivot hole (A, **Figure 32**) on the master cylinder body. Check for cracks or elongation. If damaged, replace the master cylinder body.

9. Measure the master cylinder bore inside diameter (B, **Figure 32**).

10. Check for plugged supply and relief ports (**Figure 33**) in the master cylinder. Clean with compressed air.

11. Check the brake lever assembly for the following defects:

a. Damaged brake lever. Check the pivot hole for cracks and elongation.

b. Scored or damaged pivot bolt.

Assembly

1. If installing a new piston assembly, assemble it as described under *Inspection* in this section.

2. Lubricate the piston assembly and cylinder bore with DOT 4 brake fluid. Check that the surfaces are free of dust and other particles.

CAUTION
Do not allow the piston cups to tear or turn inside out when installing the piston into the master cylinder bore. Both cups are larger than the bore.

3. Insert the piston assembly with the spring end first, into the master cylinder bore (**Figure 28**).

4. Install the washer (**Figure 28**) and seat it against the piston.

5. Secure the master cylinder in a vise as described during disassembly. Compress the piston assembly

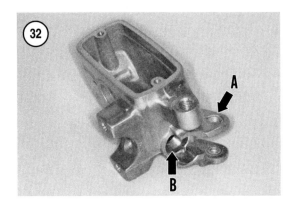

and install a new snap ring with the flat side facing out, into the bore groove (**Figure 27**).

CAUTION
The snap ring must seat in the master cylinder groove completely. Push and release the piston a few times to make sure it moves smoothly and that the snap ring does not pop out.

6. Slide the boot over the piston. Seat the large end against the snap ring and the outer lip into the groove in the end of the piston (**Figure 25**).

7. Install the brake lever assembly as follows:

a. Lubricate the pivot bolt with silicone brake grease.

b. Install the brake lever.

c. Install and tighten the brake lever pivot bolt (A, **Figure 34**) to 1 N•m (8.8 in.-lb.). Pump the brake lever to make sure it moves freely. If there is any binding or roughness, remove the pivot bolt and brake lever and inspect the parts.

d. Hold the pivot bolt, and then install and tighten the brake lever pivot nut (B, **Figure**

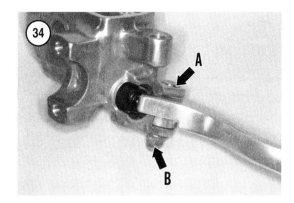

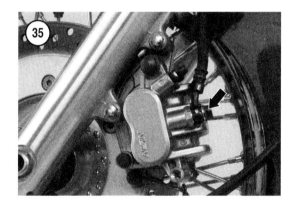

34) to 6 N•m (53 in.-lb.). Check that the brake lever moves freely.

NOTE
The piston assembly must operate smoothly when pumping the brake lever. If there is any roughness or a change in operation, the snap ring may have popped out of its groove. Remove the brake lever and check the piston and snap ring.

8. Install the deflector (**Figure 29**) into the reservoir.

NOTE
The deflector prevents brake fluid from spurting out the reservoir when operating the brake lever during brake bleeding.

9. Install the front brake light switch (A, **Figure 24**) and secure with the mounting screw.

10. Install the diaphragm, set plate and cover.

11. Install the master cylinder as described in this section.

FRONT BRAKE HOSE REPLACEMENT

Check the brake hose at the brake inspection intervals listed in Chapter Three. Replace the brake hose if it shows signs of bulging, chafing or damage. To replace the brake hose, perform the following:

1. Drape a plastic drop cloth over the front fender and fuel tank to protect them from accidental brake fluid spills.

CAUTION
Dot 4 brake fluid damages the finish on plastic, painted and plated surfaces. Immediately wash spilled brake fluid off the motorcycle. Use soapy water and rinse the area completely.

2. Drain the brake system as described in this chapter.

3. Before removing the brake hose, note the following:
   a. Record the hose routing on a piece of paper.
   b. Remove any bolts or brackets securing the brake hose to the fender, frame or suspension component.
   c. Before removing the banjo bolts, note how the end of the brake hose is positioned against the brake unit.

4. Remove the banjo bolt and the two washers at the brake caliper (**Figure 35**). Hold the open end of the hose over a container and pump the brake lever to force fluid out of the hose. Place the loose end of the hose in a plastic bag to prevent brake fluid from leaking onto the motorcycle.

CAUTION
Dispose of this brake fluid properly. Never reuse brake fluid.

5. Remove the banjo bolt and the two washers at the master cylinder (**Figure 36**).

6. Carefully remove the brake hose from the motorcycle.

7. Wash off brake fluid that may have leaked out the hose or brake units during removal.

8. Clean and dry the banjo bolts.

9. Reverse these steps to install the new brake hose, while noting the following:
   a. Compare the new and old hoses to make sure they are the same.

14

b. Clean the *new* washers, banjo bolts and hose ends to remove any contamination.

c. Referring to the notes made during removal, route the brake hose along its original path.

d. Install a *new* washer on each side of the brake hose.

e. Tighten the banjo bolts to 34 N•m (25 ft.-lb.).

10. After installation, turn the handlebars from side to side to make sure the brake hose does not rub against any part or pull away from its brake unit. Check for any twisting or interference.

11. Refill the master cylinder and bleed the front brake as described in this chapter.

> *WARNING*
> *Do not ride the motorcycle until making sure the front brake is operating properly.*

FRONT BRAKE DISC

Inspection

The front brake disc can be inspected while installed on the motorcycle. Small marks on the disc are not important, but deep scratches or other marks may reduce braking effectiveness and increase brake pad wear. If these grooves are evident and the brake pads are wearing rapidly, replace the brake disc.

Table 1 lists the new and service limit specifications for brake disc thickness. The minimum (MIN) thickness is stamped on the outside of the disc face (A, **Figure 37**). If the specification stamped on the disc differs from the service limit in **Table 1**, use the specification on the disc when inspecting it.

When servicing the brake disc, do not have the disc reconditioned (ground) to compensate for warp. The disc is thin and grinding only reduces its thickness, causing it to warp quite rapidly. If the disc is warped, refer to *Brakes* in Chapter Two.

1. Support the motorcycle with the front wheel off the ground.

2. Measure the disc thickness at several locations around the disc (**Figure 38**). Replace the disc if its thickness at any point is less than the minimum allowable specification stamped on the disc or less than the service limit in **Table 1**.

3. Make sure the disc mounting bolts are tight before checking brake disc runout.

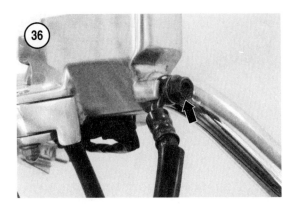

4. Turn the wheel to one side. Position a dial indicator stem against the brake disc (**Figure 39**). Zero the dial gauge and slowly turn the wheel and measure runout. If the disc runout is excessive:

a. Check for loose or missing fasteners.

b. Remove the front wheel and check the wheel bearings.

c. Check for a damaged front hub.

5. Clean the disc of any rust or corrosion, and wipe clean with brake cleaner. Never use an oil-based solvent that may leave an oil residue on the disc.

Removal/Installation

1. Remove the front wheel (Chapter Eleven).

2. Remove the bolts securing the brake disc to the wheel and remove the disc (B, **Figure 37**). Discard the mounting bolts.

3. Perform any necessary service to the front hub (wheel bearing or tire replacement) before installing the brake disc.

4. Clean the brake disc threaded holes in the front hub.

5. Clean the brake disc mounting surface on the front hub.

6. Install the brake disc with the MIN marked side (A, **Figure 37**) facing out.

7. Install *new* brake disc mounting bolts and tighten in a crossing pattern and in several steps to 42 N•m (31 ft.-lb.).

> *WARNING*
> *The disc bolts are made from a harder material than similar bolts used on the motorcycle. When replacing the bolts, use standard Honda brake disc bolts. Never compromise and use different bolts. They do **not** properly secure the disc to the hub.*

8. Clean the disc of any rust or corrosion and spray clean with brake cleaner. Never use an oil-based solvent that may leave an oil residue on the disc.

9. Install the front wheel (Chapter Eleven).

BRAKE BLEEDING

Air in the brake system increases brake lever travel while causing it to feel spongy and less responsive. Under extreme braking (heat) conditions, it can cause complete loss of the brake. Bleeding the brakes removes air from the brake system.

The brake system can be bled manually or with the use of a vacuum pump. Both methods are described in this section.

When adding brake fluid during the bleeding process, use DOT 4 brake fluid. Do not reuse brake fluid drained from the system or use DOT 5 (silicone based) brake fluid. Brake fluid damages most surfaces, so wipe up any spills immediately with soapy water and rinse completely.

> *NOTE*
> *When bleeding the brakes, check the fluid level in the master cylinder frequently to prevent it from running dry, especially when using a vacuum pump. If air enters the system, it must be rebled.*

General Bleeding Tips

When bleeding the front brake, note the following:

1. Cover all parts that could become contaminated by the accidental spilling of brake fluid. Wash any spilled brake fluid from any surface immediately, as it damages the finish. Use soapy water and rinse completely.

2. Make sure the brake system banjo bolts and hose fittings are tight.

3. Clean the bleed screw and the area around the valve of all dirt and debris. Make sure the passageway in the end of the screw is open and clear.

4. Use a box-end wrench to open and close the bleed screw to prevent damaging its hex-head. Replace the bleed screw if damaged.

5. Install the box-end wrench on the bleed screw before installing the catch hose.

6. Use a clear catch hose to allow visual inspection of the brake fluid as it leaves the caliper. Air bubbles visible in the catch hose indicate that there still may be air trapped in the brake system.

7. Turn the handlebars to level the front master cylinder and remove the screws, reservoir cap, set plate

14

and diaphragm. Fill the reservoir to about 10 mm (3/8 in.) from the top.

8. If using a vacuum pump in the following sections, continually observe the brake fluid level in the reservoir. It drops quite rapidly. Maintain the level at 10 mm (3.8 in.) from the top of the reservoir to prevent air from being drawn into the system.

9. It is possible to see air exiting through the catch hose even through there is no air in the brake system. Air can enter around a loosened bleed screw or a loose-fitting catch hose. In both cases, air is being introduced into the bleed system, not from within the brake system itself. This condition can be misleading and cause excessive brake bleeding when there is no air in the system.

10. Open the bleed screw just enough to allow fluid to pass through the valve and into the catch bottle. The farther the bleed screw is opened, the looser the valve becomes. This allows air to draw into the system from around the valve threads.

11. If air is suspected of entering from around the bleed screw, pack the area around the bleed screw threads with silicone brake grease during bleeding.

WARNING
Do not force grease into the caliper past the bleed screw threads. This can block the bleed screw passageway and contaminate the brake fluid.

12. If the system is difficult to bleed, tap the banjo bolt on the master cylinder a few times. Air bubbles can become trapped in the hose connection where the brake fluid exits the master cylinder. When a number of bubbles appear in the master cylinder reservoir after tapping the banjo bolt, air was trapped in this area. It also helps to tap the banjo bolt and hose connection at the brake caliper.

13. After bleeding the front brake so that no air bubbles appear in the catch hose, test the feel of the brake lever. It should be firm and should offer the same resistance each time it is operated. If the brake lever feels spongy, air is trapped in the system and the bleeding procedure must be continued.

14. Tighten the bleed screw to 6 N•m (53 in.-lb.).

15. If necessary, add DOT 4 brake fluid to correct the level in the master cylinder reservoir. It must be above the level line.

16. Test ride the motorcycle slowly at first to make sure that the brakes are operating correctly.

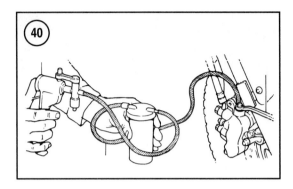

WARNING
Do not ride the motorcycle until both brakes and the brake light are working properly.

Vacuum Bleeding

Vacuum bleeding can be accomplished by using either a hand-operated or a compressed air tool. The tools described below can be used by one person to drain and bleed the front brake system.

Hand-operated vacuum pump

This procedure requires a hand-operated vacuum pump, two lengths of clear hose and a separate reservoir to drain and bleed the brake system.

1. Connect the catch hose between the bleed screw and catch bottle. Connect the other hose between the catch bottle and vacuum pump. Refer to the tool manufacturer's instructions for additional information. **Figure 40** shows a typical setup.

2. Secure the vacuum pump to the motorcycle with a length of stiff wire so it can be released when checking and refilling the master cylinder reservoir.

3. Operate the vacuum pump to create a vacuum in the catch hose connected to the bleed screw. Then open the bleed screw with a wrench to allow brake fluid to be drawn through the master cylinder and brake hose. Close the bleed screw before the brake fluid stops flowing from the system (no more vacuum in line) or before the master cylinder reservoir runs empty.

4. Refill the master cylinder and repeat Step 3 until the brake fluid running through the vacuum hose is a clear and solid stream without air bubbles.

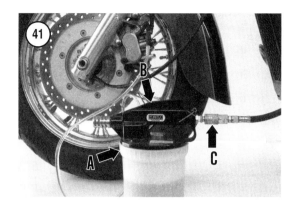

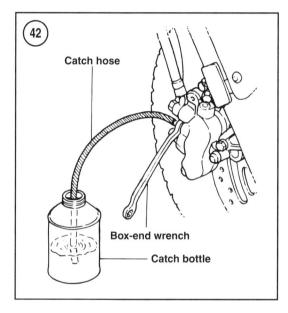

NOTE
When using a vacuum pump, observe the brake fluid level in the reservoir frequently because it drops quite rapidly.

Compressed air vacuum pump

This procedure requires a compressed air vacuum pump (A, **Figure 41**, typical) to create a powerful vacuum to drain and bleed brake systems. An air compressor (80-120 psi) is also required. The lever (B, **Figure 41**) on top of the cover allows the user to control the amount of brake fluid removed from the system.

1. Assemble the tool following the manufacturer's instructions.

2. Connect a box-end wrench onto the bleed screw. Connect the vacuum hose onto the bleed screw (**Figure 41**).

3. Connect a compressed air source (C, **Figure 41**) to the vacuum tool.

4. Depress the lever (B, **Figure 41**) on top of the pump, and then open the bleed screw slightly. As long as the lever is depressed, a vacuum is created in the canister and brake fluid evacuates from the line. Releasing the lever stops the vacuum. This tool drains the master cylinder rapidly. If an assistant is not available to refill the master cylinder during the procedure, release the lever and tighten the bleed screw. Then refill the master cylinder and continue the procedure.

NOTE
Always close the bleed screw before releasing the lever on top of the pump.

5. Continue until the brake fluid running through the vacuum hose is a clear and solid stream without air bubbles.

Manual Bleeding

This procedure requires a reservoir bottle, length of clear hose (catch hose), wrench and DOT 4 brake fluid (**Figure 42**).

1. Connect the catch hose to the bleed screw on the brake caliper. Submerge the other end of the hose into the bottle partially filled with DOT 4 brake fluid. This prevents air from being drawn into the catch hose and back into the brake caliper.

2. Apply the brake lever until it stops and hold in this position.

3. Open the bleed screw with a wrench and apply pressure against the brake lever to move it to the limit of its travel, and then close the bleed screw.

NOTE
*When bleeding the brakes manually, make sure to close the bleed screw **before** releasing the brake lever. This prevents air from being drawn back into the system.*

4. Pump the brake lever a few times and release it.

5. Repeat Steps 2-4 until the brake fluid running through the hose is a clear and solid stream without air bubbles.

14

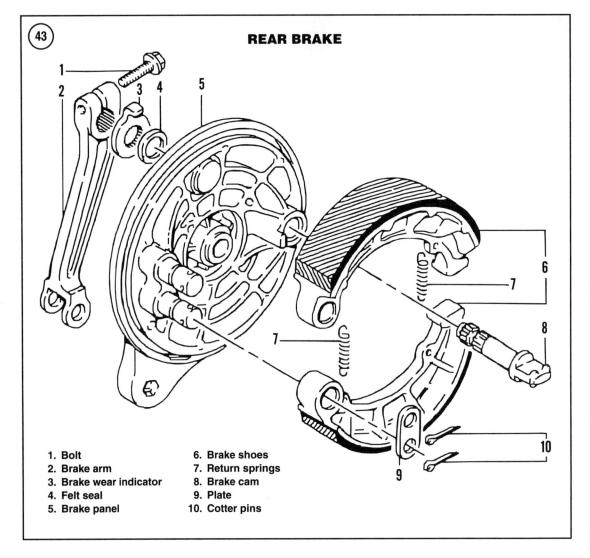

43   REAR BRAKE

1. Bolt
2. Brake arm
3. Brake wear indicator
4. Felt seal
5. Brake panel
6. Brake shoes
7. Return springs
8. Brake cam
9. Plate
10. Cotter pins

BRAKE FLUID DRAINING

Before disconnecting a brake hose, drain the brake fluid as described in this section. Doing so reduces the amount of brake fluid that can spill out when disconnecting the brake hoses and lines from the system.

1. Read the information listed under *Brake Bleeding* in this chapter for the selection, installation and operation of a brake bleeder.

2. Turn the handlebars to level the front master cylinder and remove the screws, reservoir cap, set plate and diaphragm.

3. Connect a brake bleeder to the front brake caliper bleed screw. Open the bleed screw and operate the brake bleeder until brake fluid stops flowing. Tighten the bleed screw.

4. If flushing the brake system, use DOT 4 brake fluid as a flushing fluid. Flushing consists of drawing new brake fluid into the system until new fluid appears at the caliper without the presence of any air bubbles. To flush the brake system, follow one of the bleeding procedures described under *Brake Bleeding* in this chapter.

CAUTION
Never reuse old brake fluid. Properly discard all brake fluid flushed from the system.

REAR DRUM BRAKE

All models covered in this manual use a rear drum brake (**Figure 43**). Activating the foot pedal

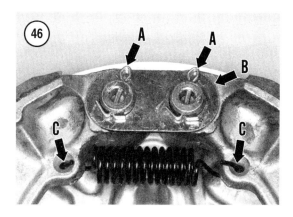

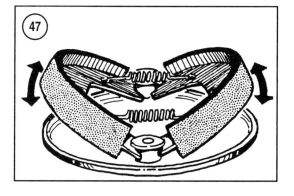

pulls the brake rods, which in turn rotates the brake cam in the brake drum. This forces the brake shoes out into contact with the drum.

Rear brake pedal free play must be maintained to minimize brake drag and premature brake wear and to maximize braking effectiveness. Refer to *Rear Brake Pedal Free Play* in Chapter Three for complete adjustment procedures.

> *WARNING*
> *When handling the rear brake assembly, do not inhale brake dust because it may contain asbestos that can cause lung injury and cancer. Wear a disposable face mask and wash hands and forearms thoroughly after completing the work. Wet down the brake dust on brake components before storing or working on them. Secure and dispose of all brake dust and cleaning materials properly. Do not use compressed air to blow off brake parts.*

Brake Shoe Replacement

Refer to **Figure 43**.

1. Remove the rear wheel (Chapter Eleven).
2. Pull the rear brake panel (**Figure 44**) out of the brake drum.

> *NOTE*
> *When measuring the brake lining thickness, measure the lining thickness only. Do not include the brake shoe thickness.*

3. Measure the brake lining thickness with a vernier caliper (**Figure 45**). Measure at several places along the brake lining. Replace the brake shoes if the lining thickness is worn to the service limit in **Table 2**.
4. Mark the web portion on both shoes so the shoes can be reinstalled in their original position.

> *NOTE*
> *When handling the brake shoes, place a clean rag over the linings to protect them from oil and grease.*

5. Remove the two cotter pins (A, **Figure 46**) and the plate (B).

14

6. Spread the brake shoes (**Figure 47**) and remove them from the brake panel.

7. Disconnect the return springs (**Figure 48**) from the brake shoes.

8. Discard the brake shoes if new shoes are going to installed.

9. Clean and dry the brake panel and springs.

10. Inspect the return springs for cracks, stretched coils or damaged spring ends. Replace both springs as a set.

> *NOTE*
> *Worn or damaged return springs may not allow the brake pads to fully retract from the drum, causing brake drag.*

11. Lubricate the brake cam and brake panel pivot shafts with a waterproof bearing grease.

12. Install the return springs onto the brake shoes with the open spring ends (C, **Figure 46**) facing away from the brake panel.

13. Spread the brake shoes (one end at a time) and install them into the brake panel (**Figure 49**). Make sure the return springs attach fully to the brake shoes.

14. Wipe excess grease from the end of the pivot shaft and brake cam.

15. Install the plate (B, **Figure 46**) and two new cotter pins. Install the cotter pins with their closed side facing out (A, **Figure 46**). Bend the cotter pin arms to lock them in place.

16. Operate the brake arm by hand, making sure it moves and returns under spring pressure.

17. Install the brake panel and rear wheel (Chapter Eleven).

Brake Arm
Removal/Installation

Refer to **Figure 43**.

1. Remove the brake shoes as described in this section.

2. Note the brake arm and brake cam alignment marks (A, **Figure 50**). Realign these marks during installation.

3. Remove the rear brake arm bolt (B, **Figure 50**) and brake arm (C).

4. Remove the brake indicator (A, **Figure 51**) and felt seal (B).

5. Remove the brake cam (**Figure 53**).

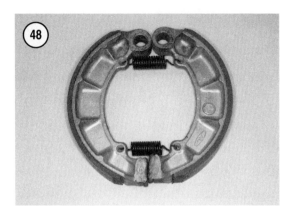

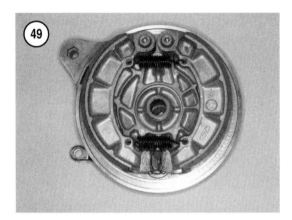

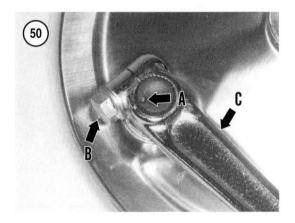

6. Clean and dry all parts (except the brake shoes and felt seal).

7. Inspect the brake arm for cracks, excessive wear or other damage.

8. Inspect the brake cam for excessive wear or damage.

9. Inspect the splines on the brake arm and brake cam for damage.

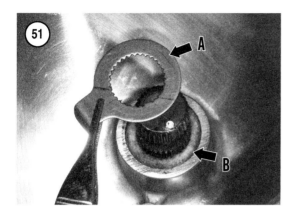

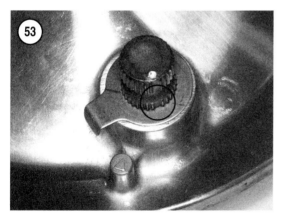

13. Install the felt seal (B, **Figure 51**) into the bore in the brake panel.

14. Install the brake indicator by aligning its wide tooth with the master spline on the brake cam (**Figure 53**).

15. Install the brake arm by aligning its punch mark with the punch mark on the end of the brake cam (A, **Figure 50**).

> *WARNING*
> *The angle between the brake arm and brake rod must not exceed 90° when the brake is applied. Installing the brake indicator and brake arm as described in the text maintains the correct operational relationship between the brake lever and brake cam. If the brake lever and brake rod angle exceeds 90°, the brake cam could pivot overcenter (turn horizontal) and lock the rear brake and wheel, causing the motorcycle to loose control. Do not reposition the brake lever on the brake cam to compensate for worn brake linings or a worn brake drum.*

16. Install the rear brake arm bolt (B, **Figure 50**) and tighten to 29 N•m (22 ft.-lb.). Pivot the brake arm, making sure it moves without any roughness or binding.

17. Install the brake shoes as described in this section.

10. Inspect the brake panel bore for cracks, wear or elongation. If damaged, replace the brake panel.

11. Replace the brake indicator and felt seal if damaged.

12. Lubricate the brake cam with a waterproof bearing grease and install it (**Figure 52**) into the brake panel. Wipe excess grease off and around the brake cam.

Rear Brake Drum Inspection

Table 2 lists the new service limit specifications for the brake drum outside diameter. The maximum (MAX) allowable outside diameter is embossed on

14

the hub near the brake drum (A, **Figure 54**). If the specification on the hub differs from the service limit in **Table 2**, use the specification on the hub when inspecting it.

When servicing the brake drum, do not have the drum machined to compensate for out-of-round or to remove wear grooves.

1. Remove the rear wheel (Chapter Eleven).
2. Clean the brake drum as follows:
    a. Turn the wheel over and pour any accumulated brake dust into a bag. Tie the bag closed and discard it.
    b. Do not clean the brake drum with compressed air. Instead spray the brake drum with a brake cleaner and allow to dry.
3. Inspect the brake drum (B, **Figure 54**) for roughness, cracks, distortion and other damage. Service the drum as follows:
    a. Remove light roughness and glaze with a fine-to-medium grade sandpaper.
    b. Replace the rear wheel if the brake drum is cracked or if the drum surface is scored heavily.
4. Measure the brake drum inside diameter with a vernier caliper (**Figure 55**). Measure at different points around the brake drum to determine any out-of-roundness. Replace the rear hub if the inner diameter exceeds the maximum allowable specification on the hub or in **Table 2**.
5. Install the rear wheel (Chapter Eleven).

REAR BRAKE PEDAL

Removal/Installation

Refer to **Figure 56** (VT750C) or **Figure 57** (VT750DC).

1. Remove the exhaust system (Chapter Fifteen).
2. Remove the adjust nut (**Figure 58**) and disconnect the brake rod from the brake arm. Remove the collar and spring.
3. Remove the middle rod joint bolt (A, **Figure 59**) and washer.
4. Disconnect the return spring (B, **Figure 59**).
5A. On VT750C models, perform the following:
    a. Remove the bolts and the right footpeg holder.
    b. Remove the brake pedal pivot bolts and washer and remove the brake pedal from the right footpeg holder.

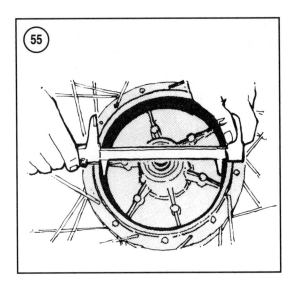

c. Disconnect the brake light switch spring at the brake rod.
    d. Refer to **Figure 56** to disconnect the brake rods from the middle rod joint.
5B. On VT750DC models, perform the following:
    a. Disconnect the brake light switch spring at the brake rod.
    b. Remove the bolts and the right footpeg mounting bracket.
    c. Refer to **Figure 57** to disconnect the middle brake rod from the rear brake pedal and middle rod joint.
6. Installation is the reverse of removal. Note the following:
    a. Clean and lubricate the pivot bolt surfaces with grease.
    b. Lubricate the joint pins with grease.
    c. On VT750DC models, replace the brake pedal dust seals if they are leaking or damaged. Lubricate the dust seal lips with grease.
    d. Install new cotter pins.
    e. On VT750C models, tighten the rear brake pedal pivot bolt to 34 N•m (25 ft.-lb.).
    f. Tighten the rear brake middle rod joint bolt to 34 N•m (25 ft.-lb.).
    g. Check the rear brake pedal height and adjust the rear brake as described under *Rear Brake* in Chapter Three.
    h. Check the rear brake light operation.

WARNING
Do not ride the motorcycle until the rear brake, brake pedal and brake light work properly.

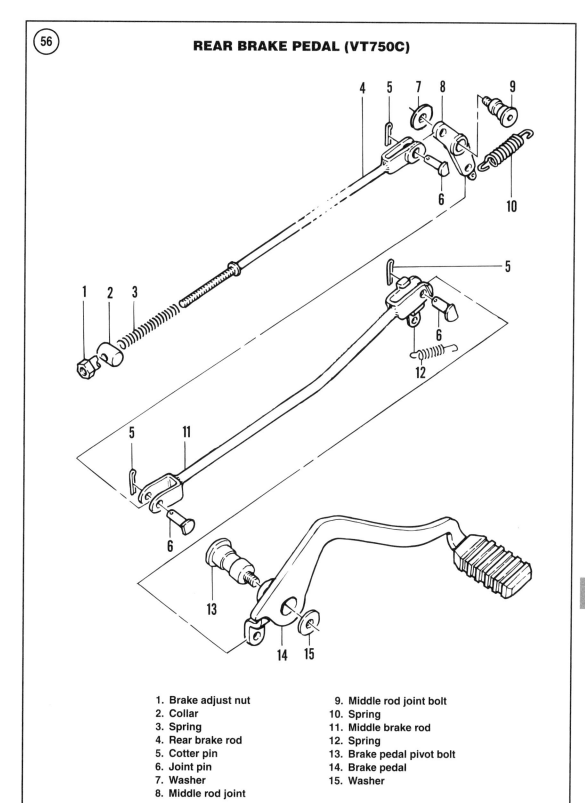

56

REAR BRAKE PEDAL (VT750C)

14

1. Brake adjust nut
2. Collar
3. Spring
4. Rear brake rod
5. Cotter pin
6. Joint pin
7. Washer
8. Middle rod joint
9. Middle rod joint bolt
10. Spring
11. Middle brake rod
12. Spring
13. Brake pedal pivot bolt
14. Brake pedal
15. Washer

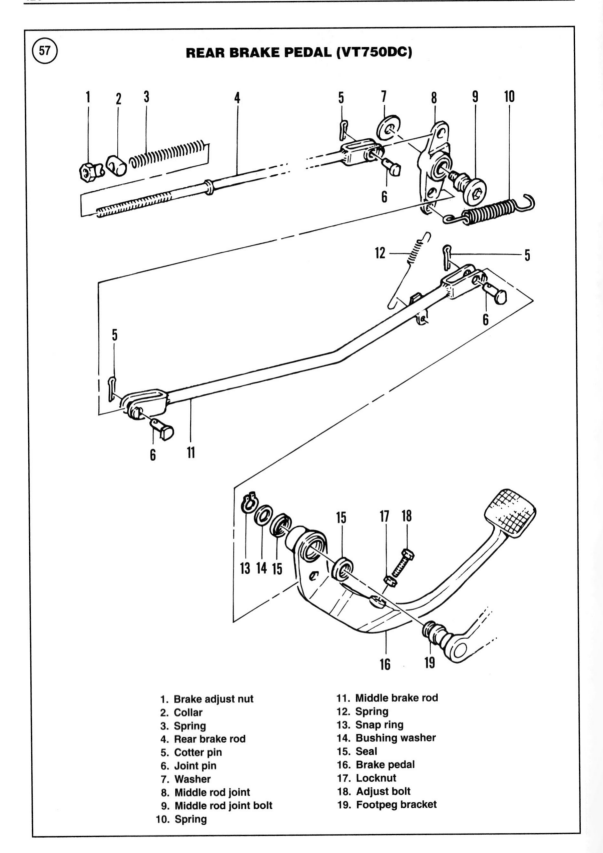

REAR BRAKE PEDAL (VT750DC)

1. Brake adjust nut
2. Collar
3. Spring
4. Rear brake rod
5. Cotter pin
6. Joint pin
7. Washer
8. Middle rod joint
9. Middle rod joint bolt
10. Spring
11. Middle brake rod
12. Spring
13. Snap ring
14. Bushing washer
15. Seal
16. Brake pedal
17. Locknut
18. Adjust bolt
19. Footpeg bracket

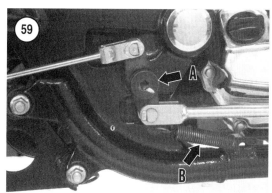

Table 1 FRONT BRAKE SERVICE SPECIFICATIONS

	New mm (in.)	Service limit mm (in.)
Brake disc runout	–	0.30 (0.012)
Brake disc thickness	5.8-6.2	5.0
	(0.23-0.24)	(0.20)
Brake caliper cylinder inside diameter	27.000-27.050	27.06
	(1.0630-1.0650)	(1.065)
Brake caliper piston outside diameter		
VT750C	26.935-26.968	26.93
	(1.0604-1.0617)	(1.060)
VT750DC	26.918-26.968	26.91
	(1.0598-1.0617)	(1.059)
Master cylinder inside diameter	11.000-11.043	11.05
	(0.4331-0.4348)	(0.435)
Master cylinder piston outside diameter	10.957-10.984	10.945
	(0.4314-0.4324)	(0.4309)

Table 2 REAR BRAKE SERVICE SPECIFICATIONS

	New mm (in.)	Service limit mm (in.)
Brake drum outside diameter	180.0-180.3	181.0
	(7.09-7.10)	(7.13)
Brake lining thickness	5.0	2.0
	(0.20)	(0.1)

Table 3 BRAKE TORQUE SPECIFICATIONS

	N•m	in.-lb.	ft.-lb.
Banjo bolt	34	–	25
Brake caliper bleed screw	6	53	–
Brake caliper mounting bolts[1]	30	–	22
Brake caliper bracket pin bolt[2]	13	115	–
Brake caliper pin bolt[2]	27	–	20
Brake disc mounting bolts	42	–	31
Front brake lever			
Pivot bolt	1	8.8	–
Nut	6	53	–
Front brake light switch screw	1	8.8	–
Master cylinder cover screw	2	18	–
Master cylinder clamp bolts	12	106	–
Pad pin plug	3	26	–
Pad pin	18	–	13
Rear brake arm bolt	29		22
Rear brake middle rod joint bolt	34	–	25
Rear brake pedal pivot bolt			
VT750C	34	–	25
Rear brake stopper arm			
Bolt (VT750C)	20	–	15
Nut (VT750DC)	20	–	15

1. ALOC fastener. Install new fastener during assembly.
2. Apply a medium strength threadlock onto fastener threads.

CHAPTER FIFTEEN

BODY AND EXHAUST SYSTEM

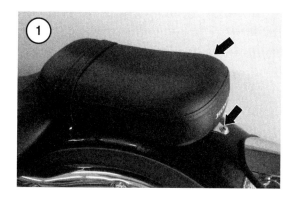

This chapter contains removal and installation procedures for the seat, side covers, fenders and exhaust system. Torque specifications are listed in **Table 1** at the end of chapter.

SEAT

Removal/Installation

VT750C

1. Remove the rear seat mounting bolt, push the rear seat forward (**Figure 1**) and remove it.

2. Remove the front seat mounting bolt and remove the seat (**Figure 2**).

3. Installation is the reverse of these steps. Note the following:

a. Install the front seat by inserting the hook on the seat pan under the lip on the front of the fuel tank (**Figure 3**) and then push the seat forward.

b. Tighten the front seat mounting bolt to 26 N•m (19 ft.-lb.).

c. Install the rear seat by hooking the seat bracket over the front seat mounting bolt (**Figure 4**). Then push the seat rearward.

d. Tighten the rear seat mounting bolt to 9 N•m (80 in.-lb.).

VT750DC

Refer to **Figure 5**.

1. Remove the seat mounting bolts, collars and strap.

2. Slide the seat rearward and remove it.

3. Installation is the reverse of these steps. Note the following:

a. Install the seat by inserting the hook on the seat pan under the lip on the front of the fuel tank and the slot in the seat with the boss on the rear fender. Push the seat forward.

b. Tighten the front seat mounting bolt to 26 N•m (19 ft.-lb.).

15

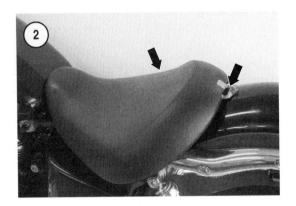

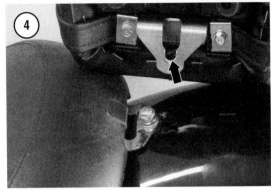

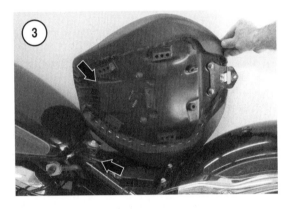

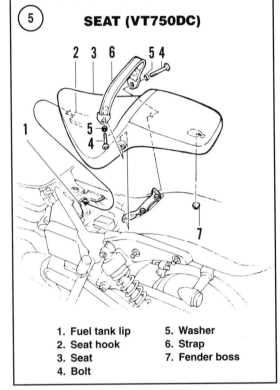

SEAT (VT750DC)

1. Fuel tank lip	5. Washer
2. Seat hook	6. Strap
3. Seat	7. Fender boss
4. Bolt	

SIDE COVERS

Removal/Installation

1. Carefully pull the side cover bosses out of the frame dampers and remove the side cover (**Figure 6**, typical).

2. Replace any missing or damaged frame dampers.

3. Install by reversing these steps.

STEERING COVERS
(VT750C)

Removal/Installation

1. Remove the fuel tank (Chapter Eight).

2. Loosen and remove the trim clip (**Figure 7**) from each steering cover.

3. Remove the left and right steering covers (**Figure 8**) as an assembly.

4. Install by reversing these steps. Check the wire harness and cable routing after installing the steering covers. Turn the handlebars to check for interference.

FRONT FENDER

Removal/Installation

1. Remove the front wheel (Chapter Eleven).
2. Remove the front brake hose mounting bracket bolt at the front fender, if so equipped. Refer to **Figure 9**, typical.
3. Remove the front fender mounting bolts, the front fender and its inner support bracket.
4. Installation is the reverse of these steps. Tighten the brake hose mounting bracket bolt securely.

REAR FENDER

Removal/Installation

1. Remove the seat(s) as described in this chapter.
2. Remove the right side cover as described in this chapter.
3. Disconnect the taillight and brake light connectors. Trace the wiring harness underneath the rear fender to the connector pouch.

NOTE
The rear part of the fender is heavy because of the taillight assembly.

When you release the rear fender in Step 4, do not let the back of the fender assembly fall against the frame.

4. Remove the bolts, washers and rear fender. Refer to **Figure 10** (VT750C) or **Figure 11** (VT750DC).
5. Installation is the reverse of these steps. Note the following:
   a. Tighten the rear fender mounting bolts to the torque specifications in **Table 1**.
   b. Check the taillight and brake light for proper operation.

GRAB RAIL

Removal/Installation

Refer to **Figure 12**.
1. Remove the rear fender as described in this chapter.
2. Left grab rail—Perform the following:
   a. Loosen the left grab rail mounting nut located between the shock absorber and frame. Do not loosen the shock absorber mounting bolt.
   b. On VT750DC models, remove the grab rail.
   c. On VT750C models, remove the bolt, washer and grab rail.

15

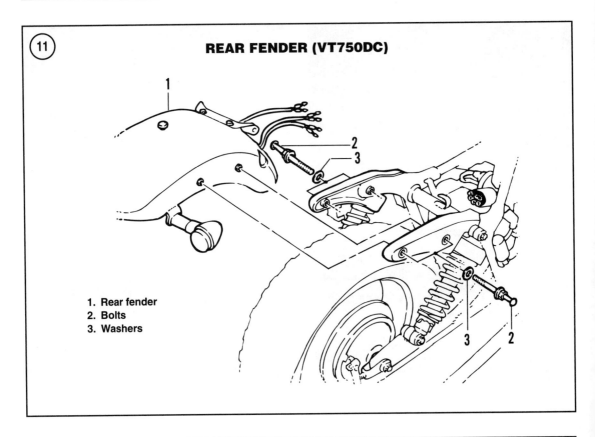

⑪ **REAR FENDER (VT750DC)**

1. Rear fender
2. Bolts
3. Washers

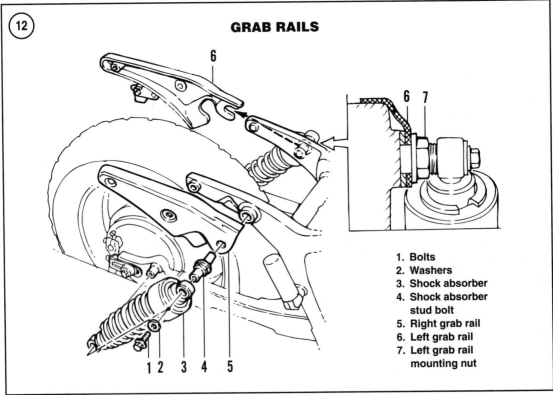

⑫ **GRAB RAILS**

1. Bolts
2. Washers
3. Shock absorber
4. Shock absorber stud bolt
5. Right grab rail
6. Left grab rail
7. Left grab rail mounting nut

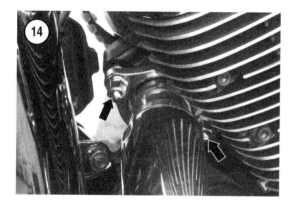

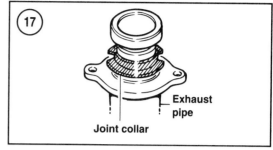

Exhaust pipe

Joint collar

3. Right grab rail—Perform the following:
   a. Remove the right side shock absorber (Chapter Thirteen).
   b. Remove the shock absorber stud bolt.
   c. Remove the rear grab rail mounting bolt, washer and grab rail.

4. Installation is the reverse of removal. Note the following:
   a. Tighten the right shock absorber stud bolt to 108 N•m (80 ft.-lb.).
   b. Tighten the left grab rail mounting nut to 88 N•m (65 ft.-lb.).
   c. Tighten the shock absorber upper and lower mounting bolts to 26 N•m (19 ft.-lb.).

EXHAUST SYSTEM

On VT750C models, the front and rear cylinder exhaust pipes and mufflers are welded together to form a single assembly. Individual replacement parts, other than the gaskets, protectors and fasteners, are not available.

On VT750DC models, the exhaust pipes can be removed as an assembly, and then disassembled as required.

Removal

1. On VT750DC models, remove the right footpeg assembly.

2. Remove the two exhaust pipe joint nuts at the front (**Figure 13**) and rear (**Figure 14**) cylinder heads.

3. Remove the muffler bracket nuts (**Figure 15**) and remove the exhaust pipe assembly.

4. Remove and discard the gasket (**Figure 16**) from each exhaust port.

5. If necessary, remove the joint collar (**Figure 17**) from each exhaust pipe.

15

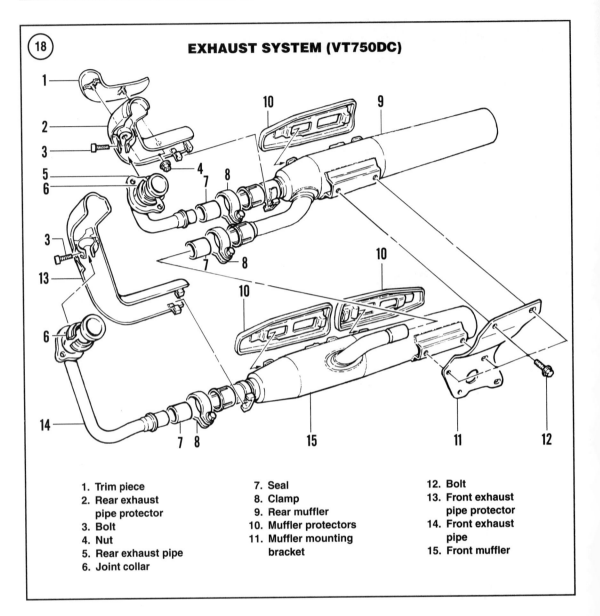

EXHAUST SYSTEM (VT750DC)

1. Trim piece
2. Rear exhaust
   pipe protector
3. Bolt
4. Nut
5. Rear exhaust pipe
6. Joint collar
7. Seal
8. Clamp
9. Rear muffler
10. Muffler protectors
11. Muffler mounting
    bracket
12. Bolt
13. Front exhaust
    pipe protector
14. Front exhaust
    pipe
15. Front muffler

Installation

1. If removed, install the joint collar (**Figure 17**) onto each exhaust pipe.

2. Install a new gasket in each exhaust port (**Figure 16**). If necessary, apply a small amount of grease onto the gasket to hold it in place.

> *NOTE*
> *If you are installing the exhaust assembly without assistance, use a jack to support and raise the exhaust system in the following steps.*

3. Lift the exhaust pipe assembly and install the two exhaust pipes into their respective cylinder heads. Make sure the gaskets seat squarely against the cylinder head gasket surfaces.

4. Install the exhaust pipe joint nuts finger-tight.

5. Install the muffler bracket nuts (**Figure 15**) finger-tight.

6. Tighten the exhaust pipe fasteners in the following order:

   a. Tighten the muffler bracket nuts (**Figure 15**) to 26 N•m (19 ft.-lb.).

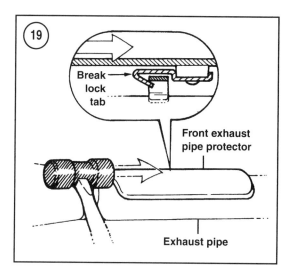

b. Tighten the rear (**Figure 14**), then the front (**Figure 13**) exhaust pipe joint nuts to 25 N•m (18 ft.-lb.).

c. On VT750DC models, tighten the right footpeg mounting bolts to 34 N•m (25 ft.-lb.).

7. Start the engine and check for exhaust leaks.

NOTE
If grease was used to hold the gaskets in place, allow the engine to run long enough to burn off the grease before suspecting an exhaust leak.

Exhaust Pipe Disassembly/Assembly (VT750DC)

Refer to **Figure 18** to disassemble and reassemble the exhaust pipe assembly. Use new joint pipe gaskets during assembly.

Exhaust Pipe and Muffler Protectors Removal/Installation

Protectors are installed on the exhaust pipe or muffler (VT750DC). The protectors can be replaced with the exhaust system mounted on the motorcycle.

NOTE
Do not remove a protector unless it is going to be replaced. During removal, lock tabs on the reverse side of the protector are broken and the protector cannot be reused.

1. Drive the protector with a plastic hammer until its lock tab breaks (**Figure 19**) and frees the protector from the exhaust pipe.
2. Discard the protector.
3. Install the new exhaust pipe protector over the exhaust pipe, and then align its holder with the flange retainer tabs on the pipe. Push it into place.

Table 1 BODY AND EXHAUST SYSTEM TORQUE SPECIFICATIONS

	N•m	in.-lb.	ft.-lb.
Exhaust system			
Exhaust pipe joint nuts	25	–	18
Exhaust pipe protector bolts	12	–	9
Muffler bracket nuts	26	–	19
Left grab rail mounting nut	88	–	65
Rear fender mounting bolts			
VT750C	26	–	19
VT750DC	64	–	47
Right footpeg mounting bolts			
VT750DC	34	–	25
Right shock absorber stud bolt	108	–	80
Seat mounting bolts			
VT750C			
Front seat	26	–	19
Rear seat	9	80	–
VT750DC	26	–	19
Shock absorber mounting bolts	26	–	19

15

INDEX

A

Air filter 59-60
  chamber 208-209
  housing 208
Alternator, specifications 309

B

Battery
  maintenance-free
    voltage readings 309
  specifications 309
  state of charge 309
Body
  and exhaust system 423
  covers
    side 424
    steering 424-425
  fender
    front 425
    rear 425
  grab rail 425-427
  seat 423-424
  torque specifications 429
Brake 396
  bleeding 411-414
  caliper 399-404

disc 410-411
drum 414-418
fluid
  draining 414
  preventing damage 396
  selection 396
hose replacement 409-410
lights
  switches
    front 303
    rear 303-304
maintenance 86-89
master cylinder 404-409
pads 397-399
pedal 418-421
service 396-397
specifications
  front 422
  rear 422
torque specifications 423
troubleshooting 55-57
Bulb specifications 310

C

Cables
  choke, replacement 232-234

throttle, replacement 230-232
Cam chains 114-116
  tensioner. 114-116
Camshafts. 102-114
Carburetor
  adjustment 226-228
  heater and air temperature switch 228-230
  maintenance and tune-up 68-72
  operation 210
  service. 211-226
  specifications 243
Charging system 252-256
  specifications 309
Choke cable
  replacement 232-234
Clutch and external shift mechanism. 172
Clutch. 175-186
  cable
    adjustment 75-76
    replacement 172-173
  crankcase, right cover 173-174
  diode 284-285
  primary drive gear. 186-188
  release lever 174-175
  specifications 192
    torque. 192
  starter 258-261, 310
  switch 302-303
  troubleshooting 47
Components
  electrical system
    location 245-246
    replacement 244
Connectors 244-245
Coolant
  capacity 96
  reserve tank 318
  temperature
    circuit troubleshooting. 295-297
    switch
      replacement 297-298
      testing 297-298
Cooling system 312
  fan. 317-318
  inspection 313-315
  maintenance 80-82
  radiator 315-317
  reserve tank 318
  specifications 324
    torque. 324

temperature warning system 312-313
thermostat. 319-321
  housing 321
water pump 321-324
Countershaft specifications 206
Crankcase
  breather system. 238
  cover
    left 256-258
    right 173-174
Cylinder 130-134
  firing order 59
  head 116-120
    covers 98-102
    service specifications 142-143
    stud replacement 141
  troubleshooting, leakdown test 46-47

D

Dimensions, general 30
Drive chain 351-354
  maintenance 89-93
  specifications 355
  sprockets
    drive 349-351
    driven 349-351
    torque specifications 355

E

Electrical system. 244
  alternator specifications 309
  battery, maintenance-free 246-252
    specifications 309
    state of charge 309
    voltage readings 309
  charging system 252-256
    specifications 309
  clutch diode 284-285
  component
    location 245-246
    replacement 244
  connectors. 244-245
  coolant temperature circuit
    switch testing and replacement 297-298
    troubleshooting 295-297
  flywheel and starter
    clutch and reduction gears 258-261
  fundamentals 20-21

16

fuses. 307-308
  specifications 311
headlight housing 289
horn 307
ignition
  coils 267-268
  control module (ICM) 269
  pulse generator 268-269
    rotor. 269
  system
    specifications 310
    troubleshooting 262-267
lighting system 285-289
neutral indicator. 300-301
oil pressure
  indicator. 299-300
  switch 299-300
sensor test specifications 311
specifications 310
  torque. 311
speedometer
  and speed sensor. 290-295
  assembly. 289-290
starter 275-283
  clutch specifications 310
  relay switch 283-284
starting system
  specifications 310
  troubleshooting 270-275
stator coil, and left crankcase cover . . . 256-258
switches
  clutch 302-303
  continuity test 305-306
  fan motor 298-299
  front brake light. 303
  handlebar. 305
  ignition 304-305
  neutral 300-301
  oil pressure 299-300
  rear brake light. 303-304
  sidestand. 301-302
testing, troubleshooting 48-54
turn signal relay 306-307
wiring diagrams. 437-445
Emission control system
  crankcase breather system 238
  evaporative 239-242
  inspection 82
Engine 146-150
  compression test 60-61

lower end. 145
  connecting rod. 162-165
    bearing selection 170
    crankshaft selection 170
  crankcase 150-159
    seal and bearing replacement. 159-160
  crankshaft 160-162
    selection 170
    specifications 170
  oil pump 165-169
    specifications 171
  servicing in frame 145-146
  torque specifications 171
lubrication
  filter 76-80
  oil 76-80
    capacity 95
serial numbers 28-29
top end. 98
  cam chain tensioner and cam chain . . . 114-116
  camshafts 102-114
  cylinder 130-134
    head 116-120
      and valve service specifications . . . 142-143
    covers 98-102
    stud replacement 141
  general specifications. 142
  piston
    rings and bore specifications 143-144
    rings 134-141
  servicing in frame 98
  torque specifications 144
  valves, components 120-130
troubleshooting 43-45
  lubrication 45-46
  operating requirements 34
  poor performance 40-42
  starting 34-40
Evaporative emission
  control system. 239-242
Exhaust system 427-429
  torque specifications 429
External shift mechanism. 188-192

                              F

Fan motor switch 298-299
Fasteners. 3-6
  inspection 93

Fender
  front 425
  rear 425
Fork
  front 361-373
    specifications 383-384
Frame
  serial numbers 28-29
Front suspension and steering 356
  troubleshooting 54-55
Fuel and emission control systems 207
Fuel system
  air filter
    housing 208
    chamber 208-209
  carburetor
    adjustment 226-228
    heater and air temperature switch . . . 228-230
    operation 210
    service 211-226
    specifications 243
  filter 234
  hose identification 207
  precautions 207
  pump 234-237
    specifications 243
  replacement cables
    choke 232-234
    throttle 230-232
  sub-air filter element 209-210
  tank 237-238
  torque specifications 243
  troubleshooting 42-43
Fuel
  filter 234
  hose
    identification 207
    inspection 72
  pump 234-237
    specifications 243
  tank 237-238
    capacity 30
  type 58-59
Fuses 307-308
  specifications 311

G

Gearshift linkage, troubleshooting 47-48
Grab rail 425-427

H

Handlebar
  grips 359-361
  suspension 356-359
  switch 305
  weights 359-361
Headlight, housing 289
Horn 307
Hose replacement 409-410
Hubs
  front 334-338
  rear 334-338

I

Ignition control module (ICM) 269
Ignition
  coils 267-268
  cut-off switch inspection 93
  pulse generator 268-269
    rotor 269
  switch 304-305
  system
    specifications 310
    troubleshooting 262-267
  timing inspection 65-66
Internal shift mechanism 204-205
  specifications, fork and shaft 206

L

Lighting system 285-289
Lights
  and horn, maintenance 93
  brake switch
    front 303
    rear 303-304
Lubrication
  and maintenance schedule 94-95
  engine oil
    and filter 76-80
    capacity 95
  periodic 58
  recommended lubricants and fuel 95

M

Mainshaft specifications 205-206
Maintenance
  air filter 59-60
  brakes 86-89

16

carburetor 68-72
clutch cable adjustment 75-76
coolant capacity 96
cooling system 80-82
crankcase breather inspection 60
drive chain 89-93
emission control system inspection 82
engine
  compression test 60-61
  oil
    and filter 76-80
    capacity 95
fastener inspection. 93
fuel
  hose inspection 72
  type. 58-59
ignition cut-off switch inspection 93
lights and horn 93
lubrication schedule 94-95
recommended lubricants and fuel 95
sidestand 93
spark plugs 61-65
specifications 96
steering, bearing inspection 85
suspension inspection
  front 85
  rear 85-86
throttle cable 73-75
tires
  and wheels 83-85
  inflation pressure 95
torque specifications 96-97
tune-up 58
valve clearance. 67-68
Master cylinder, front 404-409
Motorcycle lift. 325

N
Neutral
  indicator. 300-301
  switch 300-301

O
Oil
  capacity 95
  filter 76-80
  pressure
    indicator 299-300
    switch 299-300

P
Pistons
  bore specifications 143-144
  rings. 131-141
  specifications 143-144
Primary drive gear 186-188

R
Radiator. 315-317
  cooling system 315-317
Rear suspension 385
Recommended lubricants and fuel 95
Reduction gears. 258-261

S
Seat 423-424
Sensor test, specifications 311
Shift mechanism
  external 188-192
  internal 204-205
  specifications, fork and shaft 206
Shock absorber 385-387
Side covers 424
Sidestand
  switch 301-302
  maintenance 93
Spark plugs 61-65
Specifications
  alternator. 309
  battery 309
  brakes
    front 422
    rear 422
  bulb 310
  charging system 309
  clutch. 192
    starter. 310
  cooling system 324
  countershaft 206
  cylinder head 142-143
  drive chain 355
  electrical system 310
  engine, top end 142
  front fork 383-384
  fuel pump 243
  fuses 311
  ignition system 310
  internal shift mechanism 206
  mainshaft 205-206

pistons
  bore 143-144
  rings 143-144
sensor test 311
shift fork and shaft 206
starter clutch 310
starting system 310
steering. 383
suspension
  front 383
    fork 383-384
  rear 395
tires and wheels 354
torque 32
  body 429
  brakes 423
  clutch 192
  cooling system 324
  electrical system 311
  engine, top end 144
  exhaust system 429
  fuel system 243
  maintenance 96-97
  steering 384
  suspension
    front 384
    rear 395
  wheels and sprocket 355
transmission 205
  countershaft 206
  mainshaft 205-206
valves 142-143
wheel and axle service 354
Speed sensor 290-295
Speedometer
  and speed sensor 290-295
  assembly 289-290
  cable 328-329
  gear 328-329
Starter. 275-283
  clutch 258-261
  specifications 310
  relay switch 283-284
Starting system
  troubleshooting 270-275
  specifications 310
Stator coil 256-258
Steering
  bearing
    inspection 85

preload check 379-381
  stem race replacement 382-383
covers 424-425
front suspension, troubleshooting 54-55
head
  and stem 373-379
  bearing, replacement 381-382
specifications 383
torque 384
Storage 27-28
Sub-air filter element 209-210
Suspension
fork 361-373
  service specifications 383-384
handlebars 356-359
  grips 359-361
  weights 359-361
inspection
  front 85
  rear 85-86
shock absorber 385-387
specifications
  torque 384; 395
    front 383
    rear 395
swing arm 387-395
Swing arm 387-395
Switch continuity test 305-306

T

Thermostat 319-321
  housing 321
Throttle cable 73-75
  replacement 230-232
Tires
  and wheels 325
  maintenance 83-85
  specifications 354
  changing 343-347
  inflation pressure 95; 355
  safety 342-343
Tools
  basic 9-15
  precision measuring 15-20
  special 21
Torque
  specifications 32
    body 429
    brakes 423
    clutch 192

16

cooling system 324
electrical system 311
engine top end 144
exhaust system 429
fuel system 243
maintenance 96-97
steering 384
suspension
    front 384
    rear 395
    wheels and sprocket 355
Transmission 193-204
and internal shift mechanism 193
operation 193
specifications 205
    countershaft 206
    mainshaft 205-206
troubleshooting 48
Troubleshooting 34
brake system 55-57
clutch 47
coolant temperature, circuit 295-297
cylinder leakdown test 46-47
electrical system, ignition 262-267
    testing 48-54
engine 43-45
    lubrication 45-46
    operating requirements 34
    poor performance 40-42
    starting 34-40
front suspension, steering 54-55
fuel system 42-43
gearshift linkage 47-48
transmission 48
Tune-up 58
air filter 59-60
carburetor 68-72
cylinder

firing order 59
    identification 59
engine compression test 60-61
ignition timing inspection 65-66
spark plugs 61-65
valve clearance 67-68
Turn signal relay 306-307

V

Valves
clearance 67-68
components 120-130
service specifications 142-143

W

Water pump 321-324
Weight specifications 30
Wheels
and tires 325
    and drive chain 325
    specifications 354
axle service specifications 354
balance 347-349
driven flange 332-334
front 325-328
hubs
    front 334-338
    rear 334-338
motorcycle lift 325
rear 329-332
service 339-342
speedometer
    cable 328-329
    gear 328-329
sprocket and torque specifications 355
Wiring diagrams 437-445

WIRING
DIAGRAMS

VT750C (1998-2000)

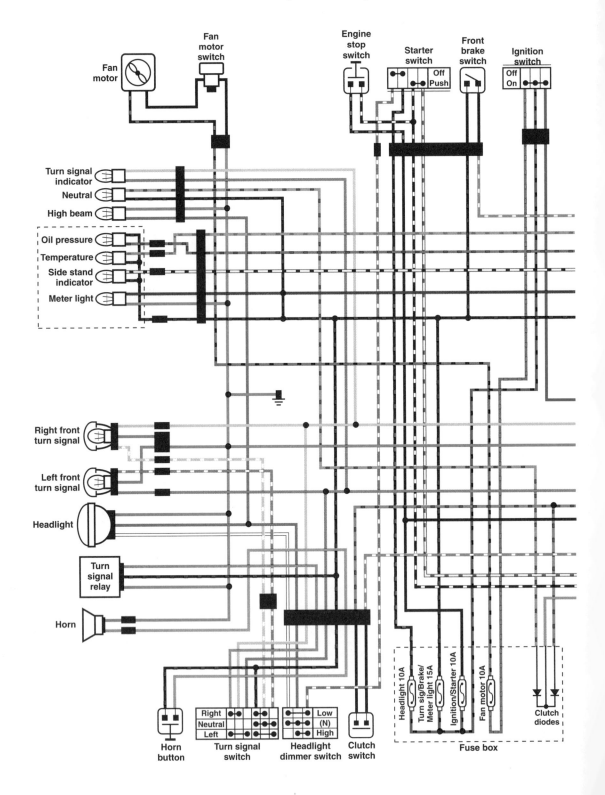

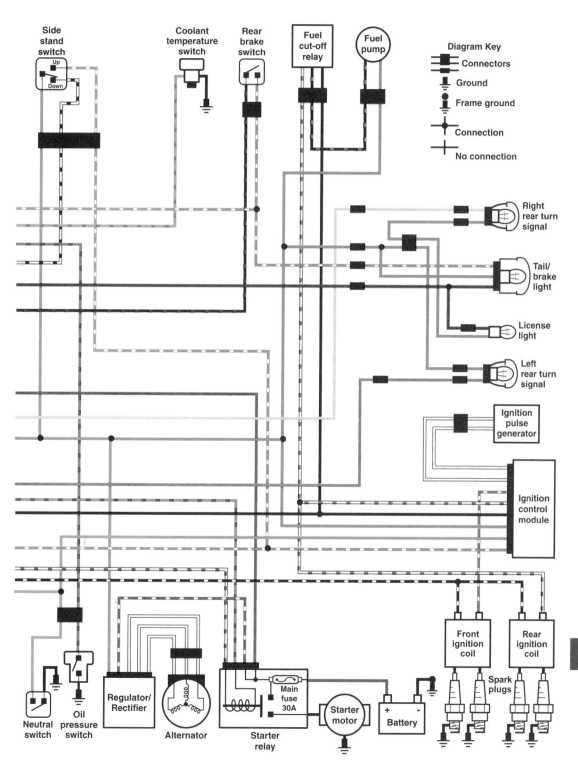

VT750C (2001-2003)

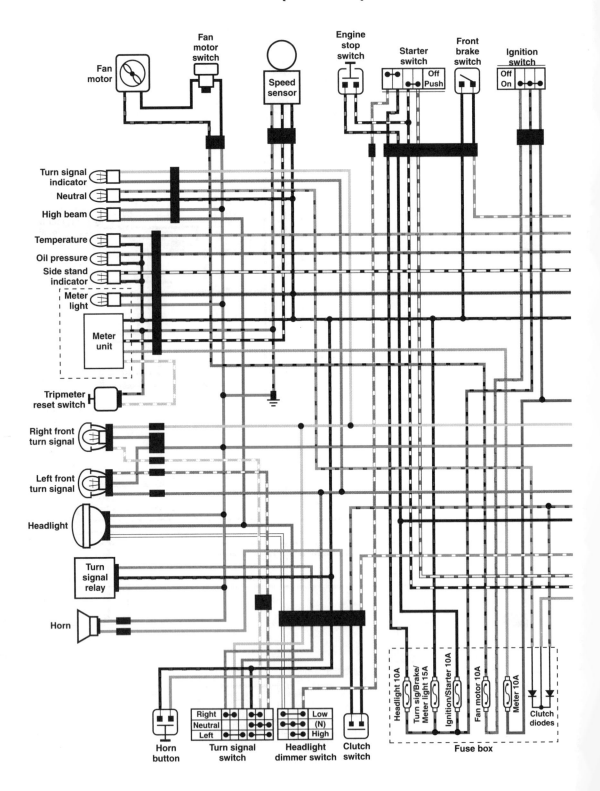

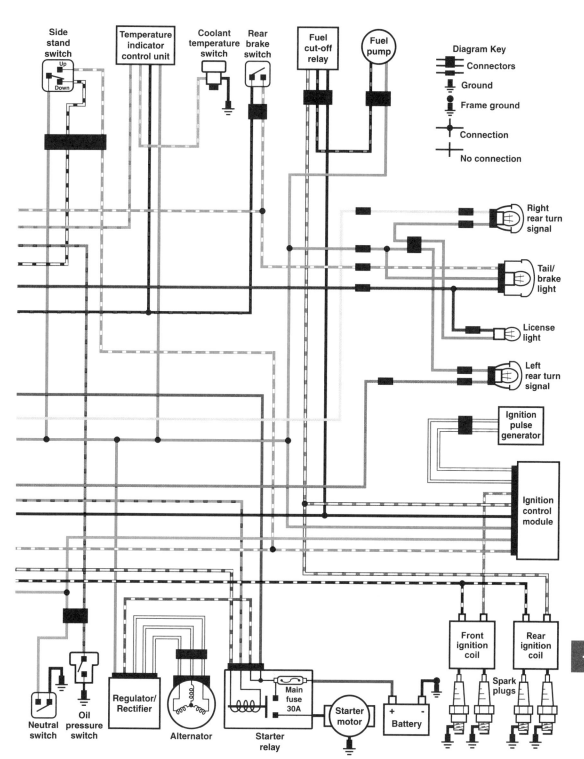

VT750DC (2001-2003)

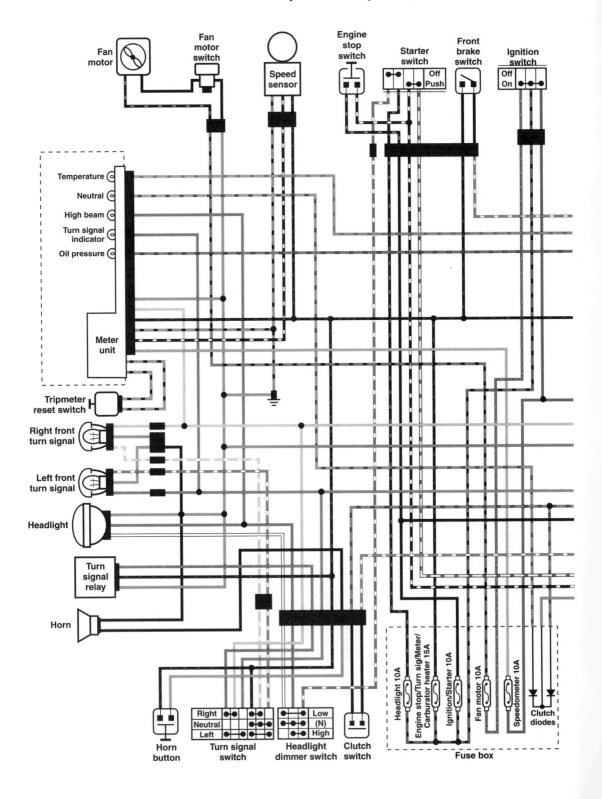

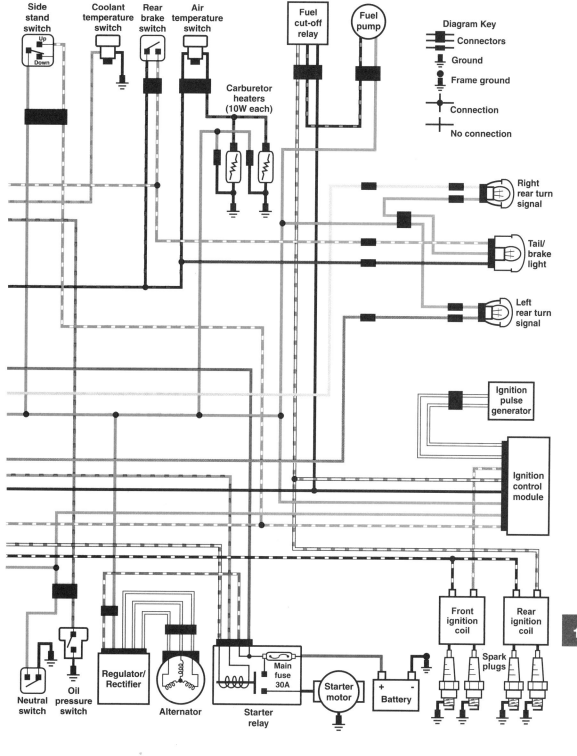

Diagram Key

- Connectors
- Ground
- Frame ground
- Connection
- No connection

Side stand switch

Coolant temperature switch

Rear brake switch

Air temperature switch

Carburetor heaters (10W each)

Fuel cut-off relay

Fuel pump

Right rear turn signal

Tail/ brake light

Left rear turn signal

Ignition pulse generator

Ignition control module

Front ignition coil

Rear ignition coil

Spark plugs

Neutral switch

Oil pressure switch

Regulator/ Rectifier

Alternator

Main fuse 30A

Starter relay

Starter motor

Battery

17

VT750DC (2004-ON)

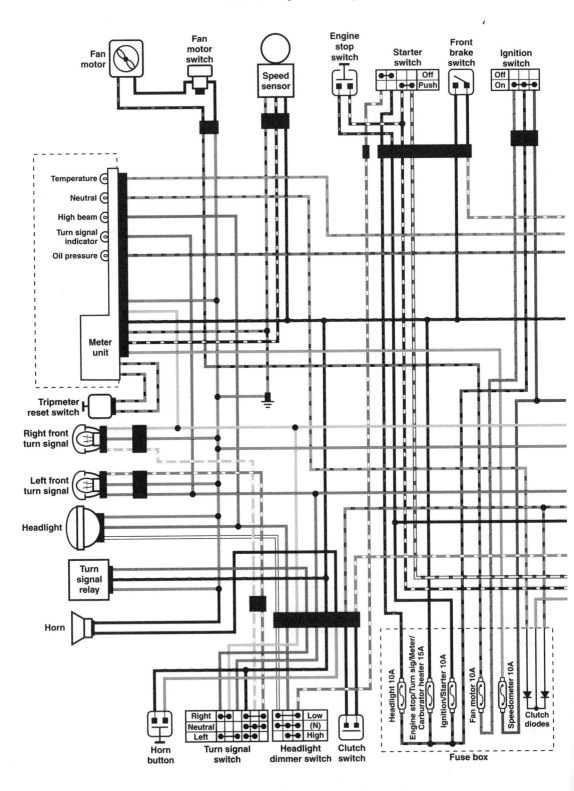

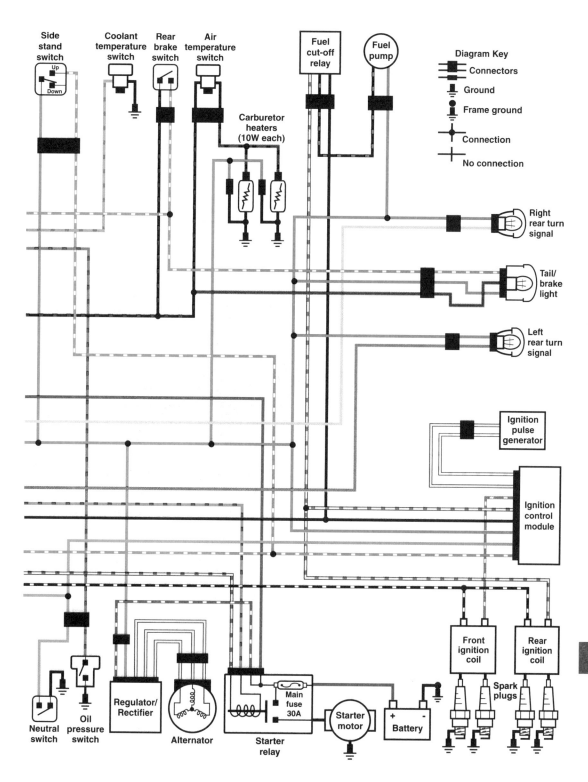

17

BMW

M308	500 & 600 CC Twins, 55-69
M309	F650, 1994-2000
M500-3	BMW K-Series, 85-97
M501	K1200RS, GT & LT, 98-05
M502-3	BMW R50/5-R100 GSPD, 70-96
M503-3	R850, R1100, R1150 and R1200C, 93-05

HARLEY-DAVIDSON

M419	Sportsters, 59-85
M428	Sportster Evolution, 86-90
M429-4	XL/XLH Sportster, 91-03
M427-1	Sportster, 04-06
M418	Panheads, 48-65
M420	Shovelheads,66-84
M421-3	FLS/FXS Evolution,84-99
M423-2	FLS/FXS Twin Cam, 00-05
M422-3	FLH/FLT/FXR Evolution,84-99
M430-4	FLH/FLT Twin Cam, 99-05
M424-2	FXD Evolution, 91-98
M425-3	FXD Twin Cam, 99-05

HONDA

ATVs

M316	Odyssey FL250, 77-84
M311	ATC, TRX & Fourtrax 70-125, 70-87
M433	Fourtrax 90 ATV, 93-00
M326	ATC185 & 200, 80-86
M347	ATC200X & Fourtrax 200SX, 86-88
M455	ATC250 & Fourtrax 200/250, 84-87
M342	ATC250R, 81-84
M348	TRX250R/Fourtrax 250R & ATC250R, 85-89
M456-3	TRX250X 87-92; TRX300EX 93-04
M215	TRX250EX, 01-05
M446-2	TRX250 Recon & ES, 97-04
M346-3	TRX300/Fourtrax 300 & TRX300FW/Fourtrax 4x4,88-00
M200-2	TRX350 Rancher, 00-06
M459-3	TRX400 Foreman 95-03
M454-3	TRX400EX 99-05
M205	TRX450 Foreman, 98-04
M210	TRX500 Rubicon, 98-04

Singles

M310-13	50-110cc OHC Singles, 65-99
M319-2	XR50R, CRF50F, XR70R & CRF70F, 97-05
M315	100-350cc OHC, 69-82
M317	Elsinore, 125-250cc, 73-80
M442	CR60-125R Pro-Link, 81-88
M431-2	CR80, 89-95, CR125R, 89-91
M435	CR80, 96-02
M457-2	CR125R & CR250R, 92-97
M464	CR125R, 1998-2002
M443	CR250R-500R Pro-Link, 81-87
M432-3	CR250R, 88-91 & CR500R, 88-01
M437	CR250R, 97-01
M352	CRF250, CRF250X & CRF450R, CRF450X, 02-05
M312-13	XL/XR75-100, 75-03
M318-4	XL/XR/TLR 125-200, 79-03
M328-4	XL/XR250, 78-00; XL/XR350R 83-85; XR200R, 84-85; XR250L, 91-96
M320-2	XR400R, 96-04
M339-7	XL/XR 500-650, 79-03

Twins

M321	125-200cc, 65-78
M322	250-350cc, 64-74
M323	250-360cc Twins, 74-77
M324-5	Twinstar, Rebel 250 & Nighthawk 250, 78-03
M334	400-450cc, 78-87
M333	450 & 500cc, 65-76
M335	CX & GL500/650 Twins, 78-83
M344	VT500, 83-88
M313	VT700 & 750, 83-87
M314-2	VT750 Shadow (chain drive), 98-05
M440	VT1100C Shadow , 85-96
M460-3	VT1100C Series, 95-04

Fours

M332	CB350-550cc, SOHC, 71-78
M345	CB550 & 650, 83-85
M336	CB650,79-82
M341	CB750 SOHC, 69-78
M337	CB750 DOHC, 79-82
M436	CB750 Nighthawk, 91-93 & 95-99
M325	CB900, 1000 & 1100, 80-83
M439	Hurricane 600, 87-90
M441-2	CBR600F2 & F3, 91-98
M445-2	CBR600F4, 99-06
M434-2	CBR900RR Fireblade, 93-99
M329	500cc V-Fours, 84-86
M438	Honda VFR800, 98-00
M349	700-1000 Interceptor, 83-85
M458-2	VFR700F-750F, 86-97
M327	700-1100cc V-Fours, 82-88
M340	GL1000 & 1100, 75-83
M504	GL1200, 84-87
M508	ST1100/PAN European, 90-02

Sixes

M505	GL1500 Gold Wing, 88-92
M506-2	GL1500 Gold Wing, 93-00
M507-2	GL1800 Gold Wing, 01-05
M462-2	GL1500C Valkyrie, 97-03

KAWASAKI

ATVs

M465-2	KLF220 & KLF250 Bayou, 88-03
M466-4	KLF300 Bayou, 86-04
M467	KLF400 Bayou, 93-99
M470	KEF300 Lakota, 95-99
M385	KSF250 Mojave, 87-00

Singles

M350-9	Rotary Valve 80-350cc, 66-01
M444-2	KX60, 83-02; KX80 83-90
M448	KX80/85/100, 89-03
M351	KDX200, 83-88
M447-3	KX125 & KX250, 82-91 KX500, 83-04
M472-2	KX125, 92-00
M473-2	KX250, 92-00
M474-2	KLR650, 87-06

Twins

M355	KZ400, KZ/Z440, EN450 & EN500, 74-95
M360-3	EX500, GPZ500S, Ninja R, 87-02
M356-4	Vulcan 700 & 750, 85-04
M354-2	Vulcan 800 & Vulcan 800 Classic, 95-04
M357-2	Vulcan 1500, 87-99
M471-2	Vulcan Classic 1500, 96-04

Fours

M449	KZ500/550 & ZX550, 79-85
M450	KZ, Z & ZX750, 80-85
M358	KZ650, 77-83
M359-3	900-1000cc Fours, 73-81
M451-3	1000 &1100cc Fours, 81-02
M452-3	ZX500 & 600 Ninja, 85-97
M453-3	Ninja ZX900-1100 84-01
M468-2	Ninja ZX-6, 90-04
M469	ZX7 Ninja, 91-98
M453-3	Ninja ZX900, ZX1000 & ZX1100, 84-01
M409	Concours, 86-04

POLARIS

ATVs

M496	Polaris ATV, 85-95
M362	Polaris Magnum ATV, 96-98
M363	Scrambler 500, 4X4 97-00
M365-2	Sportsman/Xplorer, 96-03

SUZUKI

ATVs

M381	ALT/LT 125 & 185, 83-87
M475	LT230 & LT250, 85-90
M380-2	LT250R Quad Racer, 85-92
M343	LTF500F Quadrunner, 98-00
M483-2	Suzuki King Quad/ Quad Runner 250, 87-98

Singles

M371	RM50-400 Twin Shock, 75-81
M369	125-400cc 64-81
M379	RM125-500 Single Shock, 81-88
M476	DR250-350, 90-94
M384-3	LS650 Savage, 86-04
M386	RM80-250, 89-95
M400	RM125, 96-00
M401	RM250, 96-02

Twins

M372	GS400-450 Twins, 77-87
M481-4	VS700-800 Intruder, 85-04
M482-2	VS1400 Intruder, 87-01
M484-3	GS500E Twins, 89-02
M361	SV650, 1999-2002

Triple

M368	380-750cc, 72-77

Fours

M373	GS550, 77-86
M364	GS650, 81-83
M370	GS750 Fours, 77-82
M376	GS850-1100 Shaft Drive, 79-84
M378	GS1100 Chain Drive, 80-81
M383-3	Katana 600, 88-96 GSX-R750-1100, 86-87
M331	GSX-R, 97-00
M478-2	GSX-R750, 88-92 GSX750F Katana, 89-96
M485	GSX-R750, 96-99
M377	GSX-R1000, 01-04
M338	GSF600 Bandit, 95-00
M353	GSF1200 Bandit, 96-03

YAMAHA

ATVs

M499	YFM80 Badger, 85-01
M394	YTM/YFM200 & 225, 83-86
M488-5	Blaster, 88-05
M489-2	Timberwolf, 89-00
M487-5	Warrior, 87-04
M486-5	Banshee, 87-04
M490-3	Moto-4 & Big Bear, 87-04
M493	YFM400FW Kodiak, 93-98
M280-2	Raptor 660R, 01-05

Singles

M492-2	PW50 & PW80, BW80 Big Wheel 80, 81-02
M410	80-175 Piston Port, 68-76
M415	250-400cc Piston Port, 68-76
M412	DT & MX 100-400, 77-83
M414	IT125-490, 76-86
M393	YZ50-80 Monoshock, 78-90
M413	YZ100-490 Monoshock, 76-84
M390	YZ125-250, 85-87 YZ490, 85-90
M391	YZ125-250, 88-93 WR250Z, 91-93
M497-2	YZ125, 94-01
M498	YZ250, 94-98 and WR250Z, 94-97
M406	YZ250F & WR250F, 01-03
M491-2	YZ400F, YZ426F, WR400F WR426F, 98-02
M417	XT125-250, 80-84
M480-3	XT/TT 350, 85-00
M405	XT500 & TT500, 76-81
M416	XT/TT 600, 83-89

Twins

M403	650cc, 70-82
M395-10	XV535-1100 Virago, 81-03
M495-4	V-Star 650, 98-05
M281-2	V-Star 1100, 99-05
M282	Road Star, 99-05

Triple

M404	XS750 & 850, 77-81

Fours

M387	XJ550, XJ600 & FJ600, 81-92
M494	XJ600 Seca II, 92-98
M388	YX600 Radian & FZ600, 86-90
M396	FZR600, 89-93
M392	FZ700-750 & Fazer, 85-87
M411	XS1100 Fours, 78-81
M397	FJ1100 & 1200, 84-93
M375	V-Max, 85-03
M374	Royal Star, 96-03
M461	YZF-R6, 99-04
M398	YZF-R1, 98-03
M399	FZ1, 01-05

VINTAGE MOTORCYCLES

Clymer® Collection Series

M330	Vintage British Street Bikes, BSA, 500–650cc Unit Twins; Norton, 750 & 850cc Commandos; Triumph, 500-750cc Twins
M300	Vintage Dirt Bikes, V. 1 Bultaco, 125-370cc Singles; Montesa, 123-360cc Singles; Ossa, 125-250cc Singles
M301	Vintage Dirt Bikes, V. 2 CZ, 125-400cc Singles; Husqvarna, 125-450cc Singles; Maico, 250-501cc Singles; Hodaka, 90-125cc Singles
M305	Vintage Japanese Street Bikes Honda, 250 & 305cc Twins; Kawasaki, 250-750cc Triples; Kawasaki, 900 & 1000cc Fours